The Dual-track Accounting Approach

The GASB *Statement No. 34* reporting model introduced government-wide, accrual-based financial statements to provide information that goes beyond the familiar fund accounting information. Analysts increasingly use government-wide "big picture" information in performance analysis, and some council members find that, relative to fund accounting information, accrual-based statements are better suited to demonstrate accountability for inter-period equity. For example, these statements provide the information necessary to explore critical questions such as, Has the government shifted the liability for current services to future generations? However, to date, governmental accounting software vendors have been slow to provide governments with systems that can directly produce government-wide financial statements on the required accrual basis, particularly on an interim basis, such as monthly.

Beginning with the 12th edition of this text in 2001, the authors committed themselves to the importance of providing government-wide and fund accounting information by introducing a *dual-track* approach to recording governmental transactions. The dual-track approach captures both government-wide and fund accounting information at the same time an event is recognized, thereby allowing for the direct production of both government-wide and fund financial statements. As students will learn, some transactions affect the government-wide statements only (e.g., depreciation expense) and others affect the fund financial statements only (e.g., budgetary entries). However, the majority affect both types of statements, although in different ways (e.g., expensing versus capitalizing long-lived assets). The fund financial statements reflect a short-term measurement focus that is intended to assist statement users in assessing *fiscal accountability*—how financial resources were raised and spent. The government-wide financial statements reflect a medium- to long-term measurement focus intended to assist users in assessing *operational accountability*—whether governmental services were efficiently and effectively provided. Both perspectives are important.

The dual-track approach helps students understand how two different sets of accounting records are used to collect financial data as transactions occur. One set of records collects information using the short-term measurement focus and near-cash basis of accounting traditionally used in governmental fund accounting. This set of records includes chart of accounts, general journal, general ledger, trial balances, and financial statements for each fund. The other set of records collects the same underlying information using a long-term measurement focus similar to that used by business; that is, the accrual basis of accounting. The second set of records assists in preparing statements for governmental activities and business-type activities. Each time we show what, if any, effect a transaction will have on the fund and governmental activities record.

The text does illustrate the reclassification approach in Chapter 9 since that approach is used in practice by most governments. Governments that continue to release only fund financial information throughout the year that is then converted (or reclassified) to government-wide information for the purposes of the year-end audit are not as accountable or transparent as governments that make GAAP-based information available throughout the year. Certainly the Internet and the proliferation of Web sites have dramatically changed the supply and demand for financial information. Time will tell whether there will continue to be a future demand for fund-based information in external governmental financial statements.

Governments, even small ones, are complex entities and there is no easy approach to learning the external governmental financial reporting model. But the authors believe that the dual-track approach is conceptually superior to the reclassification approach in that it gives students the tools to understand "why" and "how" financial statements are prepared and used. A greater conceptual understanding of governmental financial statements also makes it easier for students to understand the reclassification approach when it is encountered. The dual-track pedagogy can help students see the short- and long-term effects of the decisions made by government managers and oversight bodies from the perspective of all stakeholders.

Accounting for Governmental and Nonprofit Entities

Fifteenth Edition

Earl R. Wilson, Ph.D., CPA

Professor Emeritus
University of Missouri—Columbia

Jacqueline L. Reck, Ph.D., CPA

Associate Professor and James E. and C. Ellis Rooks
Distinguished Professor in Accounting
University of South Florida

Susan C. Kattelus, Ph.D., CPA, CGFM

Professor of Practice
Michigan State University

Boston Burr Ridge, IL Dubuque, IA Madison, WI New York San Francisco St. Louis
Bangkok Bogotá Caracas Kuala Lumpur Lisbon London Madrid Mexico City
Milan Montreal New Delhi Santiago Seoul Singapore Sydney Taipei Toronto

ACCOUNTING FOR GOVERNMENTAL AND NONPROFIT ENTITIES

Published by McGraw-Hill/Irwin, a business unit of The McGraw-Hill Companies, Inc., 1221 Avenue of the Americas, New York, NY, 10020.

Some ancillaries, including electronic and print components, may not be available to customers outside the United States.

This book is printed on acid-free paper.

1 2 3 4 5 6 7 8 9 0 VNH/VNH 0 9

ISBN 978-0-07-337960-9
MHID 0-07-337960-3

Vice president and editor-in-chief: *Brent Gordon*
Editorial director: *Stewart Mattson*
Publisher: *Tim Vertovec*
Senior sponsoring editor: *Alice Harra*
Developmental editor: *Emily A. Hatteberg*
Associate marketing manager: *Dean Karampelas*
Senior project manager: *Bruce Gin*
Full service project manager: *Jackie Henry, Aptara, Inc.*
Senior production supervisor: *Debra R. Sylvester*
Design coordinator: *Joanne Mennemeier*
Senior media project manager: *Greg Bates*
Cover design: *JoAnne Schopler*
Cover Image: © *Corbis Images*
Typeface: *10.5/12 Times New Roman*
Compositor: *Aptara, Inc.*
Printer: *R.R Donnelley*

Library of Congress Cataloging-in-Publication Data

Wilson, Earl Ray, 1939-
Accounting for governmental and nonprofit entities / Earl R. Wilson, Jacqueline L. Reck, Susan C. Kattelus.—Fifteenth ed.
p. cm.
Includes index.
ISBN-13: 978-0-07-337960-9 (alk. paper)
ISBN-10: 0-07-337960-3 (alk. paper)
1. Finance, Public—Accounting. 2. Nonprofit organizations—Accounting. 3. Nonprofit organizations—United States—Accounting. I. Reck, Jacqueline L. II. Kattelus, Susan C. (Susan Convery) III. Title.
HJ9733.W48 2010
657'.825—dc22

2009000175

www.mhhe.com

About the Authors

In Memoriam: This edition is dedicated to the memory and long service of **Dr. Leon E. Hay** as an author of the third through twelfth editions of *Accounting for Governmental and Nonprofit Entities*. Dr. Hay was a nationally recognized leader and educator in the field of governmental and not-for-profit accounting.

Earl R. Wilson

Is Professor Emeritus of Accountancy at the University of Missouri—Columbia. He received his BA and MBA from Chapman University and his MA and PhD in Accountancy from the University of Missouri—Columbia. He is a certified public accountant (Missouri).

Professor Wilson has contributed substantially to standards setting in governmental accounting and auditing, having served as an academic fellow with the Governmental Accounting Standards Board (GASB) and as a member of the Governmental Accounting Standards Advisory Council, the U.S. Comptroller General's Advisory Council on Governmental Auditing Standards, the American Institute of CPAs Government Accounting and Auditing Committee, and as chair of the Missouri Society of CPAs (MSCPA) Government Accounting Committee and president of the American Accounting Association Government and Nonprofit (AAA-GNP) Section. In addition, he has served on several GASB task forces and conducted financial reporting research for the GASB.

Dr. Wilson has published numerous research articles in journals such as *The Accounting Review; Journal of Accounting Research; Contemporary Accounting Research; Journal of Accounting and Public Policy; Journal of Accounting, Auditing, and Finance; Research in Governmental and Nonprofit Accounting; Public Budgeting and Finance,* and others. Many of these articles are frequently cited as influential studies of the municipal bond market. He has been an author of this text since the ninth edition in 1992. He has extensive experience teaching governmental and nonprofit accounting, including online courses.

Professor Wilson has received a number of awards for his teaching and research, including the Enduring Lifetime Contribution Award from the AAA-GNP section, the 2003 Cornelius Tierney/Ernst & Young Research Award from the Association of Government Accountants, Outstanding Teacher of the Year for 2002 from the Kansas City MU Business Alumni Association, and the 2000 Outstanding Educator of the Year and 2008 Outstanding CPA in Government awards from the MSCPA. He has chaired or served as reader of more than 30 doctoral dissertations, many in the area of governmental accounting.

Jacqueline L. Reck

Is an associate professor and the James E. and C. Ellis Rooks Distinguished Professor in Accounting for the School of Accountancy at the University of South Florida. She received a BS degree from North Dakota State University, BS and MAcc degrees from the University of South Florida, and her PhD from the University of Missouri–Columbia. She is a certified public accountant (Florida).

Dr. Reck worked for state government for several years before joining academia. Currently, she is active in several professional associations. In addition to teaching governmental and not-for-profit accounting, Dr. Reck frequently presents continuing professional education workshops and sessions. She has provided workshops on governmental and not-for-profit accounting for local accounting firms and the state auditor general's staff. Dr. Reck has received several teaching and research awards, is currently the doctoral program coordinator for the School of Accountancy, and has chaired or served on several doctoral dissertation committees.

Dr. Reck has published articles in *The Journal of Accounting and Public Policy; Research in Governmental and Nonprofit Accounting; Journal of Public Budgeting, Accounting and Financial Management;* and the *Journal of Information Systems,* among others. She joined as an author on the 14th edition.

Susan C. Kattelus

Is Professor Emeritus of Accounting at Eastern Michigan University and currently a Professor of Practice at Michigan State University. She received her BBA and PhD from Michigan State University and MSA from Eastern Michigan University. Professor Kattelus is a certified public accountant (Michigan) and a certified government financial manager.

Professor Kattelus has served on the Governmental Accounting Standards Advisory Council as the academic representative of the American Accounting Association (AAA), president of the Government and Nonprofit Section of the AAA, and chair of the Nonprofit Task Force of the Michigan Association of CPAs. She teaches the public and nonprofit accounting course for accounting majors and the principles of managerial accounting course for business students.

Dr. Kattelus has published articles in *The Accounting Review; Research in Governmental and Nonprofit Accounting; Journal of Government Financial Management; Public Budgeting and Finance; Issues in Accounting Education; Journal of Accounting Education;* and *Journal of Public Budgeting, Accounting and Financial Management,* among others. She joined as an author on the 11th edition in 1999.

Preface

For almost 60 years, *Accounting for Governmental and Nonprofit Entities* has been the leader in the market. It is a comprehensive governmental and not-for-profit accounting text written for students who will be auditing and working in public and not-for-profit sector entities. Originally published in 1951 and written by Professor R. M. Mikesell, this book—and the several subsequent editions revised by Professor Leon E. Hay—has given generations of instructors and students a comprehensive knowledge of the specialized accounting and financial reporting practices of governmental and not-for-profit organizations, as well as an understanding of how those organizations can better meet the information needs of a diverse set of financial statement users and decision makers. The vision of these original authors continues to be reflected in this 15th edition, and their strategy of providing a large and innovative set of instructional support materials prepared and tested in the classroom by the authors continues to be a guiding principle today. The current author team brings to this edition their extensive experience teaching government and not-for-profit courses as well as insights gained from scholarly writing and professional activities. The result is a relevant and accurate text that includes the most effective instructional tools.

ORGANIZATION AND CONTENT

The 15th edition of *Accounting for Governmental and Nonprofit Entities* is separated into three parts: Part I covers state and local governments (Chapters 2 through 10), Part II focuses on accountability for public funds (Chapters 11 through 13), and Part III examines not-for-profit organizations (Chapters 14 through 17). Chapter 1 continues to form a broad foundation for the more detailed material in Chapters 2–17. The order of the chapters is similar to previous editions, but some topics and chapters have been rearranged to facilitate a variety of courses and formats used by adopters of the text. For example, a course focused on state and local governments may cover Chapter 1 and Parts I and II, while a course focused on not-for-profit organizations may cover Chapter 1 and Parts II and III. Part II is a bridge between the public and not-for-profit sectors that includes accountability topics (e.g., federal government, auditing, and budgeting) applicable to all types of entities that receive public funds.

KEY CHANGES IN THIS EDITION

As always, readers can count on this edition to include authoritative changes from the Financial Accounting Standards Board, Governmental Accounting Standards Board, Federal Accounting Standards Advisory Board, American Institute of Certified Public Accountants, Office of Management and Budget, Internal Revenue Service, and Government Accountability Office. Update bulletins will be provided periodically on the text Web site as new authoritative statements are issued.

Several significant changes have been made in this edition of the text. The sample financial statements have been moved to an appendix in Chapter 1 and the management's discussion and analysis (MD&A) has been moved to an appendix in Chapter 9 for easier reference. A new appendix on managing investments has been added to Chapter 8. In a slight reorganization of coverage, what was formerly Chapter 11, "Auditing of Governmental and Not-for-Profit Organizations," is now Chapter 12. This chapter also has been modified to increase its focus on generally accepted government auditing standards. In Chapter 13, more emphasis has been placed on performance given the unique nature of governments. In addition, an appendix on cost and budget issues in grant accounting has been added to Chapter 13. Illustrative financial statements for the American Heart Association and related discussion have been incorporated into Chapter 14.

In addition to these changes, all chapters have been updated to reflect changes in the areas of accounting and auditing affecting governments and not-for-profit entities. Based on comments received and the collective experience of the authors, some items in this edition have received increased attention (e.g., major funds and postemployment benefits). A most significant enhancement is that this edition now features a second computerized practice set, the City of Bingham, which is equally as comprehensive and effective as the widely used City of Smithville practice set. Both practice sets are now downloadable from the publisher's Web site (for more information, see inside the front cover of this text).

INNOVATIVE PEDAGOGY

For state and local government accounting, the authors have found that *dual-track* accounting is an effective approach in showing the juxtaposition of government-wide and fund financial statements in GASB's integrated model of basic financial statements. It allows students to see that each transaction has an effect on the fund financial statements (that are designed to show fiscal compliance with the annual budget), on the government-wide financial statements (that demonstrate accountability for operational performance of the government as a whole), or both. This approach better serves students who will design and use accounting information systems, such as enterprise systems, to allow information to be captured once and used for several purposes. Accounting for federal agencies as well as nongovernmental, not-for-profit entities closely parallels this approach as traditional fund accounting may be appropriate for keeping track of resources with restricted purposes, but citizens and donors also need to see the larger picture provided by the entity as a whole. The dual-track approach is further described inside the front cover of this text.

Governments may continue to prepare fund-based statements throughout the year and convert to accrual-based government-wide statements at the end of the year until they invest in information systems that can deliver real-time information for decision making. We want students to think beyond being transaction-bookkeepers and aspire to design and use the systems that will make government-wide financial information available when managers and citizens need it. The City of Bingham and City of Smithville Continuous Computerized Problems are teaching tools that develop these skills and perspective. The authors feel so strongly that this general ledger software tool helps students understand the material that we again provide it with the text. Students have enthusiastically told us that they like "learning by doing" and that these continuous computerized problems helped them to understand the concepts in the book.

TARGET AUDIENCE

The text continues to be best suited for senior and graduate accounting majors who plan to sit for the certified public accountant (CPA) exam and then audit governmental or not-for-profit entities. Public administration and other students who plan to provide financial management or consulting services to government and not-for-profit entities report that the text provides a more comprehensive set of competencies than traditional public budgeting texts. Students in not-for-profit management education programs find that the coverage of accounting, financial reporting, auditing, taxation, and information systems for both governmental and not-for-profit entities provides the exposure they need to work across disciplines and sectors. Finally, students preparing for the certified government financial manager (CGFM) exam will also find Chapters 1 through 12 useful for Examination 2. We encourage all students who use this book to consider the challenges and rewards of careers in public service—in federal, state, and local governments as well as not-for-profit organizations.

SUPPLEMENT PACKAGE

The following ancillary materials are prepared by the authors to ensure consistency and accuracy and are available on the Instructor's Resource CD-ROM and the textbook's Web site, *www.mhhe.com/wilson15e.*

- Instructor's Guide and Solutions Manual.
- PowerPoint lecture presentations.
- Test Bank (including a computerized version using E-Z Test software).
- The City of Bingham and City of Smithville Continuous Computerized Problems—general ledger practice sets, downloadable from the publisher's Web site.
- The City of Bingham and City of Smithville Instructor's Version software, providing guidance for instructors, solution data files, and solution page image (.pdf) files for all required financial statements, schedules, and reports.

Students can access the PowerPoint lecture presentations, flashcards of key terms, and multiple-choice practice quizzes for each chapter at the Online Learning Center on the text's Web site, *www.mhhe.com/wilson15e.*

Acknowledgments

We are thankful for the encouragement, suggestions, and counsel provided by many instructors, professionals, and students in writing this book. They include the following professionals and educators who read portions of this book and previous editions in various forms and provided valuable comments and suggestions:

Kelli A. Bennett
City and County of Denver
Dr. Barbara Chaney
University of Montana
Mr. Jeremy Craig
Chesterfield, Missouri
Ms. Rebecca Craig
St. Charles County, Missouri
Mr. Michael Crawford
Crawford & Associates
Ms. Mary Foelster
American Institute of Certified Public Accountants
Ms. Kristen Hockman
University of Missouri—Columbia
Ms. Marie Hunniecutt
Formerly, University of South Florida
Mr. Roger P. Murphy
Iowa State University, retired
Ms. Melanie Nelson
California State University—San Marcos
Dr. David O'Bryan
Pittsburgh State University
Dr. Suzanne M. Ogilby
California State University—Sacramento
Dr. James Patton
Federal Accounting Standards Advisory Board and University of Pittsburgh
Ms. Janet Prowse
University of Nevada, Las Vegas
Dr. Walter A. Robbins
University of Alabama
Ken Schermann
Governmental Accounting Standards Board
Dr. Mark Sutter
Las Cruces, New Mexico
Dr. Relmond P. Van Daniker
Association of Government Accountants
Mr. Jay Wahlund
Minot State University
Mr. James F. White
Harvard Extension School

We acknowledge permission to quote pronouncements and reproduce illustrations from the publications of the Governmental Accounting Standards Board, American Institute of Certified Public Accountants, International City/County Management Association, and Crawford and Associates. Dr. Wilson would like to give special thanks to his wife, Florence J. Wilson, for her patience, support, and understanding in completing this and several prior editions of the book. Dr. Reck dedicates the book in memory of her husband, Albert F. Hohenstein.

Although we are extremely careful in checking the text and end-of-chapter material, it is possible that errors and ambiguities remain in this edition. As readers encounter such, we urge them to let us know so that corrections can be made. We also invite every user of this edition who has suggestions or comments about the material in the chapters to share them with one of the authors, either by regular mail or e-mail. The authors will continue the service of issuing Update Bulletins to adopters of this text that describe changes after the book is in print. These bulletins can be downloaded from the text Web site at *www.mhhe.com/wilson15e* or any of the authors' Web sites:

Dr. Earl R. Wilson
School of Accountancy
University of Missouri—Columbia
303 Cornell
Columbia, MO 65211
wilsonea@missouri.edu
http://web.missouri.edu/~wilsonea

Dr. Jacqueline L. Reck
School of Accountancy
University of South Florida
4202 East Fowler Avenue, BSN 3403
Tampa, FL 33620
jreck@coba.usf.edu
http://www.coba.usf.edu/departments/accounting/faculty/reck

Dr. Susan C. Kattelus
Department of Accounting and Information Systems
Michigan State University
N235 Business College Complex
East Lansing, MI 48824
kattelus@msu.edu
http://www.msu.edu/~kattelus

Brief Contents

Table of Contents

PART THREE
Not-for-Profit Organizations 577

Chapter 14
Accounting for Not-for-Profit Organizations 579

Chapter 15
Not-for-Profit Organizations—Regulatory, Taxation, and Performance Issues 629

Chapter 16
Accounting for Colleges and Universities 661

Chapter One

Introduction to Accounting and Financial Reporting for Governmental and Not-for-Profit Entities

Learning Objectives

After studying this chapter, you should be able to:

1. Identify and explain the characteristics that distinguish governmental and not-for-profit entities from for-profit entities.
2. Identify the authoritative bodies responsible for setting financial reporting standards for (1) state and local governments, (2) the federal government, and (3) not-for-profit organizations.
3. Contrast and compare the objectives of financial reporting for (1) state and local governments, (2) the federal government, and (3) not-for-profit organizations.
4. Explain the minimum requirements for general purpose external financial reporting for state and local governments and how they relate to comprehensive annual financial reports.
5. Explain the different objectives, measurement focus, and basis of accounting of the government-wide financial statements and fund financial statements of state and local governments.

Welcome to the strange new world of accounting for governmental and not-for-profit organizations! Initially, you may find it challenging to understand the many new terms and concepts you will need to learn. Moreover, if you are like most readers, you will question at the outset why governmental and not-for-profit organizations find it necessary to use accounting practices that are very different from those used by for-profit entities.

As you read this first chapter of the text, the reasons for the marked differences between governmental and not-for-profit accounting and for-profit accounting should become apparent. Specifically, governmental and not-for-profit organizations serve entirely different purposes in society than do business entities. Furthermore, because such organizations are largely financed by taxpayers, donors, and others who do not expect benefits proportional to the resources they provide, management has a special duty to be accountable for how those resources are used in providing services. Thus, the need to report on management's accountability to citizens, creditors, oversight bodies, and others has played a central role in shaping the accounting and reporting practices of governmental and not-for-profit organizations.

This first chapter will give you a basic conceptual foundation for understanding the unique characteristics of these organizations and how their accounting and financial reporting concepts and practices differ from those of for-profit organizations. By the time you finish subsequent chapters assigned for your course, you should have an in-depth practical knowledge of governmental and not-for-profit accounting and financial reporting.

WHAT ARE GOVERNMENTAL AND NOT-FOR-PROFIT ORGANIZATIONS?

Governmental and not-for-profit organizations are vast in number and range of services provided. In the United States, governments exist at the federal, state, and local levels and serve a wide variety of functions. The most recent census of governments reports 89,476 local governmental units, in addition to the federal government and 50 state governments. These 89,476 local governments consist of 3,033 counties, 19,492 municipalities, 16,519 towns and townships, 13,051 independent school districts, and 37,381 special district governments that derive their power from state governments.[1]

States, counties, municipalities (for example, cities and villages), and townships are **general purpose governments**—governments that provide many categories of services to their residents (such as police and fire protection; sanitation; construction and maintenance of streets, roads, and bridges; and health and welfare). Independent school districts, public colleges and universities, and special districts are **special purpose governments**—governments that provide only a single function or a limited number of functions (such as education, drainage and flood control, irrigation, soil and water conservation, fire protection, and water supply). Special purpose governments have the power to levy and collect taxes and to raise revenues from other sources as provided by state laws to finance the services they provide.

Not-for-profit organizations also exist in many forms and serve many different functions. These include private colleges and universities, various kinds of health care organizations, certain libraries and museums, professional and trade associations, fraternal and social organizations, and religious organizations. Currently, there are nearly 2 million not-for-profit organizations in the U.S.[2]

[1] U.S. Department of Commerce, Bureau of the Census, *2007 Census of Governments,* vol. 1, no. 1 (Washington, DC: U.S. Government Printing Office), p. v.

[2] The Independent Sector and Urban Institute estimate that there are about 1.8 million organizations in the not-for-profit sector. (Urban Institute, *The New Nonprofit Almanac & Desk Reference,* Washington, D.C., 2007).

DISTINGUISHING CHARACTERISTICS OF GOVERNMENTAL AND NOT-FOR-PROFIT ENTITIES

Governmental and not-for-profit organizations differ in important ways from business organizations. Not surprisingly then, accounting and financial reporting for governmental and not-for-profit organizations are markedly different from accounting and financial reporting for businesses. An understanding of how these organizations differ from business organizations is essential to understanding the unique accounting and financial reporting principles that have evolved for governmental and not-for-profit organizations.

In its *Statement of Financial Accounting Concepts No. 4,* the **Financial Accounting Standards Board (FASB)** noted the following characteristics that it felt distinguished governmental and not-for-profit entities from business organizations:

a. Receipts of significant amounts of resources from resource providers who do not expect to receive either repayment or economic benefits proportionate to the resources provided.

b. Operating purposes that are other than to provide goods or services at a profit or profit equivalent.

c. Absence of defined ownership interests that can be sold, transferred, or redeemed, or that convey entitlement to a share of a residual distribution of resources in the event of liquidation of the organization.[3]

The **Governmental Accounting Standards Board (GASB)** distinguishes governmental entities in the United States from not-for-profit entities and from businesses by stressing that governments exist in an environment in which the power ultimately rests in the hands of the people. Voters delegate that power to public officials through the election process. The power is divided among the executive, legislative, and judicial branches of the government so that the actions, financial and otherwise, of governmental executives are constrained by legislative actions, and executive and legislative actions are subject to judicial review. Further constraints are imposed on state and local governments by the existence of the federal system in which higher levels of government encourage or dictate activities by lower levels and finance the activities (partially, at least) by an extensive system of intergovernmental grants and subsidies that require the lower levels to be accountable to the entity providing the resources, as well as to the citizenry. Revenues raised by each level of government come, ultimately, from taxpayers. Taxpayers are required to serve as providers of resources to governments even though they often have very little choice about which governmental services they receive and the extent to which they receive them.[4]

In the GASB's view, accounting and financial reporting standards for governments must be separate and distinct from those for business organizations because the needs of users of financial reports are unique and different. This view is clear from a recent

[3] Financial Accounting Standards Board, *Statement of Financial Accounting Concepts No. 4,* "Objectives of Financial Reporting by Nonbusiness Organizations" (Norwalk, CT, 1980), p. 3. In 1985 the FASB replaced the term *nonbusiness* with the term *not-for-profit.* Other organizations use the term *nonprofit* as a synonym for *not-for-profit.* The term *not-for-profit* is predominantly used in this text.

[4] Based on discussion in GASB *Concepts Statement No. 1,* pars. 14–18. Governmental Accounting Standards Board, *Codification of Governmental Accounting and Financial Reporting Standards as of June 30, 2008* (Norwalk, CT, 2008), Appendix B.

GASB white paper which notes that "governments do not operate in a competitive marketplace, face virtually no threat of liquidation, and do not have equity owners."[5] Consequently, governmental financial reporting focuses on a government's stewardship of public resources, ongoing ability to raise taxes and manage resources, and compliance with legal spending limits, rather than on information about earnings. More specifically, the white paper states:

> Governmental accounting and financial reporting standards aim to address [the] need for public accountability information by helping stakeholders assess how public resources are acquired and used, whether current resources were sufficient to meet current service costs or whether some costs were shifted to future taxpayers, and whether the government's ability to provide services improved or deteriorated from the previous year.[6]

SOURCES OF FINANCIAL REPORTING STANDARDS

Illustration 1–1 shows the primary sources of accounting and financial reporting standards for business and not-for-profit organizations, state and local governments, and the federal government. Specifically, the FASB sets standards for for-profit business organizations and nongovernmental not-for-profit organizations; the GASB sets standards for state and local governments, including governmental not-for-profit organizations; and the Federal Accounting Standards Advisory Board (FASAB) sets standards for the federal government and its agencies and departments.

Authority to establish accounting and reporting standards for not-for-profit organizations is split between the FASB and the GASB because a sizeable number of

ILLUSTRATION 1–1 Primary Sources of Accounting and Financial Reporting Standards for Businesses, Governments, and Not-for-Profit Organizations

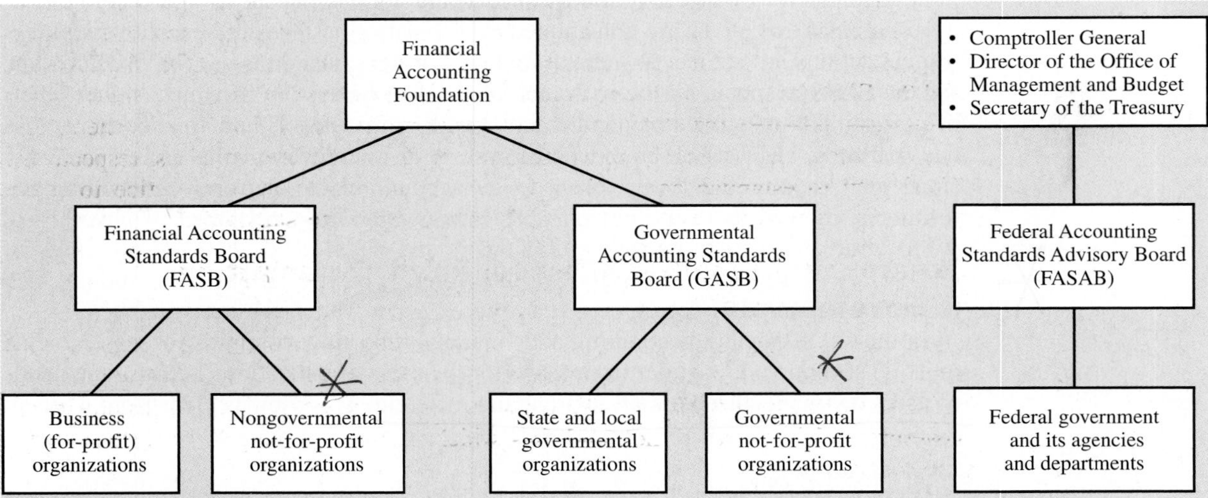

Source: *Statement on Auditing Standards (SAS) 69,* amended by *SAS 91,* April 2000, AICPA *Professional Standards,* as of June 1, 2008, v.1, Au Sec. 411.

[5] Governmental Accounting Standards Board, *White Paper "Why Governmental Accounting and Financial Reporting Is—and Should Be—Different"* (Norwalk, CT, 2006), Executive Summary, pp. 1–2.
[6] Ibid.

not-for-profit organizations are governmentally owned, particularly public colleges and universities and government hospitals. The FASB is responsible for setting accounting and reporting standards for the great majority of not-for-profit organizations, those that are independent of governments. Governmental not-for-profit organizations follow standards established by the GASB.

The GASB and the FASB are parallel bodies under the oversight of the Financial Accounting Foundation. The foundation appoints the members of the two boards and supports the boards' operations. The federal Sarbanes-Oxley Act greatly enhanced financial support for the FASB by mandating an assessed fee on corporate security offerings. The GASB, on the other hand, relies mainly on contributions from state and local government organizations and sales of publications for financial support of its operations.

Because of the breadth of support and the lack of ties to any single organization or governmental unit, the GASB and the FASB are referred to as "independent standards-setting boards in the private sector." Before the creation of the GASB and the FASB, financial reporting standards were set by groups sponsored by professional organizations: The forerunners of the GASB (formed in 1984) were the National Council on Governmental Accounting (1973–84), the National Committee on Governmental Accounting (1948–73), and the National Committee on Municipal Accounting (1934–41). The forerunners of the FASB (formed in 1973) were the Accounting Principles Board (1959–73) and the Committee on Accounting Procedure (1938–59) of the American Institute of Certified Public Accountants.

Federal statutes assign responsibility for establishing and maintaining a sound financial structure for the federal government to three officials: the Comptroller General, the Director of the Office of Management and Budget, and the Secretary of the Treasury. In 1990, these three officials created the **Federal Accounting Standards Advisory Board (FASAB)** to recommend accounting principles and standards for the federal government and its agencies. It is understood that, to the maximum extent possible, federal accounting and financial reporting standards should be consistent with those established by the GASB and, where applicable, by the FASB.

In Rule 203 of its Code of Professional Conduct, the American Institute of Certified Public Accountants (AICPA) has formally designated the GASB, the FASAB, and the FASB as the authoritative bodies to establish **generally accepted accounting principles (GAAP)** for state and local governments, the federal government, and business organizations and nongovernmental not-for-profit organizations, respectively. "Authority to establish accounting principles" is interpreted in practice to mean "authority to establish accounting and financial reporting standards."[7]

Determining Whether a Not-for-Profit Organization Is Governmental

Illustration 1–1 suggests that the kinds of organizations for which the FASB and GASB are responsible for setting standards are clearcut. Unfortunately, this is sometimes not the case. In practice, it may be difficult to determine whether some not-for-profits are governmental in nature or not, and thus which standards-setting body to look to for authoritative guidance.

[7] *Statement on Auditing Standards (SAS) 69,* as amended by *SAS 91*, April 2000, specifically establishes the FASB, the GASB, and the FASAB as the bodies to establish GAAP for their respective organizations. Other literature, such as AICPA Audit and Accounting Guides, are afforded secondary status as sources of authoritative guidance. These sources are discussed more fully in the "GAAP Hierarchy" section of Chapter 12.

The U.S. Bureau of the Census defines a *government* as:

> An organized entity which, in addition to having governmental character, has sufficient discretion in the management of its own affairs to distinguish it as separate from the administrative structure of any other governmental unit.[8]

This definition, though helpful, provides insufficient guidance because it fails to explain the meaning of "having governmental character." In order to provide additional guidance for auditors on this issue, two audit and accounting guides of the AICPA, with the tacit approval of both the FASB and the GASB, state:

> Public corporations and bodies corporate and politic are governmental organizations. Other organizations are governmental organizations if they have one or more of the following characteristics:
>
> *a.* Popular election of officers or appointment (or approval) of a controlling majority of the members of the organization's governing body by officials of one or more state or local governments,
>
> *b.* the potential for unilateral dissolution by a government with the net assets reverting to a government, or
>
> *c.* the power to enact *and* enforce a tax levy.[9]

Furthermore, organizations are presumed to be governmental if they have the ability to issue directly (rather than through a state or municipal authority) debt that pays interest exempt from federal taxation. However, organizations possessing only that ability (to issue tax-exempt debt) and none of the other governmental characteristics may rebut the presumption that they are governmental if their determination is supported by compelling, relevant evidence. Colleges and universities, hospitals, museums, and social service agencies are examples of organizations that may be either governmental or nongovernmental.

OBJECTIVES OF FINANCIAL REPORTING

GASB *Concepts Statement No. 1,* "Objectives of Financial Reporting," states that "**Accountability** is the cornerstone of all financial reporting in government. . . . Accountability requires governments to answer to the citizenry—to justify the raising of public resources and the purposes for which they are used."[10] The board elaborated:

> Governmental accountability is based on the belief that the citizenry has a "right to know," a right to receive openly declared facts that may lead to public debate by the citizens and their elected representatives. Financial reporting plays a major role in fulfilling government's duty to be publicly accountable in a democratic society.[11]

Illustration 1–2 shows several ways that state and local governmental financial reporting is used in making economic, social, and political decisions and assessing accountability. Closely related to the concept of accountability as the cornerstone of

[8] U.S. Department of Commerce, Bureau of the Census, *2007 Census of Governments,* p. ix.

[9] American Institute of Certified Public Accountants, Audit and Accounting Guide, *Health Care Organizations* (New York, 2007), par. 1.02c; and American Institute of Certified Public Accountants, Audit and Accounting Guide, *Not-for-Profit Organizations* (New York, 2008), par. 1.03.

[10] GASB, *Codification,* Appendix B, *Concepts Statement No. 1,* par. 56.

[11] Ibid.

ILLUSTRATION 1–2 Comparison of Financial Reporting Objectives—State and Local Governments, Federal Government, and Not-for-Profit Organizations

State and Local Governments[a]	Federal Government[b]	Not-for-Profit Organizations[c]
Financial reporting is used in making economic, social, and political decisions and in assessing accountability primarily by: • Comparing actual financial results with the legally adopted budget. • Assessing financial condition and results of operations. • Assisting in determining compliance with finance-related laws, rules, and regulations. • Assisting in evaluating efficiency and effectiveness.	Financial reporting should help to achieve accountability and is intended to assist report users in evaluating: • Budgetary integrity. • Operating performance. • Stewardship. • Adequacy of systems and controls.	Financial reporting should provide information useful in: • Making resource allocation decisions. • Assessing services and ability to provide services. • Assessing management stewardship and performance. • Assessing economic resources, obligations, net resources, and changes in them.

[a]Source: *GASB Concepts Statement No. 1,* par. 32.
[b]Source: *FASAB Statement of Federal Accounting Concepts No. 1,* par. 134.
[c]Source: *FASB Concepts Statement No. 4,* pp. 19–23.

governmental financial reporting is the concept the GASB refers to as **interperiod equity.** The concept and its importance are explained as follows:

> The Board believes that interperiod equity is a significant part of accountability and is fundamental to public administration. It therefore needs to be considered when establishing financial reporting objectives. In short, *financial reporting should help users assess whether current-year revenues are sufficient to pay for services provided that year and whether future taxpayers will be required to assume burdens for services previously provided.* (Emphasis added.)[12]

Accountability is also the foundation for the financial reporting objectives the FASAB has established for the federal government. The FASAB's *Statement of Accounting and Reporting Concepts Statement No. 1* identifies four objectives of federal financial reporting (see Illustration 1–2) focused on evaluating budgetary integrity, operating performance, stewardship, and adequacy of systems and controls.

Unlike the FASB and the GASB, which focus their standards on *external* financial reporting, the FASAB and its sponsors in the federal government are concerned with *both* internal and external financial reporting. Accordingly, the FASAB has identified four major groups of users of federal financial reports: citizens, Congress, executives, and program managers. Given the broad role the FASAB has been assigned, its standards focus on cost accounting and service efforts and accomplishment measures, as well as on financial accounting and reporting.

Financial reports of not-for-profit organizations—voluntary health and welfare organizations, private colleges and universities, private health care institutions, religious organizations, and others—have similar uses. However, as Illustration 1–2 shows, the reporting objectives for not-for-profit organizations emphasize decision usefulness over financial accountability needs, presumably reflecting the fact that the financial operations of not-for-profit organizations—as compared to those of governments—are generally subject to less detailed legal restrictions.

[12] Ibid., par. 61.

Note that the objectives of financial reporting for governments and not-for-profit entities stress the need for the public to understand and evaluate the financial activities and management of these organizations. Readers will recognize the impact on their lives, and on their bank accounts, of the activities of the layers of government they are obligated to support and of the not-for-profit organizations they voluntarily support. Since each of us is significantly affected, it is important that we be able to read intelligently the financial reports of governmental and not-for-profit entities. In order to make informed decisions as citizens, taxpayers, creditors, and donors, readers should make the effort to learn the accounting and financial reporting standards developed by the authoritative bodies. The standards are further explained and illustrated throughout the remainder of the text.

FINANCIAL REPORTING OF STATE AND LOCAL GOVERNMENTS

Like the FASB, the GASB continues to develop concepts statements that communicate the framework within which the Board strives to establish consistent financial reporting standards for entities within its jurisdiction. The GASB, as well as the FASB, is concerned with establishing standards for financial reporting to *external* users—those who lack the authority to prescribe the information they want and who must rely on the information management communicates to them. The Board does not intend to set standards for reporting to managers and administrators or others deemed to have the ability to enforce their demands for information.

Illustration 1–3 displays the minimum requirements for general purpose external financial reporting under the governmental financial reporting model specified by GASB *Statement No. 34 (GASBS 34).*[13] Central to the model is the **management's discussion and analysis (MD&A).** The MD&A is **required supplementary information (RSI)** designed to communicate in narrative, easily readable form the purpose of the basic financial statements and the government's current financial position and results of financial activities compared with those of the prior year.

As shown in Illustration 1–3, *GASBS 34* prescribes two categories of **basic financial statements,** government-wide and fund. **Government-wide financial statements** are intended to provide an aggregated overview of a government's net assets and changes in net assets. The government-wide financial statements report on the government as a whole and assist in assessing **operational accountability**—whether the government has used its resources efficiently and effectively in meeting operating objectives. The GASB concluded that reporting on operational accountability is best achieved by using essentially the same basis of accounting and measurement focus used by business organizations: the accrual basis and flow of economic resources measurement focus.

Fund financial statements, the other category of basic financial statements, assist in assessing whether the government has raised and spent financial resources in accordance with budget plans and in compliance with pertinent laws and regulations. Certain funds, referred to as *governmental funds,* focus on the short-term flow of current financial resources or **fiscal accountability,** rather than on the flow of economic resources.[14] Other funds, referred to as *proprietary* and *fiduciary funds,*

[13] GASB *Statement No. 34,* "Basic Financial Statements—and Management's Discussion and Analysis—for State and Local Governments" (Norwalk, CT, 1999). Hereafter, *Statement No. 34* is abbreviated as *GASBS 34.*

[14] The definition of *fund* is given in Chapter 2. For now, you can view a fund as a separate set of accounts used to account for resources segregated for particular purposes.

ILLUSTRATION 1–3 Minimum Requirements for General Purpose External Financial Reporting—GASB *Statement No. 34* Reporting Model

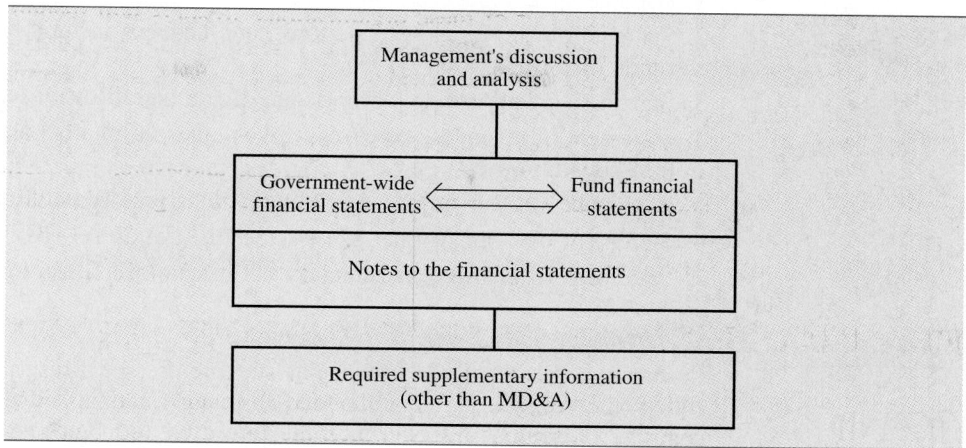

Source: GASB *Codification*, Sec. 2200.103.

account for the business-type and certain fiduciary activities of the government. These funds follow accounting and reporting principles similar to those of business organizations, although a number of GASB standards applicable to these funds differ substantially from FASB standards applicable to business organizations. These differences will be discussed in later chapters.

As shown in Illustration 1–3, the notes to the financial statements are considered integral to the financial statements. In addition, governments are required to disclose certain RSI other than MD&A. These additional information disclosures are discussed in several of the following chapters.

Illustrative Financial Statements—City and County of Denver

As mentioned at the beginning of this chapter, governmental financial reporting has evolved to meet the unique needs of citizens and other financial statement users. It should not be surprising that these financial statements are quite different from those prepared by business organizations. Real-world examples of local government financial statements—the basic financial statements of the combined City and County government of Denver, Colorado—are provided as Illustrations A1–1 through A1–11 in the appendix to this chapter. These statements should be referred to frequently while studying Chapters 1 through 9 of the text.[15] Denver's basic financial statements are those specified by *GASBS 34* and consist of:

Government-wide Financial Statements

1. Statement of net assets (see Illustration A1–1).
2. Statement of activities (see Illustration A1–2).

[15] The City and County of Denver's financial statements provided in Chapter 1, and various required and other supplementary information that are presented in later chapters, are intended for illustrative educational purposes only. Omitted in this text are the auditor's report on the financial statements, the notes to the financial statements, and other required supplementary information. Moreover, depending on the time since this text was released, more current financial statements may be available. Those who have a need for financial information for credit analysis or other evaluative or decision purposes should refer to the City and County of Denver's audited financial statements in the comprehensive annual financial report.

Fund Financial Statements

1. Balance sheet—governmental funds (see Illustration A1–3).
2. Statement of revenues, expenditures, and changes in fund balances—governmental funds (see Illustration A1–5).
3. Statement of net assets—proprietary funds (see Illustration A1–7).
4. Statement of revenues, expenses, and changes in fund net assets—proprietary funds (see Illustration A1–8).
5. Statement of cash flows—proprietary funds (see Illustration A1–9).
6. Statement of fiduciary net assets (see Illustration A1–10).
7. Statement of changes in fiduciary net assets (see Illustration A1–11).

Government-wide Financial Statements

Denver's government-wide financial statements (see Illustrations A1–1 and A1–2) follow the *GASBS 34* recommended formats; financial information is presented in separate columns for governmental activities and business-type activities of the primary government and its discretely presented component units (i.e., legally separate organizations for which the City and County of Denver is deemed financially accountable). Governmental and business-type activities are discussed in Chapter 2. Essentially, governmental activities encompass the executive, legislative, and judicial functions of the government as well as major service functions such as public safety, public works, parks and recreation, health and human services, and cultural activities. Business-type activities are largely self-supporting activities of a government that provide services to the public for a fee. Typical examples are electric, sewer, and water utilities; transportation systems; airports; toll roads and bridges; and parking facilities.

Because the financial statements display information in multiple columns, they are not fully consolidated in the manner of corporate financial statements. Receivables and payables between activities reported in the same activities column or between component units are eliminated in preparing the financial statements. However, receivables/payables between activities reported in different columns are not eliminated. For example, Denver's statement of net assets shows a receivable of $23,625 under the line item *internal balances* in the Governmental Activities column with an equal contra-asset (payable) in the Business-type Activities column. These two amounts represent the *net* receivables and payables between these two activity categories.

As mentioned earlier and discussed more fully in Chapter 2, the two government-wide financial statements are intended to report on the government's *operational accountability.* As such, the government-wide financial statements are prepared using essentially the same basis of accounting and measurement focus that are used in business accounting—that is, the accrual basis of accounting and measurement of total economic resources.

Fund Financial Statements

By contrast, governmental fund financial statements (see Illustrations A1–3 and A1–5) report on *fiscal accountability.* Therefore, these statements report only information that is useful in assessing whether financial resources were raised and expended in compliance with budgetary and other legal provisions. Thus, governmental fund statements focus on the flow of current financial resources—cash and near-cash resources that are available for expenditure. Since long-term obligations do not have to be paid in the current budgetary period, nor do noncurrent assets such as land, buildings, and equipment provide resources to pay current period obligations, neither is reported in the governmental funds. Both are reported in the Governmental Activities column of the government-wide statement of net assets, however, as shown in Illustration A1–1.

Modified accrual is the basis of accounting that has evolved for governmental funds. Under this basis, revenues are recorded only if they are measurable and available for paying current period obligations. Expenditures are generally recognized when incurred. As shown in Illustration A1–5, the governmental fund statement of revenues, expenditures, and changes in fund balances reports expenditures, since outlays to acquire goods or services are more relevant than expenses in measuring the outflow of current financial resources. Expenses, however, are more relevant at the government-wide level, as they measure the cost of services provided. Consequently, expenses, classified by program or function, are reported for both governmental and business-type activities, as shown in Denver's statement of activities (see Illustration A1–2).

Illustration 1–4 summarizes key aspects of the dual roles that governmental financial statements serve. Readers may be confused by the fact that the same underlying financial information for governmental activities is reported in two different ways: (1) using accrual basis accounting with an economic resources measurement focus in the government-wide financial statements and (2) using modified accrual basis accounting with a current financial resources focus in the fund statements. To ensure integration of these statements, GASB standards require that the total fund balances reported on the balance sheet—governmental funds (Illustration A1–3) be reconciled to total governmental activities net assets reported in the statement of net assets (Illustration A1–1). The reconciliation can be displayed on the face of the balance sheet—governmental funds or, as Denver has done, separately as a stand-alone schedule (see Illustration A1–4). Similarly, GASB requires that operating (change) statement results be reconciled for governmental activities. Accordingly, Denver presents a reconciliation (see Illustration A1–6) of the net changes in fund balances—total governmental funds reported on its statement of revenues, expenditures, and changes in fund balances—governmental

ILLUSTRATION 1–4 Dual Roles of Governmental Financial Statements in Assessing Accountability

	Operational Accountability	Fiscal Accountability
Statements	Government-wide financial statements (governmental and business-type activities) and those of proprietary funds and fiduciary funds	Governmental fund financial statements
Measurement focus	Flow of economic resources	Flow of current financial resources
Basis of accounting	Accrual basis (revenues and *expenses* are recognized when exchange of economic resources occurs or per GASB recognition rules for nonexchange transactions, such as taxes, contributions, and grants)	Modified accrual basis (revenues are recognized when resources are measurable and available for current spending; *expenditures* are recognized when an obligation to spend current financial resources is incurred)

funds (Illustration A1–5) to the change in net assets of governmental activities reported on its statement of activities (Illustration A1–2). For now, it is sufficient to just be aware that such reconciliations are required; you will learn to prepare reconciliations later in the text.

Proprietary fund financial statements present financial information for enterprise funds and internal service funds. Both types of funds operate essentially as self-supporting entities and, therefore, follow accounting and reporting practices similar to those of business organizations. Enterprise funds and internal service funds are distinguished primarily by the kinds of customers they serve. Enterprise funds provide goods or services to the public, whereas internal service funds mainly serve departments of the same government. For most governments, the information reported in the Business-type Activities column of the government-wide statements is simply the total of all enterprise funds information. Because internal service funds predominantly serve governmental activities, financial information for internal service funds is typically reported in the Governmental Activities column at the government-wide level.

As required by GASB standards, the City and County of Denver reports proprietary funds financial information in three financial statements: a statement of net assets—proprietary funds (Illustration A1–7), a statement of revenues, expenses, and changes in fund net assets—proprietary funds (Illustration A1–8), and a statement of cash flows—proprietary funds (Illustration A1–9). An astute reader will note that these are very similar to the three financial statements required for business organizations, although there are important differences, as will be discussed in later chapters.

The final two required financial statements are those for the fiduciary funds. By definition, fiduciary funds account for resources that the government is holding or managing for an external party, that is, an individual, organization, or other government. Because these resources may not be used to support the government's own programs, GASB standards require that financial information about fiduciary activities be omitted from the government-wide financial statements; however, the information must be reported in two fund financial statements: a statement of fiduciary net assets—fiduciary funds and a statement of changes in fiduciary net assets—fiduciary funds. Both statements are prepared using accrual accounting with the economic resources measurement focus. These two statements for the City and County of Denver are presented in Illustrations A1–10 and A1–11.

Major Funds

Both governmental funds and proprietary funds financial statements must provide separate columns for each **major fund** (see Chapter 2 for the definition of a major fund). The aggregate of nonmajor governmental and enterprise funds is reported in a single column of the corresponding statements. In addition to the General Fund, which is always considered a major fund, Denver identifies its Human Services and Bond Projects funds as major governmental funds (Illustration A1–3) and its Wastewater Management and Denver Airport System funds as major enterprise funds (Illustration A1–7). Major fund reporting is not applicable to internal service funds or fiduciary funds.

Reporting by major fund meets the information needs of citizens and other report users having a specific interest in the financial condition and operations of a particular fund. To meet the needs of individuals having an interest in particular *nonmajor* funds, governments should provide separate combining financial statements for nonmajor governmental and proprietary funds, as well as for discretely presented component units.

Comprehensive Annual Financial Report

Serious users of governmental financial information need more detail than is found in the MD&A, basic financial statements, and RSI (other than MD&A). For state and local governments, much of that detail is found in the governmental reporting entity's **comprehensive annual financial report (CAFR).** Although governments are not required to prepare a CAFR, most do so as a matter of public record and to provide additional financial details beyond the minimum requirements shown in Illustration 1–3. As such, the GASB provides standards for the content of a CAFR in its annually updated publication *Codification of Governmental Accounting and Financial Reporting Standards.* A CAFR prepared in conformity with these standards should contain the following sections.[16]

Introductory Section[17]

The introductory section typically includes items such as a title page and contents page, a letter of transmittal, a description of the government, and other items deemed appropriate by management. The letter of transmittal may be literally that—a letter from the chief financial officer addressed to the chief executive and governing body of the government—or it may be a narrative over the signature of the chief executive. In either event, the letter or narrative material should cite legal and policy requirements for the report.

Financial Section

The financial section of a comprehensive annual financial report should include (1) an auditor's report, (2) management's discussion and analysis (MD&A), (3) basic financial statements, (4) required supplementary information (other than MD&A), and (5) other supplementary information, such as combining statements and individual fund statements and schedules. Items (2), (3), and (4) represent the minimum requirements for general purpose external financial reporting, as depicted in Illustration 1–3. So, it should be apparent that a CAFR provides additional supplementary financial information beyond the minimum amount required by generally accepted accounting principles.

Laws regarding the audit of governments vary from state to state. Some states have laws requiring that all state agencies and all local governments be audited by an audit agency of the state government. In other states, local governments are audited by independent public accounting firms. In still other states, some local governments are audited by the state audit agency and some by independent public accounting firms. In any event, the auditor's opinion should accompany the financial statements reproduced in the report.

[16] GASB, *Codification,* Sec. 2200.104–193.

[17] For a view of the introductory section, as well as the other sections of the CAFR, you may wish to look at the City and County of Denver, Colorado's CAFR at *http://www.denvergov.org/controller/.* Click on "Financial Reports." Portions of Denver's CAFR for 2007 are included for illustrative purposes in various places in this text.

The financial section should contain sufficient information to disclose fully and present fairly the financial position and results of financial operations during the fiscal year. Laws of higher jurisdictions, actions of the legislative branch of the government itself, and agreements with creditors and others impose constraints over governments' financial activities and create unique financial accountability requirements.

Statistical Section

In addition to the introductory and financial sections of the CAFR, which were just described, a CAFR should contain a statistical section. The statistical section typically presents tables and charts showing demographic and economic data, financial trends, fiscal capacity, and operating information of the government in the detail needed by readers who are more than casually interested in the activities of the government. The GASB *Codification* suggests the content of the statistical tables usually considered necessary for inclusion in a CAFR. The statistical section is discussed at greater length in Chapter 9 of this text.

EXPANDING THE SCOPE OF ACCOUNTABILITY REPORTING

Some governments publish highly condensed popular reports. These reports usually contain selected data from the audited financial statements, statistical data, graphic displays, and narrative explanations, but the reports themselves are not audited. In addition, many state and local governments have begun to identify and report nonfinancial performance measures. For more than a decade, the GASB has encouraged state and local governments to experiment with reporting **service efforts and accomplishments (SEA)** measures to provide more complete information about a governmental entity's performance than can be provided by basic financial statements, budgetary comparison statements, and schedules. Indicators of service efforts include inputs of nonmonetary resources as well as inputs of dollars. Indicators of service accomplishments include both outputs and outcomes; outputs are quantitative measures of work done, such as the number of juvenile cases handled, and outcomes are the impacts of outputs on program objectives, such as a reduction in the high school dropout rate or incidence of juvenile crime. Chapter 13 provides additional discussion of SEA measures.

OVERVIEW OF CHAPTERS 2 THROUGH 17

GASB Principles, Standards, and Financial Reporting

Part 1 of the text (Chapters 2–10) focuses on state and local governments. The principles that underlie GASB accounting and reporting standards are presented in Chapter 2. Chapters 3 through 8 provide detailed illustrations of the effect of financial transactions on the funds and government-wide statements. Financial reporting for state and local governments, as seen in the City and County of Denver, Colorado's statements presented in the appendix to this chapter, is described in detail in Chapter 9. Analysis of the financial performance of state and local governments based on financial and other information is described in Chapter 10.

Accountability for Public Funds

Part II of the text includes three chapters that describe ways that public financial managers provide accountability over funds entrusted to them. Chapter 11 focuses on the federal government, the largest provider of public funds, and introduces federal offices that interact with state and local governments and not-for-profit organizations in a variety of ways; for example, the Government Accountability Office (GAO) and the Office of Management and Budget (OMB). Auditing techniques designed to assure the public that funds are properly accounted for and spent efficiently and effectively are described in Chapter 12, with special attention devoted to areas of auditing that are unique to federal funds, such as single audits. Chapter 13 covers tools important to managers in demonstrating accountability for funds, such as budgeting, costing, and performance measurement.

Not-for-Profit Organizations

Part III is a set of four chapters covering the unique accounting and financial reporting issues facing entities in the not-for-profit sector. Chapter 14 provides detailed illustrations of the effect of financial transactions on the financial statements of not-for-profit organizations, much like Chapter 3 through 8 does for state and local governments. The governance and regulatory issues that a not-for-profit organization faces from the time of its incorporation through merger or dissolution, if any, are presented in Chapter 15. Chapters 16 and 17 present industry-specific accounting and financial reporting requirements for colleges and universities and health care organizations, respectively.

A CAVEAT

The first edition of this text was written by the late Professor R. M. Mikesell more than 55 years ago in 1951. Some words of his bear thoughtful rereading from time to time by teachers and students in all fields, not just those concerned with accounting and financial reporting for governmental and not-for-profit entities:

> Even when developed to the ultimate stage of perfection, governmental accounting cannot become a guaranty of good government. At best, it can never be more than a valuable tool for promotion of sound financial management. It does not offer a panacea for all the ills that beset representative government; nor will it fully overcome the influence of disinterested, uninformed citizens. It cannot be substituted for honesty and moral integrity on the part of public officials; it can help in resisting but cannot eliminate the demands of selfish interests, whether in the form of individual citizens, corporations, or the pressure groups which always abound to influence government at all levels.[18]

Appendix

Illustrative Financial Statements—City and County of Denver

[18] R. M. Mikesell, *Governmental Accounting,* rev. ed., Homewood, IL: Richard D. Irwin, 1956, p. 10.

ILLUSTRATION A1–1

CITY AND COUNTY OF DENVER
Statement of Net Assets
December 31, 2007 (amounts expressed in thousands)

	Primary Government			
	Governmental Activities	**Business-type Activities**	**Total**	**Component Units**
Assets				
Cash on hand	$ 4,456	$ —	$ 4,456	$ 54
Cash and cash equivalents	442,398	160,778	603,176	52,329
Investments	—	302,979	302,979	210,759
Receivables (net of allowances):				
Taxes	300,772	—	300,772	7,414
Special assessments	956	—	956	—
Notes	80,571	—	80,571	—
Accounts	33,839	51,467	85,306	29,687
Accrued interest	2,711	5,830	8,541	61
Other	—	—	—	38,673
Due from other governments	48,853	—	48,853	—
Internal balances	23,625	(23,625)	—	—
Inventories	2,107	6,793	8,900	7,176
Prepaid items and other assets	575	427	1,002	6,404
Restricted assets:				
Cash and cash equivalents	57,423	333,494	390,917	10,087
Investments	—	759,381	759,381	123,462
Accrued interest	—	1,092	1,092	—
Other receivables	—	18,361	18,361	—
Prepaid items	—	3,108	3,108	—
Net assets held by third party	—	—	—	200,780
Capital assets:				
Land and construction in progress	348,010	561,324	909,334	340,109
Buildings, improvements, infrastructure, collections, and equipment, net of accumulated depreciation	1,858,521	3,399,042	5,257,563	1,594,557
Long-term receivables (net of allowances)	25,916	—	25,916	24,135
Bond issue cost and other assets (net of accumulated amortization)	3,850	60,142	63,992	21,104
Assets held for disposition	6,327	14,094	20,421	—
Total Assets	3,240,910	5,654,687	8,895,597	2,666,791
Liabilities				
Vouchers payable	62,405	38,287	100,692	28,450
Accrued liabilities	28,387	45,147	73,534	24,120
Deferred revenue	247,122	37,533	284,655	10,299
Advances	3,840	7,212	11,052	859
Due to taxing unit	480	—	480	—
Due to other governments	—	—	—	2,768
Liabilities payable from restricted assets	—	84,841	84,841	—
Noncurrent liabilities:				
Due within one year	112,179	120,141	232,320	41,445
Due in more than one year	1,226,795	3,938,069	5,164,864	1,147,764
Total Liabilities	1,681,208	4,271,230	5,952,438	1,255,705
Net Assets				
Invested in capital assets, net of related debt	1,170,496	317,488	1,487,984	1,156,289
Restricted for:				
Capital projects	146,735	21,189	167,924	84,785
Emergency use	31,240	—	31,240	210
Debt service	80,008	657,498	737,506	29,575
Donor restrictions:				
Expendable	9,347	—	9,347	112,742
Nonexpendable	3,387	—	3,387	103,913
Other purposes	3,442	—	3,442	—
Unrestricted	115,047	387,282	502,329	(76,428)
Total Net Assets	$1,559,702	$1,383,457	$2,943,159	$1,411,086

ILLUSTRATION A1–2

CITY AND COUNTY OF DENVER
Statement of Activities
For the year ended December 31, 2007 (amounts expressed in thousands)

		Program Revenues			Net (Expense) Revenue and Change in Net Assets			
					Primary Government			
Functions/Programs	Expenses	Charges for Services	Operating Grants and Contributions	Capital Grants and Contributions	Governmental Activities	Business-type Activities	Total	Component Units
Primary Government								
Governmental Activities:								
General government	$ 262,209	$ 51,541	$ 18,578	$ 25	$(192,065)	$ —	$(192,065)	$ —
Public safety	475,728	64,802	29,266	—	(381,660)	—	(381,660)	—
Public works	79,496	39,439	32,333	9,207	1,483	—	1,483	—
Human services	132,535	1,407	82,879	—	(48,249)	—	(48,249)	—
Health	45,345	707	7,333	—	(37,305)	—	(37,305)	—
Parks and recreation	63,778	4,803	1,341	8,839	(48,795)	—	(48,795)	—
Cultural activities	89,967	16,238	2,912	7,880	(62,937)	—	(62,937)	—
Community development	47,098	23,202	26,151	65	2,320	—	2,320	—
Economic opportunity	26,280	14,889	10,787	—	(604)	—	(604)	—
Interest on long-term debt	54,592	—	—	—	(54,592)	—	(54,592)	—
Total Governmental Activities	1,277,028	217,028	211,580	26,016	(822,404)	—	(822,404)	—
Business-type Activities:								
Wastewater management	76,298	75,750	—	9,906	—	9,358	9,358	—
Denver airport system	679,022	530,151	97,515	2,426	—	(48,930)	(48,930)	—
Environmental services	12,319	8,616	—	—	—	(3,703)	(3,703)	—
Golf course	6,570	8,157	—	—	—	1,587	1,587	—
Total Business-type Activities	774,209	622,674	97,515	12,332	—	(41,688)	(41,688)	—
Total Primary Government	$2,051,237	$839,702	$309,095	$38,348	(822,404)	(41,688)	(864,092)	
Component Units	$ 433,618	$306,353	$ 64,741	$ —				(62,524)
		General revenues:						
		Taxes:						
		Facilities development admissions			10,092	—	10,092	—
		Lodgers			49,651	—	49,651	—
		Motor vehicle ownership fee			16,963	—	16,963	—
		Occupational privilege			42,751	—	42,751	—
		Property			227,188	—	227,188	2,334
		Sales			455,436	—	455,436	—
		Public service			20,578	—	20,578	—
		Specific ownership			1,434	—	1,434	83,949
		Telephone			9,918	—	9,918	—
		Investment and interest income			39,990	87,885	127,875	20,769
		Convention center revenue			13,930	—	13,930	—
		Other revenues			26,379	33	26,412	36,879
		Transfers			2,261	(2,261)	—	—
		Total General Revenues and Transfers			916,571	85,657	1,002,228	143,931
		Change in net assets			94,167	43,969	138,136	81,407
		Net assets—January 1, as previously reported			1,465,535	1,201,635	2,667,170	1,329,679
		Restatement for correction of error			—	137,853	137,853	—
		Net assets—January 1, as restated				1,339,488	—	—
		Net assets—December 31			$1,559,702	$1,383,457	$2,943,159	$1,411,086

ILLUSTRATION A1–3

CITY AND COUNTY OF DENVER
Balance Sheet
Governmental Funds
December 31, 2007
(amounts expressed in thousands)

	General Fund	Human Services	Bond Projects	Other Governmental Funds	Total Governmental Funds
Assets					
Cash on hand	$ 2	$ 398	$ —	$ 4,056	$ 4,456
Cash and cash equivalents	94,691	11,040	143,059	171,337	420,127
Receivables (net of allowances of $71,799)					
Taxes	113,616	46,336	—	140,820	300,772
Special assessments	—	—	—	956	956
Notes	25	—	—	80,546	80,571
Accounts	14,292	18,951	—	26,004	59,247
Accrued interest	1,111	—	634	878	2,623
Interfund receivable	30,977	56	—	4,311	35,344
Due from other governments	289	4,728	—	43,836	48,853
Prepaid items and other assets	—	—	—	575	575
Restricted assets:					
Cash and cash equivalents	40,817	2,044	—	14,548	57,409
Assets held for disposition	—	—	—	6,327	6,327
Total Assets	$295,820	$83,553	$143,693	$494,194	$1,017,260
Liabilities and Fund Balances					
Liabilities:					
Vouchers payable	$13,576	$8,271	$ 10,017	$29,645	$61,509
Accrued liabilities	12,168	1,354	—	748	14,270
Due to taxing units	2	134	—	344	480
Interfund payable	2,774	5,693	395	4,641	13,503
Deferred revenue	71,706	46,702	—	154,764	273,172
Advances	3	406	—	3,431	3,840
Total Liabilities	100,229	62,560	10,412	193,573	366,774
Fund Balances:					
Reserved for:					
Notes receivable	—	—	—	80,546	80,546
Prepaid items and other assets	—	—	—	575	575
Assets held for disposition	—	—	—	6,327	6,327
Emergency use	20,101	2,000	—	9,139	31,240
Construction	—	—	—	15	15
Debt service:					
Long-term debt	20,716	44	—	39,842	60,602
Interest	—	—	—	19,450	19,450
Unreserved:					
Designated for subsequent years' expenditures, reported in:					
Capital projects funds	—	—	121,634	58,926	180,560
Undesignated, reported in:					
General Fund	154,774	—	—	—	154,774
Special revenue funds	—	18,949	—	77,190	96,139
Capital projects funds	—	—	11,647	5,224	16,871
Permanent fund	—	—	—	3,387	3,387
Total Fund Balances	195,591	20,993	133,281	300,621	650,486
Total Liabilities and Fund Balances	$295,820	$83,553	$143,693	$494,194	$1,017,260

ILLUSTRATION A1–4

CITY AND COUNTY OF DENVER
Reconciliation of the Balance Sheet—Governmental Funds to the Statement of Net Assets
December 31, 2007
(amounts expressed in thousands)

Amounts reported for governmental activities in the statement of net assets are different because:	
Total fund balance—governmental funds.	$ 650,486
Capital assets used in governmental activities, excluding internal service funds of $4,102, are not financial resources, and therefore, are not reported in the funds.	2,202,429
Accrued interest payable not included in the funds.	(13,921)
Other long-term assets are not available to pay for current-period expenditures and,therefore, are deferred in the funds.	26,050
Bond issue costs, net of accumulated amortization.	3,850
Internal service funds are used by management to charge the cost of these funds to their primary users—governmental funds. The assets and liabilities of the internal service funds are included in governmental activities in the statement of net assets.	(4,219)
Long-term liabilities, including bonds payable, are not due and payable in the current period and therefore are not reported in the governmental funds (this excludes internal service liabilities of $34,001).	(1,304,973)
Net assets of governmental activities	$1,559,702

ILLUSTRATION A1–5

CITY AND COUNTY OF DENVER
Statement of Revenues, Expenditures, and Changes in Fund Balance
Governmental Funds
For the year ended December 31, 2007
(amounts expressed in thousands)

	General Fund	Human Services	Bond Projects	Other Governmental Funds	Total Governmental Funds
Revenues					
Taxes:					
Facilities development admission	$ —	$ —	$ —	$ 10,092	$ 10,092
Lodgers	13,483	—	—	36,168	49,651
Motor vehicle ownership fee	16,963	—	—	—	16,963
Occupational privilege	21,376	—	—	21,375	42,751
Public service	18,478	2,100	—	—	20,578
Property	79,232	42,497	—	105,459	227,188
Sales	418,177	—	—	37,259	455,436
Specific ownership	—	—	—	64	64
Telephone	3,231	—	—	6,687	9,918
Special assessments	—	—	—	1,370	1,370
Licenses and permits	28,094	—	—	1,289	29,383
Intergovernmental revenues	32,861	82,644	—	95,846	211,351
Charges for services	107,519	1,406	—	47,639	156,564
Investment and interest income	18,717	23	8,888	12,362	39,990
Fines and forfeitures	34,253	—	—	2,760	37,013
Contributions	3	235	—	8,430	8,668
Other revenue	11,162	1,718	10	27,486	40,376
Total Revenues	803,549	130,623	8,898	414,286	1,357,356
Expenditures					
Current:					
General government	156,040	—	5	80,649	236,694
Public safety	400,469	—	—	70,509	470,978
Public works	84,310	—	42	11,961	96,313
Human services	—	129,451	—	—	129,451
Health	41,783	—	—	6,911	48,694
Parks and recreation	47,003	—	190	12,598	59,791
Cultural activities	31,386	—	260	41,328	72,974
Community development	17,499	—	—	36,378	53,877
Economic opportunity	—	—	—	26,122	26,122
Principal retirement	571	2,791	—	78,323	81,685
Interest	2,737	1,989	—	48,661	53,387
Bond issue costs	—	—	421	—	421
Capital outlay	—	—	56,905	38,916	95,821
Total Expenditures	781,798	134,231	57,823	452,356	1,426,208
Excess (Deficiency) of revenues over expenditures	21,751	(3,608)	(48,925)	(38,070)	(68,852)
Other Financing Sources (Uses)					
Sale of capital assets	13	—	—	5,711	5,724
General obligation bonds issued	—	—	8,861	—	8,861
Insurance recoveries	1	5	—	5	11
Transfers in	32,333	—	—	53,013	85,346
Transfers out	(44,163)	(32)	—	(38,890)	(83,085)
Total Other Financing Sources (Uses)	(11,816)	(27)	8,861	19,839	16,857
Net change in fund balances	9,935	(3,635)	(40,064)	(18,231)	(51,995)
Fund balances—January 1	185,656	24,628	173,345	318,852	702,481
Fund Balances—December 31	$195,591	$ 20,993	$133,281	$300,621	$ 650,486

ILLUSTRATION A1–6

CITY AND COUNTY OF DENVER
Reconciliation of the Statement of Revenues, Expenditures, and Changes in Fund Balance—Governmental Funds to the Statement of Activities
For the year ended December 31, 2007
(amounts expressed in thousands)

Amounts reported for governmental activities in the statement of activities are different because:	
Net change in fund balances—total governmental funds	$ (51,995)
Governmental funds report capital outlays as expenditures. However, in the statement of activities the cost of those assets is allocated over their estimated useful lives and reported as depreciation expense. This is the amount by which capital outlay exceeded depreciation expense in the current period:	
Capital outlay, including sale of assets	163,643
Depreciation expense	(109,953)
Revenues in the statement of activities that do not provide current financial resources are not reported as revenue in the funds:	
Change in revenues in fund statements previously recognized in Statement of Activities	(5,932)
Donations of capital assets	17,610
The issuance of long-term debt and other obligations (e.g., bonds, certificates of participation, and capital leases) provides current financial resources to governmental funds, while the repayment of the principal of long-term debt consumes the current financial resources of governmental funds. Neither transaction, however has any effect on change in net assets. Also, governmental funds report the effect of issuance cost, premiums, discounts, and similar items when debt is first issued, whereas these amounts are deferred and amortized in the statement of activities. These differences in the treatment of long-term debt and related items consist of:	
General obligation bonds issued	(8,861)
Principal retirement on bonds	68,265
Issuance costs, premium, discounts and deferred gain (loss) on refunding	4,425
Capital lease principal payments	13,420
Some expenses reported in the statement of activities do not require the use of current financial resources and, therefore, are not reported as expenditures in governmental funds:	
Compensated absences (excluding internal service)	(6,392)
Accrued interest payable	(1,205)
Legal liability	980
Note payable	2,044
Line of credit payable	4,474
Internal service funds are used by management to charge their cost to individual funds. The net expense of certain activities of internal service funds is reported within governmental activities.	3,644
Change in net assets of governmental activities	$ 94,167

ILLUSTRATION A1–7

CITY AND COUNTY OF DENVER
Statement of Net Assets
Proprietary Funds
December 31, 2007
(amounts expressed in thousands)

	Business-type Activities—Enterprise Funds				Governmental Activities—
	Wastewater Management	Denver Airport System	Other Enterprise Funds	Total Enterprise Funds	Internal Service Funds
Assets					
Current assets:					
Cash and cash equivalents	$ 6,834	$ 133,419	$20,525	$ 160,778	$22,271
Investments	45,991	135,544		181,535	—
Receivables (net of allowance for uncollectibles of $1,651):					
Accounts	10,753	39,225	1,489	51,467	508
Accrued interest	453	5,248	129	5,830	88
Interfund receivable	791	415		1,206	3,193
Inventories		6,658	135	6,793	2,107
Prepaid items and other assets	320	107		427	—
Restricted assets:					
Cash and cash equivalents	—	331,500	1,994	333,494	14
Investments	—	217,789		217,789	—
Accrued interest receivable	—	1,076	16	1,092	—
Other receivables	—	17,772	589	18,361	—
Prepaid items	—	3,108		3,108	—
Total Current Assets	65,142	891,861	24,877	981,880	28,181
Noncurrent assets:					
Investments—unrestricted	—	121,443	—	121,443	—
Investments—restricted	—	541,593	—	541,593	—
Capital assets:					
Land and construction in progress	86,069	466,016	9,239	561,324	—
Buildings and improvements	14,207	1,972,606	9,128	1,995,941	4,107
Improvements other than buildings	555,257	2,014,224	8,693	2,578,174	82
Machinery and equipment	13,087	603,385	4,200	620,672	8,162
Accumulated depreciation	(197,030)	(1,583,993)	(14,722)	(1,795,745)	(8,249)
Net Capital Assets	471,590	4,135,274	16,538	4,623,402	4,102
Bond issue costs and other assets, net	294	59,633	215	60,142	—
Assets held for disposition	—	14,094		14,094	—
Total Noncurrent Assets	471,884	4,209,001	16,753	4,697,638	4,102
Total Assets	$537,026	$5,100,862	$41,630	$5,679,518	$32,283

continued

ILLUSTRATION A1–7 (*Continued*)

Liabilities					
Current liabilities:					
Vouchers payable	$ 1,564	$ 32,441	$ 2,282	$ 36,287	$ 896
Revenue bonds payable	1,180	—	370	1,550	—
Accrued liabilities	665	44,839	75	45,579	211
Interfund payable	5,677	18,241	1,283	25,201	1,039
Capital lease obligations	—	—	—	—	151
Compensated absences	539	1,914	169	2,622	244
Deferred revenue	13,665		45	13,710	—
Claims reserve	—			—	11,690
Construction payable	7,212		—	7,212	—
Unearned revenue	—	23,822	—	23,822	—
Current liabilities (payable from restricted assets):					
Vouchers payable	—	24,755	1,994	26,749	—
Retainages payable	—	24,436	—	24,436	—
Notes payable	—	12,139	—	12,139	—
Accrued interest and other liabilities	—	21,517	—	21,517	—
Other accrued liabilities	—	13,708	—	13,708	—
Revenue bonds payable	—	103,830	—	103,830	—
Total Current Liabilities	30,502	321,642	6,218	358,362	14,231
Noncurrent liabilities					
Notes payable	—	49,532	—	49,532	—
Revenue bonds payable	24,323	4,095,020	6,110	4,125,453	—
Deferred loss on refunding	—	(303,121)	—	(303,121)	—
Unamortized premium (discounts)	—	58,422	59	58,481	—
Capital lease obligations	—	—	—	—	317
Other accrued liabilities	1,732	5,377	615	7,724	778
Claims reserve	—	—	—	—	20,806
Total Noncurrent Liabilities	26,055	3,905,230	6,784	3,938,069	21,901
Total Liabilities	56,557	4,226,872	13,002	4,296,431	36,132
Net Assets					
Invested in capital assets, net of related debt	439,169	(131,740)	10,058	317,487	3,634
Restricted for:					
Capital projects	—	18,773	—	18,773	—
Debt service	—	657,498	—	657,498	—
Unrestricted	41,300	329,459	18,570	389,329	(7,483)
Total Net Assets (Deficit)	$480,469	$ 873,990	$28,628	1,383,087	$(3,849)
Adjustment to reflect consolidation of internal service fund activities related to enterprise funds				370	
Net assets of business-type activities				$1,383,457	

ILLUSTRATION A1–8

CITY AND COUNTY OF DENVER
Statement of Revenues, Expenses, and Changes in Fund Net Assets
Proprietary Funds
For the year ended December 31, 2007
(amounts expressed in thousands)

	Business-type Activities—Enterprise Funds				Governmental Activities—
	Wastewater Management	Denver Airport System	Other Enterprise Funds	Total Enterprise Funds	Internal Service Funds
Operating Revenues					
Charges for services	$ 75,750	$518,229	$15,899	$ 609,878	$46,316
Other revenue	—	11,922	874	12,796	488
Total Operating Revenues	75,750	530,151	16,773	622,674	46,804
Operating Expenses					
Personnel services	18,924	104,321	6,416	129,661	9,031
Contractual services	15,382	165,044	9,362	189,788	493
Supplies and materials	1,919	21,408	807	24,134	16,370
Depreciation and amortization	11,197	159,309	678	171,184	828
Metropolitan Wastewater Reclamation District	28,777	—	—	28,777	—
Claims payments	—	—	—	—	8,648
Change in claims reserve	—	—	—	—	1,238
Other operating expenses	—	—	1,285	1,285	6,857
Total Operating Expenses	76,199	450,082	18,548	544,829	43,465
Operating income (loss)	(449)	80,069	(1,775)	77,845	3,339
Nonoperating Revenues (Expenses)					
Investment and interest income	4,240	82,249	1,396	87,885	689
Passenger facility charges	—	97,191	—	97,191	—
Disposition of assets	33	—	—	33	(2)
Grants	—	324	—	324	—
Interest expense	5	(220,064)	(312)	(220,371)	(12)
Passenger facility charge	—	(8,827)	—	(8,827)	—
Total Nonoperating Revenues (Expenses)	4,278	(49,127)	1,084	(43,765)	675
Income before contributions and transfers	3,829	30,942	(691)	34,080	—
Capital grants and contributions	9,906	2,426	—	12,332	—
Transfers out	(11)	—	(2,250)	(2,261)	—
Change in net assets	13,724	33,368	(2,941)	44,151	4,014
Net assets—January 1, as previously reported	466,745	702,769	31,569	1,201,083	(7,863)
Restatement for correction of error	—	137,853	—	137,853	—
Net assets—January 1, as restated	—	840,622	—	1,338,936	—
Net Assets (Deficit)—December 31	$480,469	$873,990	$28,628	$1,383,087	$(3,849)
Change in net assets of enterprise funds				$44,151	
Adjustment to reflect consolidation of internal service fund activities related to enterprise funds				(182)	
Change in net assets of business-type activities				$43,969	

ILLUSTRATION A1–9

CITY AND COUNTY OF DENVER
Statement of Cash Flows
Proprietary Funds
For the year ended December 31, 2007
(amounts expressed in thousands)

	Business-type Activities—Enterprise Funds				Governmental Activities—
	Wastewater Management	Denver Airport System	Other Enterprise Funds	Total Enterprise Funds	Internal Service Funds
Cash Flows from Operating Activities					
Receipts from customers	$ 77,607	$ 524,011	$16,316	$ 617,934	$ 43,790
Payments to suppliers	(32,286)	(172,191)	(6,493)	(210,970)	(23,158)
Payments to employees	(18,649)	(103,726)	(6,374)	(128,749)	(9,030)
Other receipts (payments)	—	—	—	—	426
Interfund activity	(10,437)	(13,418)	—	(23,855)	—
Sale of salvage	—	—	—	—	56
Claims paid	—	—	—	—	(8,648)
Other payments	—	—	(1,125)	(1,125)	—
Net Cash Provided by Operating Activities	16,235	234,676	2,324	253,235	3,436
Cash Flows from Noncapital Financing Activities					
Transfers out	(11)	—	(2,250)	(2,261)	—
Operating grants	—	383	—	383	—
Net Cash Provided (Used) by Noncapital Financing Activities	(11)	383	(2,250)	(1,878)	—
Cash Flows from Capital and Related Financing Activities					
Proceeds from capital debt	—	480,150	—	480,150	—
Bond issue costs	—	(2,498)	25	(2,473)	—
Principal payments	(1,135)	(172,149)	(360)	(173,644)	(143)
Passenger facility charges	—	98,242	—	98,242	—
Payments on capital assets acquired through construction payables	(13,466)	(39,670)	—	(53,136)	—
Acquisition and construction of capital assets	(57,369)	(133,132)	(6,649)	(197,150)	(1,211)
Sale of capital assets	33	503	—	536	(2)
Interest paid	(1,323)	(199,416)	(312)	(201,051)	(12)
Contributions and advances	6,257	8,260	—	14,517	—
Payments to escrow for current refunding of debt	—	(12,307)	—	(12,307)	—
Net Cash Provided (Used) by Capital and Related Financing Activities	(67,003)	27,983	(7,296)	(46,316)	(1,368)
Cash Flows from Investing Activities					
Purchases of investments	(11,923)	(7,397,239)	—	(7,409,162)	—
Proceeds from sale of investments	65,971	7,216,181	—	7,282,152	—
Sale of assets held for disposition; payments to maintain assets held	—	(24,474)	—	(24,474)	—
Insurance proceeds from Stapelton remediation	—	30,248	—	30,248	—
Interest received	3,565	66,324	1,384	71,273	675
Net Cash Provided (Used) by Investing Activities	57,613	(108,960)	1,384	(49,963)	675

ILLUSTRATION A1–9 (*Continued*)

	Business-type Activities—Enterprise Funds				Governmental Activities—
	Wastewater Management	**Denver Airport System**	**Other Enterprise Funds**	**Total Enterprise Funds**	**Internal Service Funds**
Net increase (decrease) in cash and cash equivalents	6,834	154,082	(5,838)	155,078	2,743
Cash and cash equivalents—January 1	-	310,837	28,357	339,194	19,542
Cash and Cash Equivalents—December 31	$ 6,834	$464,919	$22,519	$494,272	$22,285
Reconciliation of Operating Income (Loss) to Net Cash Provided by Operating Activities					
Operating income (loss)	$ (449)	$ 80,069	$ (1,775)	$ 77,845	$ 3,339
Adjustments to reconcile operating income (loss) to net cash provided by operating activities:					
Depreciation and amortization	11,197	159,309	678	171,184	828
Miscellaneous revenue	—	6,750	—	6,750	—
Accounts receivable, net of allowance	1,669	(12,336)	(503)	(11,170)	(379)
Interfund receivable	(225)	—	—	(225)	361
Inventories	—	(1,121)	12	(1,109)	(201)
Prepaid items	—	580	—	580	—
Vouchers payable	155	1,269	3,808	5,232	(874)
Unearned revenue	413	16,609	46	17,068	—
Accrued and other liabilities	(336)	(17,507)	43	(17,800)	1
Interfund payable	3,811	1,054	15	4,880	(877)
Claims reserve	—	—	—	—	1,238
Net Cash Provided by Operating Activities	$16,235	$234,676	$ 2,324	$253,235	$ 3,436
Noncash Activities					
Assets acquired through capital contributions	$ 3,650	$ —	$ —	$ 3,650	$ —
Unrealized gain (loss) on investments	650	18,732	—	19,382	—
Capital assets acquired through accounts payable	7,212	36,720	—	43,932	—
Amortization of bond premiums, deferred losses on bond refundings and bond costs	—	17,920	—	17,920	—

ILLUSTRATION A1–10

CITY AND COUNTY OF DENVER
Statement of Fiduciary Net Assets
Fiduciary Funds
December 31, 2007
(amounts expressed in thousands)

	Pension and Other Employee Benefit Trust Funds	Private-Purpose Trust Funds	Agency Funds
Assets			
Cash on hand	$ —	$ 782	$ 4,028
Cash and cash equivalents	40,536	573	12,960
Securities lending collateral	279,711	—	—
Receivables (net of allowance for uncollectibles of $5,987):			
Taxes	—	—	485,093
Accounts	812	—	26
Accrued interest	6,477	—	—
Investments, at fair value:			
U.S. Government obligations	158,693	—	—
Domestic stocks and bonds	1,245,363	—	—
International stocks	364,619	—	—
Annuity	428,056	—	—
Mutual funds	49,751	—	—
Real estate	238,387	—	—
Other	100,656	—	—
Total Investments	2,585,525	—	—
Capital assets, net of accumulated depreciation	1,044	—	—
Total Assets	2,914,105	1,355	502,107
Liabilities			
Vouchers payable	7,879	316	326
Securities lending obligation	279,711	—	—
Other accrued liabilities	—	—	4,213
Due to taxing units	—	782	497,568
Total Liabilities	287,590	1,098	502,107
Net Assets			
Held in trust for pension benefits and other purposes	$2,626,515	$ 257	$ —

ILLUSTRATION A1–11

CITY AND COUNTY OF DENVER
Statement of Changes in Fiduciary Net Assets
Fiduciary Funds
For the year ended December 31, 2007
(amounts expressed in thousands)

	Pension and Other Employee Benefit Trust Funds	Private-Purpose Trust Funds
Additions		
Contributions:		
City and County of Denver	$ 38,862	$ —
Denver Health and Hospital Authority	6,598	—
Plan members	47,287	—
Total Contributions	92,747	—
Investment income:		
Net appreciation in fair value of investments	156,156	—
Interest and dividends	101,988	—
Total Investment Income	258,144	—
Less investment expense	(9,453)	—
Net Income from Investments	248,691	—
Securities lending income	14,404	—
Securities lending expenses:		
Borrower rebates	(12,899)	—
Agent fees	(376)	—
Net Income from Securities Lending	1,129	—
Total net investment income	249,820	—
Other additions	—	36
Total Additions	342,567	36
Deductions		
Benefits	146,538	—
Refunds of contributions	410	—
Administrative expenses	2,604	—
Total Deductions	149,552	—
Change in net assets	193,015	36
Net assets—January 1	2,433,500	221
Net assets—December 31	$2,626,515	$257

Key Terms*

Accountability, *6*
Basic financial statements, *8*
Comprehensive annual financial report (CAFR), *13*
Federal Accounting Standards Advisory Board (FASAB), *5*
Financial Accounting Standards Board (FASB), *3*
Fiscal accountability, *8*
Fund financial statements, *8*
General purpose governments, *2*
Generally accepted accounting principles (GAAP), *5*
Governmental Accounting Standards Board (GASB), *3*
Government-wide financial statements, *8*
Interperiod equity, *7*
Major fund, *12*
Management's discussion and analysis (MD&A), *8*
Operational accountability, *8*
Required supplementary information (RSI), *8*
Service efforts and accomplishments (SEA), *14*
Special purpose governments, *2*

Questions

1–1. Explain how *general purpose governments* differ from *special purpose governments* and give a few examples of each type of government.

1–2. "Governmental and not-for-profit organizations do not differ significantly from for-profit organizations and therefore should follow for-profit accounting and reporting standards." Do you agree or disagree with this statement? Why or why not?

1–3. Which standard-setting bodies have responsibility for establishing accounting and reporting standards for (1) state and local governments, (2) business organizations, (3) not-for-profit organizations, and (4) the federal government and its agencies and departments?

1–4. How should one determine whether FASB or GASB standards should be followed by any particular not-for-profit organization?

1–5. Distinguish between *accountability* and *interperiod equity*.

1–6. "GASB financial reporting standards assist users in assessing the *operational accountability* of a government's business-type activities and the *fiscal accountability* of its governmental activities." Do you agree or disagree with this statement? Why or why not?

1–7. Why do governmental fund financial statements use a different basis of accounting and measurement focus than the Governmental Activities column of the government-wide financial statements? Also, which basis of accounting and which measurement focus applies to each?

1–8. How does the *modified accrual* basis of accounting differ from the *accrual* basis?

1–9. What are the three sections of a comprehensive annual financial report (CAFR)? What information is contained in each section? How do the minimum requirements for general purpose external financial reporting relate in scope to the CAFR?

1–10. Why does the GASB encourage state and local governments to report *service efforts and accomplishments* information in addition to a CAFR?

* See the glossary at the back of the text for a definition of each term and concept.

Cases

1–1 Internet Case—FASB. Go to the Financial Accounting Standards Board's Web site at *www.fasb.org*. List by number and name all FASB statements that specifically provide accounting and reporting guidance for not-for-profit organizations. Can you obtain a copy of the full text of these statements from this Web site? Does the FASB charge for its statements, or are they provided free of charge?

1–2 Internet Case—GASB. Examine the Governmental Accounting Standards Board's Web site (*www.gasb.org*) and prepare a brief report about its mission and structure and the representative organizations on its advisory council. Can you get a copy of the full text of a GASB statement from this Web site? If not, how would you obtain a copy of GASB *Statement No. 34,* for example? What is the cost to purchase a statement?

1–3 Internet Case—FASAB. Examine the Federal Accounting Standards Advisory Board's Web site at *www.fasab.gov* and prepare a brief report about its mission and structure and compile a list of organizations represented on its Accounting and Auditing Policy Committee. Can you obtain a copy of the full text of FASAB statements from this Web site? If not, how would you obtain a copy of a statement pertinent to federal agencies? What is the cost to purchase a statement?

1–4 Research Case—Governmental or Not-for-Profit Entity? In partnership with Jefferson County and the Mound City Visitor's Bureau, Mound City recently established a Native American Heritage Center and Museum, organized as a tax-exempt not-for-profit organization. Although the facility does not charge admission, signs at the information desk in the entry lobby encourage gifts of $3.00 for adults and $1.00 for children, 12 and under. Many visitors make the recommended contribution, some contribute larger amounts, and some do not contribute at all. Such contributions comprise 40 percent of the museum's total annual revenues, with net proceeds from fund-raising events and governmental grants comprising the remaining 60 percent. The center operates from a city-owned building for which it pays a nominal $1 per year in rent. Except for a full-time executive director and a part-time assistant, the center is staffed by unpaid volunteers. The center is governed by a seven-member board of directors, each appointed for a three-year term. Four of the directors are appointed by the Mound City Council, two by the Jefferson County Commission, and one by the Mound City Visitor's Bureau. Should the center cease to operate, its charter provides that 60 percent of its net assets will revert to the city, 25 percent to the county, and 15 percent to the Visitor's Bureau.

At the end of its first year of operation, the board of directors decided to engage a local CPA to conduct an audit of the center's financial statements. The board expects to receive an unqualified (clean) audit opinion stating that its financial statements are presented fairly in conformity with generally accepted accounting principles.

Required

Assume you are the CPA who has been engaged to conduct this audit. To which standards-setting body (or bodies) would you look for accounting and financial reporting standards to assist you in determining whether the center's financial statements are in conformity with generally accepted accounting principles? Explain how you arrived at this conclusion.

Exercises and Problems

1–1 Examine the CAFR. Download a copy of the most recent comprehensive annual financial report (CAFR) for the City and County of Denver from its Web site: *http://www.denvergov.org/controller* (click on "Financial Reports"), or that of another city or county if you wish.* Familiarize yourself with the organization by scanning the report and reread the section in this chapter entitled "Financial Reporting of State and Local Governments." Be prepared to discuss in class the items suggested below.

a. Introductory Section.

Read the letter of transmittal or any narrative that accompanies the financial statements. Does this material define the governmental reporting entity and name the primary government and all related component units included in the report? (*Note:* The reporting entity may be discussed in the notes to the financial statements rather than in the transmittal letter.) Does the introductory section discuss the financial condition of the reporting entity at the balance sheet date? Does it discuss the most significant changes in financial condition that occurred during the year? Does it alert the reader to forthcoming changes in financial condition that are not as yet reflected in the financial statements? Do the amounts reported in the letter of transmittal or other narrative agree with amounts in the statements and schedules in the financial section? Does the introductory section include a list of principal officials? An organization chart? A reproduction of a Certificate of Achievement for Excellence in Financial Reporting from the Government Finance Officers Association (GFOA)? Assuming the government follows *GASBS 34,* compare the information in the letter of transmittal with that in the management discussion & analysis (MD&A).

b. Financial Section.

(1) *Audit Report.* Are the financial statements in the report audited by an independent CPA, state auditors, or auditors employed by the government being audited? Does the auditor indicate who is responsible for preparing the financial statements? Does the auditor express an opinion that the statements are "in accordance with generally accepted accounting principles applicable to governmental entities in the United States" or some other phrase? Is the opinion qualified in some manner, disclaimed, or adverse? Does the auditor indicate that the opinion covers the basic financial statements or that plus combining statements?

(2) *Basic Financial Statements.* Does the CAFR contain the two government-wide financial statements and seven fund statements and required reconciliation?

(3) *Notes to the Financial Statements.* How many notes follow the required basic financial statements? Is there a phrase at the bottom of the basic financial statements indicating that the notes are an integral part of the financial statements?

* GASB's Web site, *http://www.gasb.org* provides a sizeable list of local governments that voluntarily report to the GASB and indicates whether their CAFRs can be downloaded. You can usually obtain a hard copy of the CAFR of any city by sending an e-mail request to the city's director of finance (or other appropriate title of the chief financial officer). Be sure to mention that you are a student and need the CAFR for a class project. Contact information for the finance director can usually be obtained by doing a search on "City of (name)" and looking for a link to the city's departments. At that link, select Finance Department or a department with a similar function, such as Accounting and Budgeting. Before you request a CAFR by e-mail, check to see if one is accessible at the department's Web site.

(4) *Individual Fund and Combining Statements.* Following the notes to the financial statements, does the CAFR provide combining and individual fund statements? Do these combining statements aggregate all the funds of a given fund type or all the nonmajor funds?

(5) *Management's Discussion and Analysis (MD&A).* Does the CAFR contain an MD&A? If so, where is it located and what type of information does it contain?

c. Statistical Tables.

Examine these tables so that you can refer to them in discussions accompanying subsequent chapters. For example, is multiyear information provided about financial trends, revenue capacity, debt capacity, demographic and economic trends, and operating activities?

1–2 Multiple Choice. Choose the best answer.

1. Special purpose governments differ from general purpose governments in that special purpose governments:
   a. Provide a single function or limited range of functions.
   b. Do not have the power to levy taxes.
   c. Derive their power from state governments.
   d. All of the above.

2. Which of the following is a true statement about accounting standard-setting bodies?
   a. The Financial Accounting Standards Board (FASB) sets accounting and reporting standards for all not-for-profit organizations, but the Governmental Accounting Standards Board (GASB) may also prescribe standards for governmental not-for-profit organizations provided they do not conflict with FASB standards.
   b. The GASB sets accounting and reporting standards for all governmental organizations; the FASB sets standards for all business and not-for-profit organizations.
   c. Only the FASB and GASB enjoy AICPA Ethics Rule 203 coverage as recognized standard-setting authoritative bodies, not the FASAB.
   d. The FASB and GASB are administratively supported by the Financial Accounting Foundation; the FASAB draws its support from the federal government.

3. A distinguishing difference between governments and not-for-profit organizations is:
   a. Lack of a profit motive.
   b. Absence of owners.
   c. Taxation as a significant source of funding.
   d. Receipt of significant amounts of funding through nonexchange transactions (i.e., resource providers do not get proportional benefits for what they pay to the organization).

4. Which of the following organizations would *most* likely meet the criteria to be classified as a *governmental* not-for-profit organization?
   a. A religion-affiliated university.
   b. A privately founded museum.

c. A public school district.
d. A city-administered community service agency.

5. The concept of *interperiod equity* refers to whether:
   a. Revenues equaled or exceeded expenditures for the year.
   b. Current year revenues were sufficient to pay for current year services.
   c. Total assets (current and noncurrent) were sufficient to cover total liabilities (current and noncurrent).
   d. Future taxpayers can expect to receive the same or higher level of services as current taxpayers.

6. Which of the following is (are) included in the minimum requirements for general purpose external financial reporting of a government?
   a. Comprehensive Annual Financial Report.
   b. Management's Discussion and Analysis (MD&A) and basic financial statements.
   c. Combining fund financial statements.
   d. Statistical section.

7. The basic financial statements of a state or local government include all of the following except:
   a. An MD&A.
   b. Government-wide financial statements.
   c. Fund financial statements.
   d. Notes to the financial statements.

8. The modified accrual basis of accounting is used to account for revenues and expenditures reported in the financial statements of:
   a. Governmental activities at the government-wide level.
   b. Business-type activities at the government-wide level.
   c. Governmental funds.
   d. Proprietary funds.

9. Separate columns for individual *major funds* should be provided in which of the following financial statements?
   a. Statement of net assets—government-wide; balance sheet—governmental funds; statement of net assets—proprietary funds.
   b. Statement of net assets—government-wide; balance sheet—governmental funds; statement of fiduciary net assets—fiduciary funds.
   c. Statement of net assets—government-wide; statement of net assets—proprietary funds; statement of fiduciary net assets—fiduciary funds.
   d. Balance sheet—governmental funds; statement of net assets—proprietary funds.

10. Under *GASBS 34,* financial information related to fiduciary activities is reported in which financial statements?

	Government-wide Financial Statements	Fund Financial Statements
a.	No	Yes
b.	Yes	No
c.	Yes	Yes
d.	No	No

1–3. Matching. Place the abbreviations corresponding to the appropriate reporting attribute(s) in the spaces provided for each financial statement. Include all that apply.

Activities or Funds
Governmental activities—GA
Business-type activities—BTA
Governmental funds—GF
Proprietary funds—PF
Fiduciary funds—FF

Basis of Accounting
Accrual—A
Modified accrual—MA

Measurement Focus
Economic resources—ER
Current financial resources—CFR

Financial Statements	Activities or Funds Reported	Basis of Accounting	Measurement Focus
Statement of net assets—government-wide			
Statement of activities—government-wide			
Balance sheet—governmental funds			
Statement of revenues, expenditures, and changes in fund balances—governmental funds			
Statement of net assets—proprietary funds			
Statement of revenues, expenses, and changes in fund net assets—proprietary funds			
Statement of cash flows—proprietary funds			
Statement of fiduciary net assets			
Statement of changes in fiduciary net assets			

PART One

STATE AND LOCAL GOVERNMENTS

Chapter Two

Principles of Accounting and Financial Reporting for State and Local Governments

Learning Objectives

After studying this chapter, you should be able to:

1. Explain the nature of the three major activity categories of a state or local government: governmental activities, business-type activities, and fiduciary activities.
2. Explain the components of GASB's integrated accounting and financial reporting model, including:
   The reporting entity.
   Government-wide financial statements.
   Fund financial statements.
   Definition of *fund* and principles of fund accounting.
   Types of funds in each fund category and characteristics of each fund type.
3. Discuss the nature of major fund reporting and the criteria used to determine whether a fund should be reported as a major fund.

Chapter 1 presented a brief overview of the minimum requirements for general purpose external financial reporting under the *GASBS 34* financial reporting model. This chapter expands on the previous discussion and focuses primarily on principles of accounting and financial reporting within the integrated reporting model framework set forth in *GASBS 34*.

When the Governmental Accounting Standards Board (GASB) was formed in 1984, it adopted 12 accounting and financial reporting principles that had been established by its predecessor standard-setting body, the National Council on Governmental Accounting (NCGA). *GASBS 34* modifies several of the original 12 principles and adds one principle for reporting long-term liabilities. A summary of these principles is presented in the appendix to this chapter. Certain of the principles are also discussed in this chapter.

ACTIVITIES OF GOVERNMENT

Chapter 1 explained that the characteristics of governmental organizations differ from those of for-profit business organizations. One key difference is that governments are not profit seeking but exist to meet citizens' demand for services, consistent with the availability of resources to provide those services. Although the types and levels of services vary from government to government, most general purpose governments provide certain core services: those related to protection of life and property (e.g., police and fire protection), public works (e.g., streets and highways, bridges, and public buildings), parks and recreation facilities and programs, and educational, cultural, and social services. Governments must also incur costs for general administrative support such as data processing, finance, and personnel. Core governmental services, together with general administrative support, comprise the major part of what GASB *Concepts Statement No. 1* refers to as governmental-type activities.[1] In its more recent pronouncements, GASB refers to these activities as simply **governmental activities.** Chapters 3 through 6 of the text focus on various aspects of accounting for governmental activities.

Some readers may be surprised to learn that governments also engage in a variety of **business-type activities.** These activities include, among others, public utilities (e.g., electric, water, gas, and sewer utilities), transportation systems, toll roads, toll bridges, hospitals, parking garages and lots, liquor stores, golf courses, and swimming pools. Many of these activities are intended to be self-supporting by charging users for the services they receive. Operating subsidies from general tax revenues are not uncommon, however, particularly for transportation systems. Accounting for business-type activities is covered in Chapter 7 of the text.

A final category of activity in which governments are involved is **fiduciary activities.** Governments often act in a fiduciary capacity, either as an agent or trustee, for parties outside the government. For example, a government may serve as agent for other governments in administering and collecting taxes. Governments may also serve as trustee for investments of other governments in the government's investment pool, for **escheat properties** that revert to the government when there are no legal claimants or heirs to a deceased individual's estate, and for assets being held for employee pension plans, among other trustee roles.

Under *GASBS 34,* only *private-purpose* agency and trust relationships—those that benefit individuals, private organizations, and other governments—are reported as fiduciary activities. *Public-purpose* agency and trust activities, those that primarily benefit the general public and the government's own programs, are treated as governmental activities for accounting and financial reporting purposes. Accounting for fiduciary activities is covered in Chapter 8 of the text.

GOVERNMENTAL FINANCIAL REPORTING ENTITY

The notion of financial accountability is basic to the definition of a governmental reporting entity. A **reporting entity** consists of the primary government and certain other organizations, identified as component units, for which the primary government is financially accountable.[2] According to GASB standards, the "financial statements of the reporting entity should provide an overview of the entity, yet allow

[1] Governmental Accounting Standards Board, *Codification of Governmental Accounting and Financial Reporting Standards as of June 30, 2008* (Norwalk, CT, 2008), Appendix B, *Concepts Statement No. 1,* par. 10.

[2] GASB, *Codification,* Sec. 2100.111.

users to distinguish between the primary government and its component units."[3] The government-wide financial statements meet this objective very well.

GASB defines a **primary government** as a state government or general purpose local government, or a special purpose government that has a separately elected governing body, is legally separate, and is fiscally independent of other state and local governments. General purpose local governments are organizations such as cities, towns, villages, counties, and townships. In many states, public school systems are legally and fiscally independent special purpose governments that are primary governments in their own right.

Component units are legally separate organizations, including organizations such as governmental hospitals, library districts, and public building authorities, for which the elected officials of the primary government are financially accountable. In addition, a component unit can be another organization for which the nature and significance of its relationship with the primary government, including its ongoing financial support of the primary government or its other component units, is such that exclusion would cause the reporting entity's financial statements to be misleading or incomplete.

Reporting the financial information of component units in a separate column of the government-wide financial statements, as shown in Illustrations A1–1 and A1–2 in Chapter 1 and Illustration 2–1, is referred to as a **discrete presentation.** Discrete presentation is the most common method used to report component units and should be used unless the financial activities of the component unit are so intertwined with those of the primary government that they are, in substance, the same as the primary government. In such cases the component unit's financial information should be reported in the same columns as the financial information of the primary government itself. This method of reporting is known as a **blended presentation.** Criteria for identification and methods of component unit reporting are covered in greater detail in Chapter 9.

The notes to the financial statements should contain a brief description of the component units of the financial reporting entity and their relationships to the primary government. This disclosure should also describe the criteria for including the component units and for reporting the component units. Information about major component units may be presented in condensed financial statements within the notes or in combining statements that provide a separate column for each component unit, along with a total column for all component units.[4] If there are only a few major component units, their financial information can be reported in separate columns of the government-wide financial statements. Under this option, aggregate financial information for all nonmajor component units is reported in an additional column of the government-wide statements. The notes should also include information about how separate financial statements for individual component units may be obtained.

INTEGRATED ACCOUNTING AND FINANCIAL REPORTING MODEL

The minimum requirements for general purpose external financial reporting for state and local governments, as well as the contents of a comprehensive annual financial report (CAFR), were briefly discussed in Chapter 1. As shown in Illustration 1–3, every state and local government should provide, in addition to its basic financial

[3] Ibid., Sec. 2100.142. Note: All definitions in this section of the text are quoted or paraphrased from GASB *Codification,* Sec. 2100.501.

[4] What constitutes a *major* component unit is a matter of professional judgment, considering each component unit's significance in relation to the other component units and to the primary government. GASB, *Codification,* Sec. 2600.108.

statements, a *management's discussion and analysis* (MD&A) and certain other required supplementary information. To understand the basic principles of accounting and financial reporting for state and local governments, one must first understand the *GASBS 34* integrated accounting and financial reporting model. This model is depicted in Illustration 2–1. Key to the integrated model is the requirement to provide two kinds of basic financial statements, government-wide and fund, each kind intended to achieve different reporting objectives. These two kinds of statements are integrated in the sense that the total fund balances of governmental funds and changes in fund balances must be reconciled to total net assets and changes in net assets of governmental activities reported in the government-wide financial statements. The necessity for these reconciliations was touched on in Chapter 1 and is further explained in the following discussion.

Government-wide and Fund Financial Statements

The government-wide financial statements report on the governmental reporting entity as a whole but focus on the primary government. As shown in Illustrations A1–1 and A1–2, as well as in Illustration 2–1, the government-wide statements present the financial information of the governmental activities and business-type activities of the primary government in separate columns, although there is a total column for the primary government.

The government-wide statements present all financial information using the **economic resources measurement focus** and the **accrual basis** of accounting—

ILLUSTRATION 2–1 **GASB *Statement No. 34* Integrated Accounting and Financial Reporting Model**

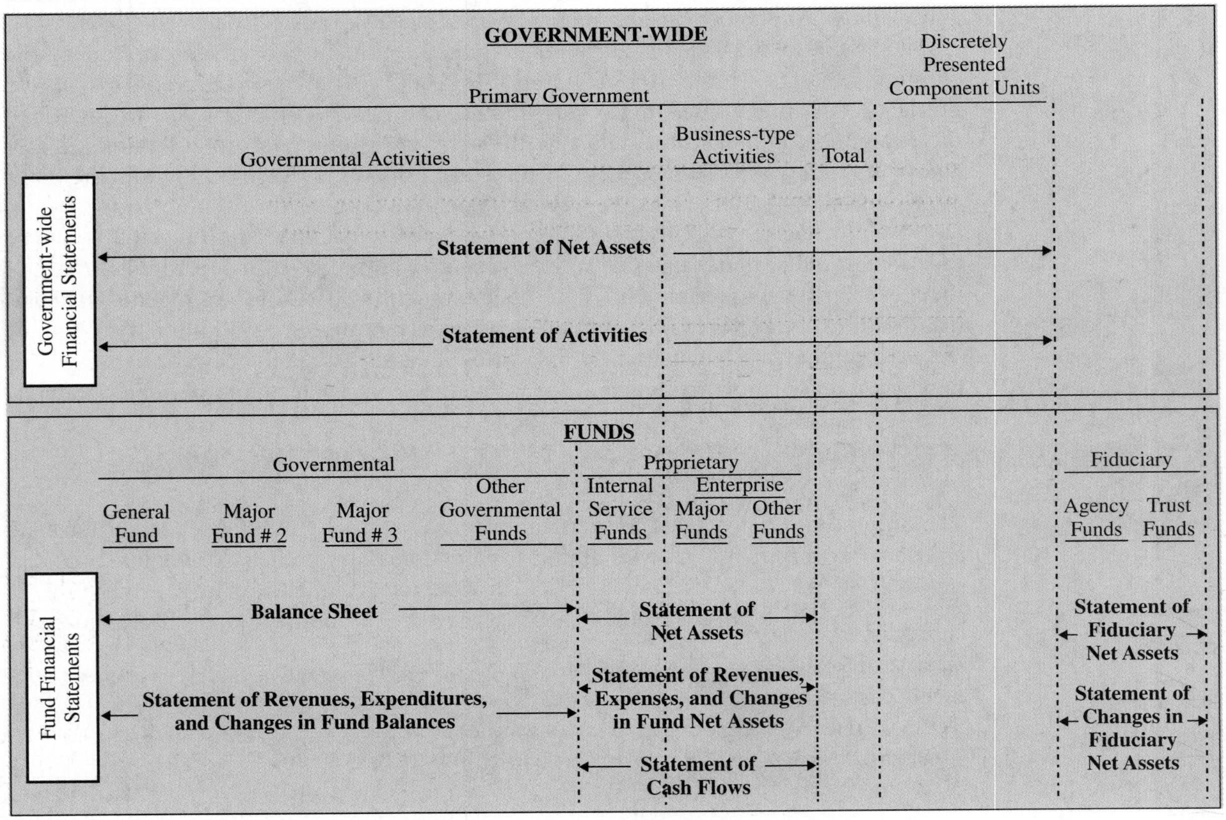

essentially the same measurement focus and basis of accounting used in the financial statements of for-profit business organizations. Thus, as discussed in Chapter 1, the government-wide financial statements report on the *operational accountability* of the government and help to assess whether the government is covering the full cost of services provided in the long run.

Governments must also present *fund* financial statements or, more precisely, three sets of fund financial statements, one set for each of the three fund categories: governmental, proprietary, and fiduciary (see the lower half of Illustration 2–1). These categories correspond closely to the governmental, business-type, and fiduciary activities described earlier in this chapter. An observant reader will note, however, that although internal service funds are included in the proprietary funds category, they are included as part of *governmental activities* in the government-wide financial statements. Thus, in most cases, only enterprise funds are reported as business-type activities in the government-wide statements. Internal service fund financial information is reported as part of governmental activities in the government-wide statements because these funds, though businesslike in operation, predominantly serve departments of the same government rather than the general public. If an internal service fund predominantly serves one or more enterprise funds, its financial information is reported in the Business-type Activities column of the government-wide statements. Financial reporting of internal service funds is discussed in depth in Chapter 7.

Another interesting aspect of the integrated accounting and reporting framework is that fiduciary activities are reported only in the two *fund* financial statements shown in Illustration 2–1 (examples of these statements are presented in Illustrations A1–10 and A1–11). Fiduciary activities are not reported at all in the government-wide financial statements because the resources held by these activities (funds) belong to external parties and cannot be used to support the services provided by the primary government or its component units.

The discussion to this point has provided a brief overview of the integrated reporting model, which requires both government-wide and fund financial statements. As the following few chapters will make clear, *governmental activities* are reported quite differently in the two types of financial statements. To fully comprehend these differences, one must first become familiar with the concept of a *fund* and the accounting characteristics associated with each fund and activity category. Fund accounting for governmental activities focuses on *fiscal accountability*—reporting on whether current financial resources were obtained from authorized sources and expended only for authorized purposes.

Fiscal Accountability and Fund Accounting

GASB's first accounting and financial reporting principle states:

> A governmental accounting system must make it possible both: (a) to present fairly and with full disclosure the funds and activities of the governmental unit in conformity with generally accepted accounting principles, and (b) to determine and demonstrate compliance with finance-related legal and contractual provisions.[5]

In the governmental environment, legal and contractual provisions often conflict with the requirements of generally accepted accounting principles (GAAP). As the first principle states, however, the accounting system must make it possible to present financial information that meets *both* requirements. Legal provisions related to budgeting revenues and expenditures, for example, often differ from GAAP accounting requirements regarding revenues and expenditures. Furthermore, revenues may be legally or contractually restricted for a particular purpose.

[5] GASB *Codification,* Sec. 1100.101.

The necessity to report on fiscal accountability creates a need for governments to account for restricted-use revenues and expenditures made from such revenues separately from unrestricted revenues and expenditures. The mechanism that has developed for segregating accountability for the inflows and outflows of restricted-use financial resources is the fund.

A **fund** is formally defined as:

> A fiscal and accounting entity with a self-balancing set of accounts recording cash and other financial resources, together with all related liabilities and residual equities or balances and changes therein, which are segregated for the purpose of carrying on specific activities or attaining certain objectives in accordance with special regulations, restrictions, or limitations.[6]

The concept of *fund* is fundamental to governmental accounting and reporting. As the definition states, a *fund* is a separate fiscal entity with its own resources, its own liabilities, and its own operating activity for the fiscal period. Furthermore, a fund conceptually has its own set of accounting records (e.g., journals and ledgers) and can have prepared for it separate financial statements. Thus, it is a separate accounting entity as well.

The latter part of the definition of fund is also worth noting: Specifically, a fund assists in *carrying on specific activities or attaining certain objectives in accordance with special regulations, restrictions, or limitations.* As this sentence implies, different funds are intended to achieve different objectives. Funds may be established by grant or contract provisions imposed by external resource providers, by state or local laws or regulations, or by the discretionary action of governing bodies. The variety of purposes that may be served by different fund categories and types will become apparent in the discussion that follows.

Fund Categories

As mentioned earlier in this chapter, there are three categories of funds: governmental, proprietary, and fiduciary (see Illustration 2–1). Accounting characteristics and principles unique to each fund category are discussed in the sections that follow.

Governmental Funds

The **governmental funds** category includes five types of funds: the General Fund, special revenue funds, debt service funds, capital projects funds, and permanent funds. Every state and local government has one and only one **General Fund**, although it may be called by a different name such as *General Revenue Fund, General Operating Fund,* or *Current Fund.* Other governmental funds will be created as needed. Most departmental operating activities, such as those of police and fire, public works, parks and recreation, culture, education, and social services, as well as general government support services, such as the city manager's office, finance, personnel, and data processing, are typically accounted for in the General Fund. Unless a financial resource is required to be accounted for in a different fund type, it is usually accounted for in the General Fund.

When tax or grant revenues or private gifts are legally restricted for particular operating purposes, such as the operation of a library or maintenance of roads and bridges, a **special revenue fund** is created. The number of special revenue funds used by state and local governments varies greatly, ranging from a few to many. Nevertheless, GASB standards recommend that governments establish only the minimum

[6] Ibid., Sec. 1100.102.

number of funds needed to comply with legal requirements and to provide sound management. An excessive number of funds creates undue complexity and contributes to inefficient financial administration.

Governments that have bond obligations outstanding and certain other types of long-term general liabilities may be required by law or bond covenants to create a **debt service fund.** The purpose of a debt service fund is to account for financial resources segregated for the purpose of making principal and interest payments on general long-term debt.[7] Some governments account for all debt service on general long-term debt in their General Fund, but governments ordinarily create one or more debt service funds if they have general long-term debt.

Governments often engage in capital projects to accommodate a growing population or to replace existing capital assets. These projects typically involve major construction of items such as buildings, highways or bridges, or parks. To account for tax or grant revenues, or bond proceeds earmarked for a capital project, as well as payments to architects, engineers, construction contractors, and suppliers, a **capital projects fund** is typically created. Multiple capital projects funds may be created if a government has multiple capital projects.

The fifth type of governmental fund is the *permanent fund.* A **permanent fund** is used to account for permanent endowments created when a donor stipulates that the principal amount of a contribution must be invested and preserved but earnings on amounts so invested can be used for some public purpose. Public purposes include activities such as maintenance of a cemetery or aesthetic enhancements to public buildings. If the earnings from a permanent fund can be used to benefit only *private* individuals, organizations, or other governments, rather than supporting a program of the government and its citizenry, a private-purpose trust fund—a fiduciary fund—is used instead of a permanent fund.

Accounting and financial reporting standards for the governmental funds category, the five fund types just described, have evolved to meet the budgetary and financial compliance needs of government. Thus, it is hardly surprising that accounting for governmental funds focuses on the inflows and outflows of **current financial resources.** Current financial resources are cash or items such as receivables that will be converted into cash during the current fiscal period or that will be **available** soon enough after the end of the period to pay current-period liabilities. With the lone exception of property tax revenues, which GASB standards require to be collectible within 60 days of the end of the current fiscal year to be deemed available, governments are free to establish their own definition of *available* and, therefore, which items to recognize in their financial statements as current financial resources and revenues.[8] In practice, the definition of *available* may range anywhere from 30 days to one year but 60 days is common.

Because governmental funds account for the inflows and outflows of current financial resources, the balance sheet for governmental funds reports only current assets and current liabilities and **fund balances** (or **fund equity**), which is the difference between current assets and current liabilities. One can readily see, for example, that no long-lived assets, such as land, buildings, and equipment,

[7] General long-term debt is distinguished from long-term debt issued and serviced by a proprietary or fiduciary fund. Interest and principal on debt issued by proprietary or fiduciary funds and payable from the revenues of those funds is accounted for in those funds rather than in a debt service fund.

[8] GASB standards require that governments disclose in the notes to their financial statements the length of time used to define *available* for purposes of revenue recognition in the governmental funds financial statements; see GASB *Codification,* Sec. 2300.106, par. a(5).

nor any long-term liabilities, such as bonds payable, are reported on the City and County of Denver's governmental funds balance sheet shown in Illustration A1–3.

Similarly, Illustrations A1–5 and 2–1 show that inflows and outflows of current financial resources of the governmental funds are reported in a statement of revenues, expenditures, and changes in fund balances. As explained previously, financial resources must be *available* to pay current-period obligations (that is, they must be expected to be received during the current period or soon thereafter) before they can be reported as a revenue of the current period. Recognizing as revenues only those inflows that are measurable and available to pay current-period obligations and recognizing as expenditures only obligations that will be paid from currently available financial resources is referred to as the **modified accrual basis** of accounting.

Accounting for financial resource inflows and outflows in the governmental funds on the modified accrual basis is much different than accounting for the corresponding *economic resource* inflows and outflows for governmental activities on the accrual basis, as they are reported in the government-wide financial statements. As puzzling as this may seem at this early point in the course, the reason for the differential accounting treatment is worth repeating: The governmental fund financial statements report on short-term fiscal accountability; the government-wide statements report on long-term operational accountability. Thus, governmental activities at the government-wide level are accounted for using principles similar to those used by for-profit business organizations.

In the next few chapters, you will become familiar with the "dual-track" approach the authors have developed to record the different effects of certain transactions on the governmental fund financial statements and the Governmental Activities column of the government-wide financial statements. The following example illustrates how certain transactions affect the fund and government-wide statements differently and thus require different accounting treatment.

The City of Princeton issued a two-year note in the amount of $2,000,000 to finance the acquisition of five new fire trucks. The proceeds of the note and the expenditure for the fire trucks are to be accounted for in the General Fund. The city maintains a general journal and general ledger for the General Fund and a separate general journal and general ledger to record the effect of transactions on governmental activities at the government-wide level.

The issuance of the two-year note by the City of Princeton has very different effects on the General Fund and governmental activities, as shown in journal entries 1a and 1b.

	General Ledger	
	Debits	**Credits**
General Fund:		
1a. Cash	2,000,000	
Other Financing Sources— Proceeds of Two-Year Note		2,000,000
Governmental Activities, Government-wide:		
1b. Cash	2,000,000	
Notes Payable		2,000,000

The credit account Other Financing Sources—Proceeds of Two-Year Note in Entry 1a is a temporary account indicating that additional financial resources (cash in this instance) have been added to the fund balance of the General Fund. Thus, the $2,000,000 proceeds of the note have the same effect on the balance of financial resources in the fund that receiving $2,000,000 of tax revenues would have. As you will learn later, other financing sources are reported in a different section of the statement of revenues, expenditures, and changes in fund balances (see Illustration A1–5) than are revenues, but beyond that the distinction is of little importance; the resources in the fund are all available to spend regardless of their source.[9] Note that Entry 1b is identical to the journal entry that a business entity would make for this transaction, reinforcing the fact that transactions affect government-wide financial statements in essentially the same manner as they do business accounting. Note also that the two-year liability is recorded only at the government-wide level since only current assets and current liabilities are recorded in governmental funds.

Journal entries 2a and 2b illustrate the dual effects on the integrated reporting model when the five fire trucks are purchased:

	General Ledger	
	Debits	**Credits**
General Fund:		
2a. Expenditures—Capital Outlay	2,000,000	
Cash		2,000,000
Governmental Activities, Government-wide:		
2b. Equipment	2,000,000	
Cash		2,000,000

Entry 2a shows that long-lived assets, fire trucks in this example, are not accounted for in the General Fund because governmental funds are used only to account for the inflows and outflows (i.e., expenditures) of current financial resources used to provide services or purchase equipment and supplies that have been approved in the budget. In the Governmental Activities column of the government-wide statement of net assets (see Illustration A1–1), the long-term effects of transactions must be reported, including general capital assets such as fire trucks that will provide service benefits in the future. Entry 2b accomplishes this objective by recording the purchase of the fire trucks in the same manner that a business entity would account for the purchase.

In addition, depreciation expense will be recognized on the fire trucks over the next several years in the government-wide financial statements. Thus, the fire trucks

[9] Some governmental accounting teachers use the example of a cookie jar or other container to illustrate the operation of a governmental fund. For example, you can visualize the General Fund, and each of the other governmental funds, as being a cookie jar. As revenues or other financing sources (cash and near-cash financial resources) flow into the cookie jar, it causes the balance of financial resources (the fund balance) in the cookie jar to rise. As financial resources (cash) are removed from the jar (or obligations are incurred to use cash later in the period or soon thereafter)—that is, as expenditures are made—the fund balance drops. It is necessary, of course, to keep an accounting record of (i.e., journalize) the inflows and outflows of financial resources as well as to maintain ledger accounts that indicate the nature of the financial resources (cash, short-term investments, receivables, and other near-cash assets), current liabilities owed by the fund, and the current fund balance. Although this is not a perfect analogy to the actual operation of a fund, it may help you to visualize its short-term, spending focus.

and all other depreciable assets used in carrying out governmental activities will be reported net of accumulated depreciation in the Governmental Activities column of the statement of net assets. Additional distinctions between expenditures and expenses will be made in Chapter 3. For now, the essential difference to note is that an **expenditure** is the amount of financial resources used to acquire an asset (i.e., the cost), and an **expense** is how much of that cost expired or was used up in producing services of the period. In the example of the City of Princeton, the expenditure was $2,000,000. If the fire trucks are being depreciated over 10 years, the expense (the portion of the cost that expired) for the year is $200,000. Note that the concept of expense, particularly depreciation expense, has no relevance in accounting for the General Fund because depreciation expense does not require the use of current financial resources.

Proprietary Funds

Proprietary funds of a government follow accounting and financial reporting principles that are similar to those for commercial business entities. As in business, if a government intends to charge users for the goods or services provided, its officials need to know the full cost of those goods and services in order to determine appropriate prices or fees. Determining the full cost is also essential in deciding whether the government should continue to produce or provide particular goods or services or to contract for them with an outside vendor. Accrual accounting, including depreciation of capital assets, is essential for governments to determine the full cost of providing business-type services and to report on the extent to which each service is covering its full cost of operation.

As Illustration 2–1 shows, there are two types of proprietary funds: *internal service funds* and *enterprise funds*. Legislative approval is ordinarily required to establish proprietary funds, although they may be required by law or contractual provisions such as debt covenants. The two funds differ primarily in terms of their objectives and the way the financial information of each type of fund is reported in the fund and government-wide financial statements. Accounting and financial reporting requirements for proprietary funds are covered in Chapter 7 of this text. Thus, only a brief overview is provided in this chapter.

Internal service funds are created to improve the management of resources and generally provide goods or services to departments or agencies of the same government and sometimes to other governments on a cost-reimbursement basis. Examples of services typically accounted for by internal service funds include central purchasing and warehousing of supplies, motor pools, centralized data processing, and self-insurance pools.

Enterprise funds *may* be used to account for activities in which goods or services are provided to the public for a fee that is the principal source of revenue for the fund. GASB standards *require* the use of an enterprise fund if:

1. The activity is financed with debt that is secured solely by a pledge of the net revenues from fees and charges of the activity.
2. Laws or regulations require that the activity's costs of providing services, including capital costs (such as depreciation or debt service), be recovered with fees and charges rather than with taxes or similar revenues.
3. The pricing policies of the activity establish fees and charges designed to recover its costs, including capital costs.[10]

To reinforce a point made previously, internal service fund financial information is generally reported in the Governmental Activities column of the government-wide

[10] GASB *Codification,* Sec. 1300.109.

statements, unless an internal service fund predominantly serves a proprietary fund, in which case it is reported in the Business-type Activities column. Thus, for most governments the information reported in the Business-type Activities column of the government-wide statements will be the same as the enterprise fund totals reported in the proprietary fund statements. Furthermore, since the business-type activity financial information is reported using the same measurement focus and basis of accounting in the proprietary fund and government-wide statements, there is no need to reconcile any differences between the statements or to use a dual-track approach.

Fiduciary Funds

Fiduciary activities of a government are reported using the same principles as proprietary fund and government-wide financial statements: the economic resources measurement focus and accrual basis of accounting. Again, it should be noted that fiduciary activities are reported *only* in the fiduciary fund statements (statement of fiduciary net assets and statement of changes in fiduciary net assets) and not in the government-wide statements (see Illustration 2–1). Examples of the two fiduciary fund statements for the City and County of Denver are provided in Illustrations A1–10 and A1–11. These statements present financial information for the City and County pension trust funds, private-purpose trust fund, and agency funds. As shown by these statements, Denver has no investment trust funds.

The fiduciary fund category consists of agency funds and three types of trust funds: investment trust funds, pension trust funds, and private-purpose trust funds. **Agency funds** generally are used when the government holds cash on a custodial basis for an external party (individual, organization, or government). An example is taxes collected by a government on behalf of other governments. There are no net assets in agency funds, since for every dollar of assets held there is a dollar of liability to the external party (total assets in the fund always equal total liabilities).

Trust funds differ from agency funds primarily in the length of time and the manner in which resources are held and managed. In most cases, trust fund assets include investments whose earnings add to the net assets of the fund and which can be used for a specified purpose. Examples of trust funds are **pension trust funds** that hold assets in trust to provide retirement benefits for employees, **investment trust funds** used to report the equity of external participants (typically other governments) in a sponsoring government's investment pool, and **private-purpose trust funds** created to benefit private individuals, such as a fund to provide scholarships for the children of firefighters and police officers killed in the line of duty.

Accounting for trust funds is typically much more complex than just accounting for investments. For example, a large, legally separate state pension plan usually has significant capital assets such as land, buildings, and equipment to report in its financial statements. The expenses of the plan include personnel, supplies, utilities, depreciation, and other items, in addition to investment-related expenses.[11] Accounting for fiduciary funds is discussed in Chapter 8 of the text.

Summary of Government-wide and Fund Characteristics

Illustration 2–2 summarizes the characteristics and principles of accounting and reporting for government-wide and fund categories. One topic not discussed in this

[11] Because fiduciary funds benefit only external parties, the account titles *revenues* and *expenses* are not used for these funds. Instead, increases in fiduciary fund net assets are called *additions* and decreases are called *deductions*.

ILLUSTRATION 2–2 Summary of Government-wide and Fund Characteristics

Characteristics	Government-wide	Governmental Funds	Proprietary Funds	Fiduciary Funds[c]
Types of funds	NA[a]	General, special revenue, debt service, capital projects, permanent	Enterprise, internal service[b]	Agency, investment trust, pension trust, private-purpose trust
Accountability focus	Operational accountability	Fiscal accountability	Operational accountability	Operational accountability
Measurement focus	Economic resources	Current financial resources	Economic resources	Economic resources
Basis of accounting	Accrual	Modified accrual	Accrual	Accrual
Required financial statements	Statement of net assets; statement of activities	Balance sheet; statement of revenues, expenditures, and changes in fund balances	Statement of net assets; statement of revenues, expenses, and changes in fund net assets; statement of cash flows	Statement of fiduciary net assets; statement of changes in fiduciary net assets
Balance sheet/statement of net assets accounts	Current and noncurrent assets, current and noncurrent liabilities, net assets	Current assets, current liabilities, fund balances (equity)	Current and noncurrent assets, current and noncurrent liabilities, net assets	Current and noncurrent assets, current and noncurrent liabilities, net assets[d]
Operating or change statement accounts	Revenues, expenses	Revenues, expenditures, other financing sources/uses	Revenues, expenses	Additions, deductions[e]
Budgetary accounting	Not formally integrated into the accounts	Formally integrated into accounts of certain funds	Not formally integrated into the accounts	Not formally integrated into the accounts

[a]Funds are not applicable to the government-wide statements.

[b]Financial information for internal service funds is usually reported in the Governmental Activities column of the government-wide statements, unless the funds predominantly benefit enterprise funds. In that case, internal service fund information would be reported in the Business-type Activities column.

[c]Fiduciary activities are reported only in the fund statements, not in the government-wide statements.

[d]Agency funds have no net assets since total assets equal total liabilities for these funds.

[e]Because fiduciary fund resources benefit external parties and cannot be used to provide governmental services, increases in fiduciary fund net assets are not revenues of the government, nor are decreases expenses of the government. Instead, increases in fiduciary net assets are reported as *additions* and decreases are reported as *deductions*. Since agency funds have no net assets, they cannot have additions or deductions.

chapter is budgetary accounting, which is a main topic of Chapter 3. As shown in Illustration 2–2, budgetary accounts are integrated into the accounts of certain governmental funds, primarily the General Fund and special revenue funds, but often other governmental funds as well. Chapter 3 also covers other important subjects such as how governmental activity revenues and expenses are classified in the government-wide statements and how revenues and *expenditures* are classified in the governmental funds.

MAJOR FUND REPORTING

GASB standards recognize that most financial statement users are unlikely to have a significant interest in all of the many funds that a government may use. Instead, it is likely that their interest will be focused on larger dollar-amount funds. Consequently, *GASBS 34* requires that financial statements prepared for governmental funds and enterprise funds include a separate column for each **major fund.**[12] An additional column is provided in each statement for the total amounts for all nonmajor funds of that type—governmental or enterprise, as applicable. For example, the governmental fund statements of the City and County of Denver, shown in Illustrations A1–3 and A1–5 in the Appendix to Chapter 1, report the General Fund and the Human Services and Bond Projects funds as major funds. Aggregate amounts for all nonmajor governmental funds are reported in the column headed *Other Governmental Funds*. Similarly, as shown in Illustrations A1–7, A1–8, and A1–9, the City and County of Denver reports its Wastewater Management and Denver Airport System funds as major enterprise funds. Aggregate amounts for all other enterprise funds are reported in the *Other Enterprise Funds* column. Major fund reporting is not applicable to internal service funds or fiduciary funds.

Determination of Major Funds

By its nature the General Fund of a government is always a major fund. In addition, any fund that a government considers of significant importance to financial statement users can be reported as major. Otherwise, *GASBS 34* requires that any fund that meets the following size criteria be designated as major:

a. Total assets, liabilities, revenues, or expenditures/expenses of that governmental or enterprise fund are at least 10 percent of the corresponding element total (assets, liabilities, and so forth) for all funds of that category or type (that is, total governmental or total enterprise funds), *and* (emphasis added)

b. The same element that met the 10 percent criterion in (*a*) is at least 5 percent of the corresponding element total for all governmental and enterprise funds combined.[13]

It is important to note that the same element of a fund must meet *both* criteria for mandatory reporting as a major fund. On occasion, a fund may meet both criteria in the preceding fiscal year but only one or perhaps neither of the criteria in the current year. In such a case, the government may elect to continue to report the fund as a major fund in the current year pending a future year determination.

[12] GASB *Codification*, Sec. 2200.152.

[13] Ibid, Sec. 2200.153

To illustrate application of the major funds criteria, consider the information given in the accompanying table for the hypothetical Town of Truesdale, which is investigating whether certain governmental funds should be reported as major funds.

Financial Statement Elements	Road Tax Fund	Debt Service Fund	Capital Projects Fund	10 Percent of Total Governmental Funds	5 Percent of Total Governmental and Enterprise Funds
Assets	$1,369,238	$3,892,020	$19,273,676	$4,492,627	$4,082,141
Liabilities	172,439	62,530	368,727	86,792	1,562,368
Revenues	4,289,876	6,836,472	6,286,240	6,073,695	3,942,318
Expenditures/Expenses	3,986,746	5,622,890	9,846,935	5,952,221	3,834,623

To determine whether a fund meets the 10 percent and 5 percent criteria, one must first calculate the threshold amounts for each element for total governmental funds and total governmental and enterprise funds, as displayed in the two rightmost columns of the table. It is then a simple matter to compare each fund's assets, liabilities, and so forth, to these threshold amounts.

Fund by fund comparisons to the 10 percent and 5 percent amounts show that for assets, only the Capital Projects Fund meets both criteria for reporting as a major fund. The Road Tax Fund meets the 10 percent criterion for liabilities but not the 5 percent criterion and meets the 5 percent criterion for both revenues and expenditures but not the 10 percent criterion. Consequently, the Road Tax Fund need not be reported as a major fund. Although the Debt Service Fund does not meet either of the criteria for its assets or liabilities and only the 5 percent criterion for its expenditures, its revenues meet both the 10 percent and 5 percent criteria. Therefore, it should be reported as a major fund. To summarize, in addition to its General Fund, the Town of Truesdale must report its Debt Service Fund and Capital Projects Fund as major governmental funds. In addition, the Town of Truesdale would use the same process to investigate whether any enterprise funds are major funds, using totals for all enterprise funds rather than governmental funds for the 10 percent comparisons.

Nonmajor Fund Reporting

Internal managers and perhaps a small number of external financial statement users may have an interest in the financial information for individual nonmajor funds. To meet these needs, many governments provide supplementary combining financial statements for nonmajor governmental and enterprise funds in their comprehensive annual financial report (CAFR). These statements provide a separate column for the financial information of each nonmajor fund as well as total column amounts that are the same as the totals reported in the Other Governmental Funds or Other Enterprise Funds columns of the basic financial statements. Such a statement, the combining balance sheet for the nonmajor governmental funds of Sioux City, Iowa, is presented in Illustration 2–3. As shown in the combining balance sheet, all of Sioux City's nonmajor governmental funds are special revenue funds except for the Cemetery Trust Fund, which is a permanent fund.

ILLUSTRATION 2–3

CITY OF SIOUX CITY, IOWA
Combining Balance Sheet
Governmental Nonmajor Funds
June 30, 2007

	Special Revenue Funds									Permanent Fund	
Assets	**Emergency Fund**	**Storm Water Drainage**	**Road Use**	**Community Development**	**Housing**	**Main Street**	**Younkers Self-Impr. District**	**Convention Center/ Auditorium**	**Transit Operations**	**Cemetery Trust**	**Total Governmental Nonmajor Funds**
Cash and cash equivalents	$4.194,297	$1,280,838	$ 615,458	$ —	$920,906	$94,935	$ —	$ —	$ —	$927,910	$ 8,034,344
Accounts receivable	—	70,884	—	—	48,337	—	—	141,342	35,693	—	296,256
Accrued interest receivable	—	—	—	141,836	—	—	—	—	—	—	141,836
Notes receivable	—	—	—	6,742,384	—	—	—	—	—	—	6,742,384
Due from other governments	545,038	—	690,666	587,838	—	133,804	—	—	1,226,574	—	3,183,920
Due from other funds	—	—	797	—	—	—	—	5,249	—	—	6,046
Inventories	—	—	—	—	—	—	—	105,754	—	—	105,754
Prepaid items	—	—	—	12,755	315,708	—	—	15,105	—	—	343,568
Notes receivable from other funds	—	—	—	11,264	—	—	—	—	—	—	11,264
Total Assets	$4,739,335	$1,351,722	$1,306,921	$7,496,077	$1,284,951	$228,739	$ —	$267,450	$1,262,267	$927,910	$18,865,372
Liabilities											
Accounts payable	$ —	$ —	$219,052	$ 57,887	$ 45,807	$ —	$ —	$665,568	$ 12,897	$ —	$ 1,001,211
Accrued wages	—	—	93,814	15,612	13,015	—	—	48,888	66,087	—	237,416
Contracts & retainers payable	—	—	—	34,220	—	—	—	—	27,859	—	62,079
Due to other governments	—	10,243	—	—	4,998	—	—	2,028	—	—	17,269
Due to other funds	—	—	2	117,134	705	—	1,587	976,797	890,615	—	1,986,840
Deferred revenue	534,992	—	—	—	—	130,061	—	—	—	—	665,053
Total Liabilities	534,992	10,243	312,868	224,853	64,525	130,061	1,587	1,693,281	997,458	—	3,969,868
Fund Balances											
Reserved for encumbrances	—	—	261,052	458,038	—	—	—	—	63,714	—	782,804
Reserved for perpetual care non-expendable	—	—	—	—	—	—	—	—	—	927,910	927,910
Reserved for inventories	—	—	—	—	—	—	—	105,754	—	—	105,754
Reserved for long-term notes	—	—	—	6,753,648	—	—	—	—	—	—	6,753,648
Reserved for prepaid items	—	—	—	12,755	315,708	—	—	15,105	—	—	343,568
Unreserved, undesignated	4,204,343	1,341,479	733,001	46,783	904,718	98,678	(1,587)	(1,546,690)	201,095	—	5,981,820
Total Fund Balances (deficit)	4,204,343	1,341,479	994,053	7,271,224	1,220,426	98,678	(1,587)	(1,425,831)	264,809	927,910	14,895,504
Total Liabilities and Fund Balances	$4,739,335	$1,351,722	$1,306,921	$7,496,077	$1,284,951	$228,739	$ —	$267,450	$1,262,267	$927,910	$18,865,372

Appendix

Summary Statement of Governmental Accounting and Financial Reporting Principles

Following is a summary statement of accounting and financial reporting principles for state and local governments, as modified by GASB *Statement No. 34.*[14] Principles summarized here that have not been discussed in Chapters 1 and 2 will be covered in depth in following chapters.

1. **Accounting and Reporting Capabilities**
   A governmental accounting system must make it possible both: (a) to present fairly and with full disclosure the funds and activities of the government in conformity with generally accepted accounting principles, and (b) to determine and demonstrate compliance with finance-related legal and contractual provisions.

2. **Fund Accounting Systems**
   Governmental accounting systems should be organized and operated on a fund basis. A fund is defined as a fiscal and accounting entity with a self-balancing set of accounts recording cash and other financial resources, together with all related liabilities and residual equities or balances, and changes therein, which are segregated for the purpose of carrying on specific activities or attaining certain objectives in accordance with special regulations, restrictions, or limitations. Fund financial statements should be used to report detailed information about the primary government, including its blended component units. The focus of governmental and proprietary fund financial statements is on major funds.

3. **Types of Funds**
   The following types of funds should be used by state and local governments to the extent that they have activities that meet the criteria for using those funds.
   a. **Governmental Funds**
   (1) *The General Fund*—to account for all current financial resources except those required to be accounted for in another fund.
   (2) *Special Revenue Funds*—to account for the proceeds of specific revenue sources (other than private-purpose trusts or for major capital projects) that are legally restricted to use for specified purposes.
   (3) *Capital Projects Funds*—to account for financial resources to be used for the acquisition or construction of major capital facilities (other than those financed by proprietary funds and trust funds).
   (4) *Debt Service Funds*—to account for the accumulation of resources for, and the payment of, general long-term debt principal and interest.
   (5) *Permanent Funds*—to account for legally restricted resources provided by trust in which the earnings but not the principal may be used for purposes that support the primary government's programs (those that benefit the government or its citizenry). [Note: Similar permanent trusts that benefit private individuals, organizations, or other governments—that is, private-purpose trust funds—are classified as fiduciary funds, as shown below.]

[14] GASB *Codification,* Sec. 1100 through 2100.

b. **Proprietary Funds**

(6) *Enterprise Funds—may* be used to report any activity for which a fee is charged to external users for goods or services. An enterprise fund *must* be used if (a) the activity is being financed with debt that is secured solely from the fees and charges for the activity, (b) laws and regulations require that the costs of providing services, including capital costs such as depreciation or debt service, be recovered from fees and charges, or (c) pricing policies of the activity are intended to recover its costs, including capital costs.

(7) *Internal Service Funds*—to account for the financing of goods or services provided by one department or agency to other funds, departments, or agencies of the governmental unit, or to other governmental units, on a cost-reimbursement basis.

c. **Fiduciary Funds** (and similar component units). These are *trust* and *agency funds* that are used to account for assets held by a governmental unit in a trustee capacity or as an agent for individuals, private organizations, and other governmental units. These include:

(8) *Agency funds.*
(9) *Pension (and other employee benefit) trust funds.*
(10) *Investment trust funds.*
(11) *Private-purpose trust funds.*

4. **Number of Funds**
Governmental units should establish and maintain those funds required by law and sound financial administration. Only the minimum number of funds consistent with legal and operating requirements should be established, however, because unnecessary funds result in inflexibility, undue complexity, and inefficient financial administration.

5. **Reporting Capital Assets**
A clear distinction should be made between general capital assets and capital assets of proprietary and fiduciary funds. Capital assets of proprietary funds should be reported in both the government-wide and fund statements. Capital assets of fiduciary funds should be reported in only the statement of fiduciary net assets. All other capital assets of the governmental unit are general capital assets. They should not be reported as assets in governmental funds but should be reported in the Governmental Activities column in the government-wide statement of net assets.

6. **Valuation of Capital Assets**
Capital assets should be reported at historical cost. The cost of a capital asset should include capitalized interest (not applicable to general capital assets) and ancillary charges necessary to place the asset into its intended location and condition for use. Donated capital assets should be reported at their estimated fair value at the time of the acquisition plus ancillary charges, if any.

7. **Depreciation of Capital Assets**
Capital assets should be depreciated over their estimated useful lives unless they are either inexhaustible or are infrastructure assets using the modified approach as set forth in *GASBS 34*, pars. 23–26. Inexhaustible assets such as land and land improvements should not be depreciated. Depreciation expense should be reported in the government-wide statement of activities; the proprietary fund statement of revenues, expenses, and changes in fund net assets; and the statement of changes in fiduciary net assets.

8. **Reporting Long-Term Liabilities**
A clear distinction should be made between fund long-term liabilities and general long-term liabilities. Long-term liabilities directly related to and expected to be paid from proprietary funds should be reported in the proprietary fund statement of net assets and in the government-wide statement of net assets. Long-term liabilities directly related to and expected to be paid from fiduciary funds should be reported in the statement of fiduciary net assets. All other unmatured general long-term liabilities of the government should not be reported in governmental funds but should be reported in the Governmental Activities column in the government-wide statement of net assets.

9. **Measurement Focus and Basis of Accounting in the Basic Financial Statements**
   a. **Government-wide Financial Statements**
   The government-wide statement of net assets and statement of activities should be prepared using the economic resources measurement focus and the accrual basis of accounting. Revenues, expenses, gains, losses, assets, and liabilities resulting from exchange and exchange-like transactions should be recognized when the exchange takes place. Revenues, expenses, assets, and liabilities resulting from nonexchange transactions should be recognized in accordance with [*Codification*] Section N50, "Nonexchange Transactions."
   b. **Fund Financial Statements**
   In fund financial statements, the modified accrual or accrual basis of accounting, as appropriate, should be used in measuring financial position and operating results.
      (1) Financial statements for governmental funds should be presented using the current financial resources measurement focus and the modified accrual basis of accounting. Revenues should be recognized in the accounting period in which they become available and measurable. Expenditures should be recognized in the accounting period in which the fund liability is incurred, if measurable, except for unmatured interest on general long-term liabilities, which should be recognized when due.
      (2) Proprietary fund statements of net assets and revenues, expenses, and changes in fund net assets should be presented using the economic resources measurement focus and the accrual basis of accounting.
      (3) Financial statements of fiduciary funds should be reported using the economic resources measurement focus and the accrual basis of accounting, except for the recognition of certain liabilities of defined benefit pension plans and certain postemployment health care plans.
      (4) Transfers between funds should be reported in the accounting period in which the interfund receivable and payable arise.

10. **Budgeting and Budgetary Control**
   a. An annual budget(s) should be adopted by every governmental unit.
   b. The accounting system should provide the basis for appropriate budgetary control.
   c. A common terminology and classification should be used consistently throughout the budget, accounts, and financial statements.

11. **Budgetary Reporting**
   a. Budgetary comparison schedules should be presented for the General Fund and each major special revenue fund that has a legally adopted budget as part of the required supplementary information (RSI). Governments may elect to present the budgetary comparisons as part of the basic financial statements.

12. **Transfer, Revenue, Expenditure, and Expense Account Classification**
    a. Transfers should be classified separately from revenues and expenditures or expenses in the basic financial statements.
    b. Proceeds of general long-term debt issues should be classified separately from revenues and expenditures in the governmental fund financial statements.
    c. Governmental fund revenues should be classified by fund and source. Expenditures should be classified by fund, function (or program), organization unit, activity, character, and principal classes of objects.
    d. Proprietary fund revenues should be reported by major sources, and expenses should be classified in essentially the same manner as those of similar business organizations, functions, or activities.
    e. The statement of activities should present *governmental* activities at least at the level of detail required in the governmental fund statement of revenues, expenditures, and changes in fund balance—at a minimum by *function.* Governments should present *business-type* activities at least by *segment.*

13. **Annual Financial Reports**
    a. A comprehensive annual financial report (CAFR) should be prepared and published, covering all activities of the primary government (including its blended component units) and providing an overview of all discretely presented component units of the reporting entity—including introductory section, management's discussion and analysis (MD&A), basic financial statements, required supplementary information other than MD&A, combining and individual fund statements, schedules, narrative explanations, and statistical section. The reporting entity is the primary government (including its blended component units) and all discretely presented component units per [*Codification*] Section 2100, "Defining the Financial Reporting Entity."
    b. The minimum requirements for general purpose external financial reporting are:
       (1) Management's discussion and analysis.
       (2) Basic financial statements. The basic financial statements should include:
          (a) Government-wide financial statements.
          (b) Fund financial statements.
          (c) Notes to the financial statements.
       (3) Required supplementary information other than MD&A.
    c. As discussed in [*Codification*] Section 2100, the financial reporting entity consists of (1) the primary government, (2) organizations for which the primary government is financially accountable, and (3) other organizations for which the nature and significance of their relationship with the primary government are such that exclusion would cause the reporting entity's basic financial statements to be misleading or incomplete. The reporting entity's government-wide financial statements should display information about the reporting government as a whole, distinguishing between the total primary government and its discretely presented component units as well as between the primary government's governmental and business-type activities. The reporting entity's fund financial statements should present the primary government's (including its blended component units, which are, in substance, part of the primary government) major funds individually and nonmajor funds in the aggregate. Funds and component units that are fiduciary in nature should be reported only in the statements of fiduciary net assets and changes in fiduciary net assets.

d. The nucleus of a financial reporting entity usually is a primary government. However, a governmental entity other than a primary government (such as a component unit, joint venture, jointly governed organization, or other stand-alone government) serves as the nucleus for its own reporting entity when it issues separate financial statements. For all of these entities, the provisions of [*Codification*] Section 2100 should be applied in layers "from the bottom up." At each layer, the definition and display provisions should be applied before the layer is included in the financial statements of the next level of the reporting government.

Key Terms

Accrual basis, *40*
Agency funds, *47*
Available, *43*
Blended presentation, *39*
Business-type activities, *38*
Capital projects funds, *43*
Component units, *39*
Current financial resources, *43*
Debt service funds, *43*
Discrete presentation, *39*
Economic resources measurement focus, *40*
Enterprise funds, *46*
Escheat properties, *38*
Expenditure, *46*
Expense, *46*
Fiduciary activities, *38*
Fund, *42*
Fund balances, *43*
Fund equity, *43*
General Fund, *42*
Governmental activities, *38*
Governmental funds, *42*
Internal service funds, *46*
Investment trust funds, *47*
Major funds, *49*
Modified accrual basis, *44*
Pension trust funds, *47*
Permanent funds, *43*
Primary government, *39*
Private-purpose trust funds, *47*
Proprietary funds, *46*
Reporting entity, *38*
Special revenue funds, *42*

Selected References

Governmental Accounting Standards Board. *Codification of Governmental Accounting and Financial Reporting Standards as of June 30, 2008.* Norwalk, CT, 2008.

Governmental Accounting Standards Board, *Statement No. 34.* Norwalk, CT, 1999.

Questions

2–1. Describe the governmental activities of a state or local government and identify the measurement focus and basis of accounting used in accounting and financial reporting for these activities.

2–2. Describe the business-type activities of a state or local government and explain how and why accounting and financial reporting for business-type activities differ from those for governmental activities.

2–3. Describe the fiduciary activities of a state or local government and explain how accounting and financial reporting for fiduciary activities differ from those for governmental and business-type activities.

2–4. What organizations does the governmental reporting entity include? Define *primary* government. How does a *component unit* differ from the primary government?

2–5. "If a discrete presentation is used for the financial data of a component unit in the statement of net assets of a governmental financial reporting entity, there is no need for the component unit to issue a separate financial report." Is this statement true or false? What other method may be allowed to include a component unit's financial information with that of the reporting entity?

2–6. What are the three categories of funds prescribed by GASB standards and which fund types are included in each? Do the three fund categories correspond precisely with the three activity categories described in Chapter 2? If not, how do they differ?

2–7. Explain what is meant by the phrase, "A *fund* is a fiscal and an accounting entity."

2–8. Which fund category uses the *modified accrual* basis of accounting? What are the recognition rules for revenues and expenditures under the modified accrual basis of accounting?

2–9. Amber City borrowed $1,000,000 secured by a 5-year mortgage note. The cash from the note was used to purchase a building for vehicle and equipment maintenance. Show how these two transactions should be recorded in the General Fund and governmental activities general journals.

2–10. Explain the criteria for determining if a governmental or enterprise fund must be reported as a *major fund*. What other funds should or may be reported as major funds?

Cases

2–1 Defining the Reporting Entity. Use the comprehensive annual financial report (CAFR) obtained for Exercise/Problem 1–1, or else locate one for a local government using either the government's own Web site or the Governmental Accounting Standards Board's Web site (follow the links "Project Pages" and "Statement 34"). Review the notes to the financial statements to find the note that describes the government's reporting entity. Prepare a brief written report summarizing the legally separate organizations that are included as component units of the governmental reporting entity and those that were excluded, and the reasons given for inclusion or exclusion. Also, indicate whether each component unit is reported by blending or by discrete presentation. How and where is financial information for individual component units reported? Describe any legally separate organizations identified as "related organizations" and why they are accorded this treatment.

2–2 Accounting and Reporting Principles. For more than 100 years, the financial statements of the Town of Brookfield have consisted of a statement of cash receipts and a statement of cash disbursements prepared by the town treasurer for each of its three funds: the General Fund, the Road Tax Fund, and the Sewer Fund. As required by state law, the town submits its financial statements to the Office of the State Auditor; however, its financial statements have never been audited by an independent auditor.

Because of its growing population (nearing 2,000) and increasing financial complexity, the town has hired Emily Eager, who recently obtained her CPA certificate, to supervise all accounting and financial reporting operations. Having worked two years for a CPA firm in a nearby town, Ms. Eager gained limited experience auditing not-for-profit organizations, as well as compiling financial statements for small businesses. Although she has little knowledge of governmental accounting, she is confident that her foundation in business and not-for-profit accounting will enable her to handle the job.

For the year ended December 31, 2011, Ms. Eager has prepared the following unaudited financial statements for the Town of Brookfield. Study these financial statements and answer the questions that follow.

TOWN OF BROOKFIELD
Balance Sheet
December 31, 2011
(unaudited)

Assets	
Cash	$ 1,740
Taxes receivable	18,555
Investments	7,468
Due from other governments	28,766
Land, buildings, and equipment (net of accumulated depreciation of $132,640)	287,580
Total assets	$344,109
Liabilities and Net Assets	
Accounts payable	$ 3,892
Due to other governments	11,943
Total liabilities	15,835
Net assets—unrestricted	299,893
Net assets—restricted	28,381
Total net assets	328,274
Total liabilities and net assets	$344,109

TOWN OF BROOKFIELD
Statement of Activities
Year Ended December 31, 2011
(unaudited)

Revenues	
Property taxes	$124,870
Sewer fees	6,859
Investment income	239
Total revenues	131,968
Expenses	
Government services	115,958
Sewer services	7,227
Miscellaneous	8,462
Total expenses	131,647
Increase in net assets	321
Net assets, January 1, 2011	327,953
Net assets, December 31, 2011	$328,274

Required

a. Assume that you are the CPA Ms. Eager has contacted about the possibility of performing an audit of the Town of Brookfield's financial statements. Based on your preliminary review, what concerns would you have about these financial statements? Do the statements appear to conform to generally accepted accounting principles (GAAP)? In what respects, if any, do the financial statements depart from GAAP?

b. Assume, instead, that you are a member of the town council or a citizen. What concerns would you have with these financial statements?

2–3 Internet Case. Locate a comprehensive annual financial report (CAFR) for a local government from some source on the Internet, perhaps the Web site of the governmental entity or the Governmental Accounting Standards Board's Web site (follow the links "Project Pages," "Statement 34," and "Implementers of Statement 34"). Print a copy of the balance sheet and the statement of revenues, expenditures, and changes in fund balance for the governmental funds.

Required

a. Which governmental funds are considered *major funds* by this government?
b. Verify by your own calculations that at least one of the financial statement elements (total assets, liabilities, revenues, or expenditures) of each major fund meets both the 10 percent and 5 percent criteria described in Chapter 2. If there is a major fund that does *not* meet the criteria, do the notes to the financial statements indicate that the fund was designated as major at the discretion of management?

Exercises and Problems

2–1 Examine the CAFR. Utilizing the CAFR obtained for Exercise/Problem 1–1, examine the financial statements included in the financial section and answer the following questions. If the CAFR you have obtained does not conform to GAAP, it is recommended that you obtain one that does.

a. Government-wide Statements. What are the titles of the two government-wide statements? Are total assets larger for governmental activities or business-type activities? Which function or program has the highest net cost? What kinds of general revenues are available to cover the net cost of governmental activities? Were business-type activities "profitable"? That is, is the excess of revenues over expenses positive? Are there any component units that are discretely presented as a column on the government-wide financial statements?
b. General Fund. What title is given to the fund that functions as the General Fund of the reporting entity? Does the report state the basis of accounting used for the General Fund? What types of assets are included on the governmental funds balance sheet? Do current and noncurrent assets appear on the balance sheet? Do current and noncurrent liabilities appear on the balance sheet? Is this reporting consistent with the basis of accounting being followed?
c. Other Governmental Fund Types. List the names of governmental funds other than the General Fund that are included as major funds in the fund financial statements. Identify which of the major funds, if applicable, are special revenue funds, debt service funds, capital projects funds, and permanent funds.
d. Proprietary Funds. List the names of the proprietary fund types included in the financial statements. Do the financial statements provide evidence that all proprietary funds use accrual accounting?
e. Fiduciary Funds. List the names of the fiduciary funds included in the fund financial statements. Identify whether each of these is an agency fund, investment trust fund, pension trust fund, or private-purpose trust fund. Do the financial statements provide evidence as to what basis of accounting these funds use?
f. Notes to the Financial Statements. Read the notes to the financial statements so that you can refer to them as needed in subsequent chapters. What significant accounting policies are discussed in the first note? Does the note describe the entities that are included as component units? Does it list entities that are not considered component units? Are there any notes that disclose (1) any material violations of legal provisions, (2) deficit fund balances or net assets, or (3) significant commitments or contingencies?

2–2 Multiple Choice. Choose the best answer.

1. Which of the following would be included as part of a governmental reporting entity?
   a. A primary government and any legally separate organization located within the geographic boundaries of the primary government.
   b. A primary government and any legally separate organization for which the primary government is financially accountable.
   c. A primary government and any legally separate organization that requests to be included.
   d. None of the above; a reporting entity consists of only a primary government.

2. Which of the following statements is true regarding the basic financial statements of a state or local government?
   a. Separate columns must be provided in the government-wide financial statements for governmental activities, business-type activities, and fiduciary activities.
   b. Discretely presented component units should be reported as a separate column on the fund financial statements.
   c. Governmental fund financial statements should provide separate columns for each major fund.
   d. All of the above.

3. In the reporting of governmental activities, fiscal accountability is demonstrated by:
   a. Government-wide financial statements.
   b. Fund financial statements.
   c. Both fund and government-wide financial statements.
   d. Neither fund nor government-wide financial statements.

4. The measurement focus and basis of accounting that should be used for the governmental *fund* financial statements are:

	Measurement Focus	**Basis of Accounting**
a.	Current financial resources	Modified accrual
b.	Current financial resources	Accrual
c.	Economic resources	Modified accrual
d.	Economic resources	Accrual

5. Which of the following statements is true regarding the definition of a fund?
   a. A fund is a fiscal and accounting entity.
   b. A fund has a self-balancing set of accounts recording cash and other financial resources, together with all related liabilities and residual equities or balances and changes therein.
   c. Resources, related liabilities, and residual equities or balances and changes therein are segregated for the purpose of carrying out specific activities or attaining certain objectives.
   d. All of the above.

6. Capital assets used for governmental activities, such as those of the police department, should be reported in:
   a. Governmental fund financial statements only.
   b. Government-wide financial statements only.

c. Neither governmental fund nor government-wide financial statements.
d. Both governmental fund and government-wide financial statements.

7. Assets and liabilities of activities for which the government is acting in either an agency or trustee capacity for individuals, organizations, or other governments should be reported in:
   a. The fiduciary column of the government-wide financial statements.
   b. The fiduciary fund financial statements.
   c. Both government-wide and fiduciary fund statements.
   d. Neither government-wide nor fiduciary fund statements.

8. Under the modified accrual basis of accounting:
   a. Revenues are recognized at the time an exchange transaction occurs.
   b. Expenditures are recognized as the cost of an asset expires or is used up in providing governmental services.
   c. Revenues are recognized when current financial resources become measurable and available to pay current-period obligations.
   d. Expenses are recognized when an obligation occurs for costs incurred in providing services.

9. Which of the following is a difference between financial reporting for internal service and enterprise funds?
   a. Internal service funds are reported in the governmental fund financial statements.
   b. Internal service funds are reported in the proprietary fund financial statements.
   c. Internal service funds are generally reported in the Business-type Activities column of the government-wide financial statements.
   d. Internal service funds are generally reported in the Governmental Activities column of the government-wide financial statements.

10. Which of the following must be reported as a *major fund*?
   a. The General Fund.
   b. A fund having total assets, liabilities, revenues, or expenditures/expenses equaling at least 10 percent of the total governmental or enterprise fund amount for the same element (assets, liabilities, and so forth), as applicable, and at least 5 percent of the combined governmental and enterprise fund total amount for the same element.
   c. Both *a* and *b*.
   d. Neither *a* nor *b*.

2–3 True or False. Write T if the corresponding statement is true. If the statement is false, write F and state what changes should be made to make it a true statement.

1. Activities of a general purpose government that provide the basis for GASB's financial accounting and reporting framework consist of governmental, business-type, and fiduciary.
2. The permanent fund is one of the several types of governmental funds.
3. Government-wide financial statements report financial transactions related to the governmental, business-type, and fiduciary activities of the government.
4. A statement of revenues, expenditures, and changes in fund balances is used to report the inflows and outflows of current financial resources of governmental funds.

5. The accounting system for proprietary funds should provide for integration of budgetary accounts.
6. Financial information for component units must be reported by discrete presentation.
7. All assets, both current and noncurrent, and all liabilities, both current and noncurrent, are reported in the government-wide financial statements.
8. All proprietary fund financial information is reported in the Business-type Activities column of the government-wide financial statements.
9. Depreciation should be reported in the financial statements of the General Fund for general capital assets accounted for in the General Fund.
10. In addition to the General Fund, in governmental and proprietary fund financial statements, the only individual funds for which financial information is reported in separate columns are major funds.

2–4 Matching Funds and Identifying Characteristics with Fund and Government-wide Financial Reporting Categories. For each fund or government-wide category listed in the left-hand column, choose the letter(s) of the applicable fund type or characteristic in the right-hand column. Multiple letters may apply to each category.

Fund or Government-wide Category	Fund Type or Characteristic
1. Governmental funds	*a.* Operational accountability
2. Proprietary funds	*b.* Modified accrual
3. Fiduciary funds	*c.* Agency funds
4. Governmental activities, government-wide	*d.* Statement of cash flows
5. Business-type activities, government-wide	*e.* Fiscal accountability
	f. Debt service funds
	g. Current and noncurrent assets and liabilities
	h. Internal service funds
	i. Integrated budgetary accounts
	j. Revenues and expenses
	k. Additions and deductions

2–5 Matching Funds with Transactions. Choose the letter of the sample transaction in the right-hand column that would most likely be reported in the fund listed in the left-hand column.

Fund	Example
1. Agency	*a.* Construction of highways, bridges, or parks.
2. Capital projects	*b.* Administrative expenses of the city manager's office.
3. Debt service	*c.* Gifts in which the principal must be invested and preserved but the investment earnings must be used to provide scholarships to children of police officers who died in the line of duty.
4. Enterprise	*d.* Costs of a central purchasing and warehouse function.
5. General	*e.* Assets held for external government participants in the government's investment pool for the purpose of earning investment income.
6. Internal service	
7. Investment trust	
8. Pension trust	
9. Permanent	
10. Private-purpose trust	
11. Special revenue	

f. Gifts in which the principal must be invested and preserved but the investment earnings can be used for public purposes.

g. Costs of operating a municipal swimming pool.

h. Grant revenues restricted for particular operating purposes.

i. Assets held in trust to provide retirement benefits for municipal workers.

j. Principal and interest payments on general long-term debt.

k. Taxes collected on behalf of another governmental unit.

2–6 General Long-term Liability and Capital Asset Transactions. The Village of Nassau issued a 3-year, 6 percent note in the amount of $100,000 to finance the purchase of vehicles for the Public Works Department.

Required

1. Record the issuance of the $100,000 note in the General Fund and the governmental activities general journals.
2. Record the purchase of vehicles in the amount of $100,000 in the General Fund and governmental activities general journals.
3. Explain why the accounting treatment is different in the General Fund and governmental activities general journals.

2–7 Major Funds. The Town of Trenton has recently implemented GAAP reporting and is attempting to determine which of the following special revenue funds should be classified as "major funds" and therefore be reported in separate columns on the balance sheet and statement of revenues, expenditures, and changes in fund balances for the governmental funds. As the town's external auditor, you have been asked to provide a rationale for either including or excluding each of the following funds as a major fund. Prepare a short report to the town manager that gives your recommendation and explanation. Selected information is provided below.

TOWN OF TRENTON
As of (for the year ended) JUNE 30, 2011

	Gas Tax Revenue Fund	Housing and Urban Development Grant Fund	Trenton Library Fund	All Governmental Funds	All Governmental and Enterprise Funds
Total assets	$160,748	$175,111	$101,549	$1,563,867	$3,497,398
Total liabilities	72,551	85,433	0	867,533	1,487,225
Total revenues	138,336	169,964	120,589	1,537,399	2,987,487
Total expenditures	124,225	130,583	119,812	1,496,223	2,684,531

Chapter Three

Governmental Operating Statement Accounts; Budgetary Accounting

Learning Objectives

After studying this chapter, you should be able to:

1. Explain how operating revenues and expenses related to governmental activities are classified and reported in the government-wide financial statements.
2. Distinguish, at the fund level, between Revenues and Other Financing Sources and between Expenditures and Other Financing Uses.
3. Explain how revenues and expenditures are classified in the General Fund.
4. Explain how budgetary accounting contributes to achieving budgetary control over revenues and expenditures, including such aspects as:
   Recording the annual budget.
   Accounting for revenues.
   Accounting for encumbrances and expenditures.
   Accounting for allotments.
   Reconciling GAAP and budgetary amounts.
5. Describe computerized accounting systems.
6. Explain the classification of revenues and expenditures of a public school system.

As discussed in Chapters 1 and 2, the GASB *Statement No. 34* financial reporting model is designed to meet the diverse needs of financial statement users and achieve the broad reporting objectives set forth in GASB *Concepts Statement No. 1.* The fund-based reporting model used for decades by state and local governments meets reasonably well the *fiscal accountability* needs of users for information about the current financial position and flows of current financial resources through the governmental funds. However, that model falls far short of meeting users' needs for information about the medium- to long-term impacts of the government's current operating and capital decisions, as well as information about the costs of conducting the government's functions and programs.

To meet users' broader needs for *operational accountability* information, the *GASBS 34* reporting model requires—in addition to traditional fund-based financial statements—a management's discussion and analysis (MD&A) and two government-wide financial statements: a statement of net assets or a balance sheet (a statement of financial position) and a statement of activities (an operating statement).[1] This chapter focuses on the latter statement as well as on the operating statement prepared for governmental funds.[2]

CLASSIFICATION AND REPORTING OF EXPENSES AND REVENUES AT THE GOVERNMENT-WIDE LEVEL

The format prescribed for the government-wide statement of activities (see Illustration 3–1) displays the net expense or revenue of each function or program reported for the governmental activities of the government. As shown in Illustration 3–1, the net expense (reported in parentheses if net expense) or net revenue for each function or program is reported in the right-hand column of the top portion of the statement. One will note from the mathematical operators between column headings that the format of the top portion of the statement is as follows:

Expenses – Program Revenues = Net (Expense) Revenue

According to the GASB, reporting in the net expense or revenue format "identifies the extent to which each function of the government draws from the general revenues of the government or is self-financing through fees and intergovernmental aid."[3] The sum of general revenues and any special or extraordinary items is then added to Net (Expense) Revenue to obtain the change in net assets for the period (see Illustrations A1–2 and 3–1).

Reporting Direct and Indirect Expenses

Except for extraordinary or special item expenses, described later in this section, expenses generally are reported by function or program (see Illustration 3–1). **Direct expenses**—those that are specifically associated with a function or program—should be reported on the line for that function or program. **Indirect expenses**—those that are not directly linked to an identifiable function or program—can be reported in a variety of ways. A typical indirect expense is interest on general long-term liabilities. In most cases, interest on general long-term liabilities should be reported as a separate line item rather than being allocated to functions or programs (observe, for example, how it is reported as the last line before total governmental activities in Illustration 3–1).

Functions and programs are discussed in more detail later in this chapter. Governments should report *at a minimum* major functions such as those described on

[1] See Chapters 1 and 2 for definitions and discussions of fiscal and operational accountability.

[2] GASB *Concepts Statement No. 4* refers to statements reporting inflows and outflows of resources as *resource flows statements*. The authors prefer the more commonly used term *operating statement* to refer to statements that report resource inflows and outflows and changes in fund balances or net assets, as appropriate. An operating statement essentially summarizes the financial operations of a government for a specified accounting period. See GASB *Concepts Statement No. 4, Elements of Financial Statements*, par. 27, Governmental Accounting Standards Board, *Codification of Governmental Accounting and Financial Reporting Standards*, as of *June 30, 2008* (Norwalk, CT, 2008), Appendix B.

[3] GASB *Codification,* Sec. 2200.126.

ILLUSTRATION 3–1 **Format of Government-wide Statement of Activities, Governmental Activities**

			Program Revenues				
Functions/Programs	Expenses	—	Charges for Services	Operating Grants and Contributions	Capital Grants and Contributions	=	Net (Expense) Revenue
Primary Government:							
Function/Program 1	$ xxx,xxx		$ xxx,xxx	$ xxx,xxx	$ xxx,xxx		$ (xxx,xxx)
Function/Program 2	xxx,xxx		xxx,xxx		xxx,xxx		(xxx,xxx)
Function/Program 3	xxx,xxx		xxx,xxx	xxx,xxx			(xxx,xxx)
Function/Program 4	xxx,xxx			xxx,xxx	xxx,xxx		(xxx,xxx)
Function/Program 5	xxx,xxx		xxx,xxx	xxx,xxx	xxx,xxx		(xxx,xxx)
Interest on long-term debt	xx,xxx						(xx,xxx)
Total governmental activities	$x,xxx,xxx		$x,xxx,xxx	$x,xxx,xxx	$x,xxx,xxx		$(x,xxx,xxx)
General Revenues:							
Taxes:							
Property taxes							xxx,xxx
Sales taxes							xxx,xxx
Other taxes							xx,xxx
Grants and contributions not restricted to particular programs							xx,xxx
Investment earnings							xx,xxx
Special item—Gain on sale of government land							xx,xxx
Extraordinary item—Loss due to volcanic eruption							(xx,xxx)
Total general revenues, special items, and extraordinary items							x,xxx,xxx
Change in net assets							xx,xxx
Net assets—beginning							xxx,xxx
Net assets—ending							$ xxx,xxx

page 79 of this chapter or those depicted in Illustration A1–2 for the City and County of Denver. The GASB encourages governments to provide additional information for more detailed programs if such information is useful and does not detract from readers' understanding of the statement.

Some readers might find it surprising that depreciation expense often is reported as a direct expense. Depreciation expense for capital assets that are clearly identified with a function or program should be included in the expenses of that function or program. Similarly, depreciation expense for infrastructure assets (such as roads and bridges) should be reported as a direct expense of the function responsible for the infrastructure assets (for example, public works or transportation). Depreciation expense for shared assets should be allocated to functions on an appropriate basis (for example, square footage of building use). If a government opts to report unallocated depreciation expense as a separate line item, it should indicate that the amount reported on that line does not include depreciation expense reported as part of direct expense of functions or programs.[4]

To achieve full costing, some governments allocate to service functions or programs certain central administrative costs that other governments may report in the general government function. If such expenses are allocated to service functions, the allocated expenses should be reported in a separate column from the direct expenses, so the direct expenses will be more comparable with the direct expenses of similar functions of other governments. On the other hand, if a government regularly assigns administrative overhead costs to functions through an internal service fund, it is not required to eliminate these costs from the direct expenses of functions or to report them in a separate column. Rather, the government should disclose in the notes to the financial statements that such overhead charges are included as part of function/program direct expenses.[5]

The foregoing discussion should make it clear that governments find it necessary to allocate depreciation and other expenses to particular functions or programs. Allocation methods are discussed in Chapters 13 and 14 of this text and in most managerial accounting texts. In addition to classification by function or program, governmental accounting computer systems typically provide classifications of expenses/expenditures in a variety of ways. These classifications are discussed later in this chapter.

Program Revenues and General Revenues

Reporting in the net (expense) revenue format requires a government to distinguish carefully between **program revenues** and **general revenues.** As shown in Illustrations A1–2 for the City and County of Denver and 3–1, *program revenues* are reported in the functions/programs section of the statement of activities, where they reduce the net expense of each function or program or produce a net revenue. *General revenues* are not directly linked to any specific function or program and thus are reported in a separate section in the lower portion of the statement.

Three categories of *program revenues* are reported in the statement of activities (see Illustrations A1–2 and 3–1): charges for services, operating grants and contributions, and capital grants and contributions. Charges for services include charges to customers or others for both governmental and business-type activities. Charges for services within the governmental activities category include items such as licenses and permits (for example, business licenses and building permits), fines and forfeits, and operating special assessments sometimes charged for services provided outside the normal service

[4] Ibid., Sec. 2200.132.

[5] Ibid., Sec. 2200.130–131.

area or beyond the normal level of services. A typical example of the latter is snow removal for or maintenance of private lanes or roads that connect with public roads normally maintained by the government. Charges to other governments for services, such as incarceration of prisoners, also are reported in the Charges for Services column.

Grants and contributions restricted by other governments, organizations, or individuals for the *operating* purposes of a particular function or program are reported in a separate column from those restricted for *capital* purposes. GASB requires that multipurpose grants and contributions be reported as *program revenues* if "the amounts restricted to each program are specifically identified in either the grant award or grant application."[6] Otherwise, multipurpose grants and contributions should be reported as *general revenue.*

Earnings from permanent funds, endowments that are restricted for a specific public purpose in the endowment contract or agreement, should be reported as program revenue in the appropriate grants and contributions category. Unrestricted earnings from such sources should be reported as general revenue. In addition, *all* taxes, even those specified by law for a particular use (for example, motor vehicle fuel taxes that can be used only for road and bridge purposes), should be reported as general revenue.

Reporting Special Items and Transfers

In the *GASBS 34* reporting model, extraordinary items and special items must be reported as separate line items below General Revenues in the statement of activities to distinguish these nonrecurring items from normal recurring general revenues, as shown in Illustration 3–1. Separate reporting of such items serves to inform citizens and other report users when governments engage in the unusual practice of balancing their budget by selling government assets or other similar practices. **Extraordinary items** are defined in the same manner as in business accounting: "transactions or other events that are both unusual in nature and infrequent in occurrence."[7] **Special items** are items *within management's control* that may be either unusual in nature or infrequent in occurrence but not both. An example of a special item is one-time revenue from the sale of a significant governmental asset. Extraordinary items should be reported as the last item on the statement of activities; special items should be reported before extraordinary items. Special items that are beyond management's control but are unusual or infrequent in nature (such as a loss due to civil riot) should be recorded as normal expenses, expenditures, or revenue, as appropriate, and be disclosed in the notes to the financial statements.

Other items that should be reported on separate lines below General Revenues (see Illustrations A1–2 and 3–1) are contributions to the principal amounts of endowments and permanent funds and transfers between funds reported as part of governmental activities and funds reported as part of business-type activities. Interfund transactions between governmental and business-type activities that involve the sale of goods or services (such as the sale of water from a water utility enterprise fund to the General Fund) are reported as program revenue and expenses, not as transfers. The reader should note that when transfers are reported, as shown in Illustration A1–2, they are reported as an inflow in one activities column and as an outflow in the other activities column, but are eliminated from the Primary Government Total column.

The preceding discussion covers the major points relating to the government-wide operating statement—the statement of activities. Some of the unique aspects of governmental fund accounting are discussed next, focusing on the General Fund.

[6] Ibid., Sec. 2200.138.

[7] Ibid., Sec. 2200.143.

STRUCTURE AND CHARACTERISTICS OF THE GENERAL FUND; CLASSIFICATION AND DESCRIPTION OF OPERATING STATEMENT ACCOUNTS

The General Fund has long been the accounting entity of a state or local government that accounts for current financial resources raised and expended for the core governmental services provided to the citizenry. The General Fund is sometimes known as an *operating fund* or *current fund;* the purpose, not the name, is the true test of identity. A typical government now engages in many activities that for legal and historical reasons are financed by sources other than those available to the General Fund. Whenever a tax or other revenue source is authorized by a legislative body to be used for a specified purpose only, a government availing itself of that source may create a special revenue fund in order to demonstrate that all revenue from that source was used for the specified purpose only. A common example of a special revenue fund is one used to account for state gasoline tax receipts distributed to a local government; in many states, the use of this money is restricted to the construction and maintenance of streets, highways, and bridges. The accounting structure specified for special revenue funds by GASB standards is identical with that specified for the General Fund.

For the sake of simplicity, and to avoid excessive repetition, the term *General Fund* will be used in the remainder of this chapter and Chapter 4 to denote all *revenue funds,* a generic name sometimes used to describe the General Fund and special revenue funds. As discussed in Chapter 2, there are three other fund types besides the General Fund and special revenue funds that are classified as governmental funds. Those other fund types are *debt service funds, capital projects funds,* and *permanent funds.* The essential characteristics of all governmental fund types were described in Chapter 2. This chapter illustrates in greater depth the manner in which generally accepted accounting principles (GAAP) are applied to the General Fund and special revenue funds. Although permanent funds usually obtain their revenues from permanent investments in financial securities, rather than taxes and other typical sources of governmental revenues, accounting for these funds is essentially the same as that for the General Fund and special revenue funds. Illustrative accounting transactions for a permanent fund are provided in Chapter 4. Accounting and reporting for capital projects funds and debt service funds are discussed in Chapters 5 and 6, respectively.

Governmental Fund Balance Sheet and Operating Statement Accounts

It should be emphasized that the General Fund and all other funds classified as governmental funds account for only current financial resources (cash, receivables, marketable securities, and, if material, prepaid items and inventories). Economic resources, such as land, buildings, and equipment utilized in fund operations, are not recorded by these funds because they are not normally converted into cash. Similarly, governmental funds account for only those liabilities incurred for normal operations that will be liquidated by use of fund assets. As discussed in Chapter 2, general capital assets and general long-term liabilities are reported only in the Governmental Activities column of the statement of net assets at the government-wide level.

The arithmetic difference between the amount of financial resources and the amount of liabilities recorded in the fund is the *fund equity,* usually referred to as fund balances. Residents of a governmental jurisdiction have no legal claim on any excess of liquid assets over current liabilities; therefore, the fund equity is not analogous to the capital accounts of an investor-owned entity. Accounts in the fund equity category of the General Fund include reserve accounts established to disclose that portions of the equity are, for reasons explained later, not available for spending, and an account called *Fund Balance* (also referred to as *Unreserved Fund Balance*), which is the portion of fund equity available for spending.[8]

In addition to the balance sheet accounts just described, the General Fund accounts for financial transactions during a fiscal year in operating statement accounts classified as Revenues, Other Financing Sources, Expenditures, and Other Financing Uses. *Revenue* is defined as increases in fund financial resources other than from financing sources such as interfund transfers and debt issue proceeds. Transfers into a fund and debt issue proceeds received by a fund are examples of inflows classified as **other financing sources** of the fund.

Expenditure is a word that represents the cost to purchase a good or service, whereas *expense* represents the cost of a good or service consumed during the period. Recall that governmental funds are concerned only with flows of current financial resources, not with determination of income or cost of services. Thus, governmental funds report expenditures, not expenses. In the case of employee payroll, utilities, professional travel, and other similar items, expenditures and expenses are essentially the same. In other cases, such as the purchase of equipment using General Fund resources, an expenditure is recorded in the General Fund for the full cost of the equipment—which differs greatly from depreciation expense, the cost of the utility of the equipment deemed to have been consumed during the year. Depreciation expense is not recorded in the General Fund because it does not represent the use of current financial resources. At the time of the purchase, the cost of the equipment is also recorded as a capital asset of government activities at the government-wide level, and the related depreciation expense is recorded as an adjusting entry at year-end.

Other financing uses, or transfers of financial resources from one fund to another fund, have the same effect on fund balance as expenditures: Both decrease the fund balance at year-end when the temporary accounts are closed. In fact, the

word *expenditure* is defined as a decrease in a fund's current financial resources other than from interfund transfers. As an example, interfund transfers occur in those jurisdictions where a portion of the taxes recognized as revenue by the General Fund is transferred to a debt service fund that will recognize an expenditure for the payment of interest and principal on general long-term debt. The General Fund would debit Other Financing Uses—Interfund Transfers Out in the appropriate amount and credit Cash. The debt service fund would debit Cash in the same amount and credit Other

[8] The GASB has issued an exposure draft of a proposed statement that, if issued, will significantly change how fund balances are reported. The exposure draft proposes to replace the current classifications of reserved and unreserved fund balances with a new classification structure that would distinguish between *nonspendable* and *spendable* fund balances. Nonspendable fund balances include balances related to long-term receivables and inventories of consumable supplies that cannot be spent during the current period. Spendable fund balances would be further classified into the four categories of *restricted, limited, assigned,* or *unassigned,* corresponding to the degree of constraint placed over how they can be spent. Restricted spendable fund balances would be those that can be spent only for specific purposes stipulated by external resource providers or a government's constitution or enabling legislation. Limited fund balances would be those that can be spent only for purposes specified by formal action of the governing body. Assigned fund balances would be those intended to be spent for specific purposes by the governing body or executive intent rather than those meeting the more constraining criteria as limited or restricted. By definition, residual fund balances will be reported in the *assigned* category for all governmental funds other than the General Fund. For the General Fund, residual fund balances will be reported as *unassigned.* If this proposal is adopted as a formal statement following due process, it will be effective for fiscal periods beginning after June 2010. Should that occur, the authors will provide an update bulletin explaining how the new standard affects various parts of the text.

ILLUSTRATION 3–2 Format of Governmental Funds Statement of Revenues, Expenditures, and Changes in Fund Balances

	General	Major Fund #2	Major Fund #3	Other Governmental Funds	Total Governmental Funds
Revenues					
Property taxes	$ xxx,xxx			$ xx,xxx	$ xxx,xxx
Sales taxes	xxx,xxx	$ xx,xxx			xxx,xxx
Fines and forfeits	xx,xxx			xx,xxx	xx,xxx
Licenses and permits	xx,xxx				xx,xxx
Other revenue sources	xx,xxx	xx,xxx	$ xx,xxx	xx,xxx	xxx,xxx
Total revenues	x,xxx,xxx	xxx,xxx	xx,xxx	xxx,xxx	x,xxx,xxx
Expenditures					
General government	xx,xxx	xx,xxx		xx,xxx	xxx,xxx
Public safety	xxx,xxx				xxx,xxx
Health and welfare	xx,xxx			xx,xxx	xxx,xxx
Other functions	xxx,xxx	xxx,xxx	xxx,xxx	xx,xxx	xxx,xxx
Total expenditures	x,xxx,xxx	xxx,xxx	xxx,xxx	xxx,xxx	x,xxx,xxx
Excess (deficiency) of revenues over expenditures	(xx,xxx)	x,xxx	(xx,xxx)	x,xxx	xx,xxx
Other Financing Sources (Uses)					
Capital-related debt issued			xxx,xxx		xxx,xxx
Transfers in	xxx,xxx				xxx,xxx
Total other financing sources (uses)	xxx,xxx		xxx,xxx		xxx,xxx
Net changes in fund balances	x,xxx	x,xxx	x,xxx	x,xxx	xx,xxx
Fund balances—beginning	xx,xxx	xx,xxx	xx,xxx	x,xxx	xxx,xxx
Fund balances—ending	$ xx,xxx	$ xx,xxx	$ xx,xxx	$ x,xxx	$ xxx,xxx

Financing Sources—Interfund Transfers In. Thus, the use of transfer accounts achieves the desired objective that revenues be recognized in the fund that raises the taxes and expenditures be recognized in the fund that expends the revenue. Illustrative journal entries are provided in Chapter 4.

Total inflows and outflows for the operating statement accounts of the governmental funds are reported each period in a statement of revenues, expenditures, and fund balances, such as the one presented in Illustration A1–5. Illustration 3–2 presents the format for such a statement in somewhat simpler form. As discussed above, both revenues and other financing sources are temporary accounts that *increase* fund balance at year-end when closing entries are made. Similarly, expenditures and other financing uses are temporary accounts that *decrease* fund balance when closing entries are made. GASB standards emphasize, however, that other financing sources (uses) should be distinguished from revenues and expenditures. The format of the operating statements shown in Illustrations A1–5 and 3–2 accomplishes this objective by reporting other financing sources (uses) in a separate section below the revenues and expenditures sections.

ILLUSTRATION 3–3 Comparison of Balance Sheet, Operating Statement, and Budgetary Accounts

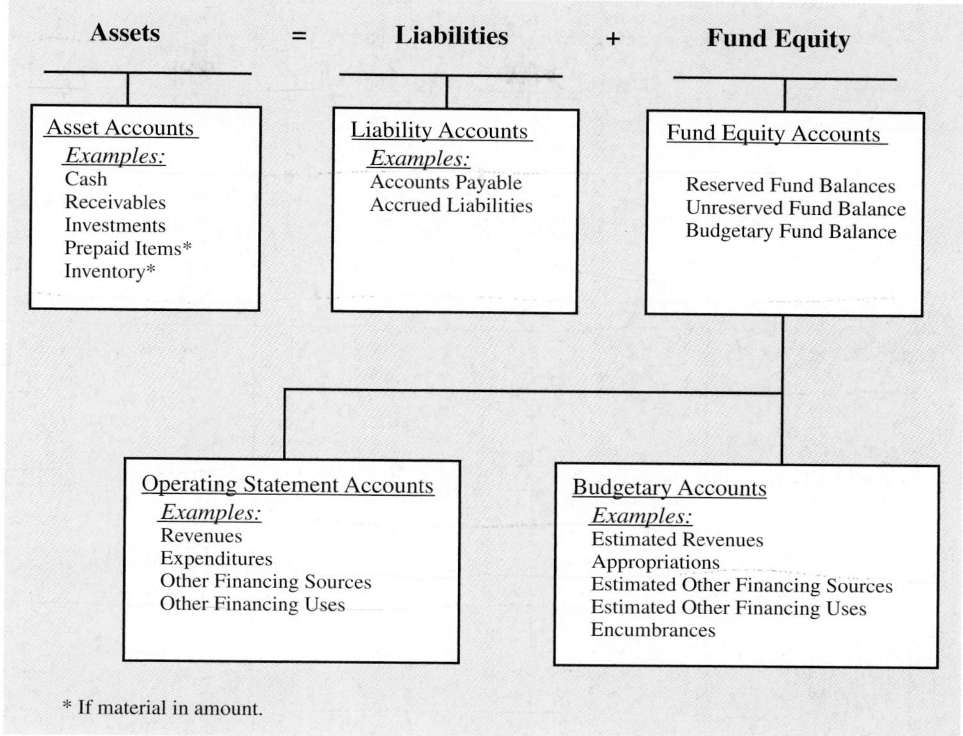

GASB standards require that the operating statement accounts of a governmental fund, such as the General Fund, be recognized on the modified accrual basis of accounting. Under this basis, revenues and other financing sources are recognized if they are *measurable* and *available.* Available means that the revenue or other financing source is expected to be collected during the current period or soon enough thereafter to pay current period obligations. In the case of property taxes, GASB requires expected collection within 60 days after the end of the current fiscal year for the taxes to be recognized as a current-period revenue.[9] Thus, if a portion of the current tax levy is not expected to be collected within 60 days, it would be recorded in the current period as a credit to Deferred Revenues (a current liability). In the following year, Deferred Revenues would be debited and Revenues would be credited. For all other categories of revenues, as well as for other financing sources, governments have the discretion to determine the length of time used to define *available* (generally not more than 90 days after the current fiscal year-end) but must disclose their policy in the notes to the financial statements.[10]

The next section introduces the use of budgetary accounts in the General Fund and certain other governmental fund types that may be included in the governmental unit's formal budget. Before beginning the discussion, it is recommended that you review Illustration 3–3, which displays the relationship between budgetary accounts and the

[9] GASB *Codification,* Sec. P70.104.

[10] GASB *Codification,* Sec. 1600.106.

ILLUSTRATION 3–4 Relationship between Budgetary and Operating Statement Accounts

Budgetary Accounts		Operating Statement Accounts		
Account Title	**Normal Balance**	**Account Title**	**Normal Balance**	**Budgetary Status**
Estimated Revenues	Debit	Revenues	Credit	Net balance indicates deficit (excess) of operating (actual) vs. budgeted revenues.
Estimated Other Financing Sources	Debit	Other Financing Sources	Credit	Net balance indicates deficit (excess) of actual OFS vs. budgeted OFS.*
Appropriations	Credit	Expenditures	Debit	Appropriations minus the sum of Expenditures and Encumbrances indicates remaining or overspent expenditure authority.
Estimated Other Financing Uses	Credit	Other Financing Uses	Debit	Net balance indicates the amount of remaining or overspent interfund transfer authority.
Encumbrances	Debit	NA	NA	See Appropriations line above. An encumbrance has a normal debit balance because it is a commitment to make an expenditure and often is considered the same as an expenditure for budgetary purposes.

NA = Not applicable, since there is no corresponding operating statement account.
*OFS = Other Financing Sources.

balance sheet and operating statement accounts of the General Fund. Two points should be noted in reviewing Illustration 3–3: (1) Both the operating statement accounts and the budgetary accounts are sub-fund equity temporary accounts that are closed to Fund Balance at year-end.[11] (2) Each operating statement account has a budgetary counterpart: Revenues and Estimated Revenues; Expenditures and both Appropriations and Encumbrances (defined in the next section); Other Financing Sources and Estimated Other Financing Sources; and Other Financing Uses and Estimated Other Financing Uses. A tip that may prove useful in understanding budgetary accounting is that, with the exception of Encumbrances, the **budgetary accounts** have normal balances that are the opposite of the corresponding operating statement accounts. For example, since the Revenues account has a normal credit balance, the Estimated Revenues account has a normal debit balance. The use of opposite account balances facilitates budgetary comparisons and makes it easy to determine whether actual amounts are under or over the budgeted amounts. The Encumbrances account has the same normal debit balance as the Expenditures account because an encumbrance represents a commitment prior to an expenditure, as discussed later in this chapter. Illustration 3–4 shows the normal balances of each budgetary account and its corresponding operating statement account.

[11] The temporary budgetary accounts are closed at year-end to Budgetary Fund Balance by reversing the original budgetary entries.

BUDGETARY ACCOUNTS

The fact that budgets are legally binding upon administrators has led to the integration of budgetary accounts into the general ledgers of the General Fund and special revenue funds, and all other funds that are required by state laws to adopt a budget. *GASBS 34* requires that a budget to actual comparison schedule be provided for the General Fund and for each *major* special revenue fund for which a budget is legally adopted.[12] *GASBS 34* recommends that these schedules be provided as required supplementary information (RSI), which should be placed immediately following the notes to the financial statements. GASB provides the option, however, for governments to report the budgetary comparison information in a budgetary comparison *statement,* a statement of revenues, expenditures, and changes in fund balances—budget and actual—which would then be part of the basic financial statements.[13]

Illustration 3–5 presents an example of a budgetary comparison schedule for the General Fund and Human Services Special Revenue Fund of the City and County of Denver. GASB standards require, at a minimum, the presentation of both the originally adopted and final amended budgets and actual amounts of inflows, outflows, and balances. A variance column, such as that included in the City and County of Denver's budgetary comparison schedule, is encouraged but not required since a financial statement user could calculate the variances himself or herself. Of particular note in this schedule is the row caption *Budget Basis Expenditures.* In a note to the required supplementary information, the City and County of Denver explains that budgets for appropriation in the general, special revenue, and capital projects funds are not adopted on a basis consistent with GAAP, as encumbrances outstanding at year-end are treated as expenditures. As explained in the following paragraph, the budget basis of some governments departs even further from GAAP.

In order to achieve meaningful budgetary comparisons, the actual amounts in the schedule should be reported using the government's budgetary basis. Some governments, for example, budget their revenues on the cash basis. If the Actual column of the budgetary comparison schedule (or statement) uses a non-GAAP budgetary basis, such as the cash basis, either the schedule captions or column heading for actual amounts should so indicate, as shown by the caption *Budget Basis Expenditures* in Illustration 3–5.

Budgetary practices of a government may differ from GAAP accounting practices in ways other than basis. GASB standards identify timing, entity, and perspective differences. Discussion of these differences is beyond the scope of this text; it is sufficient to emphasize that GASB standards require that the amounts shown in the Actual column of the budgetary comparison schedule conform in all respects with practices used to develop the amounts shown in the budget columns of the schedule so that there is a true comparison. Standards further require that either on the face of the budgetary comparison schedule or on a separate schedule, the amounts reported in the Actual column of the budgetary comparison schedule must be reconciled with the GAAP amounts shown in the statement of revenues, expenditures, and changes in fund balances. The City and County of Denver provides its reconciliation at the bottom of the budgetary comparison schedule (see Illustration 3–5).

[12] GASB *Codification,* Sec. 2200.182. See Chapter 2 or the glossary for the definition of *major fund.*

[13] Ibid., footnote 35.

ILLUSTRATION 3–5

CITY AND COUNTY OF DENVER
Required Supplementary Information
Budgetary Comparison Schedule
General Fund and Human Services Special Revenue Fund
For the year ended December 31, 2007
(amounts expressed in thousands)

	General Fund				Human Services Special Revenue Fund			
	Budget				Budget			
	Original	Final	Actual	Variance with Final Budget	Original	Final	Actual	Variance with Final Budget
Revenues								
Taxes	$546,790	$548,565	$570,940	$22,375	$ —	$ —	$44,597	$44,597
Licenses and permits	21,612	21,999	28,094	6,095	—	—	—	—
Intergovernmental revenues	25,225	27,648	32,861	5,213	—	—	82,644	82,644
Charges for services	147,455	149,214	107,519	(41,695)	—	—	1,406	1,406
Investment and interest income	11,121	11,365	18,717	7,352	—	—	23	23
Fines and forfeitures	36,832	36,125	34,253	(1,872)	—	—	—	—
Contributions	—	—	3	3	—	—	235	235
Other revenue	17,061	17,826	11,162	(6,664)	—	—	1,718	1,718
Total Revenues	806,096	812,742	803,549	(9,193)	—	—	130,623	130,623
Budget Basis Expenditures								
General government	204,026	175,025	151,486	23,539	—	—	—	—
Public safety	394,247	400,945	398,183	2,762	—	—	—	—
Public works	81,397	94,897	81,388	13,509	—	—	—	—
Human services	—	—	—	—	153,215	161,928	139,987	21,941
Health	42,649	42,756	41,061	1,695	—	—	—	—
Parks and recreation	47,804	48,012	46,903	1,109	—	—	—	—
Cultural activities	29,911	31,256	31,195	61	—	—	—	—
Community development	17,769	17,769	16,947	822	—	—	—	—
Total Budget Basis Expenditures	817,803	810,660	767,163	43,497	153,215	161,928	139,987	21,941

ILLUSTRATION 3–5 (*Continued*)

Excess (deficiency) of revenues over budget basis expenditures	(11,707)	2,082	36,386	34,304	—	—	(9,364)	9,364
Other Financing Sources (Uses)								
Insurance recoveries	—	—	1	1	—	—	5	(5)
Proceed from sale of asset	—	—	13	13	—	—	—	—
Transfers in	25,886	24,985	32,333	7,348	—	—	—	—
Transfers out	(34,611)	(44,163)	(44,163)	—	(32)	(32)	(32)	—
Total Other Financing Sources (Uses)	(8,725)	(19,178)	(11,816)	7,362	(32)	(32)	(27)	(5)
Excess of revenues and other financing sources over budget basis expenditures and other financing uses	$(20,432)	$(17,096)	24,570	$41,666	$(32)	$(32)	(9,391)	$9,359
Add outstanding encumbrances			—				—	
Less prior year encumbrances, as adjusted			(14,635)				(9,041)	
Add grantor expenditures			—				14,797	
Net change in fund balances			9,935				(3,635)	
Fund balance—January 1			185,656				24,628	
Fund Balance—December 31			$195,591				$20,993	

In order to achieve budgetary control, only three general ledger budgetary control accounts are needed in the General Fund (and other funds for which a budget is adopted): **Estimated Revenues, Appropriations,** and **Encumbrances.** Subsidiary ledger accounts should be provided in whatever detail is required by law or for sound financial administration to support each of the three control accounts. Budgeted interfund transfers and debt proceeds may be recorded in two additional budgetary control accounts: **Estimated Other Financing Sources** and **Estimated Other Financing Uses.** Again, these control accounts should be supported by subsidiary detail accounts as needed.

TERMINOLOGY AND CLASSIFICATION FOR GOVERNMENTAL FUND BUDGETS AND ACCOUNTS

Budgets may be described as legally approved plans of financial operations embodying the authorization of expenditures for specified purposes to be made during the budget period and the proposed means of financing them. The sequence of budget preparation in practice is often the same as the sequence in the preceding sentence: Expenditures are planned first; then plans are made to finance the expenditures. For that reason, the discussion in this chapter follows the same sequence. Governmental budgeting is discussed in more detail in Chapter 13.

Classification of Appropriations and Expenditures

An appropriation is a legal authorization to expend cash or other financial resources for goods, services, and facilities to be used for specified purposes, in amounts not to exceed those authorized for each purpose. When liabilities authorized by an appropriation have been incurred, the appropriation is said to be *expended.* Thus, budgeted appropriations are sometimes called *estimated expenditures*. Expenditures, then, are expended appropriations. According to GASB standards, expenditures should be classified by (1) fund, (2) function or program, (3) organization unit, (4) activity, (5) character, and (6) object.[14] A common terminology and classification should be used consistently throughout the budget, the accounts, and the financial reports of each fund.

Classification by Fund

The primary classification of governmental expenditures is by fund, since a fund is the basic fiscal and accounting entity of a government. Within each fund, the other five classifications itemized in the preceding paragraph are used to facilitate the aggregation and analysis of data to meet the objectives of financial reporting set forth in Chapter 1.

Classification by Function or Program

The GASB distinguishes between functions and programs in the following manner:

> **Functions** group related activities that are aimed at accomplishing a major service or regulatory responsibility. **Programs** group activities, operations, or organizational

[14] GASB, *Codification,* Sec. 1800.116.

units that are directed to the attainment of specific purposes or objectives.[15] [Emphasis added.]

Examples of common functional classifications are the following:

General Government
Public Safety
Highways and Streets
Health and Welfare
Culture and Recreation

A good example of program classification is found in the City of Oakland, California's FY 2007–09 Adopted Policy Budget, which classifies numerous operating objectives and programs under seven broad goals in the areas of:

Economic Development
Efficiency and Responsiveness to Citizens
Health Care
Infrastructure
Public Safety
Sustainable City
Youth and Seniors

Classification by Organization Unit

Classification of expenditures by **organization unit** is considered essential to management control, assuming the organizational structure of a given government provides clear lines of responsibility and authority. Some examples of organization units that might be found in a city are:

Police Department
Fire Department
Building Safety Department
Public Works Department
City Attorney
City Clerk
Personnel Department
Parks and Recreation Department

The key distinction between classification of expenditures by organization unit and classification by program or function is that responsibility for a department is fixed, whereas a number of departments may be involved in the performance of a program or a function. Both management control within a department and rational allocation of resources within the government require much more specific identification of expenditures (and costs and expenses) than is provided by the major classifications illustrated thus far. The next step needed is classification by activity.

Classification by Activity

An **activity** is a specific and distinguishable line of work performed by an organization unit. For example, within the public works department, activities such as the following may be performed:

Solid waste collection—residential
Solid waste collection—commercial
Solid waste disposal—landfill
Solid waste disposal—incineration

[15] Ibid. par. 117.

Activity classification is more meaningful if responsibility for the performance of each activity is fixed, performance standards are established, and a good management accounting system is installed to measure input of resources consumed (dollars, personnel time, equipment, and facilities used) relative to units of service outputs. Such information is useful to those interested in assessing the efficiency of government operations.

Classification by Character

Classification by **character,** as defined by the GASB, is based on the fiscal period that benefits from a particular expenditure. A common classification of expenditures by character recognizes three groups:

Current expenditures
Capital outlays
Debt service

Current expenditures are expected to benefit the period in which the expenditure is made. Capital outlays are expected to benefit not only the period in which the capital assets are acquired but as many future periods as the assets provide service. Debt service includes payment of interest on debt and payment of debt principal; if the debt has been wisely incurred, residents have received benefits in prior periods from the assets acquired by use of debt financing, are receiving benefits currently, and will continue to receive benefits until the service lives of the assets expire.

Character classification of expenditures is potentially important to taxpayers and other citizens. Properly used, it could give them valuable information for assessing the cost of government during a given period. Generally speaking, expenditures for debt service relate to actions incurred by previous administrations. Capital outlays are expenditures expected to provide benefits in future periods; however, as discussed earlier in this chapter, GASB standards do not allow depreciation expense to be recorded in governmental funds, but require that depreciation expense on general capital assets be reported in the government-wide statement of activities (see the section titled "Depreciation of Capital Assets" in the appendix that follows Chapter 2). It appears that expenditures in the *current* expenditures class are the most influential on the public mind, strongly influencing popular attitudes toward responsible officials.

A fourth character class, *intergovernmental,* is suggested by the GASB for use by governments that act as an intermediary in federally financed programs or that transfer "shared revenues" to other governments.

Classification by Object

The **object** of an expenditure is the thing for which the expenditure was made. Object classes may be viewed as subdivisions of character classifications. One scheme of object classification includes the following major classes:

Personal services
Supplies
Other services and charges
Capital outlays
Debt service

Many other object classifications are encountered in practice, generally more detailed than those listed above. Greater detail can, of course, be achieved by the utilization of subclasses under the major titles. Thus personal services may be subdivided on the basis of permanence and regularity of employment of the persons represented; and each subclass may be further subdivided to show whether the services performed were regular, overtime, or temporary. Employee benefits may be recorded in as much detail as desired as subclasses of the personal services class. "Other services and charges" must be subdivided if the class is to provide any useful budgeting and control information. Professional services, communication, transportation, advertising, printing and binding, insurance, public utility services, repairs and maintenance, rentals, aid to other governments, and miscellaneous are possible subdivisions.

Debt service, also listed as both an object of expenditure and a character class, should be subdivided to provide sufficient evidence that all interest payments and principal payments that should have been made in a certain fiscal period were actually made (or the appropriate liability recorded).

Classification of Estimated Revenues and Revenues

In order for administrators to determine that proposed expenditures presented in the operating budget can be financed by resources available under the laws of the budgeting jurisdiction and higher jurisdictions, revenue forecasts must be prepared. *Revenue,* in the sense in which it is customarily used in governmental budgeting, includes all financial resource inflows—all amounts that increase the net assets of a fund. Examples include interfund transfers and debt issue proceeds, as well as taxes, licenses and permit fees, fines, forfeits, and other revenue sources described in the following sections of this chapter.

It should be emphasized that a government and the funds thereof may raise revenues only from sources available to them by law. Often, the law that authorizes a government to utilize a given revenue source to finance general governmental activities, or specific activities, also establishes the maximum rate that may be applied to a specified base in utilizing the source or establishes the maximum amount that may be raised from the source during the budget period.

The primary classification of governmental revenue is by *fund.* Within each fund, the major classification is by *source.* Within each major source class, it is desirable to have as many secondary classes as needed to facilitate revenue budgeting and accounting. Secondary classes relating to each major source are discussed below under each source caption. Major revenue source classes commonly used are these:

- Taxes
- Special Assessments
- Licenses and Permits
- Intergovernmental Revenues
- Charges for Services
- Fines and Forfeits
- Miscellaneous Revenues

The operating budget and the accounting system for each governmental fund should include all revenue sources available to finance activities of that fund. The General Fund of most governments will ordinarily need all seven major classes itemized above; in some governments, additional major classes may be needed. Each special revenue fund will need to budget and account for only those revenues legally mandated for use in achieving the purpose for which the special revenue fund was created. Similarly, debt service funds budget and account for those sources of revenue that are to be used for payment of interest and principal of tax-supported and special assessment long-term debt. Revenues and other financing sources earmarked for construction or acquisition of general capital assets are budgeted and accounted for by capital projects funds.

In order to determine during a fiscal year that revenues are being realized from each budgeted source in amounts consistent with the budget, actual revenues should be accounted for on the same classification system used for estimated revenues in the operating budget.

Taxes

Taxes are of particular importance because (1) they provide a large portion of the revenue for all levels of government and (2) they are compulsory contributions to finance the cost of government, whether the affected taxpayer approves or disapproves of the taxes.

Ad valorem (based on value) **property taxes** are a mainstay of financing for many local governments but are not used as a source of revenue by many state governments or by the federal government. Ad valorem taxes may be levied against real property and personal property. Some property taxes are levied on a basis other than property values, one illustration being the tax on some kinds of financial institutions in relation to the deposits at a specified date. Other kinds of taxes are sales taxes, income taxes, gross receipts taxes, death and gift taxes, and interest and penalties on delinquent taxes.

The valuation of each parcel of taxable real property, and of the taxable personal property owned by each taxpayer, is assigned by a process known as **property assessment.** The assessment process differs state by state, and in some states by jurisdictions within the state. The tax rate is set by one of two widely different procedures: (1) The government simply multiplies the assessed valuation of property in its jurisdiction by a flat rate—either the maximum rate allowable under state law or a rate determined by the governing body—or (2) the property tax is treated as a residual source of revenue. In the latter event, revenues to be recognized from all sources other than property taxes must be budgeted; the total of those sources must be compared with the total proposed appropriations in order to determine the amount to be raised from property taxes, subject, of course, to limits set by law or legislative policy. Illustration 3–6 shows the computation of the total amount of revenues to be raised from property taxes under the assumption that property taxes are a residual source of revenues. The heading of Illustration 3–6 indicates that it is for the Town of Merrill's General Fund. A similar computation would be made for each fund for which property taxes are levied.

Note that Illustration 3–6 is a computation of the amount of revenue to be raised from property taxes six months before the beginning of the next fiscal year. This is one step in determining the tax levy for the year. A second step is the determination from historical data and economic forecasts of the percentage of the tax levy expected to be collectible. (Even though property taxes are a lien against the property, personal property may be removed from the taxing jurisdiction and some parcels of real property may not be salable or valuable enough for the taxing jurisdiction to recover accumulated taxes against the property.) Therefore, the levy must be large enough to allow for estimated uncollectible taxes. For example, assume the Town of Merrill can reasonably expect to collect only 96 percent of the year 2011 property tax levy for its General Fund. Thus, if tax revenue is to be \$3,582,000 (per Illustration 3–6), the gross levy must be \$3,582,000 ÷ 0.96, or \$3,731,250.

When the gross levy is known, the tax rate may be computed on the basis of the assessed valuation of taxable property lying within the taxing jurisdiction. The term **taxable property** is used in the preceding sentence in recognition of the fact that

ILLUSTRATION 3–6

TOWN OF MERRILL
General Fund
Calculation of Amount to Be Raised by Property Taxes
for Fiscal Year Ending December 31, 2011
As of Current Date—July 31, 2010

Estimated resource requirements:		
Estimated expenditures, remainder of FY 2010		$ 4,200,000
Appropriations proposed for FY 2011		8,460,000
Estimated working balance needed at beginning of FY 2012		510,000
Total estimated resource requirements		13,170,000
Estimated resources available and to be raised, other than from property taxes:		
Actual current balance (July 31, 2010)	$ 654,000	
From second installment of FY 2010 taxes	2,430,000	
From miscellaneous resources, remainder of FY 2010	1,960,000	
From all nonproperty tax sources in FY 2011	4,544,000	
Total estimated resources other than FY 2011 property taxes		9,588,000
Amount required from FY 2011 property taxes		$ 3,582,000

property owned by governments and property used by religious and charitable organizations are often not taxable by the local government. In addition, senior citizens, war veterans, and others may have statutory exemption from taxation for a limited portion of the assessed valuation of property. Continuing the example, assume the net assessed valuation of property taxable by the General Fund of the Town of Merrill is $214,348,000. In that case, the gross property tax levy ($3,731,250) is divided by the net assessed valuation ($214,348,000) to determine the property tax rate. The rate would be expressed as "$1.75 per $100 assessed valuation," or "$17.41 per $1,000 assessed valuation"—rounding up the actual decimal fraction (0.017407) to two places to the right of the decimal, as is customary. The latter rate is typically referred to as 17.41 mills.

Interest and Penalties on Delinquent Taxes

A **penalty** is a legally mandated addition to a tax on the day it becomes delinquent (generally, the day after the day the tax is due). Penalties should be recognized as revenue when they are assessed. *Interest* at a legally specified rate also must be added to delinquent taxes for the length of time between the day the tax becomes delinquent until the day it is ultimately paid or otherwise discharged; interest revenue should be accrued at the time financial statements are to be prepared.

Sales Taxes, Income Taxes, and Gross Receipts Taxes

GASB standards provide that revenue from sales taxes, income taxes, and gross receipts taxes be recognized, net of estimated refunds, in the accounting period in which underlying transactions (e.g., sales and earnings) occur.

Special Assessments

Special assessments differ from ad valorem real property taxes in that the latter are levied against all taxable property within the geographic boundaries of the government levying the taxes, whereas the former are levied against certain properties. The purpose of a special assessment is to defray part or all of the cost of a specific improvement or service that is presumed to be of particular benefit to the properties against which the special assessments are levied. Briefly, when routine services (street cleaning, snow plowing, and so on) are extended to property owners outside the normal service area of the government or are provided at a higher level or at more frequent intervals than for the general public, "service-type" special assessments are levied. Service-type special assessments are accounted for by the fund that accounts for similar services rendered to the general public—usually the General Fund or a special revenue fund. Special assessments for capital improvements should be accounted for by a capital projects fund during the construction phase and by a debt service or agency fund during the debt service phase if debt financing is used. (See Chapter 6 for additional details about capital improvement special assessments.)

Licenses and Permits

Licenses and permits include those revenues collected by a government from individuals or business concerns for various rights or privileges granted by the government. Some licenses and permits are primarily regulatory in nature, with minor consideration to revenue derived, whereas others are not only regulatory but also provide large amounts of revenue, and some are almost exclusively revenue producers. Licenses and permits may relate to the privilege of carrying on business for a stipulated period, the right to do a certain thing that may affect the public welfare, or the right to use certain public property. Vehicle and alcoholic beverage licenses are found extensively on the state level and serve both regulatory and revenue functions. States make widespread use of professional and occupational licenses for purposes of control. Local governments make extensive use of licenses and permits to control the activities of their citizens; and from some they derive substantial amounts of revenue. Commonly found among licenses and permits are building permits, vehicle licenses, amusement licenses, business and occupational licenses, animal licenses, and street and curb permits. Regardless of the governmental level or the purpose of a license or permit, the revenue it produces is ordinarily accounted for when cash is received.

Intergovernmental Revenue

Intergovernmental revenues include grants and other financial assistance. These may be government-mandated nonexchange transactions (for example, certain state sales taxes required by law to be shared with local governments) or voluntary nonexchange transactions (for example, federal or state grants for which local governments compete). In either case, the recipient government does not provide significant value to the grantor government for value received. GASB defines *grants and other financial assistance* as

> transactions in which one governmental entity transfers cash or other items of value to [or incurs a liability for] another governmental entity, an individual, or an organization as a means of sharing program costs, subsidizing other governments or entities, or otherwise reallocating resources to the recipients.[16]

[16] GASB *Codification,* Sec. N5O.504.

Governmental funds should recognize grants and other financial assistance as revenues in the period in which all time restrictions and eligibility requirements (such as a matching requirement) imposed by the grantor government have been met and the resources are available to pay current period obligations. Revenue recognition rules and the complexities of accounting for intergovernmental revenues are discussed in more detail in Chapter 4.

Charges for Services

As discussed earlier in this chapter, charges for services of the governmental funds (and governmental activities at the government-wide level) include all charges for goods and services provided by a governmental fund to enterprise funds, individuals and organizations, and other governments. A few of the many revenue items included in this category are court costs; special police service; solid waste collection charges; street, sidewalk, and curb repairs; receipts from parking meters; library use fees (but not fines); and tuition.

Classification of expenditures by function is discussed earlier in this chapter. The grouping of Charges for Services revenue may be correlated with the functional classification of expenditures. For example, one functional group of expenditures is named General Government, another Public Safety, and so on. In providing general government service, a government may collect revenues such as court cost charges, fees for recording legal documents, and zoning and subdivision fees. Charges for services should be recognized as revenue when measurable and available if that is prior to the collection of cash.

Fines and Forfeits

Revenue from fines and forfeits includes fines and penalties for commission of statutory offenses and for neglect of official duty; forfeitures of amounts held as security against loss or damage, or collections from bonds or sureties placed with the government for the same purpose; and penalties of any sort, except those levied on delinquent taxes. Library fines are included in this category. If desired, Fines and Forfeits may be the titles of two accounts within this revenue class, or they may be subgroup headings for more detailed breakdowns.

Revenues of this classification should be accrued to the extent practicable. Unlike property taxes, however, fines and forfeits may not be estimated with any reasonable degree of accuracy. Because of these uncertainties, revenues from fines and forfeits may be recognized when received in cash if accrual is not practicable.

Miscellaneous Revenues

Although the word *miscellaneous* is not informative and should be used sparingly, its use as the title of a revenue category is necessary. It (1) substitutes for other possible source classes that might have rather slight and infrequent usage and (2) minimizes the need for forcing some kinds of revenue into source classifications in which they do not generically belong. While miscellaneous revenues in itself represents a compromise, its existence aids in sharpening the meanings of other source classes. The heterogeneous nature of items served by the title is indicated by the diversity of items found in this category: interest earnings (other than on delinquent taxes); rents and royalties; sales of, and compensation for loss of, capital assets; contributions from public enterprises (utilities, airports, etc.); **escheats** (taking of property in default of legally qualified claimants); contributions and donations from private sources; and "other."

Some items of miscellaneous revenues, such as interest earnings on investments, might well be accrued, but mostly they are accounted for when received in cash. Also, interest earnings that are significant in amount may be reported as a separate classification.

BUDGETARY ACCOUNTING

Budgetary accounts were defined earlier in this chapter. Their use in journal entries and ledgers is described here. At the beginning of the budget period, the Estimated Revenues control account is debited for the total amount of revenues expected to be recognized, as provided in the operating budget. The amount of revenue expected from each source specified in the operating budget is recorded in a subsidiary ledger account (see Illustration 3–7) so that the total of subsidiary ledger detail agrees with the debit to the control account, and both agree with the adopted budget. If a separate entry is to be made to record Estimated Revenues, the general ledger debit to the Estimated Revenues control account is offset by a credit to Budgetary Fund Balance. In addition to estimated revenues for the year, all or part of any carryover balance in the Fund Balance account at the end of the preceding year could be available for appropriation in the operating budget. As a matter of prudent fiscal policy, however, most governments strive to maintain a *financial cushion* of around 15–25 percent of a year's expenditure requirements in their Fund Balance account to cover unforeseen expenditures or revenue shortfalls. Ordinarily, only Fund Balance amounts above the cushion level will be considered available for budgetary appropriation.

To record appropriations for the year, Budgetary Fund Balance is debited and the Appropriations control account is credited. As with Estimated Revenues, the Appropriations control account is supported by a subsidiary ledger (see Illustration 3–8 for an example of a subsidiary appropriation ledger account) kept in the same level of detail as the appropriation budget. The total of all subsidiary detail accounts must agree with the control total recorded in the Appropriations control account.[17]

ILLUSTRATION 3–7

NAME OF GOVERNMENTAL UNIT
Revenues Ledger
General Fund

Class: Licenses and Permits — Number: 351.1

Date	Item	Reference	Estimated Revenues DR.	Revenues CR.	Balance DR. (CR.)
2011					
January 1	Budget estimate	J1	$195,000		$195,000
31	Collections	CR6		$13,200	181,800

[17] As discussed later in this chapter, nearly all governments use computerized accounting systems. For learning purposes, it is helpful to understand a rudimentary manual accounting structure such as is discussed here and in many other sections of the text.

As explained earlier in this chapter, the use of budgetary accounts permits comparison of actual revenues and expenditures to budgeted amounts. Budgetary control is further enhanced by clear and logical classification of revenues and expenditures and by formally recording the budget in the accounts of the General Fund and other funds for which a budget is approved. The use of subsidiary ledgers, which permit recording revenues and expenditures—both actual and budgeted amounts—in the same level of detail as the budget, also helps to achieve sound budgetary control. Each of these topics is discussed in the remainder of this chapter.

Recording the Budget

The purpose of budgetary accounts is described earlier in this chapter. In order to illustrate entries in journal form to record a budget, assume the following amounts have been legally approved as the budget for the General Fund of a certain government for the fiscal year ending December 31, 2011. As of January 1, 2011, the first day of the fiscal year, the total Estimated Revenues should be recorded in the General Fund general ledger control account, and the amounts expected to be recognized during 2011 from each revenue source specified in the budget should be recorded in subsidiary ledger accounts. An appropriate entry would be:

		General Ledger		Subsidiary Ledger	
		Debits	***Credits***	***Debits***	***Credits***
1.	Estimated Revenues	1,277,500			
	Budgetary Fund Balance		1,277,500		
	Estimated Revenues Ledger:				
	Taxes			882,500	
	Intergovernmental Revenues			200,000	
	Licenses and Permits			195,000	

The total Appropriations and Other Financing Uses legally budgeted for 2011 for the General Fund of the same government should also be recorded in the General Fund general ledger control accounts, and the amounts appropriated for each function itemized in the budget should be recorded in subsidiary ledger accounts. An appropriate entry using assumed budget amounts would be:

		General Ledger Debits	General Ledger Credits	Subsidiary Ledger Debits	Subsidiary Ledger Credits
2.	Budgetary Fund Balance	1,636,500			
	Appropriations		1,362,000		
	Estimated Other Financing Uses . .		274,500		
	Appropriations Ledger:				
	General Government				1,150,000
	Public Safety				212,000
	Estimated Other Financing Uses Ledger:				
	Interfund Transfers Out to Other Funds				274,500

It would, of course, be acceptable to combine the two entries illustrated above and make one General Fund entry to record Estimated Revenues, Appropriations, and Estimated Other Financing Uses; in this case there would be a debit to Budgetary Fund Balance for $359,000 (the amount by which Appropriations and Estimated Other Financing Uses exceed Estimated Revenues). Even if a single combined entry is made in the General Fund general ledger accounts, that entry must provide for entry of the budgeted amounts in each individual subsidiary ledger account as shown in the illustrations of the two separate entries.

Budgetary Control of Revenues

To establish accountability for revenues and permit budgetary control, actual revenues should be recognized in the general ledger accounts of governmental funds by credits to the Revenues account (offset by debits to receivable accounts for revenues that are accrued or by debits to Cash for revenues recognized when received in cash). The general ledger Revenues account is a control account supported by Revenues subsidiary ledger accounts kept in exactly the same detail as kept for the Estimated Revenues subsidiary ledger accounts. For example, assume the General Fund of the government for which budgetary entries are illustrated in the preceding section collected revenues in cash during the month of January from Licenses and Permits, $13,200, and Intergovernmental Revenues, $61,900. In an actual case, entries should be made on a current basis and cash receipts should be deposited each working day; however, for the purpose of this chapter, the following entry illustrates the effect on the General Fund accounts of collections during the month of January 2011:

		General Ledger		Subsidiary Ledger	
		Debits	*Credits*	*Debits*	*Credits*
3.	Cash	75,100			
	Revenues		75,100		
	Revenues Ledger:				
	Licenses and Permits				13,200
	Intergovernmental Revenues				61,900

Comparability between Estimated Revenues subsidiary accounts and Revenues subsidiary accounts is necessary so that periodically throughout the fiscal year actual revenues from each source can be compared with estimated revenues from that source. Material differences between estimated and actual revenues should be investigated by administrators to determine whether (1) estimates were made on the basis of assumptions that may have appeared realistic when the budget was prepared but are no longer realistic (in that event, the budget needs to be revised so that administrators and legislators have better knowledge of revenues to be realized during the remainder of the fiscal year) or (2) action needs to be taken so that revenues estimated with reasonable accuracy are actually realized (i.e., one or more employees may have failed to understand that certain revenue items are to be collected). Illustration 3–7 shows a form of Revenues subsidiary ledger in which the Debit column is subsidiary to the Estimated Revenues general ledger control account and the Credit column is subsidiary to the Revenues general ledger control account.

A schedule of Actual and Estimated Revenues is illustrated in Chapter 4. Normally, during a fiscal year, the amount of revenue budgeted from each source will exceed the amount of revenue from that source realized to date; consequently, the Balance column will have a debit balance and may be headed Estimated Revenues Not Yet Realized, or simply Unrealized Revenues. This amount is a *budgetary resource* of the government—legally and realistically budgeted revenues that will be recognized as assets before the end of the fiscal year.

Budgetary Control of Encumbrances and Expenditures

When enacted into law, an appropriation is an authorization for administrators to expend financial resources on behalf of the government not to exceed the amounts specified in the appropriation ordinance or statute, for the purposes set forth in that ordinance or statute, during the period of time specified. An appropriation is considered *expended* when the authorized liabilities have been incurred. Penalties are imposed by law on an administrator who expends more than appropriated or who makes expenditures for any purpose not covered by an appropriation or after the authority to do so has expired. Prudence therefore dictates that each purchase order and each contract be reviewed before it is signed to determine that a valid and sufficient appropriation exists to which the expenditure can be charged when goods or services are received. If the review indicates that a valid appropriation exists and it has an available balance sufficient to cover the amount of the purchase order or contract being reviewed, the purchase order or contract legally may be issued. When a purchase order or contract has been issued, it is important to record the fact that the appropriation has been *encumbered* in the amount of the purchase order or contract. The word *encumbered* is used, rather than the word *expended*, because the amount is only an estimate of the liability that will be incurred when the purchase order is filled or the contract executed. It is reasonably common for quantities of goods received to differ from quantities ordered, and it is not uncommon for invoice prices to differ from unit prices shown on purchase orders. The use of appropriation authority may be somewhat tentative inasmuch as some suppliers are unable to fill orders or to perform as stipulated in a contract; in such cases, related purchase orders or contracts must be canceled.

Note that the issuance of purchase orders and/or contracts has two effects: (1) The encumbrance of the appropriation(s) that gave the government the authority to order goods or services and (2) the starting of a chain of events that will result in the government expending resources when the purchase orders are filled and the contracts executed. Both effects should be recorded in order to help administrators avoid overexpending appropriations and plan for payment of liabilities on a timely basis. The accounting procedure used to record the two effects is illustrated by Entry 4. The first effect is recorded by the debit to the general ledger account *Encumbrances*. Encumbrances is a control account that is related to the *Appropriations* control account discussed previously and to the *Expenditures* control account discussed in relation to Entries 5a and 5b. In order to accomplish the matching of Appropriations, Expenditures, and Encumbrances necessary for budgetary control, subsidiary account classifications of all three must correspond exactly (see Illustration 3–8). The general ledger account credited in Entry 4, *Reserve for Encumbrances*, is used to record the second effect of issuing purchase orders and contracts—earmarking a portion of Fund Balance for the estimated cost of goods or services ordered. Reserve for Encumbrances, sometimes called *Outstanding Encumbrances*, is not a control account; the balance of the account at the balance sheet date is reported as a reservation of fund balance, as illustrated in Chapter 4.

ILLUSTRATION 3–8

NAME OF GOVERNMENTAL UNIT
Appropriations, Expenditures, and Encumbrances Ledger

Code No.: 0607-03
Fund: General
Function: General Government

Year: 2011

Month and Day	Reference	Encumbrances			Expenditures		Appropriations	
		Debits	Credits	Open	Debits	Cumulative Total	Credits	Available Balance
Jan. 2	Budget (Entry 2)						$1,150,000	$1,150,000
3	Purchase orders issued (Entry 4)	$38,000		$38,000				1,112,000
17	Invoices approved for payment (Entries 5a, 5b)		$35,000	3,000	$35,100	$35,100		1,111,900

Entries 4, 5a, and 5b illustrate accounting for encumbrances and expenditures for the General Fund of the government for which entries are illustrated in previous sections of this chapter. Entry 4 is made on the assumption that early in January purchase orders are issued pursuant to the authority contained in the General Fund appropriations; assumed amounts chargeable to each function for which purchase orders are issued on this date are shown in the debits to the Encumbrances subsidiary accounts.

		General Ledger		Subsidiary Ledger	
		Debits	*Credits*	*Debits*	*Credits*
4.	Encumbrances—2011	45,400			
	Reserve for Encumbrances—2011		45,400		
	Encumbrances Ledger:				
	General Government			38,000	
	Public Safety			7,400	

When goods or services for which encumbrances have been recorded are received and the suppliers' invoices are approved for payment, the accounts should record the fact that appropriations have been *expended,* not merely encumbered, and that an actual liability, not merely an expected liability, exists. Entry 5a reverses Entry 4 to the extent that purchase orders are filled (ordinarily some of the purchase orders recorded in one encumbrance entry will be filled in one time period, and some in other time periods). It is important to note that since estimated amounts were used when encumbrances were recorded, the reversing entry must also use the estimated amounts. Thus, the balance remaining in the Encumbrances control account and in the Reserve for Encumbrances account is the *total* estimated dollar amount of purchase orders and contracts outstanding. The estimated dollar amount of purchase orders outstanding against each appropriation is disclosed by the subsidiary accounts, as shown in Illustration 3–8.

		General Ledger		Subsidiary Ledger	
		Debits	**Credits**	**Debits**	**Credits**
5a.	Reserve for Encumbrances—2011 .	42,000			
	Encumbrances—2011		42,000		
	Encumbrances Ledger:				
	General Government				35,000
	Public Safety				7,000
5b.	Expenditures—2011	42,400			
	Vouchers Payable		42,400		
	Expenditures Ledger:				
	General Government			35,100	
	Public Safety			7,300	

Expenditures and the liability account must both be recorded at the actual amount the government agrees to pay the vendors who have filled the purchase orders (see Entry 5b). The fact that estimated and actual amounts differ causes no accounting difficulties as long as goods or services are received in the same fiscal period as ordered. The accounting treatment required when encumbrances outstanding at year-end are filled, or canceled, in a following year is illustrated in Chapter 4.

The encumbrance procedure is not necessary for every type of expenditure transaction. For example, although salaries and wages of governmental employees must be chargeable against valid and sufficient appropriations in order to give rise to legal expenditures, many governments do not find it necessary to encumber the departmental personal services appropriations for estimated payrolls of recurring, relatively constant amounts. Departments having payrolls that fluctuate greatly from one season to another may follow the encumbrance procedure to make sure the personal service appropriation is not overexpended.

From the foregoing discussion and illustrative journal entries, it should be apparent that administrators of governments need accounting systems designed to provide at any given date during a fiscal year comparisons for each item in the legal appropriations budget of (1) the amount appropriated, (2) the amount of outstanding encumbrances, and (3) the cumulative amount of expenditures to this date. The net of the three items is accurately described as *Unencumbered Unexpended Appropriations* but can be labeled more simply as *Available Appropriations* or *Available Balance.*

Classification of appropriations, expenditures, and encumbrances was discussed in a preceding section of this chapter. In order to provide needed comparisons, classifications of expenditures and encumbrances must agree with the classifications of appropriations mandated by law. In many jurisdictions, good financial management may dictate all three elements be classified in greater detail than required by law. In most cases, budgetary control over expenditures follows the logical flow depicted below:

APPROPRIATION → ENCUMBRANCE → EXPENDITURE → DISBURSEMENT

At intervals during the fiscal year, a Schedule of Budgeted and Actual Expenditures and Encumbrances should be prepared to inform administrators and members of the legislative branch of the data contained in the subsidiary ledger records. An example of such a schedule is illustrated in Chapter 4 (see Illustration 4–4). Also in Chapter 4, the entries needed at year-end to close budgetary and nominal accounts are illustrated (Entries 25a, 25b, and 25c, Chapter 4).

Accounting for Allotments

In some jurisdictions, it is necessary to regulate the use of appropriations so only specified amounts may be used from month to month or from quarter to quarter. The purpose of such control is to prevent expenditure of all or most of the authorized amount early in the year without providing for unexpected requirements arising later in the year. A common device for regulating expenditures is the use of allotments. An **allotment** may be described as an internal allocation of funds on a periodic basis usually agreed upon by the department heads and the chief executive.

Allotments may be formally recorded in ledger accounts. This procedure might begin with the budgetary entry, in which Unallotted Appropriations would replace Appropriations. If this is desired, a combined entry to record the budget would be (using the numbers given in Entries 1 and 2, omitting entries in subsidiary accounts—which would be as illustrated previously with one exception—the subsidiary ledger credit accounts in Entry 2 would be designated as Unallotted Appropriations instead of Appropriations):

	General Ledger		Subsidiary Ledger	
	Debits	*Credits*	*Debits*	*Credits*
Estimated Revenues	1,277,500			
Budgetary Fund Balance	359,000			
Unallotted Appropriations		1,362,000		
Estimated Other Financing Uses		274,500		

If it is assumed that $342,000 is the amount formally allotted for the first period, the following entry could be made (amounts allotted for each function are shown in the subsidiary ledger entries):

	General Ledger Debits	General Ledger Credits	Subsidiary Ledger Debits	Subsidiary Ledger Credits
Unallotted Appropriations	342,000			
Allotments		342,000		
Allotments Ledger:				
General Government				289,000
Public Safety				53,000

Expenditures should be recorded periodically as invoices are received by using departments or divisions in the manner previously described.

Accounting Information Systems

In a computerized accounting system, an account number structure provides for appropriate classification of revenues and expenditures, as well as for the desired classification of assets, liabilities, and fund balances. Many alternative governmental accounting software systems are available. The general ledger module of most systems can easily accommodate all of the revenue and expenditure detail accounts needed for effective budgetary control.

Instead of using general ledger control accounts and related subsidiary ledgers, computerized systems often use separate files or ledgers for proprietary and budgetary reporting. For example, the general ledger module of one leading fund accounting software system includes both a general ledger and a budget ledger. Actual revenues and expenditures are posted to the general ledger, and budget amounts are posted to the budget ledger. Of course, the same account numbers and titles used in the budget ledger are used in the general ledger to permit budgetary comparison reporting. In addition, the system provides a separate encumbrance ledger to record encumbered amounts and monitor budgetary compliance. Selecting the type of transaction from a menu on the screen determines in which ledger (or ledgers) a particular transaction is posted. All such systems must provide transaction detail reports and other documentation of entries and postings in order to provide an adequate "audit trail."

In an accounting information system, the account number structure is an important design feature—one that affects the ease of financial operation and preparation of financial statements. Most account number structures provide for the multiple expenditure classifications prescribed by the GASB or similar classifications. Consider, for example, the following five-segment account number structure used by one Midwest city:

XXX – XXXX – XXX – XX – XX
(1) (2) (3) (4) (5)

The five segments of numbers represent the following classifications:

Segment	Represents
1	Fund (e.g., 110 = General Fund; 224 = Library Operating Fund; 550 = Water Fund; etc.)
2	First two positions of the segment represent department; other two positions represent divisions within a department (e.g., 2120 = Police Operations; 2125 = Police Major Crimes; 2127 = Narcotics; etc.)
3	First two positions of segment represent activity; third position represents subactivity (Note: This city uses segment 3 to indicate type of account rather than activity and subactivity. For example, 100–199 = Assets; 200–299 = Liabilities; 300–399 = Equity; 400–499 = Revenues; and 500–699 = Operating Expenses; etc.)
4	Element (broad object of expenditure category) (e.g., 01 = Personnel Services; 12 = Supplies and Materials; 75 = Debt Service, Interest; etc.)
5	Detailed object of expenditure (e.g., some detailed objects associated with Personnel Services are 01 = Salaries and Wages, Permanent Positions; 05 = Salaries and Wages, Temporary Positions; and 41 = Salaries and Wages, Overtime; etc.)

Even though the classification scheme just described does not agree precisely with the expenditure classifications required by the GASB, it conforms in all essential respects with the GASB classifications. Segment (1) accomplishes classification by fund. Segment (2) permits classification by department and division, where divisions, in most cases, represent particular activities, for example, operations, major crimes, narcotics, and other activities of the police department. Because the *Division* classification in segment (2) meets the GASB activity classification requirement, the city uses segment (3) to indicate what kind of account (asset, liability, and so forth) is being used for a particular transaction. Segments (4) and (5) permit adequate object of expenditure detail. Although the account structure provides no specific classification for functions or programs, it is relatively easy to aggregate appropriate departmental accounts to provide totals by function or program for financial reporting or management purposes. Similarly, the lack of a specific character classification is of little concern since object of expenditure accounts are provided for debt service, capital outlays, and intergovernmental activity.

To illustrate the use of this account number structure to code an actual transaction, consider how the purchase of diesel fuel by the Public Works Department, Street Cleaning activity would be coded for entry into the computer:

110	–	6023	–	534	–	12	–	40
General Fund		Public Works—Street Cleaning		Operating Expenses		Supplies and Materials		Other Supplies—Fuel, Oil, and Lubricants

If, as is likely, the diesel fuel is purchased from an internal service fund of the city, a liability account, Due to Other Funds, would also be credited. In this case, the transaction must also be recorded as a sale (Billings to Departments) and a receivable (Due from General Fund) in the internal service fund. If the fuel is purchased from an external source, either Accounts Payable or Vouchers Payable would be credited.

In actual practice, the interface programs used for most computerized accounting systems make it relatively simple to move around within the account number structure. Though systems differ markedly, department or finance personnel or accounting clerks usually enter the appropriate numbers for funds, department, activity, type of account, expenditure object, and dollar amount or choose these items from drop-down help menus. Function keys are often programmed to produce help menus for account number segments, particularly for expenditure objects.

For transactions that can be entered by department personnel, such as purchase requisitions, internal control considerations usually restrict entry and data access to only certain funds and types of accounts. For these transactions, the fund and department/division information often defaults to that applicable to a particular department or division. In addition to the information embedded in the account number, purchasing and accounts payable programs also must provide lists of vendor numbers and names, usually in drop-down menu form. Some systems automatically complete the vendor identification information as soon as a few distinguishing keystrokes are entered. Vendor detail records usually permit instant display of vendor account status, including outstanding purchase orders, invoices received, due dates, invoices paid, and payments pending. As is common in computerized accounting environments, whether business, not-for-profit, or government, the accounting clerk often has little knowledge of the actual accounting processes occurring within the information system.

Generally, any account number segments not needed for a transaction have zeros inserted or, in some systems, may be masked. For example, for the city whose account number structure was illustrated earlier, recording revenues or paying vouchers payable requires no data to be entered for segments (4) and (5), so zeros are automatically inserted for those segments. Data classified according to an entity's account number structure can easily be aggregated within any segment, or group of segments, to provide a wide variety of custom financial reports, in addition to predefined reports and financial statements.

The discussion of computerized accounting systems has focused on the systems that have evolved to meet the *fund* accounting needs of government. Governments now face the challenge of redesigning their existing systems or acquiring new systems that will accommodate government-wide accounting and financial reporting requirements, as well as preparing the fund financial statements required by *GASBS 34*. Many governments may continue for an extended period to use their present fund accounting computer systems, supplemented by spreadsheet and report writer interfaces that permit the reclassifications of fund-based information needed to prepare government-wide financial statements. The disadvantage of this approach is that government-wide statements are often not available for the use of citizens and other users until the end of the reporting period when the reconciling worksheets are prepared.

CONCLUDING REMARKS

The illustrative journal entries shown in this chapter to record the budget have no impact on the government-wide statement of activities. Operating transactions shown, however, may be treated differently at the government-wide level than in the General Fund. Because the illustrative transactions presented in this chapter were intended to illustrate budgetary control over revenues and expenditures, the possible effects of those transactions at the government-wide level were ignored. In Chapter 4, the dual effects of accounting transactions are analyzed and appropriate journal entries are made in both the general journal for the General Fund and the general journal used to record government activities at the government-wide level.

Appendix

Accounting for Public School Systems

There are about 13,000 independent public school systems in the United States. Although they are classified as special purpose governments, these school systems follow the same generally accepted accounting principles as state and local governments—the accounting and reporting standards issued by GASB.[18] The approximately 1,500 "dependent" school systems are accounted for as part of their parent general purpose government, either a state, county, municipality, or township. Public school systems, both independent and dependent, often follow specialized accounting and reporting procedures prescribed by a state oversight department or agency. Further, all state oversight departments or agencies collect revenues and expenditures data for all pre-kindergarten through grade 12 public schools in their state and provide these data to the National Center for Educational Statistics (NCES) so the NCES can prepare the annual "National Public Education Financial Survey."[19] For the sake of uniformity, most school systems follow the system of classification for revenues and expenditures recommended by the NCES. This system of classification is discussed next. In addition, independent public school systems must prepare the MD&A and basic financial statements required by *GASBS 34*.

[18] Dean Michael Mead, *What You Should Know about Your School District's Finances: A Guide to Financial Statements* (Norwalk, CT: GASB, 2000).

[19] An extensive list of NCES reports and resources is available on the Internet at *http://www.NCES.ed.gov.*

CLASSIFICATION OF EXPENDITURES OF PUBLIC SCHOOL SYSTEMS

The NCES system of expenditure classifications expands on the GASB classifications discussed in this chapter, reflecting the standardized national data collection and reporting requirements imposed by the NCES on all states. Specifically, the NCES account code structure provides for nine expenditure classification categories: fund, program, function, object, project, level of instruction, operational unit, subject matter, and job class.[20] Generally, school systems need to report data for the classifications required by the education oversight body in their state, which may vary from state to state.

The *program* classification is critically important for effective management of public education at the local, state, and federal levels. The NCES identifies several broad classes of programs, including regular elementary/secondary education programs, special programs, vocational and technical programs, other instructional programs—elementary/secondary, nonpublic school programs, adult/continuing education programs, community/junior college education programs, community service programs, and co-curricular and extracurricular activities. Numerous detailed program classifications are possible within each broad category. For example, *special programs* may include service programs related to mental retardation, physical impairment, emotional disturbance, and developmental delay, among many other services. Similarly, *vocational and technical programs* include programs intended to prepare students for careers in 16 broad-based career areas, such as agriculture and natural resources, architecture and construction, information technology, and law and public safety.

The NCES *function* classification relates to the activity for which goods or services are acquired. Functions are classified into the five broad areas of instruction, support services, operation of noninstructional services, facilities acquisition and construction, and debt service. In addition, the NCES provides account codes for 61 subfunctions, of which 14 are required for reporting to NCES. The required subfunctions are instruction; support services—students; support services—instruction; support services—general administration; support services—school administration; central services; operation and maintenance of plant; student transportation; other support services; food service operations; enterprise operations; community services operations; facilities acquisition and construction; and debt service.

Consistent with GASB standards, the NCES *object* classification describes the service or goods acquired by a particular expenditure. The NCES provides for nine major object categories: personal services—salaries; personal services—employee benefits; purchased professional and technical services; purchased property services; other purchased services; supplies; property; debt service and miscellaneous; and other items. As with programs and functions, numerous detailed object accounts are provided for each major object category, although only certain of those are identified for mandatory use and reporting to the NCES.

The *project* classification provides coding for projects that are funded from local, state, or federal sources, plus an additional code for projects that do not require specialized reporting to a local, state, or federal funding source. To meet reporting

[20] The following discussion of expenditure and revenue classifications is based on the account classification codes provided in National Center for Education Statistics, *Financial Accounting for Local and State School Systems: 2003 Edition* (Washington, DC: U.S. Department of Education, Core Finance Data Task Force, The National Forum on Education Statistics, 2003).

requirements imposed by some states on public school systems, the NCES provides a *level of instruction* classification, consisting of such categories as elementary, middle, secondary, postsecondary, and programs for adult/continuing education. Finally, there are three optional-use expenditure classifications for *operational unit, subject matter,* and *job-class.* The operational unit classification provides the option of reporting by separate attendance centers, budgetary units, or cost centers. Subject matter could include such categories as agriculture, art, business, and science. Job-class relates to classifications used for personnel, such as administrative, professional, clerical, and technical.

CLASSIFICATION OF REVENUES OF PUBLIC SCHOOL SYSTEMS

Revenues of public school systems, both those dependent upon a general purpose government and independent school systems, should be classified in the manner prescribed by the NCES, as refined by the appropriate state oversight body. Generally, public school revenues should be classified by fund, source, and project/reporting code. The NCES publication cited in footnote 20 provides the following revenue classifications:

- 1000 Revenue from local sources
  - 1100 Taxes levied/assessed by the school system
  - 1200 Revenue from local governmental units other than school districts
  - 1300 Tuition
  - 1400 Transportation fees
  - 1500 Investment income
  - 1600 Food services
  - 1700 District activities
  - 1800 Community services activities
  - 1900 Other revenue from local sources
- 2000 Revenue from intermediate sources
  - 2100 Unrestricted grants-in-aid
  - 2200 Restricted grants-in-aid
  - 2800 Revenue in lieu of taxes
  - 2900 Revenue for/on behalf of the school district
- 3000 Revenue from state sources
  - 3100 Unrestricted grants-in-aid
  - 3200 Restricted grants-in-aid
  - 3800 Revenue in lieu of taxes
  - 3900 Revenue for/on behalf of the school district
- 4000 Revenue from federal sources
  - 4100 Unrestricted grants-in-aid direct from the federal government
  - 4200 Unrestricted grants-in-aid from the federal government through the state
  - 4300 Restricted grants-in-aid direct from the federal government
  - 4500 Restricted grants-in-aid from the federal government through the state
  - 4700 Grants-in-aid from the federal government through intermediate governments
  - 4800 Revenue in lieu of taxes
  - 4900 Revenue for/on behalf of the school district
- 5000 Other financing sources
  - 5100 Issuance of bonds

5200 Fund transfers in
5300 Proceeds from the disposal of real or personal property
5400 Loan proceeds
5500 Capital lease proceeds
5600 Other long-term debt proceeds
6000 Other items
6100 Capital contributions
6200 Amortization of premium on issuance of bonds
6300 Special items
6400 Extraordinary items

Additional detail provided in the NCES revenue classification structure has been omitted from the foregoing list. For example, under classification 1100, taxes levied/assessed by the school system, are additional detail classifications for ad valorem taxes, sales and use taxes, and income taxes, among others.

"Intermediate" sources of revenue are administrative units or political subdivisions between the local school system and the state. "Grants-in-aid" from intermediate, state, or federal governments are contributions from general revenue sources of those governments, or, if related to specific revenue sources of those units, are distributed on a flat grant or equalization basis. "Revenue in lieu of taxes," analogous to payment from an enterprise fund to the General Fund discussed in Chapter 7, are payments made out of general revenues of intermediate, state, or federal governments to a local school system because the higher level governments own property located within the geographical boundaries of the local school system that is not subject to taxation. "Revenue for/on behalf of the school district" includes all payments made by intermediate, state, or federal governments for the benefit of the local system; payments to pension funds, or a contribution of fixed assets, are examples.

GASBS 34 financial reporting provides information that has not been readily available to users of public school financial statements in the past. As do other state and local governments, public school systems prepare basic financial statements, which include "district-wide" and fund financial statements, an MD&A, and other required supplementary information. Users are thus better able to assess how much the school owns and owes, its present financial status and future outlook, what it costs to educate students, and the tax burden placed on citizens and businesses to finance education.[21] District-wide statements report on traditional governmental activities of a public school district, essentially the activities related to educating students, as well as business-type activities, for example, food services or after-school latchkey programs. Accountants and auditors need to be aware of state laws and regulations affecting public schools' commercial activities, such as the sale of products, direct advertising, corporate-sponsored education materials, and exclusivity agreements with soft drink companies.[22]

[21] Ibid.

[22] General Accounting Office, *Public Educational Commercial Activities in Schools,* GAO/HEHS-00-156, September 2000.

Key Terms

Activity, *79*
Ad valorem property taxes, *82*
Allotment, *92*
Appropriations, *78*
Budgetary accounts, *74*
Character, *80*
Direct expenses, *66*
Encumbrances, *78*
Escheats, *85*
Estimated other financing sources, *78*
Estimated other financing uses, *78*
Estimated revenues, *78*
Extraordinary items, *69*
Functions, *78*
General revenues, *68*
Indirect expenses, *66*
Object, *80*
Organization unit, *79*
Other financing sources, *71*
Other financing uses, *71*
Penalty, *83*
Program revenues, *68*
Programs, *78*
Property assessment, *82*
Special items, *69*
Taxable property, *82*

Selected References

American Institute of Certified Public Accountants. *Audit and Accounting Guide. State and Local Governments.* New York, 2008.

Governmental Accounting Standards Board. *Codification of Governmental Accounting and Financial Reporting Standards as of June 30, 2008.* Norwalk, CT, 2008.

Mead, Dean Michael. *What You Should Know about Your School District's Finances: A Guide to Financial Statements.* Norwalk, CT: Governmental Accounting Standards Board, 2000.

U.S. Department of Education, National Center for Education Statistics. *Financial Accounting for Local and State School Systems: 2003 Edition* (NCES 2004–318). Core Finance Data Task Force, The National Forum on Education Statistics. Washington, DC, 2003.

Questions

3–1. Explain why governmental fund financial statements are insufficient for users seeking information about *operational accountability*.

3–2. What benefits do financial statement users derive from the net (expense) revenue format used for the government-wide statement of activities?

3–3. Why is depreciation expense typically reported as a *direct expense* in the government-wide statement of activities?

3–4. Indicate whether the following revenues would most likely be classified as *program revenues* or *general revenues* on the government-wide statement of activities.
a. Unrestricted operating grants that can be used at the discretion of the city council.
b. Capital grants restricted for highway construction.
c. Charges for building inspections.
d. A special assessment for snow removal.
e. Fines and forfeits.
f. Motor vehicle fuel taxes restricted for road repair.
g. Unrestricted investment earnings.

3–5. Explain the essential differences between *extraordinary items* and *special items* and how each of these items should be reported on the government-wide statement of activities.

3–6. Indicate whether each of the following expenditure items should be classified as a function, program, organization unit, activity, character, or object.
a. Mayor's Office.
b. Public Safety.
c. Residential trash disposal.

d. Accident investigation.
e. Salaries and wages.
f. Debt service.
g. Environmental protection.
h. Health and Welfare.
i. Police Department.
j. Printing and postage.

3–7. Distinguish between:
a. Expenditures and Encumbrances.
b. Revenues and Estimated Revenues.
c. Reserve for Encumbrances and Encumbrances.
d. Reserve for Encumbrances and Fund Balance.
e. Appropriations and Expenditures.
f. Expenditures and Expenses.

3–8. State whether each of the following items should be classified as taxes, licenses and permits, intergovernmental revenues, charges for services, fines and forfeits, or miscellaneous revenue in a governmental fund.
a. Sales and use taxes levied by the government.
b. Payments by citizens for library services.
c. Building permits to construct a garage at a residence.
d. Traffic violation penalties.
e. Federal community development block grant.
f. Royalties from an exclusivity contract with a soft drink company.
g. Charges to a local university for extra city police protection during sporting events.
h. Barbers and hairdressers' registration fees.

3–9. For which funds are budgetary comparison schedules or statements required? Should the *actual* revenues and expenditures on the budgetary comparison schedules be reported on the GAAP basis? Why or why not?

3–10. Explain how expenditure and revenue classifications for public school systems differ from those for state and local governments.

Cases

3–1 Internet Case—Revenue and Expense/Expenditure Classification. Locate a comprehensive annual financial report (CAFR) using a city's Web site, or one from the "Project Pages/Statement 34" link of the GASB's Web site, *www.gasb.org.* Examine the city's government-wide statement of activities and statement of revenues, expenditures, and changes in fund balances—governmental funds and prepare a brief report responding to the following questions.

a. Referring to the government-wide statement of activities, explain how the program revenues and expenses are classified. Are expenses and program revenues reported using a function or program classification? Do any function or program categories show net revenues, or do they all show net expenses? Is the fact that most, if not all, functions or programs show a net expense a problem? Why or why not?

b. Explain how *revenues* are classified and reported on the statement of revenues, expenditures, and changes in fund balances. Compare the amount reported for property taxes in this statement to the amount reported as general revenue on the statement of activities. Do the two amounts agree? If not, can you think of a reasonable explanation for the difference?

c. Explain how *expenditures* are classified and reported on the statement of revenues, expenditures, and changes in fund balances. Compare these amounts to the amounts reported as expenses for the same functions or programs on the statement of activities. Do the amounts agree? If not, can you think of a reasonable explanation for the differences?

3–2 Internet Case—Budgetary Comparison Statements; Budget Basis Compared with GAAP. Refer to Case 3–1 for instructions about how to obtain the CAFR for a city of your choice. Using that CAFR, go to the required supplementary information (RSI) section, immediately following the notes to the financial statements, and locate the *budgetary comparison schedule* (note: this schedule may be titled *schedule of revenues, expenditures, and changes in fund balances—budget and actual*) for the General Fund and major special revenue funds. If this schedule is not included in the RSI, then the city you have selected is one that elects to prepare an audited statement of revenues, expenditures, and changes in fund balances—budget and actual as part of the basic financial statements. Also, locate the GAAP operating statement for governmental funds called the statement of revenues, expenditures, and changes in fund balances—governmental funds in the basic statements (note: this statement does not contain any budgetary information). Examine the schedule and/or statements, as the case may be, and prepare a brief report that responds to the following questions.

a. Are revenues and/or expenditures presented in greater detail in the budgetary comparison schedule (or statement) than in the GAAP operating statement? If so, why, in your judgment, is this the case?

b. Do actual revenues on the budgetary comparison schedule agree in amount with those on the GAAP operating statement? If they differ, is there an explanation provided either in the notes to the financial statements or notes to the RSI to explain the difference? What explanations are provided, if any?

c. Do actual expenditures on the budgetary comparison schedule agree in amount with those on the GAAP operating statement? If they differ, is there an explanation provided either in the notes to the financial statements or notes to the RSI to explain the difference? What explanations are provided, if any?

d. If no differences were noted in either *b* or *c* above, go to item *e.* If differences were noted, was there a notation in the heading of the budgetary comparison schedule/statement indicating "Non-GAAP Budgetary Basis" or an indication of budget basis in the column heading for actual revenues and expenditures?

e. Does the budgetary comparison schedule/statement contain a variance column? If so, is the variance the difference between actual and original budget or the difference between actual and final budget?

3–3 Internet Case—Charter Schools. You are an accountant in a state that allows charter schools, or public school academies, to educate kindergarten through 12th grade students and receive public funds to do so. A group of parents and teachers is forming such a school and has asked for your help in establishing an accounting system. Use the Internet to identify resources that may help you in this task. For example, use your favorite search engine to look for information on "charter schools" and "accounting systems," and answer these questions:

a. Would you expect an accounting system for this type of school to be any different than that used by traditional public schools?

b. Should you incorporate budgetary accounting? (*Hint:* Try *http://www.uscharterschools.org* and look for "Budgets, Finance, and Fund-raising" under "Resources" and "Starting a Charter School.")

Exercises and Problems

3–1 Examine the CAFR. Utilizing the CAFR obtained for Exercise 1–1, in Chapter 1, review the governmental fund financial statements and related data and government-wide financial statements. Note particularly these items:

a. **Statement of Activities at the Government-wide Level.** Has the government prepared statements in compliance with the *GASBS 34* financial reporting model? Does the statement of activities appear on one page or across two pages? What is the most costly governmental function or program operated by the government? How much of the cost of governmental activities was borne by taxpayers in the form of general revenues? Did the entity increase or decrease its governmental activities unrestricted net assets this year? Did the entity increase or decrease its business-type activities unrestricted net assets this year?

b. **Statement of Revenues, Expenditures, and Changes in Fund Balances for Governmental Funds.**

(1) *Revenues and Other Financing Sources.* What system of classification of revenues is used in the governmental fund financial statements? List the three most important sources of General Fund revenues and the most important source of revenue for each major governmental fund. Does the reporting entity depend on any single source for as much as one-third of its General Fund revenues? What proportion of revenues is derived from property taxes? Do the notes clearly indicate recognition criteria for primary revenue sources?

Are charts, graphs, or tables included in the CAFR that show the changes over time in reliance on each revenue source? Are interfund transfers reported in the same section of the statement as revenues, or are they reported in other financing sources?

(2) *Expenditures and Other Financing Uses.* What system of classification of expenditures is used in the governmental fund financial statements? List the three largest categories of General Fund expenditures; list the largest category of expenditure of each major governmental fund.

Are charts, tables, or graphs presented in the CAFR (most likely in the statistical section) to show the trend of General Fund expenditures, by category, for a period of 10 years? Is expenditure data related to nonfinancial measures such as population of the government or workload statistics (e.g., tons of solid waste removed or number of miles of street constructed)?

c. **Budgetary Comparison Schedule or Statement.** Does the government present budgetary comparisons as a basic governmental fund financial statement, or as required supplementary information (RSI) immediately following the notes to the financial statements? Is the budgetary comparison title a *schedule* rather than a *statement?* Does the budgetary comparison present the original budget and the final amended budget? Does the budgetary schedule present actual data using the budgetary basis of accounting? Has the government presented one or more variance columns? Do all blended component units use the same budgetary practices as the primary government of the reporting entity? Does the CAFR state this explicitly, or does it indicate that budgetary practices differ by disclosures in the headings of statements, the headings of columns within statements, or by narrative and schedules within the notes to the financial statements?

3-2 Multiple Choice. Choose the best answer.

1. Which of the following best describes the recommended format for the government-wide statement of activities?
   a. Revenues minus expenses equals change in net assets.
   b. Revenues minus expenditures equals change in net assets.
   c. Program revenues minus expenses minus general revenues equals changes in net assets.
   d. Expenses minus program revenues minus general revenues equals change in net assets.

2. Expenses that are specifically identified with a program or function are reported in the government-wide statement of activities as:
   a. Specific expenses.
   b. Direct expenses.
   c. Incremental expenses.
   d. Program expenses.

3. An *extraordinary item* differs from a *special item* in that an extraordinary item is:
   a. Reported on a separate line below General Revenues.
   b. Within management's control.
   c. Both unusual in nature and infrequent in occurrence.
   d. Either unusual in nature or infrequent in occurrence.

4. Which of the following neither increases nor decreases fund balance of the General Fund during the current period?
   a. Deferred revenues.
   b. Revenues.
   c. Expenditures.
   d. Other financing sources.

5. One characteristic that distinguishes *other financing sources* from *revenues* is that other financing sources:
   a. Arise from debt issuances or interfund transfers in.
   b. Increase fund balance when they are closed at year-end.
   c. Provide financial resources for the recipient fund.
   d. Have a normal credit balance.

6. Under the *modified accrual* basis of accounting, expenditures generally are not recognized until:
   a. They are paid in cash.
   b. An obligation is incurred that will be paid from currently available financial resources.
   c. Goods or services are ordered.
   d. They are approved by the legislative body.

7. According to GASB standards, *expenditures* are classified by:
   a. Fund, function or program, organization unit, source, and character.
   b. Fund, function or program, organization unit, activity, character, and object.
   c. Fund, appropriation, organization unit, activity, character, and object.
   d. Fund, organization unit, encumbrance, activity, character, and object.

8. Under GASB requirements for external financial reporting, one would find the budgetary comparison schedule (or statement) in the:
   a. Required supplementary information (RSI).
   b. Basic financial statements.
   c. Either *a* or *b*, as elected by the government.
   d. Neither *a* nor *b*.

9. If supplies that were ordered by a department financed by the General Fund are received at an actual price that is less than the estimated price on the purchase order, the department's available balance of appropriations for supplies will be:
   a. Decreased.
   b. Increased.
   c. Unaffected.
   d. Either *a* or *b*, depending on the department's specific budgetary control procedures.

10. Spruce City's finance department recorded the recently adopted General Fund budget at the beginning of the current fiscal year. The budget approved estimated revenues of $1,000,000 and appropriations of $1,100,000. Which of the following is the correct journal entry to record the budget?

	Debits	Credits
a. Appropriations	1,100,000	
Budgetary Fund Balance		100,000
Estimated Revenues		1,000,000
b. Revenues Receivable	1,000,000	
Budgetary Deficit	100,000	
Appropriations		1,100,000
c. Estimated Revenues	1,000,000	
Budgetary Fund Balance	100,000	
Appropriations		1,100,000

d. Memorandum entry only.

3–3 Beginning and Ending Fund Balances. The following information is provided about the Village of Wymette's General Fund operating statement and budgetary accounts for the fiscal year ended June 30, 2010.

Estimated revenues	$3,150,000
Revenues	3,190,000
Appropriations	3,185,000
Expenditures	3,175,000
Fund balance (beginning of year)	580,000
Budgetary fund balance (after FY 2010 budget was recorded)	(35,000)

Required

a. Did the Village of Wymette engage in imprudent budgeting practice by authorizing a greater amount of expenditures than revenues estimated for the year, or potentially violate village or state balanced-budget laws?

b. Calculate the end-of-year balances for the Fund Balance and Budgetary Fund Balance accounts that would be reported on the Village's balance sheet prepared as of June 30, 2010. Show all necessary work.

3–4 Recording Adopted Budget. The City of Marion adopted the following General Fund budget for fiscal year 2011:

Estimated revenues:	
Taxes	$3,000,000
Intergovernmental revenues	1,000,000
Licenses and permits	400,000
Fines and forfeits	150,000
Miscellaneous revenues	100,000
Total estimated revenues	$4,650,000
Appropriations:	
General government	$ 950,000
Public safety	2,000,000
Public works	950,000
Health and welfare	850,000
Miscellaneous	50,000
Total appropriations	$4,800,000

Required

a. Assuming that a city ordinance mandates a balanced budget, what must be the minimum amount in the Fund Balance account of the General Fund at the beginning of FY 2011?

b. Prepare the general journal entries to record the adopted budget at the beginning of FY 2011. Show entries in the subsidiary ledger accounts as well as the general ledger accounts.

3–5 Recording Encumbrances. During July 2010, the first month of the 2011 fiscal year, the City of Marion issued the following purchase orders and contracts (see Problem 3–4):

General government	$ 50,000
Public safety	200,000
Public works	75,000
Health and welfare	65,000
Miscellaneous	4,000
Total purchase orders and contracts	$394,000

Required

a. Show the general journal entry to record the issuance of the purchase orders and contracts. Show entries in subsidiary ledger accounts as well as general ledger accounts.

b. Explain why state and local governments generally record the estimated amounts of purchase orders and contracts in the accounts of budgeted governmental funds, whereas business entities generally do not prepare formal entries for purchase orders.

3–6 Subsidiary Ledgers. The printout of the Estimated Revenues and Revenues subsidiary ledger accounts for the General Fund of the City of Salem as of February 28, 2011, appeared as follows:

PROPERTY TAXES

Date	Folio	Estimated Revenues	Revenues	Balance
01 01	45 1	9,600,000		9,600,000
02 28	45 6	(20,000)	9,580,000	0

LICENSES AND PERMITS

Date	Folio	Estimated Revenues	Revenues	Balance
01 01	45 1	1,600,000		1,600,000
01 31	27 4		640,000	960,000
02 27	27 7		200,000	760,000

INTERGOVERNMENTAL REVENUE

Date	Folio	Estimated Revenues	Revenues	Balance
01 01	45 1	3,200,000		3,200,000
02 28	27 7		1,500,000	1,700,000

CHARGES FOR SERVICES

Date	Folio	Estimated Revenues	Revenues	Balance
01 01	45 1	600,000		600,000
02 28	27 7		160,000	440,000

Required

Assuming that this printout is correct in all details and that there are no other General Fund revenue classifications, answer the following questions. *Show all necessary computations in good form.*

a. What should be the balance of the Estimated Revenues control account?

b. What was the original approved budget for Estimated Revenues for 2011?

c. (1) Was the FY 2011 Estimated Revenues budget adjusted during the year?
 (2) If so, when?
 (3) If so, by how much?
 (4) If so, was the original budget increased or decreased?

d. What should be the balance of the Revenues control account?

e. If in the Folio column of the accounts the numerals 45 stand for general journal and the numerals 27 stand for cash receipts journal, what is the most likely reason that revenues from Property Taxes are first recognized in a general journal entry, whereas revenues from the other three sources are first recognized in cash receipts journal entries?

3–7 Appropriations, Encumbrances, and Expenditures. The finance director of the Town of Liberty has asked you to determine whether the appropriations, expenditures, and encumbrances comparison for Office Supplies for a certain year (reproduced as follows) presents the information correctly. You determine that the General Fund chart of accounts describes office supplies as "tangible items of relatively short life to be used in a business office." You also determine that the transfer of stationery, at cost, to the town water utility was properly authorized; the Water Utility Fund is to pay the General Fund $330 for the supplies. The transfer of $46,000 from Office Supplies to Personal Services was made by an accounting clerk, without the knowledge of managers, to avoid reporting that the Personal Services appropriation had been overexpended.

Required

To determine whether the following budgetary comparison is correct, you need to compute each of the following. Organize and label your computations so the finance director can understand them.

a. The final amended amount of the appropriation for Office Supplies for the year.
b. The valid amount of encumbrances outstanding against this appropriation at the end of the year.
c. The net amount of expenditures made during the year that were properly chargeable to this appropriation.
d. The unencumbered unexpended balance of this appropriation.

TOWN OF LIBERTY
General Fund
Appropriation, Expenditures, and Encumbrances

Purchase No.	Explanation	Appropriations	Encumbrances Debits	Encumbrances Credits	Expenditures	Available Balance
	Budget legally approved	62,200				62,200
350	Purchase order—computer paper		600			61,600
356	Purchase order—stationery			420		62,020
	Refund of prior year expenditure	30				62,050
370	Purchase order—filing supplies		400			61,650
350	Invoice			605	605	61,045
378	Purchase order—computer		3,160			57,885
380	Contract for washing office windows		2,000			55,885
356	Invoice			420	420	55,885
	Cost of stationery issued to town's water utility	330				56,215
	Refund on P.O. 350	10				56,225
370	Invoice			400	425	55,800
380	Invoice				2,000	53,000
385	Purchase order—furniture		7,000			46,000
	Transfer to Personal Services appropriation	(46,000)				0

3–8 Computerized Accounting System—Departmental Budgetary Comparison Report. Review the computer generated budgetary comparison report presented below for the Lincoln City Parks and Recreation Department as of July 1 of its fiscal year ending December 31, 2010, and respond to the questions that follow.

LINCOLN CITY
FY 2010 Detail Report, Departmental Expenditures

Run date: July 1, 2010
08-00 Parks and Recreation Department

Account Number	Account Title	FY 2010 Budget	Expenditures 2010 to Date	Encumbrances Outstanding	Available Appropriations
01 08-00 6110	Personnel Services	$1,172,661	$533,472	$ 0	$639,189
01 08-00 7110	Materials and Supplies	376,457	207,683	27,424	141,350
01 08-00 7210	Conferences and Training	3,800	1,426	0	2,374
01 08-00 7310	Contractual Services	276,840	102,687	89,642	84,511
01 08-00 7410	Utilities	192,248	98,249	0	93,999
01 08-00 7810	Capital Outlay	57,924	21,387	3,600	32,937
01 08-00 7910	Other	248,673	172,538	6,742	69,393

Required

a. Explain the account code structure being employed by Lincoln City. Does that structure appear consistent with the expenditure classifications required by GASB standards? Does it allow for more detailed expenditure classifications, if desired? For example, could materials and supplies be further classified as recreational supplies, office supplies, building supplies, and so forth?

b. What is the likely reason there are no outstanding encumbrances for the Personnel Services, Conferences and Training, and Utilities accounts?

c. Does it appear that the Parks and Recreation Department may overexpend its appropriation for any accounts before the end of FY 2010? If so, which accounts may run short?

d. Does it appear that the Parks and Recreation Department may underexpend any of its appropriations for FY 2010? If so, which accounts may have excessive spending authority?

e. What factors may explain the expenditure patterns observed in parts *c* and *d*?

3–9 Recording General Fund Operating Budget and Operating Transactions. The Town of Bedford Falls approved a General Fund operating budget for the fiscal year ending June 30, 2011. The budget provides for estimated revenues of $2,700,000 as follows: property taxes, $1,900,000; licenses and permits, $350,000; fines and forfeits, $250,000; and intergovernmental (state grants), $200,000. The budget approved appropriations of $2,650,000 as follows: General Government, $500,000; Public Safety, $1,600,000; Public Works, $350,000; Parks and Recreation, $150,000; and Miscellaneous, $50,000.

Required

a. Prepare the journal entry (or entries), including subsidiary ledger entries, to record the Town of Bedford Falls's General Fund operating budget on July 1, 2010, the beginning of the Town's 2011 fiscal year.

b. Prepare journal entries to record the following transactions that occurred during the month of July 2010.

1. Revenues were collected in cash amounting to $31,000 for licenses and permits and $12,000 for fines and forfeits.
2. Supplies were ordered by the following functions in early July 2010 at the estimated costs shown:

General Government	$ 7,400
Public Safety	11,300
Public Works	6,100
Parks and Recreation	4,200
Miscellaneous	900
Total	$29,900

3. During July 2010, supplies were received at the actual costs shown below and were paid in cash. General Government, Parks and Recreation, and Miscellaneous received all supplies ordered. Public Safety and Public Works received part of the supplies ordered earlier in the month at estimated costs of $10,700 and $5,900, respectively.

	Actual Cost	Estimated Cost
General Government	$ 7,300	$ 7,400
Public Safety	10,800	10,700
Public Works	6,100	5,900
Parks and Recreation	4,100	4,200
Miscellaneous	900	900
Total	$29,200	$29,100

c. Calculate and show in good form the amount of budgeted but unrealized revenues in total and from each source as of July 31, 2010.

d. Calculate and show in good form the amount of available appropriation in total and for each function as of July 31, 2010.

3–10 Government-wide Statement of Activities. The following alphabetic listing displays selected balances in the governmental activities accounts of the City of Kokomo as of June 30, 2011. Prepare a (partial) statement of activities in good form. For simplicity, assume that the city does not have business-type activities or component units.

CITY OF KOKOMO
Governmental Activities
Selected Account Balances (in thousands)
For the Year Ended June 30, 2011

	Debits	*Credits*
Expenses—Culture and Recreation	12,352	
Expenses—General Government	9,571	
General Revenues—Property Taxes		56,300
General Revenues—Unrestricted Grants and Contributions		1,200
Expenses—Health and Sanitation	6,738	
Expenses—Interest on Long-term Debt	6,068	
General Revenues—Investment Earnings		1,958
Unrestricted Net Assets		126,673
Expenses—Public Safety	34,844	
Program Revenue—Culture and Recreation—Charges for Services		3,995
Program Revenue—Culture and Recreation—Operating Grants		2,450
Program Revenue—General Government—Charges for Services		3,146
Program Revenue—General Government—Operating Grants		843
Program Revenue—Health and Sanitation—Charges for Services		5,612
Program Revenue—Public Safety—Capital Grants		62
Program Revenue—Public Safety—Charges for Services		1,198
Program Revenue—Public Safety—Operating Grants		1,307
Special Item—Gain on Sale of Park Land		3,473

Chapter **Four**

Accounting for Governmental Operating Activities—Illustrative Transactions and Financial Statements

Learning Objectives

After studying this chapter, you should be able to:

1. Analyze typical operating transactions for governmental activities and prepare appropriate journal entries at both the government-wide and fund levels.
2. Prepare adjusting entries at year-end and a pre-closing trial balance.
3. Prepare closing journal entries and year-end General Fund financial statements.
4. Account for interfund and intra- and inter-activity transactions.
5. Account for transactions of a permanent fund.
6. Distinguish between exchange and nonexchange transactions, and define the classifications used for nonexchange transactions.

In Chapter 3, the use of general ledger budgetary control accounts (Estimated Revenues, Estimated Other Financing Sources, Appropriations, Estimated Other Financing Uses, and Encumbrances) and related operating statement accounts (Revenues, Other Financing Sources, Expenditures, and Other Financing Uses) was discussed and illustrated. The necessity for subsidiary ledgers, or equivalent computer files or ledgers, supporting the budgetary control accounts and related operating statement accounts was also discussed. In this chapter, common transactions and events, as well as related recognition and measurement issues, arising from the operating activities of a hypothetical local government, the Town of Brighton, are discussed, and appropriate accounting entries and financial statements are illustrated.

ILLUSTRATIVE CASE

The Town of Brighton's partial government-wide statement of net assets, showing only the governmental activities, and its General Fund balance sheet, both at the end of the 2010 fiscal year, are presented in Illustration 4–1. Because this chapter focuses on *governmental* operating activities, only the financial information for the Governmental Activities column is presented at this time. The Town of Brighton does have business-type activities, but those activities are discussed in Chapter 7 of the text. Although the Town has no discretely presented component units, the column is shown in the statement of net assets simply to illustrate the recommended financial statement format.

Measurement Focus and Basis of Accounting

As discussed at several points in the earlier chapters, the government-wide statement of net assets reports financial position using the economic resources measurement focus and the accrual basis of accounting—in short, using accounting principles similar to those used by business entities. In contrast, the General Fund balance sheet reports financial position using the current financial resources measurement focus and the modified accrual basis of accounting. Although both of these statements represent financial position at the same point in time, even a casual comparison reveals significant differences.

Perhaps the most striking difference between the two statements is that the statement of net assets reports both capital assets and long-term liabilities, whereas the General Fund balance sheet reports only current financial resources and current liabilities to be paid from current financial resources. *Current financial resources* include cash and items (such as marketable securities and receivables) expected to be converted into cash in the current period or soon enough thereafter to pay current period obligations. Prepaid items and inventories of supplies, if material, are also included in current financial resources.

Another major difference is that the information reported in the Governmental Activities column of the statement of net assets includes financial information for *all* governmental activities, not just for the General Fund. For example, the Town of Brighton also has debt service funds whose cash and receivables are combined with those of the General Fund in the Assets section of the statement of net assets. The investments reported in the statement of net assets belong to the debt service funds. In fact, it will be noted that $77,884 of net assets are restricted for purposes of paying debt service (principal and interest) on long-term debt. (*Note:* The debt service funds are discussed in Chapter 6.)

There are some other less important but still noteworthy differences. One such difference involves format. The Town's statement of net assets is in the GASB-recommended net assets format (that is, assets minus liabilities equals net assets) rather than the traditional balance sheet format (assets equals liabilities plus fund equity). This is not a *necessary* condition, however, as GASB *Statement No. 34* permits governments the option of preparing a government-wide *balance sheet* rather than a statement of net assets, if they prefer.

An alert reader may have noted that the statement of net assets reports financial information in a more condensed manner than does the General Fund balance sheet. The primary reason for reporting more aggregated financial information is that the government-wide financial statements, along with the required management's discussion and analysis (MD&A), are intended to provide a broad overview of the

ILLUSTRATION 4–1

TOWN OF BRIGHTON
Statement of Net Assets
December 31, 2010

	Primary Government			
	Governmental Activities	**Business-Type Activities**	**Total**	**Component Units (None)**
Assets				
Cash	$ 257,500	(Omitted intentionally)		
Investments	40,384			
Receivables (net)	619,900			
Inventory of supplies	61,500			
Capital assets (net)	19,330,018			
Total Assets	20,309,302			
Liabilities				
Vouchers payable	320,000			
Accrued interest payable	37,500			
Due to federal government	90,000			
Bonds payable	1,500,000			
Total Liabilities	1,947,500			
Net Assets				
Invested in capital assets, net of related debt	17,830,018			
Restricted for:				
Debt service	77,884			
Unrestricted	453,900			
Total Net Assets	$18,361,802			

TOWN OF BRIGHTON
General Fund Balance Sheet
December 31, 2010

Assets		
Cash		$220,000
Taxes receivable—delinquent	$660,000	
Less: Estimated uncollectible delinquent taxes	50,000	610,000
Interest and penalties receivable on taxes	13,200	
Less: Estimated uncollectible interest and penalties	3,300	9,900
Inventory of supplies		61,500
Total Assets		$901,400
Liabilities and Fund Balances		
Liabilities:		
Vouchers payable		$320,000
Due to federal government		90,000
Total Liabilities		410,000
Fund Balances:		
Reserved for inventory of supplies	$ 61,500	
Reserved for encumbrances—2010	127,000	
Fund balance	302,900	
Total Fund Balances		491,400
Total Liabilities and Fund Balances		$901,400

government's financial position. Additional detail is provided in the notes to the financial statements (not provided in this chapter for sake of brevity), as well as in the fund financial statements.

In the case of the Town of Brighton, the $453,900 reported for unrestricted net assets in the government-wide statement of net assets is only $37,500 less than the $491,400 reported as the total fund balances of the General Fund. In practice, these amounts may be markedly different, as many governments will have financial information for other governmental fund types that will be reported as part of the governmental activities unrestricted net assets. At any rate, neither the net assets at the government-wide level nor the fund balances (equity) at the fund level are analogous to the stockholders' equity of an investor-owned entity. Residents have no legal claim on any net assets or fund equity of the government.

A few final points should be noted about the General Fund balance sheet before discussing illustrative budgetary and operating transactions. Fund equity, usually captioned as *Fund Balances* as shown in Illustration 4–1, is the arithmetic difference between the total financial resources and the total liabilities of the General Fund. The Town of Brighton's General Fund balance sheet illustrates that at December 31, 2010, a portion of fund balances is reserved because the $61,500 inventory of supplies included in the fund's assets cannot be spent or used to pay current liabilities. In addition, some purchase orders issued in fiscal year 2010 were not filled by the end of that year. The estimated $127,000 liability that will arise when these goods or services are received in early 2011 represents a prior budgetary claim on available financial resources, as shown by the line item "Reserved for encumbrances—2010" on the General Fund balance sheet presented in Illustration 4–1. The portion of fund balances that is not reserved is shown as a fund balance of $302,900 on the balance sheet. In practice, this item is usually referred to as *unreserved fund balance*.[1]

DUAL-TRACK ACCOUNTING APPROACH

Although thousands of governments have adopted the *GASBS 34* reporting model, most have continued to use traditional fund accounting software systems. These systems record transactions that occur during the year in the appropriate governmental funds, but they are unable to directly provide account balances on the accrual basis needed for the government-wide financial statements. To compensate for this deficiency, most governments manually convert their fund-based financial information to the accrual basis by preparing spreadsheets, as illustrated in Chapter 9. Most municipal accounting software vendors have helped simplify this approach by developing report generators that selectively aggregate data needed for the government-wide statements. Nevertheless, the authors believe that the reclassification approach

[1] As explained in Chapter 3, Footnote 8, a GASB exposure draft on fund balance reporting proposes to eliminate the *reserved* and *unreserved* classifications of fund balance. If the final statement adopts the proposed classification scheme, portions of amounts reported now in the *unreserved fund balance* classification could be reported in the future as *restricted, limited, assigned*, or *unassigned* fund balances, depending on the nature of constraints that may exist on how the fund balances can be spent. When the GASB issues the final statement, the authors will provide an update bulletin explaining how the new standard affects various parts of the text.

is deficient in the sense that the general ledger accounts do not provide all the information needed to prepare government-wide financial statements. Among other problems, the reclassification approach may limit the preparation of government-wide financial statements to once a year and may present audit trail and accounting record retention problems.

In a real-world computerized accounting system, the dual effects of transactions could be captured using an extensive classification coding scheme, augmented by well-designed report writer software, to aggregate information in different ways, for example, by major fund and government-wide. In contrast, this text adopts a *dual-track* approach to analyzing and recording transactions based on manual accounting procedures. This approach is designed to facilitate ease of learning; however, as will be apparent in Chapter 9, the dual-track approach also allows preparation of both government-wide and fund financial statements.

Operating activities and transactions affect the Town of Brighton's government-wide financial statements and fund financial statements differently. Certain activities (e.g., those relating to the General Fund budget) have no effect on the government-wide financial statements. Most operating activities or transactions affect both the General Fund and governmental activities at the government-wide level, although differently. Still other activities, such as recording depreciation expense or accruing interest on general long-term debt, affect only the government-wide financial statements and are not recorded at all in the General Fund or in any other governmental fund. Examples of the latter journal entries are provided in Chapters 6 and 9.

ILLUSTRATIVE JOURNAL ENTRIES

For the illustrative journal entries that follow, if the account titles or amounts differ in any respect, *separate* journal entries are illustrated for the General Fund general journal and the governmental activities (government-wide) general journal. For activities or transactions in which the entries would be identical, only a single journal entry is illustrated. In these cases, the heading for the entry indicates that it applies to both journals.

Recording the Budget

As discussed in Chapter 3, the budget should be recorded in the accounts of each fund for which a budget is legally adopted. For purposes of review, Entry 1, which follows, illustrates an entry to record the budget in the general journal for the General Fund of the Town of Brighton for fiscal year 2011. (The entry is shown in combined form to illustrate that format. The detail shown is assumed to be the detail needed to comply with laws applicable to the Town of Brighton. Since the Estimated Revenues, Appropriations, and Estimated Other Financing Uses accounts refer only to the fiscal year 2011 budget and will be closed at the end of the year, it is not necessary to incorporate "2011" in the title of either.)

Interfund Transfer to Create a New Fund

The town council approved the creation of a new Supplies Fund, an internal service fund, effective January 1, 2011, to provide most operating and office supplies used by departments accounted for in the General Fund. The new fund was created

		General Ledger		Subsidiary Ledger	
		Debits	**Credits**	**Debits**	**Credits**
	General Fund:				
1.	Estimated Revenues	3,986,000			
	Budgetary Fund Balance	285,500			
	Appropriations		4,180,000		
	Estimated Other Financing Uses		91,500		
	Estimated Revenues Ledger:				
	Property Taxes			2,600,000	
	Interest and Penalties on Delinquent Taxes			13,000	
	Sales Taxes			480,000	
	Licenses and Permits			220,000	
	Fines and Forfeits			308,000	
	Intergovernmental Revenue			280,000	
	Charges for Services			70,000	
	Miscellaneous Revenues			15,000	
	Appropriations Ledger:				
	General Government				660,000
	Public Safety				1,240,000
	Public Works				1,090,000
	Health and Welfare				860,000
	Parks and Recreation				315,000
	Miscellaneous Appropriations				15,000
	Estimated Other Financing Uses Ledger:				
	General Government				91,500

by transferring the current inventory of supplies and $30,000 in cash from the General Fund, general government function. Appropriate journal entries are provided in Chapter 7 to create the new internal service fund. The effect on the General Fund is reflected in Entries 2 and 2a below. The transfer has no effect on governmental activities at the government-wide level since financial information for both the General Fund and the new Supplies Fund is reported in the Governmental Activities column.

		General Ledger Debits	General Ledger Credits	Subsidiary Ledger Debits	Subsidiary Ledger Credits
	General Fund:				
2.	Other Financing Uses—Interfund Transfers Out	91,500			
	Inventory of Supplies		61,500		
	Cash		30,000		
	Other Financing Uses Ledger:				
	General Government			91,500	
	General Fund:				
2a.	Reserve for Inventory of Supplies	61,500			
	Fund Balance		61,500		

Entry 2a is necessary since the General Fund no longer possesses the supplies for which the reservation of fund balance was established (see Illustration 4–1). Although the General Fund will order most operating and office supplies from the new Supplies Fund, certain special-use operating and office supplies will continue to be ordered from external vendors.

Encumbrance Entry

Interdepartmental requisitions for supplies with an estimated cost of $247,360 were submitted to the Supplies Fund, and purchase orders for certain other supplies and contracts for services were placed with outside vendors in the amount of $59,090. Entry 3 below shows the journal entry required to record the estimated cost of supplies ordered and service contracts. Since some encumbrance documents issued in 2011 may not be filled until early 2012, sound budgetary control dictates that "2011" be added to the Encumbrances general ledger control account and the corresponding Reserve for Encumbrances. The amounts chargeable to specific appropriations of 2011 are debited to detail accounts in the Encumbrances Subsidiary Ledger. (Recall that budgetary entries affect only funds for which a budget is legally adopted; they have no effect at the government-wide level.)

		General Ledger		Subsidiary Ledger	
		Debits	***Credits***	***Debits***	***Credits***
	General Fund:				
3.	Encumbrances—2011	306,450			
	Reserve for Encumbrances—2011		306,450		
	Encumbrances Ledger:				
	General Government			28,000	
	Public Safety			72,000	
	Public Works			160,000	
	Parks and Recreation			36,000	
	Health and Welfare			10,000	
	Miscellaneous Appropriations			450	

When supplies and services ordered during the current year have been received and found to be acceptable, the suppliers' or contractors' billings or invoices should be checked for agreement with the original interdepartmental requisitions, purchase orders, or contracts as to prices and terms, as well as for clerical accuracy. If all details are in order, the billing documents are approved for payment. If, as is usual practice, the estimated liability for each order was previously recorded in the Encumbrances control account in the general ledger, as well as in subsidiary Encumbrance Ledger accounts, entries must be made to reverse the encumbrances entries for the originally estimated amounts. In addition, entries are required to record the actual charges in the Expenditures control account and subsidiary Expenditures Ledger accounts. Expenses and/or assets must also be recorded in governmental activities accounts at the government-wide level, as appropriate.

Assume that goods and services ordered during 2011 by departments financed by the Town of Brighton General Fund (see Entry 3) were received as follows: All supplies ordered at an estimated cost of $247,360 from the internal service fund

(Supplies Fund) were received at an actual cost of $249,750; however, only a portion of the supplies and contracts with outside vendors were filled or completed during the year at an actual cost of $19,700, for which the estimated cost had been $22,415. For purposes of illustration, the appropriations assumed to be affected are shown in Entries 4 and 4a for the General Fund.

		General Ledger		Subsidiary Ledger	
		Debits	**Credits**	**Debits**	**Credits**
	General Fund:				
4.	Reserve for Encumbrances—2011 . . .	269,775			
	Encumbrances—2011		269,775		
	Encumbrances Ledger:				
	General Government				12,250
	Public Safety				72,000
	Public Works				150,900
	Parks and Recreation				30,000
	Health and Welfare				4,175
	Miscellaneous Appropriations				450
4a.	Expenditures—2011	269,450			
	Due to Other Funds		249,750		
	Vouchers Payable		19,700		
	Expenditures Ledger:				
	General Government			12,300	
	Public Safety			72,000	
	Public Works			150,600	
	Parks and Recreation			30,000	
	Health and Welfare			4,100	
	Miscellaneous Appropriations			450	

Although the Town of Brighton records the purchase of supplies from the Supplies Fund at the amount billed, the expenses recorded in the governmental activities accounts at the government-wide level should be the cost of the goods to the Supplies Fund. In other words, the cost to the government as a whole is what the internal service fund paid for the goods to external parties, and does not include the markup charged to departments by the Supplies Fund. As shown in Chapter 7, Entries 5a and b, the cost of the $249,750 of supplies issued to the General Fund was $185,000, so the markup is 35 percent on cost. Accordingly, the total direct expenses recorded at the government-wide level (see Entry 4b) is the $185,000 cost of supplies purchased from the Supplies Fund plus the $19,700 of goods and services purchased from external vendors, or a total of $204,700, distributed to functions based on assumed purchase patterns. It is the town's policy to include miscellaneous expenses as part of the General Government function at the government-wide level. (Note that the account credited at the government-wide level for the supplies purchased from the Supplies Fund is Inventory of Supplies since $185,000 represents supplies issued that are no longer in the Supplies Fund's inventory and thus are no longer in inventory from a government-wide perspective, assuming that substantially all supplies purchased by General Fund departments will be consumed during the year. Immaterial amounts of year-end inventory in the General Fund should be ignored.)

		General Ledger		Subsidiary Ledger	
		Debits	*Credits*	*Debits*	*Credits*
	Governmental Activities:				
4b.	Expenses—General Government	9,885			
	Expenses—Public Safety	54,889			
	Expenses—Public Works	114,148			
	Expenses—Parks and Recreation	22,741			
	Expenses—Health and Welfare	3,037			
	Vouchers Payable		19,700		
	Inventory of Supplies		185,000		

In addition to supplies, General Fund departments will make expenditures (capital outlays) for equipment or other general capital assets during the year. Although capital outlay expenditures are not illustrated in this chapter, they are recorded in the same manner as were supplies in Entries 3, 4, and 4a. At the government-wide level, an entry similar to Entry 4b would be required, except that the debit would be to Equipment (or other capital asset account as appropriate).

Payment of Liabilities

Checks were drawn to pay the $339,700 balance of vouchers payable ($320,000 balance at the end of 2010 plus the $19,700 amount from Entry 4a) and the 2010 year-end amount due to the federal government. In addition, the General Fund paid the Supplies Fund $249,750 for supplies purchased in Entry 4a. The following entries would be made for the General Fund and governmental activities at the government-wide level:

		Debits	Credits
	General Fund:		
5a.	Vouchers Payable	339,700	
	Due to Other Funds	249,750	
	Due to Federal Government	90,000	
	Cash		679,450
	Governmental Activities:		
5b.	Vouchers Payable	339,700	
	Due to Federal Government	90,000	
	Cash		429,700

Note that the entry to Due to Other Funds is omitted from Entry 5b as the transfer of cash between a governmental fund and an internal service fund has no effect on the amount of cash available within governmental activities at the government-wide level. Also, entries to subsidiary appropriation or expenditure accounts in the General Fund are unnecessary since those entries were made previously when the goods and services were received.

Some readers may question how more cash can be disbursed in Entries 5a and 5b than is available. This is no cause for concern, as the examples in this chapter are summarized transactions. Throughout the year revenues are also being collected, as illustrated in a later section. Should tax revenues be received later than needed to pay vendors on a timely basis, governments typically issue *tax anticipation notes* to meet those short-term cash needs, as discussed later in this chapter.

Payrolls and Payroll Taxes

The gross pay of employees of General Fund departments for the month of January 2011 amounted to $252,000. The town does not use the encumbrance procedure for payrolls. Deductions from gross pay for the period amount to $19,278 for employees' share of FICA tax; $25,200, employees' federal withholding tax; and $5,040, employees' state withholding tax. The first two will, of course, have to be remitted by the town to the federal government, and the last item will have to be remitted to the state government. The gross pay is chargeable to the appropriations in the General Fund as indicated by the Expenditures Ledger debits. Assuming that the liability for net pay is vouchered, the entry in the General Fund is:

		General Ledger		Subsidiary Ledger	
		Debits	***Credits***	***Debits***	***Credits***
	General Fund:				
6a.	Expenditures—2011	252,000			
	Vouchers Payable		202,482		
	Due to Federal Government		44,478		
	Due to State Government		5,040		
	Expenditures Ledger:				
	General Government			35,040	
	Public Safety			156,120	
	Public Works			29,160	
	Health and Welfare			19,080	
	Parks and Recreation			12,600	

In addition, the following entry would be required to record the payroll transaction in the governmental activities general journal at the government-wide level, using the accrual basis (expenses rather than expenditures):

		Debits	Credits		
	Governmental Activities:				
6b.	Expenses—General Government	35,040			
	Expenses—Public Safety	156,120			
	Expenses—Public Works	29,160			
	Expenses—Health and Welfare	19,080			
	Expenses—Parks and Recreation	12,600			
	Vouchers Payable		202,482		
	Due to Federal Government		44,478		
	Due to State Government		5,040		

Recording the salaries and wages expenses in the manner shown in Entry 6b permits reporting direct expenses by function, as shown in Illustration A1–2 and as described in Chapter 3 in the discussion on expense classification in the government-wide statement of activities. If a government prefers to also record the expenses by natural classification (that is, as salaries and wages expense), it will be necessary to add additional classification detail; for example, Expenses—General Government—Salaries and Wages.

Payment of the vouchers for the net pay results in the following entry in both the General Fund and governmental activities journals:

		General Ledger		Subsidiary Ledger	
		Debits	**Credits**	**Debits**	**Credits**
	General Fund and Governmental Activities:				
7.	Vouchers Payable	202,482			
	Cash		202,482		

Inasmuch as the town is liable for the employer's share of FICA taxes ($19,278), it is necessary that the town's liability be recorded, as shown in Entry 8a.

	General Fund:				
8a.	Expenditures—2011	19,278			
	Due to Federal Government		19,278		
	Expenditures Ledger:				
	General Government			2,681	
	Public Safety			11,943	
	Public Works			2,230	
	Health and Welfare			1,460	
	Parks and Recreation			964	

Entry 8b is also required to record the payroll expense on the accrual basis at the government-wide level.

	Governmental Activities:				
8b.	Expenses—General Government	2,681			
	Expenses—Public Safety	11,943			
	Expenses—Public Works	2,230			
	Expenses—Health and Welfare	1,460			
	Expenses—Parks and Recreation	964			
	Due to Federal Government		19,278		

Revenues Recognized as Received in Cash

Revenues from sources such as licenses and permits, fines and forfeits, charges for services, and certain other sources are often not measurable until received in cash. However, under the modified accrual basis of accounting, if such revenues are measurable in advance of collection and available for current period expenditure, they should be accrued by recording a debit to a receivable and a credit to Revenues. During fiscal year 2011, the Town of Brighton has collected revenues in cash from the sources shown in Entry 9a.

		General Ledger		Subsidiary Ledger	
		Debits	**Credits**	**Debits**	**Credits**
	General Fund:				
9a.	Cash	259,200			
	Revenues		259,200		
	Revenues Ledger:				
	Licenses and Permits				100,000
	Fines and Forfeits				151,000
	Charges for Services				7,000
	Miscellaneous Revenues				1,200

Of the preceding revenues, licenses and permits, fines and forfeits, and charges for services are appropriately recorded as *program revenues* at the government-wide level. Licenses and permits are attributed to the general government function. Fines and forfeits were assessed by the Public Safety function in the amount of $91,000 and by the Public Works function in the amount of $60,000. Charges for services were received from customers of the Parks and Recreation function. Miscellaneous revenues cannot be identified with a specific program and thus are recorded as *general revenues* at the government-wide level. Based on this information the entry that should be made in the journal for governmental activities is shown in Entry 9b.

		Debits	Credits		
	Governmental Activities:				
9b.	Cash	259,200			
	Program Revenues—General Government—Charges for Services		100,000		
	Program Revenues—Public Safety—Charges for Services		91,000		
	Program Revenues—Public Works—Charges for Services		60,000		
	Program Revenues—Parks and Recreation—Charges for Services		7,000		
	General Revenues—Miscellaneous		1,200		

Readers may be confused by classifying Fines and Forfeits as Charges for Services since generally we associate Charges for Services with **exchange** or **exchange-like transactions** in which value is given for value received (see the appendix to this chapter). GASB considered this issue and decided that Charges for Services does not preclude a nonexchange transaction such as Fines and Forfeits. Furthermore, Fines and Forfeits is not appropriately classified as either Operating Grants and Contributions or Capital Grants and Contributions (see program revenue classifications in Illustration A1–2 and Illustration 3–1). Thus, in substance, the GASB decided to classify Fines and Forfeits as Charges for Services to avoid the need to add a fourth category of program revenues in the government-wide statement of activities.[2]

[2] Governmental Accounting Standards Board, *Codification of Governmental Accounting and Financial Reporting Standards, as of June 30, 2008* (Norwalk, CT, 2008), Sec. 2200. 137.

ACCOUNTING FOR PROPERTY TAXES

Entry 1 of this chapter shows that the estimated revenue for fiscal year 2011 from property taxes levied for the Town of Brighton General Fund is $2,600,000. If records of property tax collections in recent years, adjusted for any expected changes in tax collection policy and changes in local economic conditions, indicate that approximately 4 percent of the gross tax levy will never be collected, the **gross tax levy** must be large enough so that the collectible portion of the levy, 96 percent, equals the needed revenue from this source, $2,600,000. Therefore, the gross levy of property taxes for the General Fund of the Town of Brighton must be $2,708,333 ($2,600,000 ÷ 0.96). In an actual situation, property situated in the Town of Brighton also would be taxed for other funds of that town; for various funds of other general purpose governments, such as the county in which the property in the Town of Brighton is located; the various funds of special purpose governments that have the right to tax the same property, such as one or more independent school districts or a hospital district; and perhaps the state in which the town is located.

Recording Property Tax Levy

The gross property tax levies for each fund of the Town of Brighton, and for each other general purpose and special purpose government, must be aggregated, and the aggregate levy for that unit divided by the assessed valuation of property within the geographical limits of that government, in order to determine the **tax rate** applicable to property within each jurisdiction. In many states, a county official prepares bills for all taxes levied on property within the county; the same official, or another, acts as collector of all property taxes levied for the county and all governments within the county. Although the billing and collecting functions may be centralized, the taxes levied for each fund must be recorded as an asset of that fund. If the accounts are to be kept in conformity with generally accepted accounting principles, the portion of the taxes expected to be collectible (0.96 of the total levy, in this example) must be recorded as revenues of that fund, and the portion expected to be uncollectible (0.04 of the total levy), must be recorded in a "contra-asset" account, as illustrated by Entries 10a and 10b.

		General Ledger		Subsidiary Ledger	
		Debits	*Credits*	*Debits*	*Credits*
	General Fund:				
10a.	Taxes Receivable—Current	2,708,333			
	Estimated Uncollectible Current Taxes		108,333		
	Revenues		2,600,000		
	Revenues Ledger:				
	Property Taxes				2,600,000
	Governmental Activities:				
10b.	Taxes Receivable—Current	2,708,333			
	Estimated Uncollectible Current Taxes		108,333		
	General Revenues—Property Taxes		2,600,000		

As Entry 10a shows, since in the General Fund the general ledger control account, Revenues, is credited, an entry must also be made in the Revenues Subsidiary Ledger. Taxes Receivable—Current is also a control account, just as is the Accounts Receivable account of a business entity; each is supported by a subsidiary ledger that shows how much is owed by each taxpayer or customer. Ordinarily, the subsidiary ledger supporting the real property taxes receivable control is organized by parcels of property according to their legal descriptions, since unpaid taxes are liens against the property regardless of changes in ownership. Because of its conceptual similarity to accounting for business receivables, taxes receivable subsidiary ledger accounting is not illustrated in this text.

Property tax revenue is an example of a **nonexchange revenue**—one in which the government receives value without directly giving equal value in exchange. More specifically, it is classified under GASB standards as an **imposed nonexchange revenue.** For imposed nonexchange revenues, a receivable should be debited when there is an enforceable claim, as in the case of a property tax levy, and a revenue should be credited in the year for which the tax was levied. The $2,600,000 credit to Revenues in Entry 10a indicates that the Town of Brighton expects to collect that amount during 2011 or within 60 days after the end of fiscal year 2011.[3] If the town expected to collect a portion of the $2,600,000 later than 60 days after fiscal year-end, it should credit that portion to Deferred Revenues (a current liability account) and reclassify it to Revenues in the period in which the deferred revenues are collected. Note, however, that even if a portion of revenues is deferred in the General Fund because of the availability criterion, the full $2,600,000 is recognized as General Revenues—Property Taxes in the governmental activities journal at the government-wide level. This is so because availability to finance current expenditures is not a revenue recognition criterion under the accrual basis used at the government-wide level.

Collection of Current Taxes

Collections of property taxes levied in 2011 for the General Fund of the Town of Brighton amount to $2,042,033. Since the revenue was recognized at the time of the levy (see Entry 10a), the following entry is made in both the General Fund and governmental activities journal.

		General Ledger		Subsidiary Ledger	
		Debits	**Credits**	**Debits**	**Credits**
	General Fund and Governmental Activities:				
11.	Cash	2,042,033			
	Taxes Receivable—Current		2,042,033		

Reclassification of Current Property Taxes

Assuming that all property taxes levied by the Town of Brighton in 2011 were legally due before the end of the year, any balance of taxes receivable at year-end is properly classified as **delinquent taxes** rather than current. The related allowance for estimated uncollectible taxes should also be reclassified as contra to the Taxes

[3] GASB *Codification,* Sec. P70.104.

Receivable—Delinquent account. The entry to accomplish the reclassification, using amounts assumed to exist in the accounts at year-end, is:

		General Ledger		Subsidiary Ledger	
		Debits	*Credits*	*Debits*	*Credits*
	General Fund and Governmental Activities:				
12.	Taxes Receivable—Delinquent	666,300			
	Estimated Uncollectible Current Taxes	108,333			
	Taxes Receivable—Current		666,300		
	Estimated Uncollectible Delinquent Taxes		108,333		

Accrual of Interest and Penalties on Delinquent Taxes

Delinquent taxes are subject to interest and penalties as discussed previously. If the amount of interest and penalties earned in 2011 by the General Fund of the Town of Brighton but not yet recognized is $13,320, and it is expected that only $10,800 of that can be collected, the following entries are necessary:

		General Ledger Debits	General Ledger Credits	Subsidiary Ledger Debits	Subsidiary Ledger Credits
	General Funds:				
13a.	Interest and Penalties Receivable on Taxes	13,320			
	Estimated Uncollectible Interest and Penalties		2,520		
	Revenues		10,800		
	Revenues Ledger:				
	Interest and Penalties on Delinquent Taxes				10,800
	Governmental Activities:				
13b.	Interest and Penalties Receivable on Taxes	13,320			
	Estimated Uncollectible Interest and Penalties		2,520		
	General Revenues—Interest and Penalties on Delinquent Taxes		10,800		

Collection of Delinquent Taxes

Delinquent taxes are subject to interest and penalties that must be paid at the time the tax bill is paid. It is possible for a government to record the amount of penalties at the time the taxes become delinquent. Interest may be computed and recorded periodically to keep the account on the accrual basis; it must also be computed and recorded for the period from the date of last recording to the date when a taxpayer pays delinquent taxes. Assume that taxpayers of the Town of Brighton have paid delinquent taxes totaling $440,000, on which interest and penalties of $8,800 had been recorded as receivable at the end of 2010. Also, assume that additional interest of $600 was paid for the period from the first day of 2011 to the dates on which the delinquent taxes were paid. Since it is common for the cashier receiving the collections to be permitted to originate source documents that result in credits only to Taxes Receivable—Current, Taxes Receivable—Delinquent, or Interest and Penalties Receivable on Taxes, the $600 interest earned in 2011 should be recorded in a separate entry, as shown in Entries 14a and b.

		General Ledger		Subsidiary Ledger	
		Debits	**Credits**	**Debits**	**Credits**
	General Funds:				
14a.	Interest and Penalties Receivable on Taxes	600			
	Revenues		600		
	Revenues Ledger:				
	Interest and Penalties on Delinquent Taxes				600

The corresponding entry at the government-wide level is:

		Debits	Credits		
	Governmental Activities:				
14b.	Interest and Penalties Receivable on Taxes	600			
	General Revenues—Interest and Penalties on Delinquent Taxes . . .		600		

Collection of the delinquent taxes as well as interest and penalties thereon is summarized in Entry 15, which is the entry that should be made in both the General Fund and governmental activities journals. Note that these collections during 2011 are from the delinquent taxes receivable reported on the 2010 General Fund balance sheet and the Governmental Activities column of the government-wide statement of net assets (see Illustration 4–1).

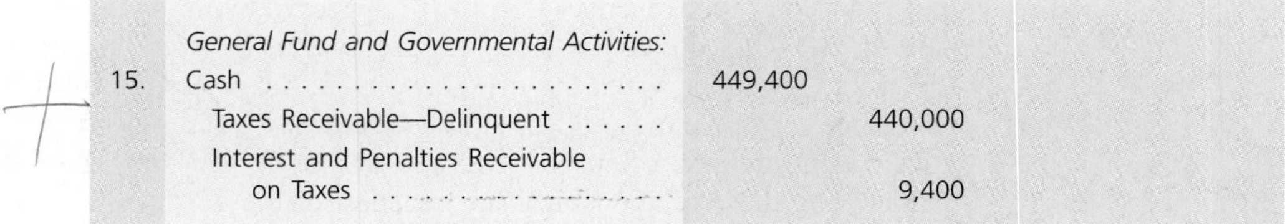

		Debits	Credits		
	General Fund and Governmental Activities:				
15.	Cash	449,400			
	Taxes Receivable—Delinquent		440,000		
	Interest and Penalties Receivable on Taxes		9,400		

Write-off of Uncollectible Delinquent Taxes

Just as officers of profit-seeking entities should review aged schedules of receivables periodically to determine the adequacy of allowance accounts and authorize the write-off of items judged uncollectible, so should officers of a government review aged trial balances of taxes receivable and other receivables. Although the levy of property taxes creates a lien against the underlying property in the amount of the tax, accumulated taxes may exceed the market value of the property, or, in the case of personal property, the property may have been removed from the jurisdiction of the government. When delinquent taxes are deemed uncollectible, the related interest and penalties must also be written off. If the treasurer of the Town of Brighton receives approval to write off delinquent taxes totaling $26,300 and related interest and penalties of $1,315, the entry for both the General Fund and governmental activities would be:

		General Ledger		Subsidiary Ledger	
		Debits	**Credits**	**Debits**	**Credits**
	General Fund and Governmental Activities:				
16.	Estimated Uncollectible Delinquent Taxes	26,300			
	Estimated Uncollectible Interest and Penalties	1,315			
	Taxes Receivable—Delinquent		26,300		
	Interest and Penalties Receivable on Taxes		1,315		

When delinquent taxes are written off, the tax bills are retained in the files in case it becomes possible to collect the amounts in the future. If collections of written-off taxes are made, it is highly desirable to return the tax bills to general ledger control by making an entry that is the reverse of the write-off entry, so that the procedures described in connection with Entries 14 and 15 can be followed.

Tax Anticipation Notes Payable

In the December 31, 2010, Statement of Net Assets and General Fund Balance Sheet of the Town of Brighton, two items, Vouchers Payable and Due to Federal Government, are current liabilities. Assuming there was a need to pay these in full within 30 days after the date of the balance sheet, the town treasurer would need to do some cash forecasting because the balance of Cash in the General Fund is not large enough to pay the $410,000 debt. In addition to this immediate problem, the treasurer, and most governmental treasurers, faces the problem that cash disbursements during a fiscal year tend to be approximately level month by month, whereas cash receipts from major revenue sources are concentrated in just a few months. For example, property tax collections may be concentrated in two separate months, such as May and November, when the installments are due. Receipts from the state or federal government of revenues collected by superior jurisdictions for distribution to a local government are also often concentrated in one or two months of the year.

Knowing these relationships, the treasurer of the Town of Brighton may, for example, forecast the need to disburse approximately one-fourth of the budgeted appropriations, or $1,045,000 (one-fourth of $4,180,000), during the first three months of fiscal year 2011, before major items of revenue are received. This amount plus current liabilities at the beginning of the year, $410,000, plus a $30,000 interfund transfer to create the new Supplies Fund, equals $1,485,000 expected cash disbursements in the period for which the forecast is made. The town's experience suggests that a conservative forecast of collections of delinquent taxes and interest and penalties thereon during the forecast period will amount to $425,000. Furthermore, assume the treasurer's review of the items in the Estimated Revenues budget indicates that at least $140,000 will be collected in the forecast period. Therefore, total cash available to meet the estimated $1,485,000 of disbursements is $785,000 ($220,000 cash as of the beginning of the period, plus the $425,000 and $140,000 items just described), leaving a deficiency of $700,000 to be met by borrowing. Determination of the $700,000 required tax anticipation note financing is summarized in Illustration 4–2.

ILLUSTRATION 4-2 Determination of Required Tax Anticipation Note Financing, January 1 through March 31, 2011

Estimated Expenditure Requirements:		
Budgeted expenditures (25% of $4,180,000),	$1,045,000	
Current liabilities payable	440,000	$1,485,000
Estimated Resources Available:		
Cash available at January 1, 2011	220,000	
Collections of delinquent taxes, interest, and penalties	425,000	
Collection of budgeted FY 2011 revenues	140,000	785,000
Estimated Amount of Required Tax Anticipation Note Financing		$ 700,000

The taxing power of the government is ample security for short-term debt; local banks customarily meet the working capital needs of a government by accepting a **tax anticipation note** from the government. Additional discussion of cash budgeting is provided in Chapter 13. If the amount of $700,000 is borrowed at this time, the necessary entries in both the General Fund and governmental activities are:

		General Ledger		Subsidiary Ledger	
		Debits	***Credits***	***Debits***	***Credits***
	General Fund and Governmental Activities:				
17.	Cash	700,000			
	Tax Anticipation Notes Payable		700,000		

Repayment of Tax Anticipation Notes

As tax collections begin to exceed current disbursements, it becomes possible for the Town of Brighton to repay the local bank for the money borrowed on tax anticipation notes. Just as borrowing the money did not involve the recognition of revenue, the repayment of the principal extinguishes the debt of the General Fund and is not an expenditure. Payment of interest, however, must be recognized as the expenditure of an appropriation because it requires a reduction in the fund balance of the fund. Assuming the interest is $13,500, and the amount is properly chargeable to Miscellaneous Appropriations, the entry is:

		General Ledger		Subsidiary Ledger	
		Debits	***Credits***	***Debits***	***Credits***
	General Fund:				
18a.	Tax Anticipation Notes Payable	700,000			
	Expenditures—2011	13,500			
	Cash		713,500		
	Expenditures Ledger:				
	Miscellaneous Appropriations			13,500	

Procedures of some governments would require the interest expenditures to have been recorded as an encumbrance against Miscellaneous Appropriations at the time the notes were issued, and the liability for the principal and interest to have been vouchered before payment. Even if these procedures were followed by the Town of Brighton, the net result of all entries is achieved by Entry 18a.

A similar entry, shown as Entry 18b, is made at the government-wide level except that an expense rather than expenditure is recorded for the interest charged on the note. This expense is deemed to be an indirect expense that benefits no single function.

		General Ledger		Subsidiary Ledger	
		Debits	*Credits*	*Debits*	*Credits*
	Governmental Activities:				
18b.	Tax Anticipation Notes Payable	700,000			
	Expenses—Interest on Tax Anticipation Notes . .	13,500			
	Cash		713,500		

Other Taxes

In addition to property taxes, many state and local governments receive sales and use taxes, income taxes, motor fuel taxes, and various other kinds of taxes, including those on businesses. These taxes, like property taxes, are **nonexchange transactions** in which one party (taxpayers in this case) does not receive (give) value proportionate to the value given (received). However, these taxes derive their valuation from underlying exchange transactions, such as selling goods, earning wages and salaries, and purchasing fuel. Thus, the GASB refers to taxes such as sales and income taxes as **derived tax revenues.**

Generally, derived tax revenues should be recognized in the period in which the underlying exchange has occurred. In practice, collections of sales and income taxes may not occur in the same period in which the underlying sales or earning transactions occurred. For example, local governments often experience delays in collecting sales taxes because in most states these taxes are collected by state governments. Moreover, businesses may only be required to file a sales tax return and remit taxes on a monthly basis. Income taxes are subject to even less frequent filings and collections. Consequently, at the end of a fiscal period, governments generally will need to estimate the amount of sales or income taxes that have accrued but have not yet been reported. Such entries will require a debit to a taxes receivable account and a credit to the Revenues control account and the appropriate Revenues Subsidiary Ledger accounts.

INTERIM FINANCIAL REPORTING

Unlike publicly traded corporations, state and local governments usually are not required to provide quarterly or other interim financial statements to external parties. Although there is no requirement for *external* interim reporting, all state and local governments should prepare interim financial schedules for the *internal* use of administrators and legislators. The frequency and nature of interim reports are at the discretion of each government. At a minimum, quarterly budgetary comparison schedules should be prepared showing actual revenues to date compared with budgeted revenues and actual expenditures and outstanding encumbrances to date compared with appropriations. Schedules such as these for the Town of Brighton, prepared as of the end of the first quarter of the 2011 fiscal year, are presented as Illustrations 4–3 and 4–4. (*Note:* The amounts of revenues, expenditures, and

ILLUSTRATION 4–3

TOWN OF BRIGHTON
General Fund
Schedule of Budgeted and Actual Revenues
For the Three Months Ended March 31, 2011

Sources of Revenues	Estimated	Actual	Estimated Revenues Not Yet Realized
Taxes:			
Property taxes	$2,600,000	$2,599,636	$ 364
Interest and penalties on taxes	13,000	600	12,400
Sales taxes	480,000	—	480,000
Total taxes	3,093,000	2,600,236	492,764
Licenses and permits	220,000	100,000	120,000
Fines and forfeits	308,000	151,000	157,000
Intergovernmental revenue	280,000	—	280,000
Charges for services	70,000	7,000	63,000
Miscellaneous revenues	15,000	1,200	13,800
Total General Fund Revenue	$3,986,000	$2,859,436	$1,126,564

encumbrances shown in these schedules are the amounts assumed to exist through March 31, 2011.) Such schedules are essential to sound budgetary control and often include an additional column showing prior year revenues and expenditures/encumbrances for the same period. So that appropriate officials can take timely action to correct unexpected revenue or expenditure/encumbrance variances, it may be necessary to prepare interim budgetary comparison schedules on a monthly, or even weekly, basis, rather than quarterly. This is particularly true for larger governments.

ILLUSTRATION 4–4

TOWN OF BRIGHTON
General Fund
Schedule of Budgeted and Actual Expenditures and Encumbrances
For the Three Months Ended March 31, 2011

Function	Appropriations	Expenditures of 2011 Appropriations	Outstanding Encumbrances	Available Appropriations
General government	$ 660,000	$ 129,100	$15,750	$ 515,150
Public safety	1,240,000	592,400	—	647,600
Public works	1,090,000	330,060	9,100	750,840
Health and welfare	860,000	67,700	5,825	786,475
Parks and recreation	315,000	72,000	6,000	237,000
Miscellaneous appropriations	15,000	450	—	14,550
Total General Fund	$4,180,000	$1,191,710	$36,675	$2,951,615

SPECIAL TOPICS

This section of the chapter presents several special topics that result in additional journal entries, either in the General Fund or governmental activities journals, or both. Many additional transactions are assumed to have occurred during 2011, the recording of which would have been redundant of the transactions already illustrated.

Correction of Errors

No problems arise in the collection of current taxes if they are collected as billed; the collections are debited to Cash and credited to Taxes Receivable—Current. Sometimes, even in a well-designed and well-operated system, errors occur and must be corrected. If, for example, the assessed valuation of a parcel of property were legally reduced but the tax bill erroneously issued at the higher valuation, the following correcting entry would be made when the error was discovered, assuming the corrected bill to be $364 smaller than the original bill. (The error also caused a slight overstatement of the credit to Estimated Uncollectible Current Taxes in Entry 10, but the error in that account is not considered material and, for that reason, does not require correction.)

		General Ledger		Subsidiary Ledger	
		Debits	**Credits**	**Debits**	**Credits**
	General Fund:				
19.	Revenues	364			
	Taxes Receivable—Current		364		
	Revenues Ledger:				
	Property Taxes			364	

An entry similar to Entry 19 would also be made at the government-wide level to correct the overstatement of General Revenues and Taxes Receivable—Current.

Postaudit may disclose errors in the recording of expenditures during the current year or during a prior year. If the error occurred during the current year, the Expenditures account and the proper Expenditures subsidiary account should be debited or credited as needed to correct the error. If it occurred in a prior year, however, the Expenditures account in error would have been closed to Fund Balance at the end of the prior year, so the correcting entry should be made to the Fund Balance account. Technically, overpayment errors of prior periods should also result in corrections to Fund Balance. However, as a practical matter, collections from suppliers of prior years' overpayments may be budgeted as Miscellaneous Revenues and recorded as credits to the Revenues account.

Receipt of Goods Ordered in Prior Year

As noted earlier in this chapter under the heading "Measurement Focus and Basis of Accounting," purchase orders and other commitment documents issued in 2010 and not filled or canceled by the end of that year total $127,000. This amount is designated as Reserved for Encumbrances—2010 in the December 31, 2010, General Fund Balance Sheet of the Town of Brighton. As stated previously, budgetary accounting has no effect on the government-wide financial statements; thus, no encumbrance is recorded at the government-wide level when goods or services are ordered or a contract is signed. When the goods on order at the end of fiscal year 2010 are received in 2011, their actual cost is considered an expenditure of the 2010 appropriations to the extent of the amount encumbered in 2010; any additional amount must be charged to the 2011 appropriations. The Appropriations account for 2010, however, was closed at the end of that year, as were the other budgetary accounts for that year.

Although other procedures may be used, the authors prefer to reestablish the Encumbrances account at the beginning of fiscal year 2011, as shown in Entry 20, assuming that the goods were ordered by the Parks and Recreation function.[4] When goods or services ordered in 2010 are received in 2011, it is convenient to debit the Expenditures—2010 account when the liability account is credited and eliminate the encumbrance in the normal manner. At year-end, the Expenditures—2010 account is closed to Fund Balance, along with Expenditures—2011 and all other operating statement accounts.

		General Ledger		Subsidiary Ledger	
		Debits	***Credits***	***Debits***	***Credits***
	General Fund:				
20.	Encumbrances—2010	127,000			
	Fund Balance		127,000		
	Encumbrances Ledger:				
	Parks and Recreation—2010			127,000	

Assuming that all goods and services for which encumbrances were outstanding at the end of 2010 were received in 2011 at a total invoice cost of $127,250, Entries 21 and 21a are necessary in the General Fund, and Entry 21b is made in the governmental activities journal. Notice that only the estimated amount, $127,000, is charged to Expenditures—2010 since this was the amount of the encumbrance against the 2010 appropriation; the difference between the amount encumbered in 2010 and the amount approved for payment in 2011 must be charged against the 2011 appropriation for Parks and Recreation.

		General Ledger Debits	General Ledger Credits	Subsidiary Ledger Debits	Subsidiary Ledger Credits
	General Fund:				
21.	Reserve for Encumbrances—2010	127,000			
	Encumbrances—2010		127,000		
	Encumbrances Ledger:				
	Parks and Recreation—2010				127,000
21a.	Expenditures—2010	127,000			
	Expenditures—2011	250			
	Vouchers Payable		127,250		
	Expenditures Ledger:				
	Parks and Recreation—2010			127,000	
	Parks and Recreation—2011			250	
	Governmental Activities:				
21b.	Expenses—Parks and Recreation	127,250			
	Vouchers Payable		127,250		

[4] State laws vary considerably regarding the treatment of appropriations and encumbrances at year-end. In some states, appropriations do not lapse at year-end. In many others, appropriations lapse and goods encumbered at year-end require a new appropriation in the next year's budget or must be charged to the next year's normal appropriation. Discussion of the methods of accounting for the various alternative laws and practices is beyond the scope of this text.

Revision of the General Fund Budget

Comparisons of budgeted and actual revenues, by sources, comparisons of departmental or program appropriations with expenditures and encumbrances, and interpretation of information that was not available at the time the budgets were originally adopted could indicate the desirability or necessity of legally amending the budget during the fiscal year. For example, the schedule of budgeted and actual revenues for the three months ended March 31, 2011 (Illustration 4–3), shows that more than 70 percent of the revenues budgeted for the General Fund of the Town of Brighton for 2011 have already been realized because revenue from property taxes was accrued when billed, whereas revenues from all other sources were recognized when collected during the three-month period for which entries are illustrated. Consequently, administrators of the town must review the information shown in Illustration 4–3 and determine whether the budget that was legally approved before the beginning of 2011 appears realistic or whether changes should be made in the Revenues budget in light of current information about local economic conditions; possible changes in state or federal laws relating to grants, entitlements, or shared revenues; or other changes relating to license and permit fees, fines, forfeits, and charges for services. Similarly, revenue collection procedures and revenue recognition policies should be reviewed to determine whether changes should be made in the remaining months of the year. Assume that the Town of Brighton's General Fund revenues budget for 2011 has been reviewed as described and that the budget is legally amended to reflect that revenues from Charges for Services are expected to be $5,000 more than originally budgeted, and that Miscellaneous Revenues are expected to be $10,000 more than originally budgeted; revenues from other sources are not expected to be materially different from the original 2011 budget. Entry 22 records the amendment of the Revenues budget, as well as the amendment of the appropriations budget, as will be discussed.

		General Ledger		Subsidiary Ledger	
		Debits	*Credits*	*Debits*	*Credits*
	General Fund:				
22.	Estimated Revenues	15,000			
	Budgetary Fund Balance	15,000			
	Appropriations		30,000		
	Estimated Revenues Ledger:				
	Charges for Services			5,000	
	Miscellaneous Revenues			10,000	
	Appropriations Ledger:				
	Public Works			50,000	
	Public Safety				80,000

Information shown in Illustration 4–4 should be reviewed by administrators of the Town of Brighton to determine whether the appropriations legally approved before the beginning of 2011 appear realistic in light of expenditures of the 2011 budget incurred in the first three months of 2011 and encumbrances outstanding on March 31 of that year. Illustration 4–4 shows that total cumulative expenditures and outstanding encumbrances exceed 29 percent of the total appropriations for 2011, which can be related to the fact that as of March 31, the year is almost 25 percent over. By function, however, cumulative expenditures and outstanding encumbrances range from 3 percent of the Miscellaneous appropriation to almost 48 percent of the Public Safety appropriation. Therefore, each appropriation should be reviewed carefully using whatever detail is available in light of current information about expenditures needed to accomplish planned services during the remainder of 2011. Assume that the Town of Brighton's General Fund appropriations for 2011 have been reviewed and are legally amended to reflect a $50,000 decrease in the appropriation for Public Works and an $80,000 increase in the appropriation for Public Safety. Entry 22 reflects the legal amendment of appropriations for 2011, as well as the amendment of the revenues budget. Note the net increase in Appropriations of $30,000 is more than the net increase in Estimated Revenues of $15,000, requiring a decrease in Budgetary Fund Balance.

Comparisons of budget and actual should be made periodically during each fiscal year. In the Town of Brighton case, it is assumed that comparisons subsequent to the ones illustrated disclosed no further need to amend either the revenues budget or the appropriations budget for 2011.

Internal Exchange Transactions

Water utilities ordinarily provide fire hydrants and water service for fire protection at a flat annual charge. A governmentally owned water utility accounted for by an enterprise fund should be expected to support the cost of its operations by user charges. Fire protection is logically budgeted as an activity of the Fire Department, a General Fund department. Assuming the amount charged by the water utility to the General Fund for hydrants and water service is $30,000, and the fire department budget is a part of the Public Safety category in the Town of Brighton example, the General Fund should record its liability as:

		General Ledger		Subsidiary Ledger	
		Debits	***Credits***	***Debits***	***Credits***
	General Fund:				
23a.	Expenditures—2011	30,000			
	Due to Other Funds		30,000		
	Expenditures Ledger:				
	Public Safety			30,000	

The corresponding entry to record the inter-activities transaction (between the governmental activities and business-type activities) at the government-wide level is given as Entry 23b.

		Debits	Credits
	Governmental Activities:		
23b.	Expenses—Public Works	30,000	
	Internal Balances		30,000

Governmental utility property is not assessed for property tax purposes, but it is common for governmental utilities to make an annual "payment in lieu of taxes (PILOT)" contribution to the General Fund in recognition of the fact the utility does receive police and fire protection and other services. In fact, an amount in lieu of taxes is often billed to the utility's customers; the aggregate amount so collected is simply passed on to the General Fund.

If the water utility of the Town of Brighton agrees to contribute $25,000 to the General Fund in lieu of taxes and that amount fairly represents the value of services received from the general government, the required journal entries for the General Fund and governmental activities are:

		General Ledger		Subsidiary Ledger	
		Debits	**Credits**	**Debits**	**Credits**
	General Fund:				
24a.	Due from Other Funds	25,000			
	Revenues		25,000		
	Revenues Ledger:				
	Miscellaneous Revenues				25,000
	Governmental Activities:				
24b.	Internal Balances	25,000			
	General Revenues—Payments in Lieu of Taxes		25,000		

Internal exchange transactions of the nature illustrated in Entries 23 and 24, and earlier in this chapter by the purchase of supplies by General Fund departments from the Supplies Fund (an internal service fund), affect both the fund and government-wide financial statements. Though the GASB refers to these transactions as *interfund services provided and used,* the authors believe that *internal exchange transactions* is a more precise term. *Internal exchange transactions* better captures the fact that these are reciprocal exchange transactions, but they occur *internally* between funds and activities rather than between the government and an external entity or person.

The funds that participate in internal exchange transactions should recognize revenues and expenditures or expenses, as appropriate, as if the transaction involved each fund and an external entity. Other types of internal transactions between funds, between governmental and business-type activities, and between the primary government and its discretely presented component units are discussed in a later section of this chapter.

Adjusting Entries

Inventories of Supplies

If a government is large enough to have sizeable inventories of consumable supplies that are used by a number of departments, it is generally recommended that the purchasing, warehousing, and distribution functions be centralized and managed by an internal service fund. This was the motivation for the Town of Brighton to create its Supplies Fund at the beginning of this year, as discussed earlier in this chapter. As is typical of small cities and towns, the town previously determined its inventories at year-end by taking a physical count of supplies on hand; for example, by periodic inventory procedures. Since establishing the Supplies Fund, the town maintains these inventories on a perpetual basis, but it will take a physical count at year-end to confirm inventory balances and adjust the inventory accounts accordingly.

Governments that account for their supplies within the General Fund can use either the *purchases method* or the *consumption method.* Using the **purchases method**, expenditures for supplies equals the total amount purchased for the year, even if the amount of supplies consumed is less than or greater than the amount purchased. Thus, the purchases method is consistent with the modified accrual basis of accounting used by the General Fund and other governmental funds. The purchases method is generally associated with a periodic inventory system, so the balance of the Inventory of Supplies account is increased or decreased as necessary at year-end to agree with the valuation based on a physical count. In addition, a Reserve for Inventory of Supplies account, having a credit balance equal in amount to the balance of the inventory account, is required to indicate that the inventory reported on the balance sheet is not available for spending.

The **consumption method** is consistent with the accrual basis of accounting, as resources (i.e., supplies) consumed in providing services is the essence of an expense. Thus, GASB standards require the use of the consumption method for government-wide and proprietary fund reporting. Using this method, the General Fund recognizes expenditures equal to the amount of supplies consumed during the year rather than the amount purchased. Accordingly, budgetary appropriations for supplies are based on estimated consumption rather than estimated purchases. When using the consumption method, reporting of a reservation of fund balance is optional, though recommended.[5]

To illustrate and contrast the purchases and consumption methods, assume the following information for supplies purchases and usage of a certain city for its 2011 fiscal year.

Balance of inventory, January 1, 2011	$ 55,000
Purchases during 2011	260,000
Supplies available for use	315,000
Less: Balance of inventory, December 31, 2011	65,000
Supplies consumed during 2011	$250,000

Purchases Method

Under the purchases method, the summary entry in the General Fund to record supplies purchased during the year, assuming all supplies are purchased from external vendors and all invoices have been paid, is (encumbrance entries and subsidiary detail omitted for simplicity):

	General Ledger		Subsidiary Ledger	
	Debits	***Credits***	***Debits***	***Credits***
General Fund:				
Expenditures	260,000			
Cash		260,000		

At year-end, a physical inventory revealed that $65,000 of inventory remained on hand. The entry to record the $10,000 increase in inventory from the beginning balance and the corresponding reservation of fund balance is given as:

General Fund:				
Inventory of Supplies	10,000			
Reserve for Inventory of Supplies		10,000		

[5] American Institute of Certified Public Accountants, Audit and Accounting Guide, *State and Local Governments* (New York: 2008), par. 10.14.

Consumption Method

Generally, the consumption method is used with a perpetual inventory system; however, because the purchases method is commonly used for General Fund accounting, many governments must convert their purchases information to the consumption basis for governmental activities at the government-wide level. Accordingly, the following examples show consumption method journal entries using periodic inventory control procedures, omitting subsidiary detail for simplicity.

If the city uses a *periodic inventory system,* but reports inventories under the consumption method in both the General Fund and governmental activities, the following entries are required. To record purchases of supplies for the year, assuming that for budgetary control purposes the city records expenditures for each purchase of supplies (encumbrance entries and subsidiary detail omitted for simplicity):

	General Ledger		Subsidiary Ledger	
	Debits	***Credits***	***Debits***	***Credits***
General Fund:				
Expenditures	260,000			
Cash		260,000		

At year-end, the city's General Fund adjusting entries will be:

	General Ledger Debits	General Ledger Credits	Subsidiary Ledger Debits	Subsidiary Ledger Credits
General Fund:				
Inventory of Supplies	10,000			
Expenditures		10,000		
Fund Balance	10,000			
Reserve for Inventory of Supplies		10,000		

The appropriate year-end adjusting entry at the government-wide level depends upon the way inventories are recorded during the year. If purchases during the year are debited to Inventory of Supplies, then the adjusting entry will require a debit to expenses and credit to the inventory account. If, on the other hand, the city records expenses at the government-wide level during the year as purchases are made, the adjusting entry will require a debit to inventory and a credit to expenses for the $10,000 increase in inventory that occurred in 2011. Assuming purchases are recorded initially as expenses, the entries that would be required for governmental activities at the government-wide level are illustrated as follows. To record purchases during the year:

	General Ledger Debits	General Ledger Credits	Subsidiary Ledger Debits	Subsidiary Ledger Credits
Governmental Activities:				
Expenses (function or program detail omitted)	260,000			
Cash		260,000		

The required governmental activities adjusting entry is:

	General Ledger Debits	General Ledger Credits	Subsidiary Ledger Debits	Subsidiary Ledger Credits
Governmental Activities:				
Inventory of Supplies	10,000			
Expenses (function or program detail omitted)		10,000		

(Note: Reservation of fund balance for inventory and other reasons applies only to governmental funds that are subject to legal budgetary control. Thus, this entry is not made at the government-wide level.)

In all of these examples, the entries in the General Fund are somewhat more complex because of the need to adjust the Reserve for Inventory of Supplies account at the fund level. One can expect that the *GASBS 34* requirement to report inventories using the consumption method at the government-wide level may lead to increased use of this method for the General Fund as well.

Pre-Closing Trial Balance

Assume that all illustrated journal entries for the transactions and events pertaining to the Town of Brighton's 2011 fiscal year have been posted to the general and subsidiary ledgers. In addition, a number of other transactions and events were journalized and posted during the year but were not shown in this chapter because they were similar to those that were illustrated. As a result of all transactions and events recorded for the year (both those that were illustrated and those that were not), the balances of all balance sheet, operating statement, and budgetary accounts before closing entries are presented in the following trial balance.

TOWN OF BRIGHTON
General Fund
Pre-Closing Trial Balance
as of December 31, 2011

	Debits	*Credits*
Cash	$ 145,800	
Taxes Receivable—Delinquent	701,813	
Estimated Uncollectible Delinquent Taxes		$ 123,513
Interest and Penalties Receivable on Taxes	13,191	
Estimated Uncollectible Interest and Taxes		3,091
Due from Other Funds	25,000	
Estimated Revenues	4,001,000	
Revenues		4,015,000
Vouchers Payable		405,800
Due to Federal Government		126,520
Due to State Government		39,740
Due to Other Funds		30,000
Appropriations		4,210,000
Estimated Other Financing Uses		91,500
Expenditures—2010	127,000	
Expenditures—2011	4,130,760	
Other Financing Uses—Interfund Transfers Out	91,500	
Encumbrances—2011	70,240	
Reserve for Encumbrances—2011		70,240
Budgetary Fund Balance	300,500	
Fund Balance		491,400
	$9,606,804	$9,606,804

Closing Entries

At fiscal year-end, all temporary accounts, both budgetary and operating, must be closed to the appropriate fund balance account. Budgetary accounts are closed by simply reversing the original budgetary entry (or entries) made at the beginning of the fiscal year, as well as any amended budget entries made during the year. Although many governments follow a more complex process for closing the Encumbrances account, we simply close any remaining balance in the Encumbrances account to the general ledger Fund Balance account.[6] In effect, this closes the Encumbrances account while leaving a balance in the Reserve for Encumbrances balance sheet account equal to the amount of undelivered goods and services. Legislators, managers, and other financial statement users understand that the amount reported as fund balance reserved for goods and services to be delivered in the following year is already committed and therefore not available for budgetary appropriation.

Closing the operating accounts increases the balance of the general ledger Fund Balance account by the excess of revenues and other financial resources over expenditures and other financing uses. If there is an operating deficit (revenues and other financing sources are less than expenditures and other financing uses), then fund balance is decreased. Entries 25a, b, and c illustrate the entries needed to close the budgetary and operating accounts, using account balances shown in the Pre-Closing Trial Balance.

Entries 25a, b, and c illustrate closing entries for the operating and budgetary *control* accounts of the General Fund but not for the detailed subsidiary ledger accounts. In a manual accounting system, such as that illustrated in this chapter, closing the

		General Ledger		Subsidiary Ledger	
		Debits	***Credits***	***Debits***	***Credits***
	General Fund:				
25a.	Appropriations	4,210,000			
	Estimated Other Financing Uses	91,500			
	Estimated Revenues		4,001,000		
	Budgetary Fund Balance		300,500		
25b.	Revenues	4,015,000			
	Fund Balance	334,260			
	Expenditures—2011		4,130,760		
	Expenditures—2010		127,000		
	Other Financing Uses—Interfund Transfers Out		91,500		
25c.	Fund Balance	70,240			
	Encumbrances		70,240		

[6] In practice, governments often use a formal account title such as Budgetary Fund Balance Reserved for Encumbrances for the credit portion of encumbrance entries recorded during the year. At year-end, the amount of outstanding encumbrances is closed by debiting Budgetary Fund Balance Reserved for Encumbrances and crediting Encumbrances. This approach requires an additional entry to record a reservation of the general ledger Fund Balance for the amount of outstanding encumbrances, assuming that outstanding purchase orders and contracts are to be honored in the following year and will not require a new appropriation. For the additional entry, Unreserved Fund Balance is debited and Fund Balance Reserved for Encumbrances, or a similarly titled account, is credited for the amount of encumbrances outstanding. For simplicity, we use the shortened account title *Reserve for Encumbrances* (see Entries 3 and 4), which is understood to represent a reservation of the general ledger Fund Balance. This approach also simplifies the closing entries since closing the Encumbrances account to Fund Balance as shown in Entry 25c leaves a balance equal to encumbrances outstanding in the Reserve for Encumbrances account.

subsidiary ledger accounts is generally unnecessary because new subsidiary ledger accounts are prepared for each fiscal year. In a computerized accounting system, closing entries may be required for detail operating and budgetary accounts, depending on the account structure employed.

Year-end Financial Statements

As discussed in earlier chapters, the General Fund of every government is considered a *major fund*. Accordingly, all governmental fund financial statements will include a separate column for the General Fund financial information, as well as for all other major governmental funds, as shown in Illustrations A1–3 and A1–5 for the City and County of Denver and Illustrations 9–6 and 9–7 for the hypothetical Town of Brighton. For internal management purposes, a government may find it useful to prepare additional financial statements for the General Fund that are more detailed than the governmental fund statements. Such financial statements prepared for the Town of Brighton's General Fund are shown in Illustrations 4–5 and 4–6.

The Town of Brighton's General Fund balance sheet includes two major sections, *Assets* and *Liabilities and Fund Balances*. Total assets should always equal total liabilities and fund balances. Note that the $25,000 receivable from the Water Utility Fund (see Entry 24a) is offset against the $30,000 payable to that fund (see Entry 23a), so that only the $5,000 net amount payable to the Water Utility Fund is reported as *Due to other funds* in the Liabilities section of the balance sheet in Illustration 4–5. It is not acceptable, however, to offset receivables or payables from one fund against those of a different fund.

ILLUSTRATION 4–5

TOWN OF BRIGHTON
General Fund Balance Sheet
As of December 31, 2011

Assets		
Cash		$145,800
Taxes receivable—delinquent	$701,813	
Less: Estimated uncollectible delinquent taxes	123,513	578,300
Interest and penalties receivable on taxes	13,191	
Less: Estimated uncollectible interest and penalties	3,091	10,100
Total Assets		$734,200
Liabilities and Fund Balances		
Liabilities:		
Vouchers payable	$405,800	
Due to federal government	126,520	
Due to state government	39,740	
Due to other funds	5,000	
Total Liabilities		$577,060
Fund Balances:		
Reserved for encumbrances—2011	70,240	
Fund balance	86,900	
Total Fund Balances		157,140
Total Liabilities and Fund Balances		$734,200

ILLUSTRATION 4–6

TOWN OF BRIGHTON
General Fund
Statement of Revenues, Expenditures, and Changes in Fund Balance
For the Year Ended December 31, 2011

Revenues:		
Property taxes	$2,599,636	
Interest and penalties on delinquent taxes	11,400	
Sales taxes	485,000	
Licenses and permits	213,200	
Fines and forfeits	310,800	
Intergovernmental revenue	284,100	
Charges for services	82,464	
Miscellaneous revenues	28,400	
Total Revenues		$4,015,000
Expenditures:		
2011:		
General government	649,400	
Public safety	1,305,435	
Public works	1,018,900	
Health and welfare	850,325	
Parks and recreation	292,500	
Miscellaneous appropriations	14,200	
Expenditures—2011	4,130,760	
2010:		
Parks and recreation	127,000	
Total Expenditures		4,257,760
Excess of Expenditures over Revenues		(242,760)
Other Financing Sources (Uses):		
Interfund transfers in	–0–	
Interfund transfers out	(91,500)	
Total Other Financing Sources		(91,500)
Change (Decrease) in Fund Balances		(334,260)
Fund Balances, January 1, 2011		491,400
Fund Balances, December 31, 2011		$ 157,140

A second financial statement should be presented for the General Fund, a statement of revenues, expenditures, and changes in fund balance (see Illustration 4–6). Illustration 4–6 presents the actual revenues and actual expenditures that resulted from transactions illustrated in this chapter and other transactions not illustrated because they were similar in nature. Note that the General Fund of the Town of Brighton reports the financial outflow resulting from the interfund transfer out as an Other Financing Use.

The Other Financing Sources (Uses) section in Illustration 4–6 shows a common means of disclosure of nonrevenue financial inflows and nonexpenditure financial outflows. Information shown as Illustration 4–6 would be presented in the General Fund column of the Statement of Revenues, Expenditures, and Changes in Fund Balances—Governmental Funds (see Illustration A1–5).

ILLUSTRATION 4–7

TOWN OF BRIGHTON
General Fund
Schedule of Revenues, Expenditures, and Changes in Fund Balance—Budget and Actual
(Non-GAAP Presentation)
For the Year Ended December 31, 2011

	Budgeted Amounts			
	Original	**Final**	**Actual Amounts Budgetary Basis**	**Variance with Final Budget Over (Under)**
Revenues:				
Taxes:				
Property taxes	$2,600,000	$2,600,000	$2,599,636	$ (364)
Interest and penalties on taxes	13,000	13,000	11,400	(1,600)
Sales taxes	480,000	480,000	485,000	5,000
Total taxes	3,093,000	3,093,000	3,096,036	3,036
Licenses and permits	220,000	220,000	213,200	(6,800)
Fines and forfeits	308,000	308,000	310,800	2,800
Intergovernmental revenue	280,000	280,000	284,100	4,100
Charges for services	70,000	75,000	82,464	7,464
Miscellaneous revenues	15,000	25,000	28,400	3,400
Total Revenues	3,986,000	4,001,000	4,015,000	14,000
Expenditures and Encumbrances:				
General government	660,000	660,000	658,850	(1,150)
Public safety	1,240,000	1,320,000	1,318,500	(1,500)
Public works	1,090,000	1,040,000	1,038,300	(1,700)
Health and welfare	860,000	860,000	858,650	(1,350)
Parks and recreation	315,000	315,000	312,500	(2,500)
Miscellaneous appropriations	15,000	15,000	14,200	(800)
Total Expenditures	4,180,000	4,210,000	4,201,000	(9,000)
Excess of Expenditures over Revenues	(194,000)	(209,000)	(186,000)	23,000
Other Financing Sources (Uses)	(91,500)	(91,500)	(91,500)	–0–
Decrease in Reserve for Encumbrances	—	—	(56,760)	(56,760)
Decrease in Fund Balance for year	(285,500)	(300,500)	(334,260)	(33,760)
Fund Balances, January 1, 2011	491,400	491,400	491,400	–0–
Fund Balances, December 31, 2011	$ 205,900	$ 190,900	$ 157,140	$(33,760)

GASBS 34 requires a budgetary comparison schedule, as shown previously in Illustration 3–5, or, alternatively, a statement of revenues, expenditures, and changes in fund balance—budget and actual for the General Fund, as well as for each *major* special revenue fund for which a budget is legally adopted. Illustration 4–7 presents a budgetary comparison schedule for the Town of Brighton General Fund. Note that columns must be provided for both the legally adopted budget amounts and the final amended amounts.

The amounts in the Revenues section of the Actual column in Illustration 4–7 present the same information as shown in the Revenues section of Illustration 4–6 because in the Town of Brighton example, the General Fund revenues budget is on a

GAAP basis, the same as actual revenues. However, the amounts in the Expenditures section of the Actual column of the budgetary comparison schedule (Illustration 4–7) differ from the expenditures shown in Illustration 4–6 because, under GAAP, expenditures chargeable to 2010 appropriations of $127,000 and expenditures of the 2011 appropriations of $4,130,760 are reported in Illustration 4–6. Also, in the GAAP operating statement, Illustration 4–6, encumbrances are not reported in the Expenditures section of the statement. In contrast, GASB standards require the amounts in the Actual column of Illustration 4–7 to conform with budgetary practices; therefore, in that statement, encumbrances outstanding at the end of fiscal 2011 are added to 2011 expenditures because both are uses of the 2011 appropriation authority.

Note that expenditures for 2010 are excluded from the budget and actual schedule because that schedule relates only to the 2011 budget. GASB standards require differences between the amounts reported in the two statements (Illustrations 4–6 and 4–7) to be reconciled in a separate schedule or in the notes to the required supplementary information. For example, the notes to the budgetary comparison schedule for the Town of Brighton might include the following reconciliation of General Fund Expenditures reported in the two operating statements illustrated:

Expenditures for 2011, budgetary basis	$4,201,000
Less: Reserve for encumbrances as of December 31, 2011	(70,240)
Expenditures for 2011, GAAP basis	$4,130,760

The presentation of Reserve for Encumbrances in Illustrations 4–5, 4–6, and 4–7 and in the illustrative reconciliation is based on the assumption that amounts encumbered at year-end do not need to be appropriated for the following year. The amounts shown in Illustration 4–7 in the Expenditures section in the Variance with Final Budget column, however, disclose the portion of each appropriation for 2011 that was neither expended nor encumbered during that year; those amounts, totaling $9,000, are said to *lapse,* that is, become unavailable for expenditure or encumbrance, in the year following 2011.

SPECIAL REVENUE FUNDS

As noted in Chapters 2 and 3, special revenue funds are needed when legal or policy considerations require separate funds to be created for current operating purposes other than those served by proprietary or fiduciary funds. An example of a special revenue fund created to demonstrate legal compliance is a Street Fund, which is largely financed by a local government's share of the motor fuel tax levied by the state to be used only for maintenance and construction of streets, roads, and bridges. A second example of a special revenue fund is a Library Operating Fund created to account for a special tax levy or a decision of the governing board to create a separate fund to account for an activity that differs from other governmental activities. A third example is a fund to account for grants received from a higher jurisdiction, such as a federal Community Development Block Grant. Grant accounting is discussed briefly in the following paragraph. A final example is a trust fund in which both the investment principal and the investment earnings are available to support a government program or the citizenry. A common example of the latter is a gift received under a trust agreement that can be used only to purchase works of art for public buildings.

Accounting for Operating Grants

Grants received by a local government from the state or federal government—or received by a state from the federal government—are often restricted for specified operating purposes. Consequently, a special revenue fund is frequently used to account for the revenues of such grants. A number of grants provide that the grantor will pay the grantee on a reimbursement basis. In such instances, GASB standards require that the grant revenue not be recognized until the expenditure has taken place.[7] As an example of appropriate accounting procedures, assume that a local government has been awarded a state grant to finance a fine arts program, but the state will provide reimbursement only after the grantee has made expenditures related to the fine arts program. This is an example of a **voluntary nonexchange transaction** in which an **eligibility requirement** (incurrence of allowable costs) must be met before the local government can recognize an asset and revenue. Assuming that the grantee government creates a special revenue fund to account for the fine arts program and has incurred qualifying expenditures, or expense at the government-wide level, the required entries in both the special revenue fund and the governmental activities journals would be:

		Debits	Credits
Special Revenue Fund and Governmental Activities:			
Expenditures (or Expense)		50,000	
Vouchers Payable (or Cash)			50,000
Cash		50,000	
Revenues			50,000

The latter entry, of course, records the reimbursement, which presumably would be a short time after the expenditures were incurred. If the grant provided instead that a specified amount would be available for the current accounting period, regardless of whether qualifying expenditures were incurred, there would be no eligibility requirement (except that the grantee be an authorized recipient). In this case, it would be appropriate for the special revenue fund to recognize an asset (Due from Federal [or State] Government) and Revenues upon notification by the state grantor agency. If the grant imposes a **time requirement,** such as specifying that the amount is intended for a future accounting period, a liability account, Deferred Revenues, would be credited upon notification of the grant rather than Revenues. In the period for which the grant is intended, an entry would be made in the special revenue fund and governmental activities journals to debit Deferred Revenues and credit Revenues.

Financial Reporting

Special revenue fund accounting and financial reporting are essentially the same as for the General Fund, as described earlier in this chapter. In addition to amounts for the General Fund, amounts for *major* special revenue funds would be included in the balance sheet and statement of revenues, expenditures, and changes in fund balances prepared for the governmental funds. A budgetary comparison schedule is

[7] GASB *Codification,* Sec. N50.112. See the appendix to this chapter for a more detailed discussion of revenue and expense/expenditure recognition for both exchange and nonexchange transactions.

also provided as required supplementary information for each major special revenue fund for which a budget is legally adopted. Elsewhere in the financial section of the government's comprehensive annual financial report (CAFR), a combining balance sheet and combining operating statement should be provided for all *nonmajor* governmental funds, including nonmajor special revenue funds. An example of a combining statement of revenues, expenditures, and changes in fund balances for nonmajor governmental funds is presented in Illustration 4–8 for the City of Sioux City, Iowa.

INTERFUND ACTIVITY

Reciprocal Interfund Activity

Internal exchange transactions—those involving the sales and purchases of goods and services in a reciprocal exchange transaction between two funds—were discussed earlier in this chapter. These transactions are termed *interfund services provided and used* in *GASBS 34.* Other interfund transactions are discussed in this section.

Interfund Loans

Interfund loans are sometimes made from one fund to another with the intent that the amount be repaid. If the loan must be repaid during the current year or soon thereafter, the lending fund should record a current receivable, and the borrowing fund should record a current liability. This is illustrated by the following journal entries, assuming that the General Fund makes a short-term loan in the amount of $100,000 to the Central Stores Fund, an internal service fund.

	General Ledger		Subsidiary Ledger	
	Debits	***Credits***	***Debits***	***Credits***
General Fund:				
Interfund Loans Receivable—Current	100,000			
Cash		100,000		
Internal Service Fund:				
Cash	100,000			
Interfund Loans Payable—Current		100,000		

If this interfund loan did not require repayment for more than one year, the word "Noncurrent" would be used rather than "Current" to signify the noncurrent nature of the loan.[8] As shown in the following entries, Noncurrent is added to each of the interfund loan receivable/payable accounts to indicate that the loan is not payable during the current year or soon thereafter.

[8] Governments also use the accounts "Due to (from) Other Funds" and "Advances from (to) Other Funds" to record current and noncurrent interfund loans, respectively. The authors prefer to reserve the use of "Due to (from) Other Funds" for operating transactions only; that is, interfund transfers and internal exchange transactions. Although used for decades, the term "Advances" is somewhat vague.

ILLUSTRATION 4–8

CITY OF SIOUX CITY, IOWA
Combining Statement of Revenues, Expenditures and Changes in Fund Balances
Governmental Nonmajor Funds
for the Year Ended June 30, 2007

	Special Revenue Funds									Permanent Fund	
Revenues	**Emergency Fund**	**Storm Water Drainage**	**Road Use**	**Community Development**	**Housing**	**Main Street**	**Younkers Self-Impr. District**	**Convention Center/ Auditorium**	**Transit Operations**	**Cemetery Trust**	**Total Governmental Nonmajor Funds**
Taxes	$ 528,056	$ —	$ —	$ —	$ —	$187,702	$ —	$ —	$ —	$ —	$ 715,758
Special assessments	—	14,203	—	—	—	—	—	—	—	—	14,203
Intergovernmental revenue	—	—	7,222,597	3,574,335	4,757,152	—	—	—	1,695,763	—	17,249,847
Revenue from use of property	—	—	—	—	—	—	—	3,011,096	50,974	72,397	3,134,467
Charges for services	—	1,270,128	4,884	—	—	—	—	1,115,766	839,618	—	3,230,396
Interest	—	9,326	—	212,376	—	—	—	24,372	—	—	246,074
Miscellaneous	—	—	48,480	61,757	64,993	—	—	372,657	29,427	17,408	594,722
Total Revenue	528,056	1,293,657	7,275,961	3,848,468	4,822,145	187,702	—	4,523,891	2,615,782	89,805	25,185,487
Expenditures											
Current											
Public works	—	91,890	7,741,877	—	—	—	—	—	3,388,565	—	11,222,332
Culture and recreation	—	—	—	—	—	—	—	7,039,061	—	—	7,039,061
Community and economic development	—	—	—	3,325,241	5,028,874	285,000	—	—	—	—	8,639,115
General government	—	1,163	—	—	—	—	—	—	—	—	1,163
Total Expenditures	—	93,053	7,741,877	3,325,241	5,028,874	285,000	—	7,039,061	3,388,565	—	26,901,671
Excess (Deficiency) of Revenues Over Expenditures	528,058	1,200,604	(465,916)	523,227	(206,729)	(97,298)	—	(2,515,170)	(772,783)	89,805	(1,716,204)
Other Financing Sources (Uses)											
Transfers in	1,500,000	—	158,899	—	—	96,633	—	2,222,092	1,302,285	—	5,279,909
Transfers out	(527,691)	(926,571)	(27,852)	(36,960)	—	—	—	—	(450,545)	—	(1,969,619)
Total Other Financing Sources (Uses)	972,309	(926,571)	131,047	(36,960)	—	96,633	—	2,222,092	851,740	—	3,310,290
Net Change in Fund Balance	1,500,365	274,033	(334,869)	486,267	(206,729)	(665)	—	(293,078)	78,957	89,805	1,594,086
Fund Balance (Deficit)—Beginning of Year	2,703,978	1,067,446	1,328,922	6,784,957	1,427,155	99,343	(1,587)	(1,132,753)	185,852	838,105	13,301,418
Fund Balance (Deficit)—End of Year	$4,204,343	$1,341,479	$ 994,053	$7,271,224	$1,220,426	$ 98,678	$(1,587)	$(1,425,831)	$ 264,809	$927,910	$14,895,504

	General Ledger		Subsidiary Ledger	
	Debits	***Credits***	***Debits***	***Credits***
General Fund:				
Interfund Loans Receivable—Noncurrent	100,000			
Cash		100,000		
Internal Service Fund:				
Cash	100,000			
Interfund Loans Payable—Noncurrent		100,000		

Because the noncurrent interfund loan receivable represents assets that are not available for the current year's appropriation in the General Fund, the Fund Balance account should be reserved for this amount, as was done for encumbered amounts and ending inventories of supplies.

General Fund:				
Fund Balance	100,000			
Reserve for Noncurrent Interfund Loans Receivable		100,000		

An interesting question is whether the illustrated interfund loans require journal entries at the government-wide level. The answer is no since *GASBS 34* requires that most internal service fund amounts be reported in the Governmental Activities column of the government-wide financial statements. Interfund receivables and payables between two funds that are both included in governmental activities have no effect on the amounts reported in the government-wide statement of net assets.

Nonreciprocal Interfund Activity

Interfund Transfers

The former reporting model identified two types of interfund transfers: *operating transfers* and *residual equity transfers,* which were reported in two different ways in governmental fund operating statements. Under *GASBS 34,* both types of transfers are described simply as **interfund transfers** and reported in the same manner—as other financing sources by the receiving fund and as other financing uses by the transferring fund. Some interfund transfers are periodic, routine transfers. For example, state laws may require that taxes be levied by a General Fund or a special revenue fund to finance an expenditure to be made from another fund (such as a debt service fund). Since the general rule is that revenues should be recorded as such only once, the transferor records the transfer of tax revenue to the expending fund as an Other Financing Use—Interfund Transfer Out, and the transferee records it as an Other Financing Source—Interfund Transfer In.

Other interfund transfers, those formerly called *residual equity transfers,* are nonroutine transactions often made to establish or liquidate a fund, such as the Town of Brighton example (Entries 2 and 2a earlier in this chapter) in which the General Fund transferred cash and inventory to create a supplies internal service fund. The creation of a fund by transfer of assets and/or resources from an existing fund to a new fund, or transfers of residual balances of discontinued funds to another fund, results in the recognition of an other financing source rather than a revenue by the new fund and an other financing use rather than an expenditure by the transferor fund.

Reimbursements

Internal exchange transactions for interfund services provided and used, described earlier in this chapter, represent the only form of interfund transactions that result in the recognition of revenue by the receiving fund. In certain instances, one fund may record as an expenditure an item that should have been recorded as an expenditure by another fund. Often this is the result of an accounting error. When the second fund reimburses the first fund, the first fund should recognize the reimbursement as a reduction of its Expenditures account, not as an item of revenue. The second fund should debit Expenditures and credit Cash, as should have been done when the transaction initially occurred. Reimbursements are not reported in the financial statements except for reporting expenditures/expenses in the correct fund.

Intra- versus Inter-Activity Transactions (Government-wide Level)

In all the preceding examples, if the interfund transaction occurs between two governmental funds (or between a governmental fund and an internal service fund) or between two enterprise funds, that is, an **intra-activity transaction,** then neither the Governmental Activities column nor the Business-type Activities column is affected at the government-wide level. Interfund loans or transfers between a governmental fund (or internal service fund) and an enterprise fund results in an **inter-activity transaction.** These transactions are reported as "Internal Balances" on the government-wide statement of net assets (see Illustration A1–1) and "Transfers" in the statement of activities (see Illustration A1–2). Except for internal exchange transactions between governmental funds and internal service funds, for which any element of profit or loss is eliminated prior to preparing the government-wide financial statements, other internal exchange transactions should be reported as revenues and expenses in the statement of activity.

Intra-Entity Transactions

Intra-entity transactions are exchange or nonexchange transactions between the primary government and its blended or discretely presented component units. Transactions between the primary government and *blended* component units follow the same standards as for reciprocal and nonreciprocal interfund activity discussed in preceding paragraphs. Transactions between the primary government and *discretely presented* component units are treated as if the component units are external entities, and thus should be reported as revenues and expenses in the statement of activities. Amounts receivable and payable resulting from these transactions should be reported on a separate line in the statement of net assets.

PERMANENT FUNDS

Governments often receive contributions under trust agreements in which the principal amount is not expendable but earnings are expendable. Most of these trusts are established to benefit a government program or function, or the citizenry, rather than an external individual, organization, or government. Trusts of the first type are called **public-purpose trusts;** trusts of the second type are called **private-purpose trusts.**

The *GASBS 34* model requires that public-purpose trusts for which the earnings are expendable for a specified purpose but the principal amount is not expendable (also referred to as *endowments*) be accounted for in a governmental fund called a **permanent fund.** Public-purpose trusts for which both principal and earnings thereon can be expended for a specified purpose are accounted for in a special revenue fund, again a governmental fund type. Accounting issues involving private-purpose trusts are discussed in Chapter 8.

Budgetary Accounts

Budgetary accounts generally should not be needed for permanent funds because transactions of the fund result in changes in the fund principal only incidentally; by definition, the principal cannot be appropriated or expended. However, public-purpose expendable trust funds may be required by law to use the appropriation procedure to ensure adequate budgetary control over the expenditure of fund assets since they are accounted for in special revenue funds. If the appropriation procedure is required, the use of the other budgetary accounts discussed earlier in this chapter is also recommended. The following paragraphs illustrate a public-purpose nonexpendable trust that is accounted for as a permanent fund.

Illustrative Case

As an illustration of the nature of accounting for permanent fund trust principal and expendable trust revenue, assume on November 1, 2010, Wilma Wexner died, having made a valid will that provided for the gift of marketable securities to the City of Concordia to be held as a nonexpendable trust. For purposes of income distribution, the net income from the securities is to be computed on the accrual basis but does not include increases or decreases in the fair value of investments. Income, so measured, is to be transferred to the City's Library Operating Fund, a special revenue fund. Accounting for the Library Operating Fund is not illustrated here because it would be very similar to General Fund accounting already covered in depth in this chapter. For the sake of brevity, corresponding entries in the general journal for governmental activities at the government-wide level are also omitted.

The gift was accepted by the City of Concordia, which established the Library Endowment Fund (a permanent fund) to account for operation of the trust. The following securities were received by the Library Endowment Fund:

	Interest Rate per Year	Maturity Date	Face Value	Fair Value as of 11/1/10
Bonds of AB Company	6%	1/1/15	$640,000	$652,000

	Number of Shares	Fair Value as of 11/1/10
Stocks:		
M Company, common	5,400	$282,000
S Company, common	22,000	214,000
Total		$496,000

Journal Entries—Permanent Fund

The Library Endowment Fund's receipt of the securities is properly recorded at the fair value of the securities as of the date of the gift because this is the amount for which the trustees are responsible. Although the face value of the bonds will be received at maturity (if the bonds are held until maturity), GASB standards require that investments in bonds maturing more than one year from receipt be reported at fair value.[9] Thus the entry in the Library Endowment Fund to record the receipt of the securities at initiation of the trust on November 1, 2010, is:

		Debits	***Credits***
	Permanent Fund:		
1.	Investment in Bonds	652,000	
	Investment in Stocks	496,000	
	Accrued Interest Receivable	12,800	
	Revenues—Contributions for Endowment		1,160,800
	[Interest accrued on the bonds of Company AB ($640,000 × 6% × 4/12 = $12,800), assuming semiannual interest was last received on July 1, 2010]		

As of January 1, 2011, semiannual interest of $19,200 is received on the AB Company bonds, of which only one-third of the total corresponding to the two months of interest earned since the endowment was created can be transferred to the Library Operating Fund. The entry for the receipt of bond interest on January 1, 2011, and the revenue earned for transfer to the Library Operating Fund is:

		Debits	Credits
	Permanent Fund:		
2.	Cash	19,200	
	Accrued Interest Receivable		12,800
	Revenues—Bond Interest		6,400

Dividends on stock do not accrue. They become a receivable only when declared by the corporation issuing the stock. Ordinarily the receivable is not recorded because it is followed in a reasonably short time by issuance of a dividend check. Assuming dividends on the stock held by the Library Endowment Fund were received early in January 2011 in the amount of $9,800, Entry 3 is appropriate:

		Debits	Credits
	Permanent Fund:		
3.	Cash	9,800	
	Revenues—Dividends		9,800

[9] GASB *Codification,* Sec. I50.105.

As the bond interest and dividends on stock were received in cash, the Library Endowment Fund has sufficient cash to pay the amount to be transferred to the Library Operating Fund for interest and dividends earned since the endowment was created. Assuming that cash is transferred as of January 3, 2011, Entry 4 is:

		Debits	**Credits**
	Permanent Fund:		
4.	Other Financing Uses—Interfund Transfers Out	16,200	
	Cash		16,200

On the advice of an investment manager, 1,800 shares of M Company stock were sold for $99,000; this amount and cash of $7,000 were invested in 4,000 shares of LH Company common stock. The M Company stock sold was one-third of the number of shares received when the trust was established; therefore, the shares sold had a carrying value of one-third of $282,000, or $94,000. The difference between the stock's carrying value and the proceeds at the time of sale is considered in this trust to belong to the corpus and does not give rise to a gain or loss that adjusts the net income to be transferred to the Library Operating Fund. Therefore, the sale of M Company stock and the purchase of LH Company stock should be recorded in the Library Endowment Fund as shown in Entries 5a and b:

		Debits	Credits
	Permanent Fund:		
5a.	Cash	99,000	
	Investment in Stocks		94,000
	Revenues—Change in Fair Value of Investments		5,000
5b.	Investment in Stocks	106,000	
	Cash		106,000

Assuming there were no further purchases or sales of stock and that dividends received on April 1, 2011, amounted to $10,800, Entry 6a is necessary, as well as Entry 6b, to make the required interfund transfer to the Library Operating Fund.

		Debits	Credits
	Permanent Fund:		
6a.	Cash	10,800	
	Revenues—Dividends		10,800
6b.	Other Financing Uses—Interfund Transfers Out	10,800	
	Cash		10,800

Interest accrued on June 30, 2011, amounted to $19,200, the same amount received early in January 2011. The fair value of the Library Endowment Fund investments as of June 30, 2011, the last day of the City of Concordia's fiscal year, is given below.

		Fair Value as of 11/1/10	Fair Value as of 6/30/11	Change in Fair Value
Bonds of AB Company		$652,000	$674,000	$22,000
Stocks	**No. of Shares**			
M Company	3,600	$188,000	$194,400	$ 6,400
S Company	22,000	214,000	220,600	6,600
LH Company	4,000	106,000*	104,500	(1,500)
Total		$508,000	$519,500	$11,500

*As of date of transaction 5 for LH Company.

Entry 7a records the accrual of interest earned for transfer to the Library Operating Fund. Entry 7b records the adjusting entry to record the change in fair value of investments at the end of the fiscal year, compared with the prior fair value recorded for the investments. Entry 7c records the liability to the Library Operating Fund.

		Debits	Credits
	Permanent Fund:		
7a.	Accrued Interest Receivable	19,200	
	Revenues—Bond Interest		19,200
7b.	Investment in Bonds	22,000	
	Investment in Stocks	11,500	
	Revenues—Change in Fair Value of Investments		33,500
7c.	Other Financing Uses—Interfund Transfers Out	19,200	
	Due to Library Operating Fund		19,200

The closing entry at the end of the fiscal year, June 30, 2011, is shown in Entry 8.

		Debits	Credits
	Permanent Fund:		
8.	Revenues—Contributions for Endowment	1,160,800	
	Revenues—Bond Interest	25,600	
	Revenues—Dividends	20,600	
	Revenues—Change in Fair Value of Investments	38,500	
	Other Financing Uses—Interfund Transfers Out		46,200
	Fund Balance—Reserved for Endowment		1,199,300

In Entry 8, one can see that $46,200, the total interest earned on bonds and dividends received on investments in stocks, was transferred during the year to the Library Operating Fund; the net change (increase) in fair value of investments, $38,500, and the original contribution are added to the Fund Balance. If the net increase in the value of investments were permitted under the trust agreement to be used for library operating purposes, the entire $84,700 (sum of earnings and increase in fair value) would have been transferred out, and the addition to Fund Balance would have been just the $1,168,300 original contribution.

At year-end, financial statements for the Library Endowment Fund would be presented in essentially the same formats as the General Fund balance sheet and General Fund statement of revenues, expenditures, and changes in fund balance shown in Illustrations 4–5 and 4–6. If the Library Endowment Fund meets the criteria for a major fund, its balance sheet and operating statement information will be included as a column in the balance sheet—governmental funds and statement of revenues, expenditures, and changes in fund balances—governmental funds, examples of which are presented in Illustrations A1–3 and A1–5 in Chapter 1. If the fund is determined to be a nonmajor fund, it would be reported in the combining balance sheet and operating statement presented in the CAFR for the nonmajor governmental funds (see Illustration 4–8 for an example of the latter type of financial statement).

As indicated previously, entries in the Library Operating Fund are omitted for the sake of brevity since accounting for special revenue funds is similar to that for the General Fund. Thus, at the beginning of the 2011 fiscal year (July 1, 2010) a budgetary entry would have been recorded; that entry would have been amended on November 1, 2010, the date the Library Endowment Fund was created, to reflect the Estimated Other Financing Sources (interfund transfers in) expected from the endowment and to authorize expenditures of all or a portion of those resources in the Library Operating Fund. Each time Other Financing Uses—Interfund Transfers Out are recorded in the Library Endowment Fund, Other Financing Sources—Interfund Transfers In would be recorded in the same amount in the Library Operating Fund.

Chapters 3 and 4 have focused on operating activities that are recorded in the General Fund, special revenue funds, permanent funds, and in governmental activities at the government-wide level. Chapter 5 discusses accounting for general capital assets and capital projects funds, while general long-term debt and debt service funds are discussed in Chapter 6.

Appendix

Concepts and Rules for Recognition of Revenues and Expenses (or Expenditures)

EXCHANGE TRANSACTIONS

Current GASB standards provide guidance for the accounting recognition of revenues and expenses on the accrual basis in the government-wide financial statements and revenues and expenditures on the modified accrual basis in the governmental fund financial statements.[10] Recognition rules for *exchange transactions* and *exchange-like transactions,* those in which each party receives value essentially equal to the value given, are generally straightforward; for operating transactions, the party selling goods or services recognizes an asset (for example, a receivable or cash) and a revenue when the transaction occurs and the revenue has been earned. The party purchasing goods or services recognizes an expense or expenditure and liability (or reduction in cash). As discussed in Chapter 2, under the *modified accrual* basis of accounting, if a governmental fund provides goods or services to another party or fund, it should recognize an asset (receivable or cash) and

[10] GASB *Codification* Secs. 1600 and N50.

a revenue if the assets (financial resources) are deemed *measurable* and *available.* If a governmental fund *receives* goods or services from another party or fund, it should recognize expenditures (not expense) when the fund liability has been incurred. In most cases, exchange transactions of governmental funds result in measurable and available assets being received or a fund liability being incurred when the transaction occurs, and thus result in immediate recognition of revenues and expenditures. For example, the General Fund should recognize a revenue immediately when a citizen is charged a fee for a building permit and an expenditure when a purchase order for supplies has been filled.

NONEXCHANGE TRANSACTIONS

Nonexchange transactions are defined as external events in which a government gives or receives value without directly receiving or giving equal value in exchange.[11] Accounting for nonexchange transactions raises a number of conceptual issues. Two key concepts that affect a resource recipient's recognition of revenues (or a resource provider's recognition of expenses/expenditures) are *time requirements* and *purpose restrictions.*[12]

Time requirements relate either to the period when resources are required to be used or to when use *may* begin. Thus, time requirements determine the *timing* of revenue or expense (expenditure) recognition—that is, whether these elements should be recognized (recorded in the accounts) in the current period or deferred to a future period. **Purpose restrictions** refer to specifications by resource providers of the purpose or purposes for which resources are required to be used. For example, a grant may specify that resources can be used only to provide transportation for senior citizens. The *timing* of revenue recognition is unaffected by purpose restrictions. Rather, the purpose restrictions should be clearly reported as restrictions of net assets in the government-wide statement of net assets or as reservations of fund balance in the governmental funds balance sheet (see Illustrations A1–1 and A1–3 in Chapter 1 for examples).

For certain classes of nonexchange transactions, discussed later in this section, revenue and expense recognition may be delayed until program *eligibility requirements* are met. Eligibility requirements may include, in addition to time requirements, specified characteristics that program recipients must possess or reimbursement provisions and contingencies tied to required actions by the recipient. GASB standards provide the example of state-provided reimbursements to school districts for special education. To meet the specified eligibility requirements, (1) the recipient must be a school district, (2) the applicable school year must have started, and (3) the district must have incurred allowable costs. Only when all three conditions are met can a school district record a revenue and the state record an expense. The school district records an asset and deferred revenue if the resources have been received in advance of meeting eligibility requirements. Otherwise, the school district does not record an asset nor does the state record a liability to provide the resources until all the eligibility requirements have been met.[13]

Nonexchange transactions are subdivided into four classes: (1) *derived tax revenues* (e.g., income and sales taxes), (2) *imposed nonexchange revenues* (e.g., property taxes and fines and penalties), (3) **government-mandated nonexchange transactions** (e.g., certain education, social welfare, and transportation services mandated and funded by a higher level of government), and (4) *voluntary nonexchange transactions* (e.g., grants and entitlements from higher levels of government and certain private donations).[14]

[11] GASB *Codification,* Sec. N50.104.
[12] Ibid., par. 109.
[13] Ibid., par. 902. Example 8.
[14] Ibid., par. 104.

RECOGNITION OF NONEXCHANGE TRANSACTIONS

Illustration A4–1 provides a summary of the recognition criteria applicable to each class of nonexchange transactions, both for the accrual basis of accounting and for modified accrual. Assets and revenues in the *derived tax revenues* category are generally recognized in the period in which the underlying exchange occurs; the period in which income is earned for income taxes and when sales have occurred for sales taxes.

For *imposed nonexchange revenues,* an asset (receivable or cash) is recognized when there is an enforceable legal claim or when cash is received, whichever is first. Revenues should be recognized in the period in which the resources are required to be used or the first period when their use is permitted. For property taxes, revenues usually are recognized in the period for which the taxes are levied. In governmental funds, the additional criterion of availability for use must be met. Current standards, as interpreted, define *available* in the context of property taxes as meaning "collected within the current period

ILLUSTRATION A4–1 Summary Chart—Classes and Timing of Recognition of Nonexchange Transactions

Class	*Recognition*
Derived tax revenues Examples: sales taxes, personal and corporate income taxes, motor fuel taxes, and similar taxes on earnings or consumption	**Assets*** Period when *underlying exchange has occurred* or when resources are received, whichever is first. **Revenues** Period when *underlying exchange has occurred*. (Report advance receipts as deferred revenues.) When modified accrual accounting is used, resources also should be "available."
Imposed nonexchange revenues Examples: property taxes, most fines and forfeitures	**Assets*** Period when an *enforceable legal claim has arisen* or when resources are received. whichever is first. **Revenues** Period when *resources are required to be used* or first period that use is permitted (for example, for property taxes, the *period for which levied*). When modified accrual accounting is used, resources *also* should be "available." (For property taxes, apply NCGA Interpretation 3, as amended.)
Government-mandated nonexchange transactions Examples: federal government mandates on state and local governments **Voluntary nonexchange transactions** Examples: certain grants and entitlements, most donations	**Assets* and Liabilities** Period when *all eligibility requirements have been met* or (for asset recognition) when resources are received, whichever is first. **Revenues and expenses or expenditures** Period when *all eligibility requirements have been met*. (Report advance receipts or payments for use in the following period as deferred revenues or advances, respectively. However, when a provider precludes the sale, disbursement, or consumption of resources for a specified number of years, until a specified event has occurred, or permanently [for example, permanent and term endowments], report revenues and expenses or expenditures when the resources are, respectively, received or paid and report resulting net assets, equity, or fund balance as restricted.) When modified accrual accounting is used for revenue recognition, resources *also* should be "available."

*If there are purpose restrictions, report restricted net assets (or equity or fund balance) or, for governmental funds, a reservation of fund balance.

Source: GASB *Statement No. 33* (Norwalk, CT, 1998), Appendix C.

or expected to be collected soon enough thereafter to be used to pay liabilities of the current period."[15] *Soon enough thereafter* means not later than 60 days after the end of the current period.[16]

A common set of recognition rules applies to the remaining two classes of nonexchange transactions: *government-mandated* and *voluntary nonexchange.* An asset (a receivable or cash) is recognized when all eligibility requirements have been met or when cash is received, whichever occurs first. For example, although cash has not been received from a grantor, when a program recipient meets matching requirements imposed by the grantor agency in order to become eligible for a social services grant, a receivable (Due from [Grantor]) would be recorded. Revenues should be recognized only when all eligibility criteria have been met. If cash is received in the period prior to intended use (that is, there is a time restriction) or before eligibility requirements have been met, deferred revenues should be reported rather than revenues. In the period when the time restriction expires, the account Deferred Revenues will be debited and Revenues will be credited.

It should be apparent that a particular nonexchange transaction may lead to recognition of revenues in one period in the government-wide statement of activities, but be reported as deferred revenues in a governmental fund because it is deemed not to be *available* to pay current period obligations.

Key Terms

Consumption method, *136*
Delinquent taxes, *124*
Derived tax revenues, *129*
Eligibility requirements, *144*
Exchange transaction, *122*
Exchange-like transaction, *122*
Government-mandated nonexchange transactions, *154*
Gross tax levy, *123*
Imposed nonexchange revenue, *124*
Inter-activity transactions, *148*
Interfund loans, *145*
Interfund transfers, *147*
Internal exchange transactions, *135*
Intra-activity transactions, *148*
Intra-entity transactions, *148*
Nonexchange revenue, *124*
Nonexchange transactions, *129*
Permanent fund, *149*
Private-purpose trusts, *148*
Public-purpose trusts, *148*
Purchases method, *135*
Purpose restrictions, *154*
Tax anticipation note, *128*
Tax rate, *123*
Time requirements, *144*
Voluntary nonexchange transactions, *144*

Selected References

American Institute of Certified Public Accountants. Audit and Accounting Guide. *State and Local Governments.* Revised. New York, 2008.

Governmental Accounting Standards Board. *Codification of Governmental Accounting and Financial Reporting Standards, as of June 30, 2008.* Norwalk, CT, 2008.

[15] GASB, *Codification,* Sec. P70.104.
[16] Ibid.

Questions

4–1. Explain why some transactions for governmental activities at the government-wide level are reported differently than transactions for the General Fund. Give some examples of transactions that would be recorded in the general journals of (*a*) only the General Fund, (*b*) only governmental activities at the government-wide level, and (*c*) both.

4–2. In what ways does the government-wide statement of net assets differ from the balance sheet for governmental funds?

4–3. How does the use of encumbrance procedures improve budgetary control over expenditures?

4–4. If the General Fund of a certain city needs $6,720,000 of revenue from property taxes to finance estimated expenditures of the next fiscal year and historical experience indicates that 4 percent of the gross levy will not be collected, what should be the amount of the gross levy for property taxes? Show all computations in good form.

4–5. "Actual revenues and expenditures reported on a budget and actual comparison schedule should be prepared on the same basis as budgeted revenues and expenditures, even if a cash basis is used." Do you agree with this statement? Why or why not?

4–6. Explain why expenses reported on the government-wide statement of activities for supplies used in conducting governmental activities may differ in amounts from expenditures for the same supplies reported on the statement of revenues, expenditures, and changes in fund balances for governmental funds.

4–7. Explain the primary differences between *ad valorem* taxes, such as property taxes, and other taxes that generate *derived tax revenues*, such as sales and income taxes. How does accounting differ between these classes of taxes?

4–8. If interim financial reporting to external parties is not required, why should a government bother to prepare interim financial statements and schedules? Give some examples of interim financial statements or schedules that a government should consider for internal management use.

4–9. How does a *permanent fund* differ from public-purpose trusts that are reported in special revenue funds? How does it differ from private-purpose trust funds?

4–10. Name the four classes of nonexchange transactions defined by GASB standards and explain the revenue and expenditure/expense recognition rules applicable to each class.

Cases

4–1 Analyzing Results of Operations. Using either a city's own Web site or the *GASBS 34* link of the GASB's Web site, download either the city's entire comprehensive annual financial report (CAFR) or, if possible, just the portion of the CAFR that contains the basic financial statements. Print a copy of the government-wide statement of activities and a copy of the statement of revenues, expenditures, and changes in fund balances—governmental funds, along with the reconciliation between these two statements, and respond to the requirements below.

The city manager is concerned that some recently elected members of the city council will get a mixed message since the change in net assets reported for governmental activities is noticeably different from the change in fund balances reported on the governmental funds statement of revenues, expenditures, and changes in fund balances. The city manager has requested that you, in your role as finance director, explain to the city council in clear, easy-to-understand terms for which purposes each operating statement is intended and how and why the operating results differ.

Required

a. Examine the two operating statements in detail, paying particular attention to the lines on which changes in net assets and changes in fund balances are reported and develop a list of reasons why the two numbers are not the same.

b. Prepare a succinct and understandable explanation of the results of operations of this government from the perspective of each operating statement, in terms that a non-accountant council member would be able to understand.

4–2 Policy Issues Relating to Property Taxes. Property owners in Trevor City were shocked when they recently received notice that assessed valuations on their homes had increased by an average 35 percent, based on a triennial reassessment by the County Board of Equalization. Like many homeowners in the city, you have often complained about the high property taxes in Trevor City, and now you are outraged that your taxes will apparently increase another 35 percent in the coming year.

After stewing all weekend about the unreasonable increase in assessed valuation, you decide to visit the county tax assessor on Monday to find out why your assessed valuation has increased so rapidly. When you finally reach the counter, the customer service representative explains that reassessment considers such factors as actual property sales in particular neighborhoods, trends in building costs, and home improvements. He also explains that heavy demand for both new and previously owned homes has skyrocketed in the Trevor City area in recent years. Moreover, you learn that the reassessment on your home is only average, with some being higher and some lower. Although this information calms you down somewhat, you ask: "But how can we possibly afford a 35 percent increase in our taxes next year?" The representative explains that actual tax rates are set by each jurisdiction having taxing authority over particular properties (in your case, these are the county government, Trevor City, the Trevor City Independent School District, the Trevor City Library, and the Trevor City Redevelopment Authority), so he cannot say how much property taxes will actually increase.

Required

a. When you have regained your composure, prepare a brief written analysis *objectively* evaluating the probability that your property taxes will actually increase by 35 percent next year. In doing so, consider factors that you feel may mitigate against such a large increase. What would have to happen to the tax rates for your taxes to remain at their current level or increase only slightly?

b. Put yourself in the position of the city manager of Trevor City. Does she view the rapid growth in property values as a windfall for the city? What are the potential economic and political risks involved with a hot real estate market such as Trevor City is experiencing?

4–3 Reporting Internal Service Fund Financial Information at the Government-wide Level. During the current fiscal year, the City of Manchester created a Printing and Sign Fund (an internal service fund) to provide custom printing and signage for city departments, predominantly those financed by the General Fund. As this is the city's first internal service fund, finance officials are uncertain how to account for the activities of the Printing and Sign Fund at the government-wide level. After much discussion, they have approached you, the audit manager, with the following questions:

1. In governmental activities at the government-wide level, should expenses for printing and signage within the various functions be the amount billed to departments or the Printing and Sign Fund's cost to provide the printing and signage service? Please explain.
2. What about the Printing and Sign Fund's operating revenues from billings to departments? Should these revenues be reported as program revenues, specifically, as charges for services of the functions receiving the services? Why or why not?
3. The Printing and Sign Fund obtains about 10 percent of its revenues from the City Electric, Sewage, and Water Fund, an enterprise fund. Should the financial information related to these transactions be reported in the Business-type Activities column of the government-wide financial statements, rather than the Governmental Activities column? Please explain in detail.

Required

a. Evaluate these questions and provide the city's finance director with a written response to each question.

b. How would your response to question 3 differ if the Printing and Sign Fund provided 60 percent of its total services to the enterprise fund?

4–4 Reporting Multipurpose Grant Transactions in the Funds and Government-wide Financial Statements of Local Government Recipients. In this case, local governments receive reimbursements from the state government's Department of Social Services Teen Assistance Program for expenditures incurred in conducting an array of locally administered programs that benefit troubled teens. The state program provides reimbursement up to a maximum amount based on grant applications submitted annually by each local government and provides notification of the amounts approved prior to the grant year. Each local government determines which kinds of teen programs and what mix of services are most appropriate for its community. Reimbursements are made only after services have been provided and documented claims for reimbursements have been submitted to the state. GASB standards relevant to this grant state:

> Multipurpose grants (those that provide financing from more than one program) should be reported as program revenue if the amounts restricted to each program are specifically identified in the grant award or grant agreement. Multipurpose grants that do not provide for specific identification of the programs and amounts should be reported as general revenues.

Required

a. In which fiscal year(s) should the grant be reported on the fund and government-wide financial statements of the local governments receiving the grant reimbursements? Please explain your answer.

b. How should the grant be reported on the fund and government-wide financial statements? Please explain your answer.

b. Equipment used by the General Fund is transferred to an internal service fund that predominantly serves departments that are engaged in governmental activities.
c. The City Airport Fund, an enterprise fund, transfers a portion of boarding fees charged to passengers to the General Fund.
d. An interfund transfer is made between the General Fund and the Debt Service Fund.

9. A special revenue fund that administers a program funded by a reimbursement-type (expenditure-driven) federal grant should recognize revenue:
a. When notified of grant approval.
b. When qualifying expenditures have been made.
c. When cash is received.
d. When the special revenue fund has paid for all of the services it has provided.

10. A city received a $1,000,000 cash contribution under a trust agreement in which investment earnings (but not the principal amount) can be used to maintain the city cemetery. This contribution should be recorded in a (an):
a. Fiduciary fund.
b. Permanent fund.
c. Special revenue fund.
d. Internal service fund.

4–3 Calculating Required Tax Anticipation Financing and Recording Issuance of Tax Anticipation Notes. The City of Perrin collects its annual property taxes late in its fiscal year. Consequently, each year it must finance part of its operating budget using tax anticipation notes. The notes are repaid upon collection of property taxes. On April 1, 2011, the City estimated that it will require $2,470,000 to finance governmental activities for the remainder of the 2011 fiscal year. On that date, it had $740,000 of cash on hand and $830,000 of current liabilities. Collections for the remainder of FY 2011 from revenues other than current property taxes and from delinquent property taxes, including interest and penalties, were estimated at $1,100,000.

Required

a. Calculate the estimated amount of tax anticipation financing that will be required for the remainder of FY 2011. Show work in good form.
b. Assume that on April 2, 2011, the City of Perrin borrowed the amount calculated in part *a* by signing tax anticipation notes bearing 5 percent per annum to a local bank. Record the issuance of the tax anticipation notes in the general journals of the General Fund and governmental activities at the government-wide level.
c. By October 1, 2011, the City had collected a sufficient amount of current property taxes to repay the tax anticipation notes with interest. Record the repayment of the tax anticipation notes and interest in the general journals of the General Fund and governmental activities at the government-wide level.

4–4 Property Tax Calculations and Journal Entries. The Village of Darby's budget calls for property tax revenues for the fiscal year ending December 31, 2011, of $2,660,000. Village records indicate that, on average, 2 percent of taxes levied are not collected. The county tax assessor has assessed the value of taxable property located in the village at $135,714,300.

Required

a. Calculate to the nearest penny what tax rate per $100 of assessed valuation is required to generate a tax levy that will produce the required amount of revenue for the year.

b. Record the tax levy for 2011 in the General Fund. (Ignore subsidiary detail and entries at the government-wide level.)

c. By December 31, 2011, $2,540,000 of the current property tax levy had been collected. Record the amounts collected and reclassify the uncollected amount as delinquent. Interest and penalties of 6 percent were immediately due on the delinquent taxes, but the finance director estimates that 10 percent will not be collectible. Record the interest and penalties receivable. (Round all amounts to the nearest dollar.)

4–5 Adjusting Entries for Inventory of Supplies. The Village of Baxter uses the *purchases* method of accounting for its inventories of supplies in the General Fund. GASB standards, however, require that the *consumption* method be used for the government-wide financial statements. Because its computer system is very limited, the Village uses a periodic inventory system, adjusting inventory balances based on a physical inventory of supplies at year-end. When supplies are received during the year, the Village records expenditures and expenses in the general journals of the General Fund and governmental activities, respectively. The Village's inventory records showed the following information for the fiscal year ending December 31, 2011:

Balance of inventory, December 31, 2010	$140,000
Purchases of inventory during 2011	720,000
Balance of inventory, December 31, 2011	155,000

Required

a. Provide the required adjusting entries at the end of 2011, assuming that the December 31, 2011, balance of Inventory of Supplies has been confirmed by physical count. Make entries in the general journals of both the General Fund (omitting subsidiary detail) and governmental activities at the government-wide level.

b. Assume that the General Fund uses the *consumption* method for reporting inventories of supplies rather than the *purchases* method. Make the required adjusting entries for the General Fund and governmental activities at the government-wide level.

4–6 Special Revenue Fund, Voluntary Nonexchange Transactions. The City of Eldon applied for a competitive grant from the state government for park improvements such as upgrading hiking trails and bike paths. On May 1, 2011, the City was notified that it had been awarded a grant of $200,000 for the program, to be received in two installments on July 1, 2011, and July 1, 2012. The grant stipulates that $100,000 is for use in each of the city's fiscal years ending June 30, 2012, and June 30, 2013. Any amounts not expended during FY 2012 can be carried over for use in FY 2013. During FY 2012, the city expended $90,000 for park improvements from grant resources.

Required

For the special revenue fund, provide the appropriate journal entries, if any, that would be made for the following:

1. May 1, 2011, notification of grant approval.
2. July 1, 2011, receipt of first installment of the grant.
3. During FY 2011 to record expenditures under the grant.
4. July 1, 2012.

4–7 Closing Journal Entries. At the end of a fiscal year, budgetary and operating statement control accounts in the general ledger of the General Fund of Dade City had the following balances: Appropriations, $6,224,000; Estimated Other Financing Uses, $2,776,000; Estimated Revenues, $7,997,000; Encumbrances, $0; Expenditures, $6,192,000; Other Financing Uses, $2,770,000; and Revenues, $7,980,000. Appropriations included the authorization to order a certain item at a cost not to exceed $65,000; this was not ordered during the year because it will not be available until late in the following year.

Required

Show in general journal form the entry needed to close all of the preceding accounts that should be closed as of the end of the fiscal year.

4–8 Interfund and Interactivity Transactions. The following transactions affected various funds and activities of the City of Atwater.

1. The Fire Department, a governmental activity, purchased $100,000 of water from the Water Utility Fund, a business-type activity.
2. The Municipal Golf Course, an enterprise fund, reimbursed the General Fund $1,000 for office supplies that the General Fund had purchased on its behalf and that were used in the course of the fiscal year.
3. The General Fund made a long-term loan in the amount of $50,000 to the Central Stores Fund, an internal service fund that services city departments.
4. The General Fund paid its annual contribution of $80,000 to the debt service fund for interest and principal on general obligation bonds due during the year.
5. The $5,000 balance in the capital projects fund at the completion of construction of a new City Hall was transferred to the General Fund.

Required

a. Make the required journal entries in the general journal of the General Fund and any other fund(s) affected by the interfund transactions described. Also make entries in the governmental activities journal for any transaction(s) affecting a governmental fund. Do not make entries in the subsidiary ledgers.

b. Why is it unnecessary to make entries in a business-type activities journal for any transaction(s) affecting proprietary funds? Are internal service funds any different?

4–9 Transactions and Budgetary Comparison Schedule. The following transactions occurred during the 2011 fiscal year for the City of Fayette. For budgetary purposes, the city reports encumbrances in the Expenditures section of its budgetary comparison schedule for the General Fund but excludes expenditures chargeable to a prior year's appropriation.

1. The budget prepared for the fiscal year 2011 was as follows:

Estimated Revenues:	
Taxes	$1,943,000
Licenses and permits	372,000
Intergovernmental revenue	397,000
Miscellaneous revenues	62,000
Total estimated revenues	2,774,000
Appropriations:	
General government	471,000
Public safety	886,000
Public works	650,000
Health and welfare	600,000
Miscellaneous appropriations	86,000
Total appropriations	2,693,000
Budgeted increase in fund balance	$ 81,000

2. Encumbrances issued against the appropriations during the year were as follows:

General government	$ 58,000
Public safety	250,000
Public works	392,000
Health and welfare	160,000
Miscellaneous appropriations	71,000
Total	$931,000

3. The current year's tax levy of $2,005,000 was recorded; uncollectibles were estimated as $65,000.
4. Tax collections from prior years' levies totaled $132,000; collections of the current year's levy totaled $1,459,000.
5. Personnel costs during the year were charged to the following appropriations in the amounts indicated. Encumbrances were not recorded for personnel costs. Since no liabilities currently exist for withholdings, you may ignore any FICA or federal or state income tax withholdings. (*Note:* Expenditures charged to Miscellaneous Appropriations should be treated as General Government expenses in the governmental activities general journal at the government-wide level.)

General government	$ 411,000
Public safety	635,000
Public works	254,000
Health and welfare	439,000
Miscellaneous appropriations	11,100
Credit to Vouchers Payable	$1,750,100

6. Invoices for all items ordered during the prior year were received and approved for payment in the amount of $14,470. Encumbrances had been recorded in the prior year for these items in the amount of $14,000. The amount chargeable to each year's appropriations should be charged to the Public Safety appropriation.
7. Invoices were received and approved for payment for items ordered in documents recorded as encumbrances in Transaction (2) of this problem. The following appropriations were affected.

	Actual Liability	Estimated Liability
General government	$ 52,700	$ 52,200
Public safety	236,200	240,900
Public works	360,000	357,000
Health and safety	130,600	130,100
Miscellaneous appropriations	71,000	71,000
	$850,500	$851,200

8. Revenue other than taxes collected during the year consisted of licenses and permits, $373,000; intergovernmental revenue, $400,000; and $66,000 of miscellaneous revenues. For purposes of accounting for these revenues at the government-wide level, the intergovernmental revenues were operating grants and contributions for the Public Safety function. Miscellaneous revenues are not identifiable with any function and therefore are recorded as General Revenues at the government-wide level.
9. Payments on Vouchers Payable totaled $2,505,000.
   Additional information follows: The General Fund Fund Balance account had a credit balance of $82,900 as of December 31, 2010; no entries have been made in the Fund Balance account during 2011.

Required

a. Record the preceding transactions in general journal form for fiscal year 2011 in both the General Fund and governmental activities general journals.

b. Prepare a budgetary comparison schedule for the General Fund of the City of Fayette for the fiscal year ending December 31, 2011, as shown in Illustration 4–7. Do not prepare a government-wide statement of activities since other governmental funds would affect that statement.

4–10 Operating Transactions, Special Topics, and Financial Statements. The City of Ashland's General Fund had the following post-closing trial balance at April 30, 2010, the end of its fiscal year:

	Debits	*Credits*
Cash	$ 97,000	
Taxes Receivable—Delinquent	583,000	
Estimated Uncollectible Delinquent Taxes		$189,000
Interest and Penalties Receivable	26,280	
Estimated Uncollectible Interest and Penalties		11,160
Inventory of Supplies	16,100	
Vouchers Payable		148,500
Due to Federal Government		59,490
Reserve for Inventory of Supplies		16,100
Fund Balance		298,130
	$722,380	$722,380

During the year ended April 30, 2011, the following transactions, in summary form, with subsidiary ledger detail omitted, occurred:

1. The budget for FY 2011 provided for General Fund estimated revenues totaling $3,140,000 and appropriations totaling $3,100,000.
2. The city council authorized temporary borrowing of $300,000 in the form of a 120-day tax anticipation note. The loan was obtained from a local bank at a discount of 6 percent per annum (debit Expenditures for discount).

3. The property tax levy for FY 2011 was recorded. Net assessed valuation of taxable property for the year was $43,000,000, and the tax rate was $5 per $100. It was estimated that 4 percent of the levy would be uncollectible.
4. Purchase orders and contracts were issued to vendors and others in the amount of $2,059,000.
5. The County Board of Review discovered unassessed properties with a total taxable value of $500,000. The owners of these properties were charged with taxes at the city's General Fund rate of $5 per $100 assessed value. (You need not adjust the Estimated Uncollectible Current Taxes account.)
6. $1,961,000 of current taxes, $383,270 of delinquent taxes, and $20,570 of interest and penalties were collected.
7. Additional interest and penalties on delinquent taxes were accrued in the amount of $38,430, of which 30 percent was estimated to be uncollectible.
8. Because of a change in state law, the city was notified that it will receive $80,000 less in intergovernmental revenues than was budgeted.
9. Total payroll during the year was $819,490. Of that amount, $62,690 was withheld for employees' FICA tax liability, $103,710 for employees' federal income tax liability, and $34,400 for state taxes; the balance was paid to employees in cash.
10. The employer's FICA tax liability was recorded for $62,690.
11. Revenues from sources other than taxes were collected in the amount of $946,700.
12. Amounts due the federal government as of April 30, 2011, and amounts due for FICA taxes, and state and federal withholding taxes during the year were vouchered.
13. Purchase orders and contracts encumbered in the amount of $1,988,040 were filled at a net cost of $1,987,570, which was vouchered.
14. Vouchers payable totaling $2,301,660 were paid after deducting a credit for purchases discount of $8,030 (credit Expenditures).
15. The tax anticipation note of $300,000 was repaid.
16. All unpaid current year's property taxes became delinquent. The balances of the current tax receivables and related uncollectibles were transferred to delinquent accounts.
17. A physical inventory of materials and supplies at April 30, 2011, showed a total of $19,100. Inventory is recorded using the purchases method in the General Fund; the consumption method is used at the government-wide level.

Required

a. Record in general journal form the effect of the above transactions on the General Fund and governmental activities for the year ended April 30, 2011. Do not record subsidiary ledger debits and credits.

b. Record in general journal form entries to close the budgetary and operating statement accounts.

c. Prepare a General Fund balance sheet as of April 30, 2011.

d. Prepare a statement of revenues, expenditures, and changes in fund balance for the year ended April 30, 2011. Do not prepare the government-wide financial statements.

4–11 Permanent Fund and Related Special Revenue Fund Transactions. Annabelle Benton, great-granddaughter of the founder of the Town of Benton, made a cash contribution in the amount of $500,000 to be held as an endowment. To account for this endowment, the town has created the Alex Benton Park Endowment Fund. Under terms of the agreement, the town must invest and conserve the principal amount of the contribution in perpetuity. Earnings, measured on the accrual basis, must be used to maintain Alex Benton Park in an "attractive manner." All changes in fair value are treated as adjustments of fund balance of the permanent fund and do not affect earnings. Earnings are transferred periodically to the Alex Benton Park Maintenance Fund, a special revenue fund. Information pertaining to transactions of the endowment and special revenue funds for the fiscal year ended June 30, 2011, follows:

1. The contribution of $500,000 was received and recorded on December 31, 2010.
2. On December 31, 2010, bonds having a face value of $400,000 were purchased for $406,300, plus three months of accrued interest of $6,000. A certificate of deposit with a face and fair value of $70,000 was also purchased on this date. The bonds mature on October 1, 2019 (105 months from date of purchase), and pay interest of 6 percent per annum semiannually on April 1 and October 1. The certificate of deposit pays interest of 4 percent per annum payable on March 31, June 30, September 30, and December 31.
3. On January 2, 2011, the town council approved a budget for the Alex Benton Park Maintenance Fund, which included estimated revenues of $13,400 and appropriations of $13,000.
4. On March 31, 2011, interest on the certificate of deposit was received by the endowment fund and transferred to the Alex Benton Park Maintenance Fund.
5. The April 1, 2011, bond interest was received by the endowment fund and transferred to the Alex Benton Park Maintenance Fund.
6. On June 30, 2011, interest on the certificate of deposit was received and transferred to the Alex Benton Park Maintenance Fund.
7. For the year ended June 30, 2011, maintenance expenditures from the Alex Benton Park Maintenance Fund amounted to $2,700 for materials and contractual services and $10,150 for wages and salaries. All expenditures were paid in cash except for $430 of vouchers payable as of June 30, 2011. Inventories of materials and supplies are deemed immaterial in amount.
8. On June 30, 2011, bonds with face value of $100,000 were sold for $102,000 plus accrued interest of $1,500. On the same date, 2,000 shares of ABC Corporation's stock were purchased at $52 per share.

Required

a. Prepare in general journal form the entries required in the Alex Benton Park Endowment Fund to record the transactions occurring during the fiscal year ending June 30, 2011, including all appropriate adjusting and closing entries. (*Note:* Ignore related entries in the governmental activities journal at the government-wide level.)

b. Prepare in general journal form the entries required in the Alex Benton Park Maintenance Fund to record Transactions 1–8.

c. Prepare the following financial statements:

(1) A balance sheet for both the Alex Benton Park Endowment Fund and the Alex Benton Park Maintenance Fund as of June 30, 2011.

(2) A statement of revenues, expenditures, and changes in fund balance for both the Alex Benton Park Endowment Fund and the Alex Benton Park Maintenance Fund for the year ended June 30, 2011.

Chapter Five

Accounting for General Capital Assets and Capital Projects

Learning Objectives

After studying this chapter, you should be able to:

1. Describe the nature and characteristics of general capital assets.
2. Account for general capital assets, including: acquisition, maintenance, depreciation, impairment, and disposition.
3. Explain the purpose, characteristics, and typical financing sources of a capital projects fund.
4. Prepare journal entries for a typical capital project, both at the fund level and within the governmental activities category at the government-wide level.
5. Prepare financial statements for capital projects funds.
6. Explain the concepts and accounting procedures for special assessment capital projects.

Chapters 3 and 4 illustrate that long-lived assets such as office equipment, police cruisers, and other items may be acquired by expenditure of appropriations of the General Fund or one or more of its special revenue funds. Long-lived assets used by activities financed by the General Fund or other governmental funds are called **general capital assets.** General capital assets should be distinguished from capital assets that are specifically associated with activities financed by proprietary and fiduciary funds. Capital assets acquired by proprietary and fiduciary funds are accounted for by those funds.

Acquisitions of general capital assets that require major amounts of money ordinarily cannot be financed from General Fund or special revenue fund appropriations. Major acquisitions of general capital assets are commonly financed by issuance of long-term debt to be repaid from tax revenues or by special assessments against property deemed to be particularly benefited by the long-lived asset. Other sources for financing the acquisition of long-lived assets include grants from other governments, transfers from other funds, gifts from individuals or organizations, capital leases, or a combination of several of these sources. If money received from these sources is restricted, legally or morally, to the purchase or construction of specified capital assets, it is recommended that a **capital projects fund** be created to account for

ILLUSTRATION 5–1 General Capital Asset Acquisition: Governmental Funds and Government-wide Governmental Activities

General Fund and/or Special Revenue Funds	Capital Projects Funds	Government-wide Governmental Activities
Used to account for capital outlay expenditures from annual budget appropriations. General capital assets acquired are recorded in the governmental activities general ledger at the government-wide level.	Used to account for construction or other major capital expenditures from debt proceeds, capital grants, special assessments, and other sources restricted for capital asset acquisition. General capital assets acquired and related long-term debt to be serviced from tax revenues or from special assessments are recorded in the governmental activities general ledger at the government-wide level.	Used to account for the cost and depreciation of general capital assets acquired by expenditures of the General Fund, special revenue funds, and capital projects funds. Also used to account for general capital assets acquired under capital leases and for those acquired by gift. Used to account for all unmatured long-term debt except debt being repaid from revenues of enterprise funds.

resources to be used for such projects. When deemed useful, capital projects funds may also be used to account for the acquisition of major general capital assets, such as buildings, under a capital lease agreement. Leases involving equipment are more commonly accounted for by the General Fund.

Illustration 5–1 summarizes the fund types and activities at the government-wide level as they relate to general capital asset acquisition. It shows that general capital assets may be acquired from expenditures of the General Fund, special revenue funds, or capital projects funds. The cost or other carrying value of general capital assets and any related long-term debt is recorded in the general ledger for the governmental activities category at the government-wide level. This chapter focuses on capital projects fund accounting and financial reporting. Chapters 3 and 4 discuss accounting and financial reporting for the General Fund, special revenue funds, and permanent funds.

ACCOUNTING FOR GENERAL CAPITAL ASSETS

Only proprietary funds routinely account for capital assets (property, plant, equipment, and intangibles) used in their operations. Fiduciary funds may use capital assets for the production of income, in which case they also account for property, plant, and equipment within the fund. Since governmental funds account only for current financial resources, these funds do not account for capital assets acquired by the funds. Rather, general capital assets purchased or constructed with governmental fund resources are recorded in the governmental activities general ledger at the government-wide level. (See Illustration 5–1.)

Governmental Accounting Standards Board (GASB) standards require that general capital assets be recorded at historical cost, or fair value at time of receipt if assets are received by donation. **Historical cost** includes acquisition cost plus ancillary costs necessary to put the asset into use.[1] Ancillary costs may include items such as freight and transportation charges, site preparation costs, and set-up costs. If the cost of a capital

[1] GASB *Codification,* Sec. 1400.102.

asset was not recorded when the asset was acquired and is unknown when accounting control over the asset occurred, it is acceptable to record an estimated cost.

Under the GASB reporting model, general capital assets are reported in the Governmental Activities column of the statement of net assets, net of accumulated depreciation, when appropriate. Any rational and systematic depreciation method is allowed. Depreciation is not reported for inexhaustible assets such as land and land improvements, noncapitalized collections of works of art or historical treasures, and infrastructure assets that are accounted for using the *modified approach.*[2] (The modified approach is explained later in this chapter.) The term amortization rather than depreciation is used when referring to intangible assets.

Management should maintain an inventory record for each asset, or group of related assets, that exceeds the minimum dollar capitalization threshold established by the government. Inventory records help achieve accountability and should provide all information needed for planning an effective maintenance program, preparing budget requests for replacements and additions, providing for adequate insurance coverage, and fixing the responsibility for custody of the assets.

Even though general capital assets are acquired for the production of general governmental services rather than for the production of services that are sold, reporting depreciation on general capital assets may provide significant benefits to users and managers alike. Reporting depreciation expense as part of the direct expenses of functions and programs in the Governmental Activities column of the government-wide statement of activities (see Illustration A1–2) helps to determine the full cost of providing each function or program. Depreciation expense on capital assets used in the operations of a government grant–financed program is often an allowable cost under the terms of a grant. In addition, depreciation expense may provide useful information to administrators and legislators concerned with the allocation of resources to programs, departments, and activities. To a limited extent, a comparison of the accumulated depreciation on an asset with the cost of the asset may assist in budgeting outlays for replacement of capital assets.

Required Disclosures about Capital Assets

GASB standards require certain disclosures about capital assets in the notes to the basic financial statements, both the general capital assets reported in the Governmental Activities column and those reported in the Business-type Activities column of the government-wide financial statements.[3] In addition to disclosure of their general policy for capitalizing assets and for estimating the useful lives of depreciable assets, governments should provide certain other disclosures in the notes to the financial statements. These disclosures should be divided into the major classes of capital assets of the primary government (as discussed in the following section) and should distinguish between general capital assets and those reported in business-type activities. Capital assets that are not being depreciated are disclosed separately from those assets that are being depreciated. Required disclosures about each major class of capital assets include:

1. Beginning-of-year and end-of-year balances showing accumulated depreciation separate from historical cost.
2. Capital acquisitions during the year.

[2] Ibid., par. 104.

[3] GASB *Codification,* Sec. 2300.111–112.

3. Sales or other dispositions during the year.
4. Depreciation expense for the current period with disclosure of the amounts charged to each function in the statement of activities.
5. Disclosures describing works of art or historical treasures that are not capitalized and explaining why they are not capitalized.[4] If collections are capitalized, they should be included in the disclosures described in items 1 through 4.

Illustration 5–2 presents capital asset note disclosures for the City and County of Denver. These disclosures conform in all respects to required items 1–4 above. In addition, the City and County of Denver capitalizes and depreciates certain collections or individual works of art or historical treasures. The first three sections of the city and county's capital asset disclosures essentially correspond to the three major columns of the government-wide statement of net assets—Governmental Activities, Business-type Activities, and Discretely Presented Component Units. Within each section, capital assets not being depreciated (land and land rights and construction in progress) are reported separately from those that are being depreciated, as required by GASB standards.

The information contained in the first three sections of the disclosure should be useful for both internal and external decision makers as it reports on beginning balances for each major class of capital assets, additions to and deletions from each class, and the ending balance of each class. The same information is provided for accumulated depreciation. Section 4 of the disclosures presents the amount of depreciation expense that was charged to each function of governmental activities at the government-wide level. Section 5 provides details of construction commitments, both for governmental activities and business-type activities.

Classification of General Capital Assets

The capital asset classifications shown in Illustration 5–2 are typical of those used by state and local governments. Additional or similarly named accounts may be needed to better describe the asset classes of any given governmental entity. As discussed previously in this chapter, general capital assets typically are those acquired using the financial resources of a governmental fund. Many of these assets, however, are not used exclusively in the operations of any one fund, nor do they belong to a fund. Consider, for example, that general capital assets include courthouses and city halls, public buildings in general, the land on which they are situated, highways, streets, sidewalks, storm drainage systems, equipment, and other tangible assets with a life longer than one fiscal year. The following paragraphs present a brief review of generally accepted principles of accounting for each category of capital assets based on applicable GASB and Financial Accounting Standards Board (FASB) standards.

[4] Even though the GASB encourages capitalization of all collections or individual works of art or historical treasures, governments can opt *not* to capitalize if the collection is (1) held for public exhibition, education, or research in furtherance of public service rather than for financial gain; (2) protected, kept unencumbered, cared for, and preserved; and (3) subject to an organizational policy that requires the proceeds from sales of collection items to be used to acquire other items for collections (GASB, *Codification,* Sec. 1400.109). These criteria, all of which must be met in order not to capitalize, are identical to those in FASB *Statement No. 116* for nongovernmental nonprofit organizations (see Chapter 14 for discussion).

ILLUSTRATION 5–2 Illustrative Capital Assets Disclosure

CITY AND COUNTY OF DENVER, COLORADO
Capital Assets Disclosure
For the Year Ended December 31, 2007

Capital asset activity for the year ended December 31, 2007, was as follows (amounts expressed in thousands):

	January 1	Additions	Deletions	December 31
1. Governmental Activities				
Capital assets not being depreciated:				
Land and land rights	$ 245,403	$ 1,009	$ (139)	$ 246,273
Construction in progress	46,487	99,200	(43,950)	101,737
Total capital assets not being depreciated	291,890	100,209	(44,089)	348,010
Capital assets being depreciated:				
Buildings and improvements	1,495,345	46,075	(7,927)	1,533,493
Equipment and other	224,135	33,935	(16,690)	241,380
Collections	75,422	4,808	(5,136)	75,094
Infrastructure	956,679	53,626	(2,896)	1,007,409
Total capital assets being depreciated	2,751,581	138,444	(32,649)	2,857,376
Less accumulated depreciation for:				
Buildings and improvements	(310,179)	(42,788)	1,918	(351,049)
Equipment and other	(157,503)	(24,732)	9,749	(172,486)
Collections	(40,489)	(4,263)	5,159	(39,593)
Infrastructure	(400,452)	(38,170)	2,895	(435,727)
Total accumulated depreciation	(908,623)	(109,953)	19,721	(998,855)
Total capital assets being depreciated, net	1,842,958	28,491	(12,928)	1,858,521
Governmental Activities Capital Assets, net	$2,134,848	$128,700	$(57,017)	$2,206,531

2. Business-type Activities

	January 1 As Restated	Additions	Deletions	December 31
Capital assets not being depreciated:				
Land and land rights	$ 305,139	$ 12,727	$ —	$ 317,866
Construction in progress	188,459	208,266	(153,267)	243,458
Total capital assets not being depreciated	493,598	220,993	(153,267)	561,324
Capital assets being depreciated:				
Buildings and improvements	1,936,449	73,769	(14,277)	1,995,941
Improvements other than buildings	2,505,160	76,071	(2,761)	2,578,470
Machinery and equipment	600,478	31,291	(11,393)	620,376
Total capital assets being depreciated	5,042,087	181,131	(28,431)	5,194,787
Less accumulated depreciation for:				
Buildings and improvements	(608,572)	(56,511)	6,495	(658,588)
Improvements other than buildings	(722,031)	(65,298)	1,031	(786,298)
Machinery and equipment	(311,273)	(49,083)	9,497	(350,859)
Total accumulated depreciation	(1,641,876)	(170,892)	17,023	(1,795,745)
Total capital assets being depreciated, net	3,400,211	10,239	(11,408)	3,399,042
Business-type Activities Capital Assets, net	$3,893,809	$231,232	$(164,675)	$3,960,366

ILLUSTRATION 5–2 (*Continued*)

3. Discretely Presented Component Units. Capital asset activity for the Water Board and Denver Convention Hotel Authority component units for the year ended December 31, 2007, was as follows (amounts expressed in thousands):

	January 1	Additions	Deletions	December 31
Capital assets not being depreciated:				
Land and land rights	$ 177,147	$ 3,263	$ (714)	$ 179,696
Construction in progress	119,506	43,180	(6,873)	155,813
Total capital assets not being depreciated	296,653	46,443	(7,587)	335,509
Capital assets being depreciated:				
Buildings and improvements	388,862	48,829	(42)	437,649
Improvements other than buildings	1,502,893	(2,474)	(1,132)	1,499,287
Machinery and equipment	196,065	13,365	(8,974)	200,456
Total capital assets being depreciated	2,087,820	59,720	(10,148)	2,137,392
Less accumulated depreciation for:				
Buildings and improvements	(50,511)	(10,563)	37	(61,037)
Improvements other than buildings	(415,353)	6,449	562	(408,342)
Machinery and equipment	(51,661)	(43,415)	7,263	(87,813)
Total accumulated depreciation	(517,525)	(47,529)	7,862	(557,192)
Total capital assets being depreciated, net	1,570,295	12,191	(2,286)	1,580,200
Discretely Presented Component	$1,866,948	$58,634	$(9,873)	$1,915,709[1]

4. Depreciation Expense. Depreciation expense that was charged to governmental activities' functions (dollars in thousands):

General government	$ 16,392
Public safety	11,592
Public works, including depreciation of infrastructure	45,569
Human services	767
Health	176
Parks and recreation	7,865
Cultural activities	26,703
Community development	56
Economic opportunity	5
Capital assets held by internal service funds	828
Total	$109,953

5. Construction Commitments. The City's governmental and business-type activities and component units have entered into construction and professional services contracts having remaining commitments under contract as of December 31, 2007, as follows (amounts expressed in thousands):

Governmental Activities:	
Bond Projects	$121,634
Entertainment and Culture	3,050
Total Governmental Activities	$124,684
Business-type Activities:	
Wastewater Management	$ 19,000
Denver Airport System	135,486
Total Business-type Activities	$154,486
Component Units:	
Denver Convention Center Hotel Authority	$ 78
Water Board	135,500
Total Component Units	$135,578

The commitments for these funds are not reflected in the accompanying financial statements. Only the unpaid amounts incurred to date for these contracts are included as liabilities in the financial statements.

[1] Excludes net capital assets of $18,957 of Other Component Units.

Source: City and County of Denver, Colorado, Notes to Basic Financial Statements, Year Ended December 31, 2007, Section III, Note D.

Land

The cost of land acquired by a government through purchase should include not only the contract price but also such other related costs as taxes and other liens assumed, title search costs, legal fees, surveying, filling, grading, draining, and other costs of preparing for the use intended. Governments are frequently subject to damage suits in connection with land acquisition, and the amounts of judgments levied are considered capital costs of the property acquired. Land acquired through forfeiture should be capitalized at the total amount of all taxes, liens, and other claims surrendered plus all other costs incidental to acquiring ownership and perfecting title. Land acquired through donation should be recorded on the basis of appraised value at the date of acquisition; the cost of the appraisal itself should not be capitalized, however.

Buildings and Improvements Other than Buildings

If a definition of assets classified as buildings is needed, they may be said to consist of those structures erected above ground for the purpose of sheltering persons or property. Improvements other than buildings consist of land attachments of a permanent nature, other than buildings, and include, among other things, walks, walls, and parking lots.

The determination of the cost of buildings and improvements acquired by purchase is relatively simple, although some peripheral costs may be of doubtful classification. The price paid for the assets constitutes most of the cost of purchased items, but legal and other costs plus expenditures necessary to put the property into acceptable condition for its intended use are proper additions. The same generalizations may be applied to acquisitions by construction under contract; that is, purchase or contract price plus positively identified incidentals, should be capitalized. The determination of the cost of buildings and improvements obtained through construction by some agency of the government (sometimes called **force account construction**) is slightly more difficult. In these cases, costs should include not only all direct and indirect expenditures of the fund providing the construction but also materials and services furnished by other funds.

The value of buildings and improvements acquired by donation should be established by appraisal. As in the case of land, one reason for setting a value on donated buildings and improvements is to aid in determining the total value of capital assets used by the government and for reports and comparisons. However, more compelling reasons exist for setting a value on buildings and certain improvements: the need for obtaining proper insurance coverage and the need to substantiate the insurance claim if loss should occur. Finally, one should not lose sight of the fact that the cost of donated general capital assets is also required to be reported in the Governmental Activities column of the government-wide financial statements.

Equipment, or Machinery and Equipment

Machinery and equipment are usually acquired by purchase. Occasionally, however, machinery and equipment may be constructed by the government, perhaps financed by an internal service fund. In such cases, the same rules will apply as for buildings and improvements constructed by governmental employees. The cost of machinery and equipment purchased should include items conventional under business accounting practice: purchase price, transportation costs if not included in purchase price, installation cost, and other direct costs of readying for use. Cash discounts on machinery and equipment purchased should be treated as a reduction of costs.

4. The present value of rental or other minimum lease payments equals or exceeds 90 percent of the fair value of the leased property less any investment tax credit retained by the lessor.

If no criterion is met, the lease is classified as an **operating lease** by the lessee. Rental payments under an operating lease for assets used by governmental funds are recorded by the using fund as expenditures of the period. In many states, statutes prohibit governments from entering into obligations extending beyond the current budget year. Because of this legal technicality, governmental lease agreements typically contain a "fiscal funding clause," or cancellation clause, which permits governmental lessees to terminate the agreement on an annual basis if funds are not appropriated to make required payments. GASB standards specify that lease agreements containing fiscal funding or cancellation clauses should be evaluated. If the possibility of cancellation is judged remote, the lease should be disclosed in financial statements and accounts in the manner specified for capital leases.[11]

As an example of accounting for the acquisition of general capital assets under a capital lease agreement, assume that a government signs a capital lease agreement to pay $10,000 on January 1, 2010, the scheduled date of delivery of certain equipment to be used by an activity accounted for by a special revenue fund. The lease calls for annual payments of $10,000 at the beginning of each year thereafter; that is, January 1, 2011, January 1, 2012, and so on, through January 1, 2019. There will be 10 payments of $10,000 each, for a total of $100,000, but GASB standards require entry in the accounts of the present value of the stream of annual payments, not their total. Since the initial payment of $10,000 is paid at the inception of the lease, its present value is $10,000. The present value of the remaining nine payments must be calculated using the borrowing rate the lessee would have incurred to obtain a similar loan over a similar term to purchase the leased asset. Assuming the rate to be 10 percent, the present value of payments 2 through 10 is $57,590. The present value of the 10 payments is, therefore, $67,590. GASB standards require a governmental fund (including, if appropriate, a capital projects fund) to record the following entry at the inception of the capital lease:

	Debits	**Credits**
Special Revenue Fund:		
Expenditures	67,590	
Other Financing Sources—Capital Lease Agreements		67,590

The corresponding entry in the governmental activities general journal at the government-wide level to record the equipment and long-term liability under the capital lease is as follows:

Governmental Activities:		
Equipment	67,590	
Capital Lease Obligations Payable		67,590

[11] Ibid., pars. 115–118.

Costs Incurred after Acquisition

Governmental accounting procedures should include clear-cut provisions for classifying costs incurred in connection with capital assets after the acquisition cost has been established. Outlays closely associated with capital assets will regularly occur in amounts of varying size, and responsible persons will be charged with deciding whether these should be recorded as additions to assets. In general, any outlay that definitely adds to the utility or function of a capital asset or enhances the value of an integral part of it may be capitalized as part of the asset. Thus, drainage of land, addition of a room to a building, and changes in equipment that increase its output or reduce its cost of operation are clearly recognizable as additions to assets. Special difficulty arises in the case of large-scale outlays that are partly replacements and partly additions or betterments. An example would be replacement of a composition-type roof with a roof of some more durable material. To the extent that the project replaces the old roof, outlays should not be capitalized unless the cost of the old roof is removed from the accounts, and to the extent that the project provides a better roof, outlays should be capitalized. The distribution of the total cost in such a case is largely a matter for managerial determination. Consistent with policy in recording original acquisition costs, some outlays unquestionably representing increases in permanent values may not be capitalized if the amount is less than some specified minimum or on the basis of any other established criterion.

Outlays that are partly replacements and partly additions or betterments create some accounting difficulty. The distribution of the outlay having been decided, the estimated amount of addition or betterment might be added to the asset. Better results are sometimes obtained by crediting the appropriate asset account for the cost of the replaced part, thus removing the amount, and then debiting the asset account for the total cost of the replacing item.

Reduction of Cost

Reductions in the cost of capital assets may relate to the elimination of the total amount expended for a given item or items, or they may consist only of removing the cost applicable to a specific part. Thus, if an entire building is demolished, the total cost of the structure should be removed from the appropriate accounts; but if the separation applies only to a wing or some other definitely identifiable portion, the cost eliminated should be the amount estimated as applying to the identifiable portion. Reductions in the recorded cost of capital assets may be brought about by sale, retirement from use, destruction by fire or other casualty, replacement of a major part, theft or loss from some other cause, and possibly other changes. The cost of capital assets recorded in the governmental activities ledger may sometimes be reduced by the transfer of an asset to an enterprise fund, or vice versa.

Accounting for cost reductions consisting of entire assets is a relatively simple matter if adequate asset records have been kept. If the reduction is only partial, the cost as shown by the capital assets record must be modified to reflect the change with a complete description of what brought about the change.

Since depreciation is recorded on general capital assets, the removal of a capital asset from the governmental activities general ledger may be accomplished by crediting the ledger account recording the asset's cost and debiting Accumulated Depreciation and Cash if the item was sold. Gains or losses should be recognized if the value received differs from the book value of the assets removed. The gains and losses are reported on the government-wide statement of activities.

Governments sometimes trade used capital assets for new items. In the governmental activities general ledger, the total cost of the old item should be removed and the total cost (not merely the cash payment) of the new one recorded.

Asset Impairments and Insurance Recoveries

GASB standards provide accounting and reporting guidance for impairment of assets, as well as for insurance recoveries. The GASB defines an **asset impairment** as a *significant, unexpected decline in the service utility of a capital asset.*[12] Impairments occur as a result of unexpected circumstances or events, such as physical damage, obsolescence, enactment of laws or regulations or other environmental factors, or change in the manner or duration of the asset's use.[13] Unless an impairment is judged to be temporary, the amount of impairment should be measured using one of three approaches: *restorative cost approach*, the estimated cost to restore the utility of the asset (appropriate for impairments from physical damage); *service units approach,* the portion of estimated service utility life of the asset that has been estimated lost due to impairment (appropriate for impairments due to environmental factors or obsolescence); and *deflated depreciated replacement cost approach,* the estimated current cost of a replacement asset with similar depreciation and deflated for the effects of inflation (appropriate for impairment due to change in the manner or duration of use).[14] Barring evidence to the contrary, asset impairments should be considered permanent.

When an asset impairment has occurred, the estimated amount of impairment is reported as a write-down in the carrying value of the asset. The loss due to impairment is recorded as a program expense in the government-wide statement of activities for the function using the asset, and as an operating expense in the statement of revenues, expenses, and changes in fund net assets of proprietary funds, if applicable. If the impairment is significant in amount and results from an event that is unusual in nature or infrequently occurring, or both, then the loss should be reported as either a special item or extraordinary item, as appropriate.

Impairment losses are reported net of any insurance recoveries that occur during the same fiscal year. Insurance recoveries occurring in a subsequent year should be reported as other financing sources in governmental fund operating statements, as program revenues in the government-wide statement of net assets, and as nonoperating revenues in proprietary fund operating statements. Finally, restorations and replacements of impaired capital assets should be reported separately from both the impairment loss and any insurance recovery.

Illustrative Entries

Acquisition of general capital assets requires a debit to the appropriate governmental activities asset account and a credit to Cash or a liability account. Thus, if office equipment is purchased for the treasurer's office from General Fund resources, the following journal entries would be made in the general journals for the General Fund (ignoring encumbrances) and governmental activities at the government-wide level:

[12] GASB, *Codification,* Sec. 1400.144.

[13] Ibid, par. 148.

[14] Ibid, par. 151.

	Debits	Cre
General Fund:		
Expenditures	450	
Vouchers Payable		450
Governmental Activities:		
Equipment	450	
Vouchers Payable		450

Assuming Vouchers Payable is paid shortly after the equipment acquisition, Vouchers Payable will be debited and Cash will be credited, both in the General Fund and the governmental activities journal at the government-wide level. General capital assets acquired with capital projects fund resources would be recorded in essentially the same manner as if they had been acquired by the General Fund. If construction of a general capital asset is in progress at the end of a fiscal year, construction expenditures to the date of the financial report should be capitalized in the governmental activities ledger. These capital asset entries will be illustrated later in this chapter in the discussion of capital projects fund transactions.

Accounting for the disposal of general capital assets is relatively simple unless cash or other assets are involved in the liquidation. Accounting for an asset disposal requires elimination of the capital asset and accumulated depreciation accounts and recognition of a gain or loss, as appropriate. Assuming a building that cost $100,000 and with $80,000 of accumulated depreciation is retired without revenue or expenditure to the General Fund, the following entry in the governmental activities general journal would be required:

Governmental Activities:		
Loss on Disposal of Building	20,000	
Accumulated Depreciation—Buildings	80,000	
Buildings		100,000

Property records for the building should receive appropriate notations about the transaction and then be transferred to an inactive file.

In the event that cash is disbursed or received in connection with the disposal of general capital assets, the Cash account would be debited or credited as part of the entry to remove the book value of the capital asset, and a gain or loss would be recorded, as appropriate. Assuming that in the preceding example the General Fund incurred $3,000 for the demolition of the building, an entry in the following form should be made on the General Fund books:

General Fund:		
Expenditures	3,000	
Vouchers Payable		3,000

The corresponding entry that should be made at the government-wide level is:

	Debits	Credits
Governmental Activities:		
Loss on Disposal of Building	23,000	
Accumulated Depreciation—Buildings	80,000	
Buildings		100,000
Vouchers Payable		3,000

If cash is received from the sale of a general capital asset, some question may arise as to its disposition. Theoretically, the cash should be directed to the fund that provided the asset, but this may not always be practicable. If the asset was provided by a capital projects fund, the contributing fund may have been liquidated before the sale occurs. Unless otherwise prescribed by law, disposition of the results of a sale will be handled as decided by the legislative body having jurisdiction over the asset and will be recorded in the manner required by the accounting system of the recipient fund. Commonly, proceeds of sales of general capital assets are budgeted as Estimated Other Financing Sources in the General Fund. In such cases, when sales actually occur, the General Fund debits Cash (or a receivable) for the selling price and credits Other Financing Sources—Proceeds of Sales of Assets.

CAPITAL PROJECTS FUNDS

The reason for creating a fund to account for capital projects is the same as the reason for creating special revenue funds—to provide a formal mechanism to enable administrators to ensure revenues and other financing sources dedicated to a certain purpose are used for that purpose and no other, as well as to enable administrators to report to creditors and other grantors of capital projects fund resources that their requirements regarding the use of the resources are being met.

Capital projects funds differ from the General Fund and special revenue funds in that the latter categories have a year-to-year life, whereas capital projects funds have a project-life focus. In some jurisdictions, governments are allowed to account for all capital projects within a single capital projects fund. In other jurisdictions, laws are construed as requiring each project to be accounted for by a separate capital projects fund. Even in jurisdictions that permit the use of a single fund, managers may prefer to use separate funds to enhance control over each project. In such cases a fund is created when a capital project or a series of related projects is legally authorized; it is closed when the project or series is completed. Appropriation accounts need not be used because the legal authorization to engage in the project is in itself an appropriation of the total amount that may be obligated for the construction or acquisition of the capital asset specified in the project authorization. Estimated revenues need not be recorded because few contractors will start work on a project until financing is ensured through the sale of bonds or the receipt of grants or gifts. To provide control over the issuance of contracts and purchase orders, which may be numerous and which may be outstanding for several years in construction projects, it is recommended that the encumbrance procedure described in Chapter 3 be used. Since the purpose of the capital projects fund is to account for the receipt and expenditure of financial resources earmarked for capital projects, its balance sheet reports only financial resources and the liabilities to be liquidated by those resources. Neither the capital assets acquired nor any long-term debt incurred for the acquisition is recorded in a capital projects fund; these items are recorded in the governmental activities general ledger at the government-wide level, as discussed earlier in this chapter and in Chapter 6.

Some jurisdictions raise annual revenues for the specific purpose of financing major repairs to existing capital assets or for replacement of components of those assets (e.g., furnaces, air conditioning systems, roofs). A **capital improvements fund** is used to account for such revenues. The specific repairs and replacements to be undertaken by the capital improvements fund in a given year are not necessarily known at the time the revenues are budgeted. The appropriation process described in previous chapters is used to authorize expenditures from capital improvement funds when the nature and approximate cost of needed repairs and replacements become known. Necessary expenditures that cannot be financed by appropriation of the fund balance of a capital improvements fund or from the General Fund or special revenue funds may result in the need to establish a capital projects fund.

Legal Requirements

Since a government's power to issue bonds constitutes an ever-present hazard to the welfare of its property owners in particular[15] and its taxpayers in general, this authority is ordinarily limited by legislation. The purpose of legislative limitation is to obtain a prudent balance between public welfare and the rights of individual citizens. In some jurisdictions, most bond issues must be approved by referendum; in others, by petition of a specified percentage of taxpayers. Not only must bond issues be approved according to law but the government must comply with other provisions, such as method and timing of payments from the proceeds and determination of validity of claims for payment. A knowledge of all details related to a bond issue is necessary to avoid difficulties and complications that might otherwise occur.

Grants or other resources provided by state and federal agencies to help finance capital acquisitions made by local governments further complicate the process. Strict control of how such grants are used is imperative for ensuring proper use of the funds. Accounting and reporting procedures must be established that can provide information showing compliance with terms of the grants. Details of the fund structure and operation should ensure that all required information is provided when it is needed and in the form in which it is needed.

The successful accomplishment of a capital acquisition project may be brought about in one or more of the following ways:

1. Outright purchase from fund cash.
2. By construction, utilizing the government's own work force.
3. By construction, utilizing the services of private contractors.
4. By capital lease agreement.

Illustrative Transactions—Capital Projects Funds

GASB standards require the use of the same basis of accounting for capital projects funds as for the other governmental fund types. Proceeds of debt issues should be recognized by a capital projects fund at the time the issue is sold rather than the time

[15] An issue of bonds to be repaid from tax revenues in essence places a lien on all taxable property within a government's jurisdiction. Responsibility for payments of principal and interest on general bonded debt provides for no consideration of a property owner's financial condition and ability or inability to pay.

it is authorized because authorization of an issue does not guarantee its sale. Proceeds of debt issues should be recorded as Proceeds of Bonds or Proceeds of Long-Term Notes rather than as Revenues, and they should be reported in the Other Financing Sources section of the statement of revenues, expenditures, and changes in fund balance. Similarly, tax revenues raised by the General Fund or a special revenue fund and transferred to a capital projects fund are recorded as Interfund Transfers In and reported in the Other Financing Sources section of the operating statement.

Taxes raised specifically for a capital projects fund would be recorded as revenues of that fund, as would special assessments to be used for the construction of assets that will be of particular benefit to certain property owners. Grants, entitlements, or shared revenues received by a capital projects fund from another government are considered revenues of the capital projects fund. Interest earned on investments of the capital projects fund is also considered revenue if the interest is available for expenditure by the capital projects fund. If, by law, the interest must be used for service of long-term capital debt, the interest should be transferred to the appropriate debt service fund.

In the following illustration of accounting for representative transactions of a capital projects fund, it is assumed that the town council of the Town of Brighton authorized an issue of $1,200,000 of 6 percent bonds as partial financing of a fire station expected to cost approximately $1,500,000; the $300,000 additional financing was to be contributed by other governments. The project, utilizing land already owned by the town, was completed partly by a private contractor and partly by the town's own workforce. Completion of the project occurred within the current year. Transactions and entries related to the project are shown here, all of which are assumed to occur in fiscal year 2011. For economy of time and space, vouchering of liabilities is omitted.

The $1,200,000 bond issue, which had been approved by voter referendum, was officially approved by the town council. No formal entry is required to record voter and town council approval. A memorandum entry may be made to identify the approved project and the means of financing it.

To defray engineering and other preliminary expenses, the sum of $50,000 was borrowed on a short-term basis from National Bank. Because this transaction affects both the Fire Station Capital Projects Fund and governmental activities at the government-wide level, the following entry is made in both journals:

		Debits	Credits
	Fire Station Capital Projects Fund and Governmental Activities:		
1.	Cash	50,000	
	Short-Term Notes Payable		50,000

Total purchase orders and other commitment documents issued for supplies, materials, items of minor equipment, and labor required for the part of the project to be performed by the town's employees amounted to $443,000. (Since the authorization is for the project, not for a budget year, it is unnecessary to include 2011, or any other year, in the account titles.) The following budgetary control entry is made in the capital projects fund but is not recorded at the government-wide level.

		Debits	Credits
	Fire Station Capital Projects Fund:		
2.	Encumbrances	443,000	
	Reserve for Encumbrances		443,000

A contract, in the amount of $1,005,000, was signed for certain work to be done by a private contractor. As with Entry 2, only the capital projects fund is affected.

		Debits	Credits
	Fire Station Capital Projects Fund:		
3.	Encumbrances	1,005,000	
	Reserve for Encumbrances		1,005,000

Special engineering and miscellaneous costs that had not been encumbered were paid in the amount of $48,000. These costs are deemed to be properly capitalized as part of the fire station.

		Debits	Credits
	Fire Station Capital Projects Fund:		
4a.	Construction Expenditures	48,000	
	Cash		48,000
	Governmental Activities:		
4b.	Construction Work in Progress	48,000	
	Cash		48,000

Entries 4a and 4b highlight a major difference between accounting for a governmental fund and governmental activities at the government-wide level. Accounting for a governmental fund focuses on the inflows and outflows of current financial resources on the modified accrual basis; accounting for governmental activities focuses on the inflows and outflows of economic resources, including capital assets, on the accrual basis used in accounting for business organizations.

When the project was approximately half finished, the contractor submitted a bill requesting payment of $495,000.

		Debits	Credits
	Fire Station Capital Projects Fund:		
5a.	Reserve for Encumbrances	495,000	
	Encumbrances		495,000
5b.	Construction Expenditures	495,000	
	Contracts Payable		495,000
	Governmental Activities:		
5c.	Construction Work in Progress	495,000	
	Contracts Payable		495,000

Entries 5a and 5b record conversion of an estimated liability to a firm liability eligible for payment upon proper authentication. Contracts Payable records the status of a claim under a contract between the time of presentation and verification for vouchering or payment.

Payment in full was received from the other governments that had agreed to pay part of the cost of the new fire station.

		Debits	Credits
	Fire Station Capital Projects Fund:		
6a.	Cash	300,000	
	Revenues		300,000
	Governmental Activities:		
6b.	Cash	300,000	
	Program Revenues—Public Safety— Capital Grants and Contributions		300,00

The National Bank loan was repaid with interest amounting to $1,000.

		Debits	Credits
	Fire Station Capital Projects Fund:		
7a.	Interest Expenditures	1,000	
	Short-Term Notes Payable	50,000	
	Cash		51,000
	Governmental Activities:		
7b.	Expenses—Interest on Notes Payable	1,000	
	Short-Term Notes Payable	50,000	
	Cash		51,000

The reader will note that the $1,000 of interest expenditure (expense) recorded in Entries 7a and 7b is not capitalized as part of the total cost of the new fire station. GASB standards prohibit capitalization of interest incurred during the construction of *general capital assets.* However, as is illustrated and discussed in Chapter 7, interest is capitalized as part of self-constructed capital assets recorded in proprietary funds.

On June 15, 2011, the Town of Brighton issued at par bonds with a par value of $1,200,000 and dated June 15, 2011. Thus, there was no accrued interest as of the date of issue. Entries 8a and 8b show the contrast between how the bond issue is recorded in the general journals for the capital projects fund and governmental activities at the government-wide level. Since the bond issue increases current financial resources in the capital projects fund, the credit in Entry 8a is to Other Financing Sources—Proceeds of Bonds rather than to a liability account. As shown in Entry 8b, the long-term liability is recorded in the governmental activities general journal as a credit to Bonds Payable, reflecting the economic resources measurement focus used at the government-wide level.

		Debits	Credits
	Fire Station Capital Projects Fund:		
8a.	Cash	1,200,000	
	Other Financing Sources—Proceeds of Bonds		1,200,000
	Governmental Activities:		
8b.	Cash	1,200,000	
	Bonds Payable		1,200,000

The contractor's initial claim was fully verified and paid (see Entries 5b and 5c).

		Debits	**Credits**
	Fire Station Capital Projects Fund and Governmental Activities:		
9.	Contracts Payable	495,000	
	Cash		495,000

Total disbursements for all costs encumbered in Entry 2 amounted to $440,000. Although the encumbrances entry only affects the capital projects fund, the disbursement affects both the capital projects fund and governmental activities at the government-wide level.

		Debits	Credits
	Fire Station Capital Projects Fund:		
10a.	Reserve for Encumbrances	443,000	
	Encumbrances		443,000
10b.	Construction Expenditures	440,000	
	Cash		440,000
	Governmental Activities:		
10c.	Construction Work in Progress	440,000	
	Cash		440,000

Billing for the balance owed on the construction contract was received from the contractor.

		Debits	Credits
	Fire Station Capital Projects Fund:		
11a.	Reserve for Encumbrances	510,000	
	Encumbrances		510,000
11b.	Construction Expenditures	510,000	
	Contracts Payable		510,000
	Governmental Activities:		
11c.	Construction Work in Progress	510,000	
	Contracts Payable		510,000

Inspection revealed only minor imperfections in the contractor's performance, and on correction of these, the liability to the contractor was paid.

		Debits	Credits
	Fire Station Capital Projects Fund and Governmental Activities:		
12.	Contracts Payable	510,000	
	Cash		510,000

All requirements and obligations related to the project having been fulfilled, the operating statement accounts were closed in the capital projects fund. Governmental activities general ledger accounts will be closed in Chapter 9.

		Debits	Credits
	Fire Station Capital Projects Fund:		
13.	Revenues	300,000	
	Other Financing Sources—Proceeds of Bonds	1,200,000	
	Construction Expenditures		1,493,000
	Interest Expenditures		1,000
	Fund Balance		6,000

Since the project has been completed, it is appropriate to terminate the capital projects fund. The only remaining asset of the fund after the 13 transactions illustrated is Cash in the amount of $6,000. State laws often require that assets no longer needed in a capital projects fund be transferred to the fund that will service the debt incurred for the project, a debt service fund. Transfers of this nature are called **interfund transfers** and are reported as other financing uses by the transferor fund and other financing sources by the transferee fund in the statement of revenues, expenditures, and changes in fund balance (see Illustration 5–3). The entries to record the transfer and termination of the Town of Brighton Fire Station Capital Projects Fund are:

		Debits	Credits
	Fire Station Capital Projects Fund:		
14a.	Other Financing Uses—Interfund Transfers Out	6,000	
	Cash		6,000
14b.	Fund Balance	6,000	
	Other Financing Uses—Interfund Transfers Out		6,000

Similar entries would be required to record the interfund transfers in by the debt service fund. No entry is required at the government-wide level since the transfer occurs *within* the governmental activities category.

The cost of the fire station constructed by the Town of Brighton is recorded in the governmental activities general journal at the government-wide level. Because all capitalizable costs have previously been recorded as construction work in progress during the period of construction, the only entry required is to reclassify the amount in that account to the Buildings account, as shown in the following entry.

		Debits	Credits
	Governmental Activities:		
15.	Buildings	1,493,000	
	Construction Work in Progress		1,493,000

ILLUSTRATION 5–3

TOWN OF BRIGHTON
Fire Station Capital Projects Fund
Statement of Revenues, Expenditures, and Changes in Fund Balance
For the Year Ended December 31, 2011

Revenues:		
From other governments		$ 300,000
Expenditures:		
Construction	$1,493,000	
Interest	1,000	1,494,000
Excess of revenues over (under) expenditures		(1,194,000)
Other financing sources (uses):		
Proceeds of bonds	1,200,000	
Interfund transfer out	(6,000)	1,194,000
Excess of revenues and other financing sources/ uses over expenditures		–0–
Fund balance, January 1, 2011		–0–
Fund balance, December 31, 2011		$ –0–

Illustrative Financial Statements for a Capital Projects Fund

Inasmuch as all balance sheet accounts of the Town of Brighton Fire Station Capital Projects Fund are closed in the case just illustrated, there are no assets, liabilities, or fund equity to report in a balance sheet. The operations of the year, however, should be reported in a statement of revenues, expenditures, and changes in fund balance, as shown in Illustration 5–3. Since it is assumed that the Town of Brighton is not required to adopt a legal budget for its capital projects funds, it does not need to prepare a budgetary comparison schedule or statement for the capital projects fund type.

At the government-wide level, the completed fire station is reported as a capital asset, net of accumulated depreciation (if any depreciation expense is recorded in the first year in which the asset is placed into service), in the Governmental Activities column of the statement of net assets (see Illustration A1–1). The $1,200,000 of tax-supported bonds issued for the project is reported as a long-term liability in the Governmental Activities column of the statement of net assets. If any depreciation expense is recorded for the portion of a year that the fire station has been in service, it would be reported as a direct expense of the Public Safety function in the statement of activities (see Illustration A1–2).

Alternative Treatment of Residual Equity or Deficits

In the example just presented, a modest amount of cash remained in the Fire Station Capital Projects Fund after the project had been completed and all liabilities of the fund were liquidated. If expenditures and other financing uses are planned and controlled carefully so that actual costs do not exceed planned costs, revenues and other financing sources of the capital projects fund should equal, or slightly exceed, the expenditures and other financing uses, leaving a residual fund equity. If, as in the example presented, long-term debt has been incurred for the purposes of the capital projects fund, the residual equity is ordinarily transferred to the fund that is to service the debt. If the residual equity has come from grants or shared revenues restricted for capital acquisitions or construction, legal advice may indicate that any residual equity must be returned to the source(s) of the restricted grants or restricted shared revenues.

Even with careful planning and cost control, expenditures and other financing uses of a capital projects fund may exceed its revenues and other financing sources, resulting in a negative fund balance, or a deficit. If the deficit is a relatively small amount, the legislative body of the government may be able to authorize transfers from one or more other funds to cover the deficit in the capital projects fund. If the deficit is relatively large, and/or if intended transfers are not feasible, the government may seek additional grants or shared revenues from other governments to cover the deficit. If no other alternative is available, the government would need to finance the deficit by issuing debt in whatever form is legally possible and feasible under market conditions then existing.

Bond Premium, Discount, and Accrued Interest on Bonds Sold

Governments that issue bonds or long-term notes to finance the acquisition of capital assets commonly sell the entire issue to an underwriter or a syndicate of underwriters on the basis of bids or negotiated terms. The underwriters then sell the bonds or notes to institutions or individuals who often have agreed in advance to purchase a specified amount of bonds from the underwriters. Statutes in some states prohibit the initial sale of an issue of local government bonds at a discount. Accordingly, it is usual to set the interest rate high enough to enable the underwriters to pay the issuer at least the par, or face, value of the bonds; it is not unusual for underwriters to pay issuers an amount in excess of par, known as a *premium*. State statutes, local ordinances, or bond indentures often require that initial issue premiums be used for debt service. In such cases only the par value of the bonds is considered as an other financing source of the capital projects fund; the premium is considered as an other financing source of the debt service fund. Therefore, the sale of bonds at a premium would require an entry in the capital projects fund for the face of the bonds (as shown in Entry 8a of this chapter) and an entry in the debt service fund for the premium. At the government-wide level, a premium would be recorded as an additional component of the general long-term liability for the bonds. As in accounting for business organizations, the premium should be amortized, using the effective-interest method, over the life of the bonds. The amount of amortization is the difference between the actual cash paid for interest and the calculated amount of effective interest expense for the period.

It may happen that the issuing government receives one check from the underwriters for the total amount of the par premium. If procedures of that government indicate that it is desirable to record the entire amount in the capital projects fund, the following entries are appropriate (using assumed amounts). (*Note:* This entry and the one that follows are not part of the Town of Brighton Fire Station Capital Projects Fund example.)

	Debits	Credits
Capital Projects Fund:		
Cash	1,509,000	
Other Financing Sources—Proceeds of Bonds		1,500,000
Due to Other Funds		9,000

This entry accounts for the bond premium as a liability of the capital projects fund because it must be remitted to the debt service fund. In the debt service fund, an entry would be made to debit Due from Other Funds and credit Other Financing Sources—Premium on Bonds. Some accountants prefer to credit Other Financing Sources—Premium on Bonds rather than Due to Other Funds in the capital projects fund, particularly if the disposition of the premium is still to be determined on the sale date. Some accountants also include the amount of the premium as part of the credit to Other Financing Sources—Proceeds of Bonds in the capital projects fund. If either of these alternative procedures is used, it is necessary to make a second entry in the Capital Projects Fund debiting Other Financing Uses—Interfund Transfers Out and crediting Due to Other Funds.

In those jurisdictions in which it is legal for bonds to be sold initially at a discount, using the same face amount as the bonds in the entry above, except the debt proceeds are less than the face amount of the bonds, the entry might be:

	Debits	***Credits***
Capital Projects Fund:		
Cash	1,491,000	
Other Financing Uses—Discount on Bonds	9,000	
Other Financing Sources—Proceeds of Bonds		1,500,000

Crediting Other Financing Sources—Proceeds of Bonds for $1,500,000 carries the implication that, if necessary, the discount is expected to be counterbalanced at a future date by receipt of money from another source, perhaps the General Fund. If it has been determined that no money from another source will be provided, the discount would be written off against Proceeds of Bonds. When the money from another source is received, the capital projects fund should debit Cash and credit either Revenues or Other Financing Sources, depending on the source of the money. When it is known in advance that the discount will not be made up by transfers from other sources, an entry debiting Cash and crediting Other Financing Sources—Proceeds of Bonds, each for par value less discount, should be made.

When bonds are sold between interest payment dates, the party buying the bonds must pay up front the amount of interest accrued from the date the bonds are issued (the starting date for purposes of calculating interest) to the date the bonds are actually sold as part of the total price of the bonds. Thus, assuming two months of interest have already accrued by the sale date, the two months of interest that bondholders pay at the sale date yields the equitable result that they earn a *net* four months of interest, although they will receive a full six months of interest only four months after the sale date. In a governmental fund, accrued interest sold should conceptually be credited to Interest Expenditure and be offset against the six-month interest expenditure recorded on the first interest payment date following the sale of the bonds. In practice, however, accrued interest sold is generally recorded as a revenue of the debt service fund. This practice simplifies budgetary control by permitting the government to budget appropriations for and record an expenditure for the full six months of interest that must be paid on the first interest payment date. At the government-wide level, however, cash received on the sale date for accrued interest would be credited either as Accrued Interest Payable or Interest Expense, as in accounting for businesses.

Retained Percentages

It is common to require contractors on large-scale contracts to give performance bonds, providing for indemnity to the government for any failure on the contractor's part to comply with terms and specifications of the agreement. Before final inspection of a project can be completed, the contractor may have moved its work force and equipment to another location, thus making it difficult to remedy possible objections to the contractor's performance. Also, the shortcoming alleged by the government may be of a controversial nature with the contractor unwilling to accede to the demands of the government. Results of legal action in such disagreements are not predictable.

To provide more prompt adjustment on shortcomings not large or convincing enough to justify legal action and not recoverable under the contractor's bond, as well as those the contractor may admit but not be in a position to rectify, it is common practice to withhold a portion of the contractor's payment until final inspection and acceptance have occurred. The withheld portion is normally a contractual percentage of the amount due on each segment of the contract.

In the Town of Brighton illustration, the contractor submitted a bill for $495,000, which, on preliminary approval, was recorded previously in Entry 5b in the Fire Station Capital Projects Fund as follows:

	Debits	Credits
Capital Projects Fund:		
Construction Expenditures	495,000	
Contracts Payable		495,000

Assuming that the contract provided for retention of 5 percent, current settlement on the billing would be recorded as follows:

	Debits	Credits
Capital Projects Fund:		
Contracts Payable	495,000	
Cash		470,250
Contracts Payable—Retained Percentage		24,750

This same entry would also be made in the governmental activities general journal at the government-wide level. Alternatively, the intention of the government to retain the percentage stipulated in the contract could be recorded at the time the progress billing receives preliminary approval. In that event, the credit to Contracts Payable in the first entry in this section would be $470,250, and the credit to Contracts Payable—Retained Percentage in the amount of $24,750 would be made at that time. The second entry, therefore, would be a debit to Contracts Payable and a credit to Cash for $470,250.

On final acceptance of the project, the retained percentage is liquidated by a payment of cash. In the event that the government that recorded the retention finds it necessary to spend money on correction of deficiencies in the contractor's performance, the payment is charged to Contracts Payable—Retained Percentage. If the cost of correcting deficiencies exceeds the balance in the Contracts Payable—Retained Percentage account, the excess amount is debited to Construction Expenditures in the Fire Station Capital Projects Fund and to Buildings (or other appropriate capital asset account) in the governmental activities general journal.

Claims and Judgments Payable

Claims and judgments often, although not always, relate to construction activities of a government. If a claim has been litigated and a judicial decision adverse to the government has been rendered, there is no question as to the amount of the liability that should be recorded. If claims have not been litigated or judgments have not been made as of the balance sheet date, liabilities may be estimated through a case-by-case review of all claims, the application of historical experience to the outstanding claims, or a combination of these methods.[16]

GASB standards specify that the amount of claims and judgments recognized as expenditures and liabilities of governmental funds is limited to the amount that would normally be liquidated with expendable resources then in the fund; however, the full known or estimated liability should be reported in the Governmental Activities column of the government-wide statement of net assets.

Bond Anticipation Notes Payable and the Problem of Interest Expenditures

Bond Anticipation Notes Payable is a liability resulting from the borrowing of money for temporary financing before issuance of bonds. Delay in perfecting all details connected with issuance of bonds and postponement of the sale until a large portion of the proceeds is needed are the main reasons for preliminary financing by use of **bond anticipation notes.** The "bond anticipation" description of the debt signifies an obligation to retire the notes from proceeds of a proposed bond issue. If two conditions specified in FASB *Statement No. 6* are met, then the liability for bond anticipation notes should be treated as a long-term liability:[17]

1. All legal steps have been taken to refinance the bond anticipation notes.
2. The intent is supported by an ability to consummate refinancing the short-term notes on a long-term basis.

In cases in which the bond anticipation notes are secured by approved but unissued bonds and the intent is to repay the notes from the proceeds of the bond issue, it would appear that the two criteria have been met and, thus, bond anticipation note issues in such cases would be reported as a long-term liability in the Governmental Activities column of the government-wide statement of net assets and as an other financing source (Proceeds of Bond Anticipation Notes) in the capital projects fund.

As an example of a bond anticipation note that meets the two criteria provided, assume that a particular city issued $500,000 of 6 percent bond anticipation notes under a written agreement that the notes will be retired within six months from the proceeds of a previously approved $5,000,000 bond issue. When the bond anticipation

[16] GASB standards (GASB *Codification,* Sec. C50.110–114) require that if information is available prior to issuance of the financial statements that indicates it is probable that an asset has been impaired or a liability has been incurred at the date of the financial statements and the amount of the loss can be estimated with a reasonable degree of accuracy, the liability should be recognized.

[17] GASB *Codification,* Sec. B50.101.

notes are issued, the journal entries for the capital projects fund and governmental activities would be as follows:

	Debits	Credits
Capital Projects Fund:		
Cash	500,000	
Other Financing Sources—Proceeds of Bond Anticipation Notes		500,000
Governmental Activities		
Cash	500,000	
Bond Anticipation Notes Payable		500,000

Six months later, the bonds are issued at par and the bond anticipation notes are retired using a portion of the bond proceeds. Cash from other sources is assumed to be used to pay interest on the bond anticipation notes. The required journal entries are as follows:

	Debits	Credits
Capital Projects Fund:		
Cash	5,000,000	
Other Financing Sources—Proceeds of Bonds		5,000,000
Other Financing Uses—Retirement of Bond Anticipation Notes	500,000	
Interest Expenditures	15,000	
Cash		515,000
Governmental Activities:		
Cash	5,000,000	
Bonds Payable		5,000,000
Bond Anticipation Notes Payable	500,000	
Expenses—Interest on Long-Term Debt	15,000	
Cash		515,000
(*Note:* Interest expense is $500,000 × .06 × 6/12 = $15,000)		

As indicated in the preceding example, interest almost always must be paid on bond anticipation notes. Both practical and theoretical problems are involved in the payment of interest on liabilities. Practically, payment of interest by the capital projects fund reduces the amount available for construction or acquisition of the assets, so the administrators of the capital projects fund would wish to pass the burden of interest payment to another fund. Logically, the debt service fund set up for the bond issue should bear the burden of interest on bond anticipation notes and possibly on judgments, but at the time this interest must be paid, the debt service fund may have no assets. It would also appeal to the capital projects fund's administrators that interest on the bond anticipation notes and judgments should be paid by the General Fund (or any other fund with available cash). If such interest payments have been included in the appropriations budget by the General Fund (or other fund), the payment is considered legal; if not, the legislative body might authorize the other fund to pay the interest.

If the capital projects fund bears the interest on bond anticipation notes or other short-term debt, either initially or ultimately, an expenditure account must be debited. In Entry 7a in the series of Fire Station Capital Projects Fund and governmental activities entries illustrated earlier in this chapter, interest paid on bond anticipation notes was debited to Interest Expenditures rather than to Construction Expenditures, reflecting the requirements of *GASBS 37*. Entry 7b showed that the $1,000 paid for interest also was not capitalized as part of the cost of the assets for the fire station project.

Investments

Interest rates payable on general long-term debt have typically been lower than interest rates that the government can earn on temporary investments of high quality, such as U.S. Treasury bills and notes, bank certificates of deposit, and government bonds with short maturities. Consequently, there is considerable attraction to the practice of selling bonds as soon as possible after a capital project is legally authorized and investing the proceeds to earn a net interest income. This practice also avoids the problems and costs involved in financing by bond anticipation notes, described in the preceding section. However, arbitrage rules under the Internal Revenue Code constrain the investment of bond proceeds to securities whose yield does not exceed that of the new debt. Application of these rules to state and local governments is subject to continuing litigation and legislative action, so competent legal guidance must be sought by governments wishing to invest bond proceeds in a manner that will avoid incurring an **arbitrage rebate** and possible difficulties with the Internal Revenue Service.

Interest earned on temporary investments is available for use by the capital projects fund in some jurisdictions; in others, laws or local practices require the interest income to be transferred to the debt service fund or to the General Fund. If interest income is available to the capital projects fund, it should be recognized on the modified accrual basis as a credit to Revenues. If it will be collected by the capital projects fund but must be transferred to another fund, an additional entry is required to record an interfund transfer out. If the interest will be collected by the debt service fund, or other fund that will recognize it as revenue, no entry by the capital projects fund is necessary.

Multiple-Period and Multiple-Project Bond Funds

Thus far, discussion of capital projects fund accounting has proceeded on the assumption that initiation and completion of projects occur in the same fiscal year. However, many projects large enough to require a capital projects fund are started in one year and ended in another. Furthermore, a single comprehensive authorization may legalize two or more purchase or construction projects as segments of a master plan of improvements. Both multiple-period and multiple-project activities require some deviations from the accounting activities that suffice for one-period, one-project accounting.

The first difference appears in the budgeting procedure. Whereas for a one-period operation a single authorization might adequately cover the project from beginning to end, annual budgets, in one form or another, may be desirable or even required for those extending into two or more periods. This practice is used as a means of keeping the project under the legislative body's control and preventing the unacceptable deviations that might result from a one-time, lump-sum approval of a long-term project. Likewise, a large bond issue, to be supplemented by grants from outside sources, may be authorized to cover a number of projects extending over a period of time but not planned in detail before initiation of the first project. Such an arrangement requires the fund administration to maintain control by giving final approval to the budget for each project only as it comes up for action.

For a multiple-projects fund, it is necessary to identify encumbrances and expenditures in a way that will indicate the project to which each encumbrance and expenditure applies in order to check for compliance with the project budget. This can be accomplished by adding the project name or other designation (e.g., City Hall or Project No. 75) to the encumbrance and expenditure account titles. This device is almost imperative for proper identification in the recording of transactions, and it facilitates preparation of cash and expenditure statements for multi-project operations.

may be paid in equal installments over a specified period of years. Commonly, the first installment is due within a relatively short period of time (say, 60 days after the assessment is levied) and, if paid by the due date, is noninterest bearing. The remainder of the installments are due annually thereafter and are interest bearing. Assume, for example, that the final installment is due five years after the levy of the special assessment. Contractors cannot be expected to wait five years to be paid for work done on the project; therefore, an issue of long-term debt is authorized in the amount of installments due in future years. The first installment and the proceeds of the long-term debt would be used to finance the capital project and would be recorded by a capital projects fund. GASB standards provide that the first installment should be recognized as revenue of the capital projects fund and governmental activities at the government-wide level at the time of the levy—providing, of course, for any estimated uncollectibles. The deferred installments, and interest thereon, are not available for expenditure by a capital projects fund. Rather, deferred installments of special assessments should be recorded as described in Chapter 6.

Long-term debt proceeds would be considered an Other Financing Source—Proceeds of Bonds (or Notes) of the capital projects fund, and as a long-term liability at the government-wide level if the primary government has an obligation to assume debt service in the event that collections of remaining installments are insufficient. If the primary government has no obligation for debt service and the creditors are payable solely from collections of the special assessment installments and interest thereon, the proceeds of special assessment long-term debt should be credited to a capital projects other financing source's account such as Contribution from Property Owners rather than as Proceeds of Bonds (or Notes).

General capital assets financed wholly or partially through collections of special assessments are recorded in the same manner as any other general capital assets in the governmental activities category at the government-wide level.

Financial Reporting for Capital Projects Funds

Each capital projects fund that meets the definition of a *major fund* (see the Glossary for a definition) must be reported in a separate column of the balance sheet—governmental funds (see Illustration A1–3) and the statement of revenues, expenditures, and changes in fund balances—governmental funds (see Illustration A1–5). Nonmajor capital projects funds would be reported in the same column as other nonmajor governmental funds in these two basic financial statements.

Governments are also encouraged but not required to provide as supplementary information combining financial statements for all nonmajor funds. Combining financial statements present each nonmajor fund as a separate column. These statements usually would not be included within the scope of the auditor's examination other than indirectly as part of the audit of the basic financial statements.

The required basic financial statements and notes thereto, along with the recommended combining financial statements, should meet most external report users' needs for information about capital projects funds. Internal management and those with oversight responsibility for capital projects may need additional information, however, of a more detailed nature. Additional information that may be useful for internal management or oversight purposes includes information about whether the amount and quality of work accomplished to date is commensurate with resources expended to date and project plans, and whether the remaining work can be accomplished within the established deadlines with remaining resources.

Key Terms

Arbitrage rebate, *195*
Asset impairment, *180*
Bond anticipation notes, *193*
Capital improvements fund, *183*
Capital leases, *177*
Capital projects fund, *169*
Force account construction, *175*
General capital assets, *169*
Historical cost, *170*
Infrastructure assets, *176*
Intangible assets, *177*
Interfund transfers, *188*
Modified approach, *176*
Operating leases, *178*
Special assessment, *197*

Selected References

Financial Accounting Standards Board. *Statement of Financial Accounting Standards No. 6,* "Classification of Short-Term Obiligations Expected to Be Refinanced." Norwalk, CT, 1975.

Statement of Financial Accounting Standards No. 13, "Accounting for Leases as Amended and Interpreted through April 2002." Norwalk, CT, 2002.

Governmental Accounting Standards Board. *Codification of Governmental Accounting and Financial Reporting Standards, as of June 30, 2008.* Norwalk, CT, 2008.

Questions

5–1. What are general capital assets? How are they reported?

5–2. Explain what disclosures the GASB requires for capital assets in the notes to the financial statements.

5–3. What is the difference between using the modified approach to accounting for infrastructure assets and depreciating infrastructure assets? Under the modified approach, what happens if infrastructure assets are not maintained at or above the established condition level?

5–4. How does one determine whether a particular lease is a capital lease or an operating lease? What entries are required in the general journals of a governmental fund and governmental activities at the government-wide level to record a capital lease at its inception?

5–5. Compare the reporting of intangible assets under GASB and FASB standards.

5–6. What is the purpose of a capital projects fund? Give some examples of projects that might be considered capital projects.

5–7. If a capital project is incomplete at the end of a fiscal year, why is it considered desirable to close Encumbrances and all operating statement accounts at year-end? Why is it desirable to reestablish the Encumbrances account as of the first day of the following year?

5–8. Which expenditures of a capital projects fund should be capitalized to Construction Work in Progress? Is Construction Work in Progress included in the chart of accounts of a capital projects fund? If not, where would it be found?

5–9. The county replaced its old office building with a new structure. Rather than destroy the old office building, the county decided to convert the old building and use it as a storage facility. Why would the old office building need to be evaluated for impairment? If it was decided the building was impaired, what would be the most appropriate method for estimating the degree of impairment?

5–10. Compare the accounting for capital projects financed by special assessment bonds when (*a*) a government assumes responsibility for debt service should special assessment collections be insufficient, as opposed to (*b*) the government assumes no responsibility whatsoever.

Cases

5–1 Using the Modified Approach or Depreciation. You are an auditor in a regional public accounting firm that does a large volume of governmental audits and consulting engagements. A large metropolitan city has asked you for assistance in determining whether it should use the modified approach or depreciate its infrastructure assets. The city is particularly interested in which accounting approach other large metropolitan cities have chosen.

Required

a. Examine several comprehensive annual financial reports (CAFRs) of large cities prepared following *GASBS 34.* (Note: The GASB provides a list of *GASBS 34* implementers classified by type of government with links to the governments' CAFRs, if available, at its Web site, *www.gasb.org*.) Create a table that lists the cities and the methods they have chosen to report their general infrastructure assets.

b. Prepare a memo to your client summarizing the results of your research. Be sure to address the city's specific concern about what other large cities are doing with respect to reporting of infrastructure assets.

c. Your client has heard that the Government Finance Officers Association (GFOA) may still award a Certificate of Achievement for Excellence in Financial Reporting if a government decides that the costs of capitalizing and depreciating (or of using the modified approach for) infrastructure assets outweighs the benefits, assuming that all other criteria are met. What other consequences can you point out to your client if it decides not to capitalize and report infrastructure assets.

5–2 Options for Financing Public Infrastructure. Desert City is a rapidly growing city in the Southwest, with a current population of 200,000. To cope with the growing vehicular traffic and the need for infrastructure expansion (e.g., streets, sidewalks, lighting, storm water drains, and sewage systems) to stay abreast of the pace of residential and commercial development, members of the city council have recently engaged in debate about the merits of alternative mechanisms for financing infrastructure expansion. The two alternatives the council is exploring are: (1) a sales tax referendum to increase an existing one-half cent capital improvement tax by one-quarter cent on every dollar of sales, and (2) a development fee of $0.50 per square foot imposed on real estate developers for new residential and commercial buildings.

Public debate at recent city council meetings has been contentious, with developers arguing that the burden for infrastructure improvements would be disproportionately placed on homeowners and businesses, whereas reliance on a sales tax increase would permit part of the infrastructure burden to be borne by nonresidents who shop in and otherwise enjoy the benefits of Desert City. Developers have also argued that more of the existing one-half-cent capital improvement tax should be spent for street and sidewalk improvements and less should be spent for improvement of public buildings, parks, and hiking trails.

Proponents of the proposed real estate development fee argue that new residential and commercial building is the main factor driving the growing demand for infrastructure development. Thus, they argue, it is most appropriate that new residents and new businesses shoulder much of the burden for expanding infrastructure. They further argue that the development fee will result in only a modest, largely invisible increase in the cost of each new building. Moreover, the incremental cost of the development fee should be recaptured as property values increase as a result of enhanced infrastructure. Finally, they argue that Desert City citizens enjoy better health and a generally higher quality life as a result of park and hiking trail improvements and that the existing one-half cent sales tax should continue to support recreational facilities.

Required

a. Evaluate the advantages and disadvantages of each potential financing option from the viewpoint of (1) a city council member, (2) the city manager, (3) current home-owners and business owners, and (4) potential new homeowners or new business owners.

b. Would accounting for infrastructure construction be impacted by the choice of financing method? Yes or No? Explain.

5–3 Recording and Reporting of Damaged Capital Assets. Recent river flooding damaged a part of the Town of Brownville Library. The library building is over 70 years old and is located in a part of the town that is on the national historic preservation register. Some of the costs related to the damage included the following:

1. The building wiring had to be replaced. Since the wiring was over 20 years old, replacing the wiring allowed the town to bring the wiring up to current code and accommodate the increasing technology needs of the library.
2. A large section of the interior walls (dry-wall) of the library had to be replaced and painted. The same type of material was used in replacing the interior walls.
3. All hardwood floors were replaced with the same materials.
4. Over 30,000 books suffered water damage.

Required

a. Discuss whether the fact that the library building is in the historic part of town has any role in determining how to record and report the damage and repairs to the library.

b. Discuss how to determine if the library should be considered impaired and, if it is impaired, how accounting and reporting should be handled.

c. Discuss whether you would classify the costs incurred to repair the building as enhancements or replacements.

d. What information would you want before determining how to record and report the damage to the books?

Exercises and Problems

5–1 Examine the CAFR. Utilizing the CAFR obtained for Exercise 1–1, answer these questions.

a. **General and Other Capital Assets:**

(1) **Reporting of Capital Assets.** Are capital assets reported as a line-item in the government-wide statement of net assets? Are nondepreciable capital assets reported on a separate line from depreciable capital assets, or are they separately reported in the notes to the financial statements? Do the notes include capital asset disclosures, such as those for the City and County of Denver shown in Illustration 5–2? Does the disclosure show beginning balances, increases and decreases, and ending balances for each major class of capital assets, as well as the same information for accumulated depreciation for each major class? Are these disclosures presented separately for the capital assets of governmental activities, business-type activities, and discretely presented component units? Do the notes specify capitalization thresholds for all capital assets, including infrastructure? Do the notes show the amounts of depreciation expense

assigned to each major function or program for governmental activities at the government-wide level? Are the depreciation policies and estimated lives of major classes of depreciable assets disclosed? Do the notes include the entity's policies regarding capitalization of collections of works of art and historical treasures? Are accounting policies disclosed for assets acquired under capital leases?

(2) **Other.** Is the accumulated cost of construction work in progress recorded as an asset anywhere? In your opinion, is the information disclosed about construction work in progress and construction commitments adequate? Which fund, or funds, account for cash received, or receivables created, from sales of general capital assets? Are the proceeds of sales of general capital assets reported as an other financing source or as revenue?

b. **Capital Projects Funds:**

(1) **Title and Content.** What title is given to the funds that function as capital projects funds, as described in this chapter? (Street Improvement Funds and Capital Improvement Funds are common titles, although these titles also are often used for special revenue funds that account for ongoing annual maintenance of roadways.) Where does the report state the basis of accounting used for capital projects funds? Is the basis used consistent with GASB standards discussed in this chapter? Are there separate capital projects funds for each project, are there several funds, each of which accounts for related projects, or is only one fund used for all projects?

(2) **Statements and Schedules.** What statements and schedules pertaining to capital projects funds are presented? In what respects (headings, arrangement, items included, etc.) do they seem similar to statements illustrated or described in the text? In what respects do they differ? Are any differences merely a matter of terminology or arrangement, or do they represent significant deviations from GASB accounting and reporting standards for capital projects funds?

(3) **Financial Resource Inflows.** What is the nature of the financial resource inflows utilized by the capital projects funds? If tax-supported bonds or special assessment bonds are the source, have any been sold at a premium? At a discount? If so, what was the accounting treatment of the bond premium or discount?

(4) **Fund Expenditures.** How much detail is given concerning capital projects fund expenditures? Is the detail sufficient to meet the information needs of administrators? Legislators? Creditors? Grantors? Interested residents? For projects that are incomplete at the date of the financial statement, does the report compare the percentage of total authorization for each project expended to date with the percentage of completion? For those projects completed during the fiscal year, does the report compare the total expenditures for each project with the authorization for each project? For each cost overrun, how was the overrun financed?

(5) **Assets Acquired under Capital Leases.** Were any general capital assets acquired by the primary government or one or more component units under a capital lease agreement during the year for which you have statements? If so, was the present value of minimum lease rentals recorded as an Expenditure and as an Other Financing Source in a capital projects fund (or in any other governmental fund)? If the primary government or one or more component units leased assets from another component unit,

how are the assets, related liabilities, expenditures, and other financing sources reported in the basic financial statements or in another section of the CAFR of the reporting entity?

5–2 Multiple Choice. Choose the best answer.

1. Under GASB standards, which of the following would be considered an example of an intangible asset?
   a. A lake located on city property.
   b. Water rights associated with the springs that supply the water to the lake.
   c. The city's irrigation system, which uses water from the lake.
   d. None of the above would be considered an intangible asset.
2. Four new desktop computers, for which the cost exceeded the city's capitalization threshold, were purchased for use in the city clerk's office using General Fund resources. Which of the following entries would be required to completely record this transaction?

		Debits	Credits
a.	*General Fund:*		
	Expenditures	8,000	
	Vouchers Payable		8,000
b.	*Governmental Activities:*		
	Expenses	8,000	
	Vouchers Payable		8,000
c.	*General Fund:*		
	Expenditures	8,000	
	Vouchers Payable		8,000
	Governmental Activities:		
	Expenses	8,000	
	Vouchers Payable		8,000
d.	*General Fund:*		
	Expenditures	8,000	
	Vouchers Payable		8,000
	Governmental Activities:		
	Equipment	8,000	
	Vouchers Payable		8,000

3. Which of the following capital assets would *not* be depreciated?
   a. The city's street lights.
   b. Purchased computer software.
   c. The partially completed city hall.
   d. The art work owned and displayed in the city parks.
4. A capital projects fund would probably not be used for which of the following assets?
   a. Construction and installation of new shelving in the mayor's office.
   b. Financing and construction of three new fire substations.
   c. Purchase and installation of an entity-wide integrated computer system (such as SAP or Oracle).
   d. Replacing a bridge.

5. Machinery and equipment depreciation expense for general capital assets totaled $163,000 for the reporting period. Which of the following correctly defines the recording of depreciation for general capital assets?

	Debits	Credits
a. Depreciation Expenditure	163,000	
Accumulated Depreciation.		163,000
b. Depreciation Expense	163,000	
Machinery and Equipment.		163,000

c. Depreciation is allocated, and recorded at the government-wide level with a debit to the functions or programs of government and a credit to accumulated depreciation.

d. Since depreciation does not involve the use of financial resources it is not necessary for the government to record it at the fund level or government-wide level.

6. Which of the following is a correct statement regarding the use of the *modified approach* for accounting for eligible infrastructure assets?

a. Depreciation on eligible infrastructure assets need not be recorded if the assets are being maintained at or above the established condition level.

b. Depreciation on eligible infrastructure assets must still be recorded for informational purposes only.

c. The government must document that it is maintaining eligible infrastructure assets at the condition level prescribed by the GASB.

d. All of the above are correct statements.

7. A government experienced significant loss of certain roadways and bridges as a result of major flooding. Which of the following estimation approaches would be most useful in estimating the amount of asset impairment that has occurred?

a. Deflated depreciated replacement cost approach.

b. Service units approach.

c. Restorative cost approach.

d. None of the above; each of these three approaches would be equally useful.

8. Callaway County issued $10,000,000 in bonds at 101 for the purpose of constructing a new County Recreation Center. State law requires that any premium on bond issues be deposited directly in a debt service fund for eventual repayment of bond principal. The journal entry to record issuance of the bonds will require a (an):

a. Credit to Bonds Payable in the capital projects fund.

b. Credit to Other Financing Sources—Proceeds of Bonds in the capital projects fund.

c. Credit to Other Financing Sources—Premium on Bonds in the debt service fund.

d. Both *b* and *c* are correct.

9. The primary reason for reestablishing the Encumbrance account balance at the beginning of the second and subsequent years of a multiple-year capital project is that:

a. The project continues beyond a single year; thus it is important that the Encumbrances account show the amount of contractual commitment remaining on the project.

b. This procedure allows the accountant to record a normal reversal of encumbrances when the next project billing is received.

c. This procedure corrects for an erroneous closure of the Encumbrances account at the end of the preceding year.
d. Failure to reestablish the Encumbrances account balance is a violation of GASB standards.

10. In 2011 the city started and completed installation of curbs and sidewalks in a new subdivision. The project was funded through special assessments. The first $500,000 installment on $2,500,000 in special assessments was received and recorded in the capital projects fund in 2011. Over the next four years the remaining special assessments are due. How would the receipt of the special assessment funds be recorded in the capital projects fund in 2011?

	Debits	Credits
a. Cash	500,000	
Special Assessments Receivable	2,000,000	
Revenues		500,000
Deferred Revenue		2,000,000
b. Cash	500,000	
Revenues		500,000
c. Cash	500,000	
Other Financing Sources—Assessments		500,000
d. Cash	2,500,000	
Revenues		500,000
Due to Debt Service Fund		2,000,000

5–3 General Capital Assets. Make all necessary entries in the appropriate governmental fund general journal and the government-wide governmental activities general journal for each of the following transactions entered into by the City of Fordache.

1. The city received a donation of land that is to be used by Parks and Recreation for a park. At the time of the donation, the land had a fair value of $5,200,000 and was recorded on the donor's books at a historical cost of $4,500,000.
2. The Public Works Department sold machinery with a historical cost of $35,100 and accumulated depreciation of $28,700 for $6,400. The machinery had originally been purchased with special revenue funds.
3. A car was leased for the mayor's use. Since the term of the lease exceeded 75 percent of the useful life of the car, the lease was capitalized. The first payment was $550 and the present value of the remaining lease payments was $30,000.
4. During the current year, a capital projects fund completed a new public safety building that was started in the prior year. The total cost of the project was $9,720,000. Financing for the project came from a $9,000,000 bond issue that was sold in the prior year, and from a $720,000 federal capital grant received in the current year. Current year expenditures for the project totaled $1,176,000. The full cost is attributed to the building since it was constructed on city-owned property.
5. Due to technological developments, the city determined that the service capacity of some of the technology equipment used by general government had been impaired. The calculated impairment loss due to technology obsolescence was $1,156,000.

5–4 Capital Asset Disclosures. Lynn County has prepared the following schedule related to its capital asset activity for the fiscal year 2011. Lynn County has governmental activities only, with no business-type activities.

LYNN COUNTY
Capital Asset Disclosures
For the Year Ended December 31, 2011

	January 1	Change	December 31
Total capital assets not being depreciated (land, infrastructure, and construction work in progress)	$61,721,000	$ 9,158,000	$70,879,000
Total capital assets being depreciated (buildings, equipment, and collections)	13,421,000	1,647,000	15,068,000
Less total accumulated depreciation	(3,464,000)	(558,000)	(4,022,000)
Capital assets, net	$71,678,000	$10,247,000	$81,925,000

Required

a. Does the above capital asset footnote disclosure comply with the GASB requirements? Explain.

b. Does the county use the modified approach to account for infrastructure assets? Explain.

c. What percentage of the useful life of the depreciable assets remains?

5–5 Capital Assets Acquired under Lease Agreements. Crystal City signed a lease agreement with East Coast Builders, Inc., under which East Coast will construct a new office building for the city at a cost of $12 million and lease it to the city for 30 years. The city agrees to make an initial payment of $847,637 and annual payments in the same amount for the next 29 years. An assumed borrowing rate of 6 percent was used in calculating lease payments. Upon completion, the building had an appraised market value of $13 million and an estimated life of 40 years.

Required

a. Using the criteria presented in this chapter, determine whether Crystal City should consider this lease agreement a capital lease. Explain your decision.

b. Provide the journal entries Crystal City should make for both the capital projects fund and governmental activities at the government-wide level to record the lease at the date of inception.

5–6 Asset Impairment. On July 20, 2011, the building occupied by Sunshine City's Parks and Recreation Department suffered severe structural damage as a result of a hurricane. It had been 48 years since a hurricane had hit the Sunshine City area, although hurricanes in Sunshine City's geographic area are not uncommon. The building had been purchased in 2001 at a cost of $2,000,000 and had accumulated depreciation of $500,000 as of July 2011. Based on a restoration cost analysis, city engineers estimate the impairment loss at $230,000; however, the city expects during the next fiscal year to receive insurance recoveries of $120,000 for the damage.

Required

a. Should the estimated impairment loss be reported as an extraordinary item? As a special item? Explain.

b. Record the estimated impairment loss in the journal for governmental activities at the government-wide level.

c. How should the insurance recovery be reported in the following fiscal year? (You need not provide the journal entry or entries here.)

5–7 Recording Capital Projects Fund Transactions. In Erikus County, the Parks and Recreation Department constructed a library in one of the county's high growth areas. The construction was funded by a number of sources. Below is selected information related to the funding and closing of the Library Capital Project Fund. All activity related to the library construction occurred within the 2011 fiscal year.

1. The county issued $6,000,000, 4 percent bonds, with interest payable semiannually on June 30 and December 31. The bonds sold for 101 on July 30, 2010. Proceeds from the bonds were to be used for construction of the library, with all interest and premiums received to be used to service the debt issue.
2. A $650,000 federal grant was received to help finance construction of the library.
3. The Library Special Revenue Fund transferred $250,000 for use in construction of the library.
4. A construction contract was awarded in the amount of $6,800,000.
5. The library was completed on June 1, 2011, four months ahead of schedule. Total construction expenditures for the library amounted to $6,890,000. When the project was completed, the cost of the library was allocated as follows: $200,000 to land, $6,295,000 to building, and the remainder to equipment.
6. The capital projects fund was closed. It was determined that remaining funds were related to the bond issue, and thus they were appropriately transferred to the debt service fund.

Required

Make all necessary entries in the capital projects fund general journal and the governmental activities general journal at the government-wide level.

5–8 Statement of Revenues, Expenditures, and Changes in Fund Balance. The pre-closing trial balance for the Annette County Public Works Capital Project Fund is provided below.

	Debits	***Credits***
Cash	$ 701,000	
Grant Receivable	500,000	
Investments	800,000	
Contract Payable		$ 835,000
Contract Payable—Retained Percentage		24,000
Reserve for Encumbrances		1,500,000
Revenues		680,000
Encumbrances	1,500,000	
Construction Expenditures	3,338,000	
Other Financing Sources—Proceeds of Bonds		3,800,000
	$6,839,000	$6,839,000

Required

a. Prepare the June 30, 2011, statement of revenues, expenditures, and changes in fund balance for the capital projects fund.

b. Has the capital project been completed? Explain your answer.

5–9 Construction Fund. During FY 2011, the voters of the Town of Dex approved constructing and equipping a recreation center to be financed by tax-supported bonds in the amount of $3,000,000. During 2011, the following events and transactions occurred.

1. Preliminary planning and engineering expenses in the amount of $60,000 were incurred. No money was immediately available for paying these costs (credit Vouchers Payable).
2. A contract was let under competitive bids for a major segment of the construction project in the amount of $2,500,000.
3. An invoice for $1,600,000 was received from a contractor for a portion of work that had been completed under the general contract.
4. The bond issue was sold at par plus accrued interest of $25,000 (the accrued interest was deposited in the fund that will service the bonded debt).
5. The contractor's bill, less a 4 percent retention, was vouchered for payment.
6. All vouchers payable, except $1,300 (about which there was some controversy), were paid.
7. Fiscal year-end closing entries were prepared.

Required

a. Prepare journal entries to record the preceding information in the Town of Dex Recreation Center Construction Fund and the governmental activities general journal at the government-wide level.

b. Prepare a Town of Dex Recreation Center Construction Fund balance sheet for the year ended December 31, 2011.

c. Prepare a Recreation Center Construction Fund statement of revenues, expenditures, and changes in fund balance for the year ended December 31, 2011.

d. How would these capital expenditures for the recreation center appear on the Town of Dex's government-wide statements of net assets and activities?

5–10 Capital Project Transactions. In 2011, Falts City began work to improve certain streets to be financed by a bond issue and supplemented by a federal grant. Estimated total cost of the project was $4,000,000; $2,500,000 was to come from the bond issue, and the balance from the federal grant. The capital projects fund to account for the project was designated as the Street Improvement Fund. The following transactions occurred in 2011:

1. Issued $100,000 of 6 percent bond anticipation notes to be repaid from the proceeds of bonds in 180 days.
2. The federal grant was recorded as a receivable; half of the grant is to be paid to Falts City in 2011 and the remainder late in 2012. The grantor specifies that the portion to be received in 2012 is not available for use until 2012 because there is no guarantee that the federal government will appropriate the 2012 portion.
3. A contract was let to Appel Construction Company for the major part of the project on a bid of $2,700,000.

4. An invoice received from the city's Stores and Services Fund for supplies provided to the Street Improvement Fund in the amount of $60,000 was approved for payment. (This amount had not been encumbered.)
5. Preliminary planning and engineering costs of $69,000 were paid to the Mid-Atlantic Engineering Company. (This cost had not been encumbered.)
6. A voucher payable was recorded for an $18,500 billing from the local telephone company for the cost of moving some of its underground properties necessitated by the street project.
7. An invoice in the amount of $1,000,000 was received from Appel for progress to date on the project. The invoice was consistent with the terms of the contract, and a liability was recorded in the amount of $1,000,000.
8. Cash received during 2011 was as follows:

From federal government	$ 750,000
From sale of bonds at par	2,500,000

9. The bond anticipation notes and interest thereon were repaid (see Transaction 1). Interest is an expenditure of the capital projects fund and, per GASB standards, will *not* be capitalized as part of the cost of street improvements.
10. The amount billed by the contractor (see Transaction 7) less 5 percent retainage was paid.
11. Temporary investments were purchased at a cost of $1,800,000.
12. Closing entries were prepared as of December 31, 2011.

Required

a. Prepare journal entries to record the preceding information in the general ledger accounts for the Street Improvement Fund. (You may ignore the entries that would also be required in the governmental activities general journal at the government-wide level.)

b. Prepare a balance sheet for the Street Improvement Fund as of December 31, 2011.

c. Prepare a statement of revenues, expenditures, and changes in fund balance for the period, assuming that the date of authorization was July 1, 2011.

Chapter **Six**

Accounting for General Long-term Liabilities and Debt Service

Learning Objectives

After studying this chapter, you should be able to:

1. Explain what types of liabilities are classified as general long-term liabilities.
2. Make journal entries in the governmental activities general journal to record the issuance and repayment of general long-term debt.
3. Prepare note disclosures for general long-term debt.
4. Describe the reasons for statutory debt limits and explain the terms *debt margin* and *overlapping debt*.
5. Explain the purpose and types of debt service funds.
6. Describe budgeting for debt service funds and make appropriate journal entries to account for activities of debt service funds.

The use of long-term debt is a traditional part of the fiscal policy of state and local governments, particularly for financing the acquisition of general capital assets. Although some governments have issued taxable debt, the interest earned on most debt issued by state and local governments is exempt from federal taxation and, in some states, from state taxation. The tax-exempt feature enables governments to raise large amounts of capital at relatively low cost. For example, from 2000 to 2007, total long-term debt outstanding for state and local governments increased by 83 percent to $2.19 trillion.[1] Because of the relative ease with which governments can issue debt, most states have acted in the public interest to impose statutory limits on the debt that can be incurred by state and local governments. Consequently, effective management of state and local governmental debt requires good legal advice and a sound understanding of public finance.

This chapter describes the types of debt and other long-term liabilities that are termed "general long-term liabilities." **General long-term liabilities** are those that arise from activities of governmental funds and that are not reported as fund liabilities of a proprietary or fiduciary fund. General long-term liabilities are

[1] U.S. Federal Reserve, *Federal Reserve Statistical Release,* "Flow of Funds Accounts of the United States," Washington, D.C., Federal Reserve, June 9, 2008, Table D.3, p. 8.

reported as liabilities in the Governmental Activities column of the government-wide statement of net assets but are not reported as liabilities of governmental funds. This chapter also discusses the concepts of direct and overlapping debt, statutory debt limit, and debt margin. Finally, the chapter explains the nature and types of debt service funds, and debt service accounting at the fund and government-wide levels for various types of general long-term liabilities, as well as accounting for refunding of debt.

GENERAL LONG-TERM LIABILITIES

Long-term liabilities include obligations arising out of financing activities, such as the issuance of bonds and notes, and capital leases. In addition, long-term liabilities can arise out of the operating activities of governments. Examples of long-term liabilities related to operating activities include claims and judgments, compensated absences, pensions and other post-employment benefits, and obligations related to landfills and pollution remediation. The primary focus of this chapter is general long-term liabilities arising from financing activities. However, since pollution remediation obligations are usually general long-term liabilities, these obligations are briefly discussed later in this section. Other types of long-term liabilities are discussed in Chapter 7 (landfill obligations) and Chapter 8 (pensions and other post-employment benefits).

Accounting for Long-term Liabilities

When studying this chapter, the reader is reminded that governmental fund types (General, special revenue, capital projects, debt service, and permanent funds) account for only short-term liabilities to be paid from fund assets.[2] Although, as described in Chapter 5, the proceeds of long-term debt may be placed in one of these fund types (usually a capital projects fund), the long-term liability itself must be recorded in the governmental activities accounting records at the government-wide level. Proprietary funds and perhaps certain private-purpose trust funds account for both long-term debt serviced by the fund and short-term debt to be repaid from fund assets.

As discussed in subsequent chapters, the liabilities of enterprise funds should be displayed on the face of the statement of the issuing fund if that fund may realistically be expected to finance the debt service; however, if the liability also is secondarily backed by the full faith and credit of the government, the contingent general obligation liability of the government should be disclosed in a note to the financial statements. The contingent obligation to assume debt service of long-term debt backed primarily by special assessments is acknowledged by reporting such debt in the government-wide financial statement as "special assessment debt with governmental commitment."[3] Any portion of such debt that will be repaid directly by the

[2] Conceivably a permanent fund could have a long-term liability, for example, if a permanent fund consisted of a gift of income-producing real property that the government accepted subject to a long-term mortgage note. In establishing the permanent fund as a governmental fund type, the GASB cited its belief that most such funds hold only financial resources (e.g., investments in financial securities and cash). Thus, it is not clear whether any permanent funds in practice hold assets other than financial assets. If not, the probability is low that any permanent funds have long-term liabilities. Moreover, *GASBS 34* provides no guidance on how income-producing real property and long-term liabilities could be accounted for as a governmental fund.

[3] GASB *Codification,* Sec. 1500.109.

government (for example, to finance the portion of a special assessment project deemed to have public benefit) should be reported like any other general long-term liabilities of the government.

Bonds and other debt of enterprise funds issued with covenants that give the debt the status, even contingently, of **tax-supported debt** may affect the government's ability to issue additional tax-supported debt. The reason for this is discussed under the heading "Debt Limit and Debt Margin" in this chapter. If the contingency clause becomes effective because resources of the enterprise fund are insufficient for debt service, the unpaid portion of the debt is recorded as a liability of the governmental activities at the government-wide level. The enterprise fund that is relieved of the liability then removes the unpaid debt from its liability accounts and recognizes an interfund transfer, which is reported after the nonoperating revenues (expenses) section of the proprietary funds statement of revenues, expenses, and changes in fund net assets.

From the discussions earlier in this section and in Chapter 5, it should be evident that entries are ordinarily made in the governmental activities general journal at the government-wide level to reflect increases or decreases in general long-term liabilities that also require entries in the accounts of one or more governmental funds. As shown in illustrative Entries 8a and 8b in Chapter 5, most increases in general long-term liabilities arising from debt issuances are recorded as an other financing source in a governmental fund and as a general long-term liability at the government-wide level. Increases in long-term liabilities that arise from operating activities, for example, estimated losses from long-term claims and judgments, are recorded at the government-wide level by debiting an expense and crediting a liability. Except for certain defeasances, as discussed later in this chapter, most general long-term liabilities are settled by the payment of cash from a governmental fund.

Pollution Remediation Obligations

The recently implemented Governmental Accounting Standards Board (GASB) *Statement No. 49* addresses accounting and reporting for pollution remediation obligations. **Pollution remediation obligations** arise from responsibilities related to the cleanup of hazardous wastes or hazardous substances resulting from existing pollution. A liability related to pollution remediation should be recognized if it is reasonably estimable and an obligating event has occurred. GASB identifies five types of obligating events: (1) the government is compelled to take remediation action due to imminent endangerment to the public health, (2) a violation of a pollution prevention permit has occurred, (3) the government is named or will be named as the responsible or potentially responsible party to a remediation, (4) the government has been or will be named in a lawsuit requiring its participation in remediation, and (5) the government commences or legally obligates itself to commence remediation.[4] Once it is deemed that an obligating event has occurred and the liability, or any component of the liability, is reasonably estimable, the liability is measured using the expected cash flow technique. Periodically, the amount of the estimated liability must be reevaluated. GASB identifies several stages or benchmarks in the remediation process where a reevaluation of the estimated liability should occur. In addition to recognizing the estimated liability, several note disclosures should be prepared to provide the reader with information concerning the liability and how the estimated liability was derived.

[4] *GASBS 49*, par. 11.

Long-term Liability Disclosures

In any given year, it is common for new debt issues to be authorized, for previously authorized debt to be issued, and for older issues to be retired. When a combination of liability events takes place, a schedule detailing changes in long-term debt is needed to inform report users of the details of how long-term liabilities have changed. The general long-term liability disclosures required by *GASBS 34* effectively meet these needs by providing detail of beginning of period long-term liabilities, additions to and reductions of those liabilities, ending liabilities, and the portion of the liabilities payable within one year. Illustration 6–1 presents this disclosure schedule for the City and County of Denver.

In addition to the disclosures about long-term liabilities presented in Illustration 6–1, information about the amount of debt principal and interest that will be due in future years is useful information to financial managers, bond analysts, and others having an interest in assessing a government's requirements for future debt service expenditures. One form of such a schedule, representing a disclosure from the notes to the financial statements for the City and County of Denver, prepared in conformity with GASB standards, is shown in Illustration 6–2. The reader should note that the interest portion of the scheduled future debt service payments is *not* a present liability and should not be presented as such. To do so would not be in conformity with generally accepted accounting principles.

Debt Limit and Debt Margin

The information provided in the debt schedules already illustrated in this chapter is primarily useful to administrators, legislative bodies, credit analysts, and others concerned with the impact of long-term debt on the financial condition and activities of the government, particularly with reference to the resulting tax rates and taxes. Another matter of importance is the legal limit on the amount of long-term indebtedness that may be outstanding at a given time, in proportion to the assessed value of property within the government's jurisdiction. This type of restriction is an important protection for taxpayers against possible confiscatory tax rates. Even though tax-rate limitation laws may be in effect for a government, the limitation on bonded indebtedness is usually needed because the prevailing practice is to exempt the claims of bondholders from any tax-rate restrictions. This is to say that, even though a law establishing maximums for tax rates is in the statutes, it will probably exclude debt service requirements from the restrictions of the law. This exclusion may be reiterated in the bond covenants.

Before continuing a discussion of debt limitation, it seems appropriate to clarify the meaning of the terms *debt limit* and *debt margin*. **Debt limit** means the total amount of indebtedness of specified kinds that is allowed by law to be outstanding at any one time. The limitation is likely to be in terms of a specified percentage of the assessed or actual valuation of property within the government's jurisdiction. It may relate to either a gross or a net valuation. The latter is logical but probably not prevalent because debt limitation exists as a device for protecting property owners from confiscatory taxation. For that reason, tax-paying property *only* should be used in regulating maximum indebtedness. In many governmental jurisdictions, certain property is legally excluded even from *assessment*. This includes property owned by governments, churches, charitable organizations, and some others, depending on state laws. Exemptions, which apply to property subject to assessment, are based on homestead or mortgage exemption laws, military service, and economic status, among others. Both exclusions and exemptions reduce the amount of tax-paying property.

Debt margin, sometimes referred to as *borrowing power,* is the difference between the amount of debt limit calculated as prescribed by law and the net amount of outstanding indebtedness subject to limitation. The net amount of outstanding indebtedness subject to limitation differs from total general long-term indebtedness because certain debt issues may be exempted from the limitation by law, and the amount available in debt service funds for debt repayment is deducted from the outstanding debt in order to determine the amount subject to the legal debt limit. Total general long-term indebtedness must, in some jurisdictions, include special assessment debt and debt serviced by enterprise funds if such debt was issued with covenants that give the debt tax-supported status in the event that collections of special assessments or enterprise fund revenues are insufficient to meet required interest or principal payments. Debt authorized but not issued as of the end of a fiscal year should be considered in evaluating debt margin, as it may be sold at any time. Although it would be in keeping with the purpose of establishing a legal debt limit to include the present value of capital lease obligations along with bonded debt in the computation of legal debt margin, state statutes at present generally do not specify that the liability for capital lease obligations is subject to the legal debt limit. The computation of the legal debt margin for the City and County of Denver is shown in Illustration 6–3. The upper portion of Illustration 6–4 shows a schedule that presents the City and County of Denver's debt burden for the past 10 years, a statistic closely watched by bond rating analysts and others.

Overlapping Debt

Debt limitation laws ordinarily establish limits that may not be exceeded by each separate governmental entity affected by the laws. This means the county government may incur indebtedness to the legal limit, a township within that county may do likewise, and a city within the township may become indebted to the legal limit, with no restriction because of debt already owed by larger territorial units in which it is located. As a result, a given parcel of real estate or object of personal property may be the basis of debt beyond the legal limit and also may be subject at a given time to assessments for the payment of taxes to retire bonds issued by two or more governments. When this situation exists, it is described as **overlapping debt.**

The extent to which debt may overlap depends on the number of governments represented within an area that are authorized to incur long-term indebtedness. These may include the state, county, township, city, and various special purpose governments. To show the total amount of indebtedness being supported by taxable property located within the boundaries of the reporting government, a statement of direct and overlapping debt should be prepared. Direct debt is the debt that is being serviced by the reporting government. To this direct debt should be added amounts owed by other governments that levy taxes against the same properties on which the direct debt is based. A statement of direct and overlapping debt for the City and County of Denver is presented in the lower portion of Illustration 6–4. Note that the overlapping debt applies to four special purpose governments, including the school district, that levy taxes on certain properties within the boundaries of the City and County of Denver.

ILLUSTRATION 6–1 **Illustrative Long-term Liabilities Disclosure**

CITY AND COUNTY OF DENVER, COLORADO
Long-term Liabilities Disclosure
For the Year Ended December 31, 2007

Long-term liability activity for the year ended December 31, 2007, was as follows (amounts expressed in thousands):

	January 1	Additions	Deletions	December 31	Due within One Year
Governmental Activities:					
Legal liability	$ 2,500	$ —	$ 980	$ 1,520	$ 1,520
Line of credit	5,209	—	4,474	735	—
Compensated absences:					
Classified service employees—3,249	54,387	35,700	26,730	63,357	5,535
Career service employees—5,666	42,757	26,176	28,725	40,208	3,637
Claims payable	31,258	9,886	8,648	32,496	11,690
General obligation bonds[1]	473,671	9,367	58,245	424,793	41,880
GID general obligation bonds	2,725	—	205	2,520	230
Excise tax revenue bonds	313,920	—	9,815	304,105	13,175
Capitalized lease obligation[2]	430,477	—	13,563	416,914	29,758
Unamortized premium	40,415	—	4,769	35,646	4,544
Unamortized gain on refunding	2,852	—	210	2,642	210
Other governmental funds—note payable	16,082	461	2,505	14,038	—
Total Governmental Activities	$1,416,253	$81,590	$158,869	$1,338,974	$112,179

The legal liability, compensated absences, claims payable, and other accrued liabilities in the governmental activities are generally liquidated by the General Fund. The other governmental funds—note payable is liquidated by the Community Development special revenue fund. The amount available for long-term debt in the debt service funds for bonds payable and in the special revenue fund was $59,292,000.

ILLUSTRATION 6–1 (*continued*)

	January 1	Additions	Deletions	December 31	Due within One Year
Business-type Activities:					
Wastewater Management:					
Revenue bonds	$ 26,565	$ —	$ 1,135	$ 25,430	$ 1,180
Unamortized premium	78	—	5	73	—
Compensated absences	2,068	1,652	1,449	2,271	539
Total Wastewater Management	28,711	1,652	2,589	27,774	1,719
Denver Airport System:					
Revenue bonds	3,869,785	860,925	531,860	4,198,850	103,830
Unamortized premium and deferred loss on refunding	(261,884)	(5,121)	22,306	(244,699)	—
Notes payable	88,985	—	27,314	61,671	12,139
Compensated absences	6,695	798	202	7,291	1,914
Total Denver Airport System	3,703,581	856,602	581,682	4,023,113	117,883
Nonmajor enterprises funds:					
Revenue bonds	6,840	—	360	6,480	370
Unamortized premium	69	—	10	59	—
Compensated absences	654	380	250	784	169
Total nonmajor enterprise funds	7,563	380	620	7,323	539
Total Business-type Activities	$3,739,855	$858,634	$584,891	$4,058,210	$120,141
Major Component Units:					
Revenue bonds[3]	$ 545,760	$100,000	$ 4,065	$ 641,695	$ 4,535
General obligation bonds[4]	86,433	—	24,982	61,451	18,820
Capitalized lease obligations	70,742	—	6,166	64,576	7,040
Increment bonds and notes payable[5]	340,091	4,847	5,975	338,963	8,087
Customer advances	45,008	22,140	15,785	51,363	—
Compensated absences	7,082	1,907	2,152	6,837	2,365
Other post employment benefits	—	3,591	—	3,591	—
Other long-term liabilities	2,421	72	—	2,493	—
Total Major Component Units	$1,097,537	$132,557	$ 59,125	$1,170,969	$ 40,947

[1] Additions and deletions to general obligation bonds include accretion of $507.
[2] Deletions include $143 paid by an internal service fund.
[3] Includes unamortized premium of $14,978: and deferred loss on refunding of ($9,518).
[4] Includes unamortized discount of ($32) and deferred loss on refunding of ($62).
[5] Includes deferred amount on refunding of ($2,414).

Source: City and County of Denver, Colorado, Notes to Basic Financial Statements, 2007. Section III, Note G.7.

ILLUSTRATION 6–2 Future Debt Service Requirements

CITY AND COUNTY OF DENVER, COLORADO
Future Debt Service Requirements
December 31, 2007

Annual debt service requirements to maturity for general obligation bonds are as follows (amounts expressed in thousands):

	Governmental Activities				Component Unit—Water Board	
	General Government		General Improvement District			
	Principal[1]	Interest	Principal	Interest	Principal[2]	Interest
2008	$ 41,880	$ 20,361	$ 230	$100	$18,820	$ 2,931
2009	35,305	18,100	415	92	11,555	2,006
2010	23,460	16,339	545	77	3,080	1,548
2011	24,380	15,184	565	59	4,265	1,391
2012	25,375	13,982	325	39	1,595	1,178
2013–2017	142,529	53,379	360	91	7,790	4,749
2018–2022	85,475	30,327	80	5	2,890	3,660
2023–2027	44,520	4,524	—	—	—	3,233
2028–2032	—	—	—	—	11,550	1,292
Total	$422,924	$172,196	$2,520	$463	$61,545	$21,988

[1] Does not include $1,578 and $291 of compound interest on the series 1999A and 2007 mini-bonds, respectively.
[2] Does not include unamortized premium of ($32) and deferred amount on refunding of ($62).
In April 2007, the City issued $8,860,500 of General Obligation Mini-Bonds, Series 2007, for the purpose of financing a portion of the City's new Justice System Facilities. The bonds are compound interest bonds that were priced at $500 per $1,000 of principal and interest due at maturity in 2022.

Source: City and County of Denver, Colorado, Notes to Basic Financial Statements, 2007, Section III, Note G.1.

ILLUSTRATION 6–3

CITY AND COUNTY OF DENVER
Computation of Legal Debt Margin
December 31, 2007
(amounts expressed in thousands)

Total Estimated Actual Valuation	$76,813,114
Maximum general obligation debt, limited to 3% of total valuation[1]	$ 2,304,393
Outstanding bonds chargeable to limit	422,924
Less: Amount reserved for long-term debt	19,930
Net chargeable to bond limit	402,994
Legal Debt Margin—December 31	$ 1,901,399

[1] Section 7.5.2, Charter of the City and County of Denver: The City and County of Denver shall not become indebted for general obligation bonds, to any amount which, including indebtedness, shall exceed three percent of the actual value as determined by the last final assessment of the taxable property within the City and County of Denver.

Source: City and County of Denver, Colorado, Comprehensive Annual Financial Report, Statistical Section, 2007, p. 151.

ILLUSTRATION 6–4

CITY AND COUNTY OF DENVER
Ratios of General Bonded Debt Outstanding
Last Ten Fiscal Years
(dollars in thousands, except per capita amount)

	1998	1999	2000	2001	2002	2003	2004	2005	2006	2007
General obligation bonds	$237,809	$303,114	$295,740	$268,226	$280,505	$424,524	$378,977	$404,667	$472,309	$422,924
Less amounts available in debt service fund	(21,187)	(28,608)	(28,607)	(25,469)	(22,029)	(18,450)	(23,485)	(23,683)	(19,288)	(19,930)
Total	$216,622	$274,506	$267,133	$242,757	$258,476	$406,074	$355,492	$380,984	$453,021	$402,994
Percentage of estimated actual taxable value of property	0.69%	0.70%	0.66%	0.46%	0.49%	0.66%	0.57%	0.58%	0.68%	0.53%
Per capita	$ 432	$ 541	$ 482	$ 430	$ 459	$ 716	$ 621	$ 657	$ 778	$ 681

Note: Details regarding the City's outstanding debt can be found in the notes to the financial statements.

ILLUSTRATION 6–4 (*continued*)

Computation of Net Direct and Overlapping Debt
December 31, 2007
(amounts expressed in thousands)

	Debt Outstanding	Percentage Applicable	City and County of Denver Share of Debt
Direct Debt			
General long-term debt	$ 740,583		
Denver Airport System bonds	3,954,151		
Wastewater Management bonds	25,503		
Golf bonds	6,539		
Water Board bonds	346,352		
Gross Bonded Debt	5,073,128		
Less self-supporting bonds:			
Gateway Village bonds	2,463		
Golf bonds	6,539		
Excise tax revenue bonds	315,196		
Denver Airport System bonds	3,954,151		
Wastewater Management bonds	25,503		
Water Board bonds	346,352		
Less amount reserved for long-term debt	19,930		
Total Net Direct Debt	402,994		
Overlapping Debt			
Denver Metropolitan Football Stadium District	145,733	29.3%[1]	$ 42,700
Regional Transportation District	994,400	29.3%[1]	291,352
Metro Wastewater Reclamation District	82,477	41.7%[2]	34,393
School District #1	638,566	100.0%	638,566
Total Overlapping Debt	1,861,176		1,007,011
Total Net Direct and Overlapping Debt	$2,264,170		$1,410,005

[1] Percentage calculated on estimated Scientific and Cultural Facilities District sales and use tax for Denver City and County compared to State total, per the Colorado Department of Revenue, Office of Research and Analysis.
[2] Percentage calculated on Denver's wastewater charges compared to the entire metro district per Metro Wastewater Reclamation District.

Source: City and County of Denver, Colorado, Comprehensive Annual Financial Report, Statistical Section, 2007, p. 153.

DEBT SERVICE FUNDS

When long-term debt has been incurred for capital or other purposes, revenues must be raised in future years to make debt service payments. Debt service payments include both periodic interest payments and the repayment of debt principal when due. Revenues from taxes that are restricted for debt service purposes are usually recorded in a *debt service fund,* as are subsequent expenditures for payments of interest and principal. A debt service fund is used only for debt service activities related to *general* long-term liabilities—those reported in the Governmental Activities column of the government-wide statement of net assets. Debt service related to long-term liabilities reported in proprietary and fiduciary funds is reported in those funds, not in a debt service fund.

Number of Debt Service Funds

In addition to debt service for bond liabilities, debt service funds may be required to service debt arising from the use of notes or warrants having a maturity more than one year after date of issue. Debt service funds may also be used to make periodic payments required by capital lease agreements. Although each issue of long-term or intermediate-term debt is a separate obligation and may have legal restrictions and servicing requirements that differ from other issues, GASB standards provide that, if legally permissible, a single debt service fund may be used to account for the service of all issues of tax-supported and special assessment debt. Subsidiary records of that fund can provide needed assurance that budgeting and accounting meet the restrictions and requirements relating to each issue. If legal restrictions do not allow for the debt service of all issues of tax-supported and special assessment debt to be accounted for by a single debt service fund, as few additional debt service funds as is consistent with applicable laws should be created. In this chapter, a separate debt service fund for each bond issue is illustrated simply as a means of helping the reader focus on the different accounting procedures considered appropriate for each type of bond issue encountered in practice.

Use of General Fund to Account for Debt Service

In some jurisdictions, laws do not require accounting for the debt service function by a debt service fund. Unless the debt service function is very simple, it may be argued that good financial management would dictate the establishment of a debt service fund even though not required by law. If neither law nor sound financial administration requires the use of debt service funds, the function may be performed within the accounting and budgeting framework of the General Fund. In such cases, the accounting and financial reporting standards discussed in this chapter should be followed for the debt service activities of the General Fund.

Budgeting for Debt Service

In addition to possible bond indenture requirements, good politics and good financial management suggest that the debt service burden on the taxpayers be spread evenly rather than lumped in the years that debt issues or installments happen to mature. To assist with good financial management, the debt service fund is considered both a budgeting and an accounting entity. As such, a budget is prepared for the debt service fund. If taxes for payment of interest and principal on long-term debt are recorded directly in the debt service fund, they are budgeted as estimated revenues of the debt service fund. Interest on the investments recorded in the debt service fund is also budgeted as estimated revenue by the debt service fund. When recognized, taxes and interest earnings are recorded as revenues. Transfers made from other funds to the debt service fund are budgeted as an estimated other financing source and when the transfers are recognized, they are recorded as *interfund transfers in*. If resources, such as taxes, are to be raised by another fund and transferred to the debt service fund, they must be included in the revenues budget of the fund that will raise the revenue (often the General Fund). The amount to be transferred to the debt service fund will be budgeted as an estimated other financing use and recorded as an *interfund transfer out* when the transfer of funds to the debt service fund is recognized.

Although the items may be difficult to budget accurately, debt service funds can often count on receiving premiums on debt issues sold and accrued interest on debt issues sold. Accrued interest on debt sold is commonly considered as revenue of the recipient debt service fund; premium on debt sold is an other financing source. Similarly, as illustrated in Chapter 5, if capital projects are completed with expenditures less than revenues and other financing sources, the residual equity may be transferred to the appropriate debt service fund. Persons budgeting and accounting for debt service funds should seek competent legal advice on the permissible use of both premiums on debt sold and interfund transfers of the residual equity of capital projects funds. In some cases, one or both of these items must be held for eventual debt repayment and may not be used for interest payments; in other cases, both premiums and interfund transfers in of equity may be used for interest payments.

The appropriations budget of a debt service fund must provide for the payment of all interest on general long-term debt that will become legally due during the budget year and for the payment of any principal amounts that will become legally due during the budget year. GASB standards require debt service fund accounting to be on the same basis as is required for general and special revenue funds. One peculiarity of the modified accrual basis used by governmental fund types (which is not discussed in Chapter 3 because it relates only to debt service funds) is that interest on long-term debt is not accrued in the debt service fund but is accrued at the government-wide level. For example, if the fiscal year of a government ends on December 31, 2010, and the interest on its bonds is payable on January 1 and July 1 of each year, the amount payable on January 1, 2011, would not be considered a liability in the balance sheet of the debt service fund prepared as of December 31, 2010. The rationale for this recommendation is that the interest is not legally due until January 1, 2011. (See Illustration 6–5.) The same reasoning applies to principal amounts that mature on the first day of a fiscal year; they are not liabilities to be recognized in statements prepared as of the day before. In the event 2010 appropriations include January 1, 2011, interest and/or principal payment, the appropriations and expenditures (and resulting liabilities) should be recognized in 2010.

Types of Serial Bonds

Several decades ago, governmental issues of long-term debt commonly matured in total on a given date. In that era, bond indentures often required the establishment of a "sinking fund," sometimes operated on an actuarial basis. Some sinking fund term tax-supported bond issues are still outstanding, but today they are dwarfed in number and amount by serial bond issues in which the principal matures in installments. Four types of serial bond issues are found in practice: regular, deferred, annuity, and irregular. If the total principal of an issue is repayable in a specified number of equal annual installments over the life of the issue, it is a **regular serial bond** issue.

ILLUSTRATION 6–5 **Modified Accrual Basis of Recognition of Expend Long-term Debt Interest and Principal**

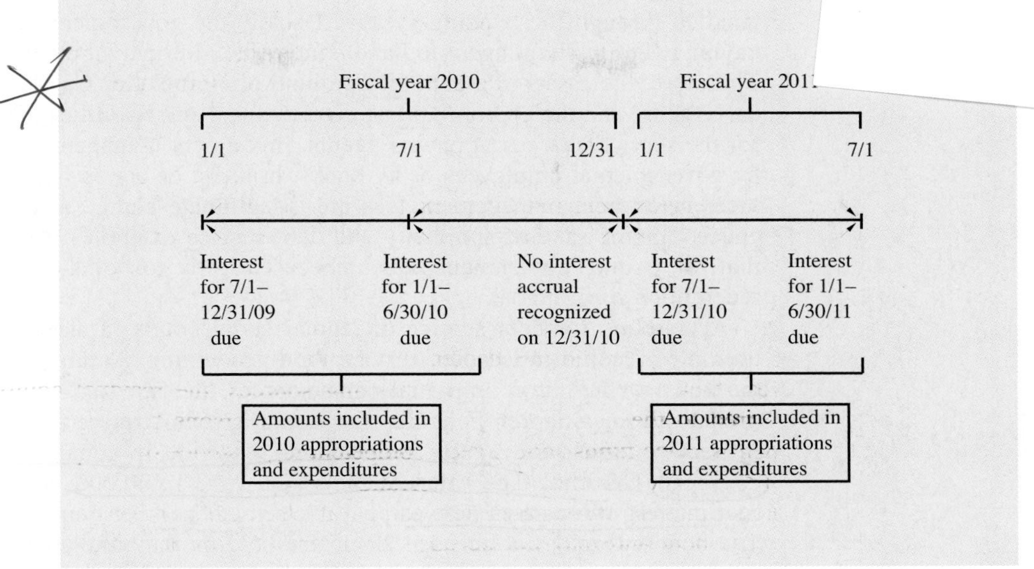

If the first installment is delayed for a period of more than one year after the date of the issue but thereafter installments fall due on a regular basis, the bonds are known as **deferred serial bonds.** If the amount of annual principal repayments is scheduled to increase each year by approximately the same amount that interest payments decrease (interest decreases because the amount of outstanding bonds decreases) so that the total debt service remains reasonably level over the term of the issue, the bonds are called **annuity serial bonds. Irregular serial bonds** may have any pattern of repayment that does not fit the other three categories.

Accounting for Regular Serial Bonds—First Year

Accounts recommended for use by debt service funds are similar to but not exactly the same as those recommended for use by the General Fund and special revenue funds. Because the number of sources of revenues and other financing sources is relatively small in a typical debt service fund, as is the number of purposes for which expenditures are made, it is generally not necessary to use control and subsidiary accounts such as those used by the General Fund. Moreover, because debt service funds do not issue purchase orders or contracts for goods and services, the use of encumbrance accounting is unnecessary. Thus, the budgetary accounts typically used for a debt service fund are Estimated Revenues, Estimated Other Financing Sources, Appropriations, Estimated Other Financing Uses, and Budgetary Fund Balance. The actual operating accounts usually include only a few revenue accounts, Other Financing Sources (for interfund transfers in and bond issue premiums), Expenditures—Bond Interest, Expenditures—Bond Principal, and, in the case of certain bond refunding transactions, Other Financing Uses. Similarly, relatively few balance sheet accounts are found in a debt service fund. Accounts typically include current asset accounts such as Cash, Investments, Taxes Receivable (and related estimated uncollectible accounts), and Due from Other Funds. Liability accounts might include

Matured Bond Interest Payable and Matured Bond Principal Payable. Fund equity typically consists of a single Fund Balance account. For the convenience of bondholders, the payment of interest and the redemption of matured bonds is ordinarily handled through the banking system. Usually the government designates a bank as paying agent or fiscal agent to handle interest and principal payments for each issue. Therefore, the assets of a debt service fund often include "Cash with Paying (or Fiscal) Agent" and the appropriations, expenditures, and liabilities may include amounts for the service charges of paying agents. Investment management may be performed by governmental employees or by banks, brokers, or others who charge for the service; investment management fees are a legitimate charge against investment revenues. For the sake of simplicity, the debt service examples in this chapter assume that the issuing government issues checks directly to bondholders for interest and redemption of principal.

Accounting for debt service of regular serial bonds furnishes the simplest illustration of recommended debt service fund accounting. Assume the bonds issued by the Town of Brighton as partial financing for the fire station construction project (discussed in Chapter 5, under the heading "Illustrative Transactions—Capital Projects Funds") are regular serial bonds maturing in equal annual amounts over 20 years. The total face value of the issue was $1,200,000; all bonds in the issue bear interest of 6 percent per year, payable semiannually on June 15 and December 15. The bonds were dated June 15, 2011, and sold on that date at par. During 2011 the only expenditure the debt service fund will be required to make will be the interest payment due December 15, 2011, in the amount of $36,000 ($1,200,000 × 0.06 × 1/2 year). Assuming that revenues to pay the first installment of bonds due on June 15, 2012, and both interest payments due in 2012 will be raised in 2012 from a special sales tax, the budget for 2011 need only provide resources in the amount of the 2011 interest expenditure. The entry to record the budget for the year ended December 31, 2011, including $6,000 residual equity to be transferred from the Fire Station Capital Projects Fund, is:

		Debits	Credits
	Serial Bond Debt Service Fund:		
1.	Estimated Revenues	30,000	
	Estimated Other Financing Sources	6,000	
	Appropriations		36,000

If sales tax revenues in the amount of $31,200 are collected in cash for debt service, the entry is:

	Serial Bond Debt Service Fund:		
2a.	Cash	31,200	
	Revenues		31,200

The corresponding entry in the governmental activities general ledger at the government-wide level is (*Note:* Entry 1 has no effect at the government-wide level since budget entries are made only in governmental funds):

		Debits	Credits
	Governmental Activities:		
2b.	Cash	31,200	
	General Revenues—Sales Taxes— Restricted for Debt Service		31,200

As illustrated in Chapter 5, the $6,000 residual equity of the Fire Station Capital Projects Fund was transferred to the debt service fund. The entry required in the latter fund is:

	Serial Bond Debt Service Fund:		
3.	Cash	6,000	
	Other Financing Sources—Interfund Transfers In		6,000

Governmental activities at the government-wide level are unaffected since the transfer is between two funds within the governmental activities category.

On December 15, 2011, when the first interest payment is legally due, the debt service fund records the expenditure of the appropriation and the corresponding entry is made to record interest expense at the government-wide level:

	Serial Bond Debt Service Fund:		
4a.	Expenditures—Bond Interest	36,000	
	Interest Payable		36,000
	Governmental Activities:		
4b.	Expenses—Interest on Long-term Debt	36,000	
	Interest Payable		36,000

Checks totaling $36,000 are written to the registered owners of these bonds. The entries to record the payment in the debt service fund and governmental activities general journals are:

	Serial Bond Debt Service Fund and Governmental Activities:		
5.	Interest Payable	36,000	
	Cash		36,000

As of December 31, 2011, an adjusting entry would be made to accrue one-half of a month's interest expense ($1,200,000 × 0.06 × 1/12 × 1/2) on the accrual basis at the government-wide level, as would be the case in accounting for business organizations. As was discussed earlier, the debt service fund recognizes an expenditure in the period the interest is legally due; it does not record an accrual at the end of the reporting period.

	Governmental Activities:		
6.	Expenses—Interest on Long-term Debt	3,000	
	Accrued Interest Payable		3,000

All budgetary and operating statement accounts are closed by the following entries:

		Debits	Credits
	Serial Bond Debt Service Fund:		
7a.	Appropriations	36,000	
	Estimated Revenues		30,000
	Estimated Other Financing Sources		6,000
7b.	Revenues	31,200	
	Other Financing Sources—Interfund Transfers In	6,000	
	Expenditures—Bond Interest		36,000
	Fund Balance		1,200

In addition, all temporary accounts of the governmental activities general ledger would be closed at year-end. Because that ledger has many temporary accounts besides those related to debt service, its closing entry is not illustrated here.

Second Year Transactions

In the second year of the Serial Bond Debt Service Fund, the fiscal year ending December 31, 2012, the following journal entries would be required.

The special sales tax for debt service is estimated to produce revenues of $135,000 for the year. From these revenues, two interest payments (the interest due on June 15, 2012, and December 15, 2012) of $36,000 and $34,200, respectively, and a principal redemption payment of $60,000 due on June 15, 2012, must be paid. Entry 8 shows the entry required at January 1, 2012, to record the budget for FY 2012.

		Debits	Credits
	Serial Bond Debt Service Fund:		
8.	Estimated Revenues	135,000	
	Appropriations		130,200
	Budgetary Fund Balance		4,800

During the year, actual revenues from the special sales tax were $134,100. Entries 9a and 9b summarize these collections.

		Debits	Credits
	Serial Bond Debt Service Fund:		
9a.	Cash	134,100	
	Revenues		134,100
	Governmental Activities:		
9b.	Cash	134,100	
	General Revenues—Sales Taxes—Restricted for Debt Service		134,100

On June 15, 2012, interest of $36,000 and the first redemption of principal in the amount of $60,000 ($1,200,000 ÷ 20 years) were paid to bondholders of record, as shown in Entries 10a and 10b.

		Debits	Credits
	Serial Bond Debt Service Fund:		
10a.	Expenditures—Bond Principal	60,000	
	Expenditures—Bond Interest	36,000	
	Cash		96,000
	Governmental Activities:		
10b.	Bonds Payable	60,000	
	Expenses—Interest on Long-term Debt	33,000	
	Accrued Interest Payable	3,000	
	Cash		96,000

The semiannual interest payment due on December 15, 2012, was paid on schedule, as reflected in Entries 11a and 11b, based on a remaining principal of $1,140,000 at 6 percent interest per annum.

		Debits	Credits
	Serial Bond Debt Service Fund:		
11a.	Expenditures—Bond Interest	34,200	
	Cash		34,200
	Governmental Activities:		
11b.	Expenses—Interest on Long-term Debt	34,200	
	Cash		34,200

On December 31, 2012, interest expense and interest payable were accrued in the amount of $2,850 ($1,140,000 × .06 × 1/12 × 1/2):

		Debits	Credits
	Governmental Activities:		
12.	Expenses—Interest on Long-term Debt	2,850	
	Accrued Interest Payable		2,850

All temporary accounts of the debt service fund were closed on December 31, 2012, as shown in Entries 13a and 13b. Closing entries for governmental activities are presented in Chapter 9 for fiscal year 2011.

		Debits	Credits
	Serial Bond Debt Service Fund:		
13a.	Appropriations	130,200	
	Budgetary Fund Balance	4,800	
	Estimated Revenues		135,000
13b.	Revenues	134,100	
	Fund Balance		3,900
	Expenditures—Bond Interest		70,200
	Expenditures—Bond Principal		60,000

In subsequent years, the pattern of journal entries will be the same as that of the preceding entries, except that actual sales taxes realized will vary from year to year and the amount of interest will decline each year as the principal is reduced. If revenues are insufficient in any year to meet debt service requirements, available fund balance can be used to augment current year revenues. If fund balance is insufficient to cover the shortfall, then an interfund transfer from the General Fund would likely be used. Making all interest and principal redemption payments by their due date is critically important, as a missed or late payment could adversely impact the entity's bond rating and significantly increase future borrowing costs.

Debt Service Accounting for Term Bonds

Term bond issues mature in their entirety on a given date, in contrast to serial bonds, which mature in installments. Required revenues of term bond debt service funds may be determined on an "actuarial" basis or on less sophisticated bases designed to produce approximately level contributions during the life of the issue. In order to illustrate the use of an actuarial basis, the following example assumes that the Town of Brighton has a term bond issue amounting to $1,500,000 with a 20-year life. The term bonds bear semiannual interest at a nominal (or stated) annual rate of 5 percent, payable on January 1 and July 1. Revenues and other financing sources of this particular debt service fund are assumed to be property taxes levied directly for this debt service fund and earnings on investments of the debt service fund. The amount of the tax levy is computed in accord with annuity tables on the assumption that revenues for principal repayment will be invested and will earn 6 percent per year, compounded semiannually. (Actuaries are usually conservative in their assumptions because they are concerned with a long time span.) Using either the annuity tables found in most intermediate accounting texts or a calculator, one will find that the future amount of $1 invested at the end of each period will amount to $75.4012597 at the end of 40 periods, if the periodic compound interest is 3 percent (as specified in this example). Since the amount needed for bond repayment at the end of 40 six-month periods is $1,500,000, the tax levy for bond principal repayment must yield $1,500,000 divided by 75.4012597, or $19,893.57, at the end of each six-month period throughout the life of the bonds. Tax revenue must be sufficient to cover each bond interest payment of $37,500 ($1,500,000, the face value of the bonds, × 5 percent, the annual nominal interest rate, × 1/2 year) plus the two required additions of $19,893.57 for sinking fund investment, for a total revenue of $114,787.14 per year.

Assuming the bonds were issued in the preceding fiscal year on January 1, 2010, and actual additions and actual earnings were both exactly as budgeted, the Term Bonds Debt Service Fund of the Town of Brighton would have the following trial balance as of December 31, 2010.[5]

[5] The computation is (all amounts rounded to nearest cent):

Year	Period	Addition at End of Period	3 Percent per Period	Balance at End of Period
2010	1	$19,893.57	$ –0–	$19,893.57
	2	19,893.57	596.81	40,383.95
2011	3	19,893.57	1,211.52	61,489.04
	4	19,893.57	1,844.67	83,227.28

The balance at the end of Period 2 is the total of investments and the total of fund balance in this case since actuarial assumptions were met exactly in 2010. The sum of the interest for Period 3 and Period 4 is $3,056.19, the required earnings for the second year.

	Debits	Credits
Cash	$37,500.00	—
Investments	40,383.95	—
Fund balance	—	$77,883.95
Totals	$77,883.95	$77,883.95

For every year of the life of the issue, the budget for the Term Bonds Debt Service Fund of the Town of Brighton, reflecting the conditions just described, will include two required additions of $19,893.57 each for investment for eventual principal repayment, and two amounts of $37,500 each for interest payment, for a total of $114,787.14. The budget will also include earnings on debt service fund investments computed in accord with actuarial requirements. For 2011, the second year of the Term Bonds Debt Service Fund's operation, the actuarial assumption is that the fund will earn 6 percent per year, compounded semiannually; the required earnings for the year amount to $3,056.19 (see footnote 5 for calculation). Therefore, Estimated Revenues is debited for $117,843.33 ($114,787.14 + $3,056.19). The appropriations budget would include only the amounts becoming due during the budget year, $75,000 (two interest payments, each amounting to $37,500). The entry to record the budget for fiscal year 2011 follows.

		Debits	Credits
	Term Bond Debt Service Fund:		
1.	Estimated Revenues	117,843.33	
	Budgetary Fund Balance		42,843.33
	Appropriations		75,000.00

If the debt service fund is to accumulate the amount needed to retire the term bond issue at maturity, both additions and earnings must be received, and invested, in accord with the actuarial assumptions. Therefore, the tax levy for this fund must yield collections in the first six months totaling at least $57,393.57, so that $19,893.57 can be invested and $37,500 can be paid in interest to bondholders, both as of the end of the first six-month period. Collections during the second six months must also total $57,393.57, for the same reason. Realistically, it is unlikely that collections would ever total exactly $57,393.57 in either six-month period. If collections were less than that amount in either period, this fund would have to borrow enough to make the required investments; there is no question that the interest would have to be paid when due, as discussed earlier in this chapter. Assuming that collection experience of the Town of Brighton indicates that a tax levy in the amount of $120,000 is needed in order to be reasonably certain that collections during each six-month period will equal the needed amount, the entries to record the levy and the expected uncollectibles amounting to $3,000 are as follows:

ILLUSTRATION 6–8

TOWN OF BRIGHTON
Debt Service Funds
Combining Schedule of Revenues, Expenditures, and Changes in Fund Balances—Budget and Actual for the Year Ended December 31, 2011
(amounts reported in dollars)

	Serial Bonds			Term Bonds			Total Debt Service Funds		
	Budget	Actual	Actual over (under) Budget	Budget	Actual	Actual over (under) Budget	Budget	Actual	Actual over (under) Budget
Revenues:									
Taxes	$30,000	$31,200	$1,200	$114,787	$117,000	$2,213	$144,787	$148,200	$3,413
Investment earnings	–0–	–0–	–0–	3,056	3,145	89	3,056	3,145	89
Total revenues	30,000	31,200	1,200	117,843	120,145	2,302	147,843	151,345	3,502
Expenditures:									
Interest on bonds	36,000	36,000	–0–	75,000	75,000	–0–	111,000	111,000	–0–
Excess of revenues over (under) expenditures	(6,000)	(4,800)	1,200	42,843	45,145	2,302	36,843	40,345	3,502
Other Financing Sources (Uses):									
Interfund transfers in	6,000	6,000	–0–	–0–	–0–	–0–	6,000	6,000	–0–
Increase in fund balance	–0–	1,200	1,200	42,843	45,145	2,302	42,843	46,345	3,502
Fund balance, January 1, 2011	–0–	–0–	–0–	77,884	77,884	–0–	77,884	77,884	–0–
Fund balance, December 31, 2011	$ –0–	$ 1,200	$1,200	$120,727	$123,029	$2,302	$120,727	$124,229	$3,502

market investments with maturities of less than one year.[6] The latter *may* be accounted for at amortized cost (interest earnings adjusted for amortization of premium or discount).[7] Often, however, premiums and discounts are not amortized for short-term investments. All long-term investments in debt and equity securities held for repayment of general long-term debt principal are reported at fair value in the debt service fund balance sheet. All *changes* in the fair value of investments during the period, both realized and unrealized, are reported as revenue in the statement of revenues, expenditures, and changes in fund balances.

Deposit and Investment Disclosures

Bond issuances and subsequent debt service activities typically result in significant deposits in financial institutions and long-term investments for principal redemption. In addition, excess cash of the General Fund and other funds, pension plan assets, self-insurance pool reserves, and investment pools are also common sources of deposits and investments. Among other concerns, deposits and investments held in the custody of financial institutions impose risks such as exposure to loss due to interest rate increases, custodial credit risk related to the underlying creditworthiness of the financial institution, credit risk related to the creditworthiness of debt security issuers, and concentration risk from holding substantial portions of investment securities of a single issuer.

Interest rate risk may be reduced by holding fixed income securities with lower term to maturity (duration) and avoiding highly interest-rate-sensitive derivative investments. Derivative securities are financial instruments or contracts whose value is dependent upon some other underlying security or market measure such as an index or interest rates.[8] Custodial credit risk for deposits may be reduced by holding other securities as collateral. Such risk may be eliminated entirely if covered by depository insurance (e.g., Federal Deposit Insurance Corporation). Credit risk can be reduced by investing in bonds with high-quality ratings or that are backed by insurance. Concentration risk can be minimized through diversification of investments by avoiding investing in securities of a single issuer that exceed 5 percent of total investments.

GASB standards require certain disclosures about *external investment pools,* as discussed in Chapter 8. For other investments, the government should describe in its notes to the financial statements (1) legal and contractual provisions for deposits and investments, including types of investments authorized to be held and any significant violations of legal or contractual provisions and (2) investment policies related to the kinds of risks described in the preceding paragraph.[9] Investment disclosures

[6] GASB standards define fair value as "the amount at which an investment could be exchanged in a current transaction between willing parties, other than in a forced or liquidation sale." GASB, *Codification,* Sec. I50.105.

[7] The reader should note that this discussion refers to amortization of premium and discount on investments purchased with the expectation of holding them until maturity. A premium or discount on bonds payable sold by a government is *not* amortized in the debt service fund but should be amortized at the government-wide level so that effective interest expense is reported in the government-wide statement of activities. Premium on bonds sold is considered as an other financing source of the debt service fund if it must be used for debt service, as discussed in Chapter 5. Accrued interest on bonds sold should be recorded as revenue of the debt service fund.

[8] For a formal definition of *derivative,* see GASB *Codification,* Sec. 2300.601, Response to Question 1.

[9] GASB *Codification,* Sec. I50.123–126.

should be organized by type of investment. Additionally, the government should provide disclosures about specific risks. These disclosures include information about:[10]

1. Interest rate risk of investments in debt securities, using one of five approved methods described in the standards.
2. Credit quality ratings of investments in debt securities, such as the ratings provided by the major national bond rating services (e.g., Moody's Investor Service, Standard & Poor's, and FitchRatings). A recommended format is to present aggregated amounts of investments by quality rating category.
3. Custodial credit risk; specifically investment securities or deposits that are not insured, deposits that are not collateralized, investments that are not registered in the name of the government, and both deposits and investments that are held by either (*a*) the counterparty (e.g., financial institution) or (*b*) the counterparty's trust department or agent but not in the government's name.
4. Concentration of credit risk, including disclosure of amount and issuer for investments in the securities of any one issuer that exceed 5 percent or more of total investments.

In addition, the government should disclose any deposits or investments that are exposed to foreign currency risk.

Debt Service Accounting for Special Assessment Debt

Special assessment projects, as discussed in Chapter 5, typically follow the same pattern as transactions of other capital projects. Specifically, construction activities are usually completed in the first year or so, using either interim financing from the government or proceeds of special assessment debt issuances (bonds or notes) to pay construction costs to contractors. Either at the beginning of the project or, more commonly, when construction is completed, assessments for debt service are levied against property owners in the defined special benefit district. Annual assessment installments receivable and interest on the balance of unpaid installments usually approximate the amount of debt principal and interest payable during the same year. If the government is obligated in some manner to make the debt service payments in the event that amounts collected from benefited property owners are insufficient, the debt should be recorded in the governmental activities journal at the government-wide level and a debt service fund should be used to account for debt service activities. If the government is not obligated in any manner for special assessment debt, the debt should *not* be recorded in any accounting records of the government. In the latter case, which is relatively rare, debt service transactions should be recorded in an *agency fund,* as explained in Chapter 8.

(see Chp. 8) Assume that special assessment bonds, secondarily backed by the general taxing authority of a certain city, were issued to complete a street-widening project. Upon completion of the project the city levied assessments amounting to $480,000, payable in 10 equal installments with 5 percent interest on unpaid installments, on owners of properties fronting on the improved streets. As shown in Entry 1, all receivables are recorded at the time of the levy, but Revenues is credited only for the amount expected to be collected within one year from the date of the levy; Deferred Revenues is credited for the amount of deferred installments. Because the entries at the government-wide level would be similar, except that interest expense would be

[10] Ibid. pars. 127–131.

reported rather than expenditures, those entries are omitted for the sake of brevity. Required budgetary entries, as shown earlier in this chapter for serial bond and term bond debt service funds, are omitted.

		Debits	Credits
1.	Assessments Receivable—Current	48,000	
	Assessments Receivable—Deferred	432,000	
	Revenues		48,000
	Deferred Revenues		432,000

All current assessments receivable due at year-end were collected along with interest of $24,000 (see Entry 2). Any amounts not collected by the due date should be reclassified by a debit to Assessments Receivable—Delinquent and a credit to Assessments Receivable—Current.

2.	Cash	72,000	
	Assessments Receivable—Current		48,000
	Revenues		24,000

Matured special assessment bond principal in the amount of $48,000 and matured bond interest payable of $24,000 were recorded and paid on schedule.

3a.	Expenditures—Bond Principal	48,000	
	Expenditures—Bond Interest	24,000	
	Bonds Payable		48,000
	Interest Payable		24,000
3b.	Bonds Payable	48,000	
	Interest Payable	24,000	
	Cash		72,000

The second installment of assessments receivable was reclassified from the deferred category to the current category. A corresponding amount of Deferred Revenues was reclassified as Revenues.

4a.	Assessments Receivable—Current	48,000	
	Assessments Receivable—Deferred		48,000
4b.	Deferred Revenues	48,000	
	Revenues		48,000

This pattern of journal entries will be repeated during each of the remaining nine years until all special assessment bonds have been retired.

Use of Debt Service Funds to Record Capital Lease Payments

In Chapter 5, under the heading "General Capital Assets Acquired under Capital Lease Agreements," an example is given of the computation of the present value of rentals under a capital lease agreement. The entry necessary in a governmental fund at the inception of the lease is illustrated in Chapter 5. The corresponding entry in the governmental activities general journal at the government-wide level is also given in Chapter 5 to show the capitalization of the asset acquired under the lease. That entry is reproduced here to illustrate how the liability is recorded.

	Debits	Credits
Governmental Activities:		
Equipment	67,590	
Capital Lease Obligations Payable		67,590

As shown in this entry, at the inception of the lease an obligation is recognized at the government-wide level in an amount equal to the present value of the stream of annual payments. Although the lease agreement calls for a $10,000 initial lease payment on January 1, 2010, the full present value should be recorded as the liability until the initial payment has been recorded. Since governmental funds do not record long-term liabilities, no journal entry is made at the fund level for the liability.

Governments may use a General Fund, a special revenue fund, or a debt service fund to record capital lease payments since the annual lease payments are merely installment payments of general long-term debt. For illustrative purposes, it is assumed that the capital lease recorded in Chapter 5 is serviced by a debt service fund. The first $10,000 lease payment, since it occurs on the first day of the lease, is entirely a payment on the principal of the lease obligation. Accordingly, the payment would be recorded as follows:

	Debits	Credits
Debt Service Fund:		
Expenditures—Principal of Capital Lease Obligation	10,000	
Cash		10,000

	Debits	Credits
Governmental Activities:		
Capital Lease Obligations Payable	10,000	
Cash		10,000

On January 1, 2011, the second lease rental payment of $10,000 is made. As the accompanying table shows, only $4,241 of that payment applies to reduction of the principal of the lease obligation (the remaining $10,000–$4,241, or $5,759, represents interest on the lease). Thus, the following entries are required at the debt service fund and government-wide level.

	Debits	Credits
Debt Service Fund:		
Expenditures—Principal of Capital Lease Obligation	4,241	
Expenditures—Interest on Capital Lease Obligation	5,759	
Cash		10,000

	Debits	Credits
Governmental Activities:		
Capital Lease Obligations Payable	4,241	
Interest Expense on Capital Leases	5,759	
Cash		10,000

The payment due on January 1, 2011, and the payment due each year thereafter, will reflect a partial payment on the lease obligation and a payment of interest on the unpaid balance of the lease obligation. GASB standards are consistent with the FASB's *SFAS 13;* both specify that a constant periodic rate of interest must be used. In the example started in Chapter 5, the present value of the obligation is computed using the rate of 10 percent per year. It is reasonable to use the same interest rate to determine what part of the annual $10,000 payment is payment of interest and what part is payment of principal. The following table shows the distribution of the annual lease rental payments:

Payment Date	Amount of Payment	Interest on Unpaid Balance at 10 Percent	Payment on Principal	Unpaid Lease Obligation
				$67,590
1/1/10	$10,000	$ -0-	$10,000	57,590
1/1/11	10,000	5,759	4,241	53,349
1/1/12	10,000	5,335	4,665	48,684
1/1/13	10,000	4,868	5,132	43,552
1/1/14	10,000	4,355	5,645	37,907
1/1/15	10,000	3,791	6,209	31,698
1/1/16	10,000	3,170	6,830	24,868
1/1/17	10,000	2,487	7,513	17,355
1/1/18	10,000	1,736	8,264	9,091
1/1/19	10,000	909	9,091	-0-

The unpaid balance of the capital lease obligation is carried in the governmental activities general ledger at the government-wide level.

Accounting for Debt Refunding

If debt service fund assets accumulated for debt repayment are not sufficient to repay creditors when the debt matures, or if the interest rate on the debt is appreciably higher than the government would have to pay on a new bond issue, or if the covenants of the existing bonds are excessively burdensome, the government may issue refunding bonds.

The proceeds of refunding bonds issued at the maturity of the debt to be refunded are accounted for as other financing sources of the debt service fund that is to repay the existing debt. The appropriation for debt repayment is accounted for as illustrated in the Town of Brighton Serial Bond Debt Service Fund second year example (see the first entry under the heading "Second Year Transactions" and related discussion).

If a government has accumulated no assets at all for debt repayment, it is possible that no debt service fund exists. In such a case, a debt service fund should be created to account for the proceeds of the refunding bond issue and the repayment of the old debt. When the debt has been completely repaid, the debt service fund relating to the liquidated issue should be closed, and a debt service fund for the refunding issue should be created and accounted for as described in this chapter. If the refunding bond issue is not sold but is merely given to the holders of the matured issue in an even exchange, the transaction does not require entries in a debt service fund or at the government-wide level but should be disclosed adequately in the notes to the financial statements.

Advance Refunding of Debt

Advance refundings of tax-exempt debt are common during periods when interest rates are falling sharply. Complex accounting and reporting issues have surfaced relating to legal issues such as whether both issues are still the debt of the issuer. If the proceeds of the new issue are to be held for the eventual retirement of the old issue, how can the proceeds be invested to avoid conflict with the Internal Revenue Service over the taxability of interest on the debt issue? (Compliance with the arbitrage rules under the Internal Revenue Code Sec. 148 and related regulations is necessary for the interest to be exempt from federal income tax and, possibly, from state and local taxes.) Full consideration of the complexities of accounting for advance refundings resulting in defeasance of debt is presented in the GASB *Codification* Section D20. Defeasance of debt can be either "legal" or "in substance." **Legal defeasance** occurs when debt is legally satisfied based on certain provisions in the debt instrument, even though the debt is not actually paid. **In-substance defeasance** occurs when debt is considered settled for accounting and financial reporting purposes, even though legal defeasance has not occurred. GASB *Codification* Section D20.103 sets forth in detail the circumstances for in-substance defeasance. Briefly, the debtor must irrevocably place cash or other assets in trust with an escrow agent to be used solely for satisfying scheduled payments of both interest and principal of the defeased debt. The amount placed in escrow must be sufficiently large so that there is only a remote possibility that the debtor will be required to make future payments on the defeased debt. The trust is restricted to owning only monetary assets that are essentially risk-free as to the amount, timing, and collection of interest and principal.

To illustrate accounting for advance refundings resulting in defeasance of debt reported in the governmental activities ledger at the government-wide level, assume that the proceeds from the sale of the refunding issue amount to $2,000,000 and that debt defeased amounted to $2,500,000. The proceeds are recorded in the fund receiving the proceeds (normally, a *debt service fund*) by an entry such as follows:

	Debits	Credits
Cash	2,000,000	
Other Financing Sources—Proceeds of Refunding Bonds		2,000,000

Payments to the escrow agent from resources provided by the new debt should be recorded in the debt service fund as an other financing use; payments to the escrow agent from other resources are recorded as debt service expenditures. Therefore, assuming $500,000 has previously been accumulated in the debt service fund for payment of the $2,500,000 bond issue, the entry to record the payment to the escrow agent is as follows:

	Debits	Credits
Other Financing Uses—Payment to Refunded Bond Escrow Agent	2,000,000	
Expenditures—Payment to Refunded Bond Escrow Agent	500,000	
Cash		2,500,000

Disclosures about Advance Refundings

The *disclosure* guidance on debt refunding in GASB *Codification* Section D20 is applicable to state and local governments, public benefit corporations and authorities, public employee retirement systems, and governmental utilities, hospitals, colleges and universities, and to all funds of those entities.

Briefly, the disclosure requirements state that all entities subject to GASB jurisdiction are to provide a general description of any advance refundings resulting in defeasance of debt in the notes to the financial statements in the year of the refunding. At a minimum, the disclosures must include (1) the difference between the cash flows required to service the old debt and the cash flows required to service the new debt and complete the refundings and (2) the economic gain or loss resulting from the transaction. Economic gain or loss is the difference between the *present value* of the old debt service requirements and the *present value* of the new debt service requirements, discounted at the effective interest rate and adjusted for additional cash paid. Section D20.901–.917 provides examples of effective interest rate and economic gain calculations and of note disclosures.

Key Terms

Annuity serial bonds, *223*
Debt limit, *214*
Debt margin, *215*
Deferred serial bonds, *223*
Fair value, *233*
General long-term liabilities, *211*
In-substance defeasance, *240*
Irregular serial bonds, *223*
Legal defeasance, *240*
Overlapping debt, *215*
Pollution remediation obligations, *213*
Regular serial bonds, *222*
Tax-supported debt, *213*
Term bonds, *228*

Selected References

American Institute of Certified Public Accountants. Audit and Accounting Guide. *State and Local Governments.* Revised. New York, 2008.

Financial Accounting Standards Board. *Statement of Financial Accounting Standards No. 13*, "Accounting for Leases as Amended and Interpreted through April 2002." Norwalk, CT, 1975.

Governmental Accounting Standards Board. *Codification of Governmental Accounting and Financial Reporting Standards, as of June 30, 2008.* Norwalk, CT, 2008.

Questions

6–1. How are *general long-term liabilities* distinguished from other long-term liabilities of the government? How does the financial reporting of general long-term liabilities differ from the financial reporting of other long-term liabilities?

6–2. What disclosures about long-term liabilities are required in the notes to the financial statements?

6–3. In the current fiscal year, St. George County issued $3,000,000 in general obligation term bonds for 102. The county is required to use any accrued interest or premiums for servicing the debt issue.

a. How would the bond issue be recorded at the fund and government-wide level?

b. How would the bond issue be reported in the fund financial statements and the government-wide financial statements?

c. What effect, if any, do interest payments have on the carrying value of the bond issue as reported in the financial statements?

6–4. If a bond ordinance provides for regular and recurring payments of interest and principal payments on a general obligation bond issue of a certain government to be made from earnings of an enterprise fund and these payments are being made by the enterprise fund, how should the bond liability be disclosed in the comprehensive annual financial report of the government?

6–5. The debt limit for general obligation debt for Milos City is 1 percent of the assessed property valuation for the city. Using the following information, calculate the city's debt margin.

Assessed property valuation	$10,863,511,000
Approved but unissued tax-supported debt	10,000,000
Revenue bonds issued	32,000,000
General obligation serial bonds issued	43,000,000
Capital leases outstanding	5,230,000

6–6. What is overlapping debt? Why would a citizen care about the amount of overlapping debt reported? Why would a government care about the amount of overlapping debt reported?

6–7. "If a certain city had six tax-supported bond issues and three special assessment bond issues outstanding, it would be preferable to operate nine separate debt service funds or, at a minimum, one debt service fund for tax-supported bonds and one for special assessment bonds." Do you agree? Explain.

6–8. Explain the essential differences between regular serial bonds and term bonds and how debt service fund accounting differs for the two types of bonds.

6–9. What are the GASB requirements for reporting investments held for the purpose of servicing government debt?

6–10. Under what circumstances might a government consider an advance refunding of general obligation bonds outstanding?

Cases

6–1 Policy Issue: Who Should Pay for Neighborhood Improvements? Related Accounting Issues.

Facts: Pursuant to its capital improvement plan, the City of Kirkland decided to make certain improvements to Oak Ridge Street, a residential thoroughfare located in the northern part of the city. Specifically, the project entailed purchasing 20 feet at the front of all private properties fronting the street to facilitate widening of the street from two to four lanes and adding sidewalks. The project was expected to cost $5 million.

After extensive and often contentious hearing presentations involving property owners, the public works director, city planners, and the city attorney, the city council decided that property owners fronting on Oak Ridge Street would be the primary beneficiaries of the street-widening project. Accordingly, as permitted by state law, the city council formed the Oak Ridge Special Improvement District and approved the issuance of $5 million in special assessment bonds to be repaid from special assessment levies on the Oak Ridge Street property owners. To reduce interest rates on the debt, the city agreed to make the bonds general obligations of the city should property owners default on debt service payments.

After the bonds had been issued and the project was well under way, all Oak Ridge Street property owners retained a local law firm and sued the City of Kirkland to make the street-widening project a publicly funded project of the city rather than a special assessment project. Attorneys for property owners argued in briefs filed with the court that (1) the property owners will not benefit from the street improvements and, in fact, had fought the project for years since they would lose valuable property and the street would be transformed from a quiet, low-density, mainly local traffic street to a noisy, high-density public thoroughfare, and (2) the property owners were not adequately informed about the special assessment financing for the project before the financing was approved and the bonds were issued.

The city attorney filed a brief with the court laying out the city's reasoning for financing the street-widening project with special assessment bonds, essentially arguing that the Oak Ridge Street Project is no different from many past city neighborhood improvement projects that have been financed with special assessments. According to the city attorney, there is strong legal precedent for requiring property owners who receive private benefit to pay for such improvements.

Required

a. Assume you are the judge in this case. After analyzing the facts of this case, decide what remedies, if any, you will order for the plaintiffs (the property owners). Prepare a written brief explaining your reasoning and verdict.

b. How would accounting for the bond issuance, street construction, and debt service differ if you (the judge) were to rule for the plaintiffs and thus require the city to repay the project bonds from tax revenues rather than from special assessments? How would accounting differ if you were to rule against the plaintiffs (assuming the city had not pledged to be secondarily liable for the bonds)?

6–2 Financial Statement Impact of Incurring General Long-term Debt on Behalf of Other Governments.

Facts: The Bates County government issued $2.5 million of tax-supported bonds to finance a major addition to the Bates County Hospital, a legally separate organization reported as a discretely presented component unit of the county. At the end of the fiscal year in which the debt was issued and the project completed, the county commission was shocked to see a deficit of more than $2 million reported for unrestricted net assets in the Governmental Activities column of the government-wide statement of net assets, compared with a surplus of over $400,000 the preceding year. The commission is quite concerned about how creditors and citizens will react to this large deficit and have asked you, in your role as county finance director, to explain how the deficit occurred and what actions should be taken to eliminate it.

Required

a. Write a brief memo to the county commission explaining how the $2.5 million bond issue for the addition to the Bates County Hospital resulted in the large and apparently unexpected deficit in unrestricted net assets.

(*Hint:* Refer to Illustration A 1–1, the City and County of Denver statement of net assets, and evaluate whether the bonds issued by Bates County would affect net assets—invested in capital assets, net of related debt or net assets—unrestricted. For additional insight, you may also wish to read the portion of Chapter 9 of this text that relates to preparation of government-wide financial statements for the Town of Brighton.)

b. In your memo, explain what actions can be taken, if any, to eliminate the deficit in governmental activities unrestricted net assets, or at least make it less objectionable.

6–3 The Case of the Vanishing Debt.

Facts: A county government and a legally separate organization—the Sports Stadium Authority—entered into an agreement under which the authority issued revenue bonds to construct a new stadium. Although the intent is to make debt service payments on the bonds from a surcharge on ticket sales, the county agreed to annually advance the Sports Stadium Authority the required amounts to make up any debt service shortfalls and has done so for several years. Accordingly, the county has recorded a receivable from the authority and the authority has recorded a liability to the county for all advances made under the agreement.

Ticket surcharge revenues that exceed $1,500,000 are to be paid to the county and to be applied first toward interest and then toward principal repayment of advances. Both parties acknowledge, however, that annual ticket surcharge revenues may never exceed $1,500,000, since to reach that level would require an annual paid attendance of 3,000,000. Considering that season ticket holders and luxury suite renters are not included in the attendance count, it is quite uncertain if the required trigger level will ever be reached.

The authority has twice proposed to raise the ticket surcharge amount, but the county in both cases vetoed the proposal. Thus, the lender in this transaction (the county) has imposed limits that appear to make it infeasible for the borrower (the authority) to repay the advances. Consequently, the authority's legal counsel has taken the position that the authority is essentially a pass-through agency with respect to the advances in that the authority merely receives the advances and passes them on to a fiscal agent for debt service payments. Moreover, they note that the bonds could never have been issued in the first place without the county's irrevocable guarantee of repayment, since all parties knew from the beginning that the authority likely would not have the resources to make full debt service payments.

Based on the foregoing considerations, the authority's legal counsel has rendered an opinion that the liability for the advances can be removed from the authority's accounts. The county tacitly agrees that the loans (advances) are worthless, since it records an allowance for doubtful loans equal to the total amount of the advances. Still, the county board of commissioners refuses to remove the receivable from its accounts because of its ongoing rights under the original agreement for repayment.

Required

a. Assume you are the independent auditor for the authority, and provide a written analysis of the facts of this case, indicating whether or not you concur with the authority's decision to no longer report the liability to the county for debt service advances.

b. Alternatively, assume you are the independent auditor for the county and, based on the same analysis you conducted for requirement *a,* indicate whether or not you concur with the county continuing to report a receivable for debt service advances on its General Fund balance sheet and government-wide statement of net assets.

6–4 Assessing General Obligation Debt Burden. This case focuses on the analysis of a city's general obligation debt burden. After examining the accompanying table that shows a city's general obligation (tax-supported) debt for the last ten fiscal years, answer the following questions.

Required

a. What is your initial assessment of the trend of the city's general obligation debt burden?

b. Complete the table by calculating the ratio of Net General Bonded Debt to Assessed Value of taxable property and the ratio of Net General Bonded Debt per Capita. In addition, you learn that the average ratio of Net General Bonded Debt to Assessed Value for comparable-size cities in 2011 was 2.13 percent, and the average net general bonded debt per capita was $1,256. Based on time series analysis of the ratios you have calculated and the benchmark information provided in this paragraph, is your assessment of the city's general obli-gation still the same as it was in part *a,* or has it changed? Explain.

Ratio of Net General Bonded Debt to Assessed Value and Net Bonded Debt per Capita (Last Ten Fiscal Years—$000s omitted)

Fiscal Year	Estimated Population	Assessed Valuation	Gross Bonded Debt	Less: Amount in Debt Service Fund	Net Bonded Debt	Net General Bonded Debt to Assessed Value	Net General Bonded Debt per Capita
2002	85,359	$1,488,391	$165,454	$101,789	$ 63,665	——	——
2003	86,935	1,552,844	164,496	100,482	64,014	——	——
2004	88,128	1,668,126	186,273	100,197	86,076	——	——
2005	90,599	1,792,747	192,151	99,545	92,606	——	——
2006	92,061	1,939,316	206,856	100,690	106,166	——	——
2007	93,524	2,057,130	212,323	106,655	105,668	——	——
2008	94,986	2,197,710	221,287	102,518	118,769	——	——
2009	96,647	2,386,169	261,519	117,212	144,307	——	——
2010	97,610	2,585,416	291,736	120,326	171,410	——	——
2011	99,208	2,843,133	280,654	106,551	174,103	——	——

Source: Adapted from City of Fargo, North Dakota, Comprehensive Annual Financial Report, 2006.

Exercises and Problems

6–1 Examine the CAFR. Utilizing the comprehensive annual financial report (CAFR) obtained for Exercise 1–1, follow the instructions below.

a. **General Long-term Liabilities.**

(1) *Disclosure of Long-term Debt.* Does the report contain evidence that the government has general long-term liabilities? What evidence is there? Does the report specify that no such debt is outstanding, or does it include

a list of outstanding tax-supported debt issues; capital lease obligations; claims, judgments, and compensated absence payments to be made in future years; and unfunded pension obligations?

Refer to the enterprise funds statement of net assets as well as note disclosures for long-term liabilities. Are any enterprise debt issues backed by the full faith and credit of the general government? If so, how are the primary liability and the contingent liability disclosed?

(2) *Changes in Long-term Liabilities.* How are changes in long-term liabilities during the year disclosed? Is there a disclosure schedule for long-term liabilities similar to Illustration 6–1? Does the information in that schedule agree with the statements presented for capital projects funds and debt service funds and the government-wide financial statements?

Are interest payments and principal payments due in future years disclosed? If so, does the report relate these future payments with resources to be made available under existing debt service laws and covenants?

(3) *Debt Limitations.* Does the report contain information as to legal debt limit and legal debt margin? If so, is the information contained in the report explained in enough detail so that an intelligent reader (you) can understand how the limit is set, what debt is subject to it, and how much debt the government might legally issue in the year following the date of the report?

(4) *Overlapping Debt.* Does the report disclose direct debt and overlapping debt of the reporting entity? What disclosures of debt of the primary government are made in distinction to debt of component units? Is debt of component units reported as "direct" debt of the reporting entity or as "overlapping debt"?

b. **Debt Service Funds.**

(1) *Debt Service Function.* How is the debt service function for tax-supported debt and special assessment debt handled—by the General Fund, by a special revenue fund, or by one or more debt service funds? If there is more than one debt service fund, what kinds of bond issues or other debt instruments are serviced by each fund? Is debt service for bonds to be retired from enterprise revenues reported by enterprise funds?

Does the report state the basis of accounting used for debt service funds? If so, is the financial statement presentation consistent with the stated basis? If the basis of accounting is not stated, analyze the statements to determine which basis is used—full accrual, modified accrual, or cash basis. Is the basis used consistent with the standards discussed in this chapter?

(2) *Investment Activity.* Compare the net assets reserved for debt service, if any, in the Governmental Activities column of the government-wide statement of net assets and the fund balance of each debt service fund at balance sheet date with the amount of interest and the amount of debt principal the fund will be required to pay early in the following year (you may find debt service requirements in the notes to the financial statements or in supplementary schedules following the individual fund statements in the Financial Section of the CAFR). If debt service funds have accumulated assets in excess of amounts needed within a few days after the end of the fiscal year, are the excess assets invested? Does the CAFR contain a schedule or list of investments of debt service funds? Does the report disclose increases or decreases in the fair value of investments realized during

the year? Does the report disclose net earnings on investments during the year? What percentage of revenue of each debt service fund is derived from earnings on investments? What percentage of the revenue of each debt service fund is derived from taxes levied directly for the debt service fund? What percentage is derived from transfers from other funds? List any other sources of debt service revenue and other financing sources, and indicate the relative importance of each source.

Are estimated revenues for term bond debt service budgeted on an actuarial basis? If so, are revenues received as required by the actuarial computations?

(3) *Management.* Considering the debt maturity dates as well as the amount of debt and apparent quality of debt service fund investments, does the debt service activity appear to be properly managed? Does the report disclose whether investments are managed by a corporate fiduciary, another outside investment manager, or governmental employees? If outside investment managers are employed, is the basis of their fees disclosed? Are the fees accounted for as additions to the cost of investments or as expenditures?

Is one or more paying agents, or fiscal agents, employed? If so, does the report disclose whether the agents keep track of the ownership of registered bonds, write checks to bondholders for interest payments and matured bonds or, in the case of coupon bonds, pay matured coupons and matured bonds presented through banking channels? If agents are employed, do the balance sheet or the notes to the financial statements disclose the amount of cash in their possession? If so, does this amount appear reasonable in relation to interest payable and matured bonds payable? Do the statements, schedules, or narratives disclose for how long a period of time debt service funds carry a liability for unpresented checks for interest on registered bonds, for matured but unpresented interest coupons, and for matured but unpresented bonds?

(4) *Capital Lease Rental Payments.* If general capital assets are being acquired under capital lease agreements, are periodic lease rental payments accounted for as expenditures of a debt service fund (or by another governmental fund)? If so, does the report disclose that the provisions of *SFAS No. 13* are being followed (see the "Use of Debt Service Funds to Record Capital Lease Payments" section of this chapter) to determine the portion of each capital lease payment considered as interest and the portion considered as payment on the principal.

6–2 Multiple Choice. Choose the best answer.

1. Which of the following would *not* be considered a general long-term liability?
   a. The estimated liability to clean up the fuel and hazard waste storage sites of the city's Public Works Department.
   b. Capitalized equipment leases of the water utility fund.
   c. Compensated absences for the city's Police Department.
   d Five-year notes payable used to acquire computer equipment for the city library.

2. Proceeds from bonds issued to construct a new county jail would most likely be recorded in the journal of the:
   a. Capital projects fund.
   b. Debt service fund.

(6) Adjusting entries were made and uncollected taxes receivable were reclassified as delinquent. At the fund level, entries were also made to close budgetary and operating statement accounts. (Ignore closing entries in the government activities journal.)

b. Prepare a statement of revenues, expenditures, and changes in fund balances for the debt service fund for the year ended December 31, 2011.

c. Prepare a balance sheet for the debt service fund as of December 31, 2011.

6–9 Term Bond Liabilities. Following are transaction data for a term bonds issue for the City of Nevin. Prepare all necessary entries for these transactions in the city's funds, and governmental activities journal at the government-wide level. Round all amounts to the nearest whole dollar.

a. On July 1, 2010, the first day of its 2011 fiscal year, the City of Nevin issued at par $2,000,000 of 6 percent term bonds to construct a new city office building. The bonds mature in five years on July 1, 2015. Interest is payable semiannually on January 1 and July 1. A sinking fund is to be established with equal semiannual additions made on June 30 and December 31, with the first addition to be made on December 31, 2010. Cash for the sinking fund additions and the semiannual interest payments will be transferred from the General Fund shortly before the due dates. Assume a yield on sinking fund investments of 6 percent per annum, compounded semiannually. Investment earnings are added to the investment principal. Based on this information:

(1) Prepare a schedule in good form showing the required additions to the sinking fund, the expected semiannual earnings, and the end-of-period balance in the sinking fund for each of the 10 semiannual periods. (*Note:* The future amount of an ordinary annuity of $1 for 10 periods at 3 percent per period is $11.4638793.)

(2) Record the issuance of the bonds.

(3) Create a term bond debt service fund and record its budget for the fiscal year ended June 30, 2011. Assume the budget has already been recorded for the General Fund. An appropriation should be provided only for the interest payment due on January 1, 2011. Also record an accrual for all interfund transfers to be received from the General Fund during the year.

b. On December 28, 2010, the General Fund transferred $234,461 to the debt service fund. The addition to the sinking fund was immediately invested in 6 percent certificates of deposit.

c. On December 28, 2010, the city issued checks to bondholders for the interest payment due on January 1, 2011.

d. On June 27, 2011, the General Fund transferred $234,461 to the debt service fund. The addition for the sinking fund was invested immediately in 6 percent certificates of deposit.

e. Actual interest earned on sinking fund investments at year-end (June 30, 2011) was the same as the amount budgeted [see *a*(1) and *a*(3)]. This interest adds to the sinking fund balance.

f. All appropriate closing entries were made at June 30, 2011 for the debt service fund.

6–10 Comprehensive Capital Assets/Serial Bond Problem. Transaction data related to the City of Chambers's issuance of serial bonds to finance street and park improvements follow. Utilizing worksheets formatted as shown at the end of the problem, prepare all necessary journal entries for these transactions in the city's capital projects fund, debt service fund, and governmental activities at the government-wide level. You may ignore related entries in the General Fund. Round all amounts to the nearest whole dollar.

a. On July 1, 2010, the first day of its fiscal year, the City of Chambers issued serial bonds with a face value totaling $5,000,000 and having maturities ranging from one to 20 years to make certain street and park improvements. The bonds were issued at 102 and bear interest of 5 percent per annum, payable semiannually on January 1 and July 1, with the first payment due on January 1, 2011. The first installment of principal in the amount of $250,000 is due on July 1, 2011. Premiums on bonds issued must be deposited directly in the debt service fund and be used for payment of bond interest. Premiums are amortized using the straight-line method in the governmental activities journal but are not amortized in the debt service fund. Debt service for the serial bonds will be provided by a one-quarter-cent city sales tax imposed on every dollar of sales in the city.

(1) Record the FY 2011 budget for the Serial Bond Debt Service Fund, utilizing worksheets formatted as shown at the end of this problem. The city estimates that the sales tax will generate $440,000 in FY 2011. An appropriation needs to be provided only for the interest payment due on January 1, 2011.

(2) Record the issuance of the bonds, again utilizing your worksheets.

b. On August 2, 2010, the city entered into a $4,800,000 contract with Central Paving and Construction. Work on street and park improvement projects is expected to begin immediately and continue until August 2011.

c. On August 10, 2010, the capital project fund paid the city's Utility Fund $42,000 for relocating power lines and poles to facilitate street widening. No encumbrance had been recorded for this service.

d. On August 20, 2010, the city's Public Works Department billed the capital projects fund $30,000 for engineering and other design assistance. This amount was paid.

e. Street and park improvement sales taxes for debt service of $248,000 were collected in the six months ending December 31, 2010.

f. On January 1, 2011, the city mailed checks to bondholders for semiannual interest on the bonds.

g. On January 15, 2011, Central Paving and Construction submitted a billing to the city for $2,500,000. The city's public works inspector agrees that all milestones have been met for this portion of the work.

h. On February 2, 2011, the city paid Central Paving and Construction the amount it had billed, except for 4 percent that was withheld as a retained percentage per terms of the contract.

i. During the six months ended June 30, 2011, sales tax collections for debt service amounted to $194,600.

j. Make all appropriate adjusting and closing entries at June 30, 2011, the end of the fiscal year. Based on authorization from the Public Works Department, $1,650,000 of construction work in progress was reclassified as infrastructure and another $250,000 was reclassified as improvements other than buildings. (Ignore closing entry for governmental activities.)

k. Reestablish the Encumbrances account balance in the capital projects fund effective July 1, 2011.

l. Record the FY 2012 budget for the debt service fund, assuming sales revenues are estimated at $492,000.

m. On July 1, 2011, the city mailed checks totaling $125,000 to all bondholders for semiannual interest and $250,000 to holders of record for bonds being redeemed.

n. On August 14, 2011, Central Paving and Construction submitted a final billing to the city for $2,300,000.

o. On August 23, 2011, the city paid the August 14 billing, except for a 4 percent retained percentage.

p. Upon final inspection by the Public Works Department, it was discovered that the contractor had failed to provide all required landscaping and certain other work for the street and park improvements. Public works employees completed this work at a total cost of $210,000. This amount was transferred to the General Fund using all retained cash and other cash of the capital projects fund.

q. The balance of the Construction Work in Progress account was reclassified as $150,000 to Improvements Other Than Buildings and the remainder to Infrastructure.

r. All remaining cash in the capital projects fund was transferred to the debt service fund and all accounts of the capital projects fund were closed.

Capital Projects Fund	***Capital Projects Fund***	***Governmental Activities***
Example: Cash 5,000,000 OFS—Proceeds of Bonds 5,000,000		

Debt Service Fund	***Debt Service Fund***	***Governmental Activities***

(Label as needed)	***(Label as needed)***	***(Label as needed)***

Chapter **Seven**

Accounting for the Business-type Activities of State and Local Governments

Learning Objectives

After studying this chapter, you should be able to:

1. Distinguish between the purposes of internal service funds and enterprise funds.
2. Describe the characteristics of proprietary funds, including those unique to internal service and enterprise funds.
3. Explain the financial reporting requirements, including the differences between the reporting of internal service and enterprise funds in the government-wide and fund financial statements.
4. Describe accounting procedures and prepare journal entries and financial statements for an internal service fund.
5. Describe accounting procedures and prepare journal entries and financial statements for an enterprise fund.

Chapters 3–6 addressed accounting and reporting for governmental funds. This chapter addresses accounting and reporting for proprietary funds. Governmental funds owe their existence to legal constraints placed on the raising of revenues and the use of resources. In contrast to the governmental funds, proprietary funds rely primarily on exchange transactions, specifically charges for services, to generate revenues. As a result, proprietary funds follow accounting principles that are similar to those of investor-owned businesses.

The focus on exchange transactions with parties outside of government is the reason that the enterprise funds are reported in a separate Business-type Activities column at the government-wide level, whereas governmental funds and internal service funds are reported as governmental activities at the government-wide level.

of a capital asset, but the proceeds of the debt have not been spent by year-end, that debt is excluded in calculating invested in capital assets, net of related debt. Restricted net assets are those net assets with restrictions on use imposed by law or external parties. For example, if a bond is issued for construction of a capital asset, but is unspent at year-end, the proceeds from the bond would be considered restricted net assets. Unrestricted net assets represent the residual amount of net assets after separately identifying investment in capital assets, net of related debt, and restricted net assets.

Statement of Revenues, Expenses, and Changes in Fund Net Assets

The period results of operations for a proprietary fund should be reported in a statement of revenues, expenses, and changes in fund net assets, which is similar to the income statement of a profit-seeking business. GASB standards state that revenues are to be reported by major revenue source. Unlike Financial Accounting Standards Board (FASB) standards, GASB standards also indicate that revenues should be shown net of any discounts or allowances. For example, rather than reporting bad debt expense, proprietary funds would record and report a contra-revenue account, such as Provision for Bad Debts, which would be netted against the Revenues account in the financial report. In the statement of revenues, expenses, and changes in fund net assets, revenues and expenses are to be identified as operating or nonoperating, with subtotals for operating revenues, operating expenses, and operating income. Operating revenues and expenses are those related to the primary functions of the proprietary fund. Management judgment is necessary when defining which revenues and expenses are primary to the operations of the fund. The distinction between operating and nonoperating revenues and expenses is important for achieving effective management control, as well as for complying with GASB requirements. If interfund transfers, special items, extraordinary items, or capital contributions are also reported in the statement of revenues, expenses, and changes in fund net assets they appear after the Nonoperating Revenues/Expenses section.

Statement of Cash Flows

GASB financial reporting standards require the preparation of a statement of cash flows as a part of the full set of financial statements for all proprietary funds. Unlike FASB, GASB requires the statement to be prepared using the direct method of presentation. Additionally, categories of cash flows provided by FASB *Statement No. 95* were deemed insufficient to meet the needs of users of governmental financial reports. Consequently, GASB standards provide four categories of cash flows: operating, noncapital financing, capital and related financing, and investing. In each category, the term *cash* also includes **cash equivalents** (defined as short-term, highly liquid investments).

Cash flows from *operating* activities include receipts from customers, receipts from sales to other funds, payments to suppliers of goods or services, payments to employees for services, payments for purchases from other funds (including payments in lieu of taxes that approximate the value of services received), and other operating cash receipts and payments.

Cash flows from *noncapital financing* activities include proceeds from debt not clearly attributable to acquisition, construction, or improvement of capital assets; receipts from grants, subsidies, or taxes other than those specifically restricted for capital purposes or those for specific operating activities; payment of interest on and repayment of principal of noncapital financing debt; and grants or subsidies paid to other governments, funds, or organizations except payments for specific operating activities of the grantor government.

Cash flows from *capital and related financing* activities include proceeds of debt and receipts from special assessments and taxes specifically attributable to acquisition, construction, or improvement of capital assets; receipts from capital grants; receipts from the sale of capital assets; proceeds of insurance on capital assets that are stolen or destroyed; payments to acquire, construct, or improve capital assets; and payment of interest on and repayment or refunding of capital and related financing debt.

Cash flows from *investing* activities include receipts from collection of loans; interest and dividends received on loans, debt instruments of other entities, equity securities, and cash management and investment pools; receipts from the sales of debt or equity instruments; withdrawals from investment pools not used as demand accounts; disbursements for loans; payments to acquire debt or equity instruments; and deposits into investment pools not used as demand accounts.

Budgetary Comparison Schedule

Unlike the General Fund and other major governmental funds for which a budget is legally adopted, proprietary funds are not required by GASB standards to record budgets in their accounting systems, nor are they required to present a budgetary comparison schedule. Some governments do, however, require all funds to operate under legally adopted budgets. In such cases GASB standards permit but do not require the integration of budgetary accounts in the manner described in Chapters 3 and 4 for the General Fund and special revenue funds.

INTERNAL SERVICE FUNDS

Although the reason for the establishment of an internal service fund is to improve financial management of scarce resources, it should be stressed that a fund is a fiscal entity as well as an accounting entity; consequently, establishment of a fund is ordinarily subject to legislative approval. The ordinance or other legislative action that authorizes the establishment of an internal service fund should also specify the source or sources of financial resources to be used for fund operations. For example, to start up an internal service fund, the General Fund or an enterprise fund may *contribute* assets to the fund, or the internal service fund may receive the assets in the form of a long-term *interfund loan* to be repaid over a number of years. Alternatively, the resources initially allocated to an internal service fund may be acquired from the proceeds of a tax-supported bond issue or by transfer from other governments that anticipate utilizing the services to be rendered by the internal service fund. Since internal service funds are established to improve the management of resources, it is generally considered that their accounting and operations should be maintained on a business basis.

The accounting and operating of a fund on a business basis can lead to conflict between managers, who want the freedom to operate the fund like a business, and legislators, who wish to exercise considerable control over funds. For example, assume that administrators request the establishment of a fund for the purchasing, warehousing, and issuing of supplies used by a number of funds and departments. Since no internal fund exists at the time of the request, each fund or department will include in its budget an appropriation for supplies, an appropriation for salaries and wages of personnel engaged in purchasing and handling the supplies, and an appropriation for any operating expense or facility costs associated with the supply function. Accordingly, legislators are likely to believe that by maintaining control over these budgets, they will be able to control the investment in supplies and the use of supplies by each fund and department. On the other hand, if they approve the establishment of the

ILLUSTRATION 7–1 Relationship between Appropriations and Internal Service Funds

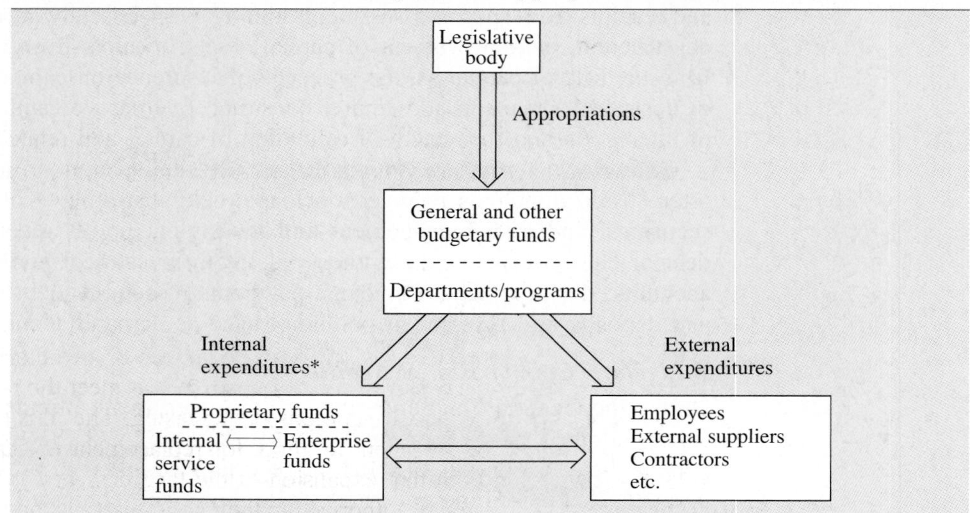

*Internal expenditures are more formally referred to as *interfund services provided and used* or, the term the authors prefer, *internal exchange transactions*.

requested supply fund, with the authority to generate operating revenues sufficient to maintain the fund, legislators may believe the supply function will no longer be subjected to annual legislative budget review and the legislature will "lose control" of the fund. Administrators are more likely to believe that if an internal service fund does not have the authority to generate operating revenues sufficient to maintain the fund and to spend those revenues at the discretion of fund management (rather than at the discretion of persons possibly more concerned with reelection than financial management), little will be gained by establishing the internal service fund.

The two opposing views should be somewhat balanced by the fact that, as shown in Illustration 7–1, the customers of an internal service fund are, by definition, other funds and departments of the government or of other governments. Therefore, each using fund and department must include in its appropriations budget request the justification for the amount to be spent (i.e., paid to the internal service fund) for supplies, so the legislative branch continues to exercise budgetary review over the amount each fund and department budgets for supplies. As shown in Illustration 7–1, departments and programs that require legislative appropriations to expend resources for goods and services should account for purchases of goods or services from internal suppliers (i.e., internal service funds or enterprise funds) in essentially the same manner as goods and services purchased from external suppliers. By setting pricing policies for the internal service fund and policies governing the use and retention of current earnings, the legislature can maintain considerable control over the function performed by the internal service fund but leave the fund managers freedom to operate at their discretion within the policies set by the legislative branch.

One of the more difficult problems to resolve to the satisfaction of persons with opposing views is the establishment of a pricing policy. "Cost" is obviously an incomplete answer: Historical cost of the supplies, whether defined as first-in, first-out; last-in, first-out; average; or specific identification, will not provide sufficient revenue to replace supplies issued if replacement prices have risen since the last purchase. Nor will it allow for an increase in the inventory quantities if the scale of governmental operations is growing. Payroll and other cash operating expenses of the internal service fund must be met; if the internal service fund has received a loan from another fund or another government, prices must be set at a level that will generate cash needed for debt retirement. If the internal service fund is to be operated on a true business basis, it must also be able to finance from its operations the replacement, modernization, and expansion of plant and equipment used in fund operations. Prices charged by the internal service fund, however, should be less than the using funds and departments would have to pay outside vendors for equivalent products and services if the existence and continued operation of the internal service fund is to be justified.

Because of the considerations mentioned in preceding paragraphs, many different approaches to internal service fund operations are found in practice. The illustrations given in the following sections of this chapter assume that the financial objective of an internal service fund is to recover from operating revenues the full cost of operations with enough net income to allow for replacement of inventories in periods of rising prices and enough increase in inventory quantities to meet the needs of using funds and departments whose scale of operations is increasing. The illustrations also assume that net income should be sufficient to allow for replacement of capital assets used by the internal service fund but that expansion of the facilities must be financed through contributions from other funds authorized in their appropriations budgets. Managers of internal service funds must prepare operating plans—budgets—as a management tool. The illustrations assume that the budgets of internal service funds are submitted to the legislative body and to the public for information but not for legal action. Therefore, the budget is not formally recorded in internal service fund accounts. Similarly, managers of businesses must be kept informed of the status of outstanding purchase orders and contracts, but encumbrances need not be recorded in the accounts to accomplish this.

Accounting for an internal service fund concerned with the functions of purchasing, warehousing, and issuing supplies is illustrated in the following section.

Illustrative Case—Supplies Fund

In prior chapters a "dual-track" approach captured transactions using both the modified accrual (governmental funds) and the accrual (government-wide) basis of accounting. Because the internal service fund uses accrual accounting, the "dual-track" approach is not needed to capture the different bases of accounting, since the basis is the same at the fund level and the government-wide level. However, the internal service fund is generally reported as a part of the Governmental Activities column of the government-wide financial statements. To ensure that double counting of revenues, expenses, and other transactions does not occur, GASB standards require the elimination of the effect of transactions between governmental funds and internal service funds.[2] For this reason, the "dual-track" approach is used in recording the following internal service fund transactions, thus ensuring that double counting does not occur at the government-wide level.

Assume that the administrators of the Town of Brighton obtain approval from the town council to centralize the purchasing, storing, and issuing functions as of January 1, 2011, and to administer and account for these functions in a Supplies Fund. The town's General Fund is to transfer to the new fund its December 31, 2010, inventory of supplies totaling $61,500 and $30,000 in cash to be used for working capital; these transfers are intended as contributions to the Supplies Fund and are not to be repaid (see Chapter 4, illustrative Entry 2). Transfers of this nature are initially recorded by the receiving fund as interfund transfers in, as shown in Entry 1. Since the transaction

[2] GASB *Codification of Governmental Accounting and Financial Reporting Standards, as of June 30, 2008* (Norwalk, CT: GASB, 2008), Sec. 1800.103.

involves two funds reported in the Governmental Activities column of the government-wide financial statements, no journal entry is made at the government-wide level.

		Debits	Credits
	Supplies Fund:		
1.	Cash	30,000	
	Inventory of Supplies	61,500	
	Interfund Transfers In		91,500

In order to provide cash to be used for acquisition of a building and the equipment needed to handle the supply function efficiently, the town's Water Utility Fund is to provide a long-term interest-free interfund loan of $130,000 to the Supplies Fund. The loan is to be repaid by the Supplies Fund in 20 equal annual installments. Entry 2 illustrates the entry to be made by the Supplies Fund for the receipt of the interfund loan; Water Utility Fund entries for this transaction are illustrated later in this chapter.

		Debits	Credits
	Supplies Fund:		
2a.	Cash	130,000	
	Interfund Loan from Water Utility Fund—Current		6,500
	Interfund Loan from Water Utility Fund—Noncurrent		123,500
	Governmental Activities:		
2b.	Cash	130,000	
	Internal Balances		130,000

Assume that a satisfactory warehouse building is purchased for $95,000; $25,000 of the purchase price is considered the cost of the land. Necessary warehouse machinery and equipment are purchased for $25,000. Delivery equipment is purchased for $10,000. If the purchases are made for cash, the acquisition of the assets would be recorded in the books of the Supplies Fund as follows:

		Debits	Credits
	Supplies Fund:		
3a.	Land	25,000	
	Buildings	70,000	
	Machinery and Equipment—Warehouse	25,000	
	Equipment—Delivery	10,000	
	Cash		130,000
	Governmental Activities:		
3b.	Land	25,000	
	Buildings	70,000	
	Equipment	35,000	
	Cash		130,000

Additional supplies would be ordered to ensure inventories can meet expected demand for supplies. During 2011, it is assumed supplies are received and related invoices are approved for payment in the amount of $192,600; the entry needed to record the asset and the liability follows:

		Debits	***Credits***
	Supplies Fund and Governmental Activities:		
4.	Inventory of Supplies	192,600	
	Vouchers Payable		192,600

The Supplies Fund should account for its inventories on the perpetual inventory basis since the information is needed for proper performance of its primary function. Accordingly, when supplies are issued, the inventory account must be credited for the cost of the supplies issued. Since the using fund will be charged an amount in excess of the inventory carrying value, the receivable and revenue accounts must reflect the selling price. The markup above cost should be determined on the basis of budgeted expenses and other items to be financed from net income, in relation to expected requisitions by using funds. If the budget for the Town of Brighton's Supplies Fund indicates a markup of 35 percent on cost is needed, issues to General Fund departments (see Chapter 4, illustrative Entry 4a) of supplies costing $185,000 would be recorded by the following entries:

		Debits	Credits
	Supplies Fund:		
5a.	Cost of Supplies Issued	185,000	
	Inventory of Supplies		185,000
5b.	Due from General Fund	249,750	
	Billings to Departments		249,750

For the effect of this transaction at the government-wide level see Chapter 4, Entry 4b.

If collections from the General Fund (see Chapter 4, illustrative Entry 5a) during 2011 totaled $249,750, the entry is as follows:

		Debits	Credits
	Supplies Fund:		
6.	Cash	249,750	
	Due from General Fund		249,750

No entry is required at the government-wide level since this transaction is between two funds that are both part of governmental activities.

Assuming that payroll and fringe benefits totaling $55,000 during the year were all paid in cash and distributed to the functional expense accounts in the amounts shown, Entry 7 is appropriate.

		Debits	Credits
	Supplies Fund:		
7a.	Administrative Expenses	11,000	
	Purchasing Expenses	19,000	
	Warehousing Expenses	12,000	
	Delivery Expenses	13,000	
	Cash		55,000
	Governmental Activities:		
7b.	Expenses—General Government	55,000	
	Cash		55,000

ILLUSTRATION 7–2

TOWN OF BRIGHTON SUPPLIES FUND
Statement of Fund Net Assets
As of December 31, 2011

Assets			
Current assets:			
Cash			$ 54,250
Inventory of supplies, at average cost			69,100
Total current assets			123,350
Capital assets:			
Land		$25,000	
Building	$70,000		
Less: Allowance for depreciation	3,500	66,500	
Machinery and equipment—warehouse	25,000		
Less: Allowance for depreciation	2,500	22,500	
Equipment—delivery	10,000		
Less: Allowance for depreciation	2,000	8,000	
Total capital assets			122,000
Total assets			245,350
Liabilities			
Current liabilities:			
Vouchers payable			28,600
Current portion of long-term liabilities			6,500
Total current liabilities			35,100
Long-term liabilities:			
Interfund loan from water utility			117,000
Total liabilities			152,100
Net Assets			
Unrestricted			$ 93,250

Statement of Net Assets

The statement of net assets for the Supplies Fund of the Town of Brighton as of December 31, 2011, is shown as Illustration 7–2. As of December 31, 2011, the Supplies Fund investment in capital assets of $122,000 is less than the balance of the interfund loan of $123,500 ($117,000 long-term liability plus $6,500 current portion due within one year). Thus, there is no net investment in capital assets to report. There also are no assets restricted as to use by external resource providers or legislative action. As a result, the Supplies Fund has only unrestricted net assets as of December 31, 2011.

Statement of Revenues, Expenses, and Changes in Fund Net Assets

Illustration 7–3 presents a statement of revenues, expenses, and changes in fund net assets for the year ended December 31, 2011, for the Town of Brighton Supplies Fund. Since interfund transfers are not a part of the primary activity of the Supplies Fund, they are shown below operating income.

Statement of Cash Flows

For the statement of cash flows (Illustration 7–4), the transactions of the Supplies Fund recorded in Entries 6, 7a, and 8 are classified as operating activities and are

ILLUSTRATION 7–3

TOWN OF BRIGHTON SUPPLIES FUND
Statement of Revenues, Expenses, and Changes in Fund Net Assets
For the Year Ended December 31, 2011

Operating revenues:		
Billings to departments		$249,750
Less: Cost of supplies issued		185,000
Gross margin		64,750
Operating expenses:		
Purchasing expenses	$19,350	
Administrative expenses	11,350	
Warehousing expenses	17,300	
Delivery expenses	15,000	
Total operating expenses		63,000
Operating income		1,750
Interfund transfers in		91,500
Change in net assets		93,250
Net assets—January 1, 2011		-0-
Net assets—December 31, 2011		$ 93,250

reported in the first section of the statement of cash flows. As required by GASB standards, the statement of cash flows is accompanied by a reconciliation of operating income with the net cash flow from operating activities. The contribution from the General Fund to the Supplies Fund (see Entry 1) is reported in the cash flows from noncapital financing activities section of the statement of cash flows. The transactions recorded in Entries 2a, 3a, and 9a are classified as capital and related financing activities and are reported in that section of the statement of cash flows. During 2011 there were no transactions that would be classified as investing activities.

External Financial Reporting of Internal Service Funds

The financial statements presented in Illustrations 7–2, 7–3, and 7–4 are prepared for internal management purposes. As indicated earlier, for external reporting purposes the Supplies Fund financial information would be reported as a separate column of the statement of net assets—proprietary funds; statement of revenues, expenses, and changes in net assets—proprietary funds; and statement of cash flows—proprietary funds, each of which is prepared for all proprietary funds (see Illustrations A1–7, A1–8, and A1–9 for examples). In the government-wide statement of net assets and statement of activities, internal service fund financial information is, in most cases, "collapsed" into and reported in the Governmental Activities column of both government-wide financial statements.

As shown by the journal entries for the Supplies Fund, collapsing information requires eliminating any interfund activity between a governmental fund and an internal service fund. Thus, under the dual-track approach those activities involving a transaction between a governmental fund (General Fund in the Town of Brighton illustration) and an internal service fund (Supplies Fund in the Town of Brighton illustration) are not recorded for governmental activities at the government-wide level.

If a portion of an internal service fund's operating income results from billings to enterprise funds, the GASB requirement to report internal service fund financial

Dissolution of an Internal Service Fund

When an internal service fund has completed the mission for which it was established or its activity is terminated for any other reason (such as outsourcing the activity to an outside vendor), dissolution must be accomplished. Liquidation may be accomplished in any one of three ways or in combinations thereof: (1) transfer the fund's assets to another fund that will continue the operation as a subsidiary activity, for example, a supply fund becoming a *department* of the General Fund; (2) distribute the fund's assets to another fund or to another government; or (3) convert all its noncash assets to cash and distribute the cash to another fund or other funds. Dissolution of an internal service fund, as for a private enterprise, would proceed by first paying outside creditors, followed by repayment of any long-term interfund loans outstanding and, finally, liquidation of remaining net assets. The entire process of dissolution should be conducted according to pertinent law and the discretion of the appropriate legislative body. Net assets contributed by another fund or government logically would revert to the contributor fund or government, but law or other regulations may dictate otherwise. If net assets have been built up from charges in excess of costs, liquidation will follow whatever regulations may govern the case; if none exist, the appropriate governing body must decide on the recipient or recipients.

ENTERPRISE FUNDS

Enterprise funds and internal service funds are both classified by the GASB as proprietary funds, although only the enterprise funds are generally reported as part of the Business-type Activities column of the government-wide financial statements. As discussed in the prior section of the chapter, internal service funds are generally reported as part of the Governmental Activities column. If only enterprise funds are included in the Business-type Activities column, there is no need to maintain a separate set of accounting records for the business-type activities at the government-wide level. Rather, the financial records of the enterprise funds can simply be added together for financial reporting purposes at the government-wide level. Any interfund transactions among enterprise funds should be eliminated because they would have no net effect on overall business-type activities.

Enterprise funds are used by governments to account for services provided to the general public on a user charge basis. Under GASB standards, a government must report certain activities in an enterprise fund if any of the following criteria are met.[4]

1. The activity is financed with debt that is secured *solely* by a pledge of the revenues from fees and charges of an activity. [Emphasis added by authors.]
2. Laws or regulations require that the activity's costs of providing services, including capital costs (such as depreciation or debt service), be recovered with fees and charges, rather than with taxes or similar revenues.
3. Pricing policies are designed to recover the costs of the activity, including capital costs.

These criteria are quite specific regarding when an enterprise fund *must* be used. For example, if debt issued is also backed by the full faith and credit of the government, even though it is intended to be repaid from revenues of a particular activity,

[4] GASB *Codification,* Sec. 1300.109.

that activity need not be reported in an enterprise fund. Similarly, if an activity is subsidized by a government's General Fund rather than fully covering its costs of providing services with fees or charges, that activity need not be reported in an enterprise fund. In either of these examples, the government could opt to report the activities in an enterprise fund. However, if governments support the activities *primarily* with general or special revenue sources rather than user charges, accounting for the activities is more appropriate in the General Fund or a special revenue fund.

Since the word *enterprise* is often used as a synonym for "business-type activity," it is logical that enterprise funds should use accrual accounting and account for all assets used in the production of goods or services offered by the fund. Similarly, if long-term debt is to be serviced by the fund, the fund does the accounting for the debt.

The most common examples of governmental enterprises are public utilities, notably water and sewer utilities. Electric and gas utilities, transportation systems, airports, ports, hospitals, toll bridges, produce markets, parking lots, parking garages, liquor stores, and public housing projects are other examples frequently found. Since services of the types mentioned are intended to be largely self-supporting, they are generally accounted for by enterprise funds.

Almost every type of enterprise operated by a government has its counterpart in the private sector. In order to take advantage of the work done by regulatory agencies and trade associations to develop useful accounting information systems for the investor-owned enterprises, *it is recommended that governmentally owned enterprises use the accounting structures developed for investor-owned enterprises of the same nature.*[5] Budgetary accounts should be used only if required by law. The accounting for debt service and construction activities of a governmental enterprise occurs within the enterprise fund rather than by separate debt service and capital projects funds. Thus, the financial statements of enterprise funds are self-contained, and creditors, legislators, or the general public can evaluate the performance of a governmental enterprise on the same bases as they can the performance of investor-owned enterprises in the same industry.

By far the most numerous and important enterprise services rendered by local governments are public utilities. In this chapter, therefore, the example used is that of a water utility fund.

[5] *GASBS 20* and *GASBS 34* provide guidance on business-type accounting and financial reporting for proprietary activities. This guidance clarifies the authoritative status of FASB pronouncements in determining generally accepted accounting principles (GAAP) for proprietary activities given the GAAP hierarchy provided in *Statement on Auditing Standards No. 69*, "The Meaning of 'Present Fairly in Conformity with Generally Accepted Accounting Principles' in the Independent Auditor's Report" (AICPA, 1992). *GASBS 20* gives governments an option between two accounting and financial reporting approaches for proprietary funds. The first approach requires consistent use of all GASB pronouncements and applicable pronouncements of FASB and its predecessors (Accounting Principles Board and Committee on Accounting Procedure) issued on or before November 30, 1989, unless those pronouncements conflict with or contradict GASB pronouncements. The second approach requires consistent use of all GASB pronouncements and all applicable pronouncements (both before and after November 30, 1989) of FASB and its predecessors unless those pronouncements conflict with or contradict GASB pronouncements. Thus, under the first approach, unless GASB directs otherwise, governments are not required to change their accounting procedures if FASB issues a standard that supersedes or amends a standard issued on or before November 30, 1989. This date (November 30, 1989) is significant as it is the date the Financial Accounting Foundation resolved a conflict over jurisdiction of the FASB and GASB.

WATER UTILITY FUNDS

The statement of net assets as of December 31, 2010, for the Town of Brighton Water Utility Fund is shown in Illustration 7–5. The statement appears fairly conventional, but terminology peculiar to utilities warrants discussion prior to proceeding to the illustrative transactions for the year ending December 31, 2011. Part of the difference in terminology relates to the fact that the Water Utility Fund is part of a regulated

ILLUSTRATION 7–5

TOWN OF BRIGHTON
Water Utility Fund
Statement of Net Assets
As of December 31, 2010

Assets			
Current and accrued assets:			
Cash		$ 126,000	
Customer accounts receivable	$69,000		
Less: Accumulated provision for uncollectibles	2,900	66,100	
Accrued utilities revenues		14,800	
Materials and supplies		28,700	
Total current and accrued assets			$ 235,600
Restricted assets:			
Cash		6,600	
Investments		556,000	562,600
Utility plant:			
Utility plant in service		3,291,825	
Less: Accumulated depreciation		440,325	
Utility plant—net		2,851,500	
Construction work in progress		125,000	
Net utility plant			2,976,500
Total assets			3,774,700
Liabilities			
Current liabilities:			
Accounts payable		33,200	
Customer advances for construction		21,000	
Total current liabilities			54,200
Liabilities payable from restricted assets:			
Customer deposits			23,700
Long-term liabilities:			
Revenue bonds payable (net of unamortized discount of $5,300)			1,744,700
Total liabilities			1,822,600
Net Assets			
Invested in capital assets, net of related debt			1,231,800
Restricted for payment of debt service			538,900
Unrestricted			181,400
Total net assets			$1,952,100

industry. As such, the primary regulatory bodies, the National Association of Regulatory Utility Commissioners (NARUC) and Federal Energy Regulatory Commission (FERC), influence the accounting for utilities.

Current and Accrued Assets

The Cash and Materials and Supplies accounts shown in Illustration 7–5 in the Current and Accrued Assets section are not peculiar to utilities and need not be discussed here. The other two asset accounts in this section—Customer Accounts Receivable and Accrued Utilities Revenues—are related. The former represents billings to customers that are outstanding at year-end (and are reduced by an accumulated provision for uncollectibles). The latter results from the fact that utilities generally prepare billings to customers on the basis of meter readings, and it is not practical for utilities to read all meters simultaneously at year-end and bill all customers as of that time. Utilities that meter their service make extensive use of cycle billing, which, in substance, consists of billing part of their customers each day instead of billing by calendar months. Under this plan, meter reading is a continuous day-by-day operation, with billings following shortly after the filing of the meter readers' reports. Individual meters are read on approximately the same day each month, or every other month, so that each bill covers approximately the same number of days of usage. Cycle billing eliminates the heavy peak load of accounting and clerical work that results from uniform billing on a calendar month basis. It does, however, result in a sizeable amount of unbilled receivables on any given date. Thus, in order to state assets and sales properly, accrual of unbilled receivables (Accrued Utilities Revenues, in regulatory terminology) is required as of the financial statement date.[6]

Restricted Assets

The section following Current and Accrued Assets in Illustration 7–5 is captioned Restricted Assets, the caption most commonly used when the use of assets is restricted by contractual agreements or legal requirements. Some governments that use regulatory terminology report restricted assets of utilities under the broader caption, Other Property and Investments. Other Property and Investments may include, in addition to restricted assets, the carrying value of property not being used for utility purposes or being held for future utility use.

Cash and Investments are the only two items reported under the Restricted Assets caption of the balance sheet shown in Illustration 7–5. Those items are restricted for return of customer deposits and for retirement of revenue bonds pursuant to the bond covenants. The amount of assets segregated, $562,600, is offset by liabilities currently payable from restricted assets (in the case of the Town of Brighton, customer deposits of $23,700) and restrictions of net assets (in this case, restricted for payment of debt service, $538,900). This *fund within a fund* approach permits segregation of assets, related liabilities, and restricted net assets within a single enterprise fund. Net assets should be restricted in the amount of the net assets of each restricted "fund" within the enterprise fund, as shown in Illustration 7–5. Other items commonly reported in the Restricted Assets section include assets set aside to fund depreciation for capital improvements or grants and contributions restricted for capital acquisition or improvement.

[6] Some governments use the same or a similar chart of accounts for utilities as those of regulated profit-seeking enterprises in the same industry.

Utility Plant

Utility Plant in Service

Utility Plant in Service is a control account, supported in whatever detail is required by regulatory agencies and by management needs. For example, water utilities commonly have six subcategories of plant assets: intangible plant, source of supply plant, pumping plant, water treatment plant, transmission and distribution plant, and general plant. Each of the six subcategories is supported by appropriate subsidiary accounts. For example, intangible plant consists of the costs of organization, franchises, and consents, and any other intangible costs necessary and valuable to the conduct of utility operations. Source of supply plant consists of land and land rights; structures and improvements; collecting and impounding reservoirs; lake, river, and other intakes; wells and springs; infiltration galleries and tunnels; supply mains; and other water source plant. Each of the accounts within each subcategory is supported by necessary subsidiary records for each individual asset detailing its description, location, cost, date of acquisition, estimated useful life, salvage value, depreciation charges, and any other information needed for management planning and control, regulatory agency reports, financial statements, or special reports to creditors.

Construction Work in Progress

The other utility plant item shown on the statement of net assets, Illustration 7–5, is Construction Work in Progress. This account represents the accumulated costs of work orders for projects that will result in items reportable as utility plant when completed and is supported by the work orders for projects in progress. Each work order, in turn, is supported by documents supporting payments to contractors and to suppliers or supporting charges for materials, labor, and overhead allocable to the project. Unlike self-constructed general capital assets, GASB requires interest capitalization for self-constructed assets of proprietary funds, except those constructed with general long-term debt that will be repaid from resources of governmental activities.[7]

Current Liabilities

Items commonly found in the Current Liabilities section of a utility statement of net assets are shown under that caption in Illustration 7–5. Accounts Payable needs no comment here. The other item, **Customer Advances for Construction**, results from utilities' practice of requiring customers to advance to the utility a sizeable portion of the estimated cost of construction projects to be undertaken by the utility at the request of the customer. If the advances are to be refunded, either wholly or in part, or applied against billings for service rendered after completion of the project, they are classified as shown in Illustration 7–5. When a customer is refunded the entire amount to which he or she is entitled according to the agreement or rule under which the advance was made, the balance retained by the utility, if any, is reported as Contributions from Customers in the statement of revenues, expenses, and changes in fund net assets. Other items commonly reported under Current Liabilities include accrued expenses, amounts due to other funds, and current portions of long-term liabilities. Some governments also report customer deposits under the Current Liabilities caption.[8]

[7] GASB requires application of FASB *Statement No. 34,* "Capitalization of Interest Cost," as amended.

[8] Generally, customer deposits should be reported as Liabilities Payable from Restricted Assets, a special category of current liabilities, as explained in the following section.

Liabilities Payable from Restricted Assets

Liabilities payable from restricted assets should be displayed separately from current liabilities, as shown in Illustration 7–5. In addition to customer deposits, the current portion of revenue bonds payable, if any, would be reported here since restricted assets have been set aside for that purpose. The Town of Brighton follows the common practice of most utilities and requires all new customers to deposit a sum of money with the utility as security for the payment of bills. In many, but not all, jurisdictions, utilities are required to pay interest on customer deposits at a nominal rate. Regulatory authorities or local policy may require utilities to refund the deposits, and interest, after a specified period of time if the customer has paid all bills on time. The utility may be required, as was the Town of Brighton Water Utility Fund, to segregate cash or investments in an amount equal to the liability for Customer Deposits. Customer Advances for Construction are contractually different from Customer Deposits and are less likely to be reported separately as restricted assets and liabilities unless agreements with developers make it necessary to restrict assets for this purpose.

Long-term Liabilities

Bonds are the customary form of long-term liabilities. Bonds issued by a utility are usually secured by the pledge of certain portions of the utility's revenue, the exact terms of the pledge varying with individual cases; bonds of this nature are called **revenue bonds.** Some utility bonds are secured not only by a pledge of a certain portion of the utility's revenues but also by an agreement on the part of the town's or city's general government to subsidize the utility in any year in which its normal revenue is inadequate for compliance with the terms of the bond indenture. Other utility bonds carry the pledge of the government entity's full faith and credit, although the intent is to service them from utility revenues rather than general taxes. The latter are, therefore, technically **general obligation bonds.** GASB standards require that general obligation bonds intended to be serviced from utility revenues be reported as a liability of the enterprise fund. Similarly, special assessment debt may be assumed by an enterprise fund if the assets constructed by special assessment financing are used in enterprise fund operations.

Governmentally owned utilities may have received long-term interfund loans from the government's General Fund or other funds. Also, enterprises may acquire assets under a capital lease arrangement. The portion of interfund loans, required lease payments, or bond or other debt issues to be paid within one year from the statement of net assets date should be reported as a current liability; the remainder is properly reported in the Long-term Liabilities section of the utility statement of net assets. Long-term bonds payable should be reported net of unamortized discount or premium, as shown in Illustration 7–5, or the unamortized discount or premium can be reported as an offset against bonds payable at par on the statement of net assets.

Net Assets

As discussed earlier in the chapter, proprietary funds report using three net asset categories: invested in capital assets, net of related debt; restricted; and unrestricted. The three categories of net assets for the Water Utility Fund are shown in Illustration 7–5. Restrictions may be placed by law, regulation, or contractual agreement with creditors or other outside parties. Illustration 7–5 shows a typical restriction: A sinking fund created pursuant to a bond indenture for repayment of revenue bond principal. Unrestricted net assets represent the residual amount of net assets after segregating investment in capital assets, net of related debt, and restricted net assets.

Bond interest in the amount of $105,000 was paid; the bonds were issued to finance the acquisition of utility plant assets. Amortization of debt discount amounted to $530.

		Debits	Credits
8.	Interest on Long-term Debt	105,530	
	Unamortized Discount		530
	Cash		105,000

Bond interest in the amount of $12,900 was properly capitalized as part of construction work in progress during the year. (The Town of Brighton does not impute interest on its own resources during construction.)

9.	Construction Work in Progress	12,900	
	Interest on Long-term Debt		12,900

Construction projects on which costs totaled $220,000 were completed and the assets placed in service were recorded:

10.	Utility Plant in Service	220,000	
	Construction Work in Progress		220,000

Collection efforts on bills totaling $3,410 were discontinued. The customers owing the bills had paid deposits totaling $2,140 to the water utility; the deposits were applied to the bills, and the unpaid remainder was charged to Accumulated Provision for Uncollectible Accounts (Entry 11a). Restricted assets (cash) is reduced by $2,140, the amount of the decrease in Customer Deposits (Entry 11b).

11a.	Customer Deposits	2,140	
	Accumulated Provision for Uncollectible Accounts	1,270	
	Customer Accounts Receivable		3,410
11b.	Cash	2,140	
	Cash—Customer Deposits		2,140

Customers' deposits amounting to $1,320 were refunded by check to customers discontinuing service (see Entry 12a). Deposits totaling $2,525 were received from new customers (see Entry 12b).

12a.	Customer Deposits	1,320	
	Cash—Customer Deposits		1,320
12b.	Cash—Customer Deposits	2,525	
	Customer Deposits		2,525

Customers' advances for construction in the amount of $14,000 were applied to their water bills; in accord with the agreement with the customers and NARUC recommendations, the remainder of the advances was transferred to Capital Contributions from Customers.

		Debits	Credits
13.	Customer Advances for Construction	21,000	
	Customer Accounts Receivable		14,000
	Capital Contributions from Customers		7,000

Payments of accounts payable for materials and supplies used in operations totaled $67,200, and payment of accounts payable for materials used in construction totaled $66,000. Payments of taxes accrued amounted to $13,500, and payments of tax collections payable amounted to $50,000.

14.	Accounts Payable	133,200	
	Taxes Accrued	13,500	
	Tax Collections Payable	50,000	
	Cash		196,700

The Water Utility Fund agreed to pay $25,000 to the town General Fund as a payment in lieu of property taxes. The entry in the General Fund is illustrated in Chapter 4 (see Chapter 4, illustrative Entry 24a). The following entry records the event in the accounts of the Water Utility Fund:

15.	Payment in Lieu of Taxes	25,000	
	Due to General Fund		25,000

During the year, interest amounting to $44,500 in cash was received on restricted investments. The amount $1,375 is allocable to investments of customer deposit assets and is unrestricted as to use; the remaining $43,125 adds to the amount restricted for revenue bond repayment.

16a.	Cash	1,375	
	Cash—Bond Repayment	43,125	
	Interest and Dividend Income		44,500
16b.	Net Assets—Unrestricted	43,125	
	Net Assets—Restricted for Bond Repayment		43,125

At year-end, entries to record depreciation expense, the provision for uncollectible accounts, and unbilled customer accounts receivable should be made as illustrated by Entry 17. In accord with regulatory terminology, Uncollectible Accounts instead of Bad Debts Expense (FASB) or Provision for Bad Debts (GASB) is debited for the amount added to Accumulated Provision for Uncollectible Accounts. Amounts are assumed.

		Debits	Credits
17.	Depreciation Expense	102,750	
	Uncollectible Accounts	3,980	
	Accrued Utility Revenues	15,920	
	Accumulated Provision for Depreciation of Utility Plant		102,750
	Accumulated Provision for Uncollectible Accounts		3,980
	Sales of Water		15,920

In accord with the revenue bond indenture, $100,000 of unrestricted cash was invested in U.S. government securities for eventual retirement of revenue bonds. Net assets are restricted in an amount equal to the increase in restricted assets. In addition, investments totaling $40,000 were made from restricted cash for eventual bond repayment.

		Debits	Credits
18a.	Investments—Bond Repayment	140,000	
	Cash		100,000
	Cash—Bond Repayment		40,000
18b.	Net Assets—Unrestricted	100,000	
	Net Assets—Restricted for Bond Repayment		100,000

Toward the end of 2011, the Supplies Fund paid its first installment of $6,500 to the Water Utility Fund as a partial repayment of the long-term advance. Entry 9a of the illustrative entries for the supply fund shown earlier in this chapter (see the section titled "Illustrative Case—Supplies Fund") illustrates the effect of the Supplies Fund on the accounts. The effect on the accounts of the Water Utility Fund is recorded by the following entry:

		Debits	Credits
19.	Cash	6,500	
	Interfund Loan to Supplies Fund—Noncurrent		6,500

Nominal accounts for the year were closed:

		Debits	Credits
20.	Sales of Water	727,120	
	Capital Contributions from Customers	7,000	
	Interest and Dividend Income	44,500	
	Source of Supply Expenses		26,200
	Pumping Expenses		36,700
	Water Treatment Expenses		41,500
	Transmission and Distribution Expenses		89,250
	Customer Account Expenses		96,550
	Sales Expenses		17,250
	Administrative and General Expenses		83,150
	Interest on Long-term Debt		92,630
	Payment in Lieu of Taxes		25,000
	Depreciation Expense		102,750
	Uncollectible Accounts		3,980
	Net Assets—Unrestricted		163,660

In addition, Net Assets—Invested in Capital Assets, Net of Related Debt, would be decreased for depreciation and amortization of the debt discount and increased for the change in utility plant during the year.

Entry 21a reflects the adjustment for depreciation (Entry 17) and amortization of the bond discount (Entry 8). The increase to capital assets (Entries 6, 7 and 9), resulting in adjustment to net assets, is shown in Entry 21b.

		Debits	Credits
21a.	Net Assets—Invested in Capital Assets, Net of Related Debt . . .	103,280	
	Net Assets—Unrestricted		103,280
21b.	Net Assets—Unrestricted	109,300	
	Net Assets—Invested in Capital Assets, Net of Related Debt . .		109,300

Illustrative Statements Using Water Utility Fund

Statement of Net Assets

The statement of net assets for a water utility, and definitions of certain statement of net assets categories and items peculiar to regulated utilities, have been explained at length in the sections of this chapter preceding the illustrative entries. The statement of net assets of the Town of Brighton Water Utility Fund as of December 31, 2011, is shown as Illustration 7–6. Similar to what was done in Chapter 4 (Illustration 4–5), and in conformance with GASB standards, internal receivables and payables are netted. That is, the amount due to the General Fund is offset against the amount due from that fund, and only the net amount of the receivable, $5,000, is shown as an asset.

Statement of Revenues, Expenses, and Changes in Fund Net Assets

The activity of the Town of Brighton's Water Utility Fund for the year ended December 31, 2011, is shown in Illustration 7–7, the statement of revenues, expenses, and changes in fund net assets. In accordance with GASB standards, operating revenues are shown net of Uncollectible Accounts and revenues and expenses are identified as operating and nonoperating. The classifications and account titles used in the statement are consistent with NARUC and FERC recommendations. If NARUC and FERC had not been used, a contra-revenue account title such as Provision for Bad Debts would have been used rather than the title Uncollectible Accounts.

Statement of Cash Flows

GASB standards require that a statement of cash flows be prepared for all proprietary funds as part of a full set of annual financial statements. As discussed earlier in this chapter, GASB standards for preparation of a cash flow statement differ from FASB standards, the main difference being that GASB standards specify four major categories of cash flows rather than three. The statement of cash flows for the Town of Brighton for the year ended December 31, 2011 (Illustration 7–8), utilizes only three of the four categories of cash flows since the town had no cash flows from noncapital financing activities. The section *Cash Flows from Operating Activities* (Illustration 7–8) was provided by receipts from customers (Entry 4) and the net increase in refundable customer deposits (Entries 12a and 12b). Note that the application of customer deposits to pay overdue bills (Entries 11a and 11b) has no effect

ILLUSTRATION 7–6

TOWN OF BRIGHTON
Water Utility Fund
Statement of Net Assets
As of December 31, 2011

Assets			
Current and accrued assets:			
Cash		$ 4,865	
Customer accounts receivable	$67,590		
Less: Accumulated provision for uncollectibles	5,610	61,980	
Accrued utilities revenues		15,920	
Due from General Fund		5,000	
Materials and supplies		24,700	
Total current and accrued assets			$ 112,465
Restricted assets:			
Cash		8,790	
Investments		696,000	704,790
Utility plant:			
Utility plant in service		3,511,825	
Less: Accumulated depreciation		543,075	
Utility plant—net		2,968,750	
Construction work in progress		14,300	
Net utility plant			2,983,050
Other noncurrent assets:			
Interfund loan to supplies fund			123,500
Total assets			3,923,805
Liabilities			
Current liabilities:			
Accounts payable		38,000	
Taxes accrued		300	
Tax collection payable		1,750	
Total current liabilities			40,050
Liabilities payable from restricted assets:			
Customer deposits			22,765
Long-term liabilities:			
Revenue bonds payable (net of unamortized discount of $4,770)			1,745,230
Total liabilities			1,808,045
Net Assets			
Invested in capital assets, net of related debt			1,237,820
Restricted for payment of debt service			682,025
Unrestricted			195,915
Total net assets			$2,115,760

ILLUSTRATION 7–7

TOWN OF BRIGHTON
Water Utility Fund
Statement of Revenues, Expenses, and Changes in Fund Net Assets
For the Year Ended December 31, 2011

Utility operating revenue:		
Sales of water (net of $3,980 for uncollectible accounts)		$ 723,140
Operating expenses:		
Source of supply expenses	$ 26,200	
Pumping expenses	36,700	
Water treatment expenses	41,500	
Transmission and distribution expenses	89,250	
Customer account expenses	96,550	
Sales expenses	17,250	
Administrative and general expenses	83,150	
Depreciation expense	102,750	
Payment in lieu of taxes	25,000	
Total operating expenses		518,350
Utility operating income		204,790
Nonoperating income and deductions:		
Interest and dividend revenue	(44,500)	
Interest on long-term debt	92,630	
Total nonoperating income and deductions		48,130
Income before contributions		156,660
Capital contributions from customers		7,000
Change in net assets		163,660
Total net assets, January 1, 2011		1,952,100
Total net assets, December 31, 2011		$2,115,760

on total cash and cash equivalents. Cash from operating activities was used to pay employees (Entries 7 and 14). As suggested in the GASB *Comprehensive Implementation Guide* on reporting cash flows,[9] all employee-related items (in this case Taxes Accrued and Tax Collections Payable) have been added to the amount actually paid to employees. Payroll taxes and fringe benefits may be included in a separate line, called cash payments for taxes, duties, fines, and other fees or penalties, if significant in amount. Cash paid to employees for services in the amount of $312,550 is calculated as the net cash paid directly to employees, $279,450, less $30,400 capitalized as Construction Work in Progress (Entry 7) plus $63,500 paid for Taxes Accrued and Tax Collections Payable (Entry 14). Finally, cash from operating activities was used to pay suppliers (Entry 14). Although suppliers were paid $133,200 in total, only $67,200 of this amount applied to operating activities.

The section *Cash Flows from Capital and Related Activities* in Illustration 7–8 shows two uses of cash. The first item, acquisition and construction of capital assets, is calculated as the sum of $30,400 (Entry 7) and $66,000 (Entry 14 where amounts

[9] Governmental Accounting Standards Board, *Comprehensive Implementation Guide—2008* (Norwalk, CT, 2008), 2.29.2.

ILLUSTRATION 7–8

TOWN OF BRIGHTON WATER UTILITY FUND
Statement of Cash Flows
For the Year Ended December 31, 2011

Cash Flows from Operating Activities:	
Cash received from customers	$680,000
Cash provided from customer deposits	1,205
Cash paid to employees for services	(312,550)
Cash paid to suppliers	(67,200)
Net cash provided by operating activities	301,455
Cash Flows from Capital and Related Financing Activities:	
Acquisition and construction of capital assets	(96,400)
Interest paid on long-term bonds	(105,000)
Net cash used for capital and related financing activities	(201,400)
Cash Flows from Investing Activities:	
Interest and dividend income	44,500
Purchases of restricted investments	(140,000)
Interfund loan	(123,500)
Net cash used for investing activities	(219,000)
Net decrease in cash and cash equivalents	(118,945)
Cash and cash equivalents—January 1, 2011	132,600
Cash and cash equivalents—December 31, 2011	$ 13,655

Reconciliation of Cash and Cash Equivalents to the Statement of Net Assets

	End of Year	Beginning of Year
Cash and cash equivalents in current and accrued assets	$ 4,865	$126,000
Restricted cash and cash equivalents	8,790	6,600
Total cash and cash equivalents	$ 13,655	$132,600

Reconciliation of Utility Operating Income to Net Cash Provided by Operating Activities

Utility operating income		$204,790
Adjustments:		
Depreciation expense	$102,750	
Increase in accounts payable	4,800	
Increase in accrued liabilities	2,050	
Decrease in customer deposits	(935)	
Decrease in inventories	4,000	
Increase in interfund receivables	(5,000)	
Increase in accrued receivables	(1,120)	
Decrease in customer accounts receivable	4,120	
Customer advances applied to customer receivables	(14,000)	
Total adjustments		96,665
Net cash provided by operating activities		$301,455

recorded in Entry 6 were paid). The other item, interest paid on long-term bonds, reflects bond interest in the amount of $105,000 paid in cash (Entry 8).

The *Cash Flows from Investing Activities* section shows cash provided by interest and dividend income (Entry 16a), cash used to purchase investments (Entry 18a), and cash used to acquire an interfund loan (Entries 2 and 19).

As shown in Illustration 7–8, two reconciliations are required. The first reconciliation is necessary because the Town of Brighton's Statement of Cash Flows reports changes in *total* cash and cash equivalents, whereas the statement of net assets shows two components of cash and cash equivalents: that included in Current and Accrued Assets and that included in Restricted Assets, respectively.[10] GASB standards also require a reconciliation of operating income to net cash provided by operating activities.

External Financial Reporting of Enterprise Funds

As shown in Illustrations A1–1 and A1–2, the totals for all enterprise funds, with interfund transactions between enterprise funds eliminated, are reported in the Business-type Activities columns of the government-wide financial statements. Governments must also prepare three fund financial statements for their major enterprise funds (see the Glossary for a definition of major funds) and the total of their internal service funds. These statements are the statement of net assets (or balance sheet), statement of revenues, expenses, and changes in fund net assets, and statement of cash flows. Illustrative proprietary fund statements are presented in Illustrations A1–7, A1–8, and A1–9. As those statements show, a separate column is provided for internal service funds. The amounts shown in this column are the totals for all internal service funds, since major fund reporting does not apply to the internal service funds.

Regulatory Accounting Principles (RAP)

Investor-owned utilities, as well as governmentally owned utilities in some states, are required to report in a prescribed manner to state regulatory commissions. Electric and certain other utilities subject to the Federal Power Act must also file reports with the FERC. As mentioned in footnote 6, both NARUC and FERC prescribe charts of accounts and uniform financial statement formats for reporting to regulatory agencies. Even though the Town of Brighton follows GAAP rather than **regulatory accounting principles (RAP)** in preparing its financial statements, the town uses some of the chart of accounts and some of the financial statement captions provided in regulatory publications. The illustrative financial statements shown earlier in this chapter are typical of those for water funds included in comprehensive annual financial reports.

For utilities that are required to report to a state rate regulatory commission or the FERC, accounting and reporting procedures under RAP are quite different from GAAP. Because plant assets and long-term debt are customarily a dominant share of the total assets and total debt of utilities and current assets and current liabilities are relatively insignificant in amount, the regulatory balance sheet format displays plant assets before current assets and long-term debt before current liabilities. In Illustration 7–5, for example, Utility Plant—Net amounts to almost 79 percent of total assets, and long-term debt is almost 96 percent of total debt.

Under regulatory reporting, Utility Plant in Service is stated at original cost. Original cost is a regulatory concept that differs from historical cost, a concept commonly used in accounting for assets of nonregulated businesses. In essence, **historical cost** is the amount paid for an asset by its present owner. In contrast,

[10] Ibid., 2.31.1.

7–5. What is the purpose of the Restricted Assets section of an enterprise fund statement of fund net assets? Provide examples of items that might be reported in the Restricted Assets section.

7–6. Explain how capitalization of interest costs differs for enterprise funds as opposed to governmental funds.

7–7. How does the statement of cash flows under GASB standards differ from the statement of cash flows under FASB standards?

7–8. What are regulatory accounting principles and how do they relate to enterprise fund accounting?

7–9. Explain the difference between operating revenues/expenses and nonoperating revenues/expenses. Why does the GASB require that operating revenues/expenses be reported separately on proprietary statements of revenues, expenses, and changes in fund net assets?

7–10. What is meant by "segment information for enterprise funds"? When is the disclosure of segment information required?

Cases

7–1 Building Maintenance Fund. The balance sheet and statement of revenues, expenditures, and changes in fund balance for the Building Maintenance Fund, an internal service fund of Coastal City, are reproduced here. No further information about the nature or purposes of this fund is given in the annual report.

COASTAL CITY BUILDING MAINTENANCE FUND
Balance Sheet
As of December 31, 2011

Assets	
Assets:	
Cash and investments	$152,879
Accounts receivable	2,116
Inventory	779,000
Prepaid expenses	19,854
Total assets	$953,849
Liabilities and Fund Equity	
Liabilities:	
Accounts payable	$ 35,675
Other accrued liabilities	109,099
Accrued annual leave	227,369
Total liabilities	372,143
Fund equity:	
Fund balance	581,706
Total liabilities and fund equity	$953,849

COASTAL CITY BUILDING MAINTENANCE FUND
Statement of Revenues, Expenditures, and Changes in Fund Balance
Year Ended December 31, 2011

Revenues:	
Billings to departments	$10,774,781
Miscellaneous	100,344
Total billings	10,875,125
Expenditures:	
Salaries and employee benefits	3,353,413
Supplies	3,409,096
Operating services and charges	495,143
Maintenance and repairs	3,536,443
Total expenditures	10,794,095
Excess of revenues over expenditures	81,030
Fund balance—January 1, 2011	500,676
Fund balance—December 31, 2011	$ 581,706

Required

a. Assuming that the Building Maintenance Fund is an internal service fund, discuss whether the financial information is presented in accordance with GASB standards.

b. If you were the manager of a city department that uses the services of the Building Maintenance Fund, what would you want to know in addition to the information disclosed in the financial statements?

7–2 Internal Service Fund. Jaffry County operates a Risk Management Pool as an internal service fund. The Risk Management Pool provides the insurance function for the county departments through the purchase of insurance policies and the investing of resources to cover uninsured losses and deductibles. The Risk Management Pool assesses the other funds of the county for the service it provides. In turn, the funds submit claims for any losses incurred to the Risk Management Pool.

Recently, the Jaffry County office building suffered fire damage that required extensive repairs. The county upgraded the materials used when repairing the building, thus extending the life of the building. The General Fund submitted all repair claims (invoices) to the Risk Management Pool, and all but $100,000 of the claims were covered by insurance. The Risk Management Pool covered the $100,000 in uninsured claims. Rather than reimbursing the General Fund for the claims, the Risk Management Pool paid the invoices. As a result, the Risk Management Pool not only recorded debits related to the expenses for the building repairs, but it also recorded debits to a Building account for those costs that added to the office building's useful life. Never before has the Risk Management Pool recognized capital assets in its financial statements, since it is not an objective of the Risk Management Pool to hold capital assets.*

Required

a. How would the General Fund and the Risk Management Pool record the assessments made by the Risk Management Pool for the services provided?

*The authors are indebted to Leanne Emm and Kathleen Askelson for providing the information from which this case was adapted.

sources furnished the original investment in fund assets? Do the notes include segment information on individual enterprise funds where applicable (see "Required Segment Information" section of this chapter)?

Are sales to other funds or other governments separately disclosed? Are there receivables from other funds or other governments? How are receivables from component units, if any, disclosed? Is there any evidence that enterprise funds contribute amounts to the General Fund in lieu of taxes to help support services received by the enterprise? Is there any evidence that enterprise funds make excessively large contributions to the General Fund or any other funds?

(2) *Utility Funds*. Is it possible to tell from the report whether utilities of this government are subject to the same regulations as investor-owned utilities in the same state? (If the utility statements use account titles prescribed by the NARUC and the FERC, as described in this chapter, there is a good chance that the governmentally owned utilities are subject to at least some supervision by a state regulatory agency.) What rate of return on sales (or operating revenues) is being earned by each utility fund? What rate of return on total assets is being earned by each utility fund?

Is depreciation taken on the utility plant? Are accounting policies and accounting changes properly disclosed? If so, what method of depreciation is being used? Does each utility account for its own debt service and construction activities in the manner described in this chapter? What special funds or restricted assets are utilized by each utility?

(3) *Nonutility Enterprise Funds*. Is the accounting for nonutility enterprise funds the same as investor-owned enterprises in the same industries? (In order to answer this, you may need to refer to publications of trade associations or to handbooks or encyclopedias of accounting systems found in business libraries.) If you cannot find information about investor-owned counterparts of the governmental nonutility enterprise funds, do the statements of the latter provide evidence that generally accepted accounting principles devised for profit-seeking businesses were used?

(4) *Government-wide Financial Statements*. What proportion of the net assets of the business-type activities are reported as invested in capital assets, restricted, and unrestricted? Were the business-type activities profitable; that is, did revenues exceed expenses?

7–2 Multiple Choice. Choose the best answer.

1. Which of the following correctly states the role of budgeting in proprietary funds?
   a. Proprietary fund managers should ensure that a valid appropriation exists before providing goods or services to other funds or departments of the same government.
   b. Proprietary fund managers should have discretion to operate within a flexible budget consistent with pricing and other policies established by the legislative body.
   c. To ensure that appropriations are not overspent, all proprietary funds should use encumbrance procedures.
   d. Expenditures from proprietary funds should not be made unless there is a valid appropriation authorizing the expenditure.

2. Which of the following would most likely be accounted for in an internal service fund?

a. City golf courses.
b. The city's investments, which are pooled with the county's and the sc district's investments.
c. An asphalt plant used to supply the asphalt needed to resurface the city's streets.
d. Proceeds from an endowment that are used to maintain the city's cemeteries.

3. The Computer Services Department operates as an internal service fund. It has billed the Parks and Recreation Department $3,000 for the services provided by its computer technicians. How would this be shown at the government-wide level?
a. It would be an increase in governmental activities expenses of $3,000.
b. It would be an increase in governmental activities internal balances of $3,000.
c. It would be an increase in business-type activities revenues of $3,000.
d. There would be no increase in governmental activities.

4. The City of Jenkins operates a central motor pool as an internal service fund for the benefit of the city's other funds and departments. In 2011, this fund billed the Community Services Department $30,000 for vehicle rentals. What account should the internal service fund use to record these billings?
a. Interfund Transfers In.
b. Interfund Exchanges.
c. Billings to Departments.
d. Cost of Providing Rentals to Other Funds and Units.

5. Which of the following events would generally be classified as nonoperating on an enterprise fund's statement of revenues, expenses, and changes in net assets?
a. Billing other funds of the same government for services.
b. Loss on the sale of a piece of equipment.
c. Depreciation expense.
d. Administrative expense.

6. During 2011 Darden City reported the following operating receipts from self-sustaining activities paid by users of the services rendered:

Operations of water supply plant	$4,000,000
Operations of transit system	800,000

What amounts should be reported as operating revenues of Darden's enterprise funds?
a. $4,800,000.
b. $4,000,000.
c. $800,000.
d. $0.

7. Under GASB standards, which of the following events would be classified as an investing activity on a proprietary fund's statement of cash flows?
a. Interest earned on certificates of deposit held by the proprietary fund.
b. Purchase of equipment for use by the proprietary fund.
c. Grant received to construct a building that will be used by the proprietary fund.
d. All of the above would be considered investing activities for reporting purposes.

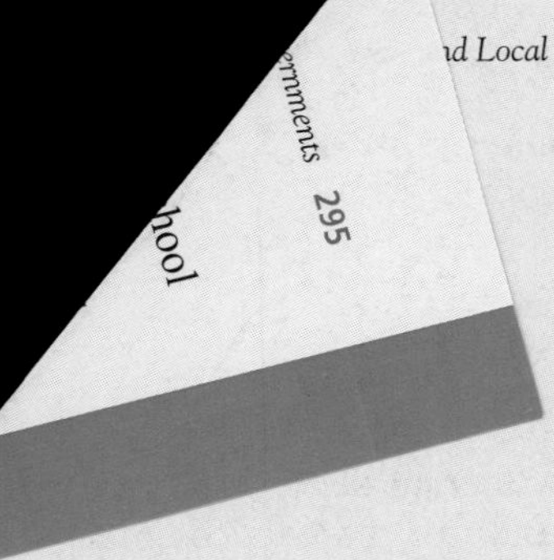

8. The proceeds of tax-supported bonds issued for the benefit of an enterprise fund and being serviced by a debt service fund:
   a. Should not be reported by the enterprise fund at all.
   b. Should be reported in the notes to enterprise fund statements but not in the body of any of the statements.
   c. Should be reported in the enterprise fund as long-term debt.
   d. Should be reported in the enterprise fund as a contribution or interfund transfer in the statement of revenues, expenses, and changes in net assets.

9. During the year an enterprise fund purchased $230,000 worth of equipment. The equipment was acquired with a cash down payment of $23,000 and a $207,000 loan. What is the net effect of this transaction on the net asset accounts of the enterprise fund?
   a. Invested in capital assets, net of related debt is increased by $23,000.
   b. Invested in capital assets, net of related debt is increased by $230,000.
   c. Invested in capital assets, net of related debt is increased by $207,000.
   d. Invested in capital assets, net of related debt is decreased by $207,000.

10. The financial statements required by GASB for a proprietary fund are:
   a. Balance sheet and statement of revenues, expenditures, and changes in net assets.
   b. Balance sheet; statement of revenues, expenditures, and changes in fund balance; statement of cash flows.
   c. Statement of net assets; statement of revenues, expenses, and changes in fund net assets; statement of cash flows.
   d. Balance sheet and statement of revenues, expenses, and changes in retained earnings.

7–3 **Central Duplicating Internal Service Fund.** As of September 30, 2010, the Central Duplicating Fund of the Town of Fredericksburg had the following post-closing trial balance:

	Debits	*Credits*
Cash	$ 15,000	
Due from Other Funds	20,200	
Service Supplies Inventory	35,300	
Machinery and Equipment	300,000	
Allowance for Depreciation		$ 90,000
Due to Federal Government		1,500
Due to Other Funds		800
Accounts Payable		12,700
Net Assets—Invested in Capital Assets		210,000
Net Assets—Unrestricted		55,500
	$370,500	$370,500

During the fiscal year ended September 30, 2011, the following transactions (summarized) occurred:

1. Employees were paid $290,000 wages in cash; additional wages of $43,500 were withheld for federal income and social security taxes. The employer's share of social security taxes amounted to $23,375.
2. Cash remitted to the federal government during the year for withholding taxes and social security taxes amounted to $65,500.

3. Utility bills received from the Town of Fredericksburg's Utility Fund during the year amounted to $23,500.
4. Office expenses paid in cash during the year amounted to $10,500.
5. Service supplies purchased on account during the year totaled $157,500.
6. Parts and supplies used during the year totaled $152,300 (at cost).
7. Charges to departments during the fiscal year were as follows:

General Fund	$308,700
Street Fund	279,300

8. Unpaid balances at year-end were as follows:

General Fund	$10,000
Street Fund	20,000

9. Payments to the Utility Fund totaled $21,800.
10. Accounts Payable at year-end amounted to $13,250.
11. Annual depreciation rate for machinery and equipment is 10 percent.
12. Revenue and expense accounts for the year were closed.

Required

a. Prepare a statement of revenues, expenses, and changes in net assets for the year.
b. Comment on the evident success of the pricing policy of this fund, assuming that user charges are intended to cover all operating expenses, including depreciation, but are not expected to provide a net income in excess of 3 percent of billings to departments.
c. Prepare a statement of net assets for the Central Duplicating Fund as of September 30, 2011.
d. Prepare a statement of cash flows for the Central Duplicating Fund for the year ended September 30, 2011.

7–4 **Central Garage Internal Service Fund.** The City of Ashville operates an internal service fund to provide garage space and repairs for all city-owned-and-operated vehicles. The Central Garage Fund was established by a contribution of $300,000 from the General Fund on July 1, 2008, at which time the land and building were acquired. The post-closing trial balance at June 30, 2010, was as follows:

	Debits	Credits
Cash	$110,000	
Due from Other Funds	9,000	
Inventory of Supplies	90,000	
Land	50,000	
Building	250,000	
Allowance for Depreciation—Building		$ 20,000
Machinery and Equipment	65,000	
Allowance for Depreciation—Machinery and Equipment		12,000
Vouchers Payable		31,000
Net Assets—Invested in Capital Assets		333,000
Nets Assets—Unrestricted		178,000
	$574,000	$574,000

The following information applies to the fiscal year ended June 30, 2011:

1. Supplies were purchased on account for $92,000; the perpetual inventory method is used.
2. The cost of supplies used during the year ended June 30, 2011, was $110,000. A physical count taken as of that date showed materials and supplies on hand totaled $72,000 at cost.
3. Salaries and wages paid to employees totaled $235,000, including related costs.
4. Billings totaling $30,000 were received from the enterprise fund for utility charges. The Central Garage Fund paid $27,000 of the amount owed.
5. Depreciation of the building was recorded in the amount of $10,000; depreciation of the machinery and equipment amounted to $9,000.
6. Billings to other departments for services provided to them were as follows:

General Fund	$270,000
Special Revenue Fund	37,000
Water and Sewer Utility Fund	90,000

7. Unpaid interfund receivable balances were as follows:

	6/30/10	*6/30/11*
General Fund	$2,500	$3,000
Special Revenue Fund	3,500	7,000
Water and Sewer Utility Fund	3,000	2,000

8. Vouchers payable at June 30, 2011, were $16,000.
9. For June 30, 2011, closing entries were prepared for the Central Garage Fund (ignore government-wide closing entry).

Required

a. Assume all expenses at the government-wide level are charged to the General Government function. Prepare journal entries to record all of the transactions for this period in the Central Garage Fund accounts and in the governmental activities accounts.

b. Prepare a statement of revenues, expenses, and changes in net assets for the Central Garage Fund for the period ended June 30, 2011.

c. Prepare a statement of net assets for the Central Garage Fund as of June 30, 2011.

d. Explain what the Central Garage Fund would need to report at the governmental activities level, and where the information would be reported.

7–5 Net Asset Classifications. During the past year, Oak City had a number of transactions that impacted net asset classifications of its produce market, which is operated as an enterprise fund. All nominal accounts for the period have been closed to unrestricted net assets. For reporting purposes, the city's finance director is trying to update the net asset categories to properly reflect current balances in each of the three net asset categories based on the following transaction information.

1. For the year, depreciation expense totaled $534,000.
2. During the year a piece of equipment with a carrying value of $2,610 was sold for its carrying value.

3. During the year $1,000,000 in deferred serial bonds was issued to construct a building to house the produce market. At the end of the year, construction work in progress for the building totaled $948,000. It is expected the building will be completed at the beginning of the next year.
4. To retire the $1,000,000 deferred serial bonds, $25,000 cash was placed in a sinking fund.
5. A $5,000 principal payment was made on a capital lease.

Required

To assist the finance director you have been asked to provide a journal entry for each of the above five items. Your journal entries should indicate the effect of each item on the net asset categories—invested in capital assets, net of related debt; restricted; and unrestricted.

7–6 Parking Facilities Fund. The City of Dalton accounts for its parking facilities as an enterprise fund. For the year ended December 31, 2011, the pre-closing trial balance for the Parking Facilities Fund is provided.

	Debits	*Credits*
Cash & Cash Equivalents	$ 869,168	
Accounts Receivable	3,607	
Allowance for Uncollectible Accounts		$ 72
Restricted Cash & Cash Equivalents	993,322	
Land	3,021,637	
Buildings and Equipment	23,029,166	
Accumulated Depreciation		5,623,315
Accounts & Accrued Payables		312,830
6-month Note Payable		360,000
Bonds Payable		15,579,325
Net Assets—Invested in Capital Assets, Net of Related Debt		4,931,749
Net Assets—Restricted		951,996
Net Assets—Unrestricted		765,893
Charges for Services		1,640,261
Interest Income		251,480
Personnel Expense	852,380	
Utilities Expense	100,726	
Repairs & Maintenance Expense	64,617	
Supplies Expense	17,119	
Depreciation Expense	578,861	
Interest Expense	874,909	
Interfund Transfer Out	11,409	
	$30,416,921	$30,416,921

Additional information concerning the Parking Facilities Fund is as follows:

1. All bonds payable were used to acquire property, plant, and equipment.
2. During the year, a principal payment of $500,000 was made to retire a portion of the bonds payable.
3. Equipment with a carrying value of $4,725 was sold for its carrying value.

4. Total cash received from customers was $1,640,155 and cash received for interest and dividends was $251,480; $150,000 of this amount is restricted cash. (*Hint:* This was the only change to restricted cash during the year.)
5. Cash payments included $750,828 to employees, $365,137 to vendors, $874,909 for interest on bonded debt, and $11,409 to subsidize public works (the General Fund).
6. The beginning balance in Accounts Receivable was $3,501, and Accounts & Accrued Payables was $393,953.
7. The net asset categories have not been updated to reflect correct balances as of the December 31, 2011, year-end.

Required

a. Prepare the statement of revenues, expenses, and changes in fund net assets for the Parking Facilities Fund as of December 31, 2011.

b. Prepare the statement of net assets for the Parking Facilities Fund as of December 31, 2011.

c. Prepare the statement of cash flows for the Parking Facilities Fund as of December 31, 2011.

7–7 **Central Station Fund.** The Town of Elizabeth operates the old train station as an enterprise fund. The train station is on the national register of historic buildings. Since the town has held the building for such a long time, the Central Station Fund has no long-term debt. The only capital assets recorded by the Central Station Fund are machinery and equipment. Businesses rent space in the building and the town provides all services related to the operation and maintenance of the building. Following is information related to the fund's 2011 operating activities.

1. Rental income of $94,444 was accrued. Subsequently, cash in the amount of $90,210 was received on accounts.
2. Cash expenses for the period included: administrative services, $25,205; maintenance and repairs, $72,882; supplies and materials, $7,792; and utilities, $30,124.
3. The Central Station Fund received a $60,000 transfer of funds from the General Fund.
4. Adjustments were made for depreciation ($3,519) and for uncollectible accounts ($667).
5. At the end of the period, nominal accounts were closed.

Required:

a. Prepare general journal entries to record the Central Station Fund's operating activities for the year.

b. Prepare a statement of revenues, expenses, and changes in fund net assets. The net asset balance at the beginning of the period was $60,129.

c. Based on the information provided, does it appear that the Central Station Fund is required to be recognized as an enterprise fund under GASB standards? Explain your answer.

d. Assuming you are the town's manager, discuss your concerns about the Central Station Fund.

7–8 **Enterprise Fund Journal Entries and Financial Statements.** Following is the June 30, 2010, statement of net assets for the City of Bay Lake Water Utility Fund.

CITY OF BAY LAKE
Water Utility Fund
Statement of Fund Net Assets
June 30, 2010

Assets		
Current assets:		
Cash and investments		$ 1,775,019
Accounts receivable (net of $13,367 provision for uncollectible accounts)		306,869
Accrued utility revenue		500,000
Due from General Fund		29,311
Accrued interest receivable		82,000
Total current assets		2,693,199
Restricted assets:		
Cash		9,193
Capital assets:		
Land	$1,780,945	
Buildings (net of $3,420,000 in accumulated depreciation)	5,214,407	
Machinery and equipment (net of $5,129,928 in accumulated depreciation)	8,488,395	
Total capital assets (net)		15,483,747
Total Assets		18,186,139
Liabilities		
Current liabilities:		
Accounts payable	532,047	
Accrued interest payable	131,772	
Current portion of long-term debt	400,000	
Total current liabilities		1,063,819
Liabilities payable from restricted assets:		
Customer deposits		9,193
Long-term liabilities:		
Revenue bond payable		11,600,000
Total Liabilities		12,673,012
Net Assets		
Invested in capital assets, net of related debt		3,483,747
Unrestricted		2,029,380
		$ 5,513,127

Required

a. For fiscal year 2011, prepare general journal entries for the Water Utility Fund using the following information.

(1) The amount in the Accrued Utility Revenue account was reversed.

(2) Billings to customers for water usage during fiscal year 2011 totaled \$2,982,557; \$193,866 of the total was billed to the General Fund.

(3) Cash in the amount of \$260,000 was received. The cash was for interest earned on investments and \$82,000 in accrued interest.

(4) Expenses accrued for the period were: management and administration, \$360,408; maintenance and distribution, \$689,103; and treatment plant, \$695,237.

(5) Cash receipts for customer deposits totaled \$2,427.

(6) Cash collections on customer accounts totaled \$2,943,401, of which \$209,531 was from the General Fund.

(7) Cash payments for the period were as follows: Accounts Payable, \$1,462,596; interest (which includes the accrued interest payable), \$395,917; bond principal, \$400,000; machinery and equipment, \$583,425; and return of customer deposits, \$912.

(8) A state grant amounting to \$475,000 was received to help pay for new water treatment equipment.

(9) Accounts written off as uncollectible totaled \$10,013.

(10) The utility fund transferred \$800,000 in excess operating income to the General Fund.

(11) Adjusting entries for the period were recorded as follows: depreciation on buildings was \$240,053 and on machinery and equipment it was \$360,079; the allowance for uncollectible accounts was increased by \$14,913; an accrual for unbilled customer receivables was made for \$700,000; accrued interest income was \$15,849; and accrued interest expense was \$61,406.

(12) The Revenue Bond Payable account was adjusted by \$400,000 to record the current portion of the bond.

(13) Closing entries and necessary adjustments were made to the net asset accounts.

b. Prepare a statement of revenues, expenses, and changes in fund net assets for the Water Utility Fund for the year ended June 30, 2011.

c. Prepare a statement of net assets for the Water Utility Fund as of June 30, 2011.

d. Prepare a statement of cash flows for the Water Utility Fund as of June 30, 2011.

7–9 Proprietary Fund Financial Statements. Von County has prepared the following statement of revenues, expenses, and changes in fund net assets for its proprietary funds. The county has three enterprise funds and two internal service funds.

VON COUNTY
Statement of Revenues, Expenses, and Changes in Fund Net Assets
Proprietary Funds
for the Year Ended December 31, 2011
(amounts expressed in thousands)

	Total Enterprise Funds	Total Internal Service Funds	Total
Revenues			
Charges for services	$ 61,309	$10,621	$ 71,930
Investment income	1,086	59	1,145
Total Revenues	62,395	10,680	73,075
Expenses			
Personnel services	24,196	5,681	29,877
Supplies and materials	11,540	3,293	14,833
Interest expense	6,904	172	7,076
Depreciation	11,213	2,076	13,289
Loss on disposal of capital assets	14		14
Interfund Transfer out	186	0	186
Total Expenses	54,053	11,222	65,275
Change in net assets	8,342	(542)	7,800
Special item—Loss on Sale	(3,794)		(3,794)
Net assets—January 1, 2011	288,611	3,337	291,948
Net assets—December 31, 2011	$293,159	$ 2,795	$295,954

Required

The statement as presented is not in accordance with GASB standards. Identify the errors and explain how the errors should be corrected in order to conform with GASB standards. Along with the information in Chapter 7, Illustration A1-8 will be helpful in identifying and correcting the errors.

7–10 Statement of Cash Flows for Proprietary Funds. From the right-hand column, choose the letter that corresponds to the section of the statement of cash flows where the activity listed in the left-hand column would be reported.

Activities	**Cash Flow Section**
1. Interest earned on investments	A. Operating Activities
2. Grants received from the state for summer interns	B. Noncapital Financing Activities
3. Payments to vendors	C. Capital & Related Financing Activities
4. Receipts from customers	D. Investing Activities
5. Interest paid on construction loans	
6. Sale of equipment	
7. Transfers to the General Fund	
8 Receipts from the General Fund for service provided	
9. Purchase of treasury notes	
10. Payment of debt principal	

Chapter Eight

Accounting for Fiduciary Activities—Agency and Trust Funds

Learning Objectives

After studying this chapter, you should be able to:

1. Explain how fiduciary funds are used to report on the fiduciary activities of a government.
2. Distinguish among agency funds and trust funds (private-purpose, investment, and pension).
3. Describe the uses for and characteristics of agency funds.
4. Explain the activities of and accounting and financial reporting for commonly used agency funds.
5. Explain the purpose, creation, operation, accounting, and financial reporting for a cash and investment pool (including an investment trust fund); a private-purpose trust fund; and a pension trust fund.
6. Describe accounting for other post-employment benefits plans.

Fiduciary activities benefit other individuals, organizations, or governments, rather than the reporting government. For this reason, Governmental Accounting Standards Board (GASB) standards exclude the reporting of fiduciary activities in the government-wide financial statements. However, fiduciary activities are reported in the fiduciary fund financial statements, the focus of this chapter.

Fiduciary funds are used to account for those activities in which a government holds assets as an agent or trustee. To account for these private-purpose fiduciary activities agency funds, investment trust funds, private-purpose trust funds, and pension trust funds are used. Resources that are held in trust for the benefit of the government's own programs or its citizenry should be accounted for using a governmental fund rather than a fiduciary fund. Such public-purpose trusts should be accounted for as special revenue funds (see Chapter 4) if the resources are expendable for the trust purpose or as permanent funds (see Chapter 4) if the trust principal is permanently restricted.

In law, there is a clear distinction between an agency relationship and a trust relationship. In accounting practice, the legalistic distinctions between trust funds and agency funds are not of major significance. The important and perhaps the sole consideration from an accounting standpoint is what can and what cannot be done with the fund's assets in accordance with laws and other pertinent regulations. The name of a particular fund is not a reliable criterion for determining the correct accounting basis for trust and agency funds.

Trust funds differ from agency funds principally in degree: Trust funds often exist over a longer period of time than an agency fund, represent and develop vested interests of a beneficiary to a greater extent, and involve more complex administration and financial accounting and reporting. Agency funds are used only if a government holds resources in a purely custodial capacity for others. As noted, specific accounting procedures and limitations depend on the enactment that brought about creation of a particular trust or agency fund, plus all other regulations under which it operates. Regulations include pertinent statutes, ordinances, wills, trust indentures, and other instruments of endowment, resolutions of the governing body, statements of purposes of the fund, kinds and amounts of assets held, and others. This aggregate of factors helps determine the transactions in which a fiduciary fund may and should engage.

AGENCY FUNDS

GASB standards identify *agency funds* as one of the four types of fiduciary funds. **Agency funds** are used to account for assets held by a government acting as an agent for one or more other governments or for individuals or private organizations. Assets that are held in an agency fund belong to the party or parties for which the government acts as agent. Therefore, *agency fund assets are offset by liabilities equal in amount; no fund equity exists.* GASB requires agency fund assets and liabilities to be recognized on the accrual basis. Revenues and expenses are not recognized in the accounts of agency funds, however.

Unless use of an agency fund is mandated by law, by GASB standards, or by decision of the governing board, an agency relationship may be accounted for within governmental and/or proprietary funds. For example, local governments act as agents of the federal and state governments in the collection and remittance of employees' withholding taxes, retirement contributions, and social security taxes. In the absence of contrary legal requirements or administrative decisions, it is perfectly acceptable to account for the withholdings, and the remittance to federal and state governments, within the funds that account for the gross pay of the employees, as is shown by the illustrative entries in Chapter 4. In general, if an agency relationship is incidental to the primary purposes for which a given fund exists, the relationship is ordinarily discharged on a current basis, and the amounts of assets held as agent are small in relation to fund assets, there is no need to create an agency fund unless required.

Agency Fund for Special Assessment Debt Service

Readers of Chapters 5 and 6 of this text should recall that GASB standards specify that a government that has *no* obligation to assume debt service on special assessment debt in the event of property owners' default but does perform the functions of billing property owners for the assessments, collecting installments of assessments and interest on the assessments, and *from the collections,* paying interest and principal on the special assessment debt, should account for those activities by use of an agency fund.

To illustrate *agency fund* accounting for special assessment debt service activities, assume the same information as used in Chapter 6 except that the government is not obligated in any manner for the special assessment debt. When the assessments in the amount of $480,000, payable in 10 equal installments, were levied on benefited property owners, the following journal entry was made in the agency fund.

		Debits	Credits
1.	Assessments Receivable—Current	48,000	
	Assessments Receivable—Deferred	432,000	
	Due to Special Assessment Bondholders—Principal		480,000

All current assessments receivable were collected (see Entry 2) along with $24,000 of interest (5 percent on the previous unpaid receivable balance). As indicated in Chapter 6, any amounts not collected by the due date should be reclassified as Assessments Receivable—Delinquent.

		Debits	Credits
2.	Cash	72,000	
	Assessments Receivable—Current		48,000
	Due to Special Assessment Bondholders—Interest		24,000

Special assessment bond principal in the amount of $48,000 and interest in the amount of $24,000 were paid during the current year.

		Debits	Credits
3.	Due to Special Assessment Bondholders—Principal	48,000	
	Due to Special Assessment Bondholders—Interest	24,000	
	Cash		72,000

The second installment of assessments receivable was reclassified at year-end from the deferred category to the current category.

		Debits	Credits
4.	Assessments Receivable—Current	48,000	
	Assessments Receivable—Deferred		48,000

This pattern of journal entries will be repeated during each of the remaining nine years until all special assessment bonds are retired.

Tax Agency Funds

An agency relationship that logically results in the creation of an agency fund is the collection of taxes or other revenues by one government for several of the funds it operates and for other governments. State governments commonly collect sales taxes, gasoline taxes, and many other taxes that are apportioned to state agencies and to local governments within the state. At the local government level, it is common for an elected county official to serve as collector for all property taxes owed by persons or corporations owning property within the county. Taxes levied by all funds and governments within the county are certified to the county collector for collection. The county collector is required by law to make periodic distributions of tax collections for each year to each fund or government in the proportion that the levy for that fund or government bears to the total levy for the year. In many jurisdictions, the law provides that governments may request advances or "draws" from the tax agency fund prior to regular distributions; advances are usually limited by law to a specified percentage, often 90 percent, of collections for the period from the last distribution until the date of the advance.

Tax agency fund accounting would be quite simple if all taxes levied for a given year were collected in that year. It is almost always true, however, that collections during any year relate to taxes levied in several prior years as well as taxes levied for the current year, and sometimes include advance collections of taxes for the following year. In many jurisdictions, not only does the total tax rate vary from year to year but the proportion that the rate of each government (and each fund) bears to the total rate also varies from year to year. Additionally, interest and penalties on delinquent taxes must be collected at statutory rates or amounts at the time delinquent taxes are collected; interest and penalties collected must be distributed to participating funds and governments in the same manner that tax collections are distributed. The following sections relate to administration of a tax agency fund.

Illustration of Composition of Total Tax Rates

Assume that the county collector of Campbell County is responsible for collecting the taxes due in 2011 for the funds and governments located within the county. Ordinarily, the taxes levied for each fund and government within the county are shown in columnar form in a newspaper advertisement as legal notice to taxpayers. In order to keep the illustrations in this text legible and comprehensible, Illustration 8–1 shows two columns of a legal advertisement. Real property tax statements are prepared for each parcel of property located within the jurisdiction for which the tax agency fund is operated. Whether each statement discloses the amount of tax that will be distributed to all of the tax agency fund's participants that levy taxes on that parcel, or shows only the total tax payable to the county collector, the collector's office must be able to compute and appropriately distribute all taxes collected to the appropriate funds and governments.

For example, Illustration 8–1 shows that a parcel of property located in Washington Township outside the City of Washington would be taxed at the rate of $7.10 per $100 of assessed valuation; if the parcel were inside the city limits, however, the tax rate would be $10.06. Therefore, if a parcel of property located in Washington Township outside the city had an assessed valuation of $10,000, the total real property tax payable in 2011 would be $710, but a parcel with the same assessed valuation located within the city would be taxed at $1,006. The subtotals in each column represent the taxes levied for each tax agency fund participant, as shown in Illustration 8–1. In turn, the taxes levied for each government are broken down into the taxes levied for funds of that government, as also shown in Illustration 8–1. The relationship between direct and overlapping debt is discussed in Chapter 6. Note that Illustration 8–1 shows that a person or organization owning property within the City of Washington is required to pay 66 cents of the total rate for debt service (20 cents to Campbell County, 38 cents to the school district, and 8 cents to the City of Washington). Illustration 8–2 summarizes the composition of each tax statement by government.

ILLUSTRATION 8–1

Composition of Taxes to Be Collected by County Collector of Campbell County for the County Funds and Other Taxing Authorities for the Year 2011

	Washington Township	City of Washington
Total state rate	$0.01	$ 0.01
County funds:		
General	1.08	1.08
Capital projects	0.09	0.09
Debt service	0.20	0.20
Welfare	0.11	0.11
Total county rate	1.48	1.48
Library Fund	0.25	0.25
Township funds:		
General	0.07	0.07
Fire protection	0.23	—
Total township	0.30	0.07
School funds:		
General	4.50	4.50
Capital projects	0.18	0.18
Debt service	0.38	0.38
Total school rate	5.06	5.06
City funds:		
General		2.53
Street		0.33
Pension		0.25
Debt service		0.08
Total city rate		3.19
Total tax rates per $100 assessed valuation	$7.10	$10.06

In those states in which taxes are levied on personal property, the funds and governments that levy the personal property taxes are generally assumed to be the ones that levy taxes on the residence of the owner unless there is convincing evidence that the legal location of the personal property is elsewhere. Inasmuch as the tax rate levied for each tax agency fund participant often varies from year to year, it is necessary that all tax collections be identified with the year for which the taxes were levied as well as with the particular parcels for which taxes were collected.

Operation of the collector's office often requires the use of substantial administrative, clerical, and computer time and provision of extensive building and computer facilities. Accordingly, it is common for the collector to be authorized to withhold a certain percentage from the collections for each government, and to remit to the county General Fund (or other fund bearing the expenditures for operating the tax agency fund) the total amount withheld from the collections of other governments.

ILLUSTRATION 8–2

2011 Taxes Payable to Campbell County Collector for Parcel with Assessed Valuation of $10,000

	Parcel Located	
Amount Levied by	**Outside City**	**In City**
State	$ 1.00	$ 1.00
County	148.00	148.00
Library	25.00	25.00
Township	30.00	7.00
School	506.00	506.00
City	—	319.00
Total	$710.00	$1,006.00

Accounting for Tax Agency Funds

Taxes levied each year should be recorded in the accounts of the appropriate funds of each government in the manner illustrated in preceding chapters. Although an allowance for estimated uncollectible current taxes would be established in each fund, the *gross* amount of the tax levy for all funds should be recorded in the Tax Agency Fund as a receivable. Note the receivable is designated as belonging to other funds and governments, and the receivable is offset in total by a liability. Assuming total real property taxes certified for collection during 2011 amounted to $9,468,000, the entry would be as follows:

		Debits	***Credits***
	Tax Agency Fund:		
1.	Taxes Receivable for Other Funds and Governments—Current . . .	9,468,000	
	Due to Other Funds and Governments		9,468,000

It would be necessary for the county collector to keep records of the total amount of 2011 taxes to be collected for each of the funds and governments in the Tax Agency Fund in order to distribute tax collections properly. Assume that the 2011 taxes were levied for the following governments (to reduce the detail in this example, a number of the governments are combined):

State	$ 10,000
Campbell County	1,480,000
Washington School District	5,060,000
City of Washington	2,552,000
Other governments (should be itemized)	366,000
	$9,468,000

If collections of 2011 taxes during a certain portion of the year amounted to $4,734,000, the Tax Agency Fund entry would be:

		Debits	Credits
	Tax Agency Fund:		
2.	Cash	4,734,000	
	Taxes Receivable for Other Funds and Governments—Current		4,734,000

The tax collections in an actual case must be identified with the parcels of property against which the taxes were levied because the location of each parcel determines the funds and governments that should receive the tax collections. Assuming for the sake of simplicity that the collections for the period represent collections of 50 percent of the taxes levied against each parcel in Campbell County and that the County General Fund is given 1 percent of all collections for governments other than the county as reimbursement for the cost of operating the Tax Agency Fund, the distribution of the $4,734,000 collections would be:

	Taxes Collected (50% of Levy)	Collection Fee (Charged) Received	Cash to Be Distributed
State	$ 5,000	$ (50)	$ 4,950
Campbell County	740,000	39,940	779,940
Washington School District	2,530,000	(25,300)	2,504,700
City of Washington	1,276,000	(12,760)	1,263,240
Other governments (should be itemized)	183,000	(1,830)	181,170
	$4,734,000	$ -0-	$4,734,000

If cash is not distributed as soon as this computation is made, the entry by the Tax Agency Fund to record the liability would be:

		Debits	Credits
	Tax Agency Fund:		
3.	Due to Other Funds and Governments	4,734,000	
	Due to State		4,950
	Due to Campbell County		779,940
	Due to Washington School District		2,504,700
	Due to City of Washington		1,263,240
	Due to Other Governments		181,170

If, as is likely, collections during 2011 include collections of taxes that were levied for 2010, 2009, and preceding years, computations must be made to determine the appropriate distribution of collections for each tax year to each fund and government that levied taxes against the property for which collections have been received.

When cash is distributed by the Tax Agency Fund, the liability accounts shown in Entry 3 should be debited and Cash credited. If cash is advanced to one or more funds or governments prior to a regular periodic distribution, the debits to the liability accounts may precede the credits. By year-end, all advances should be settled, all distributions computed and recorded, and all cash distributed to the funds and governments for which the Tax Agency Fund is being operated. Therefore, if all those events have taken place, the year-end balance sheet for the Tax Agency Fund would consist of one asset, Taxes Receivable for Other Funds and Governments—Delinquent, and one liability, Due to Other Funds and Governments.

Entries Made by Funds and Governments Participating in Tax Agency Funds

Each fund or government that receives a distribution must record the appropriate portion of it in each of the funds it maintains. In each fund it must also record the fact that cash received differs from the amount of taxes collected by the fee paid to the county General Fund. The fee paid is recorded as an expenditure. For example, the computation for the entries to be made by the various funds of Washington School District would be (using the rates shown in Illustration 8–1) as follows:

	2011 Rate	Collections of 2011 Taxes	Collection Fee Paid	Cash Received
School Funds:				
General	$4.50	$2,250,000	$22,500	$2,227,500
Capital projects	0.18	90,000	900	89,100
Debt service	0.38	190,000	1,900	188,100
Total	$5.06	$2,530,000	$25,300	$2,504,700

From the computations it can be seen that the entry made in the Washington School District General Fund for the 2011 collections distributed should be:

	Debits	Credits
Washington School District General Fund:		
Cash	2,227,500	
Expenditures	22,500	
Taxes Receivable—Current		2,250,000

Similar entries would be made in the other two funds of the Washington School District and in all the funds of governments that paid a tax collection fee to the county General Fund. The computation by the county of taxes and fees collected for the General Fund are as follows.

	2011 Rate	Collections of 2011 Taxes	Collection Fee	Cash Received
County Funds:				
General	$1.08	$540,000	$39,940	$579,940
Capital Projects	0.09	45,000	–0–	45,000
Debt Service	0.20	100,000	–0–	100,000
Welfare	0.11	55,000	–0–	55,000
Total	$1.48	$740,000	$39,940	$779,940

The entry to be made in the General Fund of Campbell County for the 2011 collections distributed should be:

	Debits	Credits
Campbell County General Fund:		
Cash	579,940	
Taxes Receivable—Current		540,000
Revenues		39,940

"Pass-through" Agency Funds

Grants, entitlements, or shared revenues from the federal or a state government often pass through a lower level of government (primary recipient) before distribution to a secondary recipient. Accounting for such "pass-through" grants depends on whether the primary recipient government is deemed to have *administrative involvement* or *direct financial involvement* in the grants. According to GASB standards:

> A recipient government has administrative involvement if, for example, it (a) monitors secondary recipients for compliance with program-specific requirements, (b) determines eligibility of secondary recipients or projects, even if using grantor-established criteria, or (c) has the ability to exercise discretion in how the funds are allocated. A recipient government has direct financial involvement if, for example, it finances some direct program costs because of a grantor-imposed matching requirement or is liable for disallowed costs.[1]

Most often, the criteria for administrative or direct financial involvement are met, in which case the primary recipient government must recognize a revenue for the receipt and an expenditure or expense for the transfer in a governmental fund, private-purpose trust fund, or proprietary fund. If, however, neither administrative nor financial involvement is deemed to exist, then a pass-through agency fund must be used and no revenue or expenditure/expense is recognized.

To illustrate accounting for a pass-through agency fund, assume that $5 million of federal financial assistance is received by a state government from the federal government, the full amount of which must be passed to local governments according to predetermined eligibility requirements and in amounts according to a predetermined formula. Since the state government is serving merely as a "cash conduit" in this case,

[1] GASB *Codification of Governmental Accounting and Financial Reporting Standards, as of June 30, 2008,* (Norwalk, CT: GASB, 2008), Sec. N50.128.

the use of a pass-through agency fund is deemed appropriate. The entry to record receipt of the $5 million in the pass-through agency fund would be:

	Debits	Credits
Cash	5,000,000	
Due to Other Governments		5,000,000

Assuming that all monies were disbursed to the secondary recipients during the current fiscal year, the pass-through agency fund entry would be:

	Debits	Credits
Due to Other Governments	5,000,000	
Cash		5,000,000

Accounting for the receipt of cash or other assets from a pass-through agency fund by the recipient should be in conformity with GASB standards discussed previously: Governmental funds are to recognize all grants as revenue when the grant proceeds are available for use for the purposes of the fund and eligibility requirements have been met. If grant proceeds are available immediately, the Revenues account is credited; if some eligibility requirement must be met, the Deferred Revenues account should be credited at the time the grant proceeds are recognized as assets, and amounts should be transferred from Deferred Revenues to Revenues as eligibility requirements are met. Proprietary funds recognize as nonoperating revenues the proceeds of grants for operating purposes or grants that may be expended at the discretion of the recipient government; if the terms of the grant restrict the use of the proceeds to the acquisition or construction of capital assets, the proceeds must be recorded as capital contributions (see Chapter 7).

Financial Reporting of Agency Funds

As mentioned earlier in this chapter, fiduciary activities are reported only in the fiduciary fund financial statements; they have no effect on the governmental or business-type activities of the primary government reported in the government-wide financial statements. As shown in Illustration A1–10, agency fund financial information is reported in a separate column of the statement of fiduciary net assets. Only those assets held for external parties are reported by agency funds in the statement of fiduciary net assets. Agency funds are not included in the statement of changes in fiduciary net assets (see Illustration A1–11) because they have no net assets (assets equal liabilities) and therefore cannot have *changes* in net assets. GASB standards do not require disclosure of the assets and liabilities of individual agency funds, but a government may optionally include in its comprehensive annual financial report a combining statement of net assets displaying the assets and liabilities of each agency fund in separate columns.

TRUST FUNDS

In addition to agency funds, the fiduciary fund classification includes investment trust funds, private-purpose trust funds, and pension trust funds.

Historically, trust funds have been created to account for assets received by the government in a trust agreement in which the assets are to be invested to produce income to be used for specified purposes (generally cultural or educational). The majority of such trusts benefit the government's own programs or its citizenry. As discussed and illustrated in Chapter 4, trusts that benefit the government's own programs or citizens at large are accounted for as either special revenue funds or *permanent funds*. The type of fund used depends on whether the principal of the gift can be spent for the specified purposes or is permanently restricted for investment, with only the earnings therefrom available to spend for the specified purposes. As discussed in Chapter 4, both special revenue funds and permanent funds are governmental fund types. GASB standards indicate that fiduciary funds are used when trusts benefit others, such as individuals, organizations, or other governments. Examples of trust funds are shown in the following sections.

INVESTMENT POOLS

Effective management of investments (and in some cases, idle cash) often is enhanced by placing the investments of the funds in a pool under the control of the treasurer or a professional investment manager, either within the treasurer's office or in a financial institution such as a bank or investment firm. For additional information on management of investments, see the appendix to this chapter.

If the investment pool is an *internal* investment pool (participating funds are all within the same government) an agency fund may be used to account for the investments in the pool. However, each participating fund is required, for financial reporting purposes, to report its proportionate share of pooled cash and investments as fund assets, and the assets and liabilities of the agency fund are not reported in the government's external financial statements.[2] For internal management purposes, it may be useful for participating funds to use the account title *Equity in Pooled Cash and Investments,* the account title used in the illustrative journal entries shown later in this section.

If the investment pool has external participants (other governments or organizations outside the government administering the pool), an **external investment pool** is used. GASB standards require that an **investment trust fund** be used to account for the assets, liabilities, net assets, and changes in net assets corresponding to the equity of the *external* participants.[3] The accounting for investment trust funds uses an economic resources measurement focus and the accrual basis of accounting.

Typically, the administering government also participates in the pool; however, its equity is considered *internal* and is not reported in the financial statements of the investment trust fund. Instead, the net assets and changes in net assets relating to the internal portion of the pool are presented in the financial statements of each participating fund and in the governmental activities and business-type activities of the sponsoring government's government-wide financial statements. Recall that the financial information for investment trust funds is reported only in the fiduciary fund financial statements (see Illustrations A1–10 and A1–11) and is not reported in the government-wide financial statements.

Accounting for an external investment pool is presented in the remainder of this section.

Creation of an Investment Pool

Earnings on pooled investments and changes in fair value of investments are allocated to the participants having an equity interest in the pool in proportion to their

[2] GASB, *Codification,* Sec. I50.112.

[3] Ibid., par. 116.

ILLUSTRATION 8–4

DREW COUNTY
Investment Pool
Trial Balance
As of January 10, 2011

Account Title	Debits	Credits
Cash	$ 1,000,000	
Investments—U.S. Treasury Notes	9,545,000	
Investments—U.S. Agency Obligations	16,385,000	
Investments—Repurchase Agreements	2,060,000	
Accrued Interest Receivable	710,000	
Due to Debt Service Fund		$14,850,000
Additions—Deposits in Pooled Investments—Town of Calvin		9,900,000
Additions—Deposits in Pooled Investments—Calvin Independent School District		4,950,000
Totals	$29,700,000	$29,700,000

the debt service fund, therefore, is increased by $150,000 (300,000 × 14,850/29,700); Additions—Change in Fair Value of Investments—Town of Calvin is credited for $100,000 (300,000 × 9,900/29,700); and Additions—Change in Fair Value of Investments—Calvin Independent School District is credited for $50,000 (300,000 × 4,950/29,700). Note that the equity of each participant in the pool remains proportionately the same (i.e., the amount due to the Town of Calvin is $10,000,000 after revaluing the investments to current fair value; total liabilities and net assets [if the Additions accounts were closed] of the pool are $30,000,000; 10,000/30,000 = 9,900/29,700, etc.). The journal entry in the investment pool summarizing the revaluation of investments and the capital projects entry into the investment pool is given as follows:

		Debits	*Credits*
	Drew County Investment Pool:		
2.	Cash	15,000,000	
	Investments—U.S. Agency Obligations	310,000	
	Investments—U.S. Treasury Notes		10,000
	Due to Debt Service Fund		150,000
	Due to Capital Projects Fund		15,000,000
	Additions—Change in Fair Value of Investments—Town of Calvin		100,000
	Additions—Change in Fair Value of Investments—Calvin Independent School District		50,000

After revaluation of investments in the pool and receipt of $15,000,000 cash from proceeds of bonds sold to finance road and bridge construction, the Drew County Trial Balance of the Investment Pool is as shown in Illustration 8–5.

ILLUSTRATION 8–5

DREW COUNTY
Investment Pool
Trial Balance
As of February 1, 2011

Account Title	Debits	Credits
Cash	$16,000,000	
Investments—U.S. Treasury Notes	9,535,000	
Investments—U.S. Agency Obligations	16,695,000	
Investments—Repurchase Agreements	2,060,000	
Accrued Interest Receivable	710,000	
Due to Debt Service Fund		$15,000,000
Due to Capital Projects Fund		15,000,000
Additions—Deposits in Pooled Investments—Town of Calvin		9,900,000
Additions—Deposits in Pooled Investments—Calvin Independent School District		4,950,000
Additions—Change in Fair Value of Investments—Town of Calvin		100,000
Additions—Change in Fair Value of Investments—Calvin Independent School District		50,000
Totals	$45,000,000	$45,000,000

Operation of a Cash and Investment Pool

Although the capital projects fund invested $15,000,000 cash, upon admission to the pool, that fund no longer has a specific claim on the cash of the pool; rather, it (and the other funds and governments that are members of the pool) has a proportionate interest in the total assets of the pool and will share in earnings, gains, and losses of the pool in that proportion. Ordinarily, it is inconvenient and unnecessary to make allocations to liability accounts and additions accounts each time dividends or interest are received and for each revaluation of the portfolio to fair value (some pools revalue to fair value daily). It is simpler to accumulate the earnings in the *Undistributed Earnings on Pooled Investments* account and the unrealized and realized gains and losses in the *Undistributed Change in Fair Value of Pooled Investments* account (both of these accounts are clearing accounts) and to make periodic distributions from these accounts to the specific liability and additions accounts for pool participants.

The frequency of distributions depends on whether all cash of all participants is pooled along with investments or whether each participant retains an operating cash account. In the former case, the pool would have frequent receipts attributable to collections of revenues and receivables of the participants and would have daily disbursements on behalf of the participants; in this case, the interest of each participant in the pool would have to be recomputed each day. If, however, a working cash balance is retained by each participant, the receipts and disbursements of pool cash would be much less frequent, and the distribution of gains and losses and earnings, as well as the recomputation of the equity of each participant in the pool, would be correspondingly less frequent.

and unrealized net gains of $450,000 should be distributed to the participants in the proportions used for the distribution of earnings in Entry 4a (3/9, 3/9, 2/9, and 1/9). The distribution is shown in the following entry:

		Debits	Credits
	Drew County Investment Pool:		
6.	Undistributed Change in Fair Value of Investments	450,000	
	Due to Debt Service Fund		150,000
	Due to Capital Projects Fund		150,000
	Additions—Change in Fair Value of Investments—Town of Calvin		100,000
	Additions—Change in Fair Value of Investments—Calvin Independent School District		50,000

At December 31, 2011, interest earnings of $720,000 had accrued and were recorded, as shown in Entry 7:

		Debits	Credits
	Drew County Investment Pool:		
7.	Accrued Interest Receivable	720,000	
	Undistributed Earnings on Pooled Investments		720,000

Assuming that the accrued interest was immediately distributed to pool participants in the same proportions listed for Entry 6, the following entry would be made to record the distribution:

		Debits	Credits
	Drew County Investment Pool:		
8.	Undistributed Earnings on Pooled Investments	720,000	
	Due to Debt Service Fund		240,000
	Due to Capital Projects Fund		240,000
	Additions—Investment Earnings—Town of Calvin		160,000
	Additions—Investment Earnings—Calvin Independent School District		80,000

Both Entries 6 and 8 would lead to entries to recognize an increase in each participant's Equity in Pooled Investments and revenue accounts. Those entries would be similar to Entry 4b and thus are not shown here.

After all earnings and changes in fair value have been recorded as in the entries illustrated, the equities and proportionate interests of the participants follow:

Debt service fund	$15,690,000, or 3/9 of total
Capital projects fund	15,690,000, or 3/9 of total
Town of Calvin	10,460,000, or 2/9 of total
Calvin Independent School District	5,230,000, or 1/9 of total
Total	$47,070,000

Withdrawal of Assets from the Pool

If a participant in a pool withdraws part of its equity from a pool, that participant's proportionate interest is decreased and all other participants' proportionate interest is increased. Before a withdrawal occurs, an allocation of proportionate shares of earnings, gains, and losses to date should be made. The same is true in the event of complete withdrawal of one or more participants from the pool.

Continuing with the Drew County Investment Pool example, assume that the debt service fund needs to withdraw $5,000,000 from the pool to retire matured bonds. Ignoring the fact that in most practical cases it would be necessary to first sell some investments, the entry in the investment trust fund for the withdrawal is given as follows:

		Debits	Credits
	Drew County Investment Pool:		
9a.	Due to Debt Service Fund	5,000,000	
	Cash		5,000,000

The corresponding entry in the debt service fund follows:

	Drew County Debt Service Fund:		
9b.	Cash	5,000,000	
	Equity in Pooled Investments		5,000,000

After withdrawal of $5,000,000 by the debt service fund, the proportionate interests in the pool become:

Debt service fund	$10,690,000, or 25.4% of total
Capital projects fund	15,690,000, or 37.3% of total
Town of Calvin	10,460,000, or 24.9% of total
Calvin Independent School District	5,230,000, or 12.4% of total
Total	$42,070,000

Closing Entry

To assist in preparing financial statements, the additions accounts (see Entries 1b, 2, 4a, 6, and 8), which reflect changes in the external participants' proportionate interest due to net new deposits/withdrawals, investment earnings, and changes in fair value, must be closed to the appropriate net asset accounts, as shown in Entry 10 below:

		Debits	Credits
	Drew County Investment Pool:		
10.	Additions—Deposits in Pooled Investments—Town of Calvin	9,900,000	
	Additions—Deposits in Pooled Investments—Calvin Independent School District	4,950,000	
	Additions—Investment Earnings—Town of Calvin	360,000	
	Additions—Investment Earnings—Calvin Independent School District	180,000	
	Additions—Change in Fair Value of Investments—Town of Calvin	200,000	
	Additions—Change in Fair Value of Investments—Calvin Independent School District	100,000	
	Net Assets Held in Trust for Participants—Town of Calvin		10,460,000
	Net Assets Held in Trust for Participants—Calvin Independent School District		5,230,000

Illustrative Financial Statements

Illustrative fiduciary fund statements, prepared for internal management purposes, are presented in Illustrations 8–6 and 8–7. These statements are prepared as of, or for the year ended, December 31, 2011, Drew County's fiscal year-end. These statements also provide the information to be reported in a column of the statement of fiduciary fund net assets (see Illustration A1–10) and statement of changes in fiduciary fund net assets (see Illustration A1–11). All assets of the pool are reported in the statement of net assets although the external participants' equity in the assets of the investment pool amounts to only the $15,690,000 reported as net assets, about 37.3 percent of the total assets. The other $26,380,000 is reported as a liability owed to the two participating funds of the Drew County government. Those funds would report their share of the investment pool as Equity in Pooled Investments rather than specific assets.

ILLUSTRATION 8–6

DREW COUNTY
Investment Pool
Statement of Net Assets
As of December 31, 2011

Assets		
Cash		$12,610,000
Investments		28,740,000
Accrued interest receivable		720,000
Total assets		42,070,000
Liabilities		
Due to internal participants		26,380,000
Total liabilities		26,380,000
Net Assets		
Held in trust for participants—		
Town of Calvin	$10,460,000	
Calvin Independent School District	5,230,000	
Total net assets		$15,690,000

ILLUSTRATION 8–7

DREW COUNTY Investment Pool Statement of Changes in Net Assets for the Year Ended December 31, 2011	
Additions	
Deposits of participants	$14,850,000
Investment earnings	540,000
Increase in fair value of investments	300,000
Total additions	15,690,000
Deductions	
Total deductions	–0–
Change in net assets	15,690,000
Net assets, January 1, 2011	–0–
Net assets, December 31, 2011	$15,690,000

PRIVATE-PURPOSE TRUST FUNDS

The fair value of assets placed in trust under a trust agreement is referred to as the *principal* or *corpus* of the trust. If the principal of the trust must be held intact (nonexpendable) to produce income, the trust is often called an *endowment*. The income from the assets of an endowment may be used only for the purposes specified by the trustor. Not all trusts require that the principal be held intact. Some trusts allow the principal to be spent (expended) for the purpose specified by the trust. Additionally, not all trusts make distinctions between the use of principal and income. For example, loan funds operated as trust funds usually require that both the principal and income be held intact, whereas public retirement systems are trusts whose principal and income are both expended for specified purposes.

Trust funds are also classified as public or private. *Public trust funds* are those whose principal or income, or both, must be used for some public purpose. The beneficiaries of *private trust funds* are private individuals, organizations, or other governments. A fund established for the purpose of holding performance deposits of licensees under a government's regulatory activities is an example of a private trust fund. A fund used to account for escheat property arising from the estate of persons who die intestate without any known heirs is another example of a private trust fund.

Because most trusts administered by governments are created for public purposes (for example, to maintain parks and cemeteries or to acquire art for public buildings), they are considered governmental rather than fiduciary activities under GASB standards. Thus, nonexpendable public-purpose trusts are accounted for as permanent funds and expendable public-purpose trusts are accounted for as special revenue funds. These governmental fund types were discussed and illustrated in Chapter 4.

There are relatively few private-purpose trust funds compared with public-purpose trust funds. Further, private-purpose trust funds follow accounting and financial reporting practices that are quite similar to those illustrated in the previous section on investment trust funds. The accounting for a private-purpose trust fund whose principal is permanently restricted for investment, with earnings available for a specified private purpose, is similar to that for the City of Concordia Library

ILLUSTRATION 8–8

JOHNSON COUNTY EMPLOYEE RETIREMENT SYSTEM Statement of Plan Net Assets June 30, 2010	
Assets	
Cash	$ 51,213
Accrued interest receivable	2,507,612
Investments (at fair value):	
Bonds	71,603,976
Common stocks	31,957,205
Commercial paper and repurchase agreements	12,570,401
Total assets	118,690,407
Liabilities	
Accounts payable and accrued expenses	401,581
Net assets held in trust for pension benefits	**$118,288,826**

a. *A statement of plan net assets* showing plan assets, liabilities, and net assets. Plan assets should be reported at fair value. (See Illustrations, 8–8 and 8–9.)

b. *A statement of changes in plan net assets* showing additions to plan net assets, deductions from plan net assets, and net increase (decrease) in plan net assets. (See Illustration 8–10.)

c. *A schedule of funding progress* showing historical data for the current year and five prior years about the actuarially determined status of plan funding. The schedule provides a long-term, ongoing perspective about the progress made in accumulating sufficient assets to pay benefits when due. (See Illustration 8–11.)

d. *A schedule of employer contributions* showing trend data for the current year and five prior years about the *annual required contributions* (*ARC*) *of the employer* and employer contributions in relation to ARC.[12] (See Illustration 8–12.)

In addition, the plan is required to provide notes to the financial statements *and* notes to the required schedules. The notes to the financial statements should disclose the following information:

a. Plan description, including:
1. Identification of the type of plan.
2. Classes of employees covered.
3. Brief description of benefit provisions.

b. Summary of significant accounting policies.

c. Description of contributions and reserves, including:
1. The authority under which contributions are made.
2. Funding policies.
3. Required contribution rates of active plan members.
4. Brief description of any long-term contracts for contributions.
5. Balances of the plan's legally required reserves at the reporting date.

[12] Ibid., par. 111.

ILLUSTRATION 8–9

JOHNSON COUNTY EMPLOYEE RETIREMENT SYSTEM
Statement of Plan Net Assets
June 30, 2011

Assets	
Cash	$ 62,434
Accrued interest receivable	4,822,076
Investments (at fair value):	
Bonds	99,965,064
Common stocks	30,627,302
Commercial paper and repurchase agreements	11,215,833
Total assets	146,692,709
Liabilities	
Accounts payable and accrued expenses	251,650
Net assets held in trust for pension benefits	$146,441,059

d. Funded status and funding progress.
e. Concentration of credit risk.[13]

The notes to the required schedules should provide:

a. Identification of actuarial methods used and significant actuarial assumptions for the most recent year covered by the required supplementary schedules.
b. Factors such as changes in benefit provisions, employees covered by the plan, or actuarial methods or assumptions used that significantly affect the trends reported in the schedules.[14]

Statement of Plan Net Assets

Illustrations 8–8 and 8–9 present the statement of plan net assets for the hypothetical Johnson County Employee Retirement System for fiscal years 2010 and 2011, respectively. Johnson County administers one pension plan. As shown, plan investments should be reported at fair value (last reported sales price) for all investments in securities that trade on active exchanges. Investments in mortgages should be based on the discounted present value of future interest and principal payments to be received. Investments in real estate should be reported at fair value based on independent appraisals. All other investments should be reported at estimated fair value, including institutional price quotes for debt securities for which trade prices are unavailable.

Depreciable assets of a pension fund, that is, capital assets held for use by the fund, should be reported at cost less accumulated depreciation. Cash, short-term investments (reported at cost), and receivables typically represent a minor part of the total assets of a pension fund. The assets of a pension fund are not classified as current and noncurrent; this distinction is not important since short-term liabilities typically are immaterial in relation to available plan assets. Fund liabilities, usually short-term (e.g., benefits due but unpaid, refunds for terminated employees, vouchers payable, accrued expenses, and payroll taxes payable), are reported as a deduction from assets; the difference is typically captioned *net assets held in trust for pension benefits.*

[13] Ibid., par. 124.
[14] Ibid., par. 132.

ILLUSTRATION 8–10

JOHNSON COUNTY EMPLOYEE RETIREMENT SYSTEM
Statement of Changes in Plan Net Assets
for the Fiscal Year Ended June 30, 2011

Additions:	
Contributions:	
Employer	$ 14,126,292
Plan members	8,009,400
Total contributions	22,135,692
Investment income:	
Net decrease in fair value of investments	(2,198,782)
Interest and dividends	14,262,845
Total investment income	12,064,063
Total additions	34,199,755
Deductions:	
Annuity benefits	3,134,448
Disability benefits	287,590
Refunds to terminated employees	2,057,265
Administrative expenses	568,219
Total deductions	6,047,522
Net increase	28,152,233
Net assets, July 1, 2010	118,288,826
Net assets, June 30, 2011	$146,441,059

Statement of Changes in Plan Net Assets

The Johnson County Employee Retirement System Statement of Changes in Plan Net Assets for fiscal year 2011 is presented in Illustration 8–10. This statement reports employer and employee contributions and investment income as additions to net assets rather than as revenues. Similarly, benefits paid, refunds of contributions, and administrative expenses are reported as deductions from net assets rather than as expenses. The net increase (decrease) in net assets is added to beginning-of-period net assets to calculate end-of-period net assets. Additions and deductions are recognized on the accrual basis.

Schedule of Funding Progress

An example of a *schedule of funding progress* for Johnson County is presented in Illustration 8–11. This schedule shows funding progress of the plan based on *actuarial* calculations. The **actuarial value of assets** is the value assigned to the plan's assets by the actuary. Generally, the actuarial value of assets should reflect "some function of market value."[15] That the actuarial value does not necessarily reflect market value is due to the fact that the actuary may use techniques that will smooth out the short-term volatility that can be present in market values. Therefore, it is unlikely that the actuarial value of plan assets will be the same as the fair value of plan assets reported in the financial statements.

[15] GASB, *Comprehensive Implementation Guide,* 5.12, June 30, 2008.

ILLUSTRATION 8–11 Required Supplementary Information

JOHNSON COUNTY EMPLOYEE RETIREMENT SYSTEM
Schedule of Funding Progress
(in thousands)

Actuarial Valuation Date	Actuarial Value of Assets (a)	Actuarial Accrued Liability (AAL)—Entry Age (b)	Unfunded (Overfunded) AAL (b − a)	Funded Ratio (a/b)	Covered Payroll (c)	Unfunded (Overfunded) AAL as a Percentage of Covered Payroll ((b − a)/c)
12/31/2005	$ 86,320	$ 80,302	($6,018)	107.49%	$59,584	(10.10)%
12/31/2006	71,756	69,436	(2,320)	103.34	59,487	(3.90)
12/31/2007	79,887	77,704	(2,183)	102.81	64,206	(3.40)
12/31/2008	88,452	88,450	(2)	100.00	50,000	0.00
12/31/2009	92,887	92,885	(2)	100.00	51,282	(0.00)
12/31/2010	111,246	111,304	58	99.95	86,567	0.07

Actuarial accrued liability (AAL) is determined by using any of several generally accepted actuarial methods (consistently applied) and is the present value of projected benefits *other than* benefits earned from current and future employee services (i.e., normal costs). The actuarial accrued liability arises primarily from past underfundng and changes in pension plan provisions.

Covered payroll is the amount on which the contributions to the pension plan are based. Examples of covered payroll include an employee's base pay and could also include employee overtime if overtime is included as part of the pension plan's coverage. As shown in Illustration 8–11 the underfunded or (overfunded) AAL, **funded ratio,** and underfunded or (overfunded) AAL as a percentage of covered payroll are derived using the actuarial value of assets, AAL, and covered payroll.

Schedule of Employer Contributions

The key information the reader should note in the *schedule of employer contributions* shown in Illustration 8–12 is the *annual required contribution* (ARC) and what percentage of the ARC the employer has contributed. **Annual required contribution** is an actuarially determined amount that the employer should contribute each year to

ILLUSTRATION 8–12

JOHNSON COUNTY EMPLOYEE RETIREMENT SYSTEM
Schedule of Employer Contributions
(in thousands)

Year Ended December 31	Annual Required Contribution	Percentage Contributed
2005	$ 2,814	100%
2006	1,702	100
2007	2,609	100
2008	5,063	100
2009	7,352	100
2010	13,615	100

		Debits	Credits
7.	Cash	1,354,568	
	Commercial Paper and Repurchase Agreements		1,354,568

Common stocks carried at fair value of $6,293,867 were sold for that amount; $1,536,364 was reinvested in common stocks and the remainder in bonds. An additional amount of $29,229,967 was also invested in bonds:

		Debits	Credits
8a.	Cash	6,293,867	
	Investment in Common Stocks		6,293,867
8b.	Investment in Bonds	33,987,470	
	Investment in Common Stocks	1,536,364	
	Cash		35,523,834

Administrative expenses for the year totaled $568,219, all paid in cash:

		Debits	Credits
9.	Deductions—Administrative Expenses	568,219	
	Cash		568,219

Nominal accounts for the year were closed:

		Debits	Credits
10.	Additions—Member Contributions	8,009,400	
	Additions—Employer Contributions	14,126,292	
	Additions—Investment Income	14,262,845	
	Deductions—Annuity Benefits		3,134,448
	Deductions—Disability Benefits		287,590
	Deductions—Refunds to Terminated Employees		2,057,265
	Deductions—Administrative Expenses		568,219
	Deductions—Change in Fair Value of Investments		2,198,782
	Net Assets Held in Trust for Pension Benefits		28,152,233

Entries 1 through 10 result in the financial statements shown as Illustrations 8–9 and 8–10, when applied to the accounts existing at the beginning of the period as shown in Illustration 8–8.

Employer's Pension Accounting

GASB standards for the employer's accounting for defined benefit pension plans provide guidance for measurement, recognition, and display of the employer's pension information. In addition to general purpose government employers, the standards apply to governmental public benefit corporations and authorities, utilities, hospitals and other health care providers, colleges and universities, and, if they are employers, to public employee retirement systems.

Many of the note and statistical disclosures applicable to defined benefit pension plans, discussed in the preceding paragraphs, apply to the employer. If the plan (or PERS) is deemed to be part of the government's reporting entity, many of the employer's required disclosures are redundant of those required of the plan (a pension trust fund). In this case, the employer need not make disclosures that would duplicate those made by the plan. If the plan issues a stand-alone financial report, however, the employer will have to make many of the same disclosures in the comprehensive annual financial report (CAFR) that the plan makes in its stand-alone report. Because of the similarity of the disclosures and supplementary information required of the employer to those enumerated previously for the plan, the reader is referred to GASB, *Codification,* Section P20.117, for specific disclosure requirements applicable to the employer.

Whether a government employer accounts for payroll in a governmental fund or proprietary fund, or both, there are three primary measures to be calculated and reported: (1) *annual required contribution* (ARC), (2) *net pension obligation* (NPO), and (3) *annual pension cost.*

Annual Required Contribution

Annual pension cost must be calculated and disclosed in the notes to the employer's financial statements. As shown in Illustration 8–13, the *annual required contribution* (ARC) is the starting point for understanding the calculation of annual pension cost. A discussion of the procedures for calculating ARC can be found in GASB, *Codification,* Section Pe5; therefore, in this chapter only the components of ARC are discussed.

ARC is calculated in accordance with certain parameters provided in GASB standards. The parameters require that for financial reporting purposes an actuarial valuation be performed at least biennially and that ARC be based on an actuarial valuation as of a date not more than 24 months prior to the beginning of the current fiscal year. A component of ARC is the **actuarial present value of total projected benefits,** allowing for projected salary increases and additional statutory or contractual agreements such as cost-of-living increases and other types of postemployment benefit increases.

The parameters used to calculate ARC also provide broad guidance regarding actuarial and economic assumptions, even though any of six actuarial methods is permitted, subject to the limitation that in most cases the same actuarial method should be used both for funding and financial reporting purposes. Both the plan and the employer should use the same actuarial method.

An employer's ARC should include **normal cost** (i.e., the actuarial present value of benefits allocated to the current year by the actuarial cost method being used) and amortization of any **unfunded actuarial liability** (same as *actuarial accrued liability* defined previously in the discussion of the required schedule of funding progress). The provision for amortization can be determined using either level dollar amounts each year or a level percentage of the projected payroll. The amortization period must fall between defined maximum and minimum amortization periods. The maximum amortization period after 2006 is 30 years.[18] If there is a significant decrease in the total unfunded actuarial liability caused by a change in actuarial cost method or a change in asset valuation method, the decrease must be amortized over a period of not less than 10 years.

[18] GASB, *Codification,* Sec. Pe5.128.

ILLUSTRATION 8–13

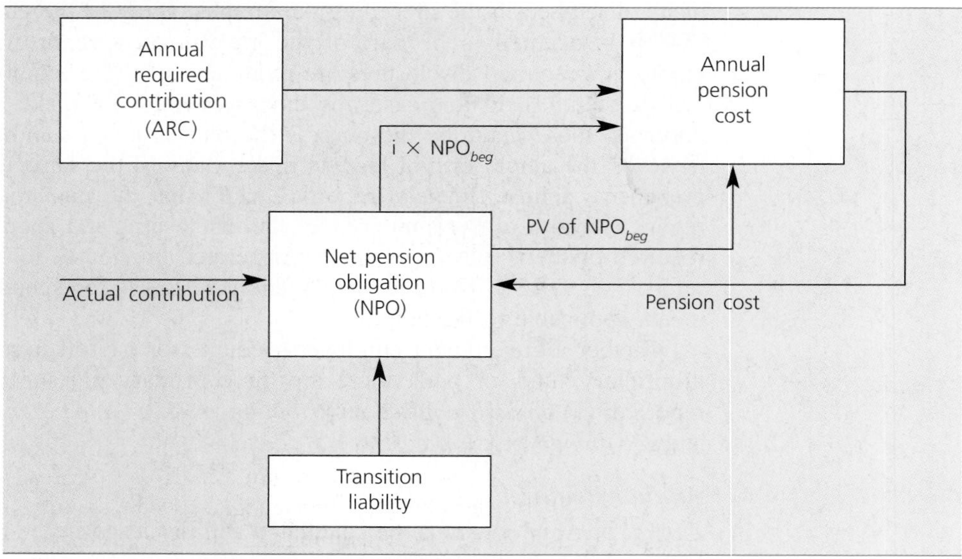

Once ARC is calculated, it becomes an input to the calculation of annual pension cost (see Illustration 8–13). If there is no *net pension obligation* (NPO), the annual pension cost is the same as ARC, and that is the amount the employer should contribute to the plan for the period in order to fully fund current-period accrued benefits. If the employer has undercontributed in the past, then ARC will contain an amount for the amortization of the unfunded actuarial liability. Moreover, if actual contributions have been less than annual pension cost, NPO will have a positive balance. Thus, annual pension cost will be affected by the existence of an NPO in addition to ARC. Before discussing the precise calculation of annual pension cost in the presence of an NPO, it will be useful to first examine the components of NPO.

Net Pension Obligation

Net pension obligation (NPO) has two components: (1) the transition pension liability (or asset), if any, existing at the date GASB *Statement No. 27* was implemented and (2) the cumulative difference from the implementation date of *Statement No. 27* to the current balance sheet date between annual pension cost (the amount that should be contributed) and the employer's actual contributions. These inputs to NPO (actual contribution, annual pension cost, and transition liability) are shown clearly in Illustration 8–13.

Annual Pension Cost

When an employer has an NPO, **annual pension cost** is equal to (1) the ARC, plus (2) one year's interest (i) on the beginning-of-year NPO, and minus or plus (3) an adjustment for any amounts already included in ARC for past amortization of contribution deficiencies or excess contributions. The adjustment is minus if the beginning balance of NPO is positive (contribution deficiencies) and plus if NPO is negative (excess contributions). As shown in Illustration 8–13, the adjustment to ARC is approximated by deducting an amount equal to the present value (PV) of the beginning balance of NPO. Illustration 8–14 provides a numerical example of how annual pension cost and NPO are related and how each is calculated.

ILLUSTRATION 8–14 Calculation of Annual Pension Cost and Net Pension Obligation

Annual required contribution (ARC)	$ 165,485
Interest on net pension obligation ($i \times NPO_{beg}$)	5,070
Adjustment to annual required contribution (PV of NPO_{beg})	(3,692)
Annual pension cost	166,863
Contributions made during the year	(157,982)
Increase in net pension obligation	8,881
Net pension obligation, January 1, 2011	67,594
Net pension obligation, December 31, 2011	$ 76,475

Source: Based on example shown in GASB, *Codification*, Sec. P20.902.

Employer Recording and Reporting of Pension Expenditure/Expense

Referring to Illustrations 8–13 and 8–14, a governmental employer that reports pension expenditures in a governmental fund should recognize the expenditures on the modified accrual basis. Thus, the amount recognized will be the actual amount contributed to the plan during the year. Assuming that the calculation in Illustration 8–14 is recognized by the General Fund of a city, the following transaction would be appropriate.

	Debits	*Credits*
General Fund:		
Expenditures—(various governmental functions)	157,982	
Cash		157,982

The governmental activities journal at the government-wide level would recognize the pension cost on the accrual basis. Therefore, if the amount contributed to the pension fund for the year is less than the annual pension cost, the difference should be added to NPO. Referring to Illustration 8–14, the appropriate journal entry for governmental activities at the government-wide level would allocate the pension cost to the various functions of government by debiting expenses.

Governmental Activities:		
Expenses—(various government functions)	166,863	
Cash		157,982
Net Pension Obligation		8,881

If the contribution is greater than the annual pension cost, the difference should be deducted from the NPO. Any cumulative positive balance of NPO, including a transition liability, should be reported in the statement of net assets at the government-wide level. A negative NPO balance should be used to reduce any other liability to the plan to zero but should not be reported as an asset. Annual pension cost should be disclosed in the notes to the financial statements. Under- or overfunding by a proprietary fund employer should be reported in the same manner except the NPO should be reported in the statement of net assets of the proprietary fund. The amount of pension expense recognized in the proprietary fund should be the same as the annual pension cost. This amount would also be recognized as program expenses in the government-wide statement of activities for business-type activities.

OTHER POSTEMPLOYMENT BENEFITS (OPEB)

In addition to accounting and reporting of pension plans, as of 2008, GASB now requires accounting and reporting for **other postemployment benefits (OPEB).** OPEB includes benefits other than pensions, such as health care, life insurance, and long-term care, among others. Due to the recency of the OPEB standards, the full impact of OPEB reporting on state and local government financial statements is not known as of the printing of this edition of the text. However, the liability for OPEB has been estimated at $1 trillion.[19] As with pension standards, GASB standards do not require that governments fund the liability associated with OPEB; however, a decision not to fund OPEB could be considered negatively by bond rating agencies and therefore affect the cost of debt.[20]

Accounting and reporting for OPEB is essentially the same as for defined benefit pension plans. The same financial reports and schedules are required, and note disclosures are essentially the same for all postemployment benefits. Therefore, the examples and information provided in the preceding section on pension funds should also be applied to OPEB. One major exception relates to transition year accounting. The employer will set the net pension obligation to zero for OPEB plans as of the beginning of the transition year. That is, the employer need not retroactively apply the OPEB standards.

TERMINATION BENEFITS

In addition to the standards on pensions and OPEB, GASB has a standard relating to accounting for **termination benefits.**[21] This standard provides guidance on expense and liability recognition for voluntary and involuntary termination benefits. Voluntary termination benefits occur when employers provide an incentive to hasten an employee's voluntary termination of employment, such as a one-time cash payout. An involuntary termination benefit could relate to layoffs or reductions in force, and include such items as career counseling and severance pay.

Appendix

Managing Investments

Wise investment is important to the success of investment trust funds and defined benefit plan funds. The managers of these funds are charged with earning the maximum return possible on the portfolio of investments within the constraints of safety and liquidity. To aid

[19] Eric S. Berman and Donald L. Rahn, "Successfully Navigating OPEB," *Journal of Accountancy*, August 2008, pp.54–60.

[20] Ibid., p. 54.

[21] GASB, *Codification*, Sec. T25.

managers, formal investment policies should be adopted by governments. A sound investment policy will:

1. Identify investment objectives.
2. Define risk tolerance.
3. Assign responsibility for the investment function.
4. Establish control over the investment process.[22]

An investment strategy that assesses liquidity needs, provides for a total return benchmark, and evaluates the success of meeting investment objectives will help maximize the return on the investment portfolio.[23] Accurately assessing liquidity needs helps ensure that short-term investments will be able to provide cash when needed. However, any cash not needed in the short term should be invested in longer term, higher yielding investments.

The benchmark selected for the targeted rates of total return or yield should be consistent with the risk tolerance defined in the investment policy. There are several types of risk that affect deposits and investments; however, two major risks the investment manager should consider are credit risk and market risk. *Credit risk* relates to the probability of loss due to the issuer or counterparty not meeting its obligations. Thus, credit risk relates to the financial viability and dependability of the issuers of the securities, any insurers of the securities, and/or the custodians of the securities or collateral. *Market risk* is the risk that the fair value of the security will decline. Periodic evaluation of the investment portfolio will help ensure that the targeted return is met while not exceeding the risk tolerance defined in the investment policy. Because risk exposure is a critical element in the management of investments, GASB requires disclosures of investment policies related to risk.[24]

To meet the investment objectives, managers can choose from a wide array of investments. Some commonly used investment securities are obligations of the federal government (e.g., U.S. Treasury bills, bonds, and notes), repurchase agreements, bankers' acceptances, commercial paper, money market funds, and state and local bonds. Additionally, some investment policies allow for investment in corporate debt and equity securities and derivatives.

In June 2008, GASB issued a standard on **derivatives** (GASB *Statement No. 53*). Governments using derivative instruments are required to implement the provisions of *GASBS 53* in periods beginning after June 15, 2009. The standard requires that derivatives be reported at fair value on the fiduciary statement of net assets. Changes in the fair value of derivative instruments used for investment purposes (or those derivatives that are deemed ineffective as hedging derivatives) are to be reported as part of investment earnings in the additions section of the statement of changes in fiduciary net assets. If the derivative is used to hedge risk (e.g., interest or foreign currency), the change in fair value will be reported as a deferred inflow or a deferred outflow on the fiduciary statement of net assets, provided the derivative meets the hedge effectiveness criteria identified in *GASBS 53*. Investment managers may want to keep the derivative standard in mind when making decisions about the best use of derivatives and the effectiveness of the derivatives.

When setting targets for rates of total return, managers need to be aware of Internal Revenue Code Sec. 148 rules on arbitrage. These rules significantly limit the ability of

[22] The preceding list is adapted from M. Corrine Larson, "Managing Your Investment Program in Today's Market," *Government Finance Review*, June 2002, p. 40.

[23] Joya C. De Foor and Kay Chandler, "Innovations in Managing Public Funds: Benchmarking and Total Return," *Government Finance Review*, August 2007, p. 16.

[24] GASB, *Codification*, Sec. I50, pars. 126–133.

a government to realize arbitrage earnings by investing tax-exempt bond proceeds (e.g., general obligation bond proceeds received for future construction of a capital asset) in taxable investments with higher yields. Interest earnings in excess of those permitted by Internal Revenue Code rules must be paid to the federal government. There are severe penalties for violating the Internal Revenue Code rules on arbitrage.

Key Terms

Actuarial accrued liability (AAL), *331*
Actuarial present value of total projected benefits, *335*
Actuarial value of assets, *330*
Agency funds, *306*
Annual pension cost, *336*
Annual required contributions, *331*
Covered payroll, *331*
Defined benefit plan, *326*
Defined contribution plan, *326*
Derivatives, *339*
External investment pool, *315*
Funded ratio, *331*
Investment trust fund, *315*
Net pension obligation (NPO), *336*
Normal cost, *335*
Other postemployment benefits (OPEB), *338*
Public Employee Retirement System (PERS), *327*
Termination benefits, *338*
Unfunded actuarial liability, *335*

Selected References

Berman, Eric S. and Donald L. Rahn, "Successfully Navigating OPEB," *Journal of Accountancy*, August 2008, pp. 54–60.

De Foor, Joya C. and Kay Chandler, "Innovations in Managing Public Funds: Benchmarking and Total Return," *Government Finance Review*, August 2007, p. 16.

Government Accountability Office. *State and Local Government Pension Plans: Current Structure and Funded Status*. July 2008. Report 08-983T. *www.gao.gov.*

———. *State and Local Government Retiree Benefits: Current Funded Status of Pension and Health Benefits*. January 2008. Report 08-223. *www.gao.gov.*

Governmental Accounting Standards Board. *Codification of Governmental Accounting and Financial Reporting Standards, as of June 30, 2008*. Norwalk, CT, 2008.

———. *Comprehensive Implementation Guide, as of June 30, 2008*. Norwalk, CT, 2008.

———, *Statement No. 53*. "Accounting and Financial Reporting for Derivative Instruments." Norwalk, CT, 2008.

Larson, M. Corrine, "Managing Your Investment Program in Today's Market," *Government Finance Review*, June 2002, p. 40.

Questions

8–1. Explain the distinction(s) between *agency funds* and *trust funds.*

8–2. Identify the different types of trust funds and explain the purpose of each type.

8–3. Must an agency fund be used to account for withholding taxes, retirement contributions, and (if applicable) social security taxes of General Fund employees? Explain.

8–4. Why do agency funds have no fund equity?

8–5. What is a "pass-through" agency fund and under what conditions is it appropriate to use such a fund?

8–6. How does the accounting for an internal investment pool differ from the accounting for an external investment pool?

8–7. GASB standards require that investments be reported at fair value. Explain the GASB reporting requirements related to fair value. How do these requirements differ from reporting requirements for corporate entities?

8–8. Explain the difference between a private-purpose trust and a public-purpose trust. How does the reporting for the two types of trusts differ?

8–9. If you were trying to assess the financial health of a government administered pension plan, which financial statements or schedules would you review and why?

8–10. What are the two types of risk that are of concern to investment managers? Define each type of risk.

Cases

8–1 Internet Case—CalPERS. While the examples in this chapter have focused on a single-employer plan, many states operate statewide plans, referred to as Public Employee Retirement Systems (PERS), to which multiple employers contribute. One of the largest PERS plans in the nation is operated in the State of California.

Required

To answer the following questions use the Web site found at *www.calpers.ca.gov*. The answers to the questions can be found in CalPERS's annual report or in the general information section provided on the site.

a. When was CalPERS established?
b. What types of employers contribute to CalPERS?
c. How many individuals are served by CalPERS?
d. How many and what types of funds are administered by CalPERS?
e. For the most recent reporting period, what is the value of total fiduciary assets?
f. For the most recent reporting period, what was the change in pension fund net assets?
g. What are the funded ratios from the schedule of funding progress and what do the funded ratios tell you?
h. What is the reporting relationship between CalPERS and the State of California?

8–2 Identification of Fiduciary Funds. Following is a list of fund names and descriptions of funds from comprehensive annual financial reports (CAFRs).

Required

For each fund, indicate which type of fund should be used to account for the activities and explain why that fund is most appropriate.

a. Tri-Centennial Fund. Accounts for money raised or contributed by several local area governments and other organizations. The purpose is to ensure availability of resources to celebrate the United States Tri-Centennial in 2076.
b. Perpetual Care Fund. Accounts for endowed gifts and investment earnings dedicated to perpetual care of the city's cemeteries.
c. Debt Service Trust Fund. The city collects special assessments from citizens in designated special benefit districts that are intended for debt service on bonds issued for projects within the district. The city bears no responsibility for this debt.
d. School Impact Fee Fund. The city collects school impact fees as part of the cost of building permits issued. Money must be remitted periodically to the local school district, a legally separate government that is not a component unit of the city.

e. *Housing Rehabilitation Fund.* Accounts for several revolving funds that provide low interest loans for housing. The collection of the loans is used to run the program and make new loans to qualified citizens. Several government sources provided the start-up funds.

f. *Payroll Fund.* The city has established a fund in which all payroll deductions are reported.

g. *Telephone Commissions Fund.* The city collects commissions on pay telephones used by jail inmates. The funds are used to provide inmates such benefits as library resources and fitness equipment.

h. *Block Grant Fund.* The state receives federal funds for the homeless which it passes through to local not-for-profit organizations. The only responsibility the state has is to contribute an additional amount of funds (match) to the federal grant.

i. *Health Benefits Fund.* The county has agreed to pay a portion of the health insurance premiums for employees when they retire. Contributions for the benefit are paid into this fund.

j. *Unclaimed Property Fund.* The state has established a fund to account for abandoned and unclaimed property. The property is held in the fund for 10 years. If a legal claimant to the property is not found within the 10-year time period, the property reverts to the state.

8–3 Other Postemployment Benefit (OPEB) Plans. GASB standards require that governments report other postemployment benefits offered to employees. A typical example of such benefits is health care provided to retirees. It is estimated that the unrecorded and unfunded liability related to OPEB is huge. To investigate the extent of the problem, examine the notes of the most recent CAFRs for the City and County of Denver (*www.denvergov.org/controller*) and the City of New York (*www.comptroller.nyc.gov*).

a. Examine the Schedule of Funding Progress in the pension plan note (section IV, note G, in Denver's 2007 CAFR) for the City and County of Denver. For the most recent year, how large is the actuarial accrued liability (AAL) for Denver's health benefits plan (titled DERP Health Benefits in the schedule) and what has been the trend in the funded ratio? Discuss how the funded ratio for the Denver Employees Retirement Plan (DERP) compares to that of the health benefits plan.

b. Examine the Schedule of Funding Progress for the health benefits plan (New York City Health Benefits Plan) for the City of New York. The schedule can be found in the Other Information note (part 3 of note E in New York City's 2007 CAFR). For the most recent year, how large is the AAL for the New York City Health Benefits Plan and what does the funded ratio indicate about the status of the plan?

c. Compare the funded status of Denver's health benefits plan to that of New York City's health benefits plan.

Exercises and Problems

8–1 Examine a CAFR. Utilizing the annual report obtained for Exercise 1–1, follow these instructions:

a. *Agency Funds*. Are employees' and employers' FICA tax contributions and contributions to other retirement funds reported in the General Fund, an agency fund, or in some other manner (describe)? Does the government operate a tax agency fund or participate in a tax agency fund operated by another government? Does the government act as agent for owners of property within a special assessment district and for the creditors of those property owners? Does the government operate one or more pass-through agency funds? If so, describe.

b. Investment Trust Funds. Does the government operate, or participate in, a cash and investments pool? If so, is the pool operated as an investment trust fund? If there is a cash and investment pool and it is not reported as an investment trust fund, how is it reported? Explain.

c. Private-purpose Trust Funds. Does the government operate one or more private-purpose trust funds? If yes, explain the purpose(s).

d. Pension Trust Funds. Are the government employees covered by a retirement fund operated by the government, by the state, by the federal Social Security Administration, or by two or more of these? If the government operates one or more pension plans, or retirement systems, are the plan statements accompanied by an actuary's report, or is a reference made to the actuary's report in the notes to the financial statements? Is a net pension obligation (NPO) reported in the government-wide statement of net assets and/or in a proprietary fund? Is all the pension information specified by GASB standards and discussed in Chapter 8 presented in the notes to the financial statements? Are all required supplementary schedules and related notes reported in the comprehensive annual financial report?

e. Fiduciary Fund Financial Statements. Are all fiduciary funds shown in a statement of fiduciary net assets and a statement of changes in fiduciary net assets? Does the financial report state the basis of accounting used for trust and agency funds? Are agency funds properly disclosed in the financial statements? Does the report contain a schedule or list of investments of trust funds? Are investments reported at fair value? Is the net increase (decrease) shown separately from interest and dividend income? If trust funds own depreciable assets, is depreciation taken? If so, is depreciation considered a charge against principal or against income?

8–2 Multiple Choice. Choose the best answer.

1. Which of the following is *not* a fiduciary fund?
   a. Permanent fund.
   b. Agency fund.
   c. Investment trust fund.
   d. Pension trust fund.
2. Which of the following is an example of a trust fund?
   a. A fund used to account for the collection and distribution of taxes to several local governments.
   b. A fund used to distribute scholarships to the children of the city's police officers.
   c. A fund used to distribute low-income housing funds received from HUD (Housing and Urban Development).
   d. A fund used to account for risk management services provided to other funds of the government.
3. Which of the following financial statements is prepared by fiduciary funds?
   a. Statement of net assets.
   b. Statement of activities.
   c. Statement of cash flows.
   d. All of the above.
4. At the government-wide level, where are fiduciary funds reported?
   a. In the Governmental Activities column.
   b. In the Business-type Activities column.

c. As a part of component units.
d. Fiduciary funds are not reported at the government-wide level.

5. The city has installed sidewalks using special assessment debt. Special assessments paid over the next 10 years will be used to retire the debt. If property owners fail to pay the assessments the city is under no obligation to pay the assessments. Debt service related to the special assessment debt used to install the sidewalks should be recorded in what fund type?
   a. Private-purpose trust fund.
   b. Debt service fund.
   c. Agency fund.
   d Capital projects fund.
6. An investment trust fund is used to report the net assets available to the:
   a. Sponsoring government only.
   b. External participants only.
   c. Financial institution that acts as custodian for the fund's investments.
   d. All of the above.
7. Which of the following fiduciary funds would account for an endowment (i.e., the principal must remain intact)?
   a. Investment trust fund.
   b. Private-purpose trust fund.
   c. Pension trust fund.
   d. Permanent fund.
8. If a county incurs the cost of monitoring grant recipients, which of the following funds would most likely account for pass-through grants to a not-for-profit organization assisting low-income individuals?
   a. Private-purpose trust fund.
   b. Agency fund.
   c. Special revenue fund.
   d. Permanent fund.
9. Arkmo City has a single pension plan for its employees, all of whose salaries and wages are paid from the General Fund. Ordinarily, the city's General Fund should report an expenditure for its annual pension contribution to a defined benefit pension plan in an amount equal to the:
   a. Annual required contribution.
   b. Annual pension cost.
   c. Net pension obligation.
   d. Actual contribution.
10. Which OPEB financial report or schedule would help in determining whether OPEB is underfunded?
    a. Statement of plan net assets.
    b. Statement of changes in plan net assets.
    c. Schedule of funding progress.
    d. Schedule of employer contributions.

8–3 Multiple Choice. Choose the best answer.

Items 1 through 3 relate to the following information.

The county administers a tax agency fund that collects taxes on behalf of the county, city, and a special purpose district. For 2011, the taxes to be levied by the government are:

County	$ 632,000
City	917,000
Special purpose district	26,000
Total	$1,575,000

1. On the date the taxes are levied, the city would debit which of the following accounts?
   a. Due from Tax Agency Fund.
   b. Equity in Tax Agency Fund.
   c. Taxes Receivable.
   d. No journal entry is recorded since the city is not collecting the taxes.
2. On the date the taxes are levied, the tax agency fund would credit which of the following accounts?
   a. Due to Other Funds and Governments.
   b. Revenues—Taxes.
   c. Additions—Other Funds and Governments.
   d. Accrued Taxes.
3. If the tax agency fund assessed a 1 percent administrative fee, it would be recorded by the agency fund as a credit to:
   a. Revenue.
   b. Transfer In.
   c. Additions—Fund Equity.
   d. Due to County.

Items 4 through 7 relate to the following information:

The city council of the City of Cadillac decided to pool the investments of its General Fund with that of Cadillac School District and Cadillac Township, each of which carried its investments at fair value as of the prior balance sheet date. All investments are revalued to current fair value at the date of the creation of the pool. At that date, the prior and current fair value of the investments of each of the participants were as follows:

	Investments	
	Prior Fair Value	Current Fair Value
General Fund	$ 600,000	$ 590,000
Cadillac School District	3,600,000	3,640,000
Cadillac Township	1,800,000	1,770,000
Total	$6,000,000	$6,000,000

4. At the date of the creation of the investment pool, each of the participants should:
   a. Debit its Fund Balance account and credit its Investments account for the prior fair value of the assets transferred to the pool.
   b. Debit or credit its Investments account as needed to adjust its carrying value to current fair value. The offsetting entry in each fund should be to Fund Balance.
   c. Debit Equity in Pooled Investments for the current fair value of investments pooled, credit Investments for the prior fair value of investments pooled, and credit or debit Revenues—Change in Fair Value of Investments for the difference.
   d. Make a memorandum entry only.

5. At the date of creation of the pool, the City of Cadillac should account for all the pooled investments in:
   a. An investment trust fund at fair value at the date the pool is created.
   b. An agency fund at fair value as of the prior balance sheet date.
   c. Its General Fund at fair value at the date the pool is created.
   d. Its General Fund at fair value as of the prior balance sheet date.
6. One day after creation of the pool, the investments that had belonged to Cadillac Township were sold by the pool for $1,760,000.
   a. The loss of $40,000 is borne by each participant in proportion to its equity in the pool.
   b. The loss of $10,000 is borne by each participant in proportion to its equity in the pool.
   c. The loss of $40,000 is considered to be a loss borne by Cadillac Township.
   d. The loss of $10,000 is considered to be a loss borne by Cadillac Township.
7. One month after creation of the pool, earnings on pooled investments totaled $59,900. It was decided to distribute the earnings to the participants, rounding the distribution to the nearest dollar. The Cadillac School District should receive:
   a. $36,000.
   b. $35,940.
   c. $36,339.
   d. $37,000.

Items 8 through 10 are based on the following information:

The City of Lindenwood contributes to and administers a single-employer defined benefit pension plan on behalf of its covered employees. The city uses a trust fund to account for and report its pension plan. Annual pension cost and actual contributions made for the past three years were as follows:

	Annual Pension Cost	Actual Contribution
2011	$32,000	$31,500
2010	31,250	30,500
2009	30,150	29,000

8. For 2011, what would be the credit to Additions—Employer Contributions in the pension trust fund?
   a. $32,000.
   b. $31,500.
   c. $1,000.
   d. $500.
9. To record the 2011 pension contribution to the pension trust fund, what account would the General Fund debit?
   a. Other Financing Uses—Interfund Transfers Out.
   b. Expenditures.
   c. Due to Pension Fund.
   d. Deductions—Employer Contributions.
10. Over the three-year time period, what has happened to the net pension obligation?
    a. It has increased.
    b. It has decreased.
    c. It has stayed the same.
    d. The reader cannot tell based on the information provided.

8–4 Tax Agency Fund. The county collector of Lincoln County is responsible for collecting all property taxes levied by funds and governments within the boundaries of the county. To reimburse the county for estimated administrative expenses of operating the tax agency fund, the agency fund deducts 1 percent from the collections for the town, the school district, and the townships. The total amount deducted is added to the collections for the county and remitted to the Lincoln County General Fund.

The following events occurred in 2011:

1. Current-year tax levies to be collected by the agency fund were:

County General Fund	$ 2,752,000
Town of Smithton General Fund	4,644,000
Lincoln Co. Consolidated School District	7,912,000
Various townships	1,892,000
Total	$17,200,000

2. $8,400,000 of current taxes was collected during the first half of 2011.
3. Liabilities to all funds and governments as the result of the first half-year collections were recorded. (A schedule of amounts collected for each participant, showing the amount withheld for the county General Fund and net amounts due the participants, is recommended for determining amounts to be recorded for this transaction.)
4. All money in the tax agency fund was distributed.

Required

a. Make journal entries for each of the foregoing transactions that affected the tax agency fund.

b. Make journal entries for each of the foregoing transactions that affected the Lincoln County General Fund. Begin with the tax levy entry, assuming 3 percent of the gross levy will be uncollectible.

c. Make journal entries for each of the foregoing entries that affected the Town of Smithton General Fund. Begin with the tax levy entry, assuming 3 percent of the gross levy will be uncollectible.

d. Which financial statements would be prepared by the tax agency fund?

8–5 Special Assessment Debt. Fawn community, located in the City of Deerville, voted to form a local improvement district to fund the construction of a new community center. The city agreed to construct the community center and administer the bond debt; however, Fawn community was solely responsible for repaying the bond issue. To administer the bond debt, the city established the Local Improvement District Fund. Following are several events connected with the Local Improvement District Fund.

1. On June 30, 2010, the city assessed levies totaling $6,000,000. The levies are payable in 10 equal annual installments with 4 1/2 percent interest on unpaid installments.
2. All assessments for the current period were collected by June 30, 2011, as was the interest due on the unpaid installments.
3. On July 1, 2011, the first principal payment of $600,000 was made to bondholders as was interest on the debt.

Required

a. What type of fund is the Local Improvement District Fund? Explain your answer.

b. Make journal entries for each of the foregoing events that affected the Local Improvement District Fund.

c. How would this fund be reported in the City of Deerville's financial statements?

8–6 Identification of Fund. St. George County has entered into a contract for the demolition and construction of a six-lane bridge. It is expected that the project will take three years to complete. The terms of the contract indicate that the county will retain 5 percent (retained percentage) from each progress billing. The contract also requires that the retained percentage be invested and accounted for in a separate fund. Investment of the retained percentage is for the benefit of the contractor, who will receive the retained percentage and investment earnings upon successful completion and acceptance of the bridge.

Required

a. What type of fund should St. George County use to account for the retained percentage? Explain your answer.

b. Record the following events in the retained percentage fund.

1. A retained percentage was withheld from a progress payment of $900,000.
2. The retained percentage was invested in certificates of deposit.
3. Interest of $675 was received.
4. At year-end, interest of $1,350 was accrued. There was no adjustment to fair value.
5. Nominal accounts were closed.

8–7 Investment Trust Fund. The Albertville City Council decided to pool the investments of its General Fund with Albertville Schools and Richwood Township in an investment pool to be managed by the city. Each of the pool participants had reported its investments at fair value as of the end of the last fiscal year. At the date of the creation of the pool, the fair value of the investments of each pool participant was as follows:

	Investments	
	Prior Fair Value	**Current Fair Value**
City of Albertville General Fund	$ 890,000	$ 900,000
Albertville Schools	4,200,000	4,230,000
Richwood Township	3,890,000	3,870,000
Total	$8,980,000	$9,000,000

Required

a. Show the entry that should be made by the City of Albertville, Albertville Schools, and Richwood Township to do the following: (1) open a new asset account, Equity in Pooled Investments, in the amount of the current fair value of the investments transferred to the pool; (2) close the existing investments account; and (3) debit or credit the revenues account of each participant as needed to adjust for changes in fair value.

b. Show in general journal form the entries to be made in the accounts of the investment pool trust fund to record the following transactions of the first year of its operations:
   (1) Record at current fair value the investments transferred to the pool; assume that the investments of the city's General Fund were in U.S. Treasury notes and the investments of both the schools and the township were in certificates of deposit (CDs).
   (2) CDs that had been recorded at a fair value of $1,000,000 matured. The pool received $1,050,000 in cash ($1,000,000 for the face of the CDs and $50,000 interest). The entire amount was reinvested in a new issue of certificates of deposit.
   (3) Interest on Treasury notes in the amount of $50,000 was collected.
   (4) Interest on CDs accrued at year-end amounted to $28,250.
   (5) At the end of the year, it was decided to compute and record the pool's liability or net assets held for each of the three participants for its proportionate share of earnings on the pooled investments. Assume that there were no changes in the fair value of investments since the investment pool was created. Carry your computation of each participant's proportionate share to two decimal places. Round the amount of the distribution to each fund or participant to the nearest dollar.

c. Record in each of the participant's funds the increase in its Equity in Pooled Investment account.

d. The City of Albertville General Fund decided to withdraw $100,000 from the investment pool to obtain the cash it needed to acquire general capital assets. The investment pool trust fund sold $50,000 of its investments in U.S. Treasury notes (no interest had accrued on these investments) to obtain the cash needed for the withdrawal. Record the sale of U.S. Treasury notes. Record the cash withdrawal in the investment pool trust fund and the City of Albertville General Fund. Recalculate each participant's proportionate share of pooled investments after the withdrawal is made.

e. Explain how the investment trust fund would report the General Fund's interest in the investment pool and the Albertville School's interest in the investment pool.

8–8 Pension Plan Calculation. The Village of Dover administers a defined benefit pension plan for its police and fire personnel. Employees are not required to contribute to the plan. The village received from the actuary and other sources the following information about the Public Safety Employees' Pension Fund as of December 31, 2011.

Item	Amount
Annual required contribution	$ 606,700
Net pension obligation, 1/1/2011	535,700
Present value of net pension obligation as of 1/1/2011	268,920
Interest rate applicable to beginning net pension obligation	7%

Required

Assuming that the Village of Dover contributes $385,000 cash to the plan on December 31, 2011, calculate the employer's

a. Annual pension cost.

b. Net pension obligation, as of December 31, 2011.

8–9 Pension Plan Financial Statements. The State of Nodak operates a Public Employees Retirement System (PERS) for all employees of the state. The preclosing trial balance of the PERS as of June 30, 2011, follows (in thousands of dollars):

	Debits	*Credits*
Cash	$ 16,000	
Accrued Interest Receivable	33,200	
Investments	2,002,000	
Equipment and Fixtures	25,200	
Accumulated Depreciation—Equipment and Fixtures		$ 3,100
Accounts Payable and Accruals		33,400
Net Assets Held in Trust for Pension Benefits, July 1, 2010		1,577,000
Member Contributions		112,100
Employer Contributions		197,800
Interest and Dividend Income		199,700
Net Change in Fair Value of Investments		58,800
Annuity Benefits	53,900	
Disability Benefits	14,000	
Refunds to Terminated Employees	28,800	
Administrative Expenses	8,800	
Total	$2,181,900	$2,181,900

Required

a. Prepare a statement of changes in plan net assets for the State of Nodak Public Employees Retirement System for the year ended June 30, 2011, in as much detail as possible.

b. Prepare a statement of plan net assets as of June 30, 2011, for the State of Nodak Public Employees Retirement System.

c. Explain how the State of Nodak (the employer) would report its participation in the state PERS at the fund level and at the government-wide level.

8–10 Fiduciary Financial Statements. Ray County administers a tax agency fund, an investment trust fund, and a private-purpose trust fund. The tax agency fund acts as an agent for the county, a city within the county, and the school district within the county. Participants in the investment trust fund are the Ray County General Fund, the city, and the school district. The private-purpose trust is maintained for the benefit of a private organization located within the county. Ray County has prepared the following statement of fiduciary net assets.

RAY COUNTY
Statement of Fiduciary Net Assets
Fiduciary Funds
June 30, 2011
(in thousands)

	Trust Funds	Agency Funds	Total
Assets			
Cash and cash equivalents	$ 104,747	$ 788	$ 105,535
Receivables	12,166	87,858	100,024
Investments:			
Short-term investments	241,645		241,645
Bonds, notes, and stock	992,226		992,226
Total assets	1,350,784	88,646	1,439,430
Liabilities			
Accounts payable	61,447		61,447
Net Assets			
Held in trust for:			
Organizations	193,400		193,400
County	219,187	10,638	229,825
City of Leetown	383,578	23,048	406,626
Leetown School District	493,172	54,960	548,132
Total net assets	$1,289,337	$88,646	$1,377,983

Required

The statement as presented is not in accordance with GASB standards. Using Illustration A1–10 as an example, identify the errors (problems) in the statement and explain how the errors should be corrected.

Chapter Nine

Financial Reporting of State and Local Governments

Learning Objectives

After studying this chapter, you should be able to:

1. Describe the concepts related to the financial reporting requirements of the GASB reporting model.
2. Explain the key concepts and terms used in describing the governmental reporting entity.
3. Apply the GASB criteria used to determine whether a potential component unit should be included in the reporting entity and, when included, the manner of reporting component units.
4. Identify and describe the contents of a comprehensive annual financial report (CAFR).
5. Understand how to reconcile governmental fund financial statements to governmental activity in the government-wide financial statements.
6. Identify and explain contemporary financial reporting issues.

Chapters 2 through 8 present extended discussions of the principles of accounting for governmental, proprietary, and fiduciary funds and governmental and business-type activities at the government-wide level. Chapters 1 and 2 provide overviews of Governmental Accounting Standards Board (GASB) financial reporting requirements, and financial reporting requirements for specific fund types are discussed in several chapters. This chapter presents the reporting requirements in more depth and discusses contemporary financial reporting issues. Prior to examining reporting requirements, a brief conceptual discussion of financial reporting is provided.

CONCEPTS RELATED TO FINANCIAL REPORTING

GASB *Concepts Statement 1*[1] identifies two objectives of government financial reports: to provide information that can be used to assess a government's accountability and to assist users in making economic, social, and political decisions. The

[1] GASB, *Codification,* Appendix B.

primary users of government financial reports are those external to government; principally, citizens, legislative and oversight bodies, and creditors. For the financial reports to be useful in meeting identified objectives, GASB indicates that the information provided in the reports should be understandable, reliable, relevant, timely, consistent, and comparable.

An important part of providing useful information is communicating the information in a manner that is helpful to the user. GASB *Concepts Statement 3*[2] provides guidance regarding where and how items of information should appear in financial reports to be the most useful. The areas identified for communicating items of information are recognition in the financial statements, disclosures in the notes to the financial statements, presentation as required supplementary information, or presentation as supplementary information. GASB indicates that an item of information that meets the definition of an element and is measurable with sufficient reliability should be recognized in the financial statements. A note should be used if it can help support an item recognized in the financial statement or provide information that is essential to the user's understanding of the item. An example of the relationship between recognized items and notes can be conveyed with the Investments account. Without a note disclosure relating information on fair values and risk exposure, the user is left without information that is relevant in assessing the quality and management of the government's investments.

Required supplementary information (RSI) and supplementary information are used to communicate information that is essential and useful, respectively. Without RSI the financial statements and related notes cannot be placed in the correct context. Examples of RSI include the budget to actual schedules (Chapter 3) and several pension disclosures (Chapter 8). Other supplementary information is useful but not essential in understanding the financial statements and related notes. Much of the supplementary information is found in the statistical section of the comprehensive annual financial report (CAFR).

As indicated, before an item can be recognized in the financial statements it must meet the definition of an element. GASB *Concept Statement 4,*[3] provides for seven financial statement elements. The elements are assets, liabilities, deferred outflows of resources, deferred inflows of resources, net position, outflows of resources, and inflows of resources. Since governments use two bases of accounting, GASB defines the elements in terms that will allow for recognition under both modified accrual and accrual accounting. For example, an outflow of resources can mean an expenditure or an expense.

The GASB concept statements primarily serve the needs of standard-setters, providing them with guidance in writing standards that form the basis for the type and display of information found in the financial reports discussed in the remainder of the chapter.

THE GOVERNMENTAL REPORTING ENTITY

The average citizen—including accountants whose only experience has been with business organizations—has only a vague knowledge and little understanding of the overlapping layers of general purpose and special purpose governments that have

[2] GASB, *Codification,* Appendix B.

[3] Ibid.

some jurisdiction over us wherever we may live and work. Illustration 8–1, for example, shows that different levels of general purpose governments can levy taxes on property. The school funds in that illustration show that taxes are also levied by special purpose governments (an independent school district in that illustration). Omitted from the illustration, for the sake of brevity, are taxes levied by any *special districts.* Special districts are defined by the Bureau of the Census as "independent special-purpose governmental units (other than school districts) that exist as separate entities with substantial administrative and fiscal independence from general-purpose local governments."[4] About 42 percent of the local governments in the United States are classified as special districts.[5]

Although the Census definition stresses the independence of special districts, in many instances they were created to provide a vehicle for financing services demanded by residents of a general purpose government that could not be financed by the general purpose government because of constitutional or statutory limits on the rates or amounts it could raise from taxes, other revenue sources, and debt. Building authorities are examples of special districts created as a financing vehicle.

In addition to independent special districts, certain governmental activities are commonly carried out by commissions, boards, and other agencies that are not considered as independent of a general purpose government by the Bureau of the Census but that may have some degree of fiscal and administrative independence from the governing board of the general purpose government. In past years, some governments included in their annual reports the financial statements of such semi-independent boards and commissions and even certain of the special districts, whereas other governments excluded them.

To improve uniformity in reporting and to promote the preparation of financial reports consistent with GASB *Concepts Statement 1,* GASB *Codification,* Section 2100 provides authoritative guidance on defining the reporting entity, and Section 2600 presents guidance on reporting entity and component unit presentations and disclosure. GASB *Codification,* Section 2100 also provides guidance for reporting certain affiliated organizations, such as fund-raising foundations. These sections provide the basis for the following discussion.

Defining the Financial Reporting Entity

Elected officials of state and local governments (*primary governments*) are accountable to their constituents. That accountability extends not only to the financial performance of the primary government, but also to any organizations that are financially dependent on the primary government or over which the primary government can impose its will. Thus, GASB takes the position that governmental financial reporting should report on all governments and organizations for which elected officials are accountable. Collectively, these governments and organizations are referred to as the *financial reporting entity*. Before proceeding further with the explanation of a financial reporting entity, it is important to more formally define the terms *primary government* and *financial reporting entity.*

A **primary government** is a state government or general purpose local government. It can also be a special purpose government that has a separately elected governing

[4] U.S. Department of Commerce, Bureau of the Census, *2002 Census of Governments,* vol. 1, no. 1 (Washington, D.C.: U.S. Government Printing Office), p. vii.

[5] http://www.census.gov/govs/cog/GovOrgTab03ss.html.

body, is *legally separate*, and is *fiscally independent* of other state or local governments. A legally separate organization has an identity of its own as an "artificial person" with a personality and existence distinct from that of its creator and others. A fiscally independent organization has the authority to determine its budget, levy its own taxes, and set rates or charges; and issue bonded debt without approval of another government.

GASB defines a **financial reporting entity** as a primary government, organizations for which the primary government is *financially accountable*, and other organizations for which the nature and significance of their relationship with the primary government are such that exclusion would cause the reporting entity's basic financial statements to be misleading. A primary government is generally the basis for the financial reporting entity. However, other types of governments can be the basis for a financial reporting entity if they issue separate financial statements. Examples of other types of governments that may serve as their own reporting entity are component units, government joint ventures, jointly governed organizations, or other stand-alone governments.

A primary government is **financially accountable** for another organization if the primary government appoints a voting majority of the organization's governing board and it is (*a*) able to impose its will on the organization *or* (*b*) there is a potential for the organization to provide specific financial benefits to, or impose specific financial burdens on, the primary government. The ability of the primary government to impose its will on an organization exists if the primary government can significantly influence the programs, projects, or activities of, or the level of services performed or provided by, the organization. A financial benefit or burden relationship exists if the primary government *(a)* is entitled to the organization's resources; *(b)* is legally obligated or has otherwise assumed the obligation to finance the deficits of, or provide financial support to, the organization; or *(c)* is obligated in some manner for the debt of the organization. Additionally, a primary government may be financially accountable for organizations with separately elected governing boards, governing boards appointed by other governments, or a jointly appointed board that is fiscally dependent on the primary government.

Component Units

Other organizations included as part of the financial reporting entity are called *component units*. Not-for-profit organizations, for-profit firms, or a nonprimary government can be component units of the financial reporting entity. A **component unit** is defined as a legally separate organization for which the elected officials of the primary government are financially accountable. A component unit can also be another organization for which the nature and significance of its relationship with the primary government is such that exclusion would cause the reporting entity's financial statements to be misleading or incomplete. Because the reporting entity must include the component unit's financial information in its financial statements, the GASB has provided that the information can be included by blending the information or discretely presenting the information.

To assist in determining whether an organization should be included as a component unit of the reporting entity, the GASB has developed the flowchart in Illustration 9–1. In addition to assisting in determining whether a component unit should be included in the financial statements, the flowchart also assists in determining whether the component unit information should be blended or discretely presented.

ILLUSTRATION 9–1 Decision Process for Inclusion or Exclusion of Potential Component Unit (PCU)

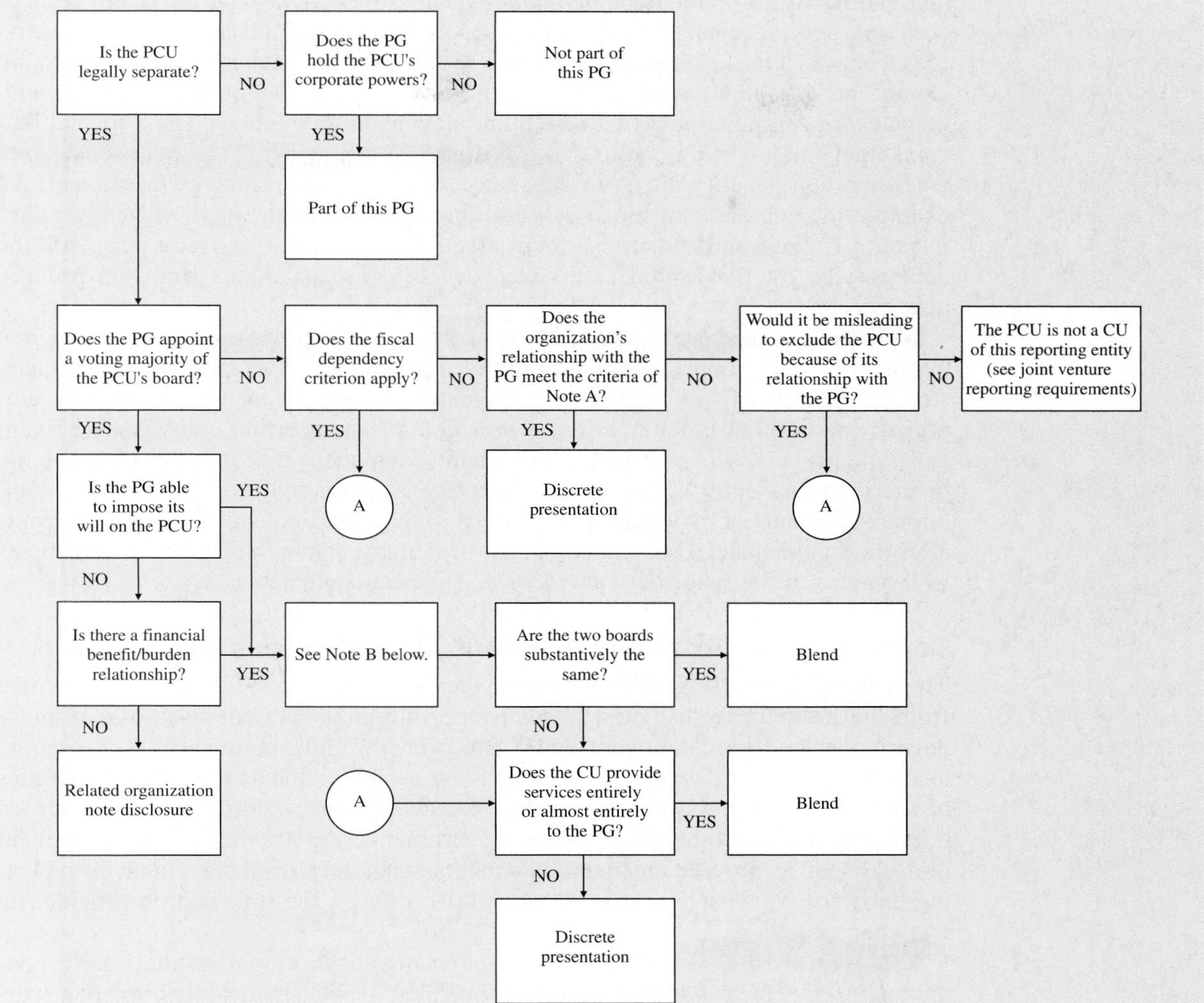

Notes:

A. A legally separate, tax-exempt organization should be reported as a component unit of a reporting entity if *all* of the following criteria are met: *(a)* The economic resources received or held by the separate organization are entirely or almost entirely for the direct benefit of the primary government, its component units, or its constituents; *(b)* the primary government or its component units is entitled to or has the ability to otherwise access a majority of the economic resources received or held by the separate organization; *(c)* the economic resources received or held by an *individual* organization that the specific primary government, or its component unit, is entitled to or has the ability to otherwise access are significant to that primary government.

B. A potential component unit (PCU) for which a primary government (PG) is financially accountable may be fiscally dependent on another government. An organization should be included as a component unit (CU) of only one reporting entity. Professional judgment should be used to determine the most appropriate reporting entity. A primary government that appoints a voting majority of the governing board of a component unit of another government should make the disclosures required for related organizations.

Source: GASB, *Codification,* Sec. 2100.901.

Blended presentation is when the component unit's financial data for its funds and activities are reported with the same fund types and activities of the primary government. For example, if a component unit has special revenue funds the funds should be reported in the same manner as special revenue funds for the primary government. A separate column should be used in the governmental funds financial statements if the fund is considered major; if the fund is not major it should be aggregated with other nonmajor funds. At the government-wide level the component unit special revenue fund data should be reported in the Governmental Activities column. One exception is that the General Fund data of a component unit cannot be combined with the General Fund data of the primary government. Instead, the component unit General Fund data should be reported as a special revenue fund (major or nonmajor).[6] As shown in the flowchart, blending is required when the component unit is, in substance, a part of the primary government. An example of such an occurrence is a building authority that was specifically established to finance and construct capital assets for the primary government, with the debt service for the capital assets provided by lease payments from the primary government.

Discrete presentation is when financial data of the component unit are reported in one or more columns, separate from the financial data of the primary government. An integral part of this method of presentation is that major component unit supporting information is required to be provided in the reporting entity's basic financial statements by *(a)* presenting each major component unit in a separate column in the reporting entity's statements of net assets and activities, *(b)* including combining statements of major component units in the reporting entity's basic statements after the fund financial statements, or *(c)* presenting condensed financial statements in the notes to the reporting entity's basic financial statements.

Reporting by Other Government Organizations

The financial reporting information in the remainder of the chapter is provided from the perspective that the financial reporting entity is composed of a primary government and its component units. However, the information would also apply to other government organizations that issue separate financial reports. Examples of such organizations would include governmental joint ventures, jointly governed organizations, and other stand-alone governments. Additionally, if a component unit chooses to provide financial statements separately from the financial reporting entity of which it is a part, it would also rely on the information provided in this chapter.

A **joint venture** is a legal entity or other organization that results from a contractual arrangement and that is owned, operated, or governed by two or more participants as a separate and specific activity subject to joint control, in which the participants retain *(a)* an ongoing financial interest or *(b)* an ongoing financial responsibility.

A **jointly governed organization** is a regional government or other multigovernmental arrangement that is governed by representatives from each of the governments that create the organization, but that is not a joint venture because the participants do not retain an ongoing financial interest or responsibility.

An **other stand-alone government** is a legally separate governmental organization that *(a)* does not have a separately elected governing body and *(b)* does not meet the definition of a component unit. Other stand-alone governments include some special purpose governments, joint ventures, jointly governed organizations, and pools.

[6] GASB, *Codification,* Sec. 2600.114.

GOVERNMENTAL FINANCIAL REPORTS

Once the reporting entity has been determined in accordance with the criteria discussed in the preceding section, persons responsible for preparing financial reports for the reporting entity should follow the guidance given in currently effective authoritative literature to determine the content of financial reports to be issued for external users. Chapter 2 contains a summary of the standards set forth for the content of the comprehensive annual financial report (CAFR) of a state or local governmental reporting entity. Chapters 3 through 8 elaborate on the application of those standards to accounting and financial reporting for each of the funds and government-wide activities. Although much of the discussion in preceding chapters concerns general purpose external financial reporting, the needs of administrators, legislators, and other users not properly classifiable as "external" have been given some attention. In the following paragraphs, the discussion in preceding chapters is briefly summarized and placed in perspective.

Need for Periodic Reports

Individuals concerned with the day-to-day operations and activities of governmental funds should be familiar with much of the data processed by the accounting information system because it results from the events and transactions with which they are involved. However, it is easy for these individuals to become overconfident of their understanding of the data with which they are daily involved. Past events are not always as remembered, and the relative significance of events changes over time. Similarly, administrators at succeedingly higher levels in the organization may feel that participation in decision making and observation of the apparent results of past decisions obviate the necessity for periodic analysis of accounting and statistical reports prepared objectively and with neutrality. The memory and perceptions of administrators at higher levels are also subject to failure. Therefore, it is generally agreed that it is useful for financial reports to be prepared and distributed at intervals throughout a fiscal period as well as at period-end.

Interim Financial Reports

Government administrators have the greatest need for interim financial reports, although members of the legislative branch of the government (particularly those on its finance committee) may also find interim reports useful. Although the particular statements and schedules that should be prepared on an interim basis are a matter of local management preference, the authors believe the following interim schedules provide the minimum useful information for budgetary and cash management purposes.

1. Schedule of actual and budgeted revenue (for the General Fund and special revenue funds and other funds for which budgets have been legally adopted).
2. Schedule of actual and budgeted expenditures (for the General Fund and special revenue funds and other funds for which budgets have been legally adopted).
3. Comparative schedule of revenue and expense (for each enterprise and internal service fund).
4. Combined schedule of cash receipts, disbursements, and balances—all funds.
5. Forecast of cash positions—all funds.

Other statements and schedules, in addition to those just listed, may be needed, depending on the complexity and scope of a government's activities. A statement of investments held and their cost and fair values is an example of an additional statement that may be useful. Schedules of past-due receivables from taxes, special assessments, and utility customers may also be needed at intervals. Interim reports of government-wide activities can be done only if the information system can capture the information.

Complete interim reports should be prepared and distributed at regular intervals throughout a fiscal period, generally monthly, although small governments that have little financial activity may find a bimonthly or quarterly period satisfactory. Partial interim reports dealing with those items of considerable current importance should be prepared and distributed as frequently as their information would be of value. For example, reports of the fair values of investments and of purchases and sales may be needed by a relatively small number of users on a daily basis during certain critical periods.

Annual Financial Reports

Governmental annual financial reports are needed by the same individuals and groups receiving interim reports. They are also often required to be distributed to agencies of higher governmental jurisdictions and to major creditors. Other users include citizens and citizen groups; news media; financial underwriters; debt insurers; debt rating agencies; debt analysts; libraries; other governments; associations of governmental administrators, accountants, and finance officers; and college professors and students.

Most larger governments prepare a comprehensive annual financial report (CAFR). The CAFR is the government's official annual report prepared and published as a matter of public record. A CAFR provides information beyond the minimum requirements of general purpose external financial reporting, which includes management's discussion and analysis (MD&A), basic financial statements and related notes (government-wide and fund), and required supplementary information (RSI). In addition, it includes individual fund and combining financial statements, schedules, narrative explanations, a statistical section, and other material management deems relevant. For CAFRs containing audited financial statements, the auditor's report should also be included.

Introductory Section

As discussed in Chapter 1, the introductory section of a CAFR generally includes the table of contents, a letter of transmittal, and other material deemed appropriate by management.

The letter of transmittal should cite legal and policy requirements for the report. The introductory section may also include a summary discussion of factors relating to the government's service programs and financial matters. Matters discussed in the introductory section should not duplicate those discussed in the MD&A. Because the MD&A is part of the information reviewed (but not audited) by the auditor, it presents information based only on facts known to exist as of the reporting date. Since the introductory section is generally not covered by the auditor's report, it may present information of a more subjective nature, including prospective information such as forecasts or expectations.

Financial Section

The financial section should contain sufficient information to disclose fully and present fairly the financial position and results of financial operations during the fiscal year. GASB *Codification,* Section 2200 identifies the minimum content for the financial section of a CAFR as consisting of the:

1. Auditor's report (discussed in Chapter 12)
2. MD&A
3. Basic financial statements
   a. Government-wide financial statements
      (1) Statement of net assets (see Illustration A1–1)
      (2) Statement of activities (see Illustration A1–2)
   b. Fund financial statements
      (1) Governmental funds
         (a) Balance sheet (see Illustration A1–3)
         (b) Statement of revenues, expenditures, and changes in fund balances (see Illustration A1–5)
      (2) Proprietary funds
         (a) Statement of net assets (see Illustration A1–7)
         (b) Statement of revenues, expenses, and changes in fund net assets (see Illustration A1–8)
         (c) Statement of cash flows (see Illustration A1–9)
      (3) Fiduciary funds (including component units that are fiduciary in nature)
         (a) Statement of fiduciary net assets (see Illustration A1–10)
         (b) Statement of changes in fiduciary net assets (see Illustration A1–11)
   c. Notes to the financial statements
4. Required supplementary information other than MD&A, including, but not limited to, the budgetary comparison schedule (see Illustration 3–5)
5. Combining statements and individual fund statements and schedules

State and local governments may provide in the financial section of the CAFR combining financial statements for nonmajor funds of each fund type and individual fund statements for the General Fund or for a nonmajor fund that is the only fund of a given type (for example, a debt service fund that is the only fund of that type). The GASB requires that all "lower" level statements, such as combining statements, be prepared and displayed in the same manner as "higher" level statements, such as the governmental funds financial statements.

Examples of all required basic financial statements were provided in Chapter 1; however, no example is provided in Chapter 1 for an MD&A. An example of an MD&A from the City and County of Denver is presented as Appendix B of this chapter. As shown in Appendix B, the MD&A should provide an overview of the government's financial activities and financial highlights for the year. The MD&A should provide a narrative explanation of the contents of the CAFR, including the nature of the government-wide and fund financial statements, and the distinctions between those statements. The remainder of the MD&A should describe the government's financial condition, financial trends of the government as a whole and of its major funds, budgetary highlights, and activities affecting capital assets and related debt. Finally, the MD&A should discuss economic factors, budget, and tax rates for the next year.

Statistical Section

In addition to the output of the accounting information system presented in the financial section of the governmental annual report, statistical information reflecting social and economic data, financial trends, and the fiscal capacity of the government are needed by users interested in better understanding the activity and condition of the government. GASB indicates that generally the statistical section should present information in five categories to assist the user in understanding and assessing a government's economic condition.[7] To be most useful, the 10 most recent years of data should generally be included (unless otherwise indicated) in the schedules used to meet the requirements of the five categories defined by the GASB. Following are descriptions of the five categories.

1. **Financial trends information** provides the user with information that is helpful in understanding and assessing how a government's financial position has changed over time. Schedules in this category are prepared at both the fund level and government-wide level. The focus is on showing the trend in fund balances and net asset categories, including changes in net asset and fund balances.
2. **Revenue capacity information** assists the user with understanding and assessing the government's ability to generate its own revenues (own-source revenues), such as property taxes and user charges. The schedules presented should focus on the government's most significant own-source revenues. Suggested schedules provide information on the revenue base (sources of revenue), revenue rates (including overlapping tax rate information), the principal revenue payors, and property tax levy and collection information.
3. **Debt capacity information** is useful in understanding and assessing the government's existing debt burden and its ability to issue additional debt. Four types of debt schedules are recommended—ratios of outstanding debt to total personal income of residents, information about direct and overlapping debt, legal debt limitations and margins, and information about pledged revenues.
4. **Demographic and economic information** assists the user in understanding the socioeconomic environment in which the government operates and provides information that can be compared over time and across governments. Governments should present demographic and economic information that will be most relevant to users, such as information on personal income, unemployment rates, and employers.
5. **Operating information** is intended to provide a context in which the government's operations and resources can be better understood. This information is also intended to assist users of financial statements in understanding and assessing the government's financial condition. At a minimum, three schedules of operating information should be presented—number of government employees, indicators of demand or level of service (*operating indicators*), and capital asset information.

Some of the information in the statistical section has been discussed previously. For example, reporting the ratio of debt per capita, as well as the computation of legal debt limit, legal debt margin, and direct and overlapping debt and future debt service requirements, are all illustrated and discussed in Chapter 6. Other information listed by the GASB as recommended for presentation in the statistical section of the CAFR is generally self-explanatory.

[7] GASB, *Codification,* Sec. 2800.

PREPARATION OF BASIC FINANCIAL STATEMENTS

The basic financial statements that must be presented to meet minimum general purpose financial reporting requirements were described earlier in this chapter. Although examples of the basic statements of the City and County of Denver are provided in the appendix of Chapter 1, it is instructive to illustrate preparation of those statements for the Town of Brighton, the hypothetical town used for illustrative purposes in several of the preceding chapters. The prior chapters provided illustrative journal entries for fund and government-wide activities for the fiscal year ending December 31, 2011, as follows:

Chapter	Illustrative Entries for
4	General Fund/governmental activities
5	Capital projects fund/governmental activities
6	Serial bond debt service fund/governmental activities
	Term bond debt service fund/governmental activities
7	Supplies fund (an internal service fund)
	Water utility fund (an enterprise fund)

Recall from Chapter 7 that the Business-type Activities column of the government-wide statements simply reports information for the enterprise funds (internal service fund information is reported in the Governmental Activities column). Further, enterprise funds report using the same measurement focus (flow of economic resources) and basis of accounting (accrual) as the government-wide financial statements. Thus, unlike governmental activities, which use a different measurement focus and basis of accounting than governmental funds, there is no need for a separate set of accounting records to record government-wide business-type transactions. The accounting information reported in enterprise funds can easily be aggregated for reporting at the government-wide level. Since, in the case of the Town of Brighton, the water utility fund is the only enterprise fund, its financial information will simply be reported in the Business-type Activities column of the government-wide financial statements. Internal service funds also use the same measurement focus and basis of accounting as the government-wide financial statements. However, internal service funds are generally reported in the Governmental Activities column. Recall that in Chapter 7 entries were made at both the fund level and the government-wide level to simplify reporting and to avoid double counting transactions (recording in the governmental fund and internal service fund) when reporting at the government-wide level.

The Governmental Activities column of the government-wide financial statements for the Town of Brighton, presented later in this section, includes all pertinent financial information, other than budget related, arising from transactions of the General Fund, the capital projects fund, the two debt service funds, and the internal service fund. In addition, the direct expenses of the functions reported in the statement of activities include depreciation on general capital assets assigned to those functions. If general capital assets are shared by functions of government, depreciation is allocated to the functions on a rational basis, such as square footage of usage for functions that share public buildings.

All changes in government-wide net assets that occurred due to transactions during fiscal year 2011 in the General Fund, capital projects fund, serial bond debt service fund, term bond debt service fund, and internal service fund are reflected in the pre-closing general ledger trial balance for governmental activities presented in Illustration 9–2. The amounts shown for certain accounts are assumed amounts that reflect many transactions that were not illustrated in Chapter 4.

Before preparing the government-wide financial statements, an adjusting entry should be made to record fiscal year 2011 depreciation expense for the general capital assets, as well as other appropriate adjusting entries. Using assumed amounts for depreciation and assuming that depreciation is assigned to functions in the amounts shown, the journal entry to record the adjusting entry for depreciation in the governmental activities general journal is as follows:

	Debits	*Credits*
Governmental Activities:		
Expenses—General Government	114,746	
Expenses—Public Safety	229,493	
Expenses—Public Works	672,288	
Expenses—Health and Welfare	95,622	
Expenses—Parks and Recreation	133,871	
Accumulated Depreciation—Buildings		527,240
Accumulated Depreciation—Equipment		428,980
Accumulated Depreciation—Improvements Other than Buildings		289,800

The pre-closing trial balance presented in Illustration 9–2 provides all of the information needed for the Governmental Activities column of the government-wide financial statements, including the effects of the preceding adjusting entry for depreciation.

ILLUSTRATION 9–2

TOWN OF BRIGHTON
Pre-Closing Trial Balance
Governmental Activities General Ledger
December 31, 2011

	Debits	*Credits*
Cash	$ 239,363	
Taxes Receivable—Delinquent	706,413	
Estimated Uncollectible Delinquent Taxes		$ 126,513
Interest and Penalties Receivable	13,191	
Estimated Uncollectible Interest and Penalties		3,091
Inventory of Supplies	69,100	
Investments	83,316	
Land	1,239,600	
Buildings	15,545,248	
Accumulated Depreciation—Buildings		10,971,847
Equipment	6,404,477	

ILLUSTRATION 9–2 (*Continued*)

	Debits	**Credits**
Accumulated Depreciation—Equipment		4,063,944
Improvements Other than Buildings	16,693,626	
Accumulated Depreciation—Improvements Other than Buildings		5,148,162
Vouchers Payable		434,400
Accrued Interest Payable		40,500
Due to Federal Government		126,520
Due to State Government		39,740
Internal Balances		128,500
Current Portion of Long-term Debt		60,000
Bonds Payable		2,640,000
Net Assets—Invested in Capital Assets, Net of Related Debt		17,830,018
Net Assets, Restricted for Debt Service		77,884
Net Assets, Unrestricted		453,900
Program Revenues—General Government—Charges for Services		213,200
Program Revenues—Public Safety—Charges for Services		186,480
Program Revenues—Public Works—Charges for Services		124,320
Program Revenues—Parks and Recreation—Charges for Services		82,464
Program Revenues—Public Safety—Operating Grants and Contributions		100,000
Program Revenues—Health and Welfare—Operating Grants and Contributions		184,100
Program Revenues—Public Safety—Capital Grants and Contributions		300,000
General Revenues—Property Taxes		2,599,636
General Revenues—Sales Taxes		485,000
General Revenues—Interest and Penalties on Delinquent Taxes		11,400
General Revenues—Miscellaneous		28,400
General Revenues—Property Taxes—Restricted for Debt Service		117,000
General Revenues—Sales Taxes—Restricted for Debt Service		31,200
General Revenues—Investment Earnings—Restricted for Debt Service		3,145
Expenses—General Government	763,096	
Expenses—Public Safety	1,534,928	
Expenses—Public Works	1,691,188	
Expenses—Health and Welfare	945,947	
Expenses—Parks and Recreation	553,371	
Expenses—Interest on Tax Anticipation Notes	13,500	
Expenses—Interest on Notes Payable	1,000	
Expenses—Interest on Long-term Debt	114,000	
Totals	$46,611,364	$46,611,364

Illustrative closing entries for the temporary accounts of the governmental activities were deferred in earlier chapters. The complete closing entry to close all temporary accounts of the governmental activities general ledger follows the pre-closing trial balance.

The governmental activities closing entry is given as follows:

	Debits	Credits
Governmental Activities:		
Program Revenues—General Government— Charges for Services	213,200	
Program Revenues—Public Safety— Charges for Services	186,480	
Program Revenues—Public Works— Charges for Services	124,320	
Program Revenues—Parks and Recreation— Charges for Services	82,464	
Program Revenues—Public Safety—Operating Grants and Contributions	100,000	
Program Revenues—Health and Welfare—Operating Grants and Contributions	184,100	
Program Revenues—Public Safety—Capital Grants and Contributions	300,000	
General Revenues—Property Taxes	2,599,636	
General Revenues—Sales Taxes	485,000	
General Revenues—Interest and Penalties on Delinquent Taxes	11,400	
General Revenues—Miscellaneous	28,400	
General Revenues—Property Taxes— Restricted for Debt Service	117,000	
General Revenues—Sales Taxes— Restricted for Debt Service	31,200	
General Revenues—Investment Earnings— Restricted for Debt Service	3,145	
Net Assets—Unrestricted	1,150,685	
Expenses—General Government		763,096
Expenses—Public Safety		1,534,928
Expenses—Public Works		1,691,188
Expenses—Health and Welfare		945,947
Expenses—Parks and Recreation		553,371
Expenses—Interest on Tax Anticipation Notes		13,500
Expenses—Interest on Notes Payable		1,000
Expenses—Interest on Long-term Debt		114,000

In addition to the closing entry just shown, entries are required to reclassify the three net asset accounts to their correct amounts as of December 31, 2011. A comparison of the pre-closing trial balance (see Illustration 9–2) to the Governmental Activities column of the statement of net assets as of December 31, 2010 (see Illustration 4–1), shows that the balances of the two accounts Net Assets—Invested in Capital Assets, Net of Related Debt and Net Assets—Restricted for Debt Service in the pre-closing trial balance are the same as those reported at the end of the prior year. The fact that the balances are the same tells the reader that these accounts have not yet been updated to reflect changes in either general capital asset transactions and related debt or changes in net assets restricted for debt service.

From the information in the trial balance, the total amount of capital assets, net of accumulated depreciation, as of December 31, 2011, is calculated as $19,698,998. Therefore, the correct balance of Net Assets—Invested in Capital Assets, Net of Related Debt is $16,998,998 ($19,698,998, less related debt of $2,700,000), a decrease of $831,020 during the year. During the year capital debt increased by $1,200,000 (from $1,500,000 to $2,700,000) and accumulated depreciation increased $1,254,020 (including $8,000 on internal service fund depreciable assets). The increase in debt and the increase in accumulated depreciation would decrease the account Net Assets—Invested in Capital Assets, Net of Related Debt a total of $2,454,020. Yet it has already been shown that the value of the account only decreased $831,020; therefore, there must have been asset acquisitions of $1,623,000 ($2,454,020 in decreases adjusted for $1,623,000 in increases equals $831,020). The amount $1,623,000 can be verified by analyzing the transactions showing that the Town of Brighton Fire Station (see Entry 15 in Chapter 5) was completed during the year at a cost of $1,493,000, and $130,000 of capital assets were acquired by the internal service fund (see Entry 3b in Chapter 7).

Based on the assets reported in the combined debt service funds balance sheet presented in Illustration 6–7, assets reported in the governmental activities trial balance must include amounts totaling $124,229 for cash, investments, and taxes receivable that are restricted for debt service. However, accrued interest payable of $40,500 will be paid from these assets. Thus, the correct balance for Net Assets—Restricted for Debt Service as of December 31, 2011, must be $83,729 ($124,229 less $40,500), an increase of $5,845 from its current balance of $77,884.

Based on the foregoing analysis, the journal entries to reclassify the governmental activities net asset accounts to the appropriate amounts are given as:

	Debits	***Credits***
Governmental Activities:		
Net Assets—Invested in Capital Assets Net of Related Debt.	831,020	
Net Assets—Unrestricted		831,020
Net Assets—Unrestricted	5,845	
Net Assets—Restricted for Debt Service		5,845

The Town of Brighton's government-wide statement of net assets and statement of activities are presented in Illustrations 9–3 and 9–4. Compared with the trial balance shown in Illustration 9–2, it is apparent that the financial statements are highly condensed. For example, taxes receivable, interest and penalties receivable, and interest receivable are reported as a single receivables amount, net of related estimated uncollectible amounts. Detail of the receivables and uncollectibles should be disclosed in the notes to the financial statements. Similarly, because the detail of capital assets, including depreciation expense and accumulated depreciation, should be disclosed in the notes to the financial statements, it is acceptable to report the aggregate net amount for capital assets on a single line. The town has also decided to report all current liabilities, except for the current portion of long-term debt, as a single amount for vouchers payable and accrued liabilities. Such highly condensed reporting is consistent with the GASB's objective to "enhance the understandability and usefulness of the general purpose external financial reports of state and local governments" by providing an overview of the financial condition and results of

ILLUSTRATION 9–3

TOWN OF BRIGHTON
Statement of Net Assets
December 31, 2011

	Primary Government			
	Governmental Activities	**Business-type Activities**	**Total**	**Component Units (None)**
Assets				
Cash	$ 239,363	$ 13,655	$ 253,018	
Receivables (net)	590,000	77,900	667,900	
Investments	83,316	696,000	779,316	
Inventory of supplies	69,100	24,700	93,800	
Capital assets (net)	19,698,998	2,983,050	22,682,048	
Total assets	20,680,777	3,795,305	24,476,082	
Liabilities				
Vouchers payable and accrued liabilities	641,160	62,815	703,975	
Internal balances	128,500	(128,500)	–0–	
Current portion of long-term debt	60,000		60,000	
Bonds payable	2,640,000	1,745,230	4,385,230	
Total liabilities	3,469,660	1,679,545	5,149,205	
Net Assets				
Invested in capital assets, net of related debt	16,998,998	1,237,820	18,236,818	
Restricted for debt service	83,729	682,025	765,754	
Unrestricted	128,390	195,915	324,305	
Total net assets	$17,211,117	$2,115,760	$19,326,877	

activities of the government as a whole, in addition to more detailed fund financial statements and detailed disclosures in the notes to the financial statements.[8]

As shown in Illustrations 9–3 and 9–4, the two government-wide financial statements should also report amounts for discretely presented component units. Because the Town of Brighton has no component units, only primary government information is presented. To minimize line-item detail in the financial statements and thus make the financial statements easier to understand, immaterial amounts for specific items may be reported with the amounts for broadly similar items. For example, in the Town of Brighton's Statement of Activities, it would have been acceptable to report the relatively small amount of revenue from interest and penalties on delinquent taxes as part of revenues from property taxes.

Fund Financial Statements

In addition to the MD&A and government-wide financial statements, the Town of Brighton would prepare several required fund financial statements. The latter include

[8] *GASBS 34,* par. 1.

ILLUSTRATION 9–4

TOWN OF BRIGHTON
Statement of Activities
For the Year Ended December 31, 2011

		Program Revenues			Net (Expenses) Revenues and Changes in Net Assets			
					Primary Government			
Functions/Programs	**Expenses**	**Charges for Services**	**Operating Grants and Contributions**	**Capital Grants and Contributions**	**Governmental Activities**	**Business-type Activities**	**Total**	**Component Units (None)**
Primary government:								
Governmental activities:								
General government	$ 763,096	$ 213,200			$ (549,896)		$ (549,896)	
Public safety	1,534,928	186,480	$100,000	$300,000	(948,448)		(948,448)	
Public works	1,691,188	124,320			(1,566,868)		(1,566,868)	
Health and welfare	945,947		184,100		(761,847)		(761,847)	
Parks and recreation	553,371	82,464			(470,907)		(470,907)	
Interest on long-term debt	114,000				(114,000)		(114,000)	
Interest on notes	14,500				(14,500)		(14,500)	
Total governmental activities	5,617,030	606,464	284,100	300,000	(4,426,466)		(4,426,466)	
Business-type activities:								
Water	614,960	727,120		7,000		$ 119,160	119,160	
Total primary government	$6,231,990	$1,333,584	$284,100	$307,000	(4,426,466)	119,160	(4,307,306)	
General revenues:								
Taxes:								
Property taxes levied for general purposes					2,599,636		2,599,636	
Property taxes levied for debt service					117,000		117,000	
Sales taxes					485,000		485,000	
Sales taxes for debt service					31,200		31,200	
Investment earnings for debt service					3,145	44,500	47,645	
Interest and penalties on delinquent taxes					11,400		11,400	
Miscellaneous					28,400		28,400	
Total general revenues					3,275,781	44,500	3,320,281	
Increase (decrease) in unrestricted net assets					(1,150,685)	163,660	(987,025)	
Net assets, January 1, 2011					18,361,802	1,952,100	20,313,902	
Net assets, December 31, 2011					$17,211,117	$2,115,760	$19,326,877	

ILLUSTRATION 9–5

TOWN OF BRIGHTON
Balance Sheet
Governmental Funds
December 31, 2011

	General Fund	Other Governmental Funds	Total Governmental Funds
Assets			
Cash	$145,800	$ 39,313	$185,113
Receivables (net)	588,400	1,600	590,000
Investments		83,316	83,316
Total assets	734,200	124,229	858,429
Liabilities and Fund Balances			
Liabilities:			
Vouchers payable	405,800		405,800
Due to other governments	166,260		166,260
Due to other funds	5,000		5,000
Total liabilities	577,060		577,060
Fund Balances:			
Reserved for encumbrances	70,240		70,240
Unreserved reported in:			
General Fund	86,900		86,900
Debt service		124,229	124,229
Total fund balances	157,140	124,229	281,369
Total liabilities and fund balances	$734,200	$124,229	$858,429

a balance sheet—governmental funds and a statement of revenues, expenditures, and changes in fund balances—governmental funds. The town would also prepare proprietary fund financial statements for the Supply Fund and the Town of Brighton Water Utility Fund. The statement of net assets; statement of revenues, expenses, and changes in fund net assets; and statement of cash flows for the funds were provided in Chapter 7 as Illustrations 7–6, 7–7, and 7–8, and thus are not shown again in this chapter.

Illustration 9–5 presents the Balance Sheet—Governmental Funds for the Town of Brighton. The Fire Station Capital Projects Fund meets the criteria of a *major fund* (see the glossary for the definition of this term and the criteria for determining whether a fund is a major fund). Since the Fire Station Capital Projects Fund has no assets or liabilities at December 31, 2011, it does not appear in the Town of Brighton Balance Sheet—Governmental Funds shown in Illustration 9–5. Therefore, no major funds are shown on the balance sheet, other than the General Fund. The nonmajor funds are combined in a single column headed Other Governmental Funds. The Town of Brighton's Statement of Revenues, Expenditures, and Changes in Fund Balances is shown in Illustration 9–6. Because all governmental funds had activity during the year, they are all included in the operating statement. The two nonmajor funds (the Serial Bond Debt Service Fund and the Term Bond Debt Service Fund) are combined under the column headed Other Governmental Funds.

ILLUSTRATION 9–6

TOWN OF BRIGHTON
Statement of Revenues, Expenditures, and Changes in Fund Balances
Governmental Funds
For Year Ended December 31, 2011

	General Fund	Fire Station Capital Projects Fund	Other Governmental Funds	Total Governmental Funds
Revenues				
Property taxes	$2,599,636		$117,000	$2,716,636
Interest and penalties	11,400			11,400
Sales taxes	485,000		31,200	516,200
Licenses and permits	213,200			213,200
Fines and forfeits	310,800			310,800
Intergovernmental	284,100	$ 300,000		584,100
Charges for services	82,464			82,464
Investment earnings			3,145	3,145
Miscellaneous	28,400			28,400
Total revenues	4,015,000	300,000	151,345	4,466,345
Expenditures				
Current:				
General government	649,400			649,400
Public safety	1,305,435			1,305,435
Public works	1,018,900			1,018,900
Health and welfare	850,325			850,325
Parks and recreation	419,500			419,500
Miscellaneous	14,200			14,200
Debt service:				
Interest		1,000	111,000	112,000
Capital outlay		1,493,000		1,493,000
Total expenditures	4,257,760	1,494,000	111,000	5,862,760
Excess (deficiency) of revenues over expenditures	(242,760)	(1,194,000)	40,345	(1,396,415)
Other Financing Sources (Uses)				
Proceeds of long-term capital debt		1,200,000		1,200,000
Interfund transfers in (out)	(91,500)	(6,000)	6,000	(91,500)
Total other financing sources (uses)	(91,500)	1,194,000	6,000	1,108,500
Net change in fund balances	(334,260)	0	46,345	(287,915)
Fund balances, January 1, 2011	491,400	0	77,884	569,284
Fund balances, December 31, 2011	$ 157,140	$ 0	$124,229	$ 281,369

Required Reconciliations

GASB requires that the financial information reported in the governmental funds balance sheet be reconciled to that reported in the Governmental Activities column of the government-wide statement of net assets. Similarly, the information reported in the governmental funds statement of revenues, expenditures, and changes in fund balances must be reconciled to that reported as governmental activities in the government-

ILLUSTRATION 9–7

TOWN OF BRIGHTON Reconciliation of the Balance Sheet—Governmental Funds to the Statement of Net Assets December 31, 2011	
Total fund balances—governmental funds	$ 281,369
Amounts reported for governmental activities in the statement of net assets are different because:	
Capital assets used in governmental activities are not financial resources and therefore are not reported in the funds.	19,698,998
Long-term liabilities, including bonds payable, are not due and payable in the current period and therefore are not reported in the funds.	(2,700,000)
The assets and liabilities of the internal service fund are included in governmental activities in the statement of net assets.	(28,750)
Accrued interest payable is not due in the current period and therefore is not included in the funds.	(40,500)
Net assets of governmental activities	$17,211,117

wide statement of activities. The need for reconciliation arises from the use of different measurement focuses and bases of accounting, as discussed at several points in prior chapters. Because enterprise funds are reported on the accrual basis, using the economic resources measurement focus, usually there will be no need for a reconciliation between the enterprise fund financial information and that of business-type activities at the government-wide level.

Items that typically differ between governmental fund statements and governmental activities at the government-wide level, and thus should be reconciled, include:

1. Capital outlays that are reported as expenditures in governmental funds but as capital assets at the government-wide level.
2. Disposition of capital assets that are reported as an other financing sources in governmental funds but as reductions of capital assets and gains/losses at the government-wide level.
3. Depreciation on capital assets that is not reported in governmental funds but is reported as expenses and contra-assets at the government-wide level.
4. Issuance of long-term debt that is reported as other financing sources in governmental funds but as an increase in general long-term liabilities at the government-wide level.
5. Retirement of long-term debt that is reported as an expenditure in governmental funds but as a reduction of general long-term liabilities at the government-wide level.
6. Some revenues that do not provide current financial resources are not recognized in governmental funds but are recognized at the government-wide level.
7. Reporting expenses on an accrual basis at the government-wide level.
8. Interfund transfers between governmental funds, which are not reported at the government-wide level.
9. Adjusting for internal service funds' assets, liabilities, operating income (loss), and transfers.

ILLUSTRATION 9–8

TOWN OF BRIGHTON
Reconciliation of the Statement of Revenues, Expenditures, and Changes in Fund Balances—Governmental Funds to the Statement of Activities
For the Year Ended December 31, 2011

Net change in fund balances—governmental funds	$ (287,915)
Amounts reported for governmental activities in the statement of activities are different because:	
Governmental funds report capital outlays as expenditures. However, in the statement of activities, the cost of those assets is allocated over their estimated useful lives as depreciation expense. This is the amount by which capital outlays exceeded depreciation.	246,980
Bond proceeds provide current financial resources to governmental funds, but issuing debt increases long-term liabilities in the statement of net assets. This is the amount of proceeds.	(1,200,000)
Some expenses reported in the statement of activities do not require the use of current financial resources and therefore are not reported as expenditures in governmental funds.	(3,000)
Interfund transfers between the governmental funds and the internal service fund are reported in governmental funds.	91,500
Internal service funds are used by management to charge the costs of certain activities to individual funds. The net revenue of the internal service fund is reported with governmental activities.	1,750
Change in net assets of governmental activities	$(1,150,685)

Illustration A1–4 reconciles the City and County of Denver's total fund balance for governmental funds to the net assets of governmental activities, while Illustration A1–6 reconciles changes in governmental fund balances to changes in governmental activities net assets. GASB standards permit reconciliations to be provided on the face of the governmental fund basic financial statements or in accompanying schedules.

The reconciliation for the Town of Brighton's balance sheet of governmental funds (Illustration 9–5) to the statement of net assets (Illustration 9–3) is presented in Illustration 9–7. Illustration 9–8 presents the reconciliation of the statement of revenues, expenditures, and changes in fund balance for the governmental funds (Illustration 9–6) to the statement of activities (Illustration 9–4).

CURRENT FINANCIAL REPORTING TOPICS AND ISSUES

The area of government financial reporting is dynamic, with new topics and issues constantly arising. For those interested in the financial topics and issues facing state and local governments, the GASB Web site (*www.gasb.org*) provides a great deal of information, including information about ongoing projects and its due process documents. Three topics not currently addressed by the GASB, but which are of interest to government entities, are popular reporting, other comprehensive basis of accounting, and international government standards. These three topics are touched on in the remainder of the chapter.

Popular Reporting

Although the CAFR has evolved to meet the diverse information needs of financial report users (i.e., citizens, legislative and oversight bodies, and investors and creditors), it is widely recognized that most citizens are unable to read and comprehend the CAFR. To better communicate financial results to citizens, a growing number of governments prepare and distribute **popular reports** that provide highly condensed financial information, budget summaries, and narrative descriptions. They are usually short in length and employ a variety of graphical techniques to enhance understandability. Popular reports are intended to supplement the CAFR, not replace it. Since they do not present minimum data required for complete and fair presentation, popular reports are considered "summary data" and are unaudited.[9] Both the GASB and the Government Finance Officers Association (GFOA), however, recognize the value of popular reports. The GASB has published a commissioned research report on popular reporting,[10] and the GFOA has established an award program for excellence in popular reporting. The award for excellence in popular reporting focuses on report characteristics such as reader appeal, understandability, distribution, and the ability of the popular report to achieve an overall goal of usefulness and quality.

Other Comprehensive Basis of Accounting (OCBOA)

Chapters 1–9 of the textbook have focused on GAAP for state and local governments. However, a large number of state and local governments do not maintain internal accounting records on a GAAP basis and many do not report using GAAP. One individual indicates that he believes that up to 75 percent of state and local governments do not use GAAP for internal and/or external reports.[11] In place of GAAP, many of these governments use an **other comprehensive basis of accounting (OCBOA).** As defined by Statement of Auditing Standards No. 62, OCBOA includes five bases of accounting other than GAAP.[12] The OCBOA most commonly used by state and local governments are cash basis, modified cash basis, and regulatory basis of accounting.

Some of the reasons given for using OCBOA instead of GAAP include: OCBOA accounting records are easier to understand and maintain, the financial statements are easier to prepare and may be easier for users to understand, and the accounting and reporting is less costly than GAAP. However, use of OCBOA does not preclude the need to present information similar to that reported under GAAP. For example, if a government is using a cash or modified cash basis of

[9] Audit standards issued by the American Institute of Certified Public Accountants permit auditors to express their opinion that a popular report (and other forms of summary data) is fairly stated *in relation to* the basic financial statements from which it is derived. Current AICPA guidance does not permit auditors to express an opinion on whether popular reports are fairly presented in conformity with GAAP.

[10] Frances H. Carpenter and Florence C. Sharp, *Research Report,* "Popular Reporting: Local Government Financial Reports to the Citizenry" (Norwalk, CT: GASB, 1992).

[11] Michael A. Crawford, AICPA Practice Aid Series, *Applying OCBOA in State and Local Governmental Financial Statements,* edited by Leslye Givarz (New York, NY: AICPA, 2003).

[12] American Institute of Certified Public Accountants, *Professional Standards,* AU section 623 (New York: AICPA, 2008).

accounting, it is expected to comply with presentation of financial statement requirements set forth in GAAP, including presentation of government-wide and fund financial statements, notes to the financial statements, and required supplementary information, such as management's discussion and analysis.[13] Readers interested in a more comprehensive discussion of OCBOA are referred to the following resources: AICPA's *Professional Standards; Applying OCBOA in State and Local Governmental Financial Statements;* and the Auditing and Accounting Guide, *State and Local Governments.*

International Accounting Standards

As in the corporate sector, the public sector also has an international accounting standards-setting body. The International Public Sector Accounting Standards Board (IPSASB) issues International Public Sector Accounting Standards (IPSAS) that have been adopted by over 60 national governments.[14] The purpose of the IPSASB is to provide high quality public sector accounting standards that can be used by governments and other public sector organizations around the world. Similar to its counterpart, the International Accounting Standards Board (IASB), the IPSASB uses due process in the issuance of standards. Prior to being issued, the proposed standard is made available for public comment in exposure draft form. Comments are considered by the Board prior to the issuance of the final standard. The IPSASB has issued over 25 standards.[15]

The IPSASB supports efforts to achieve international convergence of all accounting standards. It is the IPSASB's belief that a uniform set of standards used globally by businesses and public sector entities will increase the quality and transparency of financial reporting.[16] However, given the differences that exist in public sector entities, it may be difficult to achieve international convergence among the public sector entities, much less between the public sector and business entities.[17] As with the IASB, IPSASB faces the problem that countries may be selectively adopting and implementing IPSASs. Not adopting standards in their entirety runs counter to the IPSASB objective of providing quality and transparent reporting.

[13] American Institute of Certified Public Accountants, Audit and Accounting Guide, *State and Local Governments* (New York: AICPA, 2008).

[14] *www.ipsasb.org.*

[15] Ibid.

[16] International Federation of Accountants, "International Public Sector Accounting Standards Board," Fact Sheet issued by IFAC. Retrieved from *www.ipsasb.org.*

[17] Alan Rob and Susan Newberry, "Globalization: Governmental Accounting and International Financial Reporting Standards," *Socio-Economic Review* 5 (2007), pp. 725–754.

Appendix A

Converting Accounting Information from the Modified Accrual to the Accrual Basis of Accounting

As mentioned in Chapter 4, there are two basic approaches to obtaining the information necessary to prepare the government-wide financial statements. The first method is the dual-track approach used in this textbook, which requires an accounting information system capable of capturing two bases of accounting, the modified accrual basis and the accrual basis. The second approach, not as conceptually desirable, is to maintain one set of records on the modified accrual basis and, at the end of the reporting period, analyze all transactions occurring over the period and prepare a worksheet that converts the modified accrual basis transactions to the full accrual basis. It is this second approach that is used by a number of governments, since most existing accounting information systems only provide for reporting governmental funds on a modified accrual basis. To familiarize readers with the worksheet process, a brief introduction is provided.

The point of the worksheet is to convert account balances derived under the modified accrual basis of accounting to account balances on an accrual basis. Converting and extending the account balances provides management with the balances needed to prepare the government-wide statement of activities and statement of net assets. The conversion is accomplished through a series of adjustments to a total governmental funds pre-closing trial balance. The types of adjustments made to the modified accrual balances are similar to the adjustments found in the reconciliation process shown in Illustrations 9–7 and 9–8. Some of the transactions requiring adjustments include:

1. Converting capital acquisitions from expenditures to capital assets.
2. Recording sales of capital assets.
3. Accounting for the depreciation of capital assets.
4. Converting issuance of debt from an operating statement account to a liability.
5. Converting payment of debt from an operating statement account to a liability adjustment.
6. Recording any accruals for expenses that are deferred under modified accrual, since the payment is not legally due (e.g., interest due on long-term debt).
7. Adjusting assets and liabilities, and including the change in net assets for internal service funds.
8. Eliminating interfund receivables and payables among governmental funds (such as a special revenue fund and the General Fund) and between governmental funds and internal service funds. Any remaining balance represents activity between the governmental funds and enterprise funds (business-type activities) and is transferred to an account titled Internal Balances. Internal Balances may have a debit or credit balance. When reported in the actual *financial statement,* Internal Balances between governmental and business-type activities are offsetting.
9. Interfund transfers in and interfund transfers out occurring among governmental funds, and between governmental funds and internal service funds, must be

eliminated. Any remaining balance represents the transfers between governmental and business-type activities. When reported in the actual *financial statement,* transfers between governmental and business-type activities are offsetting.

A worksheet conversion example, using the Town of Brighton, is presented in Illustration A9–1. Since Brighton uses the dual-track approach to record keeping, it would not need to prepare a worksheet. However, the reader's familiarity with the Town of Brighton makes it easier to see how a worksheet conversion would work for a government that does not keep records on both the modified and accrual basis of accounting. The top portion of the worksheet presents the pre-closing trial balances for all governmental funds as of December 31, 2011. At the bottom of the worksheet are those accounts that would not appear in the governmental funds using the modified accrual basis but would appear under the accrual basis used by governmental activities. Examples of such accounts include capital asset and long-term debt accounts. Under the worksheet approach, the governmental activities accounts are only adjusted once a year, at the time the annual financial statements are prepared; thus the balances in the worksheet represent the beginning balances, unadjusted for any activity during the 2011 fiscal year. For ease of explanation the following liberties have been taken with the worksheet—revenue information has been consolidated since no adjustments need to be made to revenues, and capital asset accounts have been consolidated into a single capital assets (net) account. The reader should keep in mind the following points concerning the worksheet:

1. Through the conversion process expenditures are adjusted to expenses.
2. Adding the fund balance (top portion) and the net asset balance (bottom portion) yields the total net asset balance needed for the statement of net assets.
3. The total net asset balance is separated into the three components for reporting in the statement of net assets.
4. Revenues are identified as general or program for reporting in the statement of activities.
5. No worksheet entries are made in the fund journals. However, entries should be made in the worksheet to update account balances for governmental activities.

The following key provides information concerning the figures presented in the adjustment column. An identification (ID) letter is used for tracing purposes.

a. Adjusts the capital projects expenditure into a capital asset (Chapter 5).
b. Records the annual depreciation on capital assets (Chapter 9).
c. Adjusts the Other Financing Sources—Proceeds of Bonds to a long-term liability (Chapter 5).
d. Records the accrual of interest on serial bond debt (Chapter 6).
e. Incorporates the internal service fund activity (Chapter 7, Illustrations 7–2 and 7–3).
f. Transfers net Due from Other Funds and Due to Other Funds balances to Internal Balances (Chapter 4).
g. Eliminates interfund transfers between governmental funds (Chapters 4 and 6) and between governmental funds and internal service funds (Chapters 4 and 7).
h. Reclassifies miscellaneous expenditures to interest expense on notes ($13,500) and general government expense ($700). *Note:* At the government-wide level, Expenditure—Interest represents $114,000 interest on bonded debt and $14,500 interest on notes (see Chapter 4, and Chapter 5).

ILLUSTRATION A9–1

TOWN OF BRIGHTON
Conversion Worksheet
For the Year Ended December 31, 2011

Fund Accounts	Fund Balances		Adjustments				Statement of Activities		Statement of Net Assets	
	Debit	*Credit*	*ID*	*Debit*	*ID*	*Credit*	*Debit*	*Credit*	*Debit*	*Credit*
Cash	185,113		e	54,250					239,363	
Taxes Receivable—Delinquent	706,413								706,413	
Estimated Uncollectible Delinquent Taxes		126,513								126,513
Interest and Penalties Receivable	13,191								13,191	
Estimated Uncollectible Interest and Penalties		3,091								3,091
Due from Other Funds	25,000				f	25,000				
Inventory of Supplies			e	69,100					69,100	
Investments	83,316								83,316	
Vouchers Payable		405,800			e	28,600				434,400
Due to Federal Government		126,520								126,520
Due to State Government		39,740								39,740
Due to Other Funds		30,000	f	30,000						
Fund Balance		569,284								569,284
Revenues		4,463,200						4,463,200		
Revenues—Interest		3,145						3,145		
Other Financing Sources—Bond Proceeds		1,200,000	c	1,200,000						
Other Financing Sources—Interfund Transfers In		6,000	g	97,500	e	91,500				
Expenditures—General Government	649,400		b,h	115,446	e	1,750	763,096			
Expenditures—Public Safety	1,305,435		b	229,493			1,534,928			
Expenditures—Public Works	1,018,900		b	672,288			1,691,188			
Expenditures—Health and Welfare	850,325		b	95,622			945,947			
Expenditures—Parks and Recreation	419,500		b	133,871			553,371			
Expenditures—Miscellaneous	14,200				h	14,200				
Expenditures—Construction	1,493,000				a	1,493,000				
Expenditures—Interest	112,000		d,h	16,500			128,500			
Other Financing Uses—Interfund Transfers Out	97,500				g	97,500				
Total	6,973,293	6,973,293								

ILLUSTRATION A9–1 *(Continued)*

Government-wide Accounts	Government-wide Beginning Balances									
Capital Assets (net)	19,330,018		a,b,e	368,980					19,698,998	
Accrued Interest Payable		37,500			d	3,000				40,500
Bonds Payable		1,500,000			c	1,200,000				2,700,000
Net Assets		17,792,518								17,792,518
Total	19,330,018	19,330,018								
Interfund Loan Payable					e	123,500				123,500
Internal Balances					f	5,000				5,000
Total				3,083,050		3,083,050	5,617,030	4,466,345	20,810,381	21,961,066
Change in Net Assets								1,150,685	1,150,685	
Total							5,617,030	5,617,030	21,961,066	21,961,066

presented for each category? Does the information provided in each category appear to meet the purpose of the category? Explain your response.

d. GFOA Certificate of Achievement. Does the report include a copy of a GFOA Certificate of Achievement for Excellence in Financial Reporting or refer to the fact that the government has received one? If the report has been awarded a certificate, does your review indicate it was merited? If the report has not been awarded a certificate, does your review indicate that the report should be eligible for one?

e. Service Potential of the CAFR. Specify the most important information needs that a governmental annual report should fulfill for each of the following:

1. Administrators.
2. Members of the legislative branch.
3. Interested residents.
4. Creditors or potential creditors.

In what ways does the CAFR you have analyzed meet the information needs you have specified for each of the four groups, assuming that members of each group make an effort to understand reports equivalent to the effort you have made? In what way does the report fail to meet the information needs of each of the four groups?

9–2 Multiple Choice. Choose the best answer.

1. Which of the following fund type(s) uses the accrual basis of accounting?
   a. Special revenue.
   b. Internal service.
   c. Pension trust.
   d. Both *b* and *c*.
2. Which of the following items would generally be reported as a program revenue in the Governmental Activities column of the government-wide statement of net assets?
   a. Fines and forfeits.
   b. Property taxes.
   c. Sales taxes.
   d. Interest and penalties.
3. Which of the following fund type(s) utilizes the modified accrual basis of accounting?
   a. Enterprise.
   b. Permanent.
   c. Agency.
   d. Both *b* and *c*.
4. When a general obligation bond is sold at a premium, the premium should be reported:
   a. In the Governmental Activities column of the government-wide statement of net assets.
   b. In the balance sheet for governmental funds.
   c. In the Business-type Activities column of the government-wide statement of net assets.
   d. Premium on bonds sold is not reported in the financial statements of a government.

5. A general capital asset with a book value of $1,300 was sold for $1,275. Which of the following properly reflects the reporting of the sale?
   a. The cash proceeds of the sale would be reported as an other financing source on the General Fund's statement of revenues, expenditures, and changes in fund balance.
   b. The loss on the sale would be reported in the Governmental Activities column of the government-wide statement of activities.
   c. The cash proceeds of the sale would be reported in the Business-type Activities column of the government-wide statement of activities.
   d. Both *a* and *b.*
6. The members of the Library Board of the City of Fayetteville are appointed by the City of Fayetteville City Council, which has agreed to finance any operating deficits of the library. Under these conditions:
   a. The city is a primary government.
   b. The library is a component unit.
   c. Financial information of the library should be reported as part of the reporting entity by discrete presentation.
   d. All of the above.
7. Debt service for a general obligation bond would be reported in a (an):
   a. Enterprise fund.
   b. Private-purpose trust fund.
   c. Debt service fund.
   d. Permanent fund.
8. The comprehensive annual financial report (CAFR) of a governmental reporting entity should contain a statement of revenues, expenditures, and changes in fund balances for:

	Governmental Funds	Proprietary Funds
a.	Yes	No
b.	Yes	Yes
c.	No	Yes
d.	No	No

9. The comprehensive annual financial report (CAFR) of a governmental reporting entity should contain a statement of cash flows for:

	Governmental Funds	Proprietary Funds
a.	Yes	No
b.	Yes	Yes
c.	No	Yes
d.	No	No

10. The activities of a central data processing department that charges for data processing services it provides to other departments of a certain city should be recorded in:
    a. An enterprise fund.
    b. A special revenue fund.
    c. The General Fund.
    d. An internal service fund.

9–3 Multiple Choice. Choose the best answer.

1. Some governments have begun to provide highly condensed financial information, budget summaries, and narrative descriptions, in addition to their traditional CAFR. This type of report is generally referred to as a (an):
   a. Popular report.
   b. MD&A.
   c. Operating budget.
   d. General purpose financial report.
2. The City of Gourman's employee pension fund would be included in which of the following financial statements?
   a. Government-wide statement of net assets.
   b. Statement of fiduciary net assets.
   c. Statement of cash flows.
   d. Both *a* and *b.*
3. Which of the following terms would be used when describing a primary government?
   a. Fiscally independent.
   b. Legally separate organization.
   c. Separately elected governing body.
   d. All of the above.
4. Which of the following criteria regarding the relationship between a legally separate, tax-exempt organization and a primary government would lead to the separate organization being reported as a component unit?
   a. The primary government appoints the voting majority of the separate organization's board of directors.
   b. The primary government is entitled to or has the ability to otherwise access a majority of the economic resources received or held by the separate organization.
   c. The economic resources received or held by an individual organization that the specific primary government is entitled to or has the ability to otherwise access are significant to that primary government.
   d. All of the above criteria must be met.
5. Which of the following is *not* part of the minimum requirements for general purpose external financial reporting?
   a. Combining financial statement for nonmajor funds.
   b. Basic financial statements.
   c. Management's discussion and analysis (MD&A).
   d. Required supplementary information, other than MD&A.
6. A comprehensive annual financial report (CAFR) generally would include all of the following sections except:
   a. Financial section.
   b. Audit section.
   c. Statistical section.
   d. Introductory section.
7. In a governmental funds balance sheet, prepared in conformity with GAAP, a separate column is provided for each:
   a. Fund type.
   b. Major fund.
   c. Government.
   d. Significant fund.

8. Which of the following might be included as a reconciling item in reconciling governmental fund financial statements to the government-wide financial statements?
   a. Bond issuances are reported as an other financing source in a governmental fund but as a long-term liability in the government-wide financial statements.
   b. Acquisition of capital assets is reported as an expenditure in the governmental fund financial statements but as capital assets in the government-wide financial statements.
   c. Some expenses reported in the government-wide financial statements are not reported as expenditures in the governmental fund financial statements.
   d. All of the above.
9. Which of the following is *not* one of the categories of the statistical section recommended by the GASB?
   a. Demographic and economic information.
   b. Operating information.
   c. Pro forma financial information.
   d. Debt capacity information.
10. Which of the following is generally considered an other comprehensive basis of accounting (OCBOA) acceptable for governments?
   a. Cash.
   b. Budgetary.
   c. Accrual.
   d. Reserve cash.

9–4 Comprehensive Set of Transactions. The City of Lynnwood was recently incorporated and had the following transactions for the fiscal year ended December 31, 2011.

1. The city council adopted a General Fund budget for the fiscal year. Revenues were estimated at $2,000,000 and appropriations were $1,990,000.
2. Property taxes in the amount of $1,940,000 were levied. It is estimated that $9,000 of the taxes levied will be uncollectible.
3. A General Fund transfer of $25,000 in cash and $300,000 in equipment (with accumulated depreciation of $65,000) was made to establish a central duplicating internal service fund.
4. A citizen of Lynnwood donated marketable securities with a fair value of $800,000. The donated resources are to be maintained in perpetuity with the city using the revenue generated by the donation to finance an after school program for children, which is sponsored by the parks and recreation function. Revenue earned and received as of December 31, 2011, was $40,000.
5. The city's utility fund billed the city's General Fund $125,000 for water and sewage services. As of December 31, the General Fund had paid $124,000 of the amount billed.
6. The central duplicating fund purchased $4,500 in supplies.
7. Cash collections recorded by the general government function during the year were as follows:

Property taxes	$1,925,000
Licenses and permits	35,000
User charges	28,000

8. During the year the internal service fund billed the city's general government function $15,700 for duplicating services and it billed the city's utility fund $8,100 for services.
9. The city council decided to build a city hall at an estimated cost of $5,000,000. To finance the construction, 6 percent bonds were sold at the face value of $5,000,000. A contract for $4,500,000 has been signed for the project; however no expenditures have been incurred as of December 31, 2011.
10. The general government function issued a purchase order for $32,000 for computer equipment. When the equipment was received, a voucher for $31,900 was approved for payment and payment was made.

Required

Prepare all journal entries to properly record each transaction for the fiscal year ended December 31, 2011. Use the following funds and government-wide activities, as necessary:

General Fund	GF
Capital projects fund	CPF
Internal service fund	ISF
Permanent fund	PF
After School Fund (a special revenue fund)	SRF
Enterprise fund	EF
Governmental activities	GA

Each journal entry should be numbered to correspond with each transaction. Do *not* prepare closing entries.

Your answer sheet should be organized as follows:

Transaction Number	Fund or Activity	Account Title	Amounts Debits	Amounts Credits

9–5 General Fund Adjustments. The City of Allenton has engaged you to examine its June 20, 2011, financial statements. You are the first CPA ever engaged by the city and you find that the city's accounting staff is unfamiliar with GAAP accounting and reporting requirements. Following is the pre-closing trial balance of the General Fund as of June 30, 2011.

	Debits	***Credits***
Cash	$ 460,000	
Taxes Receivable—Current	169,200	
Estimated Uncollectible Taxes—Current		$ 18,000
Taxes Receivable—Delinquent	38,000	
Estimated Uncollectible Taxes—Delinquent		30,200
Equipment	66,000	
Donated Land	120,000	
Estimated Revenues	1,320,000	
Appropriations		1,378,000
Expenditures—Principal	90,000	
Expenditures—Other	1,152,000	
Bonds Payable		200,000
Revenues		1,384,000
Accounts Payable		76,000
Budgetary Fund Balance	58,000	
Fund Balance		387,000
	$3,473,200	$3,473,200

Additional information is as follows:

1. The estimated uncollectible amount of $18,000 for current-year taxes receivable was determined to be adequate. The tax year coincides with the fiscal year.
2. The city purchased $66,000 of equipment during the year.
3. The Expenditures—Principal account reflects the annual retirement of general obligation bonds issued in 2010. Interest payments of $12,000 for this bond issue are included in the Expenditures—Other account.
4. The General Fund's outstanding purchase orders as of June 30, 2011, totaled $11,300. These purchase orders were not recorded in the books.
5. The balance in the Revenues account included a credit of $100,000 for a note issued to a bank to obtain cash in anticipation of property tax collections, and a credit of $120,000 for donated land to be used by public works. As of June 30, 2011, the note was still outstanding.

Required

The foregoing information disclosed by your examination was recorded only in the General Fund even though a debt service fund is used to account for debt, using resources provided by the General Fund. Prepare the adjusting journal entries necessary to correct the General Fund and to record information for the debt service fund, assuming the financial statements are to be prepared in conformity with GAAP.

9–6 Matching. Section A provides a list of transactions or events that occurred during the year, followed by Section B, a list of the possible effects each transaction or event has on adjusting net asset accounts at year-end, assuming that all temporary accounts have already been closed to the account Net Assets—Unrestricted.

Section A

_____1. Depreciation was recorded for the year.
_____2. A fully depreciated computer was sold for $50.
_____3. Bonds issued to construct the new library were retired.
_____4. Construction expenditures were incurred for the new fire substation.
_____5. Cash was set aside for future debt retirement.

Section B

a. Restricted Net Assets is **increased** and Unrestricted Net Assets is **decreased.**
b. Restricted Net Assets is **decreased** and Unrestricted Net Assets is **increased.**
c. Invested in Capital Assets, Net of Related Debt is **increased** and Unrestricted Net Assets is **decreased.**
d. Invested in Capital Assets, Net of Related Debt is **decreased** and Unrestricted Net Assets is **increased.**
e. None of the above.

Required

Identify how the net asset categories would need to be adjusted for each of the transactions. For the statement in Section A, select the appropriate answer from Section B.

9–7 Change in Net Assets of Governmental Activities. You have been provided with the following information concerning operating activity for Leesburg County. For the year ended June 30, 2011, the net change in total governmental fund balances was $131,700, and the change in net assets of governmental activities was $(1,934,300). During the year, Leesburg issued $3,000,000 in general obligation bonds at a premium of 101. The bonds are to be used for a construction project. The county acquired $1,250,000 in capital assets and sold capital assets with a book value of $563,000 for $550,000. At the beginning of the period accrued liabilities were $470,000 and at the end of the period they totaled $446,000. Depreciation on capital assets totaled $595,000. Revenue accrued for the period but not available for use totaled $298,000.

Required

Using the information provided, prepare a reconciliation of the change in governmental fund balance to the change in net assets of governmental activities.

9–8 Governmental Funds Statement of Revenues, Expenditures, and Changes in Fund Balance. You have recently started working as the controller for a small county. The county is preparing its financial statements for the comprehensive annual financial report and you have been given the following statement for review. You know that in addition to the General Fund the county has three other funds.

Statement of Revenues, Expenses, and Changes in Fund Balances
Governmental Funds
for the Year Ended December 31, 2011
(000s omitted)

	General Fund	Other Governmental Funds
Revenue and other financing sources:		
Taxes	$10,156	
Licenses and permits	612	
Charges for services	985	
Intergovernmental revenue	2,657	$ 1,437
Fines and forfeits	422	
Debt proceeds		5,919
Miscellaneous revenues	325	23
Total Revenues and Other Financing Sources	15,157	7,379
Expenses and other financing uses:		
General government and debt service	3,187	961
Public safety and capital outlay	6,257	689
Public works and capital outlay	3,269	2,310
Parks and recreation and capital outlay	2,088	1,748
Transfers out	604	
Total Expenses and Other Financing Uses	15,405	5,708
Net Change in Fund Balances	$(248)	$1,671

Required

After reviewing the statement, you realize it is not in the GASB format. To help your staff correct the statement, please make a list of the modifications or corrections that should be made to the statement so it can be presented in the proper format.

9–9 Government-wide Financial Statements. Following is the governmental activities pre-closing trial balance for the Town of Freaz. Freaz is a relatively small town and, as a result, it has only governmental funds (i. e., it uses no proprietary funds). There are no component units. To complete the financial statements for its annual report, the town must prepare a government-wide statement of net assets and a statement of activities.

TOWN OF FREAZ
Pre-Closing Trial Balance
As of June 30, 2011
(000s omitted)

	Debits	*Credits*
Cash	$ 3,639	
Investments	7,299	
Taxes Receivable—Delinquent	5,788	
Estimated Uncollectible Delinquent Taxes		$ 49
Due from Other Funds	645	
Due from Other Governments	6,343	
Land	8,720	
Buildings	25,680	
Accumulated Depreciation—Buildings		8,021
Infrastructure	85,768	
Accumulated Depreciation—Infrastructure		45,603
Machinery & Equipment	28,720	
Accumulated Depreciation—Machinery & Equipment		13,785
Accounts Payable		7,764
Accrued Liabilities		4,765
Due to Other Funds		748
Current Portion of Long-term Debt		8,600
Bonds Payable		28,700
Net Assets—Invested In Capital Assets, Net of Related Debt		44,179
Net Assets—Restricted for Debt Service		2,123
Net Assets—Unrestricted		7,678
Program Revenues—General Government—Charges for Services		4,411
Program Revenues—Public Safety—Charges for Services		996
Program Revenues—Parks & Recreation—Charges for Services		359
Program Revenues—General Government—Operating Grants & Contributions		307
Program Revenues—Public Works—Capital Grants & Contributions		1,680
General Revenues—Property Taxes		13,665
General Revenues—Interest & Penalties		746
General Revenues—Interest Income		345
Expenses—General Government	2,468	
Expenses—Public Safety	11,577	
Expenses—Public Works	5,311	
Expenses—Parks & Recreation	1,817	
Expenses—Interest on Long-term Debt	749	
	$ 194,524	$ 194,524

Required

Using the trial balance provided by the town, prepare a government-wide statement of activities and a statement of net assets. Restricted net assets for debt service increased $87 (000s omitted) for the period.

9–10 Converting from Modified Accrual to Accrual Accounting. The Village of Rodale keeps its governmental fund accounting records on a modified accrual basis. At the end of the fiscal year, the village accountant must convert the modified accrual information to accrual information to allow for preparation of the government-wide financial statements. Following are several transactions identified by the accountant that will require conversion.

1. At the end of the year, depreciation expense of $674,300 was recorded on buildings and equipment.
2. Year-end salaries amounting to $39,123 were accrued.
3. During the year the village acquired a vehicle at a cost of $21,369 and depreciable office equipment at a cost of $7,680. (*Note:* the village uses a Buildings and Equipment account.)
4. The village made the final $50,000 payment on a long-term loan. Interest related to the loan was $2,250, half of which had been accrued at the end of the prior fiscal year.
5. The records indicate that the Due from Other Funds balance is $720. Of this amount, $480 is due from the Water Utility Fund for service provided by the general government; the remainder is due from a special revenue fund for services provided by the Police Department. The amount Due to Other Funds balance is $950, which the General Fund owes to the Water Utility Fund for water received.

Required

Prepare modified accrual to accrual adjustments for all of the transactions identified in Items 1–5. Your answer sheet should be organized as follows. In the first column, identify the account titles that will be affected by the adjustment. Use the second column to identify whether the account title provided is a modified accrual account or an accrual account. The adjustment columns should record the amount of the debit or credit that would need to be made to adjust information from modified accrual to accrual. Keep in mind that some transactions may not be recorded under modified accrual; in such cases, the debit and credit adjustments affect only accrual accounts since the adjustments are reflected at the government-wide level only.

Account Affected	Modified Accrual/ Accrual Account	Adjustment Debit	Adjustment Credit

Chapter **Ten**

Analysis of Governmental Financial Performance

Learning Objectives

After studying this chapter, you should be able to:

1. Explain the importance of evaluating governmental financial performance.
2. Distinguish among and describe key financial performance concepts, such as: financial position, financial condition, and economic condition.
3. Explain the relationships among environmental factors, organizational factors, and financial factors in determining governmental financial condition.
4. Identify, calculate, and interpret key ratios that measure financial performance.
5. Analyze financial performance using government-wide statements.
6. Describe how benchmarks can aid financial analysis.

Many of the municipal financial crises in the 20th century were caused by fiscal mismanagement, deficient financial reporting, and a lack of transparency in how governmental financial decisions were made. New York City; Cleveland, Ohio; Orange County, California; Miami, Florida; and Washington, D.C., at one time were textbook cases for what not to do. However, government managers took action and strengthened internal controls to emerge from near bankruptcies, bond defaults, or receiverships by public boards. Combined efforts on the part of users, preparers, attestors, and bond raters have led to higher quality governmental accounting principles, government auditing standards, and programs designed to recognize excellence in financial reporting and reduce the incidence of municipal financial crises.

THE NEED TO EVALUATE FINANCIAL PERFORMANCE

Despite improvements in financial accountability tools and increased public scrutiny of state and local governments, the first decade of the 21st century has brought new fiscal crises to light. Some crises continue to result from poor or criminal decisions, such as the City of San Diego's public-employee pension fund's billion-dollar deficit,[1] but other crises have resulted from natural disasters, such as Hurricane Katrina in

[1]Alan Rappeport, "SEC Settles Fraud Charges with San Diego's Auditor," *CFO.com,* Section: Today in Finance, December 11, 2007.

Another view of financial condition is provided by the International City/County

b. Determine if the ratings assigned to the City and County of Denver by the rating agencies are high, average, or low by referring to the Web sites of each of the rating agencies.

c. What information from the CAFR would the rating agencies have used in assigning a bond rating to the City and County of Denver? What other information might the rating agencies find useful?

10–3 Financial Trends. You are a new city council person for the City of Scottsdale, Arizona. You are aware that several cities have been in the news recently for financial crises for which the council or board is being held accountable. The governing bodies have been criticized for not being aware of the negative signals and trends that obviously contributed to challenging financial situations. Although you were assured at the first few council meetings that the city was overall in good financial shape, you want to be sure you "do your homework" and assess the financial condition of the city for yourself.

You know that the City of Scottsdale, Arizona, prepares a *Financial Trends* report each year based on the ICMA's Financial Trends Monitoring System and that it posts this on its Web site at *www.scottsdaleaz.gov.*

Required

a. Go to the city's Web site and view a copy of the *Financial Trends* report. (*Hint:* Look in the Finance, Demographics, Economics areas of the Web site under Budget and Finance. Examine the five-year trend information and make a list of any indicators that are negative.)

b. Prepare a list of questions for the next city council meeting. Your questions should help you focus on whether you and the other council members should be concerned about any negative trends.

10–4 Analysis of Overall Performance. The City of Edmond, Oklahoma, uses the Crawford Performeter® as a financial analysis tool and presents the results of this analysis in its Managements's Discussion and Analysis in the annual audited financial statements. For the year ended June 30, 2006, values for the following indicators were presented for the city as a whole:

	Performeter Rating Benchmark		Computation for 2006
Rating:	10	5	
Unrestricted net assets as a percentage of annual revenue	50%	30%	32%
Percentage of assets funded with outstanding debt	<10%	50%	40%
Change in net assets	10%	0%	14%
Interperiod equity—percentage of current year expenses funded by current year revenues	100%	95%	129%

Required

a. Use Illustration 10–7 in the text and assign a rating to each of the ratios provided (from 1 = lowest or worst to 10 = highest or best), calculate a score using the suggested weights provided, and compute an overall rating of the financial health and performance of this city for FY 2006.

b. Describe in your own words whether this city is in good or bad shape based on these indicators. Do the ratios point to areas to which the city should pay particular attention in the future?

c. What other information would you find useful in analyzing the financial performance of this city for this year?

Exercises and Problems

10–1 Examine the CAFR. Utilizing the CAFR obtained for Exercise 1–1 and your answers to the questions asked in Chapters 1 through 9, assess the financial condition of the government. For purposes of this project, *financial condition* is broadly defined as a city's ability to provide an adequate range of services on a continuing basis. Specifically, it refers to a city's ability to (1) maintain existing service levels, (2) withstand major economic disruptions, and (3) meet the demands of a changing society in a dynamic economy. Examine the following issues and questions.

a. Analysis of revenues and revenue sources.

(1) How stable and flexible are the city's revenue sources in the event of adverse economic conditions?

(2) Is the revenue base well diversified, or does the city rely heavily on one or two major sources?

(3) Has the city been relying on intergovernmental revenues for an excessive portion of its operating expenditures?

(4) What percentage of total expenses of governmental activities is covered by program revenues? By general revenues?

(5) Do any extraordinary or special items reported in the statement of activities deserve attention?

b. Analysis of reserves.

(1) Are the levels of financial reserves (i.e., fund balances, contingency funds, and unrestricted net assets) adequate to meet unforeseen operational requirements or catastrophic events?

(2) Is insurance protection adequate to cover losses due to lawsuits or damage to property?

(3) Is an adequate amount of cash and securities on hand, or could the city borrow quickly to cover short-term obligations?

c. Analysis of expenditures and expenses.

(1) Do any components of expenditures and, at the government-wide level, expenses exhibit sharp growth?

(2) Is adequate budgetary control being exercised over expenditures?

(3) How does the growth pattern of operating expenditures and expenses over the past 10 years compare with that of revenues?

d. Analysis of debt burden.

(1) What has been the 10-year trend in general obligation long-term debt relative to trends in population and revenue capacity?

(2) Are significant debts of other governments (e.g., a school district, a county) supported by the same taxable properties? What has been the trend for this "overlapping" debt?

(3) Are there significant levels of short-term operating debt? If so, has the amount of this debt grown over time?

(4) Are there any significant debts (e.g., lease obligations, unfunded pension liabilities, accrued employee benefits) or contingent liabilities?

(5) Are any risky investments such as derivatives disclosed in the notes to the financial statements? Are the types of investments adequately explained, and are their risks adequately disclosed?

Chapter Eleven

Accounting and Reporting for the Federal Government

Learning Objectives

After studying this chapter, you should be able to:

1. Describe the financial management structure of the federal government.
2. Describe the process for establishing generally accepted accounting principles for the federal government.
3. Explain the concepts underlying federal accounting and financial reporting.
4. Describe government-wide financial reporting for the federal government.
5. Describe federal agency performance and financial reporting requirements.
6. Contrast and compare budgetary accounting with proprietary accounting.
7. Record budgetary and proprietary journal entries and prepare financial statements for federal agencies.
8. Contrast and compare accounting for state and local governments with federal agencies.

The federal government of the United States of America is the largest reporting entity in the world and is growing. Total outlays of all federal agencies grew from $107 billion in 1962 to $2.8 trillion in 2007, and are projected to be $3.4 trillion in 2013.[1] In FY 2007 $443 billion of the federal outlays (or 16%) went to state and local governments in the form of grants.[2] Other grants are made to not-for-profit organizations to operate a wide variety of programs to meet public needs.

Federal elected officials and managers are accountable for public funds raised to meet the cost of government services today, as they have been from as far back as 1789, when a federal accounting structure was first put into place. The professional accounting consultants to the first and second Hoover Commissions generally are given credit for being among the first to provide direction to the effort to improve federal government accounting in the late 1940s to mid-1950s.

[1] A table of federal government outlays by agency for 1962–2013 (est.) is available at *www.whitehouse.gov/omb/budget/fy2009pdf/hist.pdf,* Table 4.1, p. 74.

[2] Budget of the U.S. Government, Fiscal Year 2009, State-by-State Tables, Table 8–3, Trends in Federal Grants to State and Local Governments, is available at *www.whitehouse.gov/omb/budget/fy2009/bis.html.*

Major institutional change in the last three decades is providing the impetus for even greater change in federal accounting. Among these changes are the Federal Managers Fiscal and Integrity Act (FMFIA) of 1982, the Chief Financial Officers Act (CFO) of 1990, the creation of the Federal Accounting Standards Advisory Board (FASAB) in 1990, the Government Performance and Results Act of 1993 (GPRA), the Government Management Reform Act of 1994 (GMRA), the Federal Financial Management Improvement Act of 1996, the Reports Consolidation Act of 2000, and the Accountability of Tax Dollars Act (ATDA) of 2002.

Systems put in place to demonstrate accountability for federal funds are similar to those used by state and local governments, as described in Chapters 1 through 10. Budgetary accounting is integrated with financial reporting to demonstrate compliance with annual budgets, and accrual-based entity-wide statements are also produced to give citizens information about the financial condition and sustainability of the government. In this chapter, accountability issues focusing on the federal government as a whole are discussed, followed by the unique aspects of accounting for federal agencies.

FEDERAL GOVERNMENT FINANCIAL MANAGEMENT STRUCTURE

The U.S. government is a complex set of branches, offices, and departments, as can be seen in Illustration 11–1, as well as independent establishments and government corporations, such as the U.S. Postal Service, the Securities and Exchange Commission, and the Central Intelligence Agency (not shown).[3] The United States Code (31 U.S.C. §3512) requires the head of each executive agency to establish, evaluate, and maintain adequate systems of accounting and internal control. To help ensure that federal agencies establish and maintain effective financial management systems, Congress enacted the **Federal Financial Management Improvement Act of 1996 (FFMIA).** The act states:

> To rebuild the accountability and credibility of the Federal Government, and restore public confidence in the Federal Government, agencies must incorporate accounting standards and reporting objectives established for the Federal Government into their financial management systems so that all the assets and liabilities, revenues, and expenditures or expenses, and the full costs of programs and activities of the Federal Government can be consistently and accurately recorded, monitored, and uniformly reported throughout the Federal Government.[4]

The FFMIA further requires that each agency "shall implement and maintain financial management systems that comply substantially with federal financial management systems requirements, applicable federal accounting standards, and the U.S. Government Standard General Ledger at the transaction level."[5] At the present time, 24 major agencies of the federal government must submit two reports annually to the Office of Management and Budget: (1) the audited financial statements, required by the CFO Act of 1990 (P.L. 101-576) as amended by the GMRA of 1994, and (2) performance

[3] There are also federally chartered corporations, such as the Federal Home Loan Mortgage Corporation (Freddie Mac), and the Federal National Mortgage Association (Fannie Mae), that are shareholder owned. Financial information about these entities is not included in the financial statements of the U.S. government because they do not meet the criteria for a federal entity, as described in *Statement of Federal Financial Accounting Concepts (SFFAC) No. 1,* "Entity and Display."

[4] Public Law 104-208, 104th Congress, Federal Financial Management Improvement Act of 1996, Sec. 802(a)(5).

[5] Ibid., Sec. 803(a).

ILLUSTRATION 11–1 The United States Government

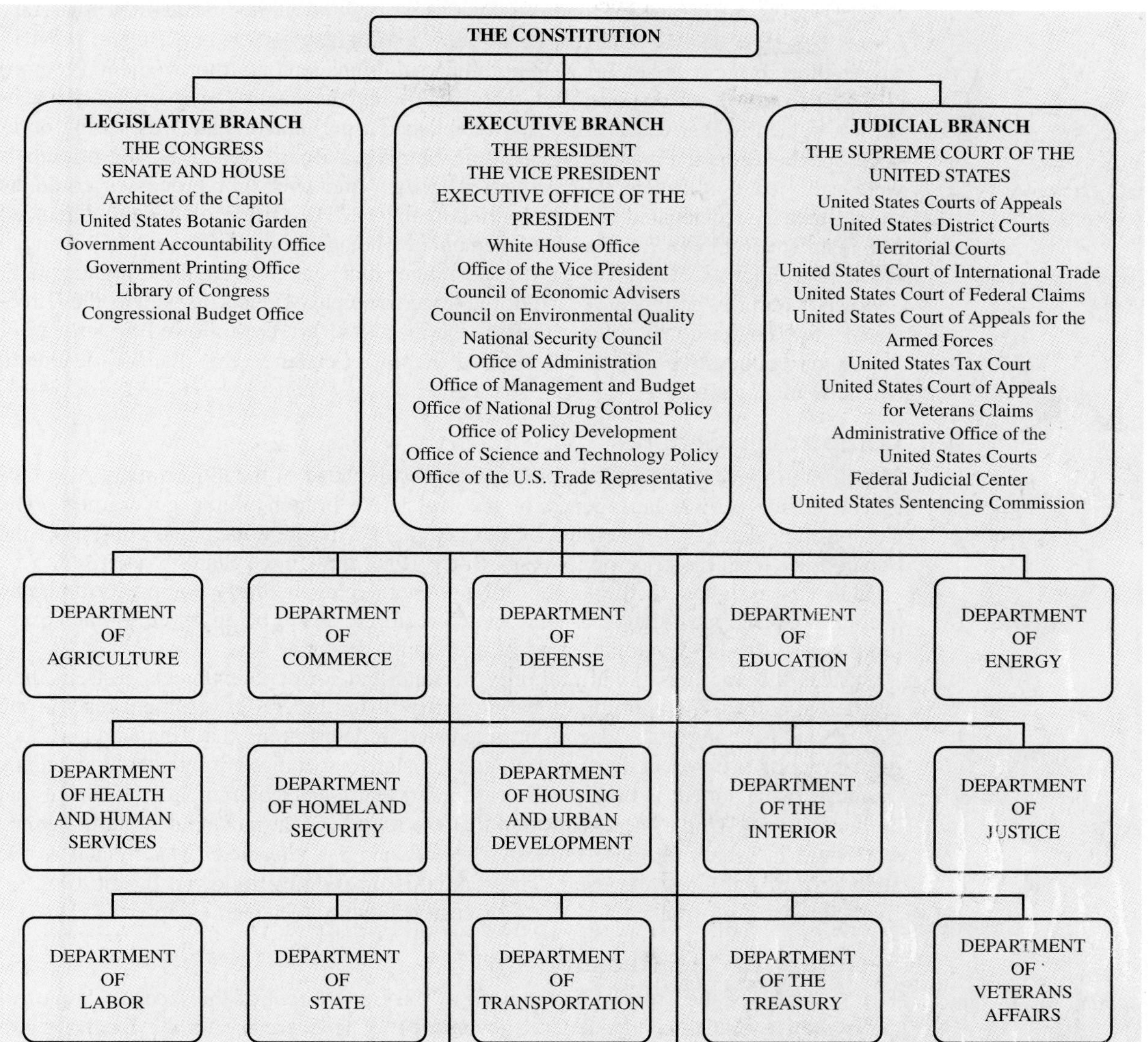

Source: 2007 *Financial Report of the United States Government,* Management's Discussion and Analysis, p. 14.

and accountability reports (PARs) that provide financial and performance information useful in assessing the agency's performance relative to its mission. For agencies not covered by the CFO Act, the Accountability of Tax Dollars Act of 2002 (P.L. 107-289), requires those entities to submit performance and accountability reports to the Office of Management and Budget (OMB). For efficiency purposes, the Reports and Consolidation Act of 2000 (P.L. 106-531) permits agencies to combine these reports.[6]

Federal statutes (Budget and Accounting Procedures Act of 1950 and the Chief Financial Officers (CFO) Act of 1990) assign responsibility for establishing and maintaining

[6] Office of Management and Budget *Circular A–136, Financial Reporting Requirements,* revised June 3, 2008.

a sound financial management structure for the federal government as a whole to three principal officials: the Comptroller General of the United States, the Secretary of the Treasury, and the Director of the Office of Management and Budget (OMB). These three principals set up a Joint Financial Management Improvement Program (JFMIP) to carry out responsibilities for improving the quality of financial management assigned to them. The principals established a permanent standards-setting organization, the Federal Financial Accounting Standards Board. By 2004, the principals were satisfied that financial management policy and oversight processes could be streamlined and delegated responsibilities to the OMB's Office of Federal Financial Management (OFFM), the Office of Personnel Management, and the Chief Financial Officers Council (CFOC). The JFMIP no longer meets as a stand-alone organization.

Responsibilities assigned to each of the three principal officials, as well as the Director of the Congressional Budget Office, are discussed briefly, followed by an examination of cooperative efforts of these officials to enhance the quality of federal financial management.

Comptroller General

The Comptroller General of the United States is the head of the Government Accountability Office (GAO), an agency of the legislative branch of the government. The Comptroller General is appointed by the President with the advice and consent of the Senate for a term of office of 15 years. Since 1950, the United States Code (31 U.S.C. §3511) has assigned to the Comptroller General responsibility for prescribing the accounting principles, standards, and related requirements to be observed by each executive agency in the development of its accounting system.

Just as the appropriational authority of state and local governments rests in their legislative bodies, the appropriational authority of the federal government rests in the Congress. The Congress is, therefore, interested in determining that financial and budgetary reports from executive, judicial, and legislative agencies are reliable; that agency financial management is timely and useful; and that legal requirements have been met by the agencies. Under the assumption that the reports of an independent audit agency would aid in satisfying these interests of the Congress, the GAO was created as the audit arm of the Congress itself. The standards of auditing followed by the GAO in financial and performance audits are discussed in some detail in Chapter 12.

Secretary of the Treasury

The Secretary of the Treasury is the head of the Department of the Treasury, a part of the executive branch of the federal government. The Secretary of the Treasury is a member of the Cabinet of the President, appointed by the President with the advice and consent of the Senate to serve an indefinite term of office. The Department of the Treasury was created in 1789 to receive, keep, and disburse monies of the United States, and to account for them. The Internal Revenue Service, Bureau of Customs, and other agencies active in the enforcement of the collections of revenues due the federal government are parts of the Department of the Treasury, as are the Bureau of the Mint, the Bureau of Engraving and Printing, the Bureau of Public Debt, the Office of Treasurer of the United States, and the Financial Management Service. The Secretary of the Treasury is responsible for the preparation of reports that will inform the President, the Congress, and the public on the financial condition and operations of the government (31 U.S.C. §3513).

An additional responsibility of the Secretary of the Treasury is the maintenance of a system of central accounts of the public debt and cash to provide a basis for consolidation of the accounts of the various executive agencies. The Department of the

Treasury's Financial Management Service (FMS) maintains the U.S. Government Standard General Ledger (USSGL) subject to the approval of the OMB. The USSGL incorporates both proprietary and budgetary accounts and is based on a standardized 4-digit coding system for assets (1000), liabilities (2000), net position (3000), budgetary (4000), revenue and other financing sources (5000), expenses (6000), and gains/losses/miscellaneous items (7000), with flexibility so that agency-specific accounts may be incorporated.[7]

Director of the Office of Management and Budget

The Director of the Office of Management and Budget is appointed by the President and is a part of the Executive Office of the President. He or she is the direct representative of the President and has the authority to control the size and nature of appropriations requested of each Congress. Congressional requirements for the budget have a number of accounting implications in addition to the explicit historical comparisons that necessitate cooperation among the OMB, the Department of the Treasury, and the GAO. Implicit in the requirements for projections of revenues and receipts is the mandate that the OMB coordinate closely with the Council of Economic Advisers in the use of macroeconomic forecasts (the study of the economic system in its aggregate). Pursuant to the Chief Financial Officers Act, an Office of Federal Financial Management was established within the OMB, headed by a controller appointed by the President. The Director of the OMB is required to prepare and update each year a five-year financial plan for the federal government. The OMB issues circulars and bulletins relating to the financial reporting and management of federal agencies.

Director of the Congressional Budget Office

The Congressional Budget and Impoundment Control Act of 1974 established House and Senate budget committees, created the Congressional Budget Office (CBO), structured the congressional budget process, and enacted a number of other provisions to improve federal fiscal procedures. The Director of the CBO is appointed to a four-year term by the Speaker of the House of Representatives and the President *pro tempore* (for the time being) of the Senate. The CBO gathers information for the House and Senate budget committees with respect to the budget (submitted by the executive branch), appropriation bills, and other bills providing budget authority or tax expenditures.[8] The CBO also provides the Congress information concerning revenues, receipts, estimated future revenues and receipts, changing revenue conditions, and any related information-gathering and analytic functions assigned to the CBO. Although not one of the three principals designated by federal statute as responsible for the quality of federal accounting and reporting, the CBO participates in and funds federal accounting standards-setting.

GENERALLY ACCEPTED ACCOUNTING PRINCIPLES FOR THE FEDERAL GOVERNMENT

Although accounting principles and standards were prescribed for many years by *Title 2* of the *General Accounting Office Policy and Procedures Manual for Guidance of Federal Agencies,* not all federal agencies complied with that guidance. To establish an

[7] Financial Management Service, *United States Government Standard General Ledger (USSGL),* August, 2008. See *www.fms.treas.gov.ussgl.*

[8] A *tax expenditure* is a revenue loss attributable to provisions of federal tax laws that allow special exclusion, exemption, or deduction from gross income, or that provide a special credit, a preferential rate of tax, or a deferral of tax liability.

improved and more generally accepted structure for setting accounting principles and standards, the three principal sponsors of the JFMIP signed a memorandum of understanding in October 1990, creating the Federal Accounting Standards Advisory Board (FASAB). The board utilizes a due process similar to that of FASB and GASB. There are four federal members and six nonfederal members on the board. Members may serve two five-year terms.

According to OMB *Circular A–134,* "Financial Accounting Principles and Standards" (par. 2):

> The role of the FASAB is to deliberate upon and make recommendations to the Principals on accounting principles and standards for the Federal Government and its agencies. The MOU [memorandum of understanding] states that if the Principals agree with the recommendations, the Comptroller General and the Director of OMB will publish the accounting principles and standards.

Since its inception, the FASAB has issued five Statements of Federal Financial Accounting Concepts (SFFAC), 32 Statements of Federal Financial Accounting Standards (SFFAS), and several reports, interpretations, technical releases, bulletins, and staff implementation guides. These statements provide general and specific accounting and financial reporting standards on a variety of topics, including assets; liabilities; inventory and related property; property, plant, and equipment; revenues and other financial sources; direct loans and loan guarantees; managerial cost accounting concepts, and supplementary stewardship reporting. This chapter provides only an overview of these standards; detailed discussion of the standards can be found at FASAB's Web site at *www.fasab.gov.* The authoritative status of SFFASs is made clear by OMB *Circular A–134* (par. 5.b):

> SFFASs shall be considered generally accepted accounting principles (GAAP) for Federal agencies. Agencies shall apply the SFFASs in preparing financial statements in accordance with the requirements of the Chief Financial Officers Act of 1990. Auditors shall consider SFFASs as authoritative references when auditing financial statements.

Hierarchy of Accounting Principles and Standards

Additional recognition of the authoritative status of FASAB standards as "federal GAAP" came in April 2000 when the American Institute of Certified Public Accountants expanded its GAAP hierarchy to include the federal government and its agencies in Rule 203 of the Code of Professional Conduct.[9] *SAS No. 91* identifies the following as federal GAAP hierarchy.

Category

a. FASAB Statements and Interpretations, plus AICPA and FASB pronouncements if made applicable to federal governmental entities by a FASAB Statement or Interpretation.

b. FASAB Technical Bulletins and the following pronouncements if specifically made applicable to federal governmental entities by the AICPA and cleared by the FASAB: AICPA Industry Audit and Accounting Guides and AICPA Statements of Position.

c. AICPA AcSEC Practice Bulletins if specifically made applicable to federal governmental entities and cleared by the FASAB and Technical Releases of the Accounting and Auditing Policy Committee of the FASAB.

[9] *Statement on Auditing Standards No. 91,* "Federal GAAP Hierarchy" (New York: American Institute of Certified Public Accountants, April 2000).

d. Implementation guides published by the FASAB staff and practices that are widely recognized and prevalent in the federal government, as well as other accounting literature.

CONCEPTUAL FRAMEWORK

Accounting standards recommended by the FASAB and issued by the Comptroller General and the OMB for federal agencies are intended to be consistent with a conceptual framework the FASAB is developing. In this respect, the FASAB is following the general pattern established by the FASB, which attempts to issue standards consistent with its several Statements of Financial Accounting Concepts, and the GASB, which looks to its concepts statements.

Concepts Statements

To date, the FASAB has issued five concepts statements: *Statement of Federal Financial Accounting Concepts (SFFAC) No. 1,* "Objectives of Federal Financial Reporting"; *SFFAC No. 2,* "Entity and Display"; *SFFAC No. 3,* "Management's Discussion and Analysis"; *SFFAC No. 4,* "Intended Target Audience and Qualitative Characteristics for the Consolidated Financial Report of the United States Government"; and *SFFAC No. 5,* "Definitions of Elements and Basic Recognition Criteria for Accrual-Basis Financial Statements."

Objectives

SFFAC No. 1 is considerably broader in scope than either the FASB's or GASB's concepts statements on objectives. The FASAB sets standards for internal management accounting and performance measurement, as well as for external financial reporting. *SFFAC No. 1* identifies four objectives of federal financial reporting: (1) budgetary integrity, (2) operating performance, (3) stewardship, and (4) adequacy of systems and controls. Budgetary integrity pertains to accountability for raising monies through taxes and other means in accordance with appropriate laws, and expenditures of these monies in accordance with budgetary authorization. Accountability for *operating performance* is accomplished by providing report users information on service efforts and accomplishments: how well resources have been managed in providing services efficiently, economically, and effectively in attaining planned goals. *Stewardship* relates to the federal government's accountability for the general welfare of the nation. To assess stewardship, report users need information about the "impact on the country of the government's operations and investments for the period and how, as a result, the government's and the nation's financial conditions have changed and may change in the future" (par. 134). Finally, financial reporting should help users assess whether financial management *systems and controls* "are adequate to ensure that (1) transactions are executed in accordance with budgetary and financial laws and other requirements, are consistent with the purposes authorized, and are recorded in accordance with federal accounting standards, (2) assets are properly safeguarded to deter fraud, waste, and abuse, and (3) performance measurement information is adequately supported" (par. 146). *SFFAC No. 1* also identifies four major groups of users of federal financial reports: citizens, Congress, executives, and program managers. Given the broad role the FASAB has been assigned, future standards recommended by the board may focus on cost accounting systems and controls, the use of financial information in service efforts and accomplishments measures, and the principles of financial accounting and reporting.

Reporting Entity

SFFAC No. 2, "Entity and Display," specifies the types of entities that should provide financial reports, establishes guidelines for defining each type of reporting entity, identifies the types of financial statements each type of reporting entity should provide, and suggests the types of information each type of statement should convey.[10]

As discussed in Chapter 9 for state and local governments, accountability reporting is facilitated by including as part of the reporting entity all separate entities for which there is financial accountability or financial interdependence. *SFFAC No. 2* discusses three perspectives from which the federal government can be viewed for accounting and reporting purposes: organizational, budget, and program. From the *organizational perspective,* the government is viewed as a collection of departments and agencies that provide governmental services. From the *budget perspective,* the government is viewed as a collection of expenditure (appropriations or funds) or receipt budget accounts. **Budget accounts** are generally quite broad in scope and are not the same as the Standard General Ledger accounts used for accounting purposes. A budget account may cover an entire organization, or a group of budget accounts may aggregate to cover an organization. From the *program perspective,* the government is viewed as an aggregation of programs (or functions) and activities.

Most programs are financed by more than one budget account, and some programs are administered by more than one organization. Similarly, some organizations administer multiple programs. Thus, in defining the reporting entity, it is necessary to consider the interacting nature of the perspectives. *SFFAC No. 2* also addresses the nature of the financial statements that should be included in the financial report of a reporting entity and the recommended format and content of the financial statements. Thus, it provides clear and strong direction to the FASAB in setting accounting and reporting standards for the federal government.

Management's Discussion and Analysis (MD&A)

SFFAC No. 3 provides guidance for the MD&A included in the Performance and Accountability Report (PAR). The MD&A is described as an "important vehicle for (1) communicating managers' insights about the reporting entity, (2) increasing the understandability and usefulness of the PAR, and (3) providing accessible information about the entity and its operations, service levels, successes, challenges, and future."[11] One difference between the FASAB's concept statement on the MD&A and the GASB's MD&A requirement is that federal agencies should address the reporting entity's performance goals and results in addition to financial activities.

Target Audience

SFFAC No. 4 expands the audiences for the consolidated financial report of the U.S. government described in *SFFAC No. 1* to include: (1) citizens, (2) citizen intermediaries, (3) Congress, (4) federal executives, and (5) program managers. The FASAB suggests the first two, citizens and their intermediaries, are the primary audiences. This statement indicates that the consolidated financial report should be "general purpose"—directed to external users and made available on a timely basis.

[10] Paraphrased from FASAB, *Report Number 1,* Reporting Relevant Financial Information, "Overview of Federal Financial Accounting Concepts and Standards" (Washington, DC: 1996), p. 11.

[11] *Statement of Federal Financial Accounting Concepts No. 3,* "Management's Discussion and Analysis," Federal Accounting Standards Advisory Board, April 1999, p. i.

Elements and Recognition Criteria

SFFAC No. 5 provides definitions of the basic elements of accrual-based financial statements—assets, liabilities, net position, revenues, and expenses. In addition, the statement establishes that for an item to be recognized on the face of a financial statement, it must meet the definition of an element and be measurable.

Funds Used in Federal Accounting

FASAB's standards do not focus on fund accounting, but Congress regularly passes laws that create, define, and modify funds for various purposes. Fund accounting is needed for federal agencies to demonstrate compliance with requirements of legislation for which federal funds have been appropriated or otherwise authorized to carry out specific activities and for financial reporting.

Two general types of funds are found in federal government accounting: (1) those used to account for resources derived from the general taxation and revenue powers of the government or from business operations of the government and (2) those used to account for resources held and managed by the government in the capacity of custodian or trustee; Six kinds of funds are specified within the two general types:

1. Funds derived from general taxing and revenue powers and from business operations:
   General Fund
   Special funds
   Revolving funds
   Management funds
2. Funds held by the government in the capacity of custodian or trustee:
   Trust funds
   Deposit funds

A brief description of each fund follows.

General Fund

The General Fund is credited with all receipts that are not dedicated by law and is charged with payments out of appropriations of "any money in the Treasury not otherwise appropriated" and out of general borrowings. Strictly speaking, there is only one General Fund in the entire federal government. The Financial Management Service of the Department of the Treasury accounts for the centralized cash balances (as it receives and disburses all public monies), the appropriations control accounts, and unappropriated balances. On the books of an agency, each appropriation is treated as a fund with its own self-balancing group of accounts; these agency "appropriation funds" are subdivisions of *the* General Fund.

Special Funds

Special funds are established to account for receipts of the government that are earmarked by law for a specific purpose but that are not generated from a cycle of operations for which there is continuing authority to reuse such receipts (as is true for revolving funds). The term and its definition are very close to that of the classification "special revenue funds" used in accounting for state and local governments.

Revolving Funds

A revolving fund is credited with collections, primarily from other agencies and accounts, that are earmarked by law to carry out a cycle of business-type operations in which the government is the owner of the activity. This type of fund is quite similar to internal service funds.

Management (Including Working) Funds

These are funds in which there are merged monies derived from two or more appropriations in order to carry out a common purpose or project but not involving a cycle of operations. Management funds include consolidated working funds that are set up to receive (and subsequently disburse) advance payments, pursuant to law, from other agencies or bureaus.

Trust Funds

Trust funds are established to account for receipts that are held in trust for use in carrying out specific purposes and programs in accordance with agreement or statute. In contrast to revolving funds and special funds, the assets of trust funds are frequently held over a period of time and may be invested in order to produce revenue. For example, the assets of the Social Security and Medicare Funds are invested in U.S. securities. The corpus of some trust funds is used in business-type operations. In such a case, the fund is called a *trust revolving fund.* Congress uses the term "trust fund" to describe some funds that in state and local governmental accounting would be called special revenue funds. An example is the Highway Trust Fund. Other federal trust funds, such as those used to account for assets that belong to Native Americans, are true trust funds.

Deposit Funds

Combined receipt and expenditure accounts established to account for receipts held in suspense temporarily and later refunded or paid to some other fund or receipts held by the government as a banker or agent for others and paid out at the discretion of the owner are classified within the federal government as deposit fund accounts. They are similar in nature to the agency funds established for state and local governments.

REQUIRED FINANCIAL REPORTING—U.S. GOVERNMENT-WIDE

In FY 1997, the Department of the Treasury began issuing an annual *Financial Report of the United States Government* that follows FASAB standards and is audited by the Government Accountability Office. Prototype "Consolidated Financial Statements" had been issued since the early 1980s; however, the Government Performance and Results Act of 1993 expanded the requirements of the Chief Financial Officers Act of 1990 and required that 24 federal agencies be audited and comprehensive government-wide financial statements be prepared within three years. The first 11 years of audits of the U.S. government's Consolidated Financial Statements resulted in a disclaimer of opinion by the Comptroller General of the United States. The most recent disclaimer (p. 32) read as follows:

> While significant progress has been made in improving financial management since the U.S. government began preparing consolidated financial statements 11 years ago, three major impediments continue to prevent us from rendering an opinion on the accrual basis consolidated financial statements: (1) serious financial management problems at the Department of Defense, (2) the federal government's inability to adequately account for and reconcile intragovernmental activity and balances between federal agencies, and (3) the federal government's ineffective process for preparing the consolidated financial statements. Until the problems outlined in our audit report are adequately addressed, they will continue to have adverse implications for the federal government and American taxpayers.[12]

[12] FY 2007 Consolidated Financial Report of the United States Government is available at *www.fms.treas.gov/fr/index.html.*

ILLUSTRATION 11–2

UNITED STATES GOVERNMENT
Balance Sheets
as of September 30, 2007, and September 30, 2006

(In billions of dollars)	2007	2006
Assets:		
Cash and other monetary assets	$ 128.0	$ 97.9
Accounts and taxes receivable, net	87.8	68.8
Loans receivable, net	231.9	220.8
Inventories and related property, net	277.1	281.3
Property, plant, and equipment, net	691.1	688.5
Securities and investments	99.8	83.8
Other assets	65.4	55.4
Total assets	1,581.1	1,496.5
Stewardship property, plant, and equipment*		
Stewardship Land* and Heritage Assets*		
Liabilities:		
Accounts payable	66.2	58.4
Federal debt securities held by the public and accrued interest	5,077.7	4,867.5
Federal employee and veteran benefits payable	4,769.1	4,679.0
Environmental and disposal liabilities	342.0	305.2
Benefits due and payable	133.7	129.3
Insurance program liabilities	70.9	72.8
Loan guarantee liabilities	69.1	66.4
Other liabilities	258.2	234.3
Total liabilities	10,786.9	10,412.9
Contingencies and Commitments*		
Net position		
Earmarked funds	614.1	419.2
Non-earmarked funds	(9,819.9)	(9,335.6)
Total net position	(9,205.8)	(8,916.4)
Total liabilities and net position	$ 1,581.1	$ 1,496.5

The notes (not shown here) are an integral part of these financial statements.
*Described in notes, no amount reported here.

Given the difficulties that agencies have experienced in complying with federal GAAP, it may be surprising that 19 of 24 agencies *did* receive unqualified opinions and all 24 CFO Act agencies reported by the 45-day financial audit deadline.

Although federal accounting has improved at a rapid rate, attributed in part to congressional mandate and the increasingly high professional skills and dedication of governmental accountants, auditors, and agency managers, serious financial management issues remain in the federal agencies, departments, and government corporations that "roll up" into the consolidated, government-wide financial statements of the U.S. government. Keeping in mind that the Comptroller General was not able to render an opinion on the federal government's consolidated financial statements, it is helpful to see the "big picture" in the government-wide statements before studying GAAP and reporting for federal agencies. The comparative balance sheets for the United States government

ILLUSTRATION 11–3

UNITED STATES GOVERNMENT
Statements of Operations and Changes in Net Position
for the Years Ended September 30, 2007, and September 30, 2006

	2007			2006		
(In billions of dollars)	Non-earmarked Funds	Earmarked Funds	Consolidated	Non-earmarked Funds	Earmarked Funds	Consolidated
Revenue:						
Individual income tax and tax withholdings	$ 1,152.6	$ 847.2	$ 1,999.8	$ 1,045.7	$ 800.4	$ 1,846.1
Corporation income taxes	367.2		367.2	350.0	—	350.0
Unemployment taxes		39.3	39.3	—	41.4	41.4
Excise taxes	15.3	52.2	67.5	24.5	49.6	74.1
Estate and gift taxes	26.0		26.0	27.4	—	27.4
Customs duties	18.2		18.2	24.7	—	24.7
Other taxes and receipts	57.9	21.7	79.6	42.8	17.2	60.0
Miscellaneous earned revenues	29.7		29.7	17.1	—	17.1
Intragovernmental interest		192.7	192.7	—	185.3	185.3
Total revenue	1,666.9	1,153.1	2,820.0	1,532.2	1,093.9	2,626.1
Eliminations			(192.7)			(185.3)
Consolidated revenue			2,627.3			2,440.8
Net cost:						
Net cost	1,622.6	1,286.9	2,909.5	1,635.6	1,265.7	2,901.3
Intragovernmental interest	192.7		192.7	185.3	—	185.3
Total net cost	1,815.3	1,286.9	3,102.2	1,820.9	1,265.7	3,086.6
Eliminations			(192.7)			(185.3)
Consolidated net cost			2,909.5			2,901.3
Intragovernmental transfers	(327.6)	327.6		(343.8)	343.8	
Other—Unmatched transactions and balances	6.7		6.7	11.0		11.0
Net operating (cost)/revenue	(469.3)	193.8	(275.5)	(621.5)	172.0	(449.5)
Net position, beginning of period	(9,335.6)	419.2	(8,916.4)	(8,714.1)	247.2	(8,466.9)
Prior period adjustments—changes in accounting principles	(15.0)	1.1	(13.9)	—	—	—
Net operating (cost)/revenue	(469.3)	193.8	(275.5)	(621.5)	172.0	(449.5)
Net position, end of period	$(9,819.9)	$ 614.1	$(9,205.8)	$(9,335.6)	$419.2	$(8,916.4)

The accompanying notes (not shown here) are an integral part of these financial statements.

for FY 2006 and FY 2007, as shown in Illustration 11–2, report a $9.2 trillion deficit in net position on September 30, 2007. The cost of government operations in FY 2007 exceeded revenues for the year by $276 billion, as seen in the Statement of Operations in Illustration 11–3, which led to the increase in the net position deficit from the prior year. Students are directed to the GAO's resource for understanding the U.S. Government's annual financial report (see references at the end of this chapter).

REQUIRED FINANCIAL REPORTING—GOVERNMENT AGENCIES

The Chief Financial Officers (CFO) Council and OMB provide guidance for federal agencies in meeting the financial and performance management requirements of various federal statutes. The form and content of these reports have changed over the years, but in a 2008 revision to OMB *Circular A–136,* "Financial Reporting Requirements," federal agencies are required to prepare a consolidated performance and accountability report (PAR) that includes the annual performance report (APR) required by the Government Performance and Results Act (GPRA) of 1994, annual financial statements, management reports on internal control and other accountability issues, and the Inspector General's assessments of management and performance challenges. Building on the experience of agencies that combined various reports (as permitted under the Reports Consolidation Act of 2000), the CFO Council and OMB felt it was most efficient to bundle required financial and performance management information in the PAR to demonstrate accountability to the President, Congress, and the public. Federal agencies prepare the PAR annually but are also required to submit unaudited interim reports to OMB on a quarterly basis within 21 days of the end of each quarter, although FY 2009 is a pilot year that substitutes business days for calendar days.

A pilot program was underway at the time of publication that allows federal agencies an alternative to the consolidated PAR. These agencies will prepare an agency financial report (AFR), an annual performance report (APR) that meets the GPRA requirements, and a citizen's report that contains key performance and financial information from the PAR presented in a concise, easy-to-understand format. All federal agencies are encouraged to prepare a citizen's report as a tool to make financial and performance information more transparent and accessible to Congress and the public.

In the sections that follow, we discuss the four sections of the PAR: (1) management's discussion & analysis, (2) performance reports, (3) financial statements, and (4) other accompanying information.

Management's Discussion and Analysis

SFFAS No. 15 (April 1999) requires that an MD&A be included in a federal agency's PAR. The conceptual basis for the role and importance of this statement was described earlier in the chapter with the discussion of the five FASAB concepts statements. This standard requires the MD&A to provide a clear description of the entity's mission and organizational structure; performance goals, objectives, and results; financial statements; and systems, controls, and legal compliance. The MD&A is considered required supplementary information and serves as a brief overview of the entire PAR.

Performance Reports

This section of the PAR contains the annual performance report (APR), which provides information on the agency's actual performance and progress in achieving the goals in its strategic plan and performance budget. There is no prescribed format for this report; however, OMB *Circular A–11,* "Preparation, Submission, and Execution of the Budget," provides guidance on what should be included in the report. The performance budget which is included in the APR is used as the basis for preparing the President's budget for the year that is then submitted to Congress for approval.

Financial Statements

OMB *Circular A–136* specifies essentially the same financial statements recommended by *SFFAC No. 2.* It also provides detailed descriptions and instructions for completing each part of each statement. These statements include the following:

1. Balance sheet
2. Statement of net cost
3. Statement of changes in net position
4. Statement of budgetary resources
5. Statement of custodial activity
6. Statement of social insurance (for specified programs)

Each of these statements is discussed briefly in the following paragraphs. The FY 2007 principal financial statements of the U.S. Department of the Interior are presented in Illustrations 11–4 through 11–9. The statements consolidate the various units of the Department of the Interior, such as the Bureau of Indian Affairs, the National Park Service, the U.S. Fish and Wildlife Service, the Bureau of Land Management, the Bureau of Land Reclamation, the U.S. Geological Survey, the Minerals Management Services, and the Office of Surface Mining. The department received an unqualified audit opinion from the public accounting firm KMPG for FY 2007.[13]

Balance Sheet

The U.S. Department of the Interior's Balance Sheet for FY 2007 is presented in Illustration 11–4. Agencies have considerable latitude regarding the level of aggregation to be used in preparing the financial statements. Agencies can use either a single-column (consolidated) format or a multicolumn format displaying financial information for component units or lines of business. If consolidated reporting is used, a separate column presenting the intraentity transactions (for example, eliminations of intercomponent unit receivables and payables) in the *consolidating* statements underlying the consolidated statements is required. As shown, when consolidated financial information is provided, comparative totals for the prior year must be presented for the balance sheet, the statement of budgetary resources, and the statement of custodial activity.

Assets A streamlined format is required in which *entity assets* are combined with *nonentity assets* but *intragovernmental assets* are reported separately from *governmental assets*. **Entity assets** are those the reporting entity has authority to use in its operations, whereas **nonentity assets** are held by the entity but are not available for the entity to spend. An example of a nonentity asset is federal income taxes collected and held by the Internal Revenue Service for the U.S. government. Nonentity assets should be disclosed in the notes. **Intragovernmental assets (liabilities)** are claims by (against) a reporting entity that arise from transactions among federal entities. **Governmental assets (liabilities)** arise from transactions of the federal government or an entity of the federal government with nonfederal entities.

SFFAS No. 1 provides specific standards relating to Cash, Fund Balance with Treasury, Accounts Receivable, Interest Receivable, and various other asset categories. In most federal agencies *Fund Balance with Treasury* is used rather than *Cash* to indicate that the agency has a claim against the U.S. Treasury on which it may draw to pay liabilities. Only a few large federal departments and agencies, such as the Department of Defense, are authorized to write and issue checks directly against their balances with the Treasury. Most departments and agencies must request that the Treasury issue checks to pay their liabilities. If a federal agency does have the right to maintain one or more bank accounts, bank balances would be reported as *Cash.*

Consistent with the manner in which business entities report inventories, *SFFAS No. 3,* "Accounting for Inventory and Related Property," distinguishes inventory from consumable supplies. Inventory is defined as "tangible personal property that is (1) held for sale, (2) in the process of production for sale, or (3) to be consumed in the production of goods for sale or in the provision of services for a fee" (p. 4). Inventory may be valued at either historical cost or latest acquisition cost. Supplies to be consumed in normal operations are reported as *operating materials and supplies.* Several SFFASs establish standards for property, plant, and equipment (PP&E). Included in this term are several items. **General PP&E** is used to provide general government goods

[13] Complete versions of these statements are available at *www.doi.gov/pfm/finstate/index.html.*

ILLUSTRATION 11–4

U.S. DEPARTMENT OF THE INTERIOR
Consolidated Balance Sheet
as of September 30, 2007 and 2006
(dollars in thousands)

	FY 2007	FY 2006
ASSETS		
Intragovernmental Assets:		
Fund Balance with Treasury	$ 34,776,671	$ 33,409,382
Investments, Net	7,322,545	8,094,833
Accounts and Interest Receivable	1,421,879	440,510
Loans and Interest Receivable, Net	2,827,301	2,631,887
Other	529	529
Total Intragovernmental Assets	46,348,925	44,577,141
Cash	756	825
Investments, Net	163,354	188,100
Accounts and Interest Receivable, Net	1,947,017	2,478,037
Loans and Interest Receivable, Net	127,285	181,137
Inventory and Related Property, Net	255,413	280,859
General Property, Plant, and Equipment, Net	17,930,798	17,491,901
Other	209,972	234,987
Total Assets	$66,983,520	$65,432,987
Stewardship Assets*		
LIABILITIES		
Intragovernmental Liabilities:		
Accounts Payable	$590,852	$44,946
Debt	858,007	1,056,572
Other		
Resources Payable to Treasury	2,030,690	2,094,244
Advances and Deferred Revenue	794,349	1,309,798
Custodial Liability	819,984	1,061,879
Other Liabilities	582,984	501,075
Total Intragovernmental Liabilities	5,676,866	6,068,514
Accounts Payable	1,076,948	1,109,655
Loan Guarantee Liability	41,434	92,380
Federal Employee and Veteran Benefits	1,363,633	1,387,423
Environmental and Disposal Liabilities	147,514	153,466
Other		
Contingent Liabilities	354,678	614,468
Advances and Deferred Revenue	741,258	747,359
Payments Due to States	639,507	812,588
Other Liabilities	937,076	952,122
Total Liabilities	10,978,914	11,937,975
Commitments and Contingencies*		
Net Position		
Unexpended Appropriations—Earmarked Funds	335,545	336,691
Unexpended Appropriations—Other Funds	3,774,190	3,890,857
Cumulative Results of Operations—Earmarked Funds	49,148,058	47,234,344
Cumulative Results of Operations—Other Funds	2,746,813	2,033,120
Total Net Position	56,004,606	53,495,012
Total Liabilities and Net Position	$66,983,520	$65,432,987

The accompanying notes (not shown here) are an integral part of these financial statements.
*Described in notes, no amounts reported here.

and services, as well as military weapon systems and space exploration equipment. **Heritage assets** are multi-use heritage assets and **stewardship land.** These include PP&E, such as the Washington Monument, that possess educational, cultural, or natural characteristics, and national parks.

Early SFFASs addressed general accounting and reporting of PP&E as well as the unique aspects of national defense PP&E, heritage assets, and stewardship land. More recent SFFASs reflect the evolution of FASAB deliberations and conclusions that information about these assets is essential to the fair presentation of the financial position of a federal agency and should be reclassified into categories that are well defined in the professional accounting literature and familiar to report users. *SFFAS No. 23,* "Eliminating the Category National Defense Property, Plant, and Equipment" (2003), does just what its title implies and reclassifies these assets as general PP&E that are capitalized and depreciated (except for land). *SFFAS No. 29,* "Heritage and Stewardship Land" (2005), requires that these assets be accounted for as basic financial information with a note on the balance sheet that discloses information about them, but without any asset dollar amount shown. The notes will disclose information such as a description of major categories of heritage, multi-use heritage, and stewardship land; physical units added and withdrawn during the year; methods of acquisition and withdrawal; and condition information.

Liabilities *SFFAS No. 1* and *SFFAS No. 2* provide specific accounting standards for Accounts Payable, Interest Payable, and Other Current Liabilities. Liabilities covered by budgetary resources (funded) and liabilities not covered by budgetary resources (unfunded) are combined on the face of the balance sheet. *Liabilities covered by budgetary resources* are those for which monies have been made available either through congressional appropriations or current earnings of the entity. *Liabilities not covered by budgetary resources* result from the receipt of goods or services in the current or prior periods but for which monies have not yet been made available through congressional appropriations or current earnings of the entity. Examples of the latter are liabilities for accrued leave, capital leases, and pensions. These should be disclosed in the notes.

SFFAS No. 5, "Accounting for Liabilities of the Federal Government," establishes standards for liabilities not covered in *SFFAS No. 1* and *No. 2.* The statement defines a *liability* as "a probable future outflow or other sacrifice of resources as a result of past transactions or events" (par. 19). *SFFAS No. 5* provides recognition criteria for liabilities arising from exchange and nonexchange transactions, government-related or acknowledged events, contingencies, capital leases, federal debt, pension and other postemployment benefits, and insurance and guarantee programs. *SFFAS No. 5* also requires disclosure in the notes to the financial statements of the condition and estimated cost to remedy deferred maintenance on PP&E. In addition, it provides standards for measurement and recognition of expenses and liabilities related to environmental cleanup and closure costs from removing general PP&E from service.

Net Position The fund balances of the entity's funds are reported in the balance sheet as **net position.** The components of net position are **unexpended appropriations,** the amount of the entity's appropriations represented by undelivered orders and unobligated balances, and **cumulative results of operations,** the net difference between expenses/losses and financing sources, including appropriations, revenues, and gains, since the inception of the activity. Cumulative results of operations would also include any other items that would affect the net position, including, for example, the fair market value of donated assets and assets (net of liabilities) transferred to or from other federal entities without reimbursement.

ILLUSTRATION 11–5

U.S. DEPARTMENT OF THE INTERIOR
Statement of Net Cost
for the years ended September 30, 2007 and 2006
(dollars in thousands)

	FY 2007	FY 2006
Resource Protection		
Costs	$ 4,459,531	$ 3,946,834
Less: Earned Revenue	793,422	1,136,759
Net Cost	3,666,109	2,810,075
Resource Use		
Costs	3,438,415	3,942,639
Less: Earned Revenue	1,294,116	1,327,167
Net Cost	2,144,299	2,615,472
Recreation		
Costs	2,593,722	1,780,694
Less: Earned Revenue	338,687	370,645
Net Cost	2,255,035	1,410,049
Serving Communities		
Costs	5,091,113	6,518,561
Less: Earned Revenue	454,591	904,395
Net Cost	4,636,522	5,614,166
Reimbursable Activity and Other		
Costs	2,626,815	3,295,714
Less: Earned Revenue	1,690,094	2,340,934
Net Cost	936,721	954,780
Total		
Costs	18,209,596	19,484,442
Less: Earned Revenue	4,570,910	6,079,900
Net Cost of Operations	$13,638,686	$13,404,542

The notes (not shown here) are an integral part of these financial statements.

Statement of Net Cost

Illustration 11–5 presents the Department of the Interior's statement of net cost. This statement shows the components of the net cost of the reporting entity's operations, both for the entity as a whole and for each of its responsibility centers or segments. Responsibility segments should align directly with the major goals and outputs described in the entity's strategic plans required by the Government Performance and Results Act. If the reporting entity has a complex organizational structure, it may need to provide supporting schedules in the notes to the financial statements to provide net cost information for its major programs and activities.

Statement of Changes in Net Position

The Department of the Interior's consolidated statement of changes in net position is shown in Illustration 11–6. The purpose of this statement is to communicate all changes in the reporting entity's net position: cumulative results of operations and unexpended appropriations. Net cost of operations is obtained from the bottom of the consolidated statement of net cost (see Illustration 11–5) and includes gross costs less any exchange (earned) revenues. Further changes in net position result from additions or deductions,

ILLUSTRATION 11–6

U.S. DEPARTMENT OF THE INTERIOR
Statement of Changes in Net Position
for the years ended September 30, 2007 and 2006
(dollars in thousands)

	Consolidated FY 2007	Consolidated FY 2006
Unexpended Appropriations		
Beginning Balance	$ 4,227,548	$ 4,179,242
Adjustments: Change in Accounting Principles	28,399	
Beginning Balance, as adjusted	4,255,947	4,179,242
Budgetary Financing Sources		
Appropriations Received, General Funds	10,315,165	10,622,534
Appropriations Transferred In/Out	3,477	115,387
Appropriations—Used	(10,443,253)	(10,531,369)
Other Adjustments	(21,601)	(158,246)
Net Change	(146,212)	48,306
Ending Balance—Unexpended Appropriations	$ 4,109,735	$ 4,227,548
Cumulative Results Of Operations		
Beginning Balance	$ 49,267,464	$ 46,274,948
Adjustments: Changes in Accounting Principles	(444,487)	
Beginning Balance, as adjusted	48,822,977	46,274,948
Budgetary Financing Sources		
Appropriations—Used	10,443,253	10,531,369
Royalties Retained	4,440,187	4,389,813
Non-Exchange Revenue	915,883	1,250,146
Transfers In/Out without Reimbursement	398,419	(194,285)
Donations and Forfeitures of Cash and Cash Equivalents	35,705	32,702
Other Budgetary Financing Sources	(14,621)	7,541
Other Adjustments	(768)	(29)
Other Financing Sources		
Donations and Forfeitures of Property	7,951	6,545
Transfers In/Out without Reimbursement	(65,622)	(99,591)
Imputed Financing from Costs Absorbed by Others	550,193	472,847
Total Financing Sources	16,710,580	16,397,058
Net Cost of Operations	(13,638,686)	(13,404,542)
Net Change	3,071,894	2,992,516
Ending Balance—Cumulative Results of Operations	51,894,871	49,267,464
Total Net Position	$ 56,004,606	$ 53,495,012

The notes (not shown here) are an integral part of these financial statements. Columns that break the consolidated totals into earmarked and all other amounts for each year are omitted for the sake of brevity.

as appropriate, of prior-period adjustments (due to material errors or accounting changes), change in cumulative results of operations, and unexpended appropriations.

Statement of Budgetary Resources

The statement of budgetary resources for the Department of the Interior (see Illustration 11–7) presents the availability of budgetary resources and the status of those resources at year-end. This statement is derived from the entity's budgetary general ledger and is designed to show consistency between budgetary information presented in the financial statement and the budget of the U.S. government. OMB *Circular A–11,*

ILLUSTRATION 11–7

U.S. DEPARTMENT OF THE INTERIOR
Combined Statement of Budgetary Resources
for the years ended September 30, 2007 and 2006
(dollars in thousands)

	Total Budgetary Accounts	
	FY 2007	**FY 2006**
Budgetary Resources:		
Unobligated Balance, Beginning of fiscal year:	$ 6,185,985	$ 5,710,929
Recoveries of Prior Year Unpaid Obligations	503,631	484,943
Budget Authority:		
Appropriation	16,405,771	16,124,453
Spending Authority from Offsetting Collections:		
Earned:		
Collected	4,804,761	5,479,124
Change in Receivables from Federal Sources	(52,531)	(2,997)
Change in Unfilled Customer Orders:		
Advance Received	(501,618)	(306,820)
Without Advance from Federal Sources	22,782	(104,540)
Total Budget Authority	20,679,165	21,189,220
Nonexpenditure Transfers, Net, Anticipated and Actual	(671,663)	438,207
Temporarily Not Available Pursuant to Public Law	—	(16,617)
Permanently Not Available	(36,895)	(186,788)
Total Budgetary Resources	$ 26,660,223	$ 27,619,894
Status of Budgetary Resources:		
Obligations Incurred:		
Direct	$ 16,457,065	$ 16,380,951
Reimbursable	4,478,735	5,052,958
Total Obligations Incurred	20,935,800	21,433,909
Unobligated Balance Available:		
Apportioned	5,499,829	5,987,182
Exempt from Apportionment	66,727	58,325
Total Unobligated Balance Available	5,566,556	6,045,507
Unobligated Balance Not Available	157,867	140,478
Total Status of Budgetary Resources	$ 26,660,223	$ 27,619,894
Obligated Balance:		
Obligated Balance, Net:		
Unpaid Obligations, Brought Forward, Beginning of Fiscal Year	$ 8,839,925	$ 8,557,216
Less: Uncollected Customer Payments from Federal Sources Brought Forward, Beginning of Fiscal Year	(1,117,227)	(1,224,762)
Total Unpaid Obligated Balances, Net, Beginning of Fiscal Year	7,722,698	7,332,454
Obligations Incurred, Net	20,935,800	21,433,909
Less: Gross Outlays	(20,178,744)	(20,666,259)
Less: Recoveries of Prior Year Unpaid Obligations, Actual	(503,631)	(484,943)
Change in Uncollected Customer Payments from Federal Sources	29,749	107,537
Total, Unpaid Obligated Balance, Net, End of Period	$ 8,005,872	$ 7,722,698

ILLUSTRATION 11–10 Summary of Key Differences between Budgetary and Proprietary Accounting in Recognition of Events That Constitute Transactions

Budgetary Accounting	Proprietary Accounting
Entries are made for commitment of funds in advance of preparing orders to procure goods and services.	Entries are not made for commitments.
Entries are made for obligation of funds at the time goods and services are ordered.	Entries are not made for obligations.
Entries are made to expend appropriations when goods and services chargeable to the appropriation are received, regardless of when they are used and regardless of when they are paid.	Goods and services that will last more than a year and otherwise meet the criteria to qualify as assets are capitalized and expensed when consumed, regardless of what appropriation funded them and when they are paid.
Entries are only made against an appropriation for transactions funded by the appropriation.	Goods and services consumed in the current period for which payment is to be made from one or more subsequent appropriations is recognized as an expense in the current period.
Entries are not made against an appropriation for transactions not funded by the appropriation.	Goods and services consumed in the current period but paid for in prior periods are expensed in the current period.

Source: U.S. General Accounting Office, *GAO Accounting Guide: Basic Topics Relating to Appropriations and Reimbursables* (Washington, DC: GAO, 1990), p. 3–2.

The accounting system of a federal agency must provide information needed for financial management as well as information needed to demonstrate that agency managers have complied with budgetary and other legal requirements. Accordingly, federal agency accounting is based on a *dual-track system,* one track being a self-balancing set of *proprietary* accounts intended to provide information for agency management and the other track being the self-balancing set of *budgetary accounts* needed (1) to ensure that available budgetary resources and authority are not overexpended or overobligated and (2) to facilitate standardized budgetary reporting requirements. Illustration 11–10 summarizes key differences between budgetary and proprietary track accounting in terms of the timing of the recognition of events and transactions. The use of the dual-track system is illustrated in the next section.

The basic budgetary authority for a federal agency can come from many different sources. Only one of those sources is illustrated here—basic operating appropriations.[14] The flow of budgetary authority generally follows a sequence of events described as follows:

1. The Congressional **appropriation** is enacted into law and provides budget authority to fund an agency's operations for the year.

[14] The illustrative journal entries shown in this section are modeled on the account titles prescribed by the U.S. Government Standard General Ledger except that we have added fiscal year designations after certain accounts for instructional purposes. The financial statements that follow are based on those specified by OMB *Circular A–136.*

ILLUSTRATION 11–11 Relationship among Budgetary Accounts

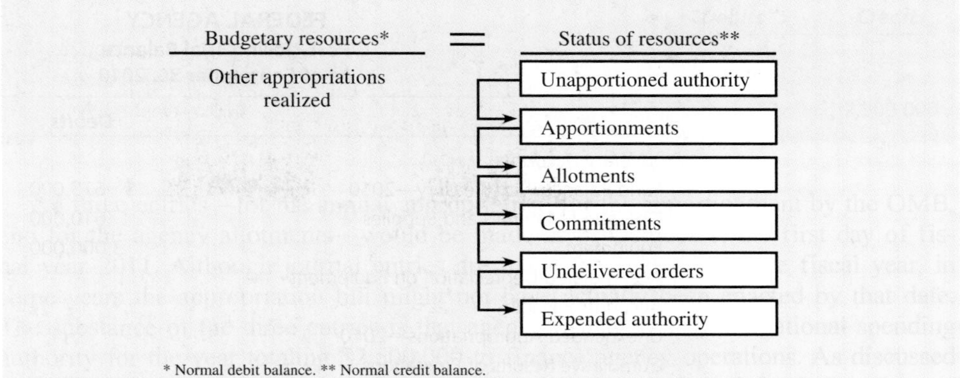

2. An **apportionment,** usually quarterly, is approved by the Office of Management and Budget and may be used by the agency to procure goods and services for the quarter.
3. The head of the agency or his or her designee authorizes an **allotment** of the apportionment for procurement of goods and services.
4. Authorized agency employees reserve allotted budget authority in the estimated amount of an order as a **commitment** prior to the actual ordering of goods and services.
5. **Obligation** of the allotment occurs when a formal order for acquisition of goods and services is placed, charging the allotment with the latest estimate of the cost of goods or services ordered.
6. An **expended appropriation** occurs when goods or services have been received.

It should be noted that the term *expended appropriation* means that the budget authority has been used and is no longer available to provide for goods and services. It does not necessarily mean that cash has been disbursed; it may be that only a liability has been incurred. A *commitment* (item 4) does not legally encumber an appropriation, but its use is recommended for effective planning and fund control. Some agencies, however, use commitments only for certain spending categories.

As shown in Illustration 11–11, the full amount of an agency's appropriation for the year is reported as a budgetary resource that, at a given point during the period, is distributed among the budgetary accounts (shown under "Status of Resources" in Illustration 11–11). As discussed earlier and in the following illustrative transactions, budgetary authority normally flows down the accounts, culminating ultimately in expended authority.

Illustrative Transactions and Entries

Consider the agency whose September 30, 2010, post-closing trial balance is shown in Illustration 11–12. If this agency receives from Congress a one-year appropriation for fiscal year 2011 (FY 2011) in the amount of $2,500,000, the Treasury's Bureau of Government Financial Operations would prepare a formal notice to the agency after the appropriation act has been signed by the President. The following entries would be made in the agency accounts:

ILLUSTRATION 11–13

FEDERAL AGENCY
Pre-closing Trial Balance
As of September 30, 2011

	Debits	Credits
Proprietary accounts:		
Fund Balance with Treasury—2011	$ 166,000	
Operating Materials and Supplies	219,000	
Equipment	3,250,000	
Accumulated Depreciation on Equipment		$ 900,000
Disbursements in Transit—2011		0
Accounts Payable		105,000
Accrued Funded Payroll and Benefits		27,000
Unexpended Appropriations—2011		34,000
Cumulative Results of Operations		3,010,000
Appropriations Used—2010		400,000
Appropriations Used—2011		2,450,000
Operating/Program Expenses	2,991,000	
Depreciation and Amortization	300,000	
	$6,926,000	$6,926,000
Budgetary accounts:		
Appropriations Realized but Withdrawn—2011	$ 16,000	
Other Appropriations Realized—2011	34,000	
Unapportioned Authority—2011		$ 0
Apportionments—2011		0
Allotments—2011		0
Commitments—2011		0
Undelivered Orders—2011		34,000
Restorations, Write-offs, and Withdrawals—2011		16,000
	$ 50,000	$ 50,000

a record of withdrawn appropriations, the second budgetary entry that follows should also be made. In addition, temporary proprietary accounts would be closed as shown in Entry 16b.

		Debits	Credits
16a.	*Budgetary:*		
	Commitments—2011	6,000	
	Allotments—2011	10,000	
	Expended Authority—2010	400,000	
	Expended Authority—2011	2,450,000	
	Other Appropriations Realized—2010		400,000
	Other Appropriations Realized—2011		2,466,000
	Appropriations Realized but Withdrawn—2011	16,000	
	Restorations, Write-offs, and Withdrawals—2011		16,000
16b.	*Proprietary:*		
	Unexpended Appropriations—2011	16,000	
	Fund Balance with Treasury—2011		16,000

Accounting procedures also exist to reverse the second entry under Entry 16a to the extent that the actual cost of goods or services received early in FY 2012 exceeds the $34,000 estimated in Undelivered Orders. Essentially, a portion of the budgetary authority that was withdrawn in Entry 16a would be *restored* in this case.

Temporary proprietary accounts should be closed to update the net position accounts so the end-of-period balance sheet can be prepared. The necessary closing entry would be:

		Debits	Credits
17.	*Proprietary:*		
	Appropriations Used	2,850,000	
	Cumulative Results of Operations	441,000	
	Operating/Program Expenses		2,991,000
	Depreciation and Amortization		300,000

The balance sheet for the example federal agency whose pre-closing trial balance is shown in Illustration 11–13 is presented in Illustration 11–14. More complex agencies usually prepare a consolidated balance sheet like the one shown in Illustration 11–4. The example federal agency is assumed to have only entity assets (those that can be used for the agency's operations) and, except for Fund Balance with Treasury, the remaining assets are governmental. All liabilities (Accounts Payable and Accrued Funded Payroll and Benefits) are assumed to be governmental. Furthermore, all liabilities are covered by budgetary resources. As discussed earlier in this chapter, the *net position* consists of only two items, Unexpended Appropriations ($34,000 reserved for goods and services on order at year-end) and Cumulative Results of Operations.

ILLUSTRATION 11–14

FEDERAL AGENCY
Balance Sheet
As of September 30, 2011

Assets	
Intragovernmental:	
Fund balance with Treasury	$ 166,000
Governmental:	
Operating materials and supplies	219,000
Equipment (net of accumulated depreciation of $900,000)	2,350,000
Total assets	$2,735,000
Liabilities	
Governmental liabilities:	
Accounts payable	$ 105,000
Accrued funded payroll and benefits	27,000
Total liabilities	132,000
Net Position	
Unexpended appropriations	34,000
Cumulative results of operations	2,569,000
Total net position	2,603,000
Total liabilities and net position	$2,735,000

ILLUSTRATION 11–15

FEDERAL AGENCY
Statement of Changes in Net Position
For the Year Ended September 30, 2011

	Cumulative Results of Operations	Unexpended Appropriations
Beginning balances	$3,010,000	$ 400,000
Prior period adjustments	0	0
Beginning balances, as adjusted	3,010,000	400,000
Budgetary financing sources:		
Appropriations received		2,484,000
Appropriations used	2,850,000	(2,850,000)
Other financing sources		
Total financing sources	5,860,000	34,000
Net cost of operations (+−) Note A	3,291,000	
Ending balances	$2,569,000	$ 34,000

Note A: These amounts are taken from the bottom line of the statement of net costs, which is not included here for sake of brevity.

A statement of net cost for the U.S. Department of the Interior was presented in Illustration 11–5. Because the federal agency used in our example is assumed to have a simple organizational structure and no earned revenues, its statement of net cost would be very simple; net cost would be the same as gross cost. Moreover, since the agency's net suborganization or program costs are reported on the first line of the statement of changes in net position presented in Illustration 11–15, a statement of net cost would

ILLUSTRATION 11–16

FEDERAL AGENCY
Statement of Budgetary Resources
For the Year Ended September 30, 2011 (Note A)

Budgetary resources:	
Budgetary authority (Note B)	$2,484,000
Status of budgetary resources:	
Obligations incurred (Note C)	$2,484,000
Total status of budgetary resources	$2,484,000
Change in obligated balance:	
Unpaid obligations, beginning of year	$ 400,000
Obligations incurred	2,484,000
Outlays (disbursements) (Note D)	(2,850,000)
Unpaid obligations, end of year	$ 34,000
(Net outlays section of statement omitted since there are no adjustments to outlays)	

Note A: Comparative totals should also be presented for the prior year. Those totals are omitted in this example.
Note B: Total available budgetary authority for the current year was the $2,500,000 appropriation less $16,000 that expired.
Note C: Obligations incurred equals the expended authority of $2,450,000 plus $34,000 obligated for undelivered orders.
Note D: Outlays for the year include all authority expended during the year, $400,000 from 2010 and $2,450,000 from 2011.

convey little additional information. Therefore, we do not include one here. While the statement of changes in net position is quite simple, it is informative nonetheless.

The final statement presented for the simple federal agency in our example is a statement of budgetary resources (see Illustration 11–16). The astute reader will note that the equation applicable to the top portion of this statement is budgetary resources = status of budgetary resources. Budgetary resources in this case are $2,884,000, consisting of current-year appropriations of $2,500,000 less expired appropriations of $16,000 plus $400,000 carried forward from prior-year appropriations to cover undelivered orders at the end of the prior year. Since there are no unobligated appropriations that can be carried forward at year-end, the *status of budgetary resources* in this case is simply the amount of budgetary resources expended ($2,450,000) plus $34,000 obligated for goods on order at the end of FY 2011 that had not yet been expended. Outlays are reported in the bottom section of the statement of budgetary resources and are the same as the total amount expended during the year, or $2,850,000 ($2,450,000 chargeable to the current-year appropriation and $400,000 chargeable to the prior-year appropriation). Subtracting the excess of outlays ($2,850,000) over obligations incurred ($2,484,000) from the beginning obligated balance of $400,000 equals the ending obligated balance of $34,000.

SUMMARY OF ACCOUNTING AND REPORTING FOR FEDERAL GOVERNMENT AGENCIES

Illustration 11–17 provides a summary comparison of budgetary and proprietary accounting procedures for state and local governments as compared with federal agencies. Although some similarities exist, there are items specific to each level of government. As shown in Illustration 11–17, state and local governments do not account for apportionments and most do not account for allotments. Federal agency accounting takes into consideration certain accruals (supplies used and depreciation) generally ignored in state and local government accounting, although as mentioned in several earlier chapters, the Governmental Accounting Standards Board (GASB) reporting model requires the use of accrual accounting by state and local governments at the government-wide level.

The head of each agency in the executive branch of the federal government has the statutory responsibility for the establishment and maintenance of systems of accounting and internal control in conformity with principles, standards, and requirements established by the Comptroller General, the Secretary of the Treasury, and the Director of the OMB. Federal agency accounting is directed at providing information for intelligent financial management of agency activities and programs to the end that they may be operated with efficiency and economy, as well as providing evidence of adherence to legal requirements. As emphasized by the headings of Illustration 11–17 and by the discussions in earlier chapters, accounting for governmental funds presently focuses on legal compliance. The focus of federal agency accounting, in contrast, is broadened to include information needed for the management of agency resources (the *proprietary* track) as well as for compliance with fund control requirements (the *budgetary* track). However, as discussed in Chapters 1–9 of this text, the authors have introduced dual-track accounting for state and local government accounting to meet the accrual accounting needs at the government-wide level while continuing to focus on legal compliance within the governmental funds. International public sector accounting standards (discussed in Chapter 9) consider funds an element of internal control and not a focal point of external reporting.

ILLUSTRATION 11–17 Comparison of Accounting for State and Local Governmental Funds and Federal Agencies (journal entries)

Item	State and Local Government Funds Compliance Track Only[1]	Federal Agency	
		Budgetary Track	Proprietary Track
1. Passage of appropriations (and for state and local governments, revenue) bills	Estimated Revenues Appropriations Budgetary Fund Balance	Other Appropriations Realized Unapportioned Authority	Fund Balance with Treasury Unexpended Appropriations
2. Revenues accrued (at expected collectible amount)	Taxes Receivable Estimated Uncollectible Taxes Revenues	No equivalent for taxes; user charges, if any, recognized as billed	Taxes Receivable Allowance for Uncollectible Taxes Earned Income from the Public
3. Apportionment by OMB	No equivalent	Unapportioned Authority Apportionments	No entry
4. Allotment by agency head	No equivalent[2]	Apportionments Allotments	No entry
5. Budget authority reserved prior to ordering goods or services	No equivalent	Allotments Commitments	No entry
6. Goods or services ordered	Encumbrances Reserve for Encumbrances	Commitments Undelivered Orders[3]	No entry
7. Goods or services received	Reserve for Encumbrances Encumbrances Expenditures Accounts Payable	Undelivered Orders Expended Authority	Expense or asset account Accounts Payable Unexpended Appropriations Appropriations Used
8. Liability paid (expenditure recorded in 7)	Accounts Payable Cash	No entry	Accounts Payable Fund Balance with Treasury[4]
9. Supplies used	No entry	No entry	Operating/Program Expenses Inventory for Agency Operations
10. Physical inventory (consumption method assumed for state and local governments)	Inventory Expenditures GF Fund Balance Reserve for Inventory	No entry	Entry for (7) assumes perpetual inventory; would need entry for (10) if physical inventory and book inventory differed
11. Depreciation computed	No entry (computation used for cost reimbursements and management information)	No entry (Not an expenditure of appropriations; will never require a check to be drawn on U.S. Treasury)	Depreciation and Amortization Accumulated Depreciation (on general property, plant, and equipment but not certain military assets and stewardship assets)
12. Closing entries	Appropriations Estimated Revenues Budgetary Fund Balance Revenues Encumbrances Expenditures Budgetary Fund Balance	Expended Authority Other Appropriations Realized; (Also must close any budgetary accounts associated with expired budget authority)	Cumulative Results of Operations Operating/Program Expenses Appropriations Used Cumulative Results of Operations

[1]Funds that use modified accrual basis of accounting.

[2]As discussed in Chapter 3, some local governments utilize allotment accounting. In such cases, the credit in Entry 1 would be to Unallotted Appropriations, and in Entry 4 it would be necessary to record the debit to that account and the credit to Allotments.

[3]As illustrated by Entry 4 earlier in this chapter, and by Entry 5, some agencies opt to use the interim account Commitments to improve planning for procurement of goods and services. If commitments are not recorded in advance of placing orders, the debit for the budgetary track would be to Allotments.

[4]As indicated in this chapter, the account credited here might be Disbursements in Transit rather than Fund Balance with Treasury.

Key Terms

Allotment, *471*
Apportionment, *471*
Appropriation, *470*
Budget accounts, *454*
Budgetary resources, *466*
Commitment, *471*
Cumulative results of operations, *462*
Entity assets, *460*
Expended appropriation (authority), *471*
Federal Financial Management Improvement Act of 1996 (FFMIA), *448*
General property, plant, and equipment, *460*
Governmental assets (liabilities), *460*
Heritage assets, *462*
Intragovernmental assets (liabilities), *460*
Net position, *462*
Nonentity assets, *460*
Obligation, *471*
Stewardship investments, *469*
Stewardship land, *462*
Unexpended appropriations, *462*

Selected References

Government Accountability Office. *Understanding the Primary Components of the Annual Financial Report of the United States Government,* GAO-05-9585P, September 2005.

Office of Management and Budget. *U.S. Government Standard General Ledger,* 2008.

———. *Circular A–136,* "Financial Reporting Requirements," 2008.

———. *Circular A–134,* "Financial Accounting Principles and Standards," 1993.

Tierney, Cornelius E., Roldan Fernandez, Edward F. Kearney, and Jeffrey W. Green. *Federal Accounting Handbook: Policies, Standards, Procedures, Practices.* New York: Wiley, 2007.

Questions

11–1. Identify the principals of the Joint Financial Management and Improvement Program (JFMIP) and identify in which branch of the federal government each operates. What role does each one play in the federal accounting standards-setting process?

11–2. Describe the institutional process for establishing generally accepted accounting principles for the federal government.

11–3. Discuss the conceptual framework of accounting for federal agencies and compare it to the conceptual framework established by the GASB for state and local governments.

11–4. Explain the differences among these accounts: (1) *Estimated Revenues* used by state and local governments, (2) *Other Appropriations Realized* used by federal agencies in their budgetary track, and (3) *Fund Balance with Treasury* used by federal agencies in their proprietary track.

11–5. "Net position for a federal agency is similar to net assets of a state or local government." Do you agree or disagree? Explain.

11–6. "The FASAB sets standards for federal agencies that relate to external financial reporting, much like the GASB sets standards for state and local governments for external financial reporting." Do you agree or disagree with this statement? Explain.

11–7. Describe financial reporting of the consolidated activities of the U.S. government. Has the federal government received an unqualified audit opinion on its consolidated financial statements? If not, provide some reasons why it has not.

11–8. Describe the dual-track system used in federal agency accounting. Compare this to the system by the same name used in the discussion of state and local government reporting under GASB standards in Chapters 1–9.

11–9. Identify the budgetary accounts used in federal agency accounting and explain the sequential flow of budgetary authority through the accounts in your own words.

11–10. Name the financial statements that should be prepared for each federal agency in conformity with OMB *Circular A–136.*

Cases

11–1 OMB Press Release. The following press release from the Office of Management and Budget was issued November 20, 2007.

FOR IMMEDIATE RELEASE
November 20, 2007
Contact: OMB Communications, 202-395-7254

Federal Agencies Continue to Improve Financial Reporting Results and Eliminate Payment Errors

Washington, DC—For the third year in row, **all** major Federal agencies successfully met the 45-day financial audit deadline as required by the rigorous reporting guidelines set by the Office of Management and Budget (OMB). Since 2001, agencies are required to complete the financial report 45 days after the end of the Fiscal Year, compared to the previous five month (150 days) window for completion. The accelerated deadline results in more immediate availability of financial information to agency decision makers and requires agencies to employ rigorous disciplines throughout the year to ensure readiness for year-end reporting.

In addition to timely reporting, the results from Fiscal Year 2007 show that the Federal government is improving the validity of its financial information.

- Of the 24 major Federal agencies, 19 received clean opinions, one more than the 18 clean opinions reported last year at this time.
- The total number of material weaknesses government-wide declined from 41 to 39. This is the fourth year in a row that material weaknesses have declined, with a more than 35% decrease in weaknesses since 2001.
- Five additional agencies received a clean opinion with no material weaknesses, including the Departments of Justice, the Interior, Energy, the Small Business Administration, and the U.S. Agency for International Development. This brings the total number of agencies realizing this important accomplishment to 13, up from just seven in 2001.

The decrease in weaknesses this year is more notable in light of recent changes to government audit guidelines that lower materiality thresholds and have the effect of characterizing more audit findings as "material weaknesses." In other words, while auditing standards are getting tougher, Federal agencies are more than keeping pace by continuing to decrease the number of material findings.

• • •

Source: *www.whitehouse.gov/omb/pubpress/index2007.html.*

Required

Choose a federal agency of the U.S. government and locate its annual financial report for the most recent fiscal year from its agency Web site or a government site such as *www.fedworld.gov* or *www.firstgov.gov.* Answer the following questions.

a. Did this agency receive an unqualified opinion for the most recent fiscal year? If not, can you determine why?

b. Examine the statements of net cost and changes in net position and determine the amount of operations that was funded by appropriations for this fiscal year. Did the agency report a positive or negative change in net position? Which elements of this financial statement were significantly different from those of the prior year and might have contributed most to the change in net position?

c. Does the agency integrate accountability reports with performance reports produced under the Government Performance and Results Act?

11–2 Internet Case—FASAB. At the cutoff date for publication of this edition of the text, 32 Statements of Federal Financial Accounting Standards (SFFASs) have been issued. In addition, OMB *Circular A–136* provides authoritative guidance for the form and content of federal agency financial statements.

Required

Using the Internet, explore the FASAB (*www.fasab.gov*) and OMB (*www.omb.gov*) Web sites and determine whether:

a. Any additional SFFASs have been issued. If so, list them by name and provide a short synopsis along with their effective dates.

b. Has the OMB updated *Circular A–136*? If so, how do the financial statements required by the later circular compare to those required by *Circular A–136,* as described and illustrated in this chapter? (*Note:* Previously issued OMB bulletins on form and content of agency financial statements were *Bulletins Nos. 01-09, 97-01,* and *94-01*. Thus, the OMB may not intend to make frequent changes in its reporting guidance.)

11–3 U.S. Government-wide Annual Report. Obtain the most recent audited annual financial report of the U.S. government. It is available from the Government Accountability Office (GAO).

Required

a. Did the U.S. Government have a surplus or deficit for this year?

b. Was there an increase or decrease in the net position of the U.S. government? How does that compare to last year?

c. Did the GAO give the federal government an unqualified, qualified, adverse, or disclaimer of opinion?

d. What weaknesses or deficiencies did the Comptroller General of the GAO note in his report?

e. What federal agencies received an unqualified opinion for this fiscal year? (*Hint:* Read page 1 of the Management's Discussion and Analysis.)

Exercises and Problems

11–1 Multiple Choice. Choose the best answer.

1. Federal statutes assign responsibility for establishing and maintaining a sound financial structure for the federal government to which of the following:
   a. Comptroller General of the United States.
   b. Comptroller General, Secretary of the Treasury, and Director of the Office of Management and Budget.
   c. Secretary of the Treasury and the Comptroller General.
   d. Federal Financial Accounting Standards Board.

2. The process for establishing generally accepted accounting principles (GAAP) for federal agencies includes:

a. A recommendation of the Federal Accounting Standards Advisory Board (FASAB) to the three principals (sponsors) to issue a statement.
b. Approval of all six federal and three nonfederal members of the FASAB.
c. Approval by the Governmental Accounting Standards Board.
d. All of the above.

3. The hierarchy of accounting principles and standards for federal government entities is described in:
a. The FASB's pronouncements, both statements and technical bulletins.
b. The FASAB's concepts statements and statements of federal financial accounting standards (SFFAS).
c. The AICPA's *Statement of Auditing Standards No. 91,* which amends *SAS No. 69.*
d. The GASB's *Statement No. 34.*

4. Objectives that are identified by *Statement of Federal Financial Accounting Concepts (SFFAC) No. 1* for federal financial reporting include all of the following except:
a. Budgetary integrity.
b. Operating performance.
c. Stewardship.
d. Transparency.

5. Which of the following is a required basic financial statement for federal agencies?
a. Statement of net cost.
b. Statement of cash flows.
c. Statement of financing.
d. Statement of budgetary revenues and expenditures.

6. Assuming that an agency's unused appropriations expire at year-end but appropriations continue in effect for obligated amounts (purchase orders, etc.), which of the following budgetary accounts would likely be found in the agency's post-closing trial balance at year-end?
a. Commitments and Other Appropriations Realized.
b. Undelivered Orders and Other Appropriations Realized.
c. Expended Authority and Undelivered Orders.
d. Commitments and Undelivered Orders.

7. Which of the following is a correct mathematical relationship among proprietary account balances?
a. Net Position equals Total Assets minus Total Liabilities.
b. Fund Balance with Treasury equals Unexpended Appropriations.
c. Cumulative Results of Operations equals Revenues and Financing Sources minus Operating/Program Expenses.
d. Disbursements in Transit equals Fund Balance with Treasury minus Accounts Payable and Other Current Liabilities.

8. Which of the following is required by OMB *Circular A–136* in the basic financial statements for a federal entity?
a. Statement of net assets.
b. Statement of changes in fund balances.
c. Statement of net cost.
d. Statement of activities.

9. Which of the following is not a true statement about the difference between accounting and reporting for federal government agencies versus state and local governments?
   a. The federal government uses a dual-track method of accounting for proprietary accounts and budgetary accounts; state and local governments also use budgetary accounting.
   b. State and local governments use accrual accounting in the government-wide statements as well as proprietary and fiduciary funds; federal agencies use only the cash basis of accounting.
   c. The budget is recorded in the general ledger of a state or local government and a federal agency.
   d. State and local governments do not account for apportionments and most do not account for allotments.

10. Which of the following statements is true about the United States government-wide financial report?
   a. Since 1997, the financial statements of the U.S. government as a whole have been audited by an external certified public accounting firm.
   b. The majority of the 24 major federal agencies required to be audited have received unqualified audit opinions by the OMB.
   c. The Comptroller General of the United States has rendered a disclaimer of opinion on the U.S. government's consolidated financial statements for as long as that office has audited those statements.
   d. None of the above statements are true.

11–2 Fund Balance with U.S. Treasury. One amount is missing in the following trial balance of proprietary accounts, and another is missing from the trial balance of budgetary accounts of a certain agency of the federal government. This trial balance was prepared before budgetary accounts were adjusted, such as returning unused appropriations. The debits are not distinguished from the credits.

FEDERAL AGENCY
Pre-closing Trial Balance
September 30, 2011

Proprietary accounts:	
Accounts Payable	$ 2,300,000
Accumulated Depreciation—Plant and Equipment	2,600,000
Appropriations Used	4,500,000
Fund Balance with Treasury—2011	?
Operating Materials and Supplies	2,700,000
Cumulative Results of Operations—10/1/10	7,700,000
Operating/Program Expenses	4,150,000
Depreciation and Amortization	1,150,000
Plant and Equipment	8,900,000
Unexpended Appropriations—2011	2,100,000
Budgetary accounts:	
Other Appropriations Realized—2011	?
Expended Authority—2011	4,500,000
Undelivered Orders—2011	1,500,000
Apportionments—2011	600,000

Required

a. Compute each missing amount in the pre-closing trial balance.

b. Compute the net additions (or reductions) to assets other than Fund Balance with Treasury during fiscal year 2011. Clearly label your computations and show all work in good form.

11–3 Federal Agency Financial Statements. Using the data from Problem 11–2, prepare the following:

a. In general journal form, entries to close the budgetary accounts as needed and to close the operating statement proprietary accounts.

b. In good form, a balance sheet for the federal agency as of September 30, 2011. (*Note:* Assume that all assets are *entity assets,* Fund Balance with Treasury is an *intragovernmental asset,* and all other assets are *governmental.*)

11–4 Statement of Net Cost. The Rural Assistance Agency operates three major programs as responsibility centers—the Food Bank, Housing Services, and Credit Counseling. Clients pay a fee for services on a sliding scale based on income. The following information is drawn from the accounting records of the agency for the year ended September 30, 2011. Earned revenue from the three programs was as follows: Food Bank, $2,611,900; Housing Services, $1,237,400; and Credit Counseling, $87,000. Costs for the same period were: Food Bank, $9,632,800; Housing Services, $7,438,500; and Credit Counseling, $2,391,000.

Required

Prepare a statement of net cost for the Rural Assistance Agency for the year ended September 30, 2011.

11–5 Statement of Budgetary Resources. The trial balance of the Federal Science Administration, as of August 31, 2011, follows:

	Debits	Credits
Budgetary Accounts		
Other Appropriations Realized—2011	$4,894,855	
Other Appropriations Realized—2010	1,210,210	
Unapportioned Authority—2011		$ 200,000
Apportionments—2011		150,000
Allotments—2011		600,000
Commitments—2011		150,000
Undelivered Orders—2011		664,131
Expended Authority—2011		3,130,724
Expended Authority—2010		1,210,210
Total Budgetary Accounts	$6,105,065	$6,105,065

Required

Prepare a statement of budgetary resources for the 11 months ended August 31, 2011, assuming that goods on order at the end of the prior year amounted to $1,210,210.

11–6 Transaction Analysis and Statements. Congress authorized the Flood Control Commission to start operations on October 1, 2011.

Required

a. Record the following transactions in general journal form as they should appear in the accounts of the Flood Control Commission. Record all expenses in the Operating/Program Expenses account.

(1) The Flood Control Commission received official notice that the one-year appropriation passed by Congress and signed by the President amounted to $7,000,000 for operating expenses.

(2) The Office of Management and Budget notified the Commission of the following schedule of apportionments: first quarter, $2,000,000; second quarter, $2,000,000; third quarter, $1,500,000; and fourth quarter, $1,500,000.

(3) The Flood Control Commissioner allotted $1,000,000 for the first month's operations.

(4) Obligations were recorded for salaries and fringe benefits, $400,000; furniture and equipment, $270,000; materials and supplies, $250,000; and rent and utilities, $50,000. The Commission does not record commitments prior to recording obligations.

(5) Payroll for the first two weeks in the amount of $170,000 was paid.

(6) Invoices approved for payment totaled $395,000; of the total, $180,000 was for furniture and equipment, $175,000 for materials and supplies, and $40,000 for rent.

(7) A liability was recorded for the payroll for the second two weeks, $160,000, and for the employer's share of FICA taxes for the four weeks, $23,000. (*Note:* Credit to Accrued Funded Payroll and Benefits.)

(8) Accounts payable totaling $189,000 were paid, which included liabilities for materials and supplies, $149,000, and rent, $40,000. Accrued Funded Payroll and Benefits in the amount of $183,000 were paid.

(9) Accruals recorded at month-end were salaries, $30,000, and utilities, $10,000. Materials and supplies costing $60,000 were used during the month. Depreciation of $2,500 was recorded on furniture and equipment for the month. (*Note:* In practice, this would likely be done in worksheet form for monthly reporting purposes.)

(10) Necessary closing entries were prepared as of October 31, 2011. (*Note:* Again, for monthly statements, this would be a worksheet entry only.)

b. Prepare the Balance Sheet of the Flood Control Commission as of October 31, 2011, assuming that all of the Commission's assets are entity assets, Fund Balance with Treasury is intragovernmental, and all other assets are governmental.

c. Prepare the Statement of Changes in Net Position of the Flood Control Commission for the month ended October 31, 2011.

d. Prepare the Statement of Budgetary Resources of the Flood Control Commission for the month ended October 31, 2011.

11–7 DOT Audit Report and Transmittal Letter. The following excerpt is from the Inspector General's transmittal letter to the Secretary of the Department of Transportation (DOT).

U.S. Department of Transportation
Office of the Secretary of Transportation Office of Inspector General

Date: November 13, 2007

Subject: ACTION: Report on Consolidated Financial Statements for Fiscal Years 2007 and 2006, DOT FI-2005-009

From: Calvin L. Scovel III, Inspector General

To: The Secretary

I respectfully submit the Office of Inspector General report on the Department of Transportation (DOT) Consolidated Financial Statements for Fiscal Years (FY) 2007 and 2006 (see Attachment). This year, our audit concluded that DOT's consolidated financial statements are fairly presented, in all material respects, in conformity with generally accepted accounting principles. The clean (unqualified) opinion signals to the public that the Department has successfully overcome last year's qualified opinion on the Construction in Progress (CIP) balance, which is a subcomponent of the Property, Plant, and Equipment line item on the Department's balance sheet.

Last year, KPMG LLP, under contract to us and under our supervision, rendered a qualified opinion on the Federal Aviation Administration's (FAA) FY 2006 financial statements because deficiencies in FAA's accounting for CIP prevented FAA from providing adequate support to verify that reported CIP balances were reliable. Since FAA's property, including CIP, represents about 95 percent of the Property, Plant, and Equipment line item on the Department's consolidated balance sheet, the Department's consolidated financial statements were similarly qualified. During FY 2007, FAA made a concerted effort to revise the CIP account balance, resulting in a clean opinion this year.

The Department's ability to regain a clean opinion on its consolidated financial statements would not have occurred without your emphasis and personal commitment to improving financial management practices, along with that of your senior leadership team, including the Acting FAA Administrator and the departmental Chief Financial Officer. During the year, you made several inquiries about FAA's CIP and financial statement audit progress. Your consistent attention to this subject helped departmental officials stay focused on their correction efforts.

The Department has undergone annual financial statement audits since FY 1992 and received the best outcome yet in FY 2007—a clean audit opinion and only one material weakness (FAA's continued challenge in managing the property account). While the Department should be commended for this accomplishment, it must remain vigilant in sustaining good financial management operations because auditors continue to find significant deficiencies associated with financial transaction processing. These deficiencies, if not properly addressed, could turn into material weaknesses in the future. The following summarizes key challenges the Department continues to face.

• • •

Source: *http://www.dot.gov/perfacc2007/igauditreport.htm.*

Required

a. Explain the role of an inspector general within a federal agency. Is an opinion from this person considered an *independent* auditor's opinion?

b. Describe how long it typically takes for financial statements to be made available to the public and where these can be found. Did the DOT present all the financial statements required by OMB *Circular A–136* on time?

c. Look at the full text of the Inspector General's report at the Web site indicated at the bottom of the excerpt. Did the Department of Transportation have any material weaknesses in internal controls or reportable conditions? If so, did they result in a qualified or adverse audit opinion for the department? Discuss.

Chapter Twelve

Auditing of Governmental and Not-for-Profit Organizations

Learning Objectives

After studying this chapter, you should be able to:

1. Explain the essential elements of financial audits by independent CPAs, including:
   The objective(s) of financial audits.
   The source and content of generally accepted auditing standards (GAAS).
   Audit report formats and opinions.
   The audit process.
2. Explain what is meant by generally accepted government auditing standards (GAGAS), the source of GAGAS, and why and how GAGAS are broader than GAAS.
3. Explain the types of audits performed under GAGAS, including financial audits, attestation engagements, and performance audits.
4. Explain the essentials of a single audit, including:
   The purpose and scope of a single audit.
   Major program identification.
   Audit work required.
   Reports that must be submitted and when and to whom.
5. Describe the implications of the Sarbanes-Oxley Act of 2002 on governments and not-for-profit organizations.

The auditing profession has undergone numerous changes in the past decade that have affected how audits are conducted and how audit results are reported to the public. Not only have the changes affected how audits are conducted under the American Institute of Certified Public Accountants's (AICPA) generally accepted auditing standards (GAAS), but they have also affected the Government Accountability Office's (GAO) generally accepted government audit standards (GAGAS) under which governments and not-for-profits may be audited.

FINANCIAL AUDITS BY INDEPENDENT CPAs

Financial statements of governmental entities, colleges and universities, health care organizations, voluntary health and welfare organizations, and other not-for-profit organizations are the representations of the officials responsible for the financial management of the entity. In order for users of the financial statements to have the assurance that the statements have been prepared in conformity with accounting and financial reporting standards established by authoritative bodies, and that all material facts have been disclosed, the statements should be accompanied by the report of an independent auditor. Audits for this purpose are called financial audits. Audits or engagements conducted for other purposes are discussed later in this section.

The auditor's objective in performing a financial audit is to render a report expressing his or her opinion that the financial statements are presented fairly. "Present fairly" means in conformity with generally accepted accounting principles. Auditors provide opinions on financial statements that are based on *reasonable assurance* that the financial statements are free from material misstatements, which is not the same as ensuring or guaranteeing that the statements are free of errors and all fraud was detected.

Three levels of audit to which governments and not-for-profit entities may be subject are discussed in this chapter. The AICPA's generally accepted auditing standards (GAAS) for financial audits are discussed first. Since most readers will be familiar with GAAS, attention will be focused on the unique aspects of auditing government and not-for-profit entities under GAAS. A broader level of financial audit is provided by GAGAS, which largely incorporate and add to the GAAS standards. Finally, the Single Audit Act is discussed. The single audit incorporates GAGAS and adds program compliance audit and internal control requirements to the financial audit standards provided by GAGAS. As can be seen, audit complexity increases as the level of the audit goes from GAAS to GAGAS to a single audit.

Generally Accepted Auditing Standards

In the case of state and local governments, audits may be performed by independent certified public accountants (CPAs) or by state or federal audit agencies. Generally, not-for-profit organizations electing or required to have an audit are audited by CPAs. In performing audits, CPAs are professionally and ethically obligated by Rule 202 of the American Institute of Certified Public Accountants's (AICPA) *Code of Professional Conduct* to follow **generally accepted auditing standards (GAAS)**—standards set by the AICPA and promulgated in *Statements on Auditing Standards*.[1] State or federal auditors, whether or not they are CPAs, are also required to follow GAAS if GAAS are prescribed by law or policy for the audits they conduct.

GAAS have been summarized by the AICPA in the three general standards, three standards of field work, and four standards of reporting shown in Illustration 12–1. These 10 standards are amplified by numerous *Statements on Auditing Standards* published in codified form in the AICPA's *Professional Standards*. Recently, *Statements on Auditing Standards* 104 through 111 have been published. These standards, referred to as the risk assessment suite, are intended to guide auditors to areas of greatest risk. The intent is to enhance auditors' application of the audit risk model.

[1] The *Public Company Accounting Reform and Investor Protection Act* (the Sarbanes-Oxley Act of 2002, H.R. 3763, July 25, 2002) creates a federal oversight board with the authority to set and enforce generally accepted auditing standards for auditors of public companies.

ILLUSTRATION 12–1 Generally Accepted Auditing Standards (GAAS)—AICPA

General Standards

1. The audit is to be performed by a person or persons having adequate technical training and proficiency as an auditor.
2. In all matters relating to the assignment, an independence in mental attitude is to be maintained by the auditor or auditors.
3. Due professional care is to be exercised in the performance of the audit and the preparation of the report.

Standards of Field Work

1. The work must be adequately planned and assistants, if any, are to be properly supervised.
2. A sufficient understanding of the entity and its environment, including its internal control, must be obtained to assess the risk of material misstatement of the financial statements whether due to error or fraud, and to design the nature, timing, and extent of further audit procedures.
3. Sufficient appropriate audit evidence must be obtained by performing audit procedures to afford a reasonable basis for an opinion regarding the financial statements under audit.

Standards of Reporting

1. The report must state whether the financial statements are presented in accordance with generally accepted accounting principles (GAAP).
2. The report must identify those circumstances in which such principles have not been consistently observed in the current period in relation to the preceding period.
3. When the auditor determines that informative disclosures are not reasonably adequate, the report must so state.
4. The report must contain either an expression of opinion regarding the financial statements, taken as a whole, or state that an opinion cannot be expressed. When an overall opinion cannot be expressed, the reasons therefore should be stated. In all cases where an auditor's name is associated with financial statements, the report should contain a clear-cut indication of the character of the auditor's work, if any, and the degree of responsibility the auditor is taking.

Source: AICPA, *Professional Standards*, 2008 AU 150.

Application of the risk model is enhanced through the standards' requirement that auditors:

1. Obtain a more in-depth understanding of the entity and its environment, including its internal control.
2. Conduct a more rigorous assessment of the risk of material misstatement.
3. Improve the link between the assessment of risk and the nature, timing, and extent of any further procedures performed.

As will be seen, properly assessing risk is important at all levels of audit.

Failure to follow GAAS can result in severe sanctions, including the loss of the auditor's license to practice as a CPA and expulsion from the AICPA. It is the auditor's duty to adhere to auditing standards, and it is his or her technical qualifications and independence from the entity being audited that add credibility to reported financial information and increase financial statement users' confidence in the information.

Format of the Audit Report

Illustration 12–2 shows an alteration to the standard audit report provided for an unqualified audit opinion on an entity's financial statements. The illustration

ILLUSTRATION 12–5 Types of Governmental Audits and Other Engagements

Financial Audits

The primary purpose of financial statement audits is to provide the reader with reasonable assurance through an independent opinion (or disclaimer of opinion) that an entity's financial statements are presented fairly in accordance with recognized criteria (e.g., GAAP).

Attestation Engagements

The primary purpose of an attestation engagement is to provide an examination, a review, or an agreed-upon procedure report on a subject matter or on an assertion about a subject matter.

- Examination—the purpose is to express an opinion on whether the subject matter examined is based on (or in conformity with) the recognized criteria or the assertion being made is presented (or fairly stated) based on the recognized criteria.
- Review—the purpose is to express a conclusion about whether any information indicates that the subject matter reviewed is not based on (or not in conformity with) the recognized criteria, or the assertion is not presented (or not fairly stated) based on the recognized criteria.
- Agreed-Upon Procedures—the purpose is specific to the procedures the auditor performs on an agreed-to subject matter.

Performance Audits

The purposes of performance audits vary widely and include assessments of program effectiveness, economy, and efficiency; internal control compliance; and prospective analyses.

- GAGAS performance audits are engagements that provide assurance or conclusions based on an evaluation of sufficient and appropriate evidence using stated criteria.
- GAGAS performance audits provide reasonable assurance concerning the conclusions the auditor reaches.

Source: *Government Auditing Standards* (Washington, DC: GAO, 2007), pars. 1.22–1.25.

Types of Audits and Engagements

The yellow book describes audits and engagements that cover a broad range of financial or nonfinancial objectives. The GAGAS framework includes three types of audits and services: financial audits, attestation engagements, and performance audits. Illustration 12–5 lists the purposes and characteristics of these auditor services. Performance audits are often performed by internal auditors or state audit agencies. An engagement letter between the auditor and the organization should clearly specify what type of audit is to be performed and which auditing standards will be followed.

Financial audits are all audits covered under GAAS, such as financial statement audits, special reports (e.g., SAS 99 fraud reports), reviews of interim financial information, letters to underwriters, compliance audits, and service organization audits. In financial audits, the auditors express an opinion on the fairness of an entity's financial statements as well as whether the statements conform to GAAP. **Attestation engagements** include services related to providing various levels of assurance on other financial or nonfinancial matters, such as internal control, compliance, MD&A presentation, allowability and reasonableness of proposed contract amounts, final contract costs, and reliability of performance measures. **Performance audits** or operational audits are independent assessments of the performance and the management of the entity, program, service, or activity against objective criteria. Objectives include assessing effectiveness and results, economy and efficiency, and internal controls and compliance with laws and regulations.

The GAGAS field work and reporting standards for performance audits are unique in that the objective of performance audits is to provide evidence to assess performance of a governmental organization, program, activity, or function rather than to render a

ILLUSTRATION 12–6 Generally Accepted Government Auditing Standards (GAGAS) for Financial Audits—GAO

General Standards

1. Independence standard: The audit organization and the individual auditor must be free from personal, external, or organizational impairments to independence.
2. Professional judgment: Auditors must use professional judgment in planning and performing audits and attestation engagements and in reporting the results.
3. Competence: The staff assigned to perform the audit or attestation engagement must collectively possess adequate professional competence for the tasks required.
4. Quality control and assurance: The audit organization must establish a system of quality and have an external peer review at least once every 3 years.

Field Work Standards That Add to the GAAS Field Work Standards

1. Information should be communicated in writing to management of the entity, those charged with governance, and those contracting for or requesting the audit. If the audit is performed pursuant to law or regulation for a legislative committee with oversight of the auditee, auditors should communicate with the legislative committee.
2. Known findings and recommendations from previous engagements that directly relate to the current audit should be considered in planning.
3. The audit should be designed to provide reasonable assurance of detecting material misstatements resulting from violations of contract or grant provisions or from abuse.
4. When the audit findings involve deficiencies, the elements (criteria, condition, cause and effect) of the findings should be developed.
5. Documentation should be provided concerning evidence of supervisory review of work performed, any departures from GAGAS that impact the audit, polices and procedures for audit documentation custody and retention, and the availability of documentation to others.

Reporting Standards That Add to the GAAS Reporting Standards

1. When audits are conducted in accordance with GAGAS, a reference to GAGAS should be made in the audit report.
2. When the financial statement audit report contains an opinion or a disclaimer of opinion, a report on internal control over financial reporting and on compliance with laws, regulations, and provisions of contracts and grants must be provided as part of the report or as a separate report.
3. Based on the audit work performed, a report should be made on significant deficiencies in internal control; all instances of fraud and illegal acts; and violations of grant or contract provisions and abuse that are material.
4. The report may communicate significant matters, such as the entity's fiscal sustainability (i.e., ability to continue operations).
5. If financial statements are restated, auditors should evaluate the timeliness and appropriateness of management's disclosures and actions regarding the restatements and report on the restatement.
6. When the report discloses deficiencies, the views of responsible officials concerning the audit report and any plans for corrective action should be included in the report.
7. When applicable, the report should indicate that confidential or sensitive information has been omitted from the report and the reason that such an omission is necessary.
8. Submission of reports should be made to appropriate officials, and audits should be made available to the public.

Source: *Government Auditing Standards* (Washington, DC: GAO, 2007).

professional opinion. Thus, testing for compliance with laws and regulations, although of critical importance in a financial audit, may be relatively less so if the audit objective in a performance audit is to assess the efficiency and effectiveness of a program and there are no laws and regulations that would have a material effect on the program.

GAGAS Financial Audits

With the changes the AICPA has been making to generally accepted auditing standards, there are fewer major differences now than ever before between financial audits conducted using GAAS and those using GAGAS. However, Illustration 12–6 shows that even though the two sets of standards may be more similar now than in the past, differences remain. GAGAS has four general standards related to independence, professional judgment, competence, and quality control and assurance. In addition to the general standards, GAGAS adds five field work standards to those required by GAAS and eight reporting standards to those required by GAAS.

General Standards

As shown in Illustrations 12–1 and 12–6, differences exist between GAAS and GAGAS in standards although they address similar concepts. For example, consider the general standards related to competence. The first GAAS general standard in Illustration 12–1and the third GAGAS general standard in Illustration 12–6 both address competency. However, the language from the GAGAS standard places responsibility on audit organizations to ensure that assignments are performed by staff that collectively have the knowledge, skills, and experience for the assignment; see GAGAS (par. 3.41). A specific GAGAS requirement to ensure that auditors conducting audits under GAGAS maintain their professional competence is that, every two years, each auditor should complete at least 80 hours of continuing professional education (CPE) that directly contributes to the auditor's professional proficiency to perform such work (par. 3.46). Of the 80 CPE hours, 24 hours should relate to government auditing, the government environment, or the specific or unique environment in which the entity operates (e.g., the not-for-profit environment). At least 20 of the CPE hours should be completed in each year of the two-year period. The GAO provides complete guidance concerning continuing education requirements in its publication *Government Auditing Standards: Guidance on GAGAS Requirements for Continuing Professional Education*, which is available through the GAO Web site (*www.gao.gov*).

To further ensure the quality of government audits, the fourth general standard in GAGAS requires each audit organization to have an "appropriate internal quality control system" and undergo an external peer review at least once every three years by an audit organization independent of the audit organization being reviewed.[7] The purpose of the standard is to ensure that the audit organization has quality control policies and procedures in place that will provide reasonable assurance that the organization and its employees are complying with applicable standards, laws, and regulations (par. 3.50). Once policies and procedures are in place, they must be monitored and analyzed at least annually to ensure that systematic improvement is being made (pars. 3.53–3.54).

Field Work Standards

The additional field work standards of financial audits contained in GAGAS emphasize the importance of communication; follow-up on prior findings and recommendations; detection of material misstatements; development of the elements of a deficiency finding; and documentation. The first additional field work standard relates to written communication. Due to the fact that more parties tend to be involved in a GAGAS audit, communication during the planning process is important.

The third additional field work standard on detection of material misstatements contains an item that is unique to GAGAS audits—abuse. According to par 4.12 of the yellow book, "abuse involves behavior that is deficient or improper when compared with behavior that a prudent person would consider reasonable and necessary business practice given the facts and circumstances. Abuse also includes misuse of authority or position for personal financial interests or those of an immediate or close family member or business associate." If abuse is detected, auditors may need to apply additional audit procedures.

[7] Ibid., pars. 3.49–3.53.

The fourth additional field work standard relates to findings in internal control, fraud, illegal acts, violations of provisions of contracts or grant agreements, or abuse. The four elements of a deficiency finding that GAGAS indicate should be developed to ensure audit objectives are met are: criteria (the basis for determining a deficiency, such as a law), condition (the deficiency as it currently exists), cause, and effect or potential effect.

The fifth additional fieldwork standard relates to documentation. This is one area that is frequently deemed deficient in reviews of GAGAS audits submitted to the Federal Audit Clearinghouse. Audit documentation needs to be sufficient to enable another auditor with no previous connection to the audit to review and understand the documentation.

Reporting Standards

GAGAS reporting standards for financial audits incorporate the GAAS reporting standards shown in Illustration 12–1. The additional GAGAS standards cover reporting on compliance, required communications, internal controls, report requirements, and distribution. Some of the additional standards relate to reporting information that is unique to government-awarded grants and contracts. For example, the yellow book permits auditors to exclude reporting certain privileged and confidential information. Other standards add to disclosure requirements. An example of additional disclosure is "when auditors detect violations of provisions of contracts or grant agreements or abuse that have an effect on the financial statements that is less than material but more than inconsequential, they should communicate those findings in writing to officials of the audited entity" (par. 5.16).

Ethics and Independence

The yellow book outlines basic ethical principles that should guide auditors who are applying GAGAS. When auditors are considering the facts and circumstances of the subject matter they are auditing, they should do so within the framework provided by the ethical principles. The five fundamental ethical principles identified by GAGAS are: public interest; integrity; objectivity; proper use of government information, resources, and position; and professional behavior. Public interest refers to consideration of the well-being of those being served by the auditor (par. 2.06). The other ethical principles outlined by GAGAS are fairly self-explanatory. Ethical principles should be considered throughout the audit.

Ethical principles are especially salient when the audit organization is considering whether it meets the GAGAS independence standard. The independence standard requires that the highest degree of integrity and objectivity be maintained by any auditor (CPA, non-CPA, government financial auditor, or performance auditor) performing audits of federal, state, and local governments and not-for-profit entities that receive federal financial assistance so that the public is best served. The standard addresses independence issues when nonaudit work is performed for audited entities. **Nonaudit work** is performed solely for the benefit of the entity requesting the work and does not provide a basis for conclusions, recommendations, or opinions as would a financial audit, attestation engagement, or performance audit.

The independence standard uses an engagement-team focus that articulates a principles-based approach with two overarching principles supplemented by seven safeguards. The principles follow:

1. Auditors should not perform management functions or make management decisions.

ILLUSTRATION 12–8 Determining Federal Awards Expended for a Hypothetical Direct Loan Program

Loan Activity	Amounts	Highest Balance
Balance, beginning of year	$400,000	
New loans during year	150,000	
		$520,000*
Loans repaid during year	(100,000)	
Balance, end of year	$450,000	

* Records indicate that $520,000 was the highest loan balance outstanding at any point during the year. Because the federal government was at risk at one point during the year for $520,000, that is the amount of federal awards deemed to have been expended.

as charges to program beneficiaries for services rendered and rental from program facilities); and the distribution or consumption of food commodities. Amounts expended would normally be determined using the entity's basis of accounting. Thus, either an expenditure or expense may enter into the calculation of federal awards expended. Federal noncash assistance received, such as free rent (if received by a nonfederal entity to carry out a federal program), food stamps, commodities, and donated property, should be valued at fair value at the time of receipt or the assessed value provided by the awarding federal agency.

If federal awards involve loan, loan guarantee, and insurance programs, the federal award expended is the amount to which the federal government is at risk for the loans. Generally this will be the amount of loans made (or received) during the year, plus any loan balances from previous years for which the federal government imposes continuing compliance requirements, plus any interest subsidy, cash, or administrative cost allowance received.[14] To the extent that new and previously issued loans may have been repaid during the year, adjustments would need to be made. This is so because the federal awards expended under a loan or insurance program represent the highest amount of risk exposure for the federal government during the year. Thus, if the total loan balance varies during the year, the highest loan balance outstanding at any point during the year is the amount of federal awards expended.

Certain federal awards are excluded from the calculation of awards expended. For example, Medicare and Medicaid payments for services provided are not included in the calculation unless required by the state.[15]

Illustration 12–8 provides an example of how federal awards expended would be calculated for a hypothetical direct loan program administered by a local government or not-for-profit organization. Although neither the beginning nor ending loan balances exceed the $500,000 single audit threshold, records showed that at one point during the year, the loan balance reached $520,000. Because at that point in time the federal government was at risk for $520,000 and the nonfederal entity had compliance duties for the $520,000 in loans outstanding, federal awards are deemed to have been expended in the same amount. If this was the only federal program for which awards were received during the year, the entity may have the option of having a single audit or a program-specific audit.

[14] Ibid., § ____. 205(b).

[15] Ibid., § ____. 205.

Single Audit Requirements

The 1996 amendments to the Single Audit Act of 1984 mandate the following audit requirements for the single audit:

1. An annual audit must be performed encompassing the nonfederal entity's financial statements and schedule of expenditures of federal awards.
2. The audit must be conducted by an independent auditor in accordance with generally accepted government auditing standards (GAGAS) and cover the operations of the entire nonfederal entity. Alternatively, a series of audits that cover departments, agencies, and other organizational units is permitted if the series of audits encompasses the financial statements and schedule of expenditures of federal awards for each such department, agency, or other organizational unit, which in aggregate are considered to be a nonfederal entity. *Independent auditor* means an external federal, state, or local auditor who meets the GAGAS independence standards or an independent public accountant.
3. The auditor must determine whether the financial statements are presented fairly in all material respects with GAAP and whether the schedule of expenditures of federal awards is presented fairly in relation to the financial statements taken as a whole.
4. For each major program, the auditor must obtain an understanding of the internal controls pertaining to the compliance requirements for the program, assess control risk, and perform tests of controls, unless the controls are deemed to be ineffective. (*Note:* OMB *Circular A–133* requires the auditor to obtain an understanding of and conduct testing of internal controls to support a low assessed level of control risk; that is, as if high reliance will be placed on the internal controls.) In addition, for each major program the auditor shall determine whether the nonfederal entity has complied with laws, regulations, and contract or grant provisions pertaining to federal awards of the program. Auditors test compliance by determining if requirements listed for each program in the *Circular A–133 Compliance Supplement* published by the OMB have been met. Auditors are required to use the *Compliance Supplement,* which details compliance auditing requirements for many federal programs, listed by *Catalog of Federal Domestic Assistance* (CFDA) title and number.
5. *Circular A–133* assigns certain responsibilities to federal awarding agencies and nonfederal entities that act as "pass-through" agents in passing federal awards to subrecipient nonfederal entities.

Compliance Audits

As noted in item (4) above, *Circular A–133* requires the auditor to express an opinion that the auditee complied with laws, regulations, and grant or contract provisions that could have a direct and material effect on each major program. To gather sufficient evidence to support his or her opinion in such **compliance audits,** the auditor tests whether each major program was administered in conformity with administrative requirements contained in OMB *Circular A–102,* "Grants and Cooperative Agreements with State and Local Governments" or OMB *Circular A–110,* "Uniform Administrative Requirements for Grants and Other Agreements with Institutions of Higher Education, Hospitals, and Other Nonprofit Organizations," as appropriate. The auditor also tests for compliance with the detailed *compliance* requirements for major programs provided in the *Circular A–133 Compliance*

Supplement or other guidance provided by federal awarding agencies. The *Compliance Supplement* identifies 14 generic compliance requirements, although not all the requirements apply to every major program. Moreover, there are additional compliance requirements specified for some programs. Generally, compliance requirements relate to matters such as allowed and unallowed activities; allowed and unallowed costs; eligibility of program beneficiaries; responsibilities of the nonfederal entity regarding matching, level of effort, and earmarking; management of equipment and real property acquired from federal awards; and required reporting.

Auditee Responsibilities

OMB *Circular A–133* also details the responsibilities of auditees (nonfederal entities). Auditees are responsible for identifying all federal awards received and expended, and the federal programs under which they were received. Identification of the federal program includes the Catalog of Federal Domestic Assistance (CFDA) title and number, award number and year, and name of the federal agency. In addition, auditees are responsible for maintaining appropriate internal controls and systems to ensure compliance with all laws, regulations, and contract or grant provisions applicable to federal awards. Finally, auditees must prepare appropriate financial statements and the schedule of expenditures of federal awards, ensure that audits are properly performed and submitted when due, and follow up and take appropriate corrective action on audit findings. The latter requirement includes preparation of a summary schedule of prior audit findings and a corrective action plan for current year audit findings.

Selecting Programs for Audit

Illustration 12–9 shows the procedures and criteria for selecting major programs for audit as described in Chapter 8 of the AICPA Audit Guide *Government Auditing Standards and Circular A–133 Audits.* A **major program** is a federal award program selected for audit using the procedures described below and shown in Illustration 12–9 or by request of a federal awarding agency. Use of a **risk-based approach** for selecting major programs for audit ensures that audit effort is concentrated on the highest risk programs. The risk-based approach is applied as follows:

1. Identify the "larger" federal programs and analyze them according to the Type A criteria. Programs not meeting Type A criteria are identified as Type B programs. Type A programs are determined using the following sliding scale:

Total Federal Awards Expended	Threshold for Type A Program
$300,000 to $100 million	Larger of $300,000 or 3% (.03) of total federal awards expended
More than $100 million to $10 billion	Larger of $3 million or .3% (.003) of total federal awards expended
More than $10 billion	Larger of $30 million or .15% (.0015) of total federal awards expended

2. Identify low-risk Type A programs: programs previously audited in at least one of the two most recent audit periods as a major program, with no audit findings in the most recent audit period; programs with no significant changes in personnel or systems that would have significantly increased risk; and programs that, in the

ILLUSTRATION 12–9 Risk-Based Approach for Selecting Major Programs for Audit

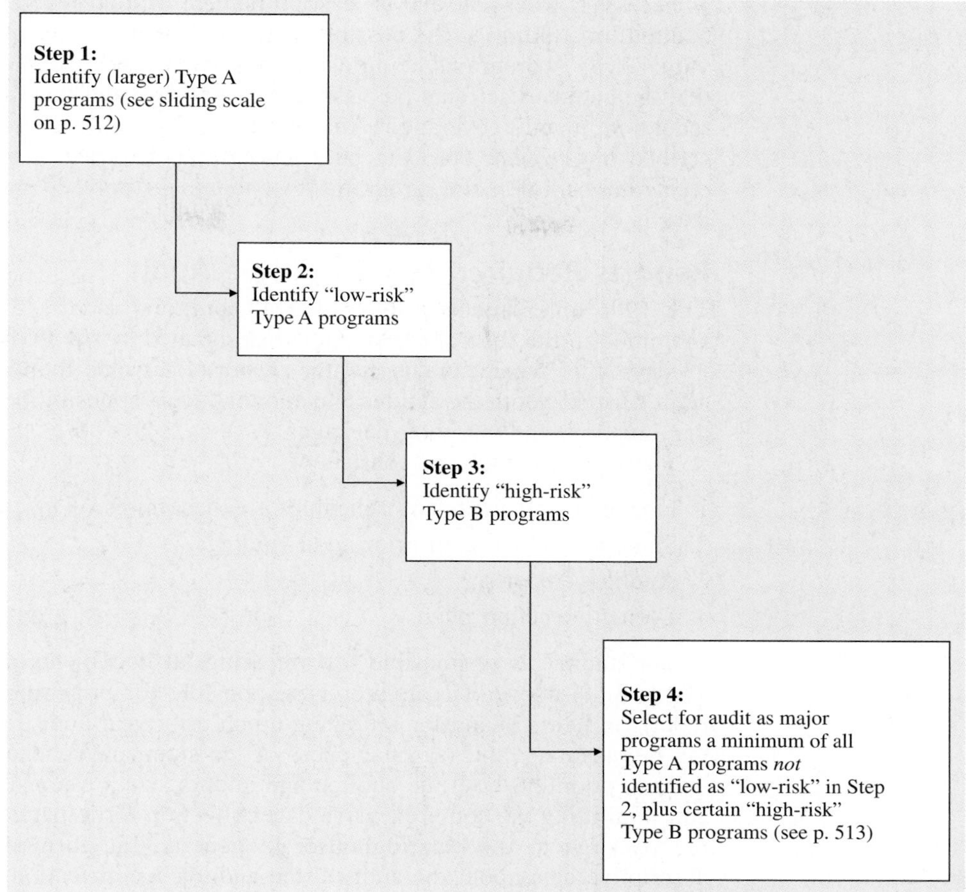
Step 1:
Identify (larger) Type A programs (see sliding scale on p. 512)
Step 2:
Identify "low-risk" Type A programs
Step 3:
Identify "high-risk" Type B programs
Step 4:
Select for audit as major programs a minimum of all Type A programs *not* identified as "low-risk" in Step 2, plus certain "high-risk" Type B programs (see p. 513)

auditor's professional judgment, are low risk, after considering such factors as the inherent risk of the program, the level of oversight exercised by federal awarding agencies and pass-through agencies, and the phase of a program in its life cycle. New programs, for example, tend to be more risky than more mature programs.

3. Identify Type B programs that, based on the auditor's professional judgment and criteria discussed above, are high risk. The auditor is not expected to perform risk assessments on relatively small federal programs. Risk assessments are performed only for those Type B programs that exceed the larger of (a) $100,000 or .3% (.003) of total federal awards expended when total federal awards expended are less than or equal to $100 million or (b) $300,000 or .03% (.0003) of total federal awards expended when total federal awards expended are more than $100 million.
4. At a minimum, audit as major programs all Type A programs *not* identified as low risk and certain high-risk Type B programs, using one of the following options:
   (*a*) audit at least half of the high-risk Type B programs, but this number need not exceed the number of Type A programs identified as low risk; or
   (*b*) audit one high-risk Type B program for each Type A program identified as low risk.

The *percentage of coverage rule* requires the auditing of as many major programs as necessary to ensure that at least 50 percent of total federal awards expended are audited. In addition to the possibility of reduced audit coverage resulting from individual Type A programs being classified as low risk, *Circular A–133* also provides that the auditee itself can be classified as low risk and thereby receive even greater reduction in audit coverage.[16] An auditee that meets the rather stringent criteria prescribed in *Circular A–133* to be a low-risk auditee needs to have audited a sufficient number of major programs to encompass only 25 percent of total federal awards expended.

Reports Required for the Single Audit

The 1996 amendments require that all auditors' reports for the single audit be submitted to the federal clearinghouse designated by the OMB within the earlier of 30 days after receipt of the auditor's report(s) or nine months after the end of the audit period.[17] Both the auditee and auditor have responsibilities for particular reports that comprise the reporting package.

The reporting package consists of:

1. Financial statements and schedule of expenditures of federal awards.
2. Summary schedule of prior audit findings.
3. Auditors' reports.
4. Corrective action plan.

The auditee is responsible for preparing all documents described in items (1), (2), and (4) above. The auditor is responsible for preparing the various auditors' reports in item (3) and for following up on prior year audit findings, including testing the accuracy and reasonableness of the summary schedule of prior audit findings. In addition, both the auditee and auditor have responsibilities for completing and submitting the comprehensive data collection form that accompanies the reporting package to the clearinghouse. In general, the form provides for extensive descriptive data about the auditee, the auditor, identification of types and amounts of federal awards and major programs, types of reports issued by the auditor, and whether the auditor identified internal control deficiencies or significant noncompliance with laws, regulations, or grant provisions. Both a senior-level representative of the auditee and auditor must sign the data collection form, certifying its accuracy and completeness.

Auditor's Reports

OMB *Circular A–133* specifies several reports that the auditor must submit for each single audit engagement. These reports can be in the form of separate reports for each requirement or a few combined reports. The auditor's report on the financial statements should indicate that the audit was conducted in accordance with GAAS and GAGAS. Other auditor's reports required by the single audit should indicate the audits were conducted in accordance with GAAS, GAGAS, and provisions of

[16] An auditee is considered "low risk" if unqualified opinions have been received on annual single audits with no deficiencies in internal control and no audit findings.

[17] A three-page data collection form (SF-SAC) is sent electronically to the Federal Audit Clearinghouse, Bureau of the Census, Department of Commerce. See *http://harvester.census.gov/fac.*

Circular A–133. The required single audit reports, whether made as separate reports or combined, must include:

1. An opinion (or disclaimer of opinion) as to whether the financial statements are presented fairly in conformity with GAAP and whether the schedule of expenditures of federal awards is presented fairly in relation to the financial statements taken as a whole.
2. A report on internal controls related to the financial statements and major programs.
3. A report and an opinion on compliance with laws, regulations, and provisions of grant or contract agreements that could have a material effect on the financial statements. The report must also include an opinion on compliance matters related to major programs audited that could have a direct and material effect on each major program. Where applicable, include findings of noncompliance in the separate schedule of findings and questioned costs, described in item (4) below.
4. A schedule of findings and questioned costs, containing the following:
   (*a*) A summary of the auditor's results, including such information as type of opinion rendered on the financial statements, significant deficiencies relating to internal control weaknesses, material noncompliance affecting the financial statements, major programs audited, type of opinion on compliance for major programs and significant deficiencies in internal control affecting major programs, and a statement as to whether the auditee qualified as low risk.
   (*b*) Findings related to the audit of the financial statements required to be reported by the yellow book (GAGAS).
   (*c*) Audit findings and questioned costs. Audit findings are discussed next.

Illustration 12–10 shows the relationship of the required auditor's reports under GAAS, GAGAS, and the Single Audit (OMB *Circular A–133*).

ILLUSTRATION 12–10 Required Auditor's Reports

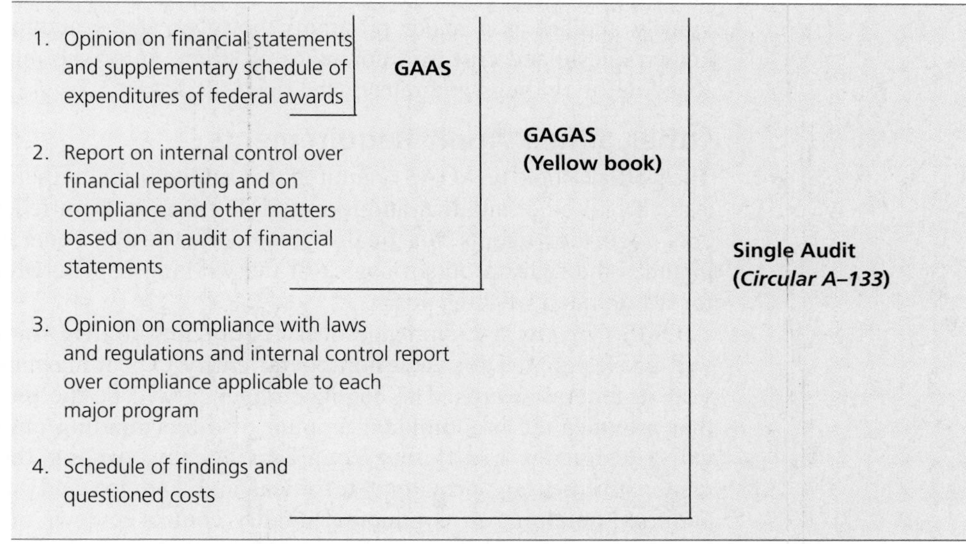

Source: Adapted from Table 12-1, AICPA Audit Guide, *Government Auditing Standards and Circular A–133 Audits* (New York: AICPA, 2008).

Reporting Audit Findings

As listed in item (4) above, auditors must prepare a schedule of findings and questioned costs. **Audit findings** reported in the schedule provide detail on matters such as internal control weaknesses, instances of noncompliance, questioned costs, fraud and illegal acts, material violations of contract and grant agreements, and material abuse.

Regarding reporting on internal controls, item (4a) above uses the term **significant deficiency.** This term is used in AICPA authoritative audit publications and has been adopted in the yellow book. In the context of GAGAS audits, a significant deficiency in the design or operation of internal control could adversely affect the entity's ability to administer a federal award program in accordance with GAAP. As a result, there is more than a remote possibility that a significant misstatement in the financial statements could occur. A **material weakness** is a significant deficiency of such magnitude that the internal control components do not reduce the risk of detection or prevention of material misstatement to an acceptably low level.

A **questioned cost** arises from an audit finding, generally relating to noncompliance with a law, regulation, or agreement, whose costs are either not supported by adequate documentation or appear unreasonable. Cost principles to be followed by nonfederal entities in the administration of federal awards are prescribed by circulars that define concepts such as direct and indirect costs, allowable and unallowable costs, and methods for calculating indirect cost rates. These circulars and cost principles are described in Chapter 13.

In auditing a major program, *Circular A–133* requires that *known questioned costs* exceeding $10,000 shall be reported in the schedule of findings and questioned costs. A known questioned cost is one that the auditor has specifically identified in performing audit procedures. In evaluating the impact of a known questioned cost, the dollar impact also includes a best estimate of "likely questioned costs." Thus, the auditor must also report known questioned costs if the likely questioned costs exceed $10,000, even if the known dollar amount is zero. Nonmajor programs are not normally audited for compliance (except for audit follow-up of a program that was previously audited as a major program); however, if the auditor becomes aware of a known questioned cost in a nonmajor program, he or she must also report it in the schedule of findings and questioned costs.

Other Single Audit Requirements

The yellow book (GAGAS) requires that auditors make their audit working papers available to other auditors and to oversight officials from federal awarding agencies and cognizant agents for quality review purposes. Federal agency access also includes the right to obtain copies of the working papers, which should be retained for a minimum of three years.

OMB *Circular A–133* provides that a **cognizant agency for audit responsibilities** will be designated for each nonfederal entity expending more than $50 million a year in federal awards. The cognizant agency will be the federal awarding agency that provides the predominant amount of direct funding unless the OMB specifically designates a different cognizant agency. Among the cognizant agency's responsibilities are providing technical audit advice and liaison to auditees and auditors, obtaining or conducting quality control reviews of selected audits made by nonfederal auditors, communicating to affected parties the deficiencies identified by quality control reviews (including, when necessary, referral of deficiencies to state licensing agencies and professional bodies for possible disciplinary action), and promptly communicating findings of irregularities and illegal acts to affected federal agencies and appropriate federal law enforcement agencies. Nonfederal entities expending less than $50 million in federal awards are assigned an **oversight agency.** The oversight agency is the agency that makes the predominant amount of direct funding to the nonfederal entity. An oversight agency has responsibilities similar to a designated cognizant agency, but they are less extensive.

Single Audit Quality[18]

In 2007 the Audit Committee of the President's Council on Integrity and Efficiency (PCIE) issued a report on the National Single Audit Sampling Project. The project was the outgrowth of Congressional testimony indicating that there were concerns about the quality of single audits. Given the large amount of taxpayer dollars that are provided by the federal government to states, local governments, and not-for-profit entities, it is imperative that quality audits be conducted to help ensure that monies are being spent as intended. To help assure quality audits of government funds, the project was charged with two purposes:

1. Determine the quality of single audits and establish a statistically based measure of audit quality.
2. Recommend changes in single audit requirements, standards, and procedures to improve the quality of single audits.

To add to the validity of the findings, a statistical sample was randomly selected from audits submitted between April 1, 2003, and March 3, 2004. Results of the statistical analysis led researchers to conclude that 48.6 percent of the single audits were of acceptable quality. Another 16.0 percent were of limited reliability (i.e., there were significant deficiencies), while 35.5 percent of the single audits were unacceptable (i.e., there were material reporting errors and/or deficiencies so severe that the opinion on at least one major program could not be relied upon). The most prevalent problems discovered related to not documenting an understanding of internal controls over compliance requirements (56.5 percent), not documenting the testing of internal controls on at least some compliance requirements (61.0 percent), and not documenting compliance testing of at least some compliance requirements (59.6 percent). As can be seen, the problem areas relate directly to and are unique to the single audit—major program compliance requirements.

The project report recommended that all parties to the single audit process become involved in helping to remedy the deficiencies found. Specifically, the first recommendation is to revise and improve the single audit standards, the criteria related to the single audit, and the guidance provided to auditors. Second, a minimum training requirement needs to be established for those conducting single audits. Finally, attention needs to be given to the consequences of conducting and submitting an unacceptable single audit. The AICPA, GAO, OMB, and other agencies are in the process of addressing the recommendations made by the report.

[18] The information in this section is from the *Report on National Single Audit Sampling Project, June 2007* (Washington, DC: President's Council on Integrity and Efficiency, 2007).

IMPACT OF SOX ON GOVERNMENTS AND NOT-FOR-PROFITS

The Sarbanes-Oxley (SOX) Act of 2002, Congress's response to corporate accounting scandals of the late 1990s and early 2000s, applies to publicly held companies, their public accounting firms, and other issuers.[19] However, some states, such as California, have passed SOX-type regulations for not-for-profit organizations (NPOs), and Congress is considering increasing the reporting requirements of NPOs.

Indirectly, SOX has impacted governments and not-for-profits as the AICPA moves to align the GAAS standards with those issued by the Public Company Accounting Oversight Board (PCAOB). This alignment is reflected in the issuance of several new auditing standards since the enactment of SOX. SOX has also indirectly affected all entities by altering the funding status of the standards-setting bodies—FASB and GASB. Finally, members of not-for-profit boards of directors and elected officials frequently have business backgrounds. As a result, board members and officials are often interested in applying SOX-related practices used in business to the not-for-profits and governments they represent. Two areas where SOX can lead to improvements in government and not-for-profit governance are audit committees and internal controls.

Best Practices—Audit Committees

The SOX legislation requires audit committees of public companies, subsets of the board of directors, to (1) appoint and oversee the auditor, (2) resolve disagreements between management and its auditor, (3) establish procedures to receive complaints from employees who "blow the whistle" on those responsible for fraud, (4) ensure auditor independence, and (5) review the audit report and other written communications. A state or local government or not-for-profit organization that establishes an audit committee, at a minimum, signals to the public that the auditors report to the board that hired them, not to management.[20]

Best Practices—Internal Controls

Section 404 of SOX requires managers of publicly traded companies to accept responsibility for the effectiveness of the entity's internal control system. The act of "certifying" requires that management present a written assertion not only that they have adopted some framework for internal controls, but also that they test these controls and can document the effectiveness of the internal control system. The OMB reexamined its internal control requirements for federal agencies in light of the Sarbanes-Oxley Act of 2002 and revised OMB *Circular A–123,* "Management's Responsibility for Internal Control." This circular "provides guidance to Federal managers on improving the accountability and effectiveness of Federal programs and operations by establishing, assessing, correcting, and reporting on internal control."[21]

Managers of government and not-for-profit entities could benefit from voluntarily adopting certain requirements of the Sarbanes-Oxley Act, such as creation of an audit committee, monitoring the independence of auditors, and certification of internal controls and financial statements by the chief executive or financial officer of the entity.

[19] For more detailed information, students are directed to the Act itself (P.L. 107–204), as well as the AICPA Web site (*http://thecaq.aicpa.org/Resources/sarbanes+oxley*), and the Public Company Accounting Oversight Board (PCAOB) Web site (*www.pcaobus.org*).

[20] The AICPA produced a *Government Audit Committee Toolkit* to provide guidance for governments in establishing and working with audit committees, available at *www.aicpa.org.*

[21] OMB *Circular A–123 revised,* "Management's Responsibility for Internal Control" (Washington, DC: OMB), December 21, 2004, effective for fiscal year 2006.

Key Terms

Attestation engagements, *502*
Audit findings, *516*
Cognizant agency for audit responsibilities, *516*
Compliance audit, *511*
Engagement letter, *499*
Financial audits, *502*
Generally accepted auditing standards (GAAS), *494*
Generally accepted government auditing standards (GAGAS), *501*
Major programs, *512*
Material weakness, *516*
Materiality, *500*
Nonaudit work, *505*
Opinion units, *500*
Oversight agency, *517*
Performance audits, *502*
Program-specific audit, *508*
Questioned cost, *516*
Risk-based approach, *512*
Significant deficiency, *516*
Single audit, *507*

Selected References

American Institute of Certified Public Accountants. Audit and Accounting Guide. *State and Local Governments.* New York: AICPA, 2008.

———. Audit Guide. *Government Auditing Standards and Circular A–133 Audits.* New York: AICPA, 2008.

Comptroller General of the United States. *Government Auditing Standards.* Washington, DC: Superintendent of Documents, U.S. Government Printing Office, 2007.

Office of Management and Budget. *Circular A–133,* "Audits of States, Local Governments, and Nonprofit Organizations." Washington, DC: Superintendent of Documents, U.S. Government Printing Office, 2003.

———. *Circular A–133, Compliance Supplement.* Washington, DC: Superintendent of Documents, U.S. Government Printing Office, March 2008.

President's Council on Integrity and Efficiency, Audit Committee. *Report on National Single Audit Sampling Project.* Washington, DC: Superintendent of Documents, U.S. Government Printing Office, June 2007.

Questions

12–1. What are the three levels of audit to which a government or not-for-profit entity may be subject? Who is responsible for setting the standards or requirements for each of the three levels identified?

12–2. What is an opinion unit and of what significance is an opinion unit to the auditor?

12–3. A new board member for the Fire Protection District (a special purpose government) was reviewing the audit report for the district and noted that, although the district received an unqualified opinion, the audit report was longer than the one received by the corporation for which he worked. Assuming that the district received only an AICPA GAAS audit, explain for the board member why the district audit report is longer than the corporate audit report.

12–4. Define GAGAS, and describe how GAGAS differ from GAAS.

12–5. What are the major types of auditor services described in the Government Accountability Office's *Government Auditing Standards* (yellow book), and how do they differ?

12–6. The director of a not-for-profit organization was overheard saying that government auditing standards (GAGAS) were developed by the federal government to ensure that local governments were spending federal funds appropriately. Therefore, her organization was not concerned with government auditing standards since the organization was only subject to a "normal" (GAAS) audit. Explain why you agree or disagree with the director.

12–7. How is an OMB *Circular A-133* audit related to a GAGAS audit? How is an OMB *Circular A-133* audit different from a GAGAS audit?

12–8. Explain how federal award programs are selected for audit under the risk-based approach.

12–9. What is the National Single Audit Sampling Project and why is it important?

12–10. What are the benefits of having an audit committee?

Cases

12–1 Audit Risk. Your firm recently signed a letter of engagement to audit CitCo, the local city and county government. Over your morning cup of coffee, you open the local newspaper and read the following:

Police are investigating how two computer servers belonging to CitCo ended up next to the commercial trash compactor of a local restaurant. The servers' property tags helped police trace them to the CitCo tax collector's office. Bob Bogus, director of the tax collector's office, said that his office had recently relinquished the servers to the property management office because the tax collector's office had purchased new servers. Ima Teller, spokesperson for the property management office, was unable to confirm whether her office had received the computer servers. It is unknown what data, such as citizen tax records and social security numbers, were on the servers at the time they were found, or whether another CitCo office was using the servers at the time of the theft. A spokesperson for the Chief Financial Officer indicated that office policy is to erase confidential data from the drives before relinquishing or disposing of servers. The investigation is ongoing.

Required

Discuss how the above information would affect the assessment and work your office does on the audit for CitCo. Include in your discussion any special considerations that may result if the audit is conducted under GAGAS.

12–2 Single Audit. *Background.* Mountain Lake Mental Health Affiliates, a non-governmental not-for-profit organization, has contacted Bill Wise, CPA, about conducting an annual audit for its first year of operations. The governing board wishes to obtain an audit of the financial statements and, having received favorable information about Mr. Wise's ability to conduct such audits, has decided not to issue a request for proposals from other audit firms. Cybil Civic, president of the board, heard from a friend associated with a similar organization that $5,000 is an appropriate price for such an audit and has offered Mr. Wise the audit for that price. Although Mr. Wise agrees that $5,000 would be reasonable for a typical financial statement audit of an organization of Mountain Lake's type and size, he refuses to contract for the audit at that price until he is able to estimate the extent of audit work that would be involved.

Facts. In discussions with Mountain Lake's controller, Mr. Wise obtains the following information about the organization for the year just ended:

1. Mountain Lake received a $200,000 grant from the City of Mountain Lake, of which 50 percent was stated as being from federal sources. Of this

amount, $150,000 was expended during the year, equally from federal and nonfederal sources.

2. Unrestricted gifts of $50,000 were received from private donors; $40,000 was spent during the year.
3. The organization received $300,000 from Medicare for mental health services rendered during the year.
4. A building owned by the U.S. Department of Health and Human Services is occupied by Mountain Lake for rent of $1 per year. The fair value of the rental has been appraised at $30,001.
5. Mountain Lake carried out a program with the Federal Bureau of Prisons to provide alcohol and drug abuse counseling services for prisoners at a nearby federal prison. Services are provided on a "units of service" reimbursement basis. Each unit of service is reimbursed at the rate of $100 and the contract provides for maximum reimbursement of $400,000. Actual units of service for the year were 4,400. Direct costs incurred for these services amounted to $250,000 in total.

Required

a. Based on the foregoing facts, is Mountain Lake Mental Health Affiliates required to have a single audit? Explain your answer.

b. Should Mr. Wise accept the audit engagement for a $5,000 fee? Why or why not?

c. Would Mr. Wise be considered independent according to *Government Auditing Standards* if he also prepares routine tax filings for the organization? Why or why not?

(*Note:* The authors are indebted to James Brown, a partner with BKD, LLP in Springfield, Missouri, for providing the example on which Case 12–2 is based.)

12–3 GAAS, GAGAS, and the Single Audit. A city has approached you concerning the audit of its 2011 financial statements. State law requires the city to have an audit and submit the audited financial report to the state. New elections at the beginning of the fiscal year resulted in a change in the administration of the city. Your firm and the audit firm that conducted the prior year's audit have been asked by the city to submit bids for the current year's audit. Since the new city administration is quite inexperienced, it has not provided you with a formal Request for Proposal (RFP). Therefore, you have the prior year's audit and financial reports, and little more information than the following for fiscal year 2011.

1. The new city controller is a certified public accountant who worked for a firm that specialized in government audits.
2. For the last three years the city has received a clean audit opinion.
3. The city is receiving grants and other aid from state and federal sources totaling $3,977,000.
4. Total budgeted revenues for the year were $20,980,000 and expenditures were $25,749,000. Approximately 48 percent of revenues are from property taxes.
5. The city has six governmental funds, three enterprise funds, and an agency fund.
6. It is five months until the end of fiscal year 2011.

Required

Prior to determining whether you would be interested in submitting a bid for the audit, you decide to use the information you have to draw up a list of factors that would affect the cost of your bid. Provide your list and explain why each item would affect your fee bid.

12–4 Single Audit, Internet Case. A not-for-profit organization has hired you to conduct an audit. The audit has been requested by the organization's board of directors. A mission of the organization is to provide for the education of children in the economically distressed area of the city. In fulfilling its mission, the organization operates a Head Start program, a K-3 elementary school, and an after-school kids program. To help fund its mission, the organization receives funds from several sources, including federal programs. The federal programs and the amount of funding expended from each program for the fiscal year are as follows:

Program	Funds Expended
Title I	$260,000
National School Lunch Program	24,320
National School Breakfast Program	8,829
Head Start	520,000
Early Reading First	55,000
Child and Adult Care Food Program	28,112

Required

It may be helpful to use the Catalog of Federal Domestic Assistance (CFDA) Web site (*www.cfda.gov*) and the OMB *Circular A-133 Compliance Supplement* (*www.whitehouse.gov/OMB/circulars*) to answer the following questions.

a. What federal departments are sponsoring the programs listed?

b. OMB allows "cluster programs" to be considered as a single program when conducting the risk-based approach to selecting programs for audits under the single audit. Of the programs listed, which (if any) are part of the same cluster?

c. Based on size alone, are there any Type A programs or other programs that would be exempt from audit under the risk-based approach?

d. Based on size alone, which programs would you select for audit and why?

e. If the not-for-profit has received an unqualified opinion in each of the last two years and the Head Start program was selected for audit in both years, would the programs you select for audit change? If not, why not? If so, what programs would you select and why?

f. Reading the objectives of the programs identified, you will notice a common underlying objective. Since the ability to obtain funds depends on meeting this underlying objective, it should be considered a major compliance issue for the auditor. What is the objective? What compliance item is particularly affected by this underlying objective? (*Hint:* There are 14 compliance items listed in *Circular A-133;* access Parts 2, 3, and 4 to help with this answer.)

12–5 Internet Case. The City of Belleview receives pass-through funds from the state's Department of Housing to assist in administering the federally funded Supportive Housing Program for the elderly. At the request of the state's

Department of Housing, the city has engaged you to perform a program-specific audit of its expenditures of federal awards for the Supportive Housing Program for the elderly. Although you are unfamiliar with the particular program, you have extensive experience in governmental auditing and have audited many other federal programs.

Required

Utilize the Internet to answer the following questions about this program.

a. What is the Catalog of Federal Domestic Assistance (CFDA) number for this program? (*Note:* The relevant Web site is *http://www.cfda.gov.*)

b. Describe the program's purpose and its eligible beneficiaries.

c. Which of the 14 compliance items (A through N) listed in the *Circular A–133 Compliance Supplement* are applicable to auditing compliance for this program? (*Hint:* Access Parts, 2, 3, and 4 of the *Compliance Supplement* at *http://www.whitehouse.gov/OMB/circulars.*)

12–6 Single Audit Quality. In this chapter, information was provided on the report of the National Single Audit Sampling project. The project was the outgrowth of concern over the quality of single audits. Based on the project's results, it would appear that there is reason for concern over the quality of audits, given that 35.5 percent of the audits were considered unacceptable. The most commonly cited problems were:

1. Failure to document an understanding of internal controls over compliance requirements.
2. Failure to document testing of internal controls on at least some compliance requirements.
3. Failure to document compliance testing on at least some compliance requirements.

Required

a. Discuss factors you believe may be contributing to the problems related to single audit quality.

b. The project report recommends that all affected parties be involved in the solution. Discuss how you think each of the following three parties could help improve single audit quality.

(1) The Office of Management and Budget (OMB).
(2) The auditee.
(3) The audit profession.

12–7 Audit Committees. The city council members of Laurel City are considering establishing an audit committee as a subset of the council. Several members work for commercial businesses that have recently established such committees in response to the Sarbanes-Oxley Act of 2002. They have asked your advice as a partner in the public accounting firm that audits the city's annual financial statements. They are especially interested in whether the benefits of such a committee outweigh any costs to establishing one.

Required

a. What resources are available to the city to help it use this audit committee efficiently and effectively?

b. Provide a short report to the council that lists the benefits and costs of establishing an audit committee. Explain what qualifications would be expected of council members who sit on this committee and the tasks in which they would be engaged.

Exercises and Problems

12–1 Examine the CAFR. Using the CAFR you obtained for Exercise 1–1, answer the following questions:

a. Auditors. Was this CAFR audited by external certified public accountants (CPAs) or by state or local governmental auditors?

b. Audit Opinion. What type of opinion did this entity receive? If it was qualified, what reason was given? Was an opinion expressed on the supplementary information as well as the basic financial statements?

c. Auditing Standards. Did the auditor use generally accepted auditing standards (GAAS), generally accepted government auditing standards (GAS or GAGAS), or both?

d. Paragraphs. How many paragraphs are there in the auditor's report? Can you identify the introductory, scope, opinion, and any explanatory paragraphs?

e. Single Audit. Can you tell whether this entity was required to have a single audit? If so, are the required single audit reports contained within the cover of the CAFR that you are examining? If the entity does receive federal financial assistance but you see no mention of the single audit in the auditor's report, where do you expect that single audit report to be?

12–2 Multiple Choice. Choose the best answer.

1. Which of the following activities would always indicate that an auditor's independence has been impaired?
   a. Providing advice on establishing an internal control system.
   b. Posting adjusting journal entries into the client's accounting records.
   c. Providing benchmarking studies to be used by management.
   d. Preparing draft financial statements based on management's trial balance.

2. An adverse opinion is most likely to be rendered when:
   a. Fund financial statements are presented along with government-wide statements in the basic financial statements.
   b. There is a violation of generally accepted accounting principles that does not cause the basic financial statements to be materially misstated.
   c. The auditor is not independent of the government being audited.
   d. The government issues a stand-alone consolidated report.

3. Which of the following is a true statement about the relationship between generally accepted government auditing standards (GAGAS) and generally accepted auditing standards (GAAS)?
   a. GAGAS and GAAS provide standards for financial audits, attestation engagements, and performance audits.
   b. GAGAS encompass GAAS and supplement certain GAAS.
   c. Single audits must be performed using GAGAS and GAAS.
   d. GAGAS are promulgated by the Government Accountability Office and GAAS are promulgated by the Government Accounting Standards Board.

4. One of the overarching principles in the GAO's standard on *independence* is:
   a. Auditors should never provide payroll or tax services to audit clients.
   b. Auditors should document an understanding with the audited entity regarding the objectives, scope of work, and product of the nonaudit service.
   c. Auditors should not perform management functions or make management decisions.
   d. Auditors should not perform nonaudit work for audit clients.

5. The goal of a performance audit is to:
   a. Provide information to improve program operations and facilitate decision making by management.
   b. Determine whether government programs and activities are meeting their stated goals and objectives.
   c. Determine whether governments are performing their duties in the most economic and efficient manner possible.
   d. All of the above.

6. Under the GASB reporting model, materiality is determined:
   a. For opinion units.
   b. At the government-wide level.
   c. At the fund level.
   d. For governmental and business-type activities and the aggregate discretely presented component units only.

7. Single audits performed pursuant to OMB *Circular A–133:*
   a. Apply to all entities that receive $500,000 or more in a fiscal year.
   b. Result in the same number of reports as a generally accepted government auditing standards (GAGAS or yellow book) audit.
   c. Must be performed in accordance with generally accepted government auditing standards.
   d. Result in a reporting package that is submitted to the Office of Management and Budget.

8. The single audit concept:
   a. Dates back to 1979 and was codified in 1984 and amended in 1996.
   b. Requires that all audits of entities receiving federal financial assistance be audited by GAO auditors.
   c. Means that each federal grant that an entity receives is audited as a single unit.
   d. Requires that all large grants and half of the small grants be audited without regard to risk.

9. OMB *Circular A–133* and the related *Compliance Supplement* provide guidance for auditors in:
   a. Conducting a financial audit of governmental entities.
   b. Conducting financial audits, attestation engagements, and performance audits of governmental entities.
   c. Conducting a single audit of a government that has expended more than $500,000 in federal financial assistance.
   d. None of the above.

10. The auditor's responsibility for required supplementary information (RSI) is:
    a. The same as with the basic financial statements.
    b. To perform certain limited procedures to ensure that RSI is fairly presented in relation to the audited financial statements.
    c. The same as for all information in the financial section of a comprehensive annual financial report.
    d. To render an opinion as to the fairness of the RSI and whether it conforms to generally accepted accounting principles.

12–3 Continuing Professional Education. As part of your audit firm's quality control policies, it maintains a record of continuing profession education (CPE) taken by professional staff members. Following is information on some of the classes, sessions, workshops, and conferences that the auditors of your firm have attended in the past year.

______1. A session dealing with the source of current revenues and three-year projections of revenues for the state.
______2. A conference on estate planning.
______3. A workshop on "Factors to Consider in Determining the Actuarial Value of Pensions".
______4. A session on the risk assessment suite (*SAS* 104-111).
______5. A session on the role of audit committees and how to form an effective audit committee.
______6. An online "Principles of Accounting" course.
______7. A workshop on "Federal Grant Administration".
______8. A session on GASB's derivative standard.
______9. A conference on "Helping Individuals Meet Their Long-Term Financial Goals" (a financial planning conference).
_____10. A session on problems associated with implementing an enterprise resource planning system (ERP).

Required

It is your responsibility to determine whether the classes, sessions, workshops, and conferences attended by the auditors could be used to meet the GAGAS requirement that auditors earn 24 hours of CPE in government-related areas every two years. In the space to the left of each item, indicate whether the item qualifies (Q) or does not quality (DNQ).

12–4 Single Audit. Quad-States Community Service Agency expended federal awards during the most recent fiscal year in the following amounts for the programs shown:

Program 1	$5,789,000	Program 6	$389,000
Program 2	350,000	Program 7	191,000
Program 3	1,069,000	Program 8	94,000
Program 4	5,963,000	Program 9	726,000
Program 5	212,000	Program 10	434,000

Additional information indicates that Programs 4 and 10 were audited as major programs in each of the two preceding fiscal years, with no audit findings reported.

Required

a. Which programs would be considered Type A programs and why? Type B programs?

b. Based on the information provided, which programs would you select for audit and why?

c. If you found out that a new manager with no previous experience was now in charge of Program 4, would your answer to part *b* change? If so how?

12–5 GAO Independence Standards. Indicate which of the following activities performed by an auditor for a governmental client are (*a*) allowable, (*b*) permitted if safeguards are in place, or (*c*) prohibited.

1. Serving as an adviser on the building subcommittee for the county.
2. Preparing a $4,000,000 indirect cost proposal.
3. Providing all payroll services for the client.
4. Converting the financial records from the cash basis to GAAP basis.
5. Providing advice on setting up the chart of accounts in a commercially purchased software package.
6. Maintaining the depreciation schedules for which management has determined the useful lives and residual values.
7. Providing appraisals and valuation of property held by the government.
8. Assessing program outcomes for three government programs.
9. Providing internal audit services.
10. Preparing draft financial statements from the client's adjusted trial balance.

12–6 Unqualified Audit Report. Following is the unqualified audit report for the City of Sand Key.

The Honorable Mayor
Members of the City Commission and
City Manager

City of Sand Key

We have audited the accompanying financial statements of the City of Sand Key (the City) as of and for the year ended September 30, 2011. These financial statements are the responsibility of the City's management. Our responsibility is to express an opinion on these financial statements based on our audit.

We conducted our audit in accordance with generally accepted auditing standards and the standards applicable to financial audits contained in the Government Audit Standards, issued by the Comptroller General of the United States. Those standards require that we plan and perform the audit to obtain a reasonable assurance about whether the financial statements are free of material misstatement. An audit includes examining, on a test basis, evidence supporting the amounts and disclosures in the financial statements. An audit also includes assessing the accounting principles used and significant estimates made by management, as well as evaluating the overall financial statement presentation. We believe that our audit provides a reasonable basis for our opinion.

In our opinion, the financial statements referred to above present fairly, in all material respects, the financial position of the City as of September 30, 2011, and the respective changes in financial position thereof for the year then ended in conformity with accounting principles generally accepted in the United States of America.

Our audit was conducted for the purpose of forming an opinion on the financial statements taken as a whole. The information presented in the Statistical Section is presented for the purpose of additional analysis and is not a required part of the basic financial statements. Such information has not been subjected to the auditing procedures applied in the audit of the basic financial statements and, accordingly, we express no opinion on it.

Steele and Steele, P.A.
January 12, 2012

Required

Based on your knowledge of audit reporting requirements for government audits, you have determined that the audit report issued by Steele and Steele does not meet requirements. Provide a list of changes that would need to be made to the audit report to bring it into conformance with audit report requirements.

Chapter Thirteen

Budgeting and Performance Measurement

Learning Objectives

After studying this chapter, you should be able to:

1. Explain the objectives of budgeting.
2. Describe methods of integrating planning, budgeting, and performance measurement.
3. Explain the differences among various budgeting approaches.
4. Describe the budgeting process for a state or local government.
5. Identify the procedures involved in specific types of budgets, including appropriation budgets, revenue budgets, cash budgets, and capital budgets.
6. Describe managerial tools used to improve performance and communicate the results of the budgeting process.
7. Describe the budget and cost issues in grant accounting.

Budgeting is an important part of a manager's planning and control responsibilities. In governments, legislators authorize managers to raise and expend resources to provide services to citizens by approving an annual budget. Legislation at the state and local government level also specifies what sanctions will be imposed if managers overspend appropriations. Chapter 3 described how fund accounting and the modified accrual basis of accounting are used to demonstrate legal compliance with the annual budget. Many state and local governments also budget resources in order to improve the quality of public services delivered to citizens. Chapter 4 illustrated how the cost of governmental activities by function is measured using accrual accounting and reported in the government-wide statement of activities. This cost information is critical in developing budgets and assessing government financial performance, as seen in Chapter 10. As described in Chapter 11, the federal government has incorporated budgeting for results (or performance or outcomes) for federal agencies in required performance and accountability reports (PARs).

Not-for-profit organizations are somewhat different in that their budgets are not legal documents reflecting plans for spending appropriations from other governments or from tax and other revenues. However, a not-for-profit entity is accountable to its resource providers, such as donors and grantors, and the Government that granted the organization its existence and tax-exempt status. The budgeting approaches described in this chapter are equally useful to not-for-profit managers, although the budgets of these organizations are most likely reviewed and approved by governing boards but not posted on public Web sites. Budgeting and performance measures in the nonprofit sector will be discussed in more detail in Chapter 15. In this chapter, the role of the budget as a communication and management tool in government and not-for-profit entities is explored.

OBJECTIVES OF BUDGETING

Budgeting may be the most important responsibility of a government legislator or manager. Citizens expect government leaders to prioritize community program and service goals, authorize the expenditure of resources to meet those goals, comply with laws over spending appropriations, improve the quality of services in the near term, and demonstrate stewardship for public funds in the long term. The budget embodies management's plans to meet public expectations. Robert Bland describes the complex set of budgeting objectives in this way:

> The budget document and its preparation and adoption express the basic political values of a government. Budgets reflect the compromises negotiated in the contentious process of budget adoption. They guide public administrators, defining government's economic and political role in a community and sanctioning, as well as limiting, administrative action. Budgets not only represent plans for the future, they also mold that future by the policies they contain . . . The budget is a tool for holding administrators accountable for performance expectations.[1]

A good budget should, at a minimum, have majority "buy-in" by all affected parties. Logistically, a budget needs to be enacted before the fiscal year begins and be integrated with the financial accounting system so that actual results can be compared to budgeted plans at regular intervals. Integrating the budget into the accounting system allows management to oversee individual unit performance and react quickly to variances between actual results and budgeted plans. Legislators can then expect an early warning should unexpected problems arise.

The legalistic view is that a budget is a plan of financial operation embodying an estimate of proposed expenditures for a given period of time and the proposed means of financing them. In a much more general sense, budgets may be regarded as devices to aid management in operating an organization more effectively. Governments build budgets to demonstrate compliance with laws and to communicate performance effectiveness. These two views of a budget are examined next.

Compliance with Laws

Budgetary principles were established by the National Committee on Governmental Accounting in the 1968 *Governmental Accounting, Auditing and Financial Reporting* guide (referred to as GAAFR or the "Blue Book"). The GASB budgeting, budgetary control, and budgetary reporting principle provides that:

a. An annual budget(s) should be adopted by every government.
b. The accounting system should provide the basis for appropriate budgetary control.

[1] Robert L. Bland, *A Budgeting Guide for Local Government* (Washington, DC: International City/County Management Association, 2007), p. 3.

c. Budgetary comparison schedules should be presented as required supplementary information for the General Fund and for each major special revenue fund that has a legally adopted annual budget. The budgetary comparison schedule should present both (*a*) the original and (*b*) the final appropriated budgets for the reporting period as well as (*c*) actual inflows, outflows, and balances, stated on the government's budgetary basis.[2]

The budgeting principle is directly related to the accounting and reporting capabilities principle, which specifies that a governmental accounting system must make it possible for a government (1) to prepare financial reports in conformity with generally accepted accounting principles (GAAP) and (2) to determine and demonstrate compliance with finance-related legal provisions. Chapter 3 is concerned with budgets as legal documents binding on the actions of administrators and with budgetary accounting needed to make it possible to prepare budgetary reports to demonstrate legal compliance. It is also concerned with budgetary comparisons required for the General Fund and major special revenue funds in conformity with the GASB reporting model.

Communicate Performance Effectiveness

Budgeting is also an important tool for achieving efficient and effective management of resources. Because of public demand for improved government performance, innovative performance measurement systems are being developed at all levels of government. Since 1997, federal agencies have submitted strategic plans to Congress, developed annual performance plans, reported annually on the results achieved in those performance plans, and integrated *accountability reports* with the Government Performance and Results Act (GPRA) performance reports.[3]

Several groups of professionals provide guidance for governments that want to communicate quality information to stakeholders about the budget and performance measures. In 1998, the National Advisory Council on State and Local Budgeting, a cooperative of organizations, issued a document that describes nearly 60 *best* budget practices covering the planning, development, adoption, and execution phases of the budget process.[4] This document recognizes that budgeting is one of the most important activities undertaken by state and local governments in allocating scarce resources to programs and services.

The Government Finance Officers Association (GFOA) reviews budgets and presents distinguished awards to those governments that not only meet the goals described in traditional government principles, but go beyond that in their presentation of the budget as a policy document, financial plan, operations guide, and communications device. For a quarter of a century, the GFOA's award program has recognized state and local governments that use the budgeting process to its fullest potential in demonstrating accountability for the use of public funds and improving the quality of government services provided. Illustration 13–1 lists the criteria the GFOA uses in its review of budget documents. Note that some of the criteria are mandatory (i.e., documents "shall" include an item) in order for a government to receive the distinguished budget presentation award. Voluntary applications for this award increased from 113 in 1984, the year the program was initiated, to 1,200 in

[2] Governmental Accounting Standards Board, *Codification of Governmental Accounting and Financial Reporting Standards,* as of June 30, 2008 (Norwalk, CT: GASB, 2008), Sec. 1100.111, 2400.

[3] See Chapter 11 for more discussion of the GPRA and performance reporting.

[4] See *www.gfoa.org,* "Recommended Practices."

ILLUSTRATION 13–1 Criteria for the GFOA's Distinguished Budget Presentation Award Program

The Budget as a Policy Document

- A coherent statement of entity-wide long-term financial policies.
- A coherent statement of entity-wide, nonfinancial goals and objectives.
- The entity's short-term initiatives that guide the development of the budget.
- Includes a budget message that articulates priorities and issues for the budget.*
- Clearly stated goals and objectives of organizational units.

The Budget as a Financial Plan

- Describes all funds that are subject to appropriation.
- Presents a summary of major revenues and expenditures and other financing sources/uses.*
- Summarizes revenues/other financing sources and expenditures/other financing uses for the prior, current, and proposed budget year.*
- Describes major revenue sources, underlying assumptions, and significant trends.*
- Includes projected changes in fund balances for appropriated governmental funds.*
- Includes budgeted capital expenditures.
- Describes significant nonroutine capital expenditures.
- Includes financial data on current debt obligations and legal debt limits.*
- Explains the basis of budgeting for all funds (e.g., cash, modified accrual, or other).*

The Budget as an Operations Guide

- Describes activities, services, or functions carried out by organizational units.*
- Provides objective measures of progress toward accomplishing goals and objectives.*
- Includes on organization chart for the entire organization.
- Provides a schedule of personnel or position counts for prior, current, and budgeted years.*

The Budget as a Communications Device

- Provides summary information on significant budgetary issues, trends, and resource choices.*
- Explains the effect, if any, of other planning processes upon the budget.
- Describes the process for preparing, reviewing, adopting, and amending the budget.*
- Uses charts and graphs to highlight financial and statistical information with narratives.*
- Provides narrative, tables, schedules, or matrices to show the relationship between functional units, major funds, and nonmajor funds in the aggregate.
- Includes a table of contents to make it easy to locate information in the document.*
- Includes a glossary for any terminology that is not readily understood.
- Includes statistical and supplemental data that describe the organization and community.
- Formatted in such a way as to enhance its understanding by the average reader.

*Indicates a mandatory criterion to receive the distinguished budget presentation award; that is, the budget "shall" include the item listed.

Source: Condensed from "Detailed Criteria Location Guide," available at *www.gfoa.org/downloads/BudgetDetailedCriteriaLocationGuide.pdf.*

2007. About 90 percent of the applicants have received the award, and many of the unsuccessful applicants have received confidential reviewer suggestions that permitted them to subsequently qualify for the award.[5]

Implications of Government Reporting for Public Budgeting

The budget has always played a role in general purpose external financial reports through the required budget-to-actual comparison statements for those funds that have a legally approved budget. At a minimum, the budget-to-actual statements are required supplementary information. However, GASB does allow governments to choose whether to present the budgetary comparison schedule after the notes to the financial statements as required supplementary information (RSI) or as a more traditional statement that compares budgeted to actual operating performance within the basic financial statements.

The addition of accrual-based government-wide statements in *GASBS 34* has a number of implications for budgeting as discussed in an article by Dr. James Chan. They include (1) emphasizing the long-term perspective in budgeting, (2) stressing budgets as a tool for demonstrating public accountability, (3) considering the government as a whole, (4) activating the debate about accrual accounting, (5) raising the need to project financial position, and (6) critically appraising budget practices.[6] It remains to be seen whether government-wide financial reporting will result in government financial managers supplying budgets for operational performance of the government as a whole and whether the public and other financial statement users will demand such budgets.

INTEGRATION OF PLANNING, BUDGETING, AND PERFORMANCE MEASUREMENT

The concept of "managing for results" has taken hold in many governments as a commonsense way to focus the activities of employees toward the needs that the government is trying to address. These goals might include safe highways, healthy children, plentiful employment opportunities, and a culturally diverse citizenry. When planning, budgeting, and performance measurement are related, good performance is rewarded, and consequences exist for substandard performance, then public employees' behaviors will change. Highway patrol officers who are judged on accident rates for their highway beat, rather than on their output of tickets written or miles covered, have changed their behavior, writing tickets strategically to slow down drivers on the most hazardous stretches of roads, and reporting potholes that cause accidents to maintenance departments more often.[7]

Illustration 13–2 is a graphic representation of the interrelations among the processes of policy setting through a strategic plan, budgeting the resources needed to deliver services that accomplish the goals of the plan, monitoring operations and reporting on performance, and assessing performance as it relates to the strategic

[5] See "Annual Report—Distinguished Budget Presentation Awards Program" of the GFOA, available at *www.gfoa.org/services/awards.shtml*.

[6] James L. Chan, "The Implications of GASB *Statement No. 34* for Public Budgeting," *Public Budgeting & Finance* (Fall 2001), p. 80.

[7] James Fountain, Wilson Campbell, Terry Patton, Paul Epstein, and Mandi Cohn, *Special Report: Reporting Performance Information: Suggested Criteria for Effective Communication* (Norwalk, CT: GASB), August 2003, p. 13.

ILLUSTRATION 13–2 Managing for Results Process

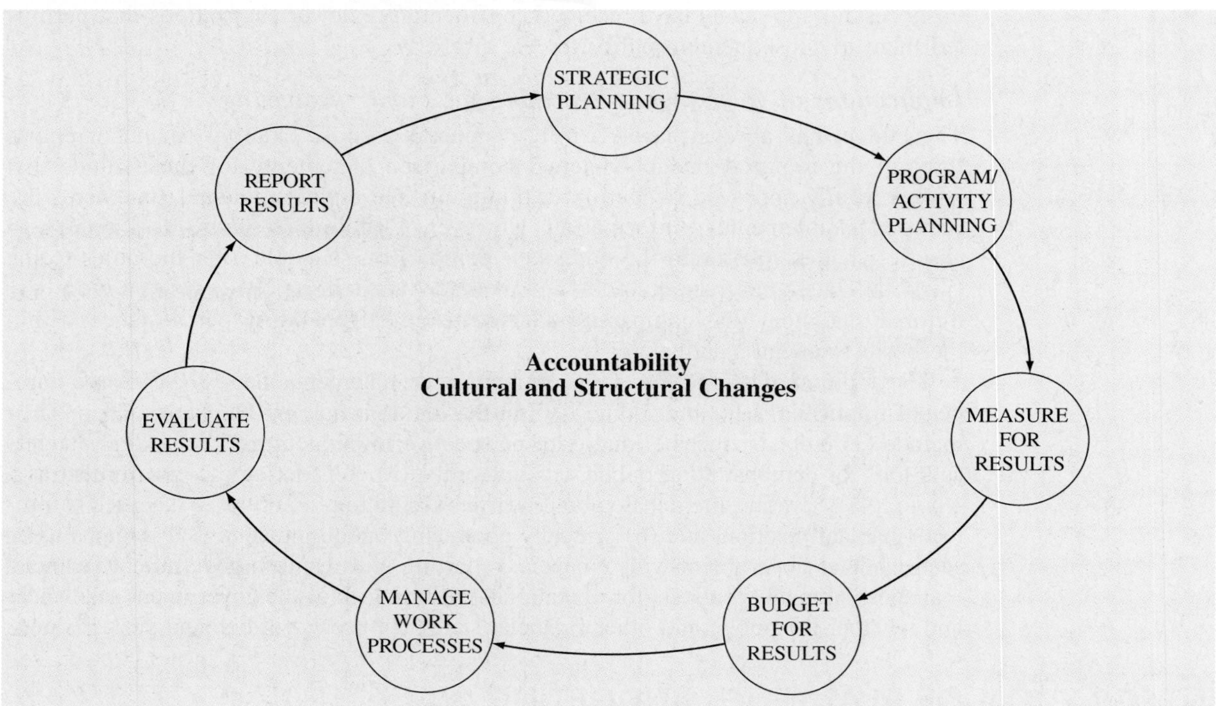

Source: Adapted from James Fountain, Wilson Campbell, Terry Patton, Paul Epstein, and Mandi Cohn, *Special Report: Reporting Performance Information: Suggested Criteria for Effective Communication* (Norwalk, CT: GASB), August 2003, p. 14.

plan. Once a government identifies the public needs it is trying to address, then it needs to develop an overall strategic plan for addressing those needs; devise policies, programs, and services to meet those needs; implement budgeting, accounting, and management systems that support the strategic plan; and track cost and performance data that allow the government to gauge its progress in reaching its goals.[8]

Certain components of a results-oriented performance measurement system are critical for effective integration with budgeting, decision making, and communication to citizens. For example, clear identification of outputs (e.g., number of lane-miles of road repaired, or the number of serious crimes reported) and outcomes (e.g., percentage of lane-miles of road maintained in excellent, good, or fair condition; or the percentage of residents rating their neighborhood as safe or very safe) is essential. These performance indicators should be transparent; that is, they should be revealed in department budget requests, the executive budget itself, operating documents, and annual reports. Government managers should report that they use performance measures over time (e.g., from budget development through the audit) and in a variety of activities (e.g., strategic planning, contract management, and personnel decisions). Leadership support and explicit, written management-for-results policies are also crucial for an integrated performance measurement system to be effective.[9]

[8] Ibid.

[9] Julia Melkers and Katherine Willoughby, "Models of Performance-Measurement Use in Local Goverments: Understanding Budgeting, Communication, and Lasting Effects," *Public Administration Review*, Vol. 65, no.2, March/April 2005.

BUDGETING APPROACHES

As the budget process has evolved from an accounting function with a control orientation to an executive tool to improve the management of operations and the assignment of priorities to public problems, so have the basic formats of budgets evolved. Governments use a variety of budgeting approaches in developing annual budgets. These budget approaches exhibit the perspective of the staff or area within the government with budget responsibilities. For example, the accounting department often focuses on line-item budgeting, the finance department can be associated with performance budgeting, an independent budget office may be concerned with program budgeting, and the chief executive office may focus on entrepreneurial budgeting.[10] These budget approaches are briefly discussed next.

Line-item Budgeting

A traditional approach to budgeting and the one that is most likely present in some portion of every government's budget today is line-item, or object-of-expenditure, budgeting. A simplistic approach to budgeting line-items is called **incremental budgeting.** In essence, an incremental budget is derived from the current year's budget by adding amounts expected to be required by line items. Examples include salary and wage increases, increases in the cost of supplies and equipment, decreases that would result from shrinkage in the scale of operations forced by pressures such as spending limitations mandated by the electorate (for example, California's Proposition 13 in 1978), and cuts in capital equipment purchases. Incremental budgeting focuses largely on controlling resource inputs and typically uses the *line-item* budget format in which the focus is on departmental expenditures for specified purposes or objects, such as personnel, supplies, equipment, and travel. The weakness of the incremental approach is that it focuses on government operations in terms of dollars spent in the prior year rather than what was accomplished by that spending.

In the 1970s, an approach to wed the legally required budget process to a rational process of allocating scarce resources among alternative uses was introduced: **zero-based budgeting,** or ZBB. As the name indicates, the basic concept of ZBB is that the very existence of each activity as well as the amounts of resources requested to be allocated to each activity must be justified each year, which is a move toward program budgeting. However, ZBB is described here as an example of line-item budgeting because it uses readily available objects of expenditures.

The ZBB approach has several advantages: It is easy to understand, uses readily available line-item data, and involves staff from the government that is going to incur the cost. Typically, staff prepare three types of budgets—one representing basic service needs, another reflecting the cost of delivering services at the current level, and a third that captures the cost of extending services to meet new demand. It is hard to argue with the basic premise of annually re-evaluating the value that a program or department adds to total government operations. However, ZBB is not widely used because it is time-intensive, and managers become skeptical of the approach when marginally successful programs continue to be funded to some degree.[11]

[10] Bland, *A Budgeting Guide for Local Government*, p. 18.

[11] Ibid., p. 20.

Performance Budgeting

The evolution of the concept of a budget from "an estimate of proposed expenditures and the proposed means of financing them" to an "operating plan" was a natural accompaniment to the development of the concept of professional management. In public administration, as in business administration, the concept of professionalism demanded that administrators or managers attempt to put the scarce resources of qualified personnel and money to the best possible uses. The legal requirement that administrators of governments submit appropriation requests to the legislative bodies in budget format provided a basis for adapting required budgetary estimates of proposed expenditures to broader management use. The legislative appropriation process has traditionally required administrators to justify budget requests. A logical justification of proposed expenditures is to relate the proposed expenditures of each governmental subdivision to the programs and activities to be accomplished by that subdivision during the budget period. The type of budgeting in which input of resources is related to output of services is sometimes known as **performance budgeting.** Performance budgeting is linked conceptually with *performance auditing* as defined in Chapter 12 of this text. Performance budgeting is a plan for relating resource inputs to the efficient production of outputs; performance auditing is the subsequent evaluation to determine that resources were in fact used efficiently and effectively in accordance with the plan.

Performance budgeting historically focused on the relation between inputs and outputs of each organizational unit rather than programs. The use of performance budgeting in governments received significant impetus from work the first Hoover Commission did for the federal government. Its report, presented to the Congress in 1949, led to the adoption in the federal government of budgets then known as *cost-based budgets* or *cost budgets.* The use of these designations suggests that a government desiring to use performance budgeting must have an accrual accounting system rather than a cash accounting system in order to routinely ascertain the costs of programs and activities. The recommendations of the second Hoover Commission led to the statutory requirement of both accrual accounting and cost-based budgeting for agencies of the executive branch of the federal government. Federal statutes also require the synchronization of budgetary and accounting classifications and the coordination of these with the organizational structure of the agencies. Entities that use performance budgeting consider it a financial management tool and not a subfield of accounting.[12]

Program Budgeting

Program budgeting is a term sometimes used synonymously with performance budgeting. However, the term is more generally used to refer to a budget format that discloses the full costs of programs or functions without regard to the number of organizational units that might be involved in performing the various aspects of the program or functions. Program budgets address the fundamental issues of whether programs should exist at all and how to allocate scarce resources among competing programs. The integration of planning, programming, budgeting, and accounting has considerable appeal to persons concerned with public administration because an integrated system should, logically, provide legislators and administrators with much better information for the management of governmental resources than has been provided by separate systems. In the late 1960s, there was

[12] Ibid., p. 21.

a concentrated effort to introduce a **planning-programming-budgeting system,** called PPBS, throughout the executive branch of the federal government, and to adapt the concept to state and local governments and other complex organizations. The advantage that program and PPBS budgeting offer compared to performance budgeting is the ability to address fundamental policy questions about whether the government or not-for-profit is better off operating certain programs.

As state and local governments have experimented with program budgeting, they have developed stand-alone budget offices to analyze the costs and benefits of programs that cut across department or division lines. These budget offices report directly to the highest level administrator, so budgeting is neither a subfield of accounting nor a responsibility of the finance department.[13]

Entrepreneurial Budgeting

Another evolution of budgeting that removes it even further from the purview of the accounting department is **entrepreneurial budgeting,** an approach that positions budgeting so that it is the responsibility of the highest level person in the government, most often the chief executive officer. In this approach, strategic plans, incentives, and accountability are merged into the budget and communicated to citizens as a package. The balanced scorecard, discussed later in this chapter, is a tool that links financial and nonfinancial indicators of financing, customer satisfaction, internal operations, and the learning and growth of employees in a clear graphic that can be shared with councils and governing boards and posted on the government's Web site. Budgeting for outcomes is a different type of entrepreneurial budgeting that articulates government-wide goals, such as "improve community safety" or "improve environmental health," and all departments or units cast their budget requests in terms of advancing those goals.[14] An advantage of integrating strategic planning into a government's daily activities is that units (or departments or programs) remain focused on outcomes that improve the government's services to its citizens. A disadvantage is that market-based concepts, such as competition among units for scarce resources, are often seen as being at odds in a nonbusiness entity. Managers may find that the department and program personnel continue to operate in a traditional legalistic budget environment.

It is important to realize that a government does not choose a single budgeting approach to the exclusion of the others. An entity-wide budget may be constructed from program or department budgets using different approaches.[15] Over time, changes in leadership, technological advances in data availability, and other circumstances will also result in variations on budget approaches for a government.

BUDGETING PROCESS IN A STATE OR LOCAL GOVERNMENT

Budgeting Governmental Appropriations

Appropriations budgets are an administration's requests for authorization to incur liabilities for goods, services, and facilities for specified purposes. The preparation of appropriations budgets for any one year is related to the administration's budget of revenues since the revenues budget is the plan for financing the proposed

[13] Ibid.

[14] Ibid., pp. 22–23.

[15] More details about these specific budgeting techniques and their application to industries, such as service, not-for-profit, higher education, and health care, can be found in William R. Lalli, ed., *Handbook of Budgeting,* 5th ed. (New York: John Wiley & Sons, 2003, with 2006 Supplement).

appropriations. If the program or performance budget concept is followed, appropriations budgets are prepared for each existing and continuing work program or activity of each governmental subdivision; for each program authorized or required by action of past legislative bodies but not yet made operative; and for each new program the administration intends to submit to the legislative body for approval.

In budgeting, each ongoing program should be subjected to rigorous management scrutiny at budget preparation time to make sure there is a valid reason for continuing the program at all: This is the fundamental idea of zero-based budgeting. If the program should be continued, management must decide whether the prior allocation of resources to the program is optimal or whether changes should be made in the assignment of personnel, equipment, space, and money. In a well-managed government, the same sort of review is given to each continuing program. The mere fact that the program was authorized by a past legislative body does not mean that the administration may shirk its duty to recommend discontinuance of a program that has ceased to serve a real need. If, in the judgment of the administration, the program should be continued, the appropriate level of activity and the appropriate allocation of resources must be determined; this determination takes far more political courage and management skill than the common practice of simply extrapolating the trend of historical activity and historical cost.

If the administration is convinced that a program should be continued and the prior allocation of resources is reasonable, the preparation of the appropriations budget is delegated to the persons in charge of the program. In the case of a new program, the administration states the objectives of the program and sets general guidelines for the operation of the program and then delegates budget preparation to individuals who are expected to be in charge of the program when legislative authorization and appropriations are secured. State laws or local ordinances typically require that certain steps be followed in the budgeting process and may prescribe dates by which each step must be completed. These requirements are referred to as the **budget calendar.** A budget calendar (or cycle) for Eugene, Oregon, is presented in Illustration 13–3. The budget calendar could span a 10-month period. Many governments are implementing multiyear budgeting to enhance long-range planning, decrease staff time, and improve program evaluation.[16] In these cases, the budget calendar should span the two-year period (or appropriate time frame) and refer to dates when mid-period forms and reports are due.

To ensure that administrative policies are actually used in budget preparation and that the budget calendar and other legal requirements are met, it is customary to designate someone in the central administrative office as budget officer. In addition to the responsibilities enumerated, the **budget officer** is responsible for providing technical assistance to the operating personnel who prepare the budgets. The technical assistance provided may include clerical assistance with budget computations as well as the maintenance of files for each program containing (1) documents citing the legal authorization and directives, (2) relevant administrative policies, (3) historical cost and workload data, (4) specific factors affecting program costs and workloads, and (5) sources of information to be used in projecting trends.

Budgets prepared by departmental administrators should be reviewed by the central administration before submission to the legislative branch because the total

[16] Andrea Jackson, "Taking the Plunge: The Conversion to Multi-Year Budgeting," *Government Finance Review* (August 2002), p. 24.

ILLUSTRATION 13–3 City of Eugene Budget Cycle for FY09

October–December 2007

Executive Managers review and approve FY09 budget rates and budget development timeline. City Council and Budget Committee provide guidance on the new "budgeting for outcomes" budget development process. Vision Teams are formed and departments prepare service offers for consideration by the Vision Teams. Fund forecasts are updated. FY07 Financial Audit is completed. ⓘSupplemental budget #1, amending the FY08 budget for unanticipated revenues and expenditures and audited beginning working capital, is advertised and presented to the City Council for review and approval.

January–March 2008

ⓘBudget Committee reviews the General Fund Six-Year Forecast, Multi-Year Financial Plan, other fund forecasts and issues, and the Capital Improvement Program (biennially). ⓘPublic Workshop to review budgeting for outcomes process and provide feedback on Council visions. Executive Managers review departmental service offers and vision team recommendations, make funding recommendations. Funds are balanced and reviewed. The Proposed Budget Document is prepared for print. ⓘSupplemental Budget #2, amending the FY08 Budget for unanticipated revenues and expenditures, is advertised and presented to the City Council for review and approval.

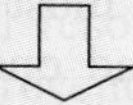

April–May 2008

City Manager presents the Budget Message to the Budget Committee. ⓘBudget Committee Reviews the Proposed Budget during several work sessions, conducts a public hearing, and prepares their recommendation to the City Council for the City of Eugene and the Urban Renewal Agency. Public comment is received during the first 30-minutes of most work sessions.

June 2008

ⓘCity Council conducts public hearing and adopts the annual budgets for the City and the Urban Renewal Agency. The approved FY09 Budget is moved to the General Ledger. ⓘSupplemental Budget #3, amending the FY08 Budget for unanticipated revenues and expenditures, is advertised and presented to the City Council for review and approval.

July 2008

Staff prepares and publishes the FY09 Annual Budget. Tax levies are certified with the county assessor by July 15. FY08 financial audit begins.

ⓘIndicates public input opportunity.

Source: City of Eugene, OR, FY09 Proposed Budget, p. B.16, available at *www.eugene-or.gov.*

of departmental requests frequently exceeds the total of estimated revenues, and it is necessary to trim the requests in some manner. Central review may also be necessary to make sure that enough is being spent on certain programs. Good financial management of the taxpayers' dollars is a process of trying to determine the optimum dollar input to achieve the desired service output, not a process of minimizing input. Even though the appropriations budget is a legally prescribed document, the administration should not lose sight of its managerial usefulness.

Budgeting Capital Expenditures

Accounting principles for business enterprises and for proprietary funds of governments require the cost of assets expected to benefit more than one period to be treated as a balance sheet item rather than as a charge against revenues of the period. No such distinction exists for governmental fund types. Expenditures for long-lived assets to be used in the general operations of a government are treated in the appropriations process in the same manner as are expenditures for salaries, wages, benefits, materials, supplies, and services to be consumed during the accounting period. Accounting control over long-lived assets used in governmental activities is established at the government-wide level.

Effective financial management requires the plans for any one year to be consistent with intermediate-and long-range plans. Governmental projects such as the construction or improvement of streets; construction of bridges and buildings; acquisition of land for recreational use, parking lots, and future building sites; and urban renewal may require a consistent application of effort over a span of years. Consequently, administrators need to present to the legislative branch and to the public a multiyear capital improvements program, as well as the budget for revenues, operating expenditures, and capital outlays requested for the forthcoming year.

Effective financial management also requires nonfinancial information such as physical measures of capital assets, their service condition, and their estimated replacement cost. Nonfinancial information of these types is useful for purposes of forecasting future asset repair and replacement schedules, repair and replacement costs, and financing requirements, and is required for certain eligible infrastructure assets.

Budgeting Cash Receipts

Revenues and expenditures budgets would best be prepared on the same basis as the accounts and financial reports: modified accrual, in the case of governmental funds—particularly the General Fund and special revenue funds. Although it is highly desirable for persons concerned with the financial management of governments (or any other organization) to foresee the effects of operating plans and capital improvement plans on receivables, payables, inventories, and facilities, it is absolutely necessary to foresee the effects on cash. An organization must have sufficient cash to pay employees, suppliers, and creditors the amounts due at the times due, or it risks labor troubles, an unsatisfactory credit rating, and consequent difficulties in maintaining its capacity to render services at levels acceptable to its residents. An organization that maintains cash balances in excess of needs fails to earn interest on temporary investments; therefore, it is raising more revenues than would otherwise be needed or failing to offer services.

In Chapter 4 it was noted that in a typical government, cash receipts from major sources of revenues of general and special revenue funds are concentrated in a few months of each fiscal year, whereas cash disbursements tend to be approximately level month by month. Under the heading "Tax Anticipation Notes Payable" in Chapter 4, reference is made to cash forecasting done by the treasurer of the Town of Brighton in order to determine the amount of **tax anticipation notes** to be issued. The cash forecasting method illustrated in that chapter is quite crude but often reasonably effective if done by experienced persons. Sophisticated cash budgeting methods used in well-managed governments require additional data, such as historical records of monthly collections from each revenue source, including percentage of billings where applicable. In addition to the historical record of collections, the budget files should contain analyses of the factors affecting the collections from each source so that adjustments to historical patterns may be made, if needed, for the budget year.

Property taxes are often the largest recurring cash receipt in a government; however, all other expected cash receipts must be included in the cash budget. More difficult to project are self-assessed taxes, such as income taxes; nonrecurring receipts, such as those from the sale of assets; and income earned on **sweep accounts,** arrangements by which a bank automatically "sweeps" cash that exceeds the target balance into short-term cash investments.

Managing cash flows involves accelerating the flow of cash receipts. This can be done by using techniques such as earlier billing, prompt payment discounts, and late payment penalties. Lockbox systems, electronic fund transfers, and accepting credit cards for payment all help to reduce the time between when the payment is converted to cash and the government has the use of the funds.[19]

Budgeting Cash Disbursements

Except for modified accrual provisions regarding expenditures of debt service funds, the expenditures of all other governmental funds (and of all proprietary funds) are to be recognized and budgeted on the accrual basis for governments that follow generally accepted accounting principles (GAAP) for budgeting. Therefore, the conversion of the approved appropriations budget into a cash disbursements budget involves the knowledge of personnel policies, purchasing policies, and operating policies and plans, which should govern the timing of expenditures of appropriations and the consequent payment of liabilities. Information as to current and previous typical time intervals between the ordering of goods and contractual services, their receipt, and the related disbursements should be available from the appropriation expenditures ledgers and cash disbursement records. In the case of salaries and wages of governmental employees, the cash disbursements budget for each month is affected by the number of paydays that fall in the month rather than the number of working days in the month.

Monthly cash receipts budgets are prepared for all sources of revenues of each fund, and cash disbursements budgets are prepared for all organizational units. Management should then match the two in order to determine when and for how long cash balances will rise to unnecessarily high levels or fall to levels below those prudent management would require. Note that the preceding sentence concerns cash receipts and disbursements of all funds of a government, not of a single fund. There is no reason for bank accounts and fund cash accounts to agree, except in total. Effective cash planning and control suggests that *all* cash be put under control of the treasurer of the government.

Managing cash flows also involves minimizing or decelerating cash disbursements. Techniques that can be used include pooling cash balances into a central concentration account to permit better monitoring of payables and balances, using zero-balance accounts to reduce the amount of idle cash, and implementing expenditure controls to track and brake unnecessary early payments. Standard payment periods that are as long apart as possible can reduce processing costs and increase the predictability of payment amounts.[20]

As shown in Illustration 13–5, cash receipts for the Town of Brighton are highest in April, May, and November, presumably when taxes are collected. Disbursements are

[19] William R. Voorhees and Jeongwoo Kim, "Cash Flow Forecasting: Principles," *Encyclopedia of Public Administration and Public Policy*, Taylor and Francis, 2008, p. 285.

[20] Ibid.

7. Productivity and quality measures and standards that are meaningful to the government.
8. Written vision or mission statements that are linked directly to team-established targets or goals.[21]

The elements of TQM are obviously consistent with those of the program budgeting approaches (particularly PPBS) previously discussed. Thus governments that have implemented one of those budgeting approaches may find it less costly to implement a TQM structure. On the other hand, few governments possess adequate data on customer satisfaction. Moreover, the traditional emphases of government on line-item budgeting, rigid personnel classifications, restrictive procurement regulations, and so on, tend to reduce management autonomy and thus may be inconsistent with the need under TQM to empower employees to be "entrepreneurial" in improving processes and meeting customer demand. It should also be noted that the objective of TQM is not necessarily to reduce cost but to increase "value for the dollar." Insofar as a TQM program successfully adds value, it has the potential to improve the public perception of government in addition to improving service delivery.

Element 7 from the preceding list of TQM elements requires that the government develop meaningful standards for and measures of performance in terms of productivity and quality. In the government and not-for-profit context, the analogous performance terms more typically used are *efficiency* and *effectiveness,* the former relating efforts (resource inputs) to outputs of a service process and the latter relating efforts to outcomes or the results produced by service.

Customer Relationship Management

Customer relationship management (CRM) systems, developed in the 1990s for businesses, have great potential for governments as they provide services to their customers—citizens. CRM systems create an integrated view of a customer to coordinate services from all channels of the organization with the intent to improve the long-term relationship the organization has with its customer.

At first glance, it might seem that the high cost of CRM technology that would allow citizens to interact with their government electronically for public services, and the traditional government culture where information resides in departments or agencies that often do not share data, would prove to be insurmountable obstacles for governments in establishing a CRM system. However, a 2001 Accenture study found that government managers are realistic about the challenges and interested and eager to put CRM principles to work as they strive to become more effective and efficient at providing public services.[22] Examples some governments are using include obtaining licenses and making tax payments through a government Web site. Choosing to apply CRM to strategically selected narrow projects with modest goals may be the most realistic way for governments to realize benefits from this innovative business tool.[23]

[21] Adapted from James J. Kline, "Total Quality Management in Local Government," *Government Finance Review,* August 1992, p. 7. See also International City/County Management Association, MIS Report: Performance Measurement for Accountability and Service Improvement, September 1997.

[22] Accenture, *Customer Relationship Management—A Blueprint for Government,* November 2001, pp. 6–13; see *www.accenture.com.*

[23] Darrell K. Rigby and Dianne Ledingham, "CRM Done Right," *Harvard Business Review,* November 2004, p. 2.

Service Efforts and Accomplishments (SEA)

The Governmental Accounting Standards Board's (GASB) accountability reporting objective includes reporting on the efficient and effective use of resources. GASB *Codification* Appendix B, *Concepts Statement 1,* par. 77c. states:

> Financial reporting should provide information to assist users in assessing the service efforts, costs, and accomplishments of the governmental entity.

The lack of a bottom-line measure of performance for a governmental entity, such as "profit" for a business, means that *nonfinancial* measures of **service efforts and accomplishments (SEA)** and related costs are necessary for informed decision making by citizens, elected officials, appointed officials, investors and creditors, and others having an interest in the government's performance. The GASB has sponsored and conducted extensive research on SEA measures for several service areas, including, among others, elementary and secondary education, higher education, fire departments, police departments, and hospitals, as well as public health, mass transit, road maintenance, and sanitation collection and disposal organizations.

GASB identifies three broad categories of SEA measures: (1) measures of service efforts, (2) measures of service accomplishments, and (3) measures that relate efforts to accomplishments.[24] Measures of service efforts, or **input measures,** relate to the amount of financial and nonfinancial resources (such as money and materials) used in a program or process.[25] Measures of service accomplishments are of two types: outputs and outcomes. **Output measures** are quantity measures that reflect either the quantity of a service provided, such as the number of lane-miles of road repaired, or the quantity of service provided that meets a specified quality requirement, such as the number of lane-miles of road repaired to a specified minimum condition. **Outcome measures** gauge accomplishments, or the results of services provided, such as the percentage of lane-miles of road in excellent, good, or fair condition. Such measures are particularly useful when compared with established objectives or norms or with results from previous years. Finally, measures that relate efforts to accomplishments are essential to assessing efficiency and effectiveness. **Efficiency measures** relate the quantity or cost of resources used to unit of output (e.g., cost per lane-mile of road repaired). Measures that relate resource costs to outcomes are useful in evaluating how effectively service objectives are being met and at what cost (e.g., the cost per lane-mile of road maintained in excellent, good, or fair condition). Additional quantitative and narrative explanation may be necessary to help users fully assess the entity's performance. **Effectiveness measures** relate costs to outcomes; for example, cost for each percentage reduction in traffic accidents or percentage increase in citizens who report feeling safe in the neighborhood.

Illustration 13–6 shows performance indicators for the fire department in Bellevue, Washington. The input measures (not shown) are the quantities and dollar amounts of resources used in providing fire suppression services. The output and outcome indicators collectively indicate service accomplishments where outputs are workload (such as number of fire service requests and responses) and outcomes indicate the effectiveness of activities in achieving desired objectives (such as the percentage of fires confined to room of orgin). The city presents trend information and

[24] Governmental Accounting Standards Board, *Concepts Statement No. 2,* "Service Efforts and Accomplishments Reporting" (Norwalk, CT: April 1994).

[25] The discussion of SEA measures in this paragraph is paraphrased from the discussion in *Concepts Statement No. 2,* pars. 50–53.

ILLUSTRATION 13–6 Performance Indicators for the City of Bellevue, Washington, Fire Department

Annual Scorecard of Fire Department Performance Measures

Key Performance Measures	2005 Actual	2006 Actual	2007 Actual	2007 Target	2007 Target Met or Exceeded
Program: Fire Suppression and Rescue/Emergency Medical Services					**Budget: $30,257,000**
Effectiveness					
1. Percent of fires confined to room of origin	90%	88%	**82%**	85%	
2. Cardiac arrest survival rate	50%	63%	**64%**	45%	✓
3. Emergency Response Time—Benchmark					
a. % of incidents where Call Processing time is 1 minute or less	64%	65%	**68%**	90%	
b. % of incidents where Turnout time is 1 minute or less	19%	28%	**30%**	90%	
c. % of incidents where Travel time is 4 minutes or less	68%	71%	**72%**	90%	
d. % of incidents where Total Emergency Response time is 6 minutes or less	51%	59%	**61%**	90%	
Workload					
4*a.* Number of Fire services requests/unit responses generated	3,550/ 9,194	4,302/ 10,038	**3,352/ 8,356**	4,000/ 10,000	
4*b.* Number of EMS services requests/unit responses generated	13,156/ 19,525	14,002/ 20,976	**13,525/ 19,976**	13,000/ 19,500	
5. Number of annual Fire Company fire inspections	5,215	4,840	**4,917**	4,000	
6. Number of annual individual training hours	37,274	26,419	**38,762**	32,000	
Program: Fire Prevention					**Budget: $1,909,000**
Efficiency					
7. Percent of Annual Fire and Life Safety Inspections completed	93%	100%	**100%**	100%	✓
Effectiveness					
8. Fire Loss in Inspected Buildings ($000)	$469	$236	**$1,801**	$500	
Program: Emergency Preparedness					**Budget: $1,112,000**
Effectiveness					
9. Emergency Preparedness Response hands-on-skilled training programs	11	4	**8**	25	
Workload					
10. Emergency Preparedness audiences reached—general education	4,124	2,946	**2,911**	4,000	

Source: City of Bellevue 2007 Performance Measures. See *www.ci.bellevue.wa.us/pdf/finance/2007_Annual_Performance_Report.0110i.arc.pdf,* p. 62.

target values to assist users in the analysis of effectiveness and efficiency measures. Presumably, some of these measures correspond to standard measures used nationally by fire-fighting agencies, further increasing the comparability value of this service efforts and accomplishments (SEA) report.

In 2003, GASB published 16 suggested criteria for use in preparing reports on service efforts and accomplishment measures presented in three broad categories. Illustration 13–7 shows these measures and categories. It is important to note that these are criteria that suggest characteristics of performance reports and measures that are expected to lead to their usefulness by users. There is no suggestion as to what values of these measures would be considered good or bad.

ILLUSTRATION 13–7 Suggested Criteria and Purpose for Reporting Performance Information

Category I: The External Report on Performance Information

1. *Purpose and scope:* To inform users of the intent of the report and to identify the programs and services that are included.
2. *Statement of major goals and objectives:* To provide users with the goals and objectives and their source so users can determine how they were established.
3. *Involvement in establishing goals and objectives:* To help users identify who established the goals and objectives and whether that includes those responsible for achieving results.
4. *Multiple levels of reporting:* To allow specific users to find the appropriate level of detail performance information for their needs.
5. *Analysis of results and challenges:* To present performance results with a discussion of challenges facing the organization.
6. *Focus on key measures:* To ensure that reports provide users with enough (and not too much) information to develop their own conclusions about the organization's performance.
7. *Reliable information:* To assist users in assessing the credibility of the reported performance information.

Category II: What Performance Information to Report

8. *Relevant measures of results:* To ensure that performance measures reflect the degree to which those goals and objectives have been accomplished.
9. *Resources used and efficiency:* To facilitate an assessment of resources used and the efficiency, cost-effectiveness, and economy of programs and services.
10. *Citizen and customer perceptions:* To ensure that a more complete view of the results of programs and services results than is captured in other "objective" measures of outputs and outcomes.
11. *Comparisons for assessing performance:* To provide a clear frame of reference for assessing the performance of the organization, its programs, and its services.
12. *Factors affecting results:* To help users understand the factors that might have an effect on performance, including relevant conditions in the state, region, or community.
13. *Aggregation and disaggregation of information:* To provide performance information that is not misleading and is relevant to users with different interests and needs.
14. *Consistency:* To allow users to compare an organization's performance from period to period and to better understand changes in measures and reasons why measures changed.

Category III: Communication of Performance Information

15. *Easy to find, access, and understand:* To ensure that a broad group of potential users can access, understand, and use various forms of performance reports to reach conclusions.
16. *Regular and timely reporting:* To ensure that organizations report performance information on a regular and timely basis to be useful in decision making.

Source: Paul Epstein, James Fountain, Wilson Campbell, Terry Patton, and Kimberly Keaton, *Government Service Efforts and Accomplishment Performance Reports: A Guide to Understanding* (Norwalk, CT: GASB) July 2005, App. A, pp. 37–41.

Since these suggested criteria were published, many state and local governments have experimented with issuing performance information and reports. In July 2005, the GASB issued *Government Service Efforts and Accomplishments Performance Reports: A Guide to Understanding* that provides users and preparers with a basis for understanding and using an SEA performance report. Included in this user guide are several excerpts from performance reports issued by local governments, including one from the Prince William County, Virginia's *FY 2004 Service Efforts and Accomplishments Report.* Illustration 13–8 presents an updated graphic of what Prince William County calls its Results Oriented Government System. As can be seen, this county builds its system on the characteristics of the accountability model presented earlier in this chapter in Illustration 13–2. Because of its efforts in the area

ILLUSTRATION 13–8 Prince William County (PWC), Virginia, Results Oriented Government System

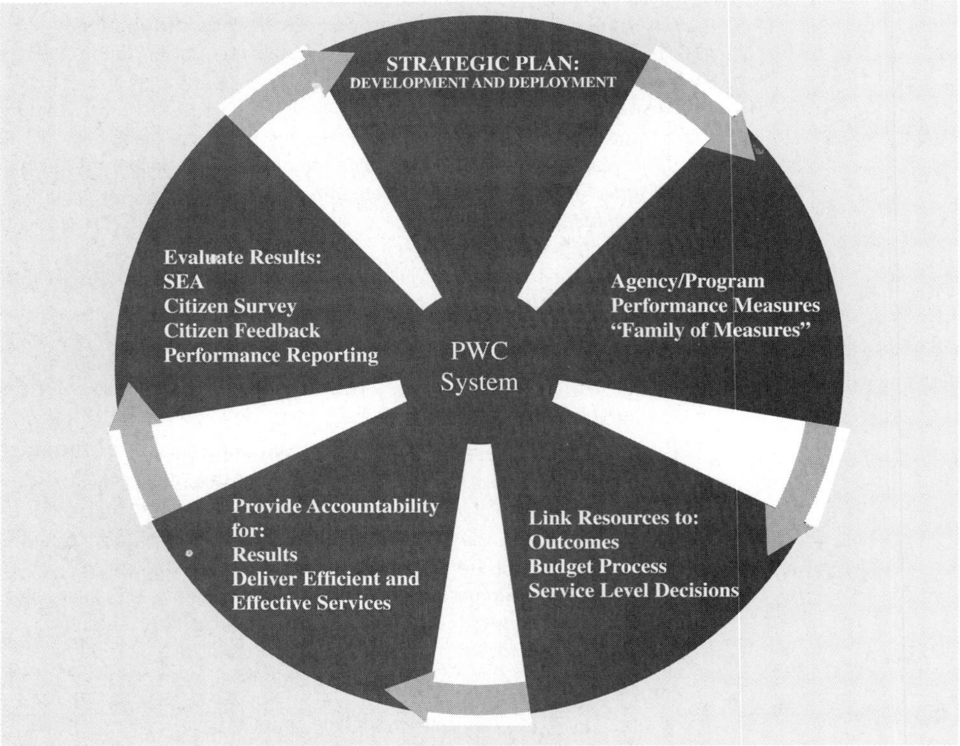

Source: Prince William County, VA, *FY 2006 Service Efforts & Accomplishments Report,* p. u. See *www.pwcgov.org/accountability.*

of SEA, Prince William County has been the recipient of the Association of Government Accountants's (AGA) Certificate for Excellence in Service Efforts and Accomplishments Reporting each year.

Activity-based Costing

Budgeting for performance requires sophisticated cost accounting systems to determine the full cost of programs or functions. Better managed state and local governments are therefore actively developing improved cost accounting systems. One costing approach being implemented by some governments is activity-based costing (ABC). **Activity-based costing (ABC)** was developed for use by manufacturing companies when it became apparent that traditional cost accounting systems were producing distorted product costs. Thus, some products that were thought to be profitable were, on closer inspection, found to be unprofitable, and vice versa. Two Harvard University professors, Robin Cooper and Robert S. Kaplan, made convincing arguments that typical cost accounting systems often understate profits on high-volume products and overstate profits on low-volume specialty items.[26] This problem is attributable, in part, to greater product diversity, shorter product life cycles, the shift in production technology from labor to automation, more diverse distribution

[26] Robin Cooper and Robert S. Kaplan, "Measure Costs Right: Make the Right Decisions," *Harvard Business Review,* September–October 1988, pp. 96–103.

channels, and greater quality demands, all of which are driven by the need to more effectively compete in the global marketplace. The net effect of these trends (which are also applicable to government, at least to some extent) is to create a larger infrastructure of "production support" activities and, thus, to shift costs from direct cost categories to indirect cost, or overhead, categories. Because a larger proportion of these costs is allocated to products, product cost distortions become a larger problem and may result in poor product decisions.

ABC essentially attempts to determine the cost of specific process-related activities, the "drivers" of those costs (e.g., labor-hours, machine-hours, or units of material), and the consumption of cost drivers in producing outputs of goods or services. Emphasis is placed on tracing the specific activities performed to specific outputs of goods or services rather than on allocating average costs to units of output as is done in conventional cost accounting systems.

Determining the amount of each activity that is consumed in each product or service utilizes materials usage records, observation, and timekeeping systems, but is often augmented with estimates obtained through employee interviews and other means. The cost of designing a system that totally eliminates the need for overhead allocation is likely to be prohibitive. If allocation of "residual" unassigned costs is not potentially distortive, it may be more cost effective to focus ABC design on major activities and cost drivers and to allocate any remaining costs on an appropriate basis.

An article by Bridget Anderson explains the objectives of ABC in a governmental environment as follows:

> The objectives of ABC are to preserve, at a minimum, the present quality and availability of core services but to acknowledge that some of the forces for greater expenditures have not been controlled. It seeks to reduce the costs of service outcomes by:
> - reducing the number of service units through program redesign,
> - finding lower cost alternatives,
> - making volume increases dependent on cost reductions, and
> - understanding and controlling the delivery/program design interaction.[27]

A simplified diagram of an ABC cost model used by the City of Grahamston for its revenue collection process for personal property taxes on vehicles is shown in Illustration 13–9. This program involves four activities that identify vehicle owners who need to renew their auto registration: (1) sending a mailing by which owners can automatically renew their auto registration, (2) mailing information requests to car dealers and repair shops, (3) having officers put flyers on cars during a night patrol, and (4) placing ads in the local paper and at community events. The resources required and cost drivers associated with each of these activities are also presented in Illustration 13–9.

A quick review of the total cost per registration by activity (shown in Illustration 13–10) suggests that night surveys are the most expensive way to identify residents who have not registered their vehicles and, therefore, represent the greatest potential for cost-cutting measures. The costs associated with this activity appear to be all variable; that is, if surveys are conducted less frequently, costs would be reduced proportionately. Advertising is the least expensive method of collecting revenue for personal property taxes on vehicles. Although it is tempting to shift resources to increase this activity, the advertising campaign will likely not reach all residents contacted through

[27] Bridget M. Anderson, "Using Activity-Based Costing for Efficiency and Quality," *Government Finance Review,* June 1993, pp. 7–9.

ILLUSTRATION 13–9 Identification of Components in an Activity-based Costing System: Grahamston Revenue Collection Program

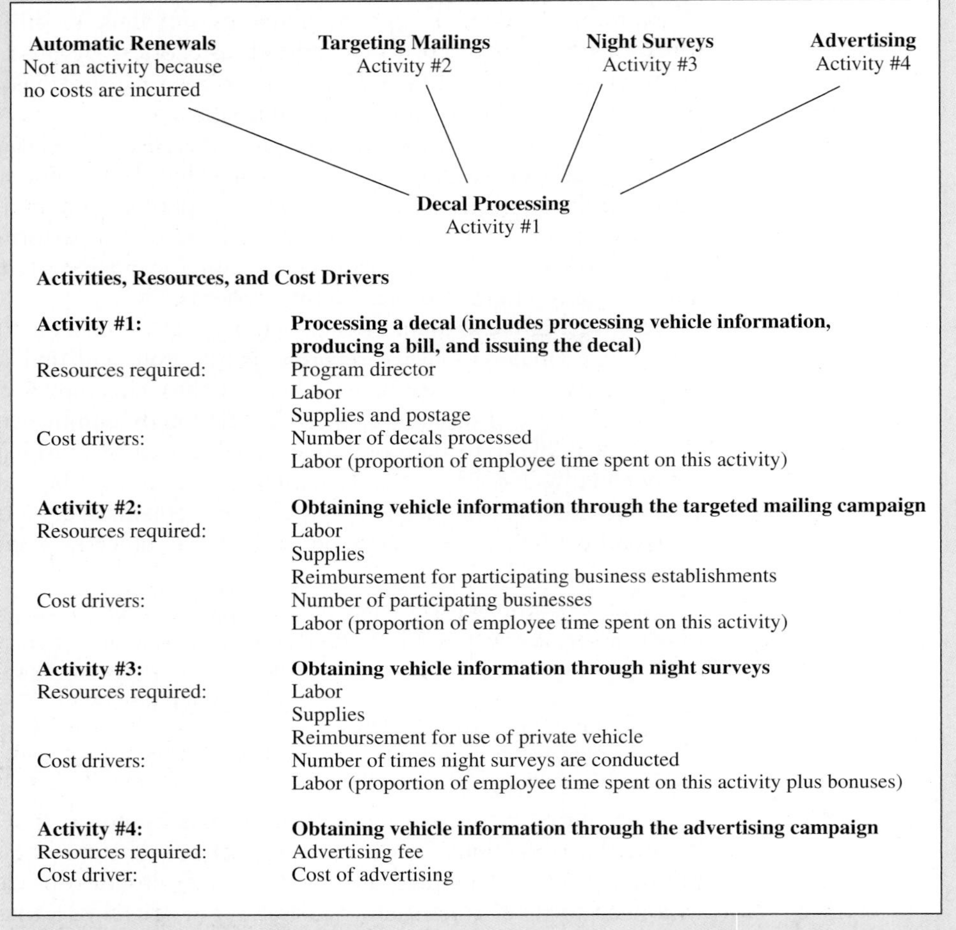

Automatic Renewals
Not an activity because
no costs are incurred
Targeting Mailings
Activity #2
Night Surveys
Activity #3
Advertising
Activity #4
Decal Processing
Activity #1
Activities, Resources, and Cost Drivers
Activity #1: **Processing a decal (includes processing vehicle information, producing a bill, and issuing the decal)**
Resources required: Program director
Labor
Supplies and postage
Cost drivers: Number of decals processed
Labor (proportion of employee time spent on this activity)
Activity #2: **Obtaining vehicle information through the targeted mailing campaign**
Resources required: Labor
Supplies
Reimbursement for participating business establishments
Cost drivers: Number of participating businesses
Labor (proportion of employee time spent on this activity)
Activity #3: **Obtaining vehicle information through night surveys**
Resources required: Labor
Supplies
Reimbursement for use of private vehicle
Cost drivers: Number of times night surveys are conducted
Labor (proportion of employee time spent on this activity plus bonuses)
Activity #4: **Obtaining vehicle information through the advertising campaign**
Resources required: Advertising fee
Cost driver: Cost of advertising

Source: International City/County Management Association, Service Report: *Introduction to Activity-Based Costing,* February 1998. Reprinted with permission of ICMA.

other approaches. The targeted mailings, while twice as costly as the advertising approach, are probably effective because correspondence is sent personally addressed to the resident whose address was obtained by a participating car dealer or repair shop. Activity-based costing is a managerial tool that can enhance decision making by creating a clearer picture of the costliest activities of a service. However, ABC only supplements traditional accounting systems; it does not replace them.

Administrative Costs

A very large part of governmental expenditures are incurred for administrative services of a general nature (such as the costs of the chief executive's office, costs of accounting and auditing, and costs of boards and commissions), which are somewhat remote from the results any given subdivision is expected to accomplish. Furthermore,

ILLUSTRATION 13–10 **Cost Analysis of Revenue Collection Program**

Activity	1 Decal Processing	2 Targeted Mailings	3 Night Surveys	4 Advertising	Total
Program director	$ 40,000				$ 40,000
Labor	89,600	$19,200	$19,200		128,000
Employee bonuses for night work			6,000		6,000
Employee reimbursement for use of their personal vehicles			600		600
Supplies and postage	6,000	1,500	500		8,000
Annual advertising costs				$ 500	500
Reimbursements for participating businesses		4,800			4,800
Total annual costs	$135,600	$25,500	$26,300	$ 500	$187,900
Divided by number of decals processed as a result of this activity	15,300	2,700	1,260	540	
Equals cost per decal	$ 8.86	$9.44	$ 20.87	$0.93	
Additional cost of Activity 1		8.86	8.86	8.86	
Total cost per decal by activity	$ 8.86	$ 18.30	$ 29.73	$9.79	

Source: International City/County Management Association, Service Report: *Introduction to Activity-Based Costing,* February 1998. Reprinted with permission of ICMA.

in smaller units of government, many offices or departments perform such a variety of services that separating their costs is practically impossible under their present schemes of organization.

Given the importance and magnitude of key administrative offices, government officials should attempt to measure the efficiency and effectiveness of the activities of these offices just as they would other service activities. The primary difference is that many of these activities, such as those of the finance and legal departments for example, mainly serve customers within the government rather than the general public. Activity-based costing would seem to be a useful tool for measuring the cost of such activities. Possible activities and cost drivers for selected offices follow.

Office	Activities	Cost Drivers
Tax collector	Preparing tax bills.	Number of bills prepared.
	Collecting tax bills.	Number of bills collected.
	Preparing receipts.	Number of receipts prepared.
	Mailing receipts.	Number of receipts mailed.
	Preparing deposits.	Number of deposits prepared.
Accounting	Recording revenues.	Number of revenue transactions.
	Recording expenditures.	Number of expenditure transactions.
	Processing payroll.	Number of employees.
	Recording purchase orders.	Number of orders.
Public recorder	Recording documents.	Number of documents or number of lines.

This table is intended to be illustrative of the types of activities and cost drivers that

personnel, procurement of goods and services, and disposal of scrap or surplus materials related to the performance of a federal award. Some of the cost items are *unallowable,* including items such as alcoholic beverages, bad debt expenses, contributions and donated services, fund-raising and investment management costs, entertainment, general expenses of the state or local government (e.g., salaries of the chief executive, legislatures, and judicial department officials), and lobbying. Similar prohibitions apply to colleges and universities under the provisions of *Circular A–21.*

Direct Costs

Direct costs are those that can be identified specifically with a particular cost objective.[33] A **cost objective,** in federal terminology, is an organizational unit, function, activity, project, cost center, or pool established for the accumulation of costs. A final, or ultimate, cost objective is a specific grant, project, contract, or other activity (presumably one of interest to the federal agency that provides resources for the activity under a grant, contract, or other agreement). A cost may be direct with respect to a given function or activity but indirect with respect to the grant or other final cost objective of interest to the grantor or contractor. Typical direct costs chargeable to grant programs include compensation of employees for the time and efforts devoted specifically to the execution of grant programs; cost of materials acquired, consumed, or expended specifically for the purpose of the grant; and other items of expense incurred specifically to carry out the grant agreement. If approved by the grantor agency, equipment purchased and other capital expenditures incurred for a certain grant or other final cost objective would be considered direct costs.

Indirect Costs

Indirect costs, according to *Circular A–87,* are those (1) incurred for a common or joint purpose benefiting more than one cost objective and (2) not readily assignable to the cost objectives specifically benefited without effort disproportionate to the results achieved.[34] The term *indirect costs* applies to costs originating in the grantee department as well as to those incurred by other departments in supplying goods, services, and facilities to the grantee department. To facilitate equitable distribution of indirect expenses to the cost objectives served, it may be necessary to establish a number of "pools" of indirect cost within the grantee department. Indirect cost pools should be distributed to benefited cost objectives on bases that produce an equitable result in consideration of relative benefits derived. In certain instances, grantees may negotiate annually with the grantor a predetermined fixed rate for computing indirect costs applicable to a grant or a lump-sum allowance for indirect costs, but generally grantees must prepare a cost allocation plan that conforms with instructions issued by the U.S. Department of Health and Human Services. Cost allocation plans of local governments will be retained for audit by a designated federal agency. (Audit of federal grants is discussed in some detail in Chapter 12 of this text.)

NONFEDERAL GRANTS

States make grants to local governments, and both states and local governments make grants to not-for-profit organizations. It is important for the recipient organization to know if funds received are actually federal funds being passed through to them or nonfederal grants. If so, when the recipient entity spends these funds, the entity must consider them federal funds expended for the purpose of the Single Audit Act (described in Chapter 12).

[33] Ibid., Attachments A, E.

[34] Ibid., Attachments A, F.1.

Private foundations and community foundations also make grants to state and local governments and other not-for-profit organizations. A common grant application may be required, such as the one created by and accessible from the Council of Michigan Foundations's Web site at *www.cmif.org*. The advantage of a form agreed upon by grantors is that applicants are more likely to provide the information required in a format and with the level of detail desired, resulting in a more efficient grant process for all concerned. Grantors may not have specific cost requirements, as seen in the discussion of federal grants; however, they may explicitly deny or limit indirect cost recovery or grants for capital assets (e.g., computers or buildings). The more familiar the applicant is with the funding policies of the grantor, the more likely the organization will be successful it its bid for funds.

ACCOUNTING INFORMATION SYSTEMS

Whether funds come from federal or nonfederal sources, the recipient is expected to have an accounting information system with adequate internal controls that can deliver reliable information to compare the actual amount spent with budgeted amounts. Illustration A13–2 shows the relationship between programs and grantors and indicates some of the challenges for grantees in accounting for grants. A cost must be classified by these two dimensions, as well as by line-item (or object-of-expenditure), in order to prepare appropriate cost reports to the funding organizations. For example, an organization may receive one grant to support a single program that has no other source of funds (e.g., Program A and Grant 1), or a program may be supported by multiple sources of funds (e.g., Program B and Grants 2 and 3), or a grant may support more than one program (e.g., Programs B and C and Grant 3). A computerized accounting information system can be designed to allow reporting by grantor, by program (as is needed in a statement of functional expenses for an organization, described in Chapter 14), or by line-item. A well-structured chart of accounts is the key to reporting along multiple dimensions. Illustration A13–3 shows a chart of accounts for a not-for-profit organization that operates seven programs (e.g., Programs A through G) and receives funding from federal, state, local government, foundation, and church sources. Reports can then be generated based on the account numbering systems for revenues and expenses.

ILLUSTRATION A13–2 Relationship of Programs and Grantors in an Organization

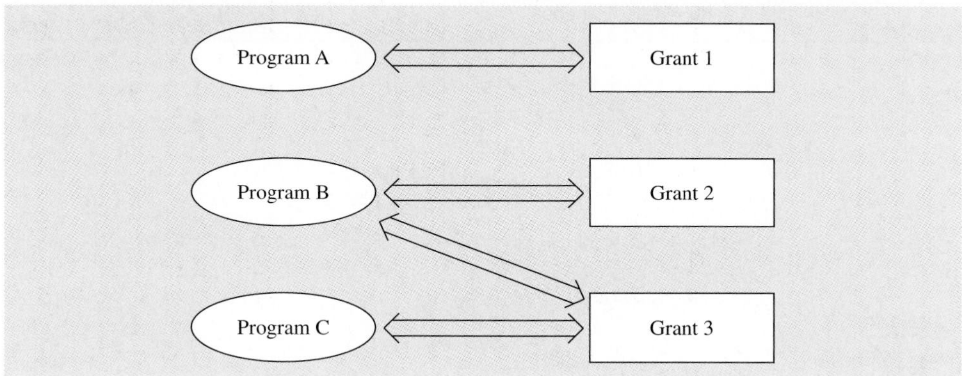

ILLUSTRATION A13–3 Chart of Accounts for a Not-for-Profit Organization Account Number (X)–(XX)–(X)–(XX)

Type of Account X	Object XX	Program X	Funding Source XX
1 = Assets	10 = Cash		
	20 = Accounts receivable		
	30 = Inventory		
	40 = Prepaid expenses		
	50 = Investments		
	60 = Property, plant, and equipment		
	70 = Accumulated depreciation		
2 = Liabilities	10 = Accounts payable		
	20 = Accrued payroll		
	30 = Other accrued liabilities		
3 = Net assets	10 = Unrestricted net assets		
	20 = Unrestricted, designated net assets		
	30 = Temporarily restricted net assets		
	40 = Permanently restricted net assets		
4 = Revenues	10 = Contributions	A = Community Impact	01 = Federal grant
	20 = Grants	B = Youth Commission	02 = Community development block grant
	30 = Charges for services	C = Juvenile Court Advocacy	21 = State grant
	40 = Dues	D = Student Outreach	22 = County grant
	50 = Investment income	E = Safe Schools	23 = City grant
	60 = Special events	F = Parent Effectiveness Training	24 = City Housing Commission grant
	70 = Miscellaneous	G = Advocacy	30 = Ford Foundation grant
5 = Cost of programs	11 = Salaries and wages		31 = Kellogg Foundation grant
6 = Expenses (general and administrative; fund-raising)	12 = Fringe benefits and payroll taxes		32 = Smith Foundation grant
	20 = Travel		33 = Brown Foundation grant
	30 = Supplies, phone, postage, printing		43 = Universal Church
	40 = Occupancy costs		50 = United Way
	60 = Equipment maintenance		
	61 = Depreciation		
	70 = Legal and professional services		
	80 = Miscellaneous		

Key Terms

Activity-based costing (ABC), *550*
Allowable costs, *556*
Balanced scorecard, *554*
Budget calendar, *538*
Budget officer, *538*
Cost objective, *558*
Customer relationship management (CRM), *546*
Direct costs, *558*
Effectiveness measures, *547*
Efficiency measures, *547*
Entrepreneurial budgeting, *537*
Incremental budgeting, *535*
Indirect costs, *558*
Input measures, *547*
Outcome measures, *547*
Output measures, *547*
Performance budgeting, *536*
Planning-programming-budgeting system (PPBS), *537*
Program budgeting, *536*
Service efforts and accomplishments (SEA), *547*
Sweep accounts, *543*
Tax anticipation notes, *542*
Total quality management (TQM), *545*
Zero-based budgeting, *535*

Selected References

Bland, Robert L. *A Budgeting Guide for Local Government.* Washington, DC: International City/County Management Association, 2007.

Epstein, Paul, James Fountain, Wilson Campbell, Terry Patton, and Kimberly Keaton. *Government Service Efforts and Accomplishments Performance Reports: A Guide to Understanding.* Norwalk, CT: Government Accounting Standards Board, July 2005.

Fishbein, John. *Preparing High Quality Budget Documents.* Chicago, IL: GFOA, 2006.

Fountain, James, Wilson Campbell, Terry Patton, Paul Epstein, and Mandi Cohn. *Special Report: Reporting Performance Information: Suggested Criteria for Effective Communication.* Norwalk, CT: Government Accounting Standards Board, August 2003.

Government Finance Officers Association. *Best Practices in Public Budgeting.* Chicago, IL: GFOA, 2000 (on CD-ROM) at *www.gfoa.org.*

Lalli, William, ed., *Handbook of Budgeting,* 5th ed. New York: John Wiley & Sons, 2005, with 2006 Supplement.

Meyers, Roy T. *Handbook of Government Budgeting.* San Francisco, CA: Jossey-Bass, 1998.

National Advisory Council on State and Local Budgeting. *Recommended Budget Practices: A Framework for Improved State and Local Government Budgeting.* Chicago, IL: NACSLB, 1998.

Questions

13–1. "The sole objective of budgeting in a governmental entity is to demonstrate compliance with appropriation legislation." Do you agree or disagree? Explain.

13–2. Explain how strategic planning, budgeting, and performance measurement can be integrated in a government and why this integration is desirable.

13–3. What is the difference between two types of line-item budgeting approaches—incremental budgeting and zero-based budgeting? Which of the two approaches is more widely used by governments?

13–4. Describe the advantages of performance budgeting and program budgeting over incremental budgeting in a governmental entity.

13–5. Identify some essential components of an annual budget process for a state or local government.

13–6. What advantages does total quality management (TQM) offer a government? Is it fundamentally a budget approach?

13–7. Discussion at a local meeting of government financial officers centered on using a balanced scorecard to present information to the public on the government's Web site. Describe the components of a balanced scorecard and its advantages in communicating performance results to citizens.

13–8. What are the three broad categories of service efforts and accomplishments (SEA) measures? Explain the GASB's role in developing standards for SEA reporting.

13–9. Explain why conventional cost accounting systems have become less useful in both business and government settings. How does activity-based costing (ABC) reduce the problems created by conventional cost accounting systems?

13–10. The finance officer of a small city has heard that certain items of cost may be allowable under federal grants, even though they were not incurred specifically for the grant. To what source could the finance officer go to determine what costs are allowable under federal grants?

Cases

13–1 Distinguished Budget Presentation Award. You are a governmental accountant for a large municipality, and you have recently been assigned to the Budget office and charged with building a better budget document—one that will be of the highest quality so that citizens and others with an interest in the government's finances will be fully informed.

Required

a. Find out which other local governments in your state have received the GFOA's Distinguished Budget Presentation Award (*Hint:* the GFOA posts an annual report on award winners of the Distinguished Budget Presentation Program on its Web site at *www.gfoa.org*.)

b. What components of the budget must exist for the GFOA to award the "Distinguished Budget Presentation Award"?

c. Provide some examples from an award-winning budget in your state that you can model in preparing the budget for your own municipality. Locate examples of budgets that excel in each of these categories: (1) as a policy document, (2) as a financial plan, (3) as an operations guide, and (4) as a communications device.

13–2 Budgeting Process and Policies. The City of Topeka, Kansas, has received a Distinguished Budget Presentation Award for at least 12 years. An excerpt from the 2008 Budget is presented on the next page:

Financial Policies, Guidelines, and Practices

Budgeting, Accounting, and Audit Practices. Kansas law prescribes the policies and procedures by which the cities prepare annual budgets. By August 25th of each year, prior to commencement of the new fiscal year on the following January 1st, the governing body of the City must adopt a budget, which is filed with the City Clerk and the State Director of Accounts and Reports. The budget itemizes anticipated revenues and proposed expenditures, detailed by program and object of expenditures, for the next fiscal year. Funds must be balanced so that total resources equal obligations in accordance with Kansas law (K.S.A. 79-2927), which requires that, "The budget of expenditures for each fund shall balance with the budget of revenues for such fund. . . ." The level of budgetary control or expenditure limit is at the fund level, except for the General Fund, which also has established expenditure limits for each Department financed. However, statutes allow for the transfer of budgeted amounts between line items within a fund. Departments are responsible for managing their budgets to the fund or department total level. Changes from expenditure category to expenditure category may be made administratively. Transfers of $15,000 or more from department to department within the General Fund may only be made with the approval of the City Council. The City maintains a financial and budgetary control system. Expenditures and revenues are tracked to ensure adherence to the budget and awareness of the financial environment. Monthly reports are prepared that compare actual revenues and expenditures to budgeted amounts and provide a picture of the City's cash position.

Kansas statutes require that the budget be prepared for the next fiscal year by August 1st of each year. The proposed budget must then be published along with a notice of public hearing on or before August 5th. The public hearing is held by August 15th, but must be at least ten days after publication. The budget is to be adopted on or before August 25th. The statutes allow for the governing body to increase the originally adopted budget if that increase is financed with previously unbudgeted revenue other than ad valorem property taxes. A notice of public hearing to amend the budget must be published in the local newspaper. At least ten days after publication, the hearing may be held and the City Council may amend the budget.

In order to ensure that Kansas municipalities conduct their affairs in a fiscally responsible manner, the State Legislature enacted a cash basis law in 1933 (K.S.A. 10-1101 et seq.) which states in part that it is unlawful, except where bonds, temporary notes, or no-fund warrants are authorized, "for the governing body of any municipality to create any indebtedness in excess of the amount of funds actually on hand in the treasury of such municipality, or to authorize the issuance of any order, warrant or check, or other evidence of such indebtedness of such municipality in excess of the amount of funds actually on hand in the treasury of such municipality at the time for such purpose." The purpose of the cash basis law is to prevent municipalities from spending more than they receive annually in operating revenues, and to prevent the issuance of short-term debt to cover operating expenditures.

Kansas statutes and regulations of the Kansas Board of Accountancy provide for municipal accounting in conformance with generally accepted accounting principles (GAAP). Separate funds are maintained by the City for specific purposes and projects, in compliance with GAAP, State laws and regulations, bond covenants, tax levies, grant agreements, and City ordinances and resolutions. The City prepares a Comprehensive Annual Financial Report (CAFR), disclosing the financial position, results of operations, and changes in fund equities or retained earnings for all funds and accounts groups in accordance with GAAP. An independent firm of certified public accountants performs annual audits of this information. The audited CAFR is filed in the Office of the City Clerk and with the Nationally Recognized Municipal Securities Information Repositories (NRMSIRs), among other agencies.

Source: City of Topeka, Kansas, 2008 Budget, pp. 31–32. Full text available at *www.topeka.org/pdfs/2008budget.pdf*.

Required

a. Evaluate whether this passage from the budget could be clearly understood by the average reader.

b. What changes can you recommend in the content or presentation of this section on budgeting, accounting, and audit practices that the city's financial managers may consider to improve the usefulness of this section for members of the city council? For citizens?

13–3 Indirect Costs. As a cost reimbursement accountant in a large public research university, you are aware that federal agencies have increased auditing efforts in the area of federal research grants to higher education institutions. In particular, OMB *Circular A–21* detailing allowable costs for colleges and universities receiving federal funds. The administration has asked you whether it is appropriate to include certain overhead costs in the pool of indirect costs (facilities and administrative costs) that are recovered in most federal research awards. Items include (1) holiday lights put on the president's university-owned home, (2) library books in the research section of the undergraduate library, (3) the cost of a large boat used by higher administration in meeting with faculty and outside researchers for social events, (4) advertising new graduate programs in the large urban newspaper, (5) clerical salaries in the academic departments where a large amount of research is conducted, and (6) utility bills in the research wing of one of the buildings.

Required

Write a short professional memo to the administration giving your opinion about whether these costs would be allowable "indirect costs" to be recovered in part by federal research grants. Defend your position.

Exercises and Problems

13–1 Examine the Budget. Obtain a copy of a recent operating budget document of a government.* Familiarize yourself with the organization of the operating budget document; read the letter of transmittal or any narrative that accompanies the budget.

Budgetary practices may differ from the GAAP reporting model as to *basis, timing, perspective,* and *entity.* GASB standards (*Codification,* Section 2400.110–199) define these differences as:

1. *Basis* differences arising through the employment of a basis of accounting for budgetary purposes that differs from the basis of accounting applicable to the fund type when reporting on the operations in accordance with GAAP.
2. *Timing* differences that can result in significant variances between budgetary practices and GAAP may include continuing appropriations, project appropriations, automatic reappropriations, and biennial budgeting.
3. *Perspective* differences resulting from the structure of financial information for budgetary purposes. The perspectives used for budgetary purposes include fund structure and organizational or program structure. In addition, some subsidiary perspective, such as nature of revenue source, special projects, or capital and operating budgets, may also be used. The fund structure

*Contact the budget officer of the city, town, or county of your choice and request a copy of the most recent available operating budget document.

and individual fund definitions establish which assets, liabilities, equities, and revenue and expenditure/expense flows are recorded in a fund. In the traditional view, budgeting, accounting, financial reporting, and auditing would follow the fund perspective.

4. *Entity* differences occur when "appropriated budget" either includes or excludes organizations, programs, activities, and functions that may or may not be compatible with the criteria defining the governmental reporting entity.

Required

Answer the following questions, which aid in assessing the quality of the budget document you are reviewing.†

Policy Document. Does the operating budget you are reviewing include a coherent statement of entity-wide long-term financial policies and nonfinancial goals and objectives? Does the budget document describe the entity's short-term initiatives that guide budget development for the upcoming year? Does the budget document include a coherent statement of goals and objectives of organizational units? Does the document include a budget message that articulates priorities and issues for the budget for the new year? Does the message describe significant changes in priorities from the current year and the factors that led to those changes?

Financial Plan. Does the budget document describe all funds that are subject to appropriation? Does the document present a summary of major revenues and expenditures as well as other financing sources and uses? Does the document include summaries of revenues, other financing sources, and expenditures and other financing uses for prior-year actual, current-year budget and/or estimated current-year actual, and proposed budget year? Are major revenue sources described? Are the underlying assumptions for revenue estimates and significant revenue trends explained? Does the document include projected changes in fund balances for governmental funds included in the budget presentation, including all balances potentially available for appropriation?

Does the budget document include budgeted capital expenditures (even if these are authorized in a separate capital budget)? Does the document describe whether, and to what extent, significant and nonroutine capital expenditures or other major capital spending will impact the entity's current and future operating budget? Are financial data on current debt obligations provided, describing the relationship between current debt levels and legal debt limits, and explaining the effects of existing debt levels on current and future operations? Is the basis of budgeting explained for all funds, whether cash, modified accrual, or some other statutory basis?

Operations Guide. Does the operating budget document describe activities, services, or functions carried out by organizational units? Are objective measures of progress toward accomplishing the government's mission, as well as goals and objectives, provided for specific units or programs? Does the budget document include an organizational chart for the entire organization? Is a schedule(s) or summary table provided giving personnel or position counts for prior, current, and budget years?

†These questions are paraphrased from the awards criteria established by the Government Finance Officers Association for its Distinguished Budget Presentation Awards Program.

Communication Device. Does the budget document provide summary information, including an overview of significant budgetary issues, trends, and resource choices? Does the budget document explain the effect, if any, of other planning processes (e.g., strategic plans, long-range financial plans, capital improvement plans) on the budget and budget process? Is the process used to prepare, review, adopt, and amend the budget explained? Are charts and graphs used, where appropriate, to highlight financial and statistical information? Is narrative information provided when the messages conveyed by the charts and graphs are not self-evident? Does the document provide narrative, tables, schedules, or matrices to show the relationship between functional units, major funds, and nonmajor funds in the aggregate? Is a table of contents provided to make it easy to locate information in the document? Is there a glossary to define terms (including abbreviations and acronyms) that are not readily understood by a reasonably informed lay reader? Does the document include statistical and supplemental data that describe the organization and the community or population it serves and provide other pertinent background information related to services provided? Finally, is the document produced and formatted in such a way as to enhance understanding by the average reader? Is it attractive, consistent, and oriented to the reader's needs?

13–2 Multiple Choice. Choose the best answer.

1. An often used approach to budgeting that simply derives the new year's budget from the current year's budget is called:
   a. Planning-programming-budgeting.
   b. Incremental budgeting.
   c. Zero-based budgeting.
   d. Performance budgeting.
2. Which of the following steps would *not* usually be part of the budgeting process?
   a. Heads of operating departments prepare budget requests.
   b. Budget officer and other central administrators review and make adjustments to departmental requests.
   c. One or more public budget hearings are held.
   d. The chief executive (mayor or city manager, as appropriate) formally adopts the budget, thus giving it the force of law.
3. The budgeting principle in generally accepted accounting principles (GAAP) for state and local governments states that:
   a. The accounting system should provide the basis for appropriate budgetary control.
   b. Budgetary comparison schedules should be presented as required supplementary information for the General Fund and each major special revenue fund that has a legally adopted budget.
   c. Annual budgets should be adopted by each government.
   d. All of the above.
4. The budgetary comparison schedule required of state and local governments by *GASBS 34*:
   a. Can be presented as required supplementary information (RSI) or as a statement in the basic financial statements.
   b. Must be a schedule included as part of RSI.
   c. Continues to be a statement included in the basic financial statements.
   d. Is no longer required.

5. All of the following are true statements about budgeting for performance in a governmental entity *except*:
   a. There are few examples of successful improvements in budgeting processes that have resulted in higher quality and performance of governments.
   b. The GFOA's Distinguished Budget Presentation Award Program has spurred many governments to improve their budgeting processes and be recognized for it.
   c. Some states have passed legislation that requires performance measures, both financial and nonfinancial.
   d. Governments have adapted many private sector budgeting tools in an attempt to improve efficiency and deliver higher quality services to taxpayers.
6. An approach to budgeting that requires the very existence of each program and the amount of resources requested to be allocated to that program to be justified each year is called:
   a. Incremental budgeting.
   b. Zero-based budgeting.
   c. Performance budgeting.
   d. Planning-programming-budgeting.
7. A benefit of using activity-based costing in a government is:
   a. Understanding and controlling the delivery/program design interaction.
   b. Finding lower cost alternatives.
   c. Reducing the cost of service outcomes.
   d. All of the above.
8. Total quality management (TQM), a process designed to continuously improve the government's ability to meet customer demands, incorporates all of the following elements *except*:
   a. Productivity and quality measures and standards that are meaningful to the government.
   b. Adherence to a line-item budgeting and centralized management system.
   c. Support and commitment of top-level officials.
   d. Employee involvement in productivity and quality improvement efforts.
9. Efficiency measures, as the term is used in the service efforts and accomplishments (SEA) literature, can be described as:
   a. Measures that relate the quantity or cost of resources used to units of output.
   b. Measures that relate to the amount of financial and nonfinancial resources used in a program or process.
   c. Measures that relate costs to outcomes.
   d. Measures that reflect either the quantity or quality of a service provided.
10. Which of the following provides guidance to government managers and auditors in determining appropriate and allowable costs chargeable to federal grants and contracts for not-for-profit organizations?
   a. OMB *Circular A–102,* "Grants and Cooperative Agreements with State and Local Governments."
   b. OMB *Circular A–110,* "Uniform Administrative Requirements for Grants and Other Agreements with Institutions of Higher Education, Hospitals, and Other Non-Profit Organizations."

SOUTHWEST CITY

Annual Budget | **General Fund**
FY 2010–2011 | **Description**
Department Description *(concluded)* | **Streets**

Streets

Account Number	Account Description	FY 2009 Actual	FY 2010 Budget	FY 2010 Estimated	FY 2011 Budget
02-13-00-0101	Salaries—Administrative	$ 4,827.90	$ 4,910.00	$ 4,910.00	$ 4,910.00
02-13-00-0102	Salaries—Operations	27,445.47	29,834.00	29,834.00	36,617.00
02-13-00-0103	Salaries—Supervisory	67,951.32	70,081.00	59,231.00	58,577.00
02-13-00-0104	Salaries—Skilled	42,957.99	42,944.00	55,175.00	69,443.00
02-13-00-0107	Salaries—Overtime	6,584.77	6,854.00	7,604.00	6,500.00
02-13-00-0108	Part-time and hourly	0	1,800.00	0	0
02-13-00-0116	TMRS retirement	12,159.21	11,847.00	12,169.00	11,665.00
02-13-00-0117	Employer's FICA	11,249.99	1,581.00	11,208.00	11,707.00
02-13-00-0118	Hospitalization insurance	12,203.21	13,532.00	13,090.00	15,544.00
02-13-00-0119	Workers' compensation	20,351.76	32,987.00	33,941.00	33,941.00
02-13-00-0120	Unemployment compensation	403.38	378.00	111.00	1,096.00
	Total personnel	$206,135.00	$226,748.00	$227,273.00	$250,000.00
02-13-00-0210	Chemical supplies	$ 760.95	$ 250.00	$ 0	$ 1,500.00
02-13-00-0220	Clothing supplies	1,638.28	2,164.00	1,520.00	1,600.00
02-13-00-0260	General office supplies	14.79	50.00	6.00	25.00
02-13-00-0270	Janitorial supplies	143.43	50.00	72.00	75.00
02-13-00-0280	Minor tools	609.32	300.00	496.00	400.00
02-13-00-0285	Fuel and vehicle supplies	6,938.49	8,500.00	8,861.00	8,900.00
02-13-00-0290	Other supplies	543.74	400.00	863.00	500.00
	Total supplies	$ 10,649.00	$ 11,714.00	$ 11,818.00	$ 13,000.00
02-13-00-0302	Building maintenance	$ 0	$ 50.00	$ 93.00	$ 50.00
02-13-00-0304	Street maintenance	17,520.75	20,950.00	20,950.00	18,950.00
02-13-00-0305	Seal coating and overlays	37,457.21	35,488.00	24,481.00	35,275.00
02-13-00-0306	Sidewalks	5,085.75	1,048.00	1,048.00	1,000.00
02-13-00-0307	Street sweeping	0	10,500.00	10,500.00	9,575.00
02-13-00-0401	Heating and air conditioning maintenance	60.00	50.00	225.00	50.00
02-13-00-0420	Machine tools maintenance	1,928.05	1,500.00	1,978.00	1,500.00
02-13-00-0430	Motor vehicle maintenance	5,000.00	5,000.00	5,000.00	3,500.00
02-13-00-0460	Radio maintenance	0	100.00	0	100.00
02-13-00-0480	Signs	3,572.24	3,000.00	2,092.00	3,000.00
	Total maintenance	$ 70,624.00	$ 77,686.00	$ 66,367.00	$ 73,000.00

13–4 Police Department Budget. The police chief of the Town of Meridian submitted the following budget request for the police department for the forthcoming budget year 2011–12.

Item	Actual FY 2010	Budget FY 2011	Forecast FY 2011	Budget FY 2012
Personnel	$1,051,938	$1,098,245	$1,112,601	$1,182,175
Supplies	44,442	61,971	60,643	64,450
Maintenance	47,163	45,310	46,139	47,422
Miscellaneous	34,213	36,272	32,198	37,723
Capital outlay	65,788	69,433	67,371	102,210
Totals	$1,243,544	$1,311,231	$1,318,952	$1,433,980

Upon questioning by the newly appointed town manager, a recent masters graduate with a degree in public administration from a nearby university, the police chief explained that he had determined the amounts in the budget request by multiplying the prior year's budget amount by 1.04 (to allow for the expected inflation rate of 4 percent). In addition, the personnel category includes a request for a new uniformed officer at an estimated $40,000 for salary, payroll expenses, and fringe benefits. Capital outlay includes a request for a new patrol vehicle at an estimated cost of $30,000. The amount of $300 was added to the maintenance category for estimated maintenance on the new vehicle. The police chief is strongly resisting instructions from the town manager that he justify the need not only for the new uniformed position and additional vehicle but also for the existing level of resources in each category. The town manager has stated she will not request any increase in the police department's budget unless adequate justification is provided.

Required

a. Evaluate the strengths and weaknesses of the police chief's argument that his budget request is reasonable.

b. Are the town manager's instructions reasonable? Explain.

c. Would the town council likely support the town manager or the police chief in this dispute, assuming the police chief might take his case directly to the town council?

d. What other improvements could be made to the town's budgeting procedures?

13–5 Budgeting Cash Flows. Eagleview City prepares a quarterly forecast of cash flows for its water service department. Data for the upcoming quarter (in alphabetical order) measured on the cash basis are presented below.

Bond interest expense	$ 1,950,000
Current month's collections on receivables	4,349,350
Interest income on excess cash from previous months	1,849
Investment income	11,250
Materials and supplies disbursements	925,000
Nonoperating revenue	479,030
Other fees and services disbursements	4,070,000
Previous months' collections on receivables	4,582,425
Personal services disbursements	1,991,000
Transfers in	50,000
Transfers out	540,000

The city maintains no more than the minimum cash balance of $100,000 on hand.

Required

a. What are the projected cash flows from operating activities, noncapital financing activities, capital and related financing activities, and investing activities? Indicate whether the balance is a positive cash flow or a negative cash flow. (*Hint:* Consider using a cash flows statement format in analyzing the data.)

b. What is the projected amount the city will have to borrow at the end of the quarter to maintain the minimum balance, or what is the amount the city has to invest that exceeds the minimum balance?

c. What steps can the city take to prevent being in a position where it will have to borrow at the end of the quarter?

This problem is adapted from an example in William R. Voorhees and Jeongwoo Kim, "Cash Flow Forecasting: Principles," *Encyclopedia of Public Administration and Public Policy,* Taylor & Francis, 2008, pp. 285–290.

13–6 SEA Reporting. The City of Ankeny, Iowa, has produced a Service Efforts and Accomplishments report since 2003 in an attempt to answer the question, "Am I getting my money's worth?" for its citizens. The city received the Association of Governmental Accountants Certificate of Excellence in Service Efforts & Accomplishments Reporting for 2005 and 2006. Reproduced below is an excerpt from the Fall 2006–07 SEA report that details Library Services.

New in the 2006–07 report is library programming and participation. This measure shows the efforts of library staff to offer more library programs to the

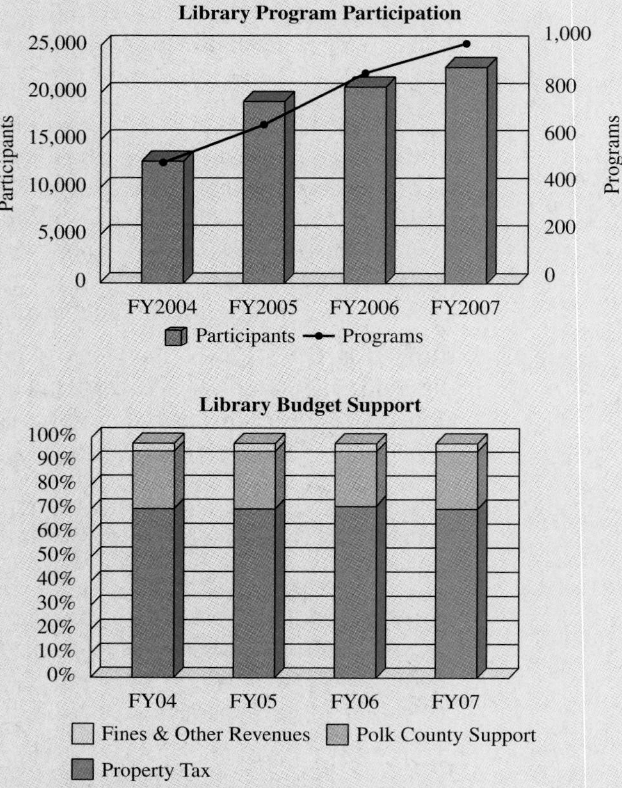

increasing population and customer base in the city. As shown in the graph, program participation has seen steady increases over the past four years, with some programs so high in demand waiting lists to participate are starting to occur.

Citizen Perceptions

The 2005 Community survey reported that 84 percent of city residents rated Library services as "good" or "excellent," only marginally down from 86 percent in 2003. For the variety of materials at the library, 79 percent of citizens rated the variety as "good" or "excellent," unchanged from 2003.

Library Budget

The owner of a house with a total assessed valuation of $150,000 paid property taxes of $33 in FY 2007 to support the Library. Twenty-six percent (26%) of the Library's FY 2007 budget depends upon support from Polk County in return for services provided to rural Polk County residents. Polk County's support is expected to decrease after FY 2007. Options being considered to offset the loss of county funding include allocation of General Fund monies and/or reduction in library services.

Library Performance Measures	2003–04 Actual	2004–05 Actual	2005–06 Actual	2006–07 Actual
Authorized FT Positions	7	7	7	7
Total Visitations	296,441	299,405	302,399	317,518
City Resident Cardholders	19,805	23,161	25,607	25,318
Non-Resident Cardholders	6,761	6,114	6,655	6,559
Average Visits per Cardholder	11	10	9	10
Number of Circulations	316,117	320,910	350,213	367,723
Number of Items for Circulation	75,411	78,697	82,955	86,273
Number of Reference Desk Inquiries	21,949	25,266	26,051	27,353
Number of PC Users	32,250	39,400	41,704	58,815
Number of PC Users per Available PC	1,194	1,359	1,438	1,837
Number of Special Programs	475	629	856	955
Number of Participants per Program	25	30	24	24
Cost per Registered Borrower	$35	$34	$ 32	$ 33
Cost per Circulation	$2.96	$3.09	$2.91	$2.85
Cost per Visitation	$3.16	$3.32	$3.37	$3.31

Source: City of Ankeny, Iowa, 2006–07 Service Efforts and Accomplishments Report, pp. 24 and 35.

Required

a. Which of the performance measures best represents inputs, outputs, and outcomes?

b. How does the city demonstrate efficiency with respect to the General Fund budget it receives?

c. How would you address a citizen who feels he or she is not getting his or her money's worth?

13–7 **Activity-based Costing in a Government.** The midsize City of Orangeville funds an animal control program intended to minimize the danger stray dogs pose to people and property. The program is under scrutiny because of current budgetary constraints and constituency pressure.

An animal control warden responds to each complaint made by citizens about dogs running loose. Approximately one in six complaints results in the capture of a dog. When a dog is caught, the warden must drive it to a kennel 20 miles from the center of the city. Donna's Kennels, a privately owned animal boarding establishment, is under contract with the city to board, feed, and care for the impounded dogs. It is a no-kill shelter (i.e., it does not euthanize healthy animals), and dogs remain there until they are claimed by their owners or adopted. The program's complaint and impoundment data for the past four years follow:

	Year 1	Year 2	Year 3	Year 4
Complaints	2,330	2,410	2,540	2,730
Impoundments	376	398	414	440
Impoundment rate	16.1%	16.5%	16.3%	16.1%

Costs of Orangeville's animal control program are as follows. The city employs two animal control wardens, a clerk, and a program director. The task of the wardens is to respond to complaints, drive to the site, search for the dog, and deliver it (if it is found) to Donna's Kennels. The clerk is responsible for issuing licenses to dogs that are returned to their owners or are adopted, as well as tracking correspondence between Donna's Kennels and the city. The clerk also tracks program statistics and provides support to the program director.

The city owns and operates two vehicles specially designed for impounding and transporting stray dogs. For $10 per dog per day, Donna's Kennels provides shelter, food, and routine veterinary care. On average, 60 percent of impounded dogs are returned to their owners in seven days. The other 40 percent stay at Donna's Kennels for an average of 14 days before being adopted. Summarized program costs follow:

Salaries (annual):	
Program director	$40,000
Animal wardens (2)	$56,000 ($28,000 × 2)
Clerk	$27,000
Vehicles:	
Cost	$48,000 ($24,000 × 2)
Expected life	7 years
Operating costs	$0.30 per mile
Dog care:	
Shelter, food, medical care	$10 per dog per day (according to the contract)
Revenues:	
Fees received for adoptions	$35 per adoption
Fees received from owners:	
Fines	$75 per dog
Boarding expense reimbursement	$10 per dog per day

Critics of the animal control program argue that it costs too much to drive to the distant kennel to deliver an impounded dog. They have suggested that the city convert a vacant building within the city limits into an animal shelter to save on transportation costs. Prompted by the need to cut the city budget and address the public outcry, city officials are reviewing the budget proposal for the animal control program and are looking for ways to reduce the program's costs.

Required

a. Prepare a diagram that identifies (1) the activities related to the animal control program, (2) the relationship among each of the activities, (3) the resources required for each activity, and (4) the cost drivers for each activity. Use the format of Illustration 13–9.

b. Calculate the cost of each activity. Show your work. Use the format of Illustration 13–10.

c. Interpret the results of the activity based-costing example.

This problem is taken from the International City/County Management Association *Service Report: Introduction to Activity-Based Costing,* February 1998, pp. 9–13.

13–8 Total Program Costs. On the basis of the following data, prepare a statement for the Town of Chippewa for the year ended June 30, 2011, showing the total cost of solid waste removal and the cost per ton of residential solid waste removed or cubic yard of commercial solid waste removed (carry unit costs to three decimal places).

	Residential	Commercial
By town employees:		
Salaries and wages	$702,000	$481,000
Materials and supplies	$ 39,000	$ 36,090
Equipment use	$300,840	$201,470
Tons collected	165,000	—
Cubic yards collected	—	248,000
Labor-hours	90,000	68,000
By contractors:		
Cost	$ 78,900	$ 48,000
Tons collected	23,000	—
Cubic yards collected	—	30,000

Overhead for town collection of residential solid waste is $0.948 per labor-hour; for commercial solid waste collection it is $0.924 per labor-hour. Overhead for contract residential solid waste collection is 20 percent of cost (exclusive of overhead); for commercial solid waste collection it is 15 percent of cost (exclusive of overhead).

PART Three

NOT-FOR-PROFIT ORGANIZATIONS

Chapter Fourteen

Accounting for Not-for-Profit Organizations

Learning Objectives

After studying this chapter, you should be able to:

1. Distinguish not-for-profit organizations (NPOs) from entities in the governmental and commercial sectors of the U.S. economy.
2. Identify the authoritative standards-setting body for establishing GAAP for nongovernmental NPOs.
3. Explain financial reporting and accounting for NPOs, including required financial statements; classification of net assets; accounting for revenue, gains, and support; accounting for expenses; and accounting for assets.
4. Identify the unique accounting issues of financially interrelated organizations.
5. Describe optional fund accounting.
6. Prepare financial statements using *SFAS No. 117.*

The not-for-profit sector serves a critically important role in the United States by providing a vast array of community services, including emergency and disaster assistance; health and human services; education and research; furthering the arts, sciences, and human development; and protecting the environment. In 2006, not-for-profit organizations (NPOs)[1] numbered over 1.9 million in the United States, of which about 1.5 million were in the *independent sector*, separate from government and business.[2] The number of NPOs that were required to register with the Internal Revenue Service (IRS) in 2005 (religious organizations and those with annual revenues of less than $5,000 are not required to register) doubled over the past 25 years and grew at twice the business sector growth rate from 1987 to 2006.[3] Estimated paid employment in the not-for-profit sector was 12.9 million in 2005.[4] The more

[1] The Financial Accounting Standards Board (FASB) and the American Institute of CPAs (AICPA) prefer to call these organizations *not-for-profit organizations*, which is the term we use in this text. Within the industry and among the general public, however, the term *nonprofit organizations* is more commonly used, along with the abbreviations NPO, ONPO (other nonprofit organizations), and NGO (nongovernmental organizations, used in an international context). We use the abbreviation NPO interchangeably with the term *not-for-profit organization*.

[2] *Facts and Figures About Charitable Organizations* (Washington, DC: Independent Sector, 2007), p. 1. Available at http://independentsector.org/programs/research/Charitable_Fact_Sheet.pdf.

[3] Ibid., p. 2.

[4] *The Nonprofit Almanac 2008* (Washington, DC: The Urban Institute Press, 2008), p. 20.

than 500,000 NPOs that met the requirements to submit annual reports to the IRS reported expenses of $1.4 trillion and held assets of nearly $3.3 trillion.[5]

CHARACTERISTICS OF THE NOT-FOR-PROFIT SECTOR

This chapter focuses primarily on NPOs referred to as **voluntary health and welfare organizations (VHWO)** or **human service organizations,** such as the American Cancer Society, Girl Scouts, and Boy Scouts. These organizations receive contributions from the public at large and provide health and welfare services for a nominal or no fee. There are many other kinds of not-for-profit organizations, such as cemetery organizations, civic organizations, fraternal organizations, labor unions, libraries, museums, cultural institutions, performing arts organizations, political parties, private schools, professional and trade associations, social and country clubs, research and scientific organizations, and religious organizations. These organizations are classified by Internal Revenue Code Sections (discussed further in Chapter 15). The National Center for Charitable Statistics (NCCS) of the Urban Institute developed a National Taxonomy of Exempt Entities (NTEE) that divides the largest set of tax-exempt entities, Internal Revenue Code Sec. 501(c)(3) and (c)(4) organizations, into 10 functional categories (arts, culture, and humanities; education and research; environment/animals; health; human services; international/foreign affairs; public/society benefit; religion related; mutual/membership benefit; and others) and 26 major group areas.[6]

Illustration 14–1 shows various organizational forms that comprise the not-for-profit sector of the U.S. economy. The terms *public* and *private* that appear in illustration 14–1 can be confusing; for example, *public* charities are in the not-for-profit sector, *public* schools are in the governmental sector, and *publicly* traded companies are in the for-profit sector of our economy. Distinguishing between for profit, not-for-profit, and *governmental/nongovernmental* is more useful. "Governmental" not-for-profit organizations may receive tax revenue or be owned or controlled by a government but are not governments.[7] Examples of entities that receive special tax revenue include libraries and transportation authorities. Governments often control museums, cemeteries, development authorities, housing authorities, public hospitals, public colleges and universities, and other public benefit corporations. Some such organizations are reported as a department or unit of a general purpose government.

GAAP FOR NONGOVERNMENTAL NPOs

The Financial Accounting Standards Board (FASB) assumed primary responsibility for providing guidance on generally accepted accounting principles for not-for-profit entities in 1979.[8] The Governmental Accounting Standards Board

[5] *The Nonprofit Almanac* 2008, table 1–1, p. 5. See Chapter 15 of this text for IRS reporting requirements applicable to NPOs.

[6] This set of organizations, representing 75 percent of all tax-exempt organizations, is referred to as the *independent sector* because it includes private, self-governing organizations founded to serve a public purpose and foster volunteerism and philanthropy. Classifications available at http://nccs.urban.org/classification/index.cfm.

[7] See pp. 5–6 for the definition of a governmental NPO.

[8] Financial Accounting Standards Board, *Statement of Financial Accounting Standards No. 32,* "Specialized Accounting and Reporting Principles in AICPA Statements of Position and Guides on Accounting and Auditing Matters" (New York, 1979).

ILLUSTRATION 14–1 Organizational Forms

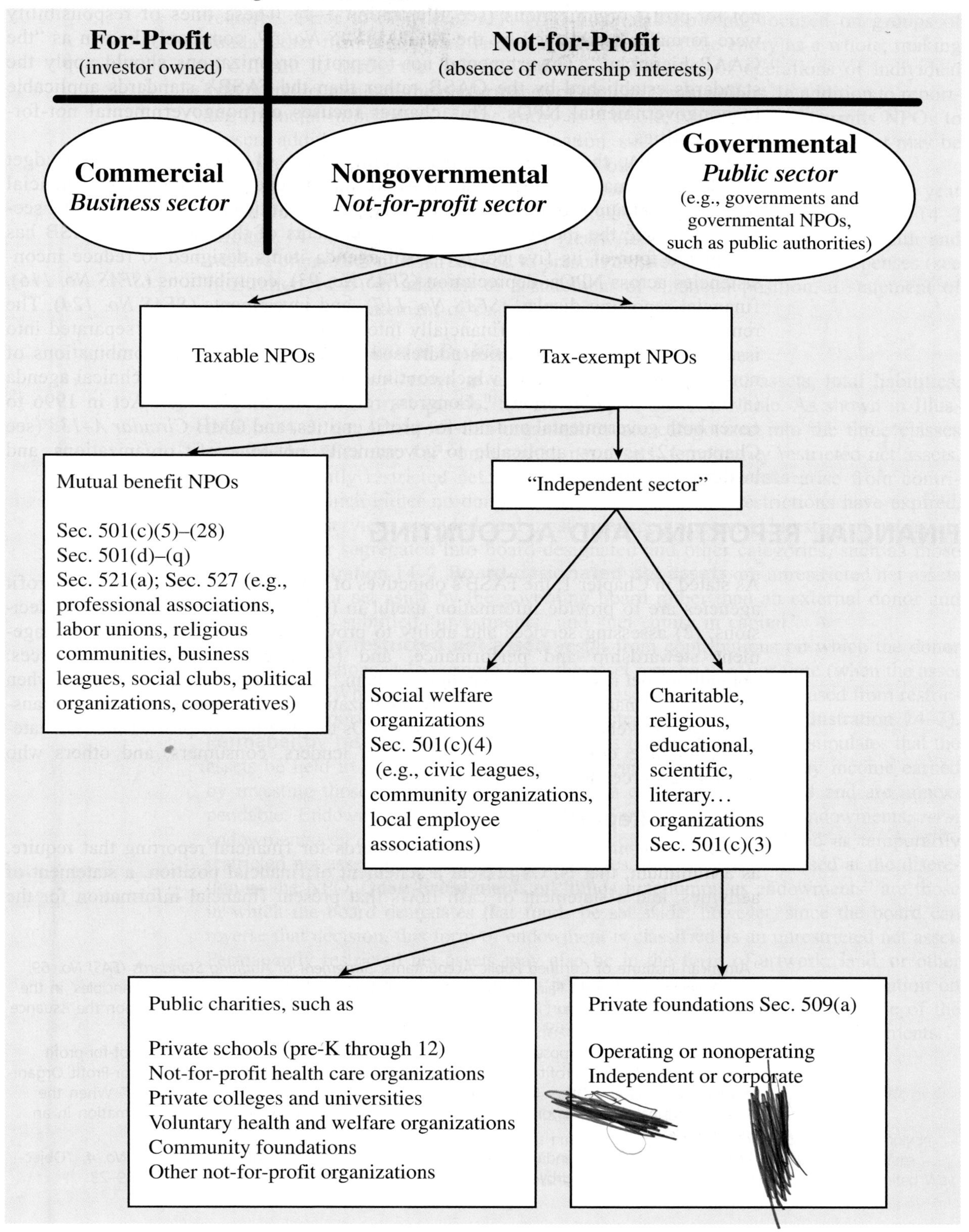

ILLUSTRATION 14–2

AMERICAN HEART ASSOCIATION, INC.
Statement of Financial Position
Year ended June 30, 2007
with summarized comparative totals for the year ended June 30, 2006

Assets	Unrestricted	Temporarily Restricted	Permanently Restricted	2007 Total	2006 Total
Current Assets:					
Cash and cash equivalents	$152,036,764	$ 3,796,837	$ 294,151	$ 156,127,752	$ 136,630,376
Short-term investments	46,168,490	129,664	201,767	46,499,921	53,742,365
Accrued investment income	1,049,230	36,261	7,888	1,093,379	1,094,413
Accounts receivable:					
Federated and nonfederated	—	7,398,430	—	7,398,430	7,204,846
Pledges, net	3,622,756	59,456,185	1,170,271	64,249,212	50,698,537
Bequest/split-interest agreements	20,832,127	4,046,826	—	24,878,953	29,320,714
Exchange transactions	3,877,678	—	—	3,877,678	13,865,900
Other	6,867,238	41,500	—	6,908,738	5,145,447
Inventory	8,345,393	—	—	8,345,393	6,980,974
Interfund receivable (payable)	(35,367,589)	35,884,565	(516,976)	—	—
Prepaid expense and other assets	7,789,852	—	—	7,789,852	8,073,578
Total current assets	215,221,939	110,790,268	1,157,101	327,169,308	312,757,150
Noncurrent Assets:					
Long-term investments	467,255,768	8,501,773	34,162,359	509,919,900	432,274,264
Beneficial interest in perpetual trusts	—	—	129,391,047	129,391,047	113,461,222
Land, buildings, and equipment, net	78,991,381	—	—	78,991,381	80,418,535
Accounts receivable:					
Federated and nonfederated, net	—	—	—	—	280,000
Bequests, net	948,012	7,434	—	955,446	1,624,302
Pledges, net	45,000	41,587,241	2,487,640	44,119,881	25,428,600
Split-interest agreements, net	—	114,234,691	474,184	114,708,875	119,859,678
Prepaid expenses and other assets	3,304,392	3,363,750	—	6,668,142	8,922,757
Total noncurrent assets	550,544,553	167,694,889	166,515,230	884,754,672	782,269,358
Total assets	$765,766,492	$278,485,157	$167,672,331	$1,211,923,980	$1,095,026,508

ILLUSTRATION 14–2 (*Continued*)

AMERICAN HEART ASSOCIATION, INC.
Statement of Financial Position
Year ended June 30, 2007
with summarized comparative totals for the year ended June 30, 2006

Liabilities and Net Assets	Unrestricted	Temporarily Restricted	Permanently Restricted	2007 Total	2006 Total
Current Liabilities:					
Accounts payable and accrued expense	$ 50,595,994	—	—	$ 50,595,994	$ 47,999,384
Current portion of long-term debt	234,560	—	—	234,560	230,829
Research awards payable	138,737,260	$ 6,710,856	—	145,448,116	141,574,487
Deferred revenue and support	7,937,740	—	—	7,937,740	9,935,956
Other liabilities	994,670	—	—	994,670	976,359
Total current liabilities	198,500,224	6,710,856	—	205,211,080	200,717,015
Noncurrent Liabilities:					
Long-term debt	2,428,946	—	—	2,428,946	6,380,051
Research awards	153,240,207	7,524,093	—	160,764,300	153,287,399
Other noncurrent liabilities	26,979,662	1,506,879	$ 52,305	28,538,846	22,941,977
Total noncurrent liabilities	182,648,815	9,030,972	52,305	191,732,092	182,609,427
Total liabilities	381,149,039	15,741,828	52,305	396,943,172	383,326,442
Net Assets:					
Net investment in land, buildings, and equipment	73,395,747	—	—	73,395,747	74,738,236
Programs and operations for the ensuing fiscal year	285,784,180	—	—	285,784,180	220,563,860
Capital expenditures	632,936	174,575	—	807,511	1,770,483
Research designated for future years	20,511,235	27,638,274	—	48,149,509	41,477,591
Specific programs and support activities	—	91,338,571	—	91,338,571	80,417,518
Split-interest agreements	4,293,355	78,212,869	129,391,047	211,897,271	201,250,060
Time restrictions	—	65,379,040	—	65,379,040	57,903,591
Endowment funds	—	—	38,228,979	38,228,979	33,578,727
Total net assets	384,617,453	262,743,329	167,620,026	814,980,808	711,700,066
Total liabilities and net assets	$765,766,492	$278,485,157	$167,672,331	$1,211,923,980	$1,095,026,508

Notes (not provided here) are an integral part of the financial statements.

ILLUSTRATION 14–3

AMERICAN HEART ASSOCIATION, INC.
Statement of Activities
Year ended June 30, 2007
with summarized comparative totals for the year ended June 30, 2006

	Unrestricted	Temporarily Restricted	Permanently Restricted	2007 Total	2006 Total
Revenue:					
Public support:					
Received directly:					
Contributions	$ 94,238,156	$ 61,721,184	$ 3,311,140	$159,270,480	$138,135,699
Contributed materials	181,988	—	—	181,988	5,229,108
Contributed services	68,722,155	—	—	68,722,155	87,490,666
Special events	245,740,303	59,693,642	—	305,433,945	281,050,552
Direct donor benefits	(36,043,729)	—	—	(36,043,729)	(38,381,673)
Bequests	76,662,983	10,723,583	228,401	87,614,967	74,711,682
Charitable gift annuities	593,148	—	—	593,148	974,241
Other split-interest agreements	—	877,887	—	877,887	3,035,675
Perpetual trusts	—	—	1,123,551	1,123,551	393,130
Total received directly	450,095,004	133,016,296	4,663,092	587,774,392	552,639,080
Received indirectly:					
Federated and nonfederated fund-raising organizations	6,731,717	7,310,653	—	14,042,370	15,703,533
Total public support	456,826,721	140,326,949	4,663,092	601,816,762	568,342,613
Other Revenue:					
Program fees	20,448,094.	—	—	20,448,094	18,622,632
Sales of educational materials	66,697,435	—	—	66,697,435	49,740,997
Membership dues	2,072,301	—	—	2,072,301	1,846,924
Fees and grants	6,900	29,170	—	36,070	342,682
Interest and dividends, net of fees	18,099,223	864,424	(12,566)	18,951,081	17,077,807
Net unrealized gains/losses on investment transactions	30,472,052	(162,967)	1,003,632	31,312,717	(3,550,296)
Net realized gains on investment transactions	18,778,360	2,433,684	(36,272)	21,175,772	18,672,406
Perpetual trust revenue	4,323,928	1,232,689	—	5,556,617	5,013,555
Net unrealized gains on beneficial interest in perpetual trusts	—	—	14,458,607	14,458,607	4,152,728
Change in value of split-interest agreements	569,654	(3,436,045)	(37,082)	(2,903,473)	(8,679,187)
Gains on disposal of fixed assets	2,213,284	—	—	2,213,284	2,417,279
Royalty revenue	15,287,514	—	—	15,287,514	14,614,810
Miscellaneous revenue (losses)	4,934,053	(2,693,469)	(3,752)	2,236,832	8,629,865
Total other revenue	183,902,798	(1,732,514)	15,372,567	197,542,851	128,902,202

ILLUSTRATION 14–3 (*Continued*)

Net assets released from restrictions:					
Satisfaction of research restrictions	$ 17,696,056	$ (17,696,056)	—	—	—
Satisfaction of other program restrictions	51,036,742	(51,036,742)	—	—	—
Expiration of time restrictions	42,581,285	(42,581,285)	—	—	—
Satisfaction of equipment acquisition restrictions	90,274	(90,274)	—	—	—
Satisfaction of geographic restrictions	8,876,954	(8,876,954)	—	—	—
Total net assets released from restrictions	120,281,311	(120,281,311)	—	—	—
Total of public support and other revenue	761,010,830	18,313,124	20,035,659	799,359,613	697,244,815
Expenses:					
Program services:					
Research—to acquire new knowledge through biomedical investigation by providing financial support to academic institutions and scientists	150,665,604	—	—	150,665,604	145,679,263
Public health education—to inform the public about the prevention and treatment of cardiovascular diseases and stroke	271,530,685	—	—	271,530,685	276,586,862
Professional education and training—to improve the knowledge, skills, and techniques of health professionals	87,916,834	—	—	87,916,834	79,828,219
Community services—to provide organized training in emergency aid, blood pressure screening, and other community-wide activities	43,888,390	—	—	43,888,390	41,558,816
Total program services	554,001,513	—	—	554,001,513	543,653,160
Supporting services:					
Management and general providing executive direction, financial management, overall planning, and coordination of the Association's activities	49,167,728	—	—	49,167,728	48,933,347
Fundraising—activities to secure vital financial support from the public	88,218,143	—	—	88,218,143	88,515,327
Total supporting services	137,385,871	—	—	137,385,871	137,448,674
Total program and supporting services expenses	691,387,384	—	—	691,387,384	681,101,834
Change in net assets before effect of adoption of *FASB Stmt No. 158*	69,623,446	18,313,124	20,035,659	107,972,229	16,142,981
Effect of adoption of *FASB Stmt No. 158*	(4,691,487)	—	—	(4,691,487)	—
Change in net assets	64,931,959	18,313,124	20,035,659	103,280,742	16,142,981
Net assets, beginning of year	319,685,494	244,430,205	147,584,367	711,700,066	695,557,085
Net assets, end of year	$384,617,453	$262,743,329	$167,620,026	$814,980,808	$711,700,066

Notes (not provided here) are an integral part of the financial statements.

SFAS No. 117 requires that assets and liabilities be reported in reasonably homogeneous groups and that information about liquidity be provided by either listing assets and liabilities by nearness to cash or by classifying them as current or noncurrent, or both, as presented on the American Heart Association statement of financial position (Illustration 14–2). Alternately, relevant information about liquidity can be disclosed in the notes to the financial statements. In general, donor-imposed restrictions apply to net assets; however, if restrictions also apply to particular assets or liabilities, those assets and liabilities should be reported separately from unrestricted assets and liabilities. Restrictions on asset use are more common than the requirement to pay liabilities from restricted assets. As Illustration 14–2 shows, the American Heart Association reports a temporarily restricted liability for research awards it has approved but not yet funded. Asset and liability restrictions may also be disclosed in the notes to the financial statements rather than segregating them on the face of the statements.

Statement of Activities

The statement of activities is an operating statement that presents, in aggregated fashion, all changes in unrestricted net assets, temporarily restricted net assets, permanently restricted net assets, and total net assets for the reporting period. These changes take the form of revenues, gains, expenses, and losses. As seen in Illustration 14–3, for the American Heart Association, a section titled "Net Assets Released from Restrictions" indicates the reclassification of temporarily restricted support to unrestricted support in the year in which the donor stipulations were met. Reclassifications are made for (1) satisfaction of program or purpose restrictions, (2) satisfaction of equipment acquisition restrictions, sometimes measured by depreciation expense, and (3) satisfaction of time restrictions, either actual donor or implied restrictions.

NPOs have considerable flexibility in presenting financial information as long as it is useful and understandable to the reader. *SFAS No. 117* does not preclude the NPO from using additional classifications, such as operating and nonoperating, expendable and nonexpendable, earned and unearned, and recurring and nonrecurring.

Although some NPOs may use the cash basis as a simple method of internal accounting, external financial statements must be prepared on the accrual accounting basis to be in conformity with GAAP. In general, revenues and expenses should be reported at their gross amounts. Exceptions include activities peripheral to the entity's central operations and investment revenue, which may be reported net of related expenses, if properly disclosed. Although revenues are categorized into three classes, all expenses are reported as reductions of unrestricted net assets. In addition, expenses must be reported by their functional classification (e.g., program or supporting) either in this statement or in the notes to the financial statements. Gains and losses on investments and other assets are reported as changes in unrestricted net assets unless their use is temporarily or permanently restricted.

Statement of Cash Flows

SFAS No. 117 requires a statement of cash flows by amending *SFAS No. 95* to extend its coverage to not-for-profit organizations.[14] As Illustration 14–4 shows, the American Heart Association reports its cash flows in three categories: operating, investing, and

[14] Financial Accounting Standards Board, *Statement of Financial Accounting Standards No. 95,* "Statement of Cash Flows" (Norwalk, CT, 1987).

ILLUSTRATION 14–4

AMERICAN HEART ASSOCIATION, INC.
Statement of Cash Flows
Year ended June 30, 2007
with summarized comparative totals for the year ended June 30, 2006

	2007	2006
Cash flows from operating activities:		
Change in net assets	$ 103,280,742	$ 16,142,981
Adjustments to reconcile change in net assets to net cash provided by operating activities:		
Depreciation and amortization	10,911,151	10,263,673
Net unrealized (gains) losses on investments	(31,312,717)	3,550,296
Net realized gains on investments	(21,175,772)	(18,672,406)
Net unrealized gains on beneficial interest in perpetual trusts	(14,458,607)	(4,152,728)
Change in value of split-interest agreement	2,903,473	8,679,187
Gains on disposal of equipment	(2,213,284)	(2,417,279)
Losses on uncollectible accounts and settlement of receivables	4,476,359	3,474,361
Contributions to endowment	(4,663,092)	(1,225,880)
Decrease in accrued investment income	1,034	241,525
Increase in accounts receivable	(22,653,665)	(15,839,125)
Increase in educational and campaign materials inventory	(1,364,419)	(1,287,118)
Decrease (increase) in prepaid expenses and other assets	2,538,341	(8,813,790)
Increase in beneficial interest in perpetual trusts	(1,471,218)	(393,130)
(Increase) decrease in split-interest agreements	1,604,637	(1,313,689)
Increase in accounts payable, accrued expenses, and other liabilities	8,713,700	12,205,822
Decrease in research awards payable	11,350,530	11,244,130
(Decrease) increase in deferred revenue and support	(1,998,216)	1,632,953
Net cash provided by operating activities	44,468,977	13,319,783
Cash flows from investing activities:		
Purchases of equipment	(10,566,092)	(14,354,052)
Proceeds from sale of equipment	3,937,315	2,744,076
Purchases of investments	(259,486,302)	(233,476,167)
Proceeds from sales/maturities of investments	241,555,344	218,945,863
Net cash used in investing activities	(24,559,735)	(26,140,280)
Cash flows from financing activities:		
Payments on mortgage notes payable and capital leases	(5,074,958)	(1,169,410)
Borrowings on mortgage notes payable and capital leases	—	3,714,671
Contributions to endowment	4,663,092	1,225,880
Net cash (used in) provided by financing activities	(411,866)	3,771,141
Net increase (decrease) in cash and cash equivalents	19,497,376	(9,049,356)
Cash and cash equivalents, beginning of year	136,630,376	145,679,732
Cash and cash equivalents, end of year	$ 156,127,752	$ 136,630,376
Supplemental cash flow information:		
Interest paid	$148,783	$127,563
Contributed materials	181,988	5,229,108
Equipment purchased by capital lease	625,674	1,482,506

Notes (not provided here) are an integral part of the financial statements.

financing. Although the American Heart Association uses the indirect method for reporting its cash flows from operating activities, either the direct or indirect method may be used. If the direct method is used, a reconciliation showing the change in total net assets from the statement of activities to net cash used for operating activities must be presented at the bottom of the statement.

Donor-imposed restrictions are not separately reported in the cash flows statement; however, the statement does have some unique aspects. Unrestricted gifts are included with the operating activities, whereas the receipt of temporarily and permanently restricted net assets given for long-term purposes are included in the financing activities section, as is the related income. The financing activities section also includes the issuance and repayment of long-term debt. Noncash gifts or in-kind contributions (discussed later) are disclosed as noncash investing and financing activities in a separate section.

Notes to the Financial Statements

Although the notes to the financial statements for the American Heart Association have been omitted for brevity, the notes are an integral part of the financial statements of NPOs. Disclosures include principles applicable to for-profit entities unless there is a specific exemption for not-for-profit organizations. Examples of required disclosures are those relating to financial instruments, commitments, contingencies, extraordinary items, prior-period adjustments, changes in accounting principles, employee benefits, and credit risks. In addition, the nature and amounts of unrestricted, temporarily restricted, and permanently restricted net assets must be disclosed if not displayed on the face of the financial statements. Notes are encouraged to report the detail of reclassifications, investments, and promises to give. Policy statements regarding whether restricted gifts received and expended in the same period are reported first as temporarily restricted must also be disclosed.

Statement of Functional Expenses

VHWOs must prepare a statement of functional expenses along with their other financial statements. Illustration 14–5 for the American Heart Association shows the usual format with functional expenses reported in the columns and the natural classification of expenses shown as rows. *Functional expenses* are those that relate to either the program or mission of the organization (*program expenses*) or the management and general and fund-raising expenses required to support the programs (*support expenses*). The natural classification of expenses, or object of expense, includes salaries, supplies, occupancy costs, interest, and depreciation, among other categories the organization considers useful to the readers. Watchdog agencies, donors, and others often use the ratio of program expenses to total expenses as a measure of an NPO's performance. Natural expenses that apply to more than one function must be allocated across program, general and administrative, and fund-raising using a systematic method. Allocation of fund-raising costs is discussed later in this chapter, and performance measurement is discussed in Chapter 15.

Accounting for Revenues and Gains

Not-for-profit organizations have traditionally distinguished revenues, gains, and support. **Revenues** in the traditional sense, represent increases in unrestricted net assets arising from bilateral **exchange transactions** in which the other party to the transaction is presumed to receive direct tangible benefit commensurate with the resources provided. Examples are membership dues, program service fees, sales of

ILLUSTRATION 14–5

AMERICAN HEART ASSOCIATION, INC.
Statement of Functional Expenses
Year ended June 30, 2007
with summarized comparative totals for the year ended June 30, 2006

	Direct Donor Benefits	Research	Public Health Education	Professional Education/ Training	Community Services	Subtotal Program Services	Management and General	Fund-raising	Subtotal Supporting Services	2007 Total	2006 Total
Salaries	—	$ 2,358,467	$ 85,203,394	$22,432,397	$15,228,088	$125,222,346	$25,813,995	$35,613,102	$61,427,097	$186,649,443	$175,924,189
Payroll taxes	—	167,032	6,331,393	1,682,403	1,201,698	9,382,526	2,455,416	2,761,489	5,216,905	14,599,431	14,161,858
Employee benefits	—	470,925	13,713,419	3,340,087	2,483,645	20,008,076	5,852,925	5,880,160	11,733,085	31,741,161	31,477,461
Occupancy	—	160,333	7,418,489	1,311,888	1,510,778	10,401,488	2,042,140	3,231,759	5,273,899	15,675,387	15,286,097
Telephone	—	52,838	2,744,906	776,680	580,597	4,155,021	665,790	1,454,412	2,120,202	6,275,223	6,469,386
Supplies	—	36,022	2,939,828	628,081	418,036	4,021,967	470,214	1,695,084	2,165,298	6,187,265	6,187,862
Rental and maintenance of equipment	—	55,161	3,015,117	798,829	500,746	4,369,853	977,119	1,623,239	2,600,358	6,970,211	6,538,079
Printing and publication	—	35,677	22,785,109	14,409,187	9,437,017	46,666,990	263,078	10,467,657	10,730,735	57,397,725	52,148,990
Postage and shipping	—	53,214	10,781,598	537,357	339,989	11,712,158	381,156	5,518,166	5,899,322	17,611,480	16,501,470
Conferences and meetings	—	403,277	3,566,645	12,489,613	1,471,086	17,930,621	939,518	1,519,309	2,458,827	20,389,448	18,605,254
Travel	—	944,791	8,492,123	4,184,908	2,229,045	15,850,867	1,613,256	5,487,112	7,100,368	22,951,235	22,678,485
Professional fees	—	4,450,627	96,851,198	18,219,296	3,629,971	123,151,092	4,016,741	8,682,683	12,699,424	135,850,516	151,775,187
Awards and grants	—	140,628,161	1,696,702	2,233,279	1,410,342	145,968,484	15,369	2,152	17,521	145,986,005	140,776,155
Other expenses	—	663,192	1,392,794	3,260,204	2,434,484	7,750,674	2,078,483	2,362,546	4,441,029	12,191,703	12,307,688
Depreciation and amortization	—	185,887	4,597,970	1,612,625	1,012,868	7,409,350	1,582,528	1,919,273	3,501,801	10,911,151	10,263,673
Total functional expenses before direct donor benefits	—	150,665,604	271,530,685	87,916,834	43,888,390	554,001,513	49,167,728	88,218,143	137,385,871	691,387,384	681,101,834
Direct donor benefit	$36,043,729	—	—	—	—	—	—	—	—	36,043,729	38,381,673
Total functional expenses and direct donor benefits	$36,043,729	$150,665,604	$271,530,685	$87,916,834	$43,888,390	$554,001,513	$49,167,728	$88,218,143	$137,385,871	$727,431,113	$719,483,507

Notes (not provided here) are an integral part of the financial statements.

c. Fair value.
d. Replacement value.

10. A particular organization functions as an intermediary between donors and other beneficiary organizations. The intermediary organization must report contribution revenue from donors if:
a. The organization has variance power.
b. The organization elects to consistently report such donor gifts as contribution revenue.
c. The beneficiary organization requests a delay in receiving the contribution from the intermediary organization.
d. All of the above are correct.

14–2. Classification of Revenues/Support and Expenses. For each of the independent transactions listed in the left-hand column below, indicate which of the revenue/support or expense classifications apply by choosing one or more of the letters from the listed items in the right-hand column. Choose all that apply.

Transaction	Revenue/Support and Expense Classifications
1. A museum gift shop sold prints of famous paintings.	*a.* Exchange revenue *b.* Unrestricted support
2. An NPO incurred a cost for its annual financial statement audit.	*c.* Temporarily restricted support *d.* Permanently restricted support
3. A registered nurse volunteered 10 hours a week for a local agency for disabled persons.	*e.* Released from restriction *f.* Program services expense *g.* Management and general expense
4. A donor contributed $1 million to a not-for-profit hospital for a new clinic.	*h.* Fund-raising expense
5. An art association hosted a $100-per-plate dinner attended by members, donors, and potential donors.	
6. A donor contributed securities valued at $10 million to be permanently invested. Earnings thereon are stipulated by the donor to be used for eye research.	
7. An NPO job training center incurred payroll expenses of $500,000 for instructors and mechanics and $100,000 for the center director and clerical staff. Of this amount, $400,000 was spent from temporarily restricted federal and state grants.	
8. The Older Adult Transportation Service received $8,000 from riders for the year and $52,000 from temporarily restricted grant sources.	

14–3 Donated Services. Indicate whether each of the following donated services situations would require a journal entry for contribution revenue and a related expense or asset by circling Y for yes or N for no.

Y N 1. Volunteers worked as sales assistants in a not-for-profit hospital snack shop.

Y N 2. An architect provided *pro bono* design services for the planned remodeling of a local museum.

Y N 3. A member of a church volunteered to repaint the church's activities room to make it more attractive. Church leaders had not planned to repaint the room.

Y N 4. Several local persons used their cars to deliver meals to senior citizens for Meals on Wheels.

Y N 5. A psychiatrist volunteered several hours each week at a not-for-profit counseling center to assist persons with alcohol and drug addiction.

Y N 6. A local CPA performed the regular annual financial statement audit for a local youth development camp, an NPO.

Y N 7. A local church pastor donated several hours weekly to work with troubled youths in an after-school activities program run by a local NPO.

Y N 8. Helpful citizens served as "bell ringers" at the entrances of local businesses to collect money for the Salvation Army.

14–4 Joint Activities with a Fund-Raising Appeal. Consider the following scenarios relating to activities that include a fund-raising appeal:

1. The Green Group's mission is to protect the environment by increasing the portion of waste recycled by the public. The group conducts a door-to-door canvass of communities that recycle a low portion of their waste. The canvassers share their knowledge about the environmental problems caused by not recycling with households, asking them to change their recycling habits. The canvassers also ask for charitable contributions to continue this work, although these canvassers have not participated in fund-raising activities before.
2. Central University's mission is to educate students in various academic pursuits. The political science department holds a special lecture series in which prominent world leaders speak about current events. Admission is priced at $250, which is above the $50 fair value of other lectures on campus, resulting in a $200 contribution. Invitations are sent to previous attendees and donors who have contributed significant amounts in the past.
3. The mission of Kid's Camp is to provide summer camps for economically disadvantaged youths. It conducts a door-to-door solicitation campaign for its camp programs by sending volunteers to homes in upper-class neighborhoods. The volunteers explain the camp's programs and distribute leaflets explaining the organization's mission. Solicitors say, "Although your own children most likely are not eligible to attend this camp, we ask for your financial support so that children less fortunate can have this summer camp experience."

Required

Determine for each scenario whether its purpose, audience, and content meet the criteria described in this chapter and Chapter 13 of the *AICPA,* Audit and Accounting Guide, Not-For-Profit Organizations so that the joint costs can be allocated between programs and support expenses. Explain your reasons.

14–5 Identify Departures from GAAP. The balance sheet and statement of activities for the Central Area Disadvantaged Youth Center for fiscal year 2011, prepared by a volunteer accountant with business experience, are presented on the following page.

CENTRAL AREA DISADVANTAGED YOUTH CENTER
Balance Sheet
As of December 31, 2011

Assets	
Cash	$ 26,802
Investments	71,143
Contributions receivable	16,372
Supplies and other prepaid expenses	13,258
Land	70,000
Buildings (net of accumulated depreciation of $63,420)	249,750
Equipment (net of accumulated depreciation of $87,642)	184,230
Total assets	$631,555
Liabilities and net assets	
Liabilities	
Accounts payable	$ 25,722
Accrued liabilities	4,963
Total liabilities	30,685
Net assets	
Invested in property, plant, and equipment	503,980
Other net assets	96,892
Total net assets	600,870
Total liabilities and net assets	$631,555

CENTRAL AREA DISADVANTAGED YOUTH CENTER
Statement of Activities
For Year Ended December 31, 2011

Revenues and contributions	
Contributions from donors	$ 69,250
Grants:	
From United Way	15,000
From state government	22,000
Contributed goods and services	43,500
Interest on investments	3,200
Miscellaneous—Sale of refurbished goods	6,900
Total revenues and contributions	159,850
Expenses	
Payroll	62,580
Payroll taxes	4,605
Travel and conferences	2,795
Promotion and advertising	1,430
Cost of donated goods and services	32,600
Food, recreational, and other supplies	18,310
Postage, printing, and copying	1,057
Building and equipment maintenance	3,100
Utilities	4,378
Depreciation	12,700
Miscellaneous	10,380
Total expenses	153,935
Increase in net assets	5,915
Net assets, December 31, 2010	625,640
Net assets, December 31, 2011	$ 631,555

Required

a. Assume that you are the independent auditor performing a financial statement audit of the center. Identify and make a list of your concerns based on your review of the center's financial statements. Would you feel comfortable issuing an unqualified (i.e., "clean") opinion on the Central Area Disadvantaged Youth Center's financial statements?

b. What actions would you require of the center's management to address your concerns before you would be willing to perform this audit? What would be your recourse if the center refused to take the recommended actions? (You may wish to refer to Chapter 12 in forming your answer to these questions.)

14–6 Statement of Activities. The Atkins Museum recently hired a new controller. His experience with managerial accounting and strong communication skills were extremely attractive. The new controller sent each member of the Board of Trustees' Finance Committee a set of the monthly financial statements one week before the monthly meeting for their review. The set included the following statement of activities.

THE ATKINS MUSEUM
Statement of Activities
For the Eleven Months Ended February 28, 2011
(in hundreds of dollars)

	Public Exhibits	Abstract Exhibit	Mgt. & General	Total
Revenues:				
Contributions	$ 61,400	$50,000	$ 0	$111,400
Charges for services	478,800	0	0	478,800
Interest income	0	0	2,500	2,500
Total revenues	540,200	50,000	2,500	592,700
Expenses:				
Salaries and wages	381,900	24,700	44,200	450,800
Occupancy costs	38,100	12,000	14,900	65,000
Supplies	7,100	2,300	8,300	17,700
Equipment	5,000	0	6,500	11,500
Travel and development	2,800	0	6,900	9,700
Depreciation	12,000	1,500	6,300	19,800
Interest	0	0	3,700	3,700
Total variable expenses	456,900	40,500	90,800	588,200
Allocated management and general expenses	85,300	5,500	(90,800)	0
Total costs	542,200	46,000	0	588,200
Excess of revenues over expenses	$ (2,000)	$ 4,000	$ 2,500	$ 4,500

Other information: The management and general expenses are first allocated to the programs to which they directly relate; for example, the executive director's salary is allocated to the Public Exhibit Program according to the percentage of time spent working on the program. Remaining unallocated management and general expenses are allocated to the programs as indirect costs based on the relative amount of salaries and wages to total salaries and wages for the programs.

Required

As a member of The Atkins Museum's Board of Directors Finance Committee, review this statement and answer the following questions:

a. Is the statement in proper form according to *SFAS No. 117?*
b. What questions do you have for the controller?
c. The Atkins Museum would like to open an Impressionists exhibit. If its operating expenses are expected to be similar to that of the Abstract Exhibit, how much should the organization solicit in contributions or grants to cover the full cost of the program?
d. If you were a potential contributor to the Atkins Museum, do you think you have enough information from this statement on which to base your decision to donate?

14–7 Notes on Net Assets. The following items are taken from the financial statements of the Kids Clubs of America for the years ending December 31, 2011, and 2010, with related notes.

KIDS CLUBS OF AMERICA
Statement of Financial Position (selected items)
For the Years Ended December 31, 2011 and 2010

	2011	2010
Net assets:		
Unrestricted		
Undesignated	$ 878,901	$ 882,912
Board designated (Note 11)	66,540,051	57,479,525
Temporarily restricted (Note 9)	74,789,227	47,668,565
Permanently restricted (Note 9)	18,675,644	16,183,950
Total net assets	$160,883,823	$122,214,952

Note 9: Restricted Net Assets

Temporarily restricted net assets at December 31, 2011 and 2010, are available for the following purposes or periods:

	2011	2010
Gifts and other unexpended revenues available for on-site assistance to member clubs and establishment of new clubs	$ 4,469,136	$ 5,266,823
Gifts and other unexpended revenues available for leadership training, development, and support of youth programs	35,864,678	27,915,087
Gifts available for future periods	34,455,413	14,486,655
	$74,789,227	$47,668,565

Permanently restricted net assets consist of the following at December 31, 2011 and 2010:

	2011	2010
Endowments	$18,675,644	$16,183,950

Note 11: Unrestricted Net Assets—Board Designated

Board-designated net assets consist of the following at December 31, 2011 and 2010:

	2011	2010
Reserve fund (functioning as quasi-endowment)	$44,762,573	$39,203,909
Gains on endowments	12,051,815	10,678,020
Land, buildings, and equipment	9,010,568	6,924,643
Other board designated	715,095	72,953
	$66,540,051	$57,479,525

The authors would like to thank Michelle Richards of the Center for Empowerment and Economic Development, Ann Arbor, MI, for sharing the model on which this statement is built.

Required

a. Explain what the term *board-designated, unrestricted net assets* means. What does the board plan to do with these net assets? Can board members change their minds in future years?

b. Describe the types of restrictions that donors have placed on net assets. How much of those gifts are restricted for a period of time as opposed to purpose?

c. If an unexpected need arises, can the board of directors decide to spend donor-restricted funds in ways other than the donor indicated when the contribution was made?

14–8 Prepare Financial Statements. The Children's Counseling Center was incorporated as a not-for-profit voluntary health and welfare organization 10 years ago. Its adjusted trial balance as of June 30, 2011, follows.

	Debits	***Credits***
Cash	$126,500	
Pledges Receivable—Unrestricted	41,000	
Estimated Uncollectible Pledges		$ 4,100
Inventory	2,800	
Investments	178,000	
Furniture and Equipment	210,000	
Accumulated Depreciation—Furniture and Equipment		160,000
Accounts Payable		13,520
Unrestricted Net Assets		196,500
Temporarily Restricted Net Assets		50,500
Permanently Restricted Net Assets		100,000
Contributions—Unrestricted		338,820
Contributions—Temporarily Restricted		48,100
Investment Income—Unrestricted		9,200
Net Assets Released from Restrictions—Temporarily Restricted	22,000	
Net Assets Released from Restrictions—Unrestricted		22,000
Salaries and Fringe Benefit Expense	286,410	
Occupancy and Utility Expense	38,400	
Supplies Expense	6,940	
Printing and Publishing Expense	4,190	
Telephone and Postage Expense	3,500	
Unrealized Loss on Investments	2,000	
Depreciation Expense	21,000	
Totals	$942,740	$942,740

1. Salaries and fringe benefits were allocated to program services and supporting services in the following percentages: counseling services, 40%; professional training, 15%; community service, 10%; management and general, 25%; and fund-raising, 10%. Occupancy and utility, supplies, printing and publishing, and telephone and postage expense were allocated to the programs in the same manner as salaries and fringe benefits. Depreciation expense was divided equally among all five functional expense categories. Unrealized loss on investments was charged to the management and general function.

2. The organization had $153,314 of cash on hand at the beginning of the year. During the year, the center received cash from contributors: $310,800 that was unrestricted and $48,100 that was restricted for the purchase of equipment for the center. It had $9,200 of income earned and received on long-term investments. The center spent cash of $286,410 on salaries and fringe benefits, $22,000 on the purchase of equipment for the center, and $86,504 for operating expenses. Other pertinent information follows: net pledges receivable increased $6,000, inventory increased $1,000, accounts payable decreased $102,594, and there were no salaries payable at the beginning of the year.

Required

a. Prepare a statement of financial position as of June 30, 2011, following the format in Illustration 14–7.

b. Prepare a statement of functional expenses for the year ended June 30, 2011, following the format in Illustration 14–10.

c. Prepare a statement of activities for the year ended June 30, 2011, following the format in Illustration 14–8.

d. Prepare a statement of cash flows for the year ended June 30, 2011, following the format in Illustration 14–9.

Chapter Fifteen

Not-for-Profit Organizations—Regulatory, Taxation, and Performance Issues

Learning Objectives

After studying this chapter, you should be able to:

1. Identify oversight bodies and the source of their authority over not-for-profit organizations (NPOs).
2. Describe how and why states regulate NPOs and describe the following:
   Not-for-profit incorporation laws.
   Registration, licenses, and tax exemption.
   Lobbying and political influence.
3. Identify how the federal government regulates NPOs and describe the following:
   Tax-exempt status—public charities and private foundations.
   Unrelated business income tax.
   Restricting political activity.
   Intermediate sanctions.
   Reorganization and dissolution.
4. Describe governance issues of NPO boards, including incorporating documents and board membership.
5. Identify how benchmarks and performance measures can be used to evaluate NPOs.
6. Describe uniform policies and practices for NPOs across states.

As seen in the beginning of Chapter 14 (and Illustration 14–1), the not-for-profit sector is a very large and diverse sector of the U.S. economy. In 1848, Alexis de Tocqueville, chronicler of democratic life in America, wrote that

> Americans of all ages, all stations in life, and all types of disposition are forever forming associations . . . if they want to proclaim a truth or propagate some feeling by the encouragement of a great example, they form an association.[1]

[1] Alexis de Tocqueville, *Democracy in America,* translated by George Lawrence, edited by J. P. Mayer (New York: Harper & Row, 1969) (from works of de Tocqueville written around 1848), p. 513.

The process that has evolved for individuals who wish to operate a not-for-profit organization (NPO) is to first request recognition from a state as a legal entity separate from an association of individuals, and then to apply to the Internal Revenue Service for exemption from federal taxes. With these two steps, the association accepts oversight, transparency, and accountability for performance. Watchdog organizations, not-for-profit organizations themselves, have sprung up to ensure that data are available for stakeholders to evaluate the effectiveness and efficiency of not-for-profit organizations in meeting their public purpose.

Sometimes the line between businesses and not-for-profit organizations is fuzzy, but a widely accepted definition of a not-for-profit entity is one whose goals involve something other than earning a profit for owners, usually the provision of services.[2] Lack of a profit motive presents control and reporting problems for not-for-profit managers. Success becomes measured by how much the organization contributes to the public well being with the resources available to it.[3] In this chapter, the role of accounting data in helping NPO managers and governing bodies to comply with regulations and respond to the information needs of various stakeholders is examined. While the term *not-for-profit* encompasses the governmental entities described in Chapters 2 through 11, the focus in Chapters 14 and 15 is on nongovernmental, not-for-profit organizations. Not-for-profit entities in higher education and health care industries are described in Chapters 16 and 17, along with public and for-profit entities that provide specialized services.

OVERSIGHT AUTHORITY

The compassion and generosity of people supplies charities with tremendous amounts of resources to meet the public demand, particularly in the early days following natural and man-made disasters. Although during times of disaster (and other times) new organizations are created to meet the health and welfare needs of people in crisis, more often donors provide resources to large and well-established not-for-profit organizations that have proven track records of effective and efficient delivery of services to the needy, such as the American National Red Cross and the Salvation Army.

Inevitably, disasters are followed by unscrupulous fundraisers and illegal scams that result in public outcry for accountability regarding how public funds were used. In addressing who is responsible for charitable spending decisions, it is important to understand the legal and governance structure of an organization. For example, the American National Red Cross is a federally chartered instrumentality of the U.S. government (established in 1881, chartered in 1905) whose mission includes disaster preparedness and relief. The Salvation Army is an international Christian church established in London in 1881 that has adopted a quasi-military command structure in serving the needy. Neither of these organizations receive not-for-profit and tax-exempt status through the channels most nongovernmental not-for-profit organizations take; however, information about these organizations (or related offices) is available on Internal Revenue Service (IRS) Form 990s at *www.guidestar.org,* along with other public charities.

[2] David W. Young, *Management Control in Nonprofit Organizations,* 8th ed. (Cambridge, MA: The Crimson Press, 2008), p. 20.

[3] Ibid.

In general, NPOs are accountable to the state government that grants them their legal existence, the federal government for granting them tax-exempt status, their own governing board, individual donors and grantors, consumers of their services, and the public at large. It is important to note that churches, while certainly part of the nongovernmental, not-for-profit sector, do not require states and the federal government to grant them legal and tax-exempt status because of the historic constitutional separation of church and state in the United States. However, many activities in which churches engage are subject to state and federal regulations.

Accountants and auditors play a critical role in assuring stakeholders that all not-for-profit organizations have complied with applicable laws and regulations, and, in the process, have efficiently and effectively used the assets with which they were entrusted. Various state and federal regulations are examined next; however, many of these topics have complex legal aspects that are not accounting-related. For the interested reader, additional references are provided at the end of the chapter.

STATE REGULATION

Oversight responsibility derives from a state's power to give legal life to a not-for-profit organization, either in the form of a not-for-profit corporation or limited liability company, or in the state's recognition of a charitable trust.

The state monitors NPO managers whom the public entrusts with funds and grants economic privileges, such as exemption from taxes. The state has responsibility to represent public beneficiaries of charities and contributors and to detect cases when managers or directors have mismanaged, diverted, or defrauded the charity and the public.

Legislation regulating NPOs varies greatly across states. However, there are some common methods used by states and sometimes adopted by local governments to ensure that the public good is protected as NPOs solicit charitable contributions and conduct business. The audited annual financial statements are not always sufficient to satisfy the oversight body that the NPO has complied with laws. The accountant often serves the NPO client in preparing specialized reports required by the oversight body.

Not-for-Profit Incorporation Laws

A group of individuals who share a philanthropic or other vision may operate as an unincorporated association if it is small or if they expect the endeavor to have a limited life; however, organizers are treated as partners and share liability for any debts incurred by the association. If the organization plans to grow into a long-lived operation, organizers may choose to file articles of incorporation with a state under the not-for-profit corporation statutes or charitable trust laws to create a legal entity and limit the liability of the incorporators and directors. These laws differ across the 50 states, but states generally have built into the not-for-profit corporation laws the requirement that organizers (1) choose a name that is not misleading or in use by another corporation, (2) designate a resident agent and address, (3) state a clear purpose for the entity, (4) appoint a board of directors, (5) write by-laws that delineate board responsibilities and operating structure, (6) call at least one board meeting a year, and (7) require management to report on financial condition and operations at least once a year. Not-for-profit incorporation statutes also state the extent to which directors are individually liable for the misapplication of assets through neglect or failure to exercise reasonable care and prudence in administration of the affairs of the corporation. Upon conferring the NPO legal status separate from the incorporators, the state bears oversight responsibility for the NPO.

ILLUSTRATION 15–1 **Regulations over Not-for-Profit Organizations (varies by state)**

State and/or Local Government Regulations
Application to operate under an assumed name.
Application to incorporate as a not-for-profit corporation or a limited liability company.
Annual compliance reporting.
Special licenses with particular state departments to operate a health care facility (public health), housing corporation (housing authority), residential care facility (social service), school (education), or to handle food.
Application for exemption from income, franchise, sales, use, real, and personal property taxes.
Employer registration, including payroll tax returns, withholding of state taxes, and unemployment.
License to solicit charitable contributions.
Registration of political lobbyists, lobbying agents, or lobbying activities.
License for one-day beer, wine, and liquor sales.
License to conduct charitable games (e.g., bingo, raffles, millionaire parties).
Policies on conflict of interest and self-dealing with directors.
License to collect sales and use taxes as a vendor.
Freedom of Information Act (FOIA) (if a substantial amount of funds are public).
Open Meetings Act (if governmental in nature).
Notice of plans to merge with another agency.
Notice of plans to dissolve, including tax clearance.

FEDERAL REGULATION

Because charities serve the common good, the federal government has encouraged not-for-profit associations and charitable contributions since the first revenue act in 1894. The public expects the federal government to monitor those organizations receiving tax benefits to ensure that these privileges are not abused. NPOs must follow general laws that govern businesses (such as fair labor standards, older workers' benefits protection, equal employment opportunities acts, disabilities acts, civil rights laws, drug-free workplace laws, immigration laws, antidiscrimination and harassment laws, and veterans and whistleblowers' protection), unless they are specifically exempted. This section describes federal laws that are unique to NPOs.

Illustration 15–2 is a chart depicting how a public charity interacts with the IRS during its existence.

Tax-exempt Status

Even though a state may have conferred not-for-profit corporation status on an organization, that NPO must still apply to the Internal Revenue Service (IRS) for exemption from federal income tax.[8] Churches (including synagogues, temples, and mosques), integrated auxiliaries of churches, and any organization that has gross receipts in each taxable year of normally not more than $5,000 do not have to file Form 1023 to be considered tax-exempt under Sec. 501(c)(3).

As shown in Illustration 14–1, not all not-for-profit organizations are tax exempt. A common reason that an NPO is not exempt from income taxes is that its mission is primarily to influence legislation. The stated purpose of the NPO and the services

[8] Application for income tax exemption is made on Form 1023 for public charities and Form 1024 for all other organizations. NPOs may also qualify for exemption from certain federal excise taxes (e.g., communications, manufacturers, diesel, and motor fuels taxes). See also IRS Pub. 557 *Tax-Exempt Status for Your Organization.*

ILLUSTRATION 15–2 Life Cycle of a Public Charity

Starting Out

- Organizing documents, articles, trust, or charter
- By-laws
- Employer identification number (EIN)
- Charitable solicitation registration

Applying to IRS

- Application for tax-exempt status (Forms 1023 and 1024)
- IRS processing (rulings and determination letter)

Required Annual Filings

- Annual exempt organizations information return (Forms 990, 990-EZ, 990-N)
- Unrelated business income tax (UBIT)

Ongoing Compliance

- Jeopardizing exemption (private benefit, political activity)
- Intermediate sanctions
- Employment taxes
- Substantiation and disclosure (e.g., noncash contributions)
- Public disclosure requirements
- Charitable contributions—what's deductible?
- *Charitable Contributions. Substantiation and Disclosure Requirements* (Pub. 1771)
- Customer account services
- Compliance Guide (Pub. 4221)

Significant Events

- Notifying the IRS of significant changes (e.g., mergers)
- Private letter ruling
- Audits of exempt organizations
- Termination of an exempt organization

Source: Internal Revenue Service "Life Cycle of a Public Charity" with examples and links to appropriate forms, available at *www.irs.ustreas.gov/charities/charitable/article/0,,id= 122670,00.html.*

it will perform determine under which section of the Internal Revenue Code (IRC) of 1986 the NPO requests exemption. Illustration 15–3 shows some of the more than 35 classifications of statutory exemptions under which tax-exempt organizations fall. The most common classification under IRC Section 501 is Sec. 501(c)(3), which is an organization operated for philanthropic, educational, or similar purposes. The **organizational test** for tax-exempt status is that the articles of incorporation must limit the organization's purposes to those described in the categories in IRC Sec. 501 and must not empower it to engage in activities that are not in furtherance of those purposes. Alternatively, some not-for-profit organizations, such as hospitals, have been criticized for not providing an adequate amount of free services as a benefit to society, as stated in their application for tax-exempt status.

An individual can receive a charitable contribution deduction by making a donation to a Sec. 501(c)(3) organization (and certain other exempt organizations), but only if the gift is used for charitable purposes. Gifts are nonexchange transactions (discussed in Chapters 4 and 14) for which the donor receives no benefit in exchange for the contribution. Many categories of tax-exempt organizations, such as business leagues, social clubs, and cooperatives, cannot offer donors the advantage of a charitable deduction from income taxes because they operate primarily for the benefit of members, not the public at large. Another advantage of tax exemption under Sec. 501(c)(3) is the opportunity to apply for grants from foundations and government agencies, which

ILLUSTRATION 15–3 Tax-Exempt Status According to the Internal Revenue Code (selected)

Section of 1986 Internal Revenue Code	Description of Organization and Its Activities
501(c)(1)	Corporations organized under acts of Congress, such as the Federal Deposit Insurance Corporation
501(c)(2)	Title-holding corporation for exempt organizations
501(c)(3)	Charitable, religious, scientific, literary, educational, testing for public safety
501(c)(4)	Civic leagues, social welfare organizations, local employee associations, community organizations
501(c)(5)	Labor unions, agricultural and horticultural organizations, farm bureaus
501(c)(6)	Business leagues, trade associations, chambers of commerce, real estate boards
501(c)(7)	Social and recreational clubs, hobby clubs, country clubs
501(c)(8)	Fraternal beneficiary society and associations; lodges providing for payment of insurance benefits to members
501(c)(9)	Voluntary employees' beneficiary associations to provide insurance benefits to members
501(c)(13)	Cemetery companies; burial activities
501(c)(14)	State-chartered credit unions, mutual reserve fund
501(c)(17)	Supplemental unemployment benefit trusts
501(c)(19)	Veterans' organizations or armed forces members' posts
501(c)(20)	Group legal service plans provided by a corporation for its members
501(d)	Religious and apostolic associations; religious communities
501(e)	Cooperative hospital service organizations
501(f)	Cooperative service organization of operating educational organizations
501(k)	Child care organizations
521(a)	Farmers; cooperative associations
527	Political parties, campaign committees, political action committees
529	Qualified state tuition programs

often limit funding to public charities. An organization that is not a Sec. 501(c)(3) organization must disclose to donors that contributions are *not* tax deductible.

Independent charitable organizations may voluntarily join together as a **federated fund-raising organization** to raise and distribute money among themselves. Examples of such federations are the United Way and community chests.

Annual Compliance Reporting

Form 990 is the primary tool the federal government uses to collect information about the NPO and its activities. The IRS expands the form as Congress requires more information to be furnished by tax-exempt organizations. The form must be made available to the public for three years.[9] Failure to file this form brings significant

[9] Public disclosure regulations issued in 1999 require that tax-exempt organizations provide a copy of their three most recently filed Form 990s and exempt application immediately upon personal request or within 30 days for a written request. Penalties for not doing so are $20 per day up to a maximum of $10,000 but can be avoided if the organization makes these forms widely available on the Internet [Treas. Reg. §1.6104]. Similar regulations were passed for private foundations and their Form 990-PFs in 2000.

ILLUSTRATION 15–4 Parts of the revised IRS Form 990 (for the 2008 tax year and beyond)

	Core Form
Part I	Summary
Part II	Signature block
Part III	Statement of program service accomplishments
Part IV	Checklist of required schedules
Part V	Statements regarding other IRS filings and tax compliance
Part VI	Governance, management, and disclosure
Part VII	Compensation of officers, directors, trustees, key employees, highest compensated employees, and independent contractors
Part VIII	Statement of revenue
Part IX	Statement of functional expenses
Part X	Balance sheet
Part XI	Financial statements and reporting
	Schedules
A	Public charity status and public support
B	Schedules of contributors
C	Political campaign and lobby activities
D	Supplemental financial statements
E	Schools
F	Statement of activities outside the United States
G	Supplemental information regarding fund-raising or gaming activities
H	Hospitals
I	Grants and other assistance to organizations, governments, and individuals in the U.S.
J	Compensation information
K	Supplemental information on tax-exempt bonds
L	Transactions with interested persons
M	Noncash contributions
N	Liquidation, termination, dissolution, or significant disposition of assets
O	Supplemental information to Form 990
R	Related organizations and unrelated partnerships

penalties, unless an extension is granted. Annual reporting requirements do not apply to federal agencies and churches and their affiliates.

The IRS has overhauled the Form 990 effective for returns filed for the 2008 tax year, the first substantive change in annual reporting for tax-exempt organizations since 1979. The changes are designed to enhance transparency about the organization, allow the IRS to efficiently assess noncompliance, and minimize the burden of filing on tax-exempt organizations. The form is comprised of an 11-page core return and 16 schedules that may apply to only some organizations (increased from a 9-page core return and 2 schedules). Some information is new, some information has been deleted, and much of it has been reorganized. Illustration 15–4 delineates the information that is required on the new annual reporting Form 990.

Those tax-exempt organizations required to file a Form 990 will file one of three forms, depending on the size of the organization. For the tax year 2008 and beyond, small tax-exempt entities with gross receipts normally under $25,000 a year will file a Form 990-N "postcard." For 2008, Form 990-EZ will be filed by mid-sized tax-exempt entities with annual gross receipts between $25,000 and $1,000,000 and total assets less than $2.5 million. All other tax-exempt public charities will file Form 990. After a three-year transition period (2008–2010) that allows a large number of organizations to file a Form 990–EZ, the maximum annual gross receipts for filing a Form 990-EZ will be reduced to $200,000 (down from $1 million) and $500,000 in total assets (down from $2.5 million). Private foundations, discussed in the next section, will prepare an annual Form 990-PF.

Public Charities versus Private Foundations

IRC Sec. 501(c)(3) encompasses private foundations and public charities. A **private foundation** is one that receives its support from a small number of individuals or corporations and investment income rather than from the public at large. It exists to make grants to public charities. Private foundations file an annual Form 990-PF and are subject to several excise taxes: (1) for failure to take certain actions (such as distribute a minimum amount to public charities), (2) for prohibited behavior (such as speculative investing, self-dealing transactions with disqualified persons, and excess business holdings), and (3) on net investment income (this tax is then used to support the costs of auditing tax-exempt organizations).[10]

Public charities are funded, operated, and monitored by the public at large rather than by a limited number of donors. Public charities receive preferential treatment over private foundations because of their broad base of support. They are not subject to the excise taxes mentioned for private foundations, and donors do not face the same limitations when giving to a public charity.

New tax-exempt organizations are presumed to be public charities for their first five years. In their sixth year, they must meet the public support test (described below) in order to avoid being classified as a private foundation. Generally, an IRC Sec. 501(c)(3) organization is considered to be a public charity if it meets one of the exclusions to the private foundation definition: For example, it is broadly supported by the public, government, or other public charities; it operates to support another public charity; or it tests products for public safety.

Two parts of the *broad public support test* must be satisfied. The **external support test** is met if at least one-third of the organization's total revenue comes from the government, general public (e.g., individuals, private foundations, corporations), or other public charities in the form of contributions, grants, membership dues, charges for services, or sales of merchandise. If gross receipts from any person or governmental agency exceed $5,000 or 1 percent of the organization's support for the taxable year, the excess is not counted in public support for the purposes of the external support test. Investment income and gains from sales of capital assets are *not* considered public support. Private foundations try not to give a grant to a not-for-profit organization that might cause the public charity to fail the support test and be reclassified as a private foundation. If that happens, the foundation must exercise **expenditure responsibility** and monitor whether the grant was used exclusively for the purpose for which it was made. The private foundation can require the grantee to provide assurance that the grant will not *tip* the grantee into private foundation status before it is granted. The **internal support test** requires that the NPO *not* receive more than one-third of its total support from investment income and unrelated business income. Once an organization is in its sixth year, classification as a public charity must be redetermined on an annual basis.

[10] IRC Sec. 509(a) and T. D. 9423, September 08, 2008, which eliminated the advance ruling period.

Unrelated Business Income Tax

Owners of small businesses have long complained that NPOs compete with them in businesslike activities with the unfair advantage of lower costs due to exemption from income taxes. For example, college bookstores sell clothing, credit unions operate travel agencies, YMCAs run health clubs, and universities operate veterinary clinics.[11] In 1950 Congress passed the first unrelated business income tax (UBIT), which assesses tax at corporate rates on income that NPOs derive from activities not substantially related to their charitable or tax-exempt mission.[12] UBIT requirements apply to all not-for-profit organizations and public colleges and universities except federal corporations and certain charitable trusts.

The IRS is primarily interested in how the unrelated business income was earned, not in how it is used, even if it is used to further the organization's tax-exempt purpose. **Unrelated business income (UBI)** is calculated as the gross income from an unrelated trade or business engaged in on a *regular* basis less directly connected expenses, certain net operating losses, and qualified charitable contributions. The first $1,000 of unrelated business income is excluded from taxation. Unrelated trade or business activities are those that are *substantially* unrelated to carrying out the organization's exempt purpose. Stated differently, unless activities make an important contribution to the accomplishment of the organization's exempt purpose, they will be considered unrelated. The activities that must be carefully examined include sponsorships, advertising, affinity credit card arrangements, sale of mailing lists, travel tour services, and fund-raising events. The UBIT is reported on a Form 990-T, which must be publicly available as is the Form 990.

To determine whether the business activity is substantially related to the organization's exempt purpose, the relationship between the business activity and the exempt purpose is examined. Unrelated business income does not include dividends, interest, royalties, fees for use of intangible property, gains on the sale of property (unless that property was used in an unrelated trade or business), or income from activities in which substantially all of the work is done by volunteers, income from the sale of donated merchandise, income from legally conducted games of chance, rents from real property, or when the trade is conducted primarily for the convenience of its members, such as a laundry in a college dorm. However, rents from debt-financed property, rents based on a percentage of net income rather than gross income, and rents on personal property are considered to be unrelated business income. Excluded from UBI is income from advertising done in the form of corporate sponsorships for particular events if (1) the corporate sponsor does not get any substantial benefit in return for its payment other than the promotion of its name, (2) the display does not advertise the company's products or services, and (3) the amount of payment is not contingent on the level of attendance at the event.[13] Corporate sponsorships that appear in regularly published periodicals are still UBI. Special rules apply to bingo and distribution of low-cost items, such as pens or stickers.

Feeder Organizations

NPOs may control a **feeder organization** that is organized to carry on a trade or business for the benefit of the exempt organization and remit its profits to the NPO. The income passed from the feeder to the not-for-profit organization in the form of

[11] See *www.irs.gov/charities,* then search for "UBIT" for general rules and current developments.

[12] IRC Secs. 511–513. Unrelated business income is also subject to the alternative minimum tax.

[13] This change came about in the Taxpayer Relief Act of 1997 and was a codification of proposed IRS regulations from prior years.

mentoring, among others. Although a not-for-profit program will never be able to show that its actions were entirely responsible for outcomes, the attempt to measure and draw correlations is a valiant effort at accountability for the scarce dollars entrusted to NPOs to make a difference.

UNIFORM POLICIES ACROSS STATES

States' attorneys general and others involved in the regulation of the not-for-profit sector have collaborated over the years with model acts that can be adapted by states in establishing policies and best practices in the areas of incorporation, investments, solicitation, and volunteers. The Volunteer Protection Act of 1997 (P.L. 105-19) is an example of federal legislation that affects all NPOs. A model not-for-profit corporation act developed by the American Bar Association and a model charitable solicitation act prepared by the National Association of Attorneys General provide a basic framework of best practices that have been used by many states and by many not-for-profit organizations.

The Uniform Prudent Management of Investment Funds Act (UPMIFA) of 2006 relates to not-for-profit organizations that manage charitable funds—both investing those funds and spending endowment income. This act was approved at the June 2006 annual meeting of the national Conference of Commissioners on Uniform State Laws to revise its predecessor, the Uniform Management of Institutional Funds Act (UMIFA). Both acts are designed to provide guidance in the absence of explicit donor stipulations. The commissioners revised the UMIFA for three primary reasons:

- To provide stricter guidelines regarding endowment fund expenditures and give organizations the ability to cope more easily with fluctuating endowment fund values.
- To adopt the approach of the Uniform Trust Code (2005) regarding the release and modification of restrictions on charitable funds.
- To adopt language similar to the Uniform Prudent Investors Act (1994) and the Revised Model Nonprofit Corporation Act (1987).

At least 25 states have already enacted the UPMIFA and more have introduced bills for its adoption. More information about the act is available at *www.upmifa.org.*

National nonprofit support groups, such as Boardsource, facilitate the sharing of policies and procedures for NPOs across states. For example, publications are available with sample conflict of interest policies, whistle-blower protection policies, and other policies that auditors and the public now expect to be in place.

SUMMARY

This chapter provides a general description of tax laws and other state and federal regulations so that accountants and decision makers using financial information are familiar with the environment within which tax-exempt organizations operate. It should be clear that a thorough understanding of current case law about exempt organizations is also important. More specific details are available in Internal Revenue Service literature available on its Web site (*www.irs.ustreas.gov*) and books on taxation of tax-exempt organizations. In the future, NPOs can expect increased scrutiny and accountability for performance outcomes as a more well-informed public demands it and as technology enables government agencies, such as the IRS, to audit and monitor tax-exempt organizations.

Key Terms

Advocacy, *633*
Charitable solicitation, *632*
Debt-financed income, *640*
Direct lobbying, *633*
Disqualified person, *641*
Due diligence, *642*
Economic size, *642*
Excess benefit transaction, *641*
Expenditure responsibility, *638*
External support test, *638*
Federated fund-raising organization, *636*
Feeder organization, *639*
Grass-roots lobbying, *633*
Influencing, *633*
Intermediate sanctions, *641*
Internal support test, *638*
Legislation, *640*
Lobbying, *633*
Organizational test, *635*
Political activity, *633*
Political organization, *641*
Private foundation, *638*
Propaganda, *640*
Public charity, *638*
Unrelated business income, (UBI), *639*

Selected References

Gross, Malvern J., Jr., John H. McCarthy, and Nancy E. Shelmon. *Financial and Accounting Guide for Not-for-Profit Organizations*, 7th ed. New York: John Wiley & Sons, 2005, with 2008 Cumulative Supplement.

Internal Revenue Service, Department of Treasury. *Application for Recognition of Exemption under Sec. 501(c)(3) of the Internal Revenue Code.* Package 1023.

_______. Pub. 78. *Cumulative List of Exempt Organizations.*

_______. Pub. 557. *Tax-Exempt Status for Your Organization.*

_______. Pub. 598. *Tax on Unrelated Business Income of Exempt Organizations.*

_______. Pub. 1771. *Charitable Contributions Substantiation & Disclosure Requirements.*

_______. Pub. 4221-PC. *Compliance Guide for 501(c)(3) Public Charities.*

Michigan Nonprofit Association (and Accounting Aid Society). *Michigan Nonprofit Management Manual*, 4th ed. Lansing, MI. Available at *www.mnaonline.org.*

Ober Kaler. *The Nonprofit Legal Landscape*. Washington, DC: Boardsource, 2005.

Wing, Kennard T., Thomas H. Pollak, and Amy Blackwood. *The Nonprofit Almanac*. Washington, DC: The Urban Institute Press, 2008.

Young, David. *Managerial Control in Nonprofit Organizations*. Cambridge, MA: Crimson Press, 2008.

Web Sites for Not-for-Profit Support Organizations

American Institute of Philanthropy, *www.charitywatch.org*
BBB Wise Giving Alliance, *www.give.org*
Boardsource, Inc., *www.boardsource.org*
Guidestar, Inc., *www.guidestar.org*
Independent Sector, *www.independentsector.org*
National Center for Charitable Statistics, at the Urban Institute, *www.nccs.urban.org*

Periodicals

Chronicle of Philanthropy, http://philanthropy.com.
Nonprofit Management and Leadership, Jossey-Bass.
Nonprofit and Voluntary Sector Quarterly, Association for Research on Nonprofit Organizations and Voluntary Action (ARNOVA), *www.arnova.org.*
Exempt Organization Tax Review. Tax Analysts.
The Nonprofit Times, http://www.nptimes.com.

Questions

15–1. Explain why a state has regulatory authority over a not-for-profit organization. When does the federal government have regulatory authority over a not-for-profit organization?

15–2. A local not-for-profit organization that provides shelter for the homeless favors proposed legislation in the state that would facilitate converting an old hotel into a transitional living facility. What actions can the organization take to ensure this legislation gets approved?

15–3. Using Illustration 15–3 as a guide, indicate under which Internal Revenue Code section each of the following public charities is most likely to be exempt from federal income tax.

a. Ottowa County Credit Union.
b. Midwest Rheumatoid Arthritis Association.
c. Peaceful Place Cemetery.
d. Blacksberry Civic League.
e. Delta Gamma Epsilon sorority.
f. Landscapers Professional Association.

15–4. What are the distinguishing characteristics between a public charity and a private foundation? Why do these differences result in different federal reporting requirements?

15–5. Describe the general ways that the revised Form 990, applicable for tax year 2008 and beyond, is different from previous versions.

15–6. How can a not-for-profit museum ensure that its gift shop activities will not result in an unrelated business income tax liability?

15–7. A new not-for-profit board member suggests that the NPO create a separate audit committee to work with the external auditors. The other board members feel that it is already difficult to find community people with financial expertise who have the time to serve on boards, so they do not support creating a new committee. Do you agree with the new board member or the other board members? Why?

15–8. Why are the intermediate sanction regulations an important tool for the IRS to use in curbing abuses such as excessive management compensation?

15–9. The financial manager of a not-for-profit child care center wants to improve the monthly report to the board and has decided to include performance measures. What issues should the manager consider in calculating and reporting measures of performance? What resources are available to use in benchmarking the performance of this child care center to similar organizations?

15–10. What incorporating documents should an auditor examine in conducting an audit or preparing an annual Form 990 tax return of a not-for-profit organization? What information in these documents is most useful to stakeholders external to the not-for-profit organization?

Cases

15–1 Establishing a Not-for-Profit Organization. As a certified public accountant, you have been asked by a group of local citizens to assist in establishing a not-for-profit organization for the purpose of raising funds to keep their neighborhood safe and clean. These people are concerned about the growing crime rate and increased amount of trash and traffic in their community. They believe that a collaborative effort is needed to address these problems. The citizens are not sure how large the organization will be.

Required

a. Prepare a memo to the group that outlines the process involved in creating a tax-exempt not-for-profit entity. Be sure to point out particular alternative strategies, including the advantages and disadvantages you believe the incorporating officers should spend time considering.

b. What resources are available on the Internet to help this group understand the regulatory, taxation, and performance measure issues that they will face as officers of a tax-exempt, not-for-profit organization?

15–2 Unrelated Business Income Tax. Dan Smith is a certified human resource manager who serves on the board of a local professional association of human resource managers. The association puts on an annual conference for its members at which there are educational workshops, keynote speakers, and a display of vendors that serve the needs of human resource managers. This year, the association has decided to allow vendors to advertise in the annual meeting publication for a fee. Mr. Smith is unsure whether the benefits of allowing this advertising outweigh the potential costs if this income is subject to unrelated business income tax. As a result, Mr. Smith has asked your assistance, as an accounting student, in analyzing the costs and benefits of this proposal.

Required

a. Create a list of questions to pose to the executive director of the association about the proposed advertising so that the board has all the relevant facts on hand.

b. What resources are available to investigate whether income from advertising is subject to unrelated business income tax?

c. Prepare a memo to Mr. Smith that outlines the key issues involved in the proposal and suggest an approach to analyzing whether the proposal is in the best interests of the professional association.

15–3 Internet Case—Performance Measures. Go to the Internet Web sites of five of the largest charitable organizations listed in Illustration 15–7 and search for financial information and performance measures they may disclose on their Web sites.

Required

a. Locate a comparable organization for each of these five NPOs, perhaps a competitor. From information provided on the Web sites, calculate the amount that each organization spent on its program (as a percentage of income and of total expenses) as well as the number of dollars it raised for each dollar spent on fund-raising.

b. Select other financial performance measures from Illustration 15–6, calculate those measures, and compare pairs of organizations. Where could you get other useful information?

c. Prepare a table showing the five charities, their counterparts, and performance measures for each. Which charity would you consider the most efficient and effective? Why?

15–4 Nonfinancial Performance Measures. The Little Feet Dance Association is a performing arts program in an urban area. It was established to increase appreciation for dance among youth and strengthen social bonds in the community. The association has been in existence for several years, and it has recently attracted the attention of several governmental, foundation, and private donors who support its cause. Prior to making a financial commitment, however, these funders have asked for documentation that the association is effective in accomplishing its goals. As a managerial accountant on the board of the Little Feet Dance Association, you have been asked to assist in responding to the funders' request.

Required

a. Prepare a graphic or chart showing possible outputs and outcomes that could be expected from activities and expenditures of a not-for-profit organization such as Little Feet Dance Association. (*Hint:* See the common outcomes and indicators framework of the Urban Institute and The Center for What Works for this type of program, available at *www.urban.org/nonprofits/index.cfm,* for an example of an outcomes sequence chart).

b. List two indicators that could be used to measure whether the association met each of its intermediate and end outcomes.

c. What questions do you anticipate potential funders will have when reviewing the outcomes sequence chart and indicators that the association has put together?

Exercises and Problems

15–1 Multiple Choice. Choose the best answer.

1. State regulation of not-for-profit organizations derives from the state's power to:
   a. Grant exemption from income taxes.
   b. Give legal life to a not-for-profit corporation.
   c. Grant exemption from sales taxes.
   d. Grant licenses for charitable solicitation.
2. A typical reason why an NPO might not be exempt from federal taxes is:
   a. The NPO expects to spend all of its annual revenue and, therefore, will have no "income" on which to be taxed.
   b. The NPO is primarily organized to influence political legislation.
   c. The NPO chooses not to apply to the federal government for tax-exempt status.
   d. All of the above.
3. The "ongoing compliance" stage of the life cycle of a tax-exempt organization that interacts with the IRS includes:
   a. Intermediate sanctions.
   b. Application for exempt status with Form 1023.
   c. Notifying the IRS about a merger.
   d. Filing unrelated business income tax returns.
4. Federal regulation of not-for-profit organizations derives from the federal government's power to:
   a. Grant licenses for charitable solicitation.
   b. Grant exemption from federal income taxes.
   c. Grant exemption from sales taxes.
   d. Give legal life to a not-for-profit corporation.
5. A term used to indicate that a not-for-profit organization is communicating directly with a public official in either the executive or legislative branch of the state government for the purpose of influencing legislation is:
   a. Influencing.

b. Grass-roots lobbying.
c. Direct lobbying.
d. Propagandizing.

6. A not-for-profit organization that is exempt from federal income taxes under IRC Sec. 501(c)(3), exists to make grants to public charities, and receives its support from a small number of individuals or corporations and investment income rather than from the public at large is called a:
   a. Private foundation.
   b. Public charity.
   c. Nongovernmental organization.
   d. Governmental, not-for-profit organization.
7. A measure of performance of a not-for-profit organization that captures whether contributions received are appropriately higher than the cost of raising those funds is:
   a. Unrestricted net assets divided by operating expenses.
   b. Revenues divided by expenses.
   c. Public support divided by fund-raising expenses.
   d. Program expenses divided by total expenses.
8. An example of unrelated business income for which a tax-exempt entity may have to pay taxes at corporate rates is:
   a. An environmental organization that offers advertising to nonmembers in its annual catalog.
   b. A university that offers health club memberships in its intramural facilities to local residents.
   c. A credit union that offers insurance and travel agency services to members and nonmembers.
   d. All of the above.
9. The tool the IRS most likely will use when key officers in a tax-exempt entity receive excess economic benefits from transactions with the not-for-profit organization is:
   a. Fines and forfeits.
   b. Revocation of the organization's tax-exempt status.
   c. Intermediate sanctions.
   d. Public display on the IRS's Web site.
10. When a tax-exempt organization dissolves, the managers must ensure that:
   a. All assets are appropriately transferred to another tax-exempt organization.
   b. All creditors get paid.
   c. All federal, state, and local taxes are paid.
   d. All of the above.

15–2 Public Charity. The Kids Club of Clare County is a public charity under IRC Sec. 501(c)(3). It had total support last year of the following:

United Way support	$ 80,000
Grant from Clare County	70,000
Contributions	350,000
Investment income	75,000
	$575,000

Of the $350,000 received from contributors, $250,000 came from five contributors, each of whom gave more than $5,000; the other $100,000 came from small individual contributors.

Required

a. Calculate the total amount of support that qualifies as "public support" in meeting the external support test to escape private foundation status.

b. Is the organization considered a public charity or a private foundation? Why?

c. If the organization had received an additional $140,000 grant from one individual during the year, would the NPO still be classified the same as in your response to part *b* (assuming that the previous five gifts still represent more than 1 percent of the new total)?

15–3 Lobbying Expenses. EarthFriendly, Inc., an IRC Sec. 501(c)(3) organization, incurred lobbying expenses of $150,000 and exempt purpose expenditures of $1.2 million in carrying out its exempt mission.

Required

a. What are the tax consequences if the organization does not elect to participate in lobbying activities on a limited basis?

b. Discuss the factors involved in the association's decision to elect to participate in lobbying activities under IRC Sec. 501(h).

15–4 Unrelated Business Income Tax. The Silverton Symphony Orchestra Hall is a well-established not-for-profit organization exempt under IRC Sec. 501(c)(3) that owns a facility that is home to the local symphony orchestra. Its mission is to increase access to the arts for the community of Silverton. The facility is used throughout the year for many activities. Which of the following regularly conducted activities of Silverton Symphony Hall are subject to unrelated business income tax? (*Hint:* IRS Publication 598 may be helpful in answering this question, available at *www.irs.gov* under "Charities and Non-Profits" and "UBIT.")

	Subject to UBIT	**Not Subject to UBIT**
1. Sale of Silverton Symphony Orchestra Concert CDs in the facility's gift shop.		
2. Rental of the facility to the high school drama club.		
3. Rental of two apartments in the facility to the symphony.		
4. Sale of the season ticket membership list to a local music store.		
5. Rental of the facility to the state CPA association for continuing professional education events.		
6. Internet sales of gift shop items with the Silverton Symphony Orchestra logo.		
7. Lease of the facility's parking lot to the local university on football game days.		

15–5 Gift Shop UBIT. A local exempt organization that trains at-risk youth for employment has an annual operating budget of $300,000, which includes revenue from operating a gift shop in a nearby hotel lobby. Gift shop sales result in a profit of $15,000. The organization has $6,500 of endowment income that it earns on permanently restricted net assets. The income from both the gift shop and the endowment is used to support the organization's exempt purpose. The balance of $278,500 required for annual operations is provided through public support and charges for services.

Required

a. Calculate the UBIT if the corporate tax rate is 15 percent on the first $50,000 of net income and 25 percent on the next $25,000 of income.

b. Assume that the endowment income is reinvested rather than being used to support annual operations. Calculate the amount of unrelated business income.

15–6 Intermediate Sanctions. For each of the following independent situations, determine whether the organization is at risk for receiving intermediate sanctions from the Internal Revenue Service for conferring excess economic benefits on disqualified persons. If so, indicate how the organization can minimize those sanctions.

1. Jane is president of an IRC Sec. 501(c)(3) public charity and personally owns a building that she has decided to sell to the not-for-profit organization. The appraisal value is $200,000, and the agreed-upon selling price is $250,000.
2. A large public charity is very happy with its president's performance and offers him a new compensation agreement for the coming year. He will receive a base salary plus a percentage of the increase in the gross revenues of the organization with no limitation as to the maximum amount.
3. Ann is a member and the director of a symphony association. She receives 20 free admission tickets as a member of the organization.
4. The local chapter of the United Way recently hired Joe Curtis as its new president at a salary of $200,000. The outgoing president was paid $150,000. Mr. Curtis had other offers that ranged from $95,000 to $190,000. The minutes of the meeting reflected that he was exceptionally talented and would not have accepted the position for a lower salary.

15–7 Investment Performance and UPMIFA. Crossroads University is a tax-exempt, private university. An excerpt from Note 5 "Endowment Fund" of its 2007 audited financial statements is as follows:

State law allows the board to appropriate investment income and as much of the net appreciation as is prudent considering the University's needs and general economic conditions. Under the University's endowment spending policy, approximately 4 percent of the value of fixed income investments and 4.5 percent of the value of equity investments is appropriated to support current operations.

. . .

The state adopted the 1972 Uniform Management of Institutional Funds Act (the Act). Under the provisions of the Act, appreciation of permanently restricted

ILLUSTRATION 16–3

MIDWEST UNIVERSITY
Statement of Cash Flows
For the Year Ended June 30, 2011
(in thousands)

	Primary Institution	Component Unit Hospital
Cash Flows from Operating Activities		
Cash received from students for tuition and fees	$ 2,775	—
Research grants and contracts	35	—
Cash received from auxiliary activities	2,300	—
Cash received from patients and third-party payors	—	$1,858
Cash received from Medicaid and Medicare	—	3,164
Payments to suppliers and others	(1,322)	(1,308)
Payments to students—scholarships	(135)	—
Payments to employees	(6,344)	(3,299)
Payments to annuitants	(250)	—
Other payments	(447)	(100)
Net cash provided (used) by operating activities	(3,388)	315
Cash Flows from Noncapital Financing Activities		
Federal appropriations	438	—
State appropriations	4,170	—
Gifts and grants received for endowment purposes	4,192	—
Net cash flows provided by noncapital financing activities	8,800	—
Cash Flows from Capital and Related Financing Activities		
Capital grants and gifts received	220	71
Proceeds from capital debt	500	—
Purchase of capital assets	(1,490)	(195)
Principal paid on capital debt	(550)	(13)
Interest paid on capital debt	(1,850)	(3)
Net cash used by capital and related financing activities	(3,170)	(140)
Cash Flows from Investing Activities		
Proceeds from sales and maturities of investments	2,664	284
Investment income	975	7
Loans	(163)	—
Purchase of investments	(4,825)	(454)
Net cash provided (used) by investing activities	(1,349)	(163)
Net Increase in Cash and Cash Equivalents	893	12
Cash and cash equivalents—beginning of year	675	86
Cash and cash equivalents—end of year	$ 1,568	$ 98
Reconciliation of Net Operating Revenues (Expenses) to Net Cash Provided (Used) by Operating Activities		
Operating income (loss)	$(6,182)	$ 2
Adjustments to reconcile net income (loss) to net cash provided (used) by operating activities:		
Depreciation expense	3,000	297

ILLUSTRATION 16–3 (*Continued*)

	Primary Institution	Component Unit Hospital
Change in assets and liabilities:		
Receivables, net	70	33
Inventories	(15)	(16)
Short-term investments	(128)	—
Deposit with bond trustee	(23)	—
Prepaid expenses	(9)	8
Accounts payable	119	(8)
Deferred revenue	15	—
Deposits held in custody for others	15	—
Annuities payable	(250)	(1)
Net cash provided (used) by operating activities	$(3,388)	$ 315

Source: Adapted from GASB, *Codification*, Sec. Co5.902.

Chapter 14. The reader is directed to that chapter for more information on the definitions of net asset classifications and the considerable discretion that is allowed by *SFAS No. 117* in presenting financial information, including optional display of supplementary fund accounting information, if desired. Later in this chapter, Illustrations 16–4, 16–5, and 16–6 present the statement of financial position, statement of activities, and statement of cash flows, respectively, for Valley College, a hypothetical private not-for-profit college. These statement formats are generally the same as those illustrated in Chapter 14.

Some of the major differences that do exist between the financial statements of private and public institutions of higher education are in the areas of classification of net assets, format of the operating statement, the cash flows statement, investments, pension disclosures, and compensated absences. Several of the accounting and reporting differences are discussed in the next section of this chapter.

Fund Accounting

Many private and public colleges and universities may continue to use fund accounting for internal purposes. For these institutions, a worksheet can then be used to convert fund accounting information to institution-wide information necessary for the basic financial statements. Fund information may also be included as supplementary information in the financial report. The most commonly used funds are unrestricted current funds, restricted current funds, plant funds, loan funds, endowment funds, annuity and life-income funds, and agency funds. As can be seen, several of the funds have similar counterparts under government fund accounting; these include unrestricted current funds (similar to a General Fund), restricted current funds (similar to special revenue funds), endowment funds, and agency funds. Additional information concerning funds can be found in the AICPA Audit and Accounting Guide, *Not-for-Profit Organizations*. In this chapter, our focus is on basic external financial reporting for the majority of colleges and universities expected to report as "engaged in business-type activities only"; consequently, there is little discussion of fund accounting in this chapter.

ILLUSTRATION 16–6

VALLEY COLLEGE
Statement of Cash Flows
Year Ended June 30, 2011

Cash Flows from Operating Activities	
Increase in net assets	$ 3,524,940
Adjustments to reconcile increase in net assets to net cash provided by operating activities:	
Depreciation	300,000
Increase in pledges receivable (net)	(845,000)
Decrease in tuition and fees receivable (net)	112,000
Increase in accounts payable and accrued expenses	99,460
Increase in deposits and agency funds	10,000
Increase in annuities payable	135,000
Increase in prepaid expenses	(9,000)
Increase in inventories	(15,000)
Gains restricted for long-term purpose	(7,800)
Contributions restricted for long-term investment	(2,673,000)
Net cash provided for operating activities	631,600
Cash Flows from Investing Activities	
Purchases of investments	(2,500,000)
Purchases of property, plant, and equipment	(2,350,000)
Loans to students and faculty	(260,000)
Collections of loans to students and faculty	95,000
Net cash used for investing activities	(5,015,000)
Cash Flows from Financing Activities	
Proceeds from contributions restricted for long-term investment	2,673,000
Issuance of long-term debt	2,000,000
Repayment of long-term debt	(550,000)
Net cash provided by financing activities	4,123,000
Net decrease in cash and cash equivalents	(260,400)
Cash and cash equivalents, beginning of year	675,000
Cash and cash equivalents, end of year	$ 414,600

The financial community, through bond rating agencies, financial analysts, underwriters, and investors, has always evaluated financial performance and the creditworthiness of institutions that issue debt. Some key ratios they use to evaluate viability, return, and leverage are (1) expendable resources to debt, (2) unrestricted resources to operations, (3) expendable resources to total net assets, (4) total resources per full-time-equivalent student, and (5) maximum debt service coverage.[24]

[24] See Engstrom and Esmond-Kiger, "Different Formats," pp. 24–25.

Auditing Colleges and Universities

Most colleges and universities, whether private or public, publish audited financial statements. More and more often, financial statements appear on their Web sites. At a minimum, audits of colleges and universities are performed in conformity with the generally accepted auditing standards (GAAS) promulgated by the AICPA, as discussed in Chapter 12. Additionally, many colleges and universities, as a condition of accepting federal financial awards, are audited under the auditing standards established by the U.S. Government Accountability Office in its publication *Government Auditing Standards* (GAS), also known as the "yellow book," as discussed in Chapter 12. Specifically, if a college or university expends $500,000 or more in federal awards in a given fiscal year, it must have a "single audit" in accordance with the provisions of Office of Management and Budget (OMB) *Circular A–133,* "Audits of States, Local Governments and Nonprofit Organizations." Since the audit requirements for the single audit are described in considerable detail in Chapter 12, they need not be reiterated here.

Due to the large number of dollars involved and decentralized controls, an item of special concern in auditing colleges and universities is ensuring that only costs allowable under OMB *Circular A–21,*[25] "Cost Principles for Educational Institutions," are charged, either as direct costs or indirect costs, to federal grants or contracts. The federal government devotes considerable resources to auditing educational institutions that receive federal assistance, in particular their compliance with OMB *Circular A–21,* as well as unrelated business income. The cost principles and administrative requirements under OMB *Circular A–110*[26] are discussed more fully in Chapter 13. The tax issues involving unrelated business income are discussed in Chapter 15. As with single audits of state and local governments, *Circular A–133* audits place heavy emphasis on evaluating the system of internal controls and compliance with applicable laws and regulations in addition to the traditional audit of the financial statements.

Federal Financial Assistance

The federal government supports institutions of higher learning in the form of research grants and student loan funds. As mentioned in the previous section on auditing issues, acceptance of federal funds requires reporting to the grantor and conformance with various cost accounting rules as well as administrative requirements.

Sponsored Research Funds

Research funds received from the federal government are most likely to be in the form of contracts and grants in which the government is expecting periodic activity reports and a report at the end of the grant period as to how the funds were used. In some instances, the organization may contract with the federal government for a specific product for the funds paid. The terms of the grant or contract are critical factors in determining whether it is an exchange or a nonexchange transaction. Some colleges and universities may have a policy to classify all federal grants as exchange transactions, but the facts and circumstances of each grant should be examined.

[25] OMB *Circular A–21* has been relocated to Title 2 of the Code of Federal Regulations (2CFR), Subtitle A, Chapter II, Part 220.

[26] OMB *Circular A–110* has been relocated to 2CFR, Subtitle A, Chapter II, Part 215.

Student Grants and Loans

Student assistance takes various forms: loans or grants, subsidized or unsubsidized, held by the institution or given directly to the student. A Pell Grant is one in which the federal government provides funds to the institution, which then selects the recipient.[27]

Related Entities

Public and private colleges and universities can be complex in their organizational structure, including majority-owned subsidiaries for intellectual property and businesslike enterprises; clinical and research facilities; financing corporations; and controlled affiliates for fund-raising, alumni relations, and management of assets. At issue is whether there is sufficient control of one organization over another to combine their financial information under one reporting entity.

Most institutionally related fund-raising, clinical, and athletic foundations are legally separate organizations independent of the college or university they serve. However, it may be misleading to exclude the foundation from the college or university's financial report if the foundation operates essentially as an agent of the institution. GASB provides guidance for public colleges and universities in determining whether certain organizations such as those just described are component units of the institution.[28] Organizations that raise and hold economic resources for the direct benefit of a governmental unit, are legally separate, tax-exempt entities, and meet *all* of the following criteria should be discretely presented as component units:

1. The economic resources received or held by the separate organization are entirely or almost entirely for the direct benefit of the primary government, its component units, or its constituents.
2. The primary government or its component units are entitled to or have the ability to otherwise access a majority of the economic resources received or held by the separate organization.
3. The economic resources received or held by an individual organization that the specific primary government or its component units are entitled to or has the ability to otherwise access are significant to that primary government.

If a college or university has a relationship with an organization that does not meet each of these criteria and for which it is not financially accountable, professional judgment should be exercised to determine whether exclusion would render the financial statements of the reporting entity misleading or incomplete.[29] At a minimum, note disclosures of the existence of these affiliated organizations should be made in the public college or university's financial report.

Private colleges and universities, although less likely to have independent fund-raising foundations, may have related entities that require preparation of consolidated financial reports. Generally, consolidated financial reports are needed when a college or university has a controlling financial interest in a for-profit or not-for-profit entity. Controlling financial interest can occur when the college or university has direct or indirect ownership of a majority voting interest in the for-profit or not-for-profit entity or it can occur under other circumstances, such as through a contract.

[27] Catalog of Federal Domestic Assistance (CFDA) #84.063. See: *http://www.cfda.gov.*

[28] GASB, *Codification,* Sec. 2100, pars. 119–141.

[29] Ibid., par. 141.

Key Terms

Annuity agreements, *671*
Collections, *669*
Endowments, *670*
Gifts in kind, *674*
Permanent endowments, *670*
Pooled (life) income fund, *671*
Spending rate, *670*
Split-interest agreements, *671*
Term endowments, *670*
Total return, *670*

Selected References

American Institute of Certified Public Accountants. Audit and Accounting Guide. *Not-for-Profit Organizations.* New York: AICPA, 2008.

Financial Accounting Standards Board. *Statement of Financial Accounting Standards No. 116,* "Accounting for Contributions Received and Contributions Made." Norwalk, CT, 1993.

———. *Statement of Financial Accounting Standards No. 117,* "Financial Statements of Not-for-Profit Organizations." Norwalk, CT, 1993.

Governmental Accounting Standards Board. *Codification of Governmental Accounting and Financial Reporting Standards as of June 30, 2008.* Norwalk, CT, 2008.

National Association of College and University Business Officers. *Financial Accounting and Reporting Manual for Higher Education* (*e-FARM*). Washington, DC. In electronic form.

Questions

16–1. What are restricted assets and how are they shown in the financial statements?

16–2. Explain how restricted gifts and grants are reported by a public college or university. How would such restricted gifts and grants be recorded and reported by a private college or university?

16–3. Private colleges and universities report temporarily and permanently restricted net assets. What, if any, comparable reporting is provided by public universities?

16–4. What are some of the accounting and reporting differences between endowments and split-interest agreements?

16–5. Compare the reporting of contributed services by private and public colleges and universities.

16–6. A private college has received a multi-year unconditional pledge from a major supporter. How will the college report the pledge in its financial statements?

16–7. Explain the conditions that must exist for a public or private college or university to avoid accounting recognition of the value of its collections of art, historical treasures, and similar assets.

16–8. What is an annuity agreement and how does it differ from a life income fund?

16–9. What is a revocable split-interest agreement and how is it recorded by a private college?

16–10. Describe some measures of performance that can be used in assessing whether a university operates effectively.

Cases

16–1 Institutionally Related Foundations. Review each of the following cases that describe a public university and a foundation related to it (i.e., an institutionally related foundation). Explain whether the GASB criteria are met so that the organizations should be discretely presented in the financial statements of the public university. (*Hint:* See Illustration 9–1 and related discussion in Chapter 9.) If the criteria are not met, explain why.

1. *University Alumni Association.* KMH University Alumni Association was established as a legally separate, tax-exempt organization to support both KMH University and its students. Generally, when the university awards a scholarship to a student who meets the criteria established by the Alumni Association, the university requests funds from the Alumni Association's resources. Normally, the Alumni Association honors the request and transfers the funds to the university. In the current year, the Alumni Association has endowed a chair and financed 14 scholarships for the KMH University School of Business and has donated funds for these purposes to KMH University. The funds donated directly to the university and the resources held by the association are significant to the university's financial statements.
2. *University Fund-Raising Foundation.* CCB University Foundation is a legally separate, tax-exempt organization whose bylaws state that it exists solely to provide financial support to CCB University. The foundation regularly makes distributions directly to the university and pays certain maintenance expenses by making payments directly to vendors and contractors rather than the university. Separately, the direct cash payments to the university and the maintenance expenses of the university paid by the foundation are not significant to the university; however, they are significant when combined. The economic resources of the foundation that are restricted for the benefit of the university are significant.
3. *University Research Foundation.* Ten years ago, the State University Research Foundation was established as a legally separate, tax-exempt organization to provide the buildings, laboratory facilities, and administrative support necessary for the faculty of State University to competitively attract and carry out research grants, principally from the federal government and corporations. The foundation's total research and administrative costs were significant to the university in the current year. The foundation occupies two buildings that it constructed on campus on land leased from the university. A significant portion of the instructional faculty in the School of Engineering, Science, and Technology carry out research at the foundation, and the annual university performance evaluations and merit increases of these faculty are based to a certain extent on the research they perform at the foundation.

   The completion of a research grant typically results in the submittal of a report of research findings and recommendations to the grantor, and often the publication of results in academic and professional journals. This research activity is deemed integral to the duties of faculty and is consistent with the university's mission.

   A formal agreement between the university and the foundation requires the foundation to make its general lecture and meeting rooms available, upon request, to the university, and to make certain research laboratories available for special lectures and seminars. The university's personnel office provides administrative support for hiring foundation personnel, including research technicians who typically are selected by faculty committees. The relationship between the university and the foundation is disclosed in a brochure for prospective faculty of the university.

Students enrolled in university graduate courses work at the foundation as research assistants. They are compensated through stipends paid by research grants through financial aid work-study programs administered by the university. Faculty are required to periodically report their research, instructional, and other efforts through a reporting system administered jointly by the foundation and the university. Faculty working on research grants typically receive a portion of their compensation from grant funds.

Note: The preceding cases were taken from Appendix C of *GASBS 39*.

16–2 Comparison of Public and Private Universities. Following are the operating statements for a public and private university. The operating statements have been adapted from the annual reports of a public and a private university. As would be expected, the reports are somewhat different. Boca Bay State College has an enrollment of 28,980 students and Von College has an enrollment of 20,100 students.

VON COLLEGE
Statement of Activities
for Year Ended June 30, 2011
(amounts in thousands)

	Unrestricted	Temporarily Restricted	Permanently Restricted	Totals
Revenues				
Tuition and fees	$494,729	—	—	$ 494,729
Less: Scholarships	(173,659)	—	—	(173,659)
Net tuition and fees	321,070	—	—	321,070
Contributions	28,121	$17,443	$ 45,135	90,699
Grants and contracts	66,730	—	—	66,730
Investment revenue	21,361	112	403	21,876
Net realized and unrealized gains on investments	83,655	—	168	83,823
Auxiliary enterprises	141,910	—	—	141,910
Other	16	—	—	16
Net assets released from restrictions	14,508	(14,508)	—	—
Total revenues	677,371	3,047	45,706	726,124
Expenses				
Instruction	265,946	—	—	265,946
Sponsored research	48,331	—	—	48,331
Academic support	77,969	—	—	77,969
Student services	40,541	—	—	40,541
Institutional support	67,475	—	—	67,475
Auxiliary enterprises	144,013	—	—	144,013
Total expenses	644,275	—	—	644,275
Change in net assets before cumulative effect of change in accounting principle	33,096	3,047	45,706	81,849
Cumulative effect of change in accounting principle	(24,083)	—	—	(24,083)
Change in net assets	9,013	3,047	45,706	57,766
Net assets at beginning of year	845,610	35,936	358,121	1,239,667
Net assets at end of year	$854,623	$38,983	$403,827	$1,297,433

4. A college expended $2,475,000 on a new parking facility. How would this be reported in the statement of cash flows?
   a. As an investing activity by a public college.
   b. As a capital and related financing activity by a private college.
   c. As an investing activity by a private college.
   d. Both *a* and *c* are correct.
5. Funds that the governing board of a public university has set aside so that only the income earned on the assets is expendable are called:
   a. Term endowments.
   b. Designated, unrestricted net assets.
   c. Life income fund agreements.
   d. Permanently restricted net assets.
6. If during the year a college or university expends federal awards such as research grants, it is required to:
   a. Have a single audit in accordance with the provisions of OMB *Circular A–133* if expenditures have exceeded $500,000.
   b. Follow OMB *Circular A–21,* "Cost Principles for Educational Institutions."
   c. Follow federal uniform administrative requirements under OMB *Circular A–110.*
   d. Do all of the above.
7. Accounting for public colleges and universities and private colleges and universities differs in that:
   a. Net assets are classified differently.
   b. Depreciation is reported differently.
   c. Collections are reported differently.
   d. Only private colleges and universities report investments at fair value.
8. Under generally accepted accounting principles applicable to public universities, the monies resulting from a new library construction fund drive would be recorded as increases to:
   a. Unrestricted net assets.
   b. Permanently restricted net assets.
   c. Temporarily restricted net assets.
   d. Restricted net assets.
9. Funds received from an external donor that are to be retained and invested, with the related earnings restricted to the purchase of library books, would be accounted for as an increase to:
   a. Temporarily restricted net assets in a private university.
   b. Nonexpendable, restricted net assets in a public university.
   c. Unrestricted net assets in either a public or private university.
   d. Permanently restricted net assets in a public university.
10. Which of the following statements helps define an irrevocable split-interest agreement?
   a. The college is sharing the income from investments with a donor.
   b. The college is maintaining the donation indefinitely.
   c. The college is reporting the donation as a liability.
   d. The college is receiving all of the income from the investments.

16–3 Private College Transactions. Elizabeth College, a small private college, had the following transactions in fiscal year 2011.

1. Billings for tuition and fees totaled $5,600,000. Tuition waivers and scholarships of $61,500 were granted. Students received tuition refunds of $101,670.
2. During the year the college received $1,891,000 cash in unrestricted private gifts, $575,200 cash in temporarily restricted grants, and $1,000,000 in securities for an endowment.
3. A pledge campaign generated $626,000 in unrestricted pledges, payable in fiscal year 2012.
4. Auxiliary enterprises provided goods and services that generated $94,370 in cash.
5. Collections of tuition receivable totaled $5,380,000.
6. Unrestricted cash of $1,000,000 was invested.
7. The college purchased computer equipment at a cost of $10,580.
8. During the year the following expenses were paid:

Instruction	$3,866,040
Academic support	1,987,000
Student services	87,980
Institutional support	501,130
Auxiliary enterprises	92,410

9. Instruction provided $450,000 in services related to the temporarily restricted grant recorded in transaction 2.
10. At year-end, the allowance for uncollectible tuition and fees was increased by $7,200. The fair value of investments had increased $11,540; of this amount, $3,040 was allocated to permanently restricted net assets, the remainder was allocated to unrestricted net assets. Depreciation on plant and equipment was allocated $34,750 to instruction, $41,000 to auxiliary enterprises, and $12,450 to academic support.
11. All nominal accounts were closed.

Required

a. Prepare journal entries in good form to record the foregoing transactions for the fiscal year ended June 30, 2011.

b. Prepare a statement of activities for the year ended June 30, 2011. Assume beginning net asset amounts of $7,518,000 unrestricted, $200,000 temporarily restricted, and $5,000,000 permanently restricted.

16–4 Public University Transactions. The Statement of Net Assets of Green Tree State University, a governmentally owned university, as of the end of its fiscal year June 30, 2010, follows.

GREEN TREE STATE UNIVERSITY
Statement of Net Assets
June 30, 2010

Assets		
Cash		$ 340,000
Accounts receivable (net of doubtful accounts of $15,000)		370,000
Investments		250,000
Capital assets	$1,750,000	
Accumulated depreciation	275,000	1,475,000
Total assets		2,435,000

Liabilities	
Accounts payable	105,000
Accrued liabilities	40,000
Deferred revenue	25,000
Bonds payable	600,000
Total liabilities	770,000
Net Assets	
Invested in capital assets, net of related debt	875,000
Restricted	215,000
Unrestricted	575,000
Total net assets	$1,665,000

The following information pertains to the year ended June 30, 2011:

1. Cash collected from students' tuition totaled $3,000,000. Of this $3,000,000, $362,000 represented accounts receivable outstanding at June 30, 2010; $2,500,000 was for current-year tuition; and $138,000 was for tuition applicable to the semester beginning in August 2011.
2. Deferred revenue at June 30, 2010, was earned during the year ended June 30, 2011.
3. Notification was received from the federal government that up to $50,000 in funds could be received in the current year for costs incurred in developing student performance measures.
4. During the year, the University received an unrestricted appropriation of $60,000 from the state.
5. Equipment for the student computer labs was purchased for cash in the amount of $225,000.
6. During the year, $200,000 in cash contributions was received from alumni. The contributions are to be used for construction of a new library.
7. Interest expense on the bonds payable in the amount of $48,000 was paid.
8. During the year, investments with a carrying value of $25,000 were sold for $31,000. Investments were purchased at a cost of $40,000. Investment income of $18,000 was earned and collected during the year.
9. General expenses of $2,500,000 related to the administration and operation of academic programs, and research expenses of $37,000 related to the development of student performance measures were recorded in the voucher system. At June 30, 2011, the accounts payable balance was $75,000.
10. Accrued liabilities at June 30, 2010, were paid.
11. At year-end, adjusting entries were made. Depreciation on capital assets totaled $90,000. Accrued interest on investments was $1,250. The fair value of investments at year-end was $262,000. The Allowance for Doubtful Accounts was adjusted to $17,000.
12. Nominal accounts were closed and net asset amounts were reclassified as necessary.

Required

a. Prepare journal entries in good form to record the foregoing transactions for the year ended June 30, 2011.

b. Prepare a statement of net assets for the year ended June 30, 2011.

16–5 Various Unrelated Transactions. Following are several unrelated transactions involving a university.

1. In fiscal year 2011, the university was notified by the federal government that in 2012 it would receive a $500,000 grant for wetlands research.
2. The university received $234,000 in contributed services from nurses providing services in its community outreach clinics. The services were part of the regular operation of the clinics.
3. During the year, the university constructed a new street, to allow for the expansion of its student housing efforts. The cost of the street was $1,980,000.
4. The university extended $325,000 in loans to students. During the year, $196,000 in loans was collected, along with $2,450 in interest.
5. At year-end, the Allowance for Doubtful Accounts was increased by $1,670.

Required

a. Prepare journal entries to record the foregoing transactions, assuming the university is a private institution.

b. Prepare journal entries to record the foregoing transactions, assuming the university is a public institution.

16–6 Financial Statements—Private University. The following is the pre-closing trial balance for Horton University as of June 30, 2011. Additional information related to net assets and the statement of cash flows is also provided.

HORTON UNIVERSITY
Pre-Closing Trial Balance
June 30, 2011

	Debits	***Credits***
Cash and Cash Equivalents	$1,516,600	
Investments	3,200,000	
Tuition and Fees Receivable	372,400	
Allowance for Doubtful Accounts		$ 75,600
Pledges Receivable	223,000	
Allowance for Doubtful Pledges		79,000
Property, Plant, and Equipment	1,996,160	
Accumulated Depreciation		658,720
Accounts Payable		103,000
Accrued Liabilities		37,500
Deposits Held in Custody for Others		17,570
Bonds Payable		792,000
Deferred Revenue		62,150
Liabilities Under Split-Interest Agreements		40,510
Net Assets—Unrestricted		4,051,410
Net Assets—Temporarily Restricted		200,600
Net Assets—Permanently Restricted		980,000
Net Assets Released from Restrictions—Temporarily Restricted	26,850	
Net Assets Released from Restrictions—Unrestricted		26,850
Tuition and Fees		290,750
Tuition and Fees Discounts and Allowances	98,000	

Contributions—Unrestricted		310,200
Contributions—Temporarily Restricted		77,000
Grants and Contracts—Unrestricted		324,000
Grants and Contracts—Temporarily Restricted		121,800
Investment Income—Unrestricted		11,500
Other Revenue		13,250
Auxiliary Enterprise Sales and Services		53,560
Unrealized Gain on Investments		280,400
Instruction Expense	629,750	
Research Expense	269,600	
Academic Support Expense	100,400	
Student Services Expense	46,500	
Institutional Support Expense	68,910	
Auxiliary Enterprise Expenses	58,700	
Loss on Sale of Equipment	500	
Total	$8,580,520	$8,580,520

Additional information

Net assets released from temporary restrictions totaled $26,850. There were no restrictions on the investment income earned. Twenty percent of the unrealized gain is related to permanently restricted net assets and 10 percent is related to temporarily restricted net assets, with the remainder related to unrestricted net assets.

The differences between the beginning and ending balances were as follows:

Tuition and Fees Receivable increased by $10,230.
Pledges Receivable decreased by $1,560.
Allowance for Doubtful Accounts was increased by $770 (the bad debt was netted against Tuition and Fees).
Accounts Payable decreased by $2,900.
Accrued Liabilities decreased by $1,120.
Deferred Revenue increased by $6,200.
Depreciation Expense was $30,070.
Cash of $100,000 was used to retire bonds.
Investments were sold for $1,500,000 and others were purchased for $1,250,000.

Required

a. Prepare a statement of activities for the year ended June 30, 2011.
b. Prepare a statement of financial position for June 30, 2011.
c. Prepare a statement of cash flows for the year ended June 30, 2011.

16–7 Financial Statements—Public College. The following balances come from the trial balance of Sherlock State College as of the end of the 2011 fiscal year.

SHERLOCK STATE COLLEGE
Pre-Closing Trial Balance
June 30, 2011
(000s omitted)

	Debits	***Credits***
Cash and Cash Equivalents	$ 3,278	
Investments	29,387	
Accounts Receivable	1,957	
Allowance for Uncollectible Receivables		$ 137
Due from State	79,626	
Cash and Cash Equivalents—Restricted	26,716	
Investments—Restricted	2,383	
Depreciable Capital Assets	149,714	
Accumulated Depreciation		28,850
Nondepreciable Assets	55,481	
Other Noncurrent Assets	26	
Accounts Payable		2,306
Accrued Liabilities		2,039
Deferred Revenue		13,789
Bonds Payable—Current Portion		1,538
Bonds Payable		92,116
Net Assets—Invested in Capital Assets, Net of Related Debt		82,692
Net Assets—Restricted for Debt Service—Expendable		1,157
Net Assets—Restricted for Capital Projects—Expendable		49,272
Net Assets—Unrestricted		70,954
Tuition and Fees		30,095
Tuition and Fees Discounts and Allowances	7,565	
Grants and Contracts Revenue		18,196
Auxiliary Enterprise Sales		14,595
Investment Income		1,745
State Appropriations		44,894
Capital Appropriations		12,785
Institutional Support Expenses	26,268	
Academic Support Expenses	58,940	
Scholarships and Fellowships Expense	7,664	
Depreciation Expense	5,580	
Interest Expense	378	
Auxiliary Enterprise Expenses	12,197	
Totals	$467,160	$467,160
Information on Cash and Cash Equivalents Activity		
Beginning Cash Balance	$ 28,067	
Received Tuition and Fees (net)	23,609	
Received Grants and Contracts	12,940	
Received from Auxiliary Enterprises	13,765	
Payments to Employees	58,220	
Payments to Vendors	21,711	
Payments to Students for Scholarships and Fellowships	7,664	
Received State Appropriations	39,894	
Received Capital Appropriations	20,540	
Purchase of Capital Assets	20,634	
Interest Paid on Debt	2,095	
Interest Income	1,503	

Required

a. Prepare a statement of revenues, expenses, and changes in net assets for the year ended June 30, 2011, in good form. See Illustration 16–2; however, display expenses using functional classifications as shown in Illustration 16–6.

b. Prepare a statement of net assets as of June 30, 2011, in good form. For the period, net assets restricted for capital projects increased by $3,000, and net assets restricted for debt service increased by $150; all bonded debt relates to capital assets. See Illustration 16–1.

c. Prepare a statement of cash flows for the year ended June 30, 2011. Information on changes in assets and liabilities is as follows: Accounts Receivable (net) increased by $2,574; Due from State decreased by $14,842; Accounts Payable and Accrued Liabilities increased by $1,962; and Deferred Revenue decreased by $1,763. See Illustration 16–3.

Chapter **Seventeen**

Accounting for Health Care Organizations

Learning Objectives

After studying this chapter, you should be able to:

1. Identify the different organizational forms and the related authoritative accounting literature for health care organizations.
2. Describe financial reporting for health care organizations.
3. Explain unique accounting and measurement issues in health care organizations, including accounting for revenues, assets, expenses, and liabilities.
4. Journalize transactions and prepare the basic financial statements for not-for-profit and governmental health care organizations.
5. Describe other accounting issues in the health care industry, including budgeting and costs, auditing, taxation and regulation, prepaid health care services, and continuing care retirement communities.
6. Explain financial and operational analysis of health care organizations.

The health care industry in the United States changed dramatically in the last century. In the early 1900s health care was provided primarily by not-for-profit hospitals affiliated with communities or religious organizations, major projects were funded by donations, and hospital managers had little financial expertise and faced few regulations. Today, health care organizations are complex entities that cross the private, public, and not-for-profit sectors; spiraling costs outpace inflation; capital construction requires extensive financing; and professional managers face increasing public scrutiny and government oversight. Technological advances brought dramatic changes in the delivery and quality of health care services but also contributed greatly to rising costs. Health care spending in 2007 was \$2.3 trillion, representing 16 percent of gross domestic product. It is projected to grow to \$4.2 trillion by 2016.[1]

Political, social, and economic factors explain the tremendous change in the health care industry. For example, in the 1940s and 1950s, health insurance coverage became a common employee fringe benefit, and health care providers began to look to employers and third parties for payment for services. The Hill-Burton Program in 1944 encouraged growth in the industry by making federal funds available for the construction of health care facilities.[2] The initiation of entitlement programs, such as Medicare and Medicaid in the 1960s, reflected public policy efforts to make health

[1] National Coalition on Health Care, *Health Insurance Cost.* see *www.nchc.org.*

[2] The Hospital Survey and Construction Act of 1946 (P.L. 79-725).

care a basic right to be regulated at the federal level. In the 1980s, employers and insurance companies initiated managed care systems in an attempt to bring down the cost of providing health care coverage. In the 1990s, comprehensive health care reform became a political issue at the federal level.

Health care continues to be a political issue in the first decade of the 21st century, with soaring health care costs running two to five times the rate of inflation since 2000.[3] Today, roughly half of *hospital* health care is provided by not-for-profit organizations, although most *providers* of health care are for-profit groups of medical professionals who are associated with governmental or not-for-profit health care organizations. Illustration 17–1 shows classifications of health care organizations by legal structure as well as by the nature of services they provide. This chapter focuses on the financial reporting and accounting issues of primarily not-for-profit and governmental organizations that charge patients or third parties for the services provided. Voluntary health and welfare organizations, which are nonbusiness oriented and provide more general social services funded primarily by contributions and grants rather than charges for services, are discussed in Chapter 14.

GAAP FOR HEALTH CARE PROVIDERS

Generally accepted accounting principles (GAAP) for hospitals and other health care organizations have evolved through the efforts of the American Hospital Association (AHA), the Healthcare Financial Management Association (HFMA), and the American Institute of Certified Public Accountants (AICPA). More recently, statements of the Financial Accounting Standards Board (FASB) and the Governmental Accounting Standards Board (GASB) have directly impacted accounting and reporting for health care providers. The AICPA Audit and Accounting Guide *Health Care Organizations* applies to health care organizations that are either (1) investor-owned businesses, (2) not-for-profit enterprises that, although they have no ownership interests, are essentially business-oriented and self-sustaining from fees charged for goods and services, or (3) governmental entities. These organizations are often classified by the nature of the services provided, as listed in Illustration 17–1. Since 1990, the AICPA Audit and Accounting Guide has covered *all* providers of health care services, not just hospitals. The guide covers *governmental* providers that use proprietary accounting, as well as private and not-for-profit health care organizations.[4]

Governmental hospitals and health care providers are considered special purpose governments, that is, legally separate entities that may be either component units of another government or stand-alone governmental entities. GASB standards provide guidance for organizations that may be engaged in either governmental or business-type activities or both. The AICPA Audit and Accounting Guide is considered category (b) authority for both governmental and nongovernmental entities, which means that GASB and FASB statements take precedence.[5] Consequently, even though there is only one audit guide for all health care entities, accounting and reporting rules may

[3] National Coalition on Health Care, *Health Insurance Cost.* See *www.nchc.org*.

[4] American Institute of Certified Public Accountants, Audit and Accounting Guide, *Health Care Organizations* (AAG-HCO) (New York: AICPA, 2007).

[5] American Institute of Certified Public Accountants, *SAS No. 69,* "The Meaning of 'Present Fairly in Conformity with Generally Accepted Accounting Principles' in the Independent Auditor's Report" (New York: AICPA, 1991), as amended by *SAS No. 91,* "Federal GAAP Hierarchy," 2001.

ILLUSTRATION 17–1 Classification of Health Care Organizations

Sponsorship or Legal Structure

For-profit (Proprietary)	**Not-for-profit: Business-oriented**	**Governmental: Public**
– Investor-owned	– Community-based	– Federal
	– Religion affiliated	– State
	– Private university sponsored	– County
		– City
		– Public university sponsored

Types of Health Care Organizations

Clinics, medical group practices, individual practice associations, individual practitioners, and other ambulatory care organizations.

Continuing care retirement communities (CCRCs).

Health maintenance organizations (HMOs) and similar prepaid health care plans.

Home health agencies.

Hospitals.

Nursing homes that provide skilled, intermediate, and a less-intensive level of health care.

Drug and alcohol rehabilitation centers and other rehabilitation facilities.

Parent companies and other organizations that primarily plan, organize, and oversee health care services.

Source: Adapted from the American Institute of Certified Public Accountants, Audit and Accounting Guide, *Health Care Organizations* (New York: AICPA, 2007), Preface.

differ, depending on whether the health care provider is legally structured as an investor-owned, not-for-profit, or governmental organization. Some of the differences relate to accounting and reporting for contributions and financial reporting display, cash flows, and investments, as seen in Illustration 17–2. This chapter illustrates financial accounting and reporting for not-for-profit health care organizations, the largest segment of the in-patient health care industry, and points out differences unique to

ILLUSTRATION 17–2 GAAP for Health Care Entities in Different Sectors

Accounting and Reporting Issue	Health Care Providers		
	Investor-Owned	**Not-for-Profit**	**Governmental**
Reporting entity	APB *Opinion No. 18, SFAS No. 94*	AICPA *SOP 94-3*	GASB *Codification,* Sec. 2100 (see Footnote 9 for citation)
Contributions and financial statement display	*SFAS No. 116*	*SFAS Nos. 116* and *117*	GASB *Codification,* Secs. N50 and 2200
Cash flows	*SFAS No. 95*	*SFAS No. 95*	GASB *Codification,* Sec. 2450
Deposits with financial institutions	*SFAS No. 105*	*SFAS No. 105*	GASB *Codification,* Sec. C20
Investments	*SFAS No. 115* and AAG-HCO, Chapter 4	*SFAS No. 124*	GASB *Codification,* Sec. I50
Operating leases	*SFAS No. 13*	*SFAS No. 13*	GASB *Codification,* Sec. C20
Prepaid health care arrangements and self-insurance programs	AAG-HCO, Chapters 8 and 14	AAG-HCO, Chapters 8 and 14	GASB *Codification,* Secs. C50 and Po20
Compensated absences	*SFAS Nos. 43* and *112*	*SFAS Nos. 43* and *112*	GASB *Codification,* Sec. C60
Debt refundings	APB *Opinion No. 26, SFAS Nos. 4* and *125*	APB *Opinion No. 26, SFAS Nos. 4* and *125*	GASB *Codification,* Sec. D20
Pensions	*SFAS Nos. 87, 132* (revised), and *158*	*SFAS Nos. 87, 132* (revised), and 158	GASB *Codification,* Sec. P20
Risks and uncertainties	AICPA *SOP 94-6*	AICPA *SOP 94-6*	GASB *Codification,* Sec. C50
Post-retirement benefits	*SFAS Nos. 106* and *132* (revised)	*SFAS Nos. 106* and *132* (revised)	GASB *Codification,* Sec. P50
Fair value measurements	*SFAS No. 157*	*SFAS No. 157*	None

Source: Adapted from the AICPA, *Audit Risk Alert, Health Care Industry Developments—2001/02* (New York: AICPA, 2002), par. 121, updated for new standards.

governmental health care providers. The reader is directed to Chapter 14 for a more thorough discussion of *SFAS Nos. 116* and *117* for not-for-profit organizations, and to Chapter 7 for a discussion of business-type enterprises of government.

FINANCIAL REPORTING

The financial statements of a health care entity serve a broad set of users and consequently include: (1) a balance sheet (statement of financial position) or statement of net assets; (2) a statement of operations or statement of revenues, expenses, and changes in net assets; and (3) a statement of cash flows, as well as notes to the financial statements. Additionally, proprietary and not-for-profit entities prepare a statement of changes in equity (net assets), which can be issued as a separate statement or combined with the statement of operations. The FASB and AICPA allow considerable flexibility in displaying financial information.

A health care organization may choose to use fund accounting for internal purposes, in part, to account for revenues and expenses associated with grants (or because it is a governmental entity). For organizations using fund accounting, the fund structure should include general unrestricted funds and donor-restricted funds (e.g., specific

ILLUSTRATION 17–3

SIERRA REGIONAL HOSPITAL
Balance Sheet
As of September 30, 2011

Assets		**Liabilities and Net Assets**	
Current assets:		Current liabilities:	
Cash	$ 172,100	Accounts payable	$ 259,000
Accounts and notes receivable, net of allowance for uncollectibles of $135,000	353,000	Accrued expenses payable	173,500
Pledges receivable, net of allowance for uncollectibles of $114,300	548,700		
Accrued interest receivable	44,000		
Inventory	160,000		
Prepaid expenses	8,000		
Short-term investments	1,778,000		
Total current assets	3,063,800	Total current liabilities	432,500
Assets limited as to use:		Long-term debt:	
Internally designated for capital acquisition—cash	6,500	Mortgages payable	6,000,000
		Total liabilities	6,432,500
Internally designated for capital acquisition—investments	778,000		
Total assets limited as to use	784,500	Net assets:	
Long-term investments	146,000	Unrestricted—undesignated	8,536,600
Property, plant, and equipment:		Unrestricted—designated	784,500
		Temporarily restricted—plant	2,392,700
Land	1,080,000	Temporarily restricted—programs	25,000
		Permanently restricted	178,000
Buildings, net of accumulated depreciation of $1,365,000	9,685,000	Total net assets	11,916,800
Equipment, net of accumulated depreciation of $1,702,000	3,590,000		
Total property, plant, and equipment	14,355,000		
Total assets	$18,349,300	Total liabilities and net assets	$18,349,300

purpose, plant replacement and expansion, and endowment). Comparative statements for a not-for-profit hospital are presented in Illustrations 17–3 through 17–5.

Balance Sheet or Statement of Net Assets

The balance sheet presented in Illustration 17–3 is for Sierra Regional Hospital, a hypothetical not-for-profit health care entity. Not-for-profit organizations are required to present information about the liquidity of their assets and liabilities. The net asset section of a not-for-profit organization balance sheet should classify net assets into unrestricted, temporarily restricted, and permanently restricted categories, as described in Chapter 14. Governmental organizations classify net assets into invested in capital assets, net of related debt; restricted; and unrestricted, as illustrated in Chapters 1 through 9. The equity section of an investor-owned health care provider should show stockholders' equity separated into capital stock and retained earnings.

Operating Statement

The principal sources of revenue for a health care organization are (1) patient service revenue, (2) premium revenue derived from **capitation fees,** which are fixed fees per person paid periodically, regardless of services provided, by a health maintenance organization, (3) resident service revenue, such as maintenance or rental fees in an extended care facility, and (4) other revenue or gains. Service revenue is shown net of contractual adjustments, discussed later in this chapter. Other revenue includes sales (e.g., medical supplies and cafeteria meals), fees (e.g., for educational programs or transcripts), rental of facilities other than to residents, investment income and gains, contributions, and grants. Additionally, some governmental health care organizations may be supported, at least in part, by taxes or intergovernmental revenue. Research grants or contracts may be considered exchange transactions or nonexchange transactions (i.e., contributions), as discussed in Chapters 14 and 16. Not-for-profit health care entities show net assets released from temporary restrictions as increases to unrestricted net assets and also indicate how the restriction was met, such as passage of time, satisfaction of purpose, or through acquisition of equipment. Sierra Regional Hospital, as shown in Illustration 17–4, reports some of these sources of income.

Considerable flexibility is allowed not-for-profits in displaying the results of operations, such as classifying them as operating and nonoperating, earned and unearned, or recurring and nonrecurring. FASB concepts statements provide guidance on distinguishing operating items (i.e., those arising from ongoing major activities, such as service revenue) from nonoperating items (i.e., those arising from transactions peripheral or incidental to the delivery of health care, such as investment income and unrestricted contributions).[6] Unlike not-for-profits, governmental health care entities are required to display operating and nonoperating activity on the operating statement.

As required, Sierra Regional Hospital reports all expenses as decreases in unrestricted net assets. Functional expenses must be displayed or disclosed in the notes and can be as simple as distinguishing between health care services and support services, such as general/administrative expenses. If functional expenses are displayed, all natural expenses (e.g., depreciation, interest, and provision for bad debts) should be allocated to the functional expenses.

Not-for-profit health care organizations should include a **performance indicator** to report the results of operations. The intent of the performance indicator is to provide an operating measure that is equivalent to income from continuing operations of for-profit health care organizations. The principal components of a performance indicator are unrestricted revenues, gains, and other support; expenses; and other income. Examples include excess of revenues over expenses, revenues and gains over expenses and losses, earned income, and performance earnings. Investment income, realized gains and losses, and unrealized gains and losses on trading securities should be reported in the performance indicator; however, the following items should be reported separately from the performance indicator:

- Transactions with owners acting in that capacity.
- Equity transfers involving other related entities.
- Receipt of temporarily and permanently restricted contributions.
- Contributions of (and assets released from donor restrictions related to) long-lived assets.

[6] Financial Accounting Standards Board, *Concepts Statement No. 6,* "Elements of Financial Statements" (Norwalk, CT: FASB, 1985).

ILLUSTRATION 17–4 Illustration of a Two-Part Statement of Operations

SIERRA REGIONAL HOSPITAL
Statement of Operations
Year Ended September 30, 2011

Unrestricted revenues, gains, and other support:		
Net patient service revenue		$ 9,161,000
Other revenue		48,800
Contributions		297,900
Investment income		36,100
Total revenues and gains		9,543,800
Expenses and losses:		
Nursing services	$4,667,500	
Other professional services	1,311,620	
General services	2,056,260	
Fiscal and administrative services	1,332,320	
Total expenses		9,367,700
Loss on disposal of equipment		1,500
Total expenses and losses		9,369,200
Excess of revenue and gains over expenses and losses		174,600
Net assets released from restrictions:		
Satisfaction of equipment acquisition restrictions		100,000
Increase in unrestricted net assets		$ 274,600

Statement of Changes in Net Assets
Year Ended September 30, 2011

Unrestricted net assets (see Part 1 above):	
Total unrestricted revenues, gains, and other support	$ 9,543,800
Net assets released from restrictions	100,000
Total unrestricted expenses and losses	(9,369,200)
Increase in unrestricted net assets	274,600
Temporarily restricted net assets:	
Contributions	25,000
Investment income	77,000
Increase in provision for uncollectible pledges	(66,300)
Loss on sale of investments	(26,000)
Net assets released from restrictions	(100,000)
Decrease in temporarily restricted net assets	(90,300)
Permanently restricted net assets:	
Contributions	24,000
Increase in permanently restricted net assets	24,000
Increase in net assets	208,300
Net assets at beginning of year	11,708,500
Net assets at end of year	$11,916,800

- Unrealized gains and losses on investments other than trading securities.
- Investment returns restricted by donors or by law.
- Other items that are required by GAAP to be reported separately, such as extraordinary items, the effect of discontinued operations, or the cumulative effect of accounting changes.[7]

Statement of Changes in Net Assets

Illustration 17–4 shows increases and decreases in the three classes of net assets for a not-for-profit organization: unrestricted, temporarily restricted, and permanently restricted. Net assets released from restrictions increase unrestricted net assets and decrease temporarily restricted net assets. Net gains on permanently restricted endowments are shown as increases to the permanently restricted net assets in Illustration 17–4; however, the accounting treatment of net gains will depend on donor stipulations, state law, and organizational policy. Note that this statement may be combined with the statement of activities or operations. Governmental health care entities do not have a statement comparable to the statement of changes in net assets.

Statement of Cash Flows

The statement of cash flows in Illustration 17–5 is that required by *SFAS No. 95* (as amended).[8] The direct method is presented with a reconciliation of changes in net assets to net cash provided by operating activities, although the indirect method is also acceptable. Note that Illustration 17–6, presented later in this chapter, shows the statement of cash flows required by GASB standards for a governmental health care organization. That statement includes a fourth section, cash flows from noncapital financing activities. The FASB statement can be prepared using either the direct method or the indirect method, but under GASB standards, governmental entities must use the direct method.[9] The statements differ primarily in terms of which cash flows are reported as part of each activity. In the GASB statement, interest paid and interest received are reported as investing activities, whereas the same items are reported as operating activities in the FASB statement except for investment income added to temporarily or permanently restricted net assets. Such restricted income is reported in the FASB statement as a financing activity. Acquisitions of property and equipment are reported as capital and related financing activities in the GASB statement but as investing activities in the FASB statement. Unrestricted gifts are reported as cash flows from noncapital financing activities in the GASB statement but as cash flows from operating activities in the FASB statement. A final, and major, difference is that the reconciliation schedule in the GASB statement reconciles operating income (loss) to cash flows from operating activities, whereas in the FASB statement the schedule reconciles changes in net assets to cash flows from operating activities. In preparing either cash flow statement, the worksheet or T-account approaches explained in most intermediate accounting texts may be useful.

[7] AAG-HCO, pars. 4.07, 10.20–21.

[8] Financial Accounting Standards Board, *Statement No. 95,* "Statement of Cash Flows" (Norwalk, CT: FASB, 1987), as amended by *SFAS No. 117,* "Financial Statements of Not-for-Profit Organizations" (Norwalk, CT: FASB, 1993), par. 30.

[9] Governmental Accounting Standards Board, *Codification of Governmental Accounting and Financial Reporting Standards as of June 30, 2008* (Norwalk, CT, 2008), Sec. 2200. 174.

ILLUSTRATION 17–5 Illustration of Statement of Cash Flows—Not-for-Profit Organizations

SIERRA REGIONAL HOSPITAL
Statement of Cash Flows
Year Ended September 30, 2011

Cash Flows from Operating Activities	
Cash received from patients and third-party payors	$ 8,842,000
Other receipts from operations	48,800
Interest received on assets limited as to use	36,100
Receipts from unrestricted gifts	297,900
Cash paid to employees and suppliers	(8,014,200)
Interest paid	(160,000)
Net cash provided by operating activities	1,050,600
Cash Flows from Investing Activities	
Purchase of property and equipment	(400,000)
Purchase of long-term investments	(737,000)
Proceeds from sale of securities	59,000
Proceeds from sale of equipment	500
Net cash used by investing activities	(1,077,500)
Cash Flows from Financing Activities	
Proceeds from contributions restricted for:	
Investment in plant	292,000
Future operations	5,000
	297,000
Other financing activities:	
Interest and dividends restricted to endowment	69,000
Repayment of long-term debt	(400,000)
	(331,000)
Net cash used by financing activities	(34,000)
Net increase (decrease) in cash	(60,900)
Cash and cash equivalents, September 30, 2010	239,500
Cash and cash equivalents, September 30, 2011	$ 178,600

Reconciliation of Changes in Net Assets to Net Cash Provided by Operating Activities

Changes in net assets	$ 208,300
Adjustments to reconcile change in net assets to net cash provided by operating activities:	
Depreciation	783,000
Loss on disposal of equipment	1,500
Increase in patient accounts receivable, net	(139,000)
Increase in supplies	(80,000)
Increase in accounts payable and accrued expenses	306,500
Decrease in prepaid expenses	4,000
Gifts, grants, and bequests restricted for long-term investment	(49,000)
Interest restricted for long-term investment	(77,000)
Loss on sale of investments	26,000
Increase in provision for uncollectible pledges	66,300
Net cash provided by operating activities	$ 1,050,600

17–7. What are *assets limited as to use* and how do they differ from restricted assets?

17–8. What contingent liabilities arise from a health care organization's relations with third-party payors?

17–9. Explain the importance of diagnosis-related groups (DRGs) in the cost accounting systems of a health care provider.

17–10. What are some taxation and regulatory issues affecting health care organizations?

Cases

17–1 **Charity Care.** The local newspaper of a large urban area printed a story titled "Charity Care by Hospitals Stirs Debate." The story quotes one legislator who wants "to ensure that the state's nonprofit hospitals are fulfilling their obligation; that is to provide charity care at least equal to the tax exemption they receive as a nonprofit entity." The following table is provided:

Comparison of Selected Factors in Three Nonprofit Hospitals (dollars in millions)

	Hope Hospital	St. Pat's Hospital	Capitol Hospital
Estimated taxes the hospitals would pay if they were not tax-exempt	$6.8	$2.2	$4.5
Charity and other uncompensated care	$17.8, of which $3.8 is bad debts	$3.1, not including bad debts	$6.7
Community service programs*	$1.6	$1.0	n.a.
Unpaid cost of Medicaid and Medicare	$3.4	$0.6	n.a.
Nonreimbursed research and graduate medical education	$2.0	$0.7	n.a.

n.a. = Not available.
*Including such programs as activity sponsorships, playground equipment, neighborhood outreach, and scholarships for at-risk students.

Required

a. What are the obligations of IRC Sec. 501(c)(3) organizations to provide charity care?

b. Do you agree that the hospitals are not fulfilling their obligations? Why or why not?

c. What additional information would you like to have? Do you expect to find this information in the audited annual financial statements?

17–2 **Organizational Form.** Responding to a growing need for medical care as its population grew in the early 1900s, Suffolk County founded the Suffolk County Hospital in 1920, financing construction of the original hospital building and equipment with a $500,000 general obligation bond issue. Over the next 75 years, the hospital was able to sustain its own operations from patient service, federal and state grants, and other revenues, but it relied on the Suffolk County government to finance construction of needed expansions. In 1995, Suffolk County issued $10 million of general obligation bonds to finance a new hospital building. A special property tax levy has paid principal and interest on this debt issue and will continue to do so until 2020.

In 1998, the hospital board of trustees signed a 10-year lease and management contract under which the hospital became an affiliate of ABC Medical Group, a for-profit organization. Under the contract, ABC agreed to provide capital financing for plant expansion and equipment modernization, in addition to providing the county with 15 percent of net income, as defined in the contract. Over the past 10 years, the county has received an average of about $1.5 million each year, but it has had no involvement with the operations of the hospital, except for continuing oversight by the elected board of trustees.

As the lease contract nears its renewal date, two of the five members of the hospital board are openly questioning ABC's quality of care and pricing structures. In addition, these members argue that the hospital has not been sufficiently responsive to county patients and has not provided adequate charity care. The other three members of the board believe that ABC is performing well under the lease contract and that the contract should be renewed for another 10 years. These three members of the board believe, however, that the contract should not be renewed unless a higher share of net income can be negotiated with ABC. A target share of 20 percent has been mentioned by one of the board members.

As might be expected in such circumstances, the local print and broadcast media have devoted extensive coverage to this issue and public feelings are running strong both for and against renewing the lease contract with ABC. For the most recent year, ABC reported $10.9 million of net income on revenues of $17.4 million and expenses of $6.5 million.

Required

a. Assume you are the county finance director and have been asked to evaluate the arguments for and against renewing the lease contract with ABC Medical Group. What financial and nonfinancial factors would you consider in conducting your analysis and preparing recommendations to share with the hospital board of trustees?

b. What factors, in your judgment, are most important in deciding whether or not to renew the lease contract?

17–3 Internet Case—Medicare and Medicaid. The federal government through the Medicare and Medicaid programs is one of the largest providers of patient service revenues to health care organizations. Information concerning these programs is available through the Department of Health and Human Services Web site.

Required

Accessing the Web site at *www.cms.hhs.gov,* answer the following questions:

a. Who are the recipients of Medicare and Medicaid program benefits?

b. What were the annual outlays (expenditures) for each program for the most recent year?

c. What is CMS?

d. What is the National Program on Integrity and what are the objectives of its program reviews?

e. What factors do you believe contribute to fraud in Medicare and Medicaid programs?

17–4 Internet Case—Evaluating the Quality of Health Care. The U.S. Department of Health and Human Services maintains the Web site *www.hospitalcompare.hhs.gov,* which provides an array of *process of care* and *outcome of care* measures that report on how well individual hospitals are caring for their patients, compared with state and national benchmarks.

Required

a. Access the Web site shown above and describe the medical and surgical categories for which process of care and outcome of care quality measures are reported.

b. At the Web site, click on "Find and Compare Hospitals" and locate quality of care data for two hospitals in your city or geographic area. Evaluate that data and explain how the quality of care scores of each of those hospitals compares with the average scores for your state and the nation.

c. Explain how such factors as patient mix, occupancy rate, average length of stay, payor mix (i.e., Medicare, Medicaid, third-party insurers, self-pay, and charity care), and the hospital's financial condition may affect the quality of care. Did any of these factors impact, in your judgment, the quality of care scores received by the two hospitals you selected for analysis?

Exercises and Problems

17–1 Multiple Choice. Choose the best answer.

1. The organization assigned primary responsibility for establishing accounting and financial reporting standards for health care organizations is the:
   a. American Institute of CPAs (AICPA).
   b. Financial Accounting Standards Board (FASB) for for-profit and nongovernmental not-for-profit health care organizations.
   c. Governmental Accounting Standards Board (GASB) for governmental health care organizations.
   d. Both *b* and *c* are correct.
2. A not-for-profit hospital would present all of the following financial statements, *except* a:
   a. Balance sheet or statement of financial position.
   b. Statement of functional expenses.
   c. Statement of operations.
   d. Statement of cash flows.
3. Which of the following is a true statement regarding a *performance indicator*?
   a. All health care organizations are required to report a performance indicator.
   b. Only governmental health care organizations are required to report a performance indicator.
   c. The purpose of reporting a performance indicator is to make it easier to compare the results of operations of not-for-profit health care organizations to those of for-profit health care organizations.
   d. The purpose of reporting a performance indicator is to assist in evaluating the efficiency and effectiveness of a health care organization's operating activities.
4. Which of the following is *not* a correct statement about the statement of cash flows presented by a health care organization?
   a. Governmental health care organizations must report cash flows from operating activities using the direct method.
   b. For-profit and not-for-profit health care organizations may report cash flows from operating activities using either the direct or indirect method.

c. All health care organizations report acquisition of capital assets in the cash flows from investing activities section of the statement of cash flows.
d. All of the above are correct statements.

5. How should charity service be reported in the operating statement?
a. Receivables and revenues should *not* be reported for these services.
b. Receivables and revenues should be reported at the regular self-pay amount.
c. Receivables and revenues should be reported at the regular self-pay amount, less the estimated cost of collection efforts.
d. None of the above.

6. Contractual adjustments are reported as:
a. Additions to the cost of providing medical services.
b. Reductions to receivables and revenue for medical services provided to insured patients.
c. Reductions to receivables and revenues for charity care medical services.
d. Contingent liabilities.

7. Assets that are set aside under a bond covenant for future debt service payments are reported by a not-for-profit health care organization as:
a. Assets limited as to use.
b. Temporarily restricted net assets.
c. Restricted for debt service.
d. Assets held by trustee.

8. Fees received by a hospital for medical record transcripts should be reported as:
a. Patient service revenue.
b. Administrative service revenue.
c. Other revenue.
d. Nonoperating gains.

9. A governmental health care organization, depending on its legal form, may be required to prepare which of the following financial statements?
a. Statement of revenues, expenses, and changes in net assets.
b. Statement of revenues, expenditures, and changes in fund balances.
c. Statement of cash flows.
d. All of the above.

10. Which of the following would be most useful for evaluating the financial liquidity of a not-for-profit health care organization?
a. Current ratio.
b. Debt-to-capitalization.
c. Capital expense.
d. Debt services coverage.

17–2 Revenue Classifications. Rosemont Hospital, a not-for-profit hospital, recorded the following transactions. For each transaction, indicate the appropriate revenue or gain classification by selecting the letter or letters of that (those) classification(s) from the list in the right-hand column.

1. Received $100 as co-pay from a patient for an out-patient visit. Billed $500 to insurance.	*a.* Patient service revenue *b.* Contractual adjustments *c.* Other revenue
2. Gift shop sales amounted to $1,500.	*d.* Nonoperating gain

	2011	2010		2011	2010
Deferred bond issue costs, less accumulated amortization of $4,783,225 in 2011 and $3,868,295 in 2010	14,429	15,423	Unrestricted net assets	298,457	363,740
Investment in affiliates	13,065	11,723			
Pledges receivable	2,963	3,801			
Other	13,867	17,896			
	124,604	190,158			
Property and equipment:					
Land	15,157	16,038			
Buildings and improvements	304,856	318,465			
Equipment	332,685	282,762			
Construction in progress	33,599	23,854			
	686,297	641,119			
Accumulated depreciation	(317,144)	(280,220)			
	369,153	360,899			
Total assets	$872,178	$960,173	Total liabilities and net assets	$872,178	$960,173

OAK VALLEY HOSPITAL
Consolidated Statements of Operations and Changes in Net Assets
Year Ended December 31
(in thousands)

	2011	2010
Unrestricted revenue, gains and other support:		
Net patient service revenue	$553,152	$555,579
Other revenue	72,800	75,867
Total revenue	625,952	631,447
Expenses:		
Salaries and wages	297,248	283,800
Employee benefits	52,071	54,845
Services, supplies, and other	215,719	206,097
Bad debts	43,329	32,096
Depreciation and amortization	46,141	39,859
Interest	20,592	21,020
Impairment and restructuring	28,725	
Total expenses	703,825	637,718
Operating loss	(77,873)	(6,271)
Nonoperating gains (losses):		
Investment income	23,537	19,308
Interest expense	—	(410)
Share of net income (loss) of affiliates	377	(77)
Excess of (expenses over revenue)	(53,959)	12,548
Other changes in net assets:		
Change in unrealized appreciation in fair value of investments	(11,326)	16,466
(Decrease) increase in net assets, before extraordinary item	(65,283)	29,015
Extraordinary loss	—	(1,032)
(Decrease) increase in net assets	(65,283)	27,983
Net assets, beginning of year	363,740	335,757
Net assets, end of year	$298,457	$363,740

OAK VALLEY HOSPITAL
Consolidated Statements of Cash Flows
Year Ended December 31
(in thousands)

	2011	2010
Operating activities:		
(Decrease) increase in unrestricted net assets	$(65,282)	$ 27,983
Adjustments to reconcile (decrease) increase in unrestricted net assets to net cash provided by operating activities and nonoperating gains and losses:		
Extraordinary loss	—	1,032
Depreciation and amortization	46,141	39,859
Impairment of long-lived assets	24,940	2,000
Change in unrealized depreciation (appreciation) in fair market value of investments	11,330	(16,466)
Decrease in accounts receivable	23,872	5,211
(Increase) decrease in inventories	(501)	170
Decrease (increase) in other current assets	1,019	(7,361)
Decrease in pledges receivable	836	418
(Decrease) increase in accounts payable and other accrued expenses	(15,966)	13,629
Increase in accrued compensation and amounts withheld	7,058	32
(Decrease) increase in deferred revenue	(29)	1,005
(Decrease) increase in claims liability	(5,014)	1,425
Share of net (gain) loss in equity transactions of affiliate	(383)	77
Cash provided by operating activities and nonoperating gains and losses	28,022	69,017
Investing activities:		
Purchase of property and equipment	(78,421)	(58,082)
Decrease (increase) in investments, marketable securities with limited use	70,676	(63,726)
Increase in investment in affiliates	(958)	(4,097)
Decrease (increase) in other assets	4,109	(2,425)
Cash used in investing activities	(4,594)	(128,331)
Financing activities:		
Proceeds from issuance of long-term debt	—	124,472
Payments and refunding of long-term debt	(8,762)	(66,886)
Cash (used in) provided by financing activities	(8,762)	57,586
Increase (decrease) in cash and cash equivalents	14,666	(1,728)
Cash and cash equivalents at beginning of year	623	2,351
Cash and cash equivalents at end of year	$ 15,289	$ 623

17–8 Not-for-Profit Hospital. The Phelps Community Hospital balance sheet as of December 31, 2010, follows.

PHELPS COMMUNITY HOSPITAL
Balance Sheet
December 31, 2010

Assets			Liabilities and Net Assets	
Current:			Current:	
Cash		$ 65,000	Accounts payable	$ 65,000
Accounts and notes receivable	$ 140,000		Accrued payroll	110,000
Less: Allowance for uncollectibles	12,000	128,000		
Inventory		71,000		
Total current assets		264,000	Total current liabilities	175,000
Assets limited as to use:				
Cash	11,500		Long-term debt:	
Investments	210,000		Mortgage payable	3,500,000
Total assets			Total liabilities	3,675,000
limited as to use		221,500	Net assets:	
Property, plant, and equipment:			Unrestricted, undesignated	1,782,000
Land		208,000	Unrestricted, designated for plant replacements	221,500
Buildings, at cost	4,516,000			
Less: Accumulated			Total net assets	2,003,500
depreciation	1,506,000	3,010,000		
Equipment, at cost	2,871,000			
Less: Accumulated depreciation	896,000	1,975,000		
Total property, plant, and equipment		5,193,000		
Total assets		$5,678,500	Total liabilities and net assets	$5,678,500

Required

a. Record in general journal form the effect of the following transactions during the fiscal year ended December 31, 2011, assuming that Phelps Community Hospital is a not-for-profit hospital.

(1) Summary of revenue journal:

Patient services revenue, gross	$3,584,900
Adjustments and allowances:	
Contracting agencies	162,000

(2) Summary of cash receipts journal:

Interest on investments in Assets Limited as to Use	7,350
Unrestricted grant from United Fund	300,000
Collections of receivables	3,520,600

(3) Purchases journal:

Administration expenses	167,900
General services expenses	181,200
Nursing services expenses	278,800
Other professional services expenses	263,100

(4) Payroll journal:

Administration expenses	253,700
General services expenses	179,200
Nursing services expenses	659,200
Other professional services expenses	422,400

5) Summary of cash payments journal:

Interest expense	280,000
Payment on mortgage principal	500,000
Accounts payable for purchases	936,800
Accrued payroll	1,579,500
Transfer to Assets Limited as to Use	30,000

(6) The following additional information relates to assets limited as to use:
  (*a*) $10,000 in CDs matured on which $590 in interest was earned.
  (*b*) $30,000 was reinvested in CDs.
  (*c*) $12,300 in equipment was purchased.

(7) Depreciation charges for the year amounted to $117,000 for the buildings and $128,500 for equipment.

(8) Other information:
  (*a*) Provision for uncollectible receivables was increased by $3,800.
  (*b*) Supplies inventory:

	12/31/2010	12/31/2011
Administration expenses	$ 8,000	$ 7,300
General services expenses	8,700	9,000
Nursing services expenses	17,000	16,800
Other professional services expenses	37,300	40,000
Totals	$71,000	$73,100

  (*c*) Portion of mortgage payable due within one year, $500,000.

(9) Assume that there was no change in fair value of investments at year-end.

(10) Provisions for bad debts, interest expense, and depreciation expense were allocated to functional expense accounts in proportion to their preallocation balances. Nominal accounts were closed.

(11) Reflecting the net increase in Assets Limited as to Use of $25,640 (see transactions 2, 5, and 6), record the increase in Net Assets—Unrestricted, Designated for Plant Replacement.

b. Prepare a balance sheet as of December 31, 2011.

c. Prepare a statement of operations for the year ended December 31, 2011.

Glossary

Some of these definitions were adapted from publications of the Government Finance Officers Association. Others were taken from specialized publications cited in the text; the remainder were supplied by the authors. The letters *q.v.* signify "which see"; that is, the preceding word is defined elsewhere in the glossary.

A

Abatement A complete or partial cancellation of a levy imposed by a government. Abatements usually apply to tax levies, special assessments, and service charges.

Accountability Being obliged to explain one's actions, to justify what one does; the requirement for government to answer to its citizenry—to justify the raising of public resources and expenditure of those resources. Also, in the GASB's view, the obligation to report whether the government operated within appropriate legal constraints; whether resources were used efficiently, economically, and effectively; whether current-year revenues were sufficient to pay for the services provided in the current year; and whether the burden for services previously provided will be shifted to future taxpayers.

Accounting Period A period at the end of which and for which financial statements are prepared. See also Fiscal Period.

Accounting System The total structure of records and procedures that discover, record, classify, and report information on the financial position and operations of a government or any of its funds, and organizational components.

Accounts Receivable Amounts owing on open account from private persons, firms, or corporations for goods and services furnished by a government. Taxes Receivable and Special Assessments Receivable are recorded separately. Amounts due from other funds or from other governments should be reported separately.

Accrual Basis The basis of accounting under which revenues are recorded when earned and expenditures (or expenses) are recorded as soon as they result in liabilities for benefits received, notwithstanding that the receipt of cash or the payment of cash may take place, in whole or in part, in another accounting period. See also Accrue and Levy.

Accrue To record revenues when earned and to record expenditures (or expenses) as soon as they result in liabilities for benefits received, notwithstanding that the receipt of cash or payment of cash may take place, in whole or in part, in another accounting period. See also Accrual Basis, Accrued Expenses, and Accrued Revenue.

Accrued Expenses Expenses incurred during the current accounting period but not payable until a subsequent accounting period. See also Accrual Basis and Accrue.

Accrued Interest on Investments Purchased Interest accrued on investments between the last interest payment date and the date of purchase.

Accrued Interest Payable A liability account that represents the amount of interest expense accrued at the balance sheet date but not due until a later date.

Accrued Revenue Revenue earned during the current accounting period but not to be collected until a subsequent accounting period. See also Accrual Basis and Accrue.

Accrued Taxes Payable A liability for taxes that have accrued since the last payment date.

Accrued Wages Payable A liability for wages earned by employees between the last payment date and the balance sheet date.

Acquisition Adjustment Difference between amount paid by a utility for plant assets acquired from another utility and the original cost (*q.v.*) of those assets less depreciation to date of acquisition.

Activity A specific and distinguishable line of work performed by one or more organizational components of a government for the purpose of accomplishing a function for which the government is responsible. For example, food inspection is an activity performed in the discharge of the health function. See also Function, Subfunction, and Subactivity.

Activity-Based Costing (ABC) A cost accounting system that identifies specific factors (cost drivers) that drive the costs of service or production activities and tracks the consumption of cost drivers in producing outputs of goods or services. See also Cost Determination.

Activity Classification A grouping of expenditures on the basis of specific lines of work performed by organization units. For example, sewage treatment and disposal, solid waste collection, solid waste disposal, and street cleaning are activities performed in carrying out the function of sanitation, and the segregation of the expenditures made for each of these activities constitutes an activity classification.

Actuarial Accrued Liability (AAL) A liability arising from past unfunding and ad hoc changes in pension plan provisions. AAL is determined by using any of several generally accepted actuarial methods, for example, entry age method.

Actuarial Basis A basis used in computing the amount of contributions to be made periodically to a fund so that the total contributions plus the compounded earnings thereon will equal the required payments to be made out of the fund. The factors taken into account in arriving at the amount of these contributions include the length of time over which each contribution is to be held and the rate of return compounded on such contribution over its life.

Actuarial Present Value of Total Projected Benefits A component of the annual required contribution that allows for projected salary increases and additional statutory or contractual agreements.

Actuarial Value of Assets The value of a pension plan's assets used by an actuary for purposes of determining annual required contributions and other actuarial aspects of a defined benefit pension plan.

Ad Valorem Property Taxes In proportion to value. A basis for levy of taxes on property.

Advance Refunding The issuance of debt instruments to refund existing debt before the existing debt matures or is callable.

Advocacy Speaking up for the mission of an organization or needs of a group of people.

Agency Funds Funds consisting of resources received and held by the government as an agent for others; for example, taxes collected and held by a municipality for a school district. *Note:* Sometimes resources held by a government for other organizations are handled through an agency fund known as a *pass-through agency fund.*

Allocate To divide a lump-sum appropriation into parts that are designated for expenditure by specific organization units and/or for specific purposes, activities, or objects.

Allotment A part of an appropriation (or, in federal usage, parts of an apportionment) that may be encumbered (obligated) or expended during an allotment period.

Allotments Available for Commitment/Obligation The portion of a federal agency's allotments not yet obligated by issuance of purchase orders, contracts, or other evidence of commitment.

Allowable Costs Costs that meet specific criteria determined by the resource provider, generally used in the context of federal financial assistance.

Allowance for Amortization The account in which the amounts recorded as amortization (*q.v.*) of the intangible asset are accumulated.

Allowance for Depreciation The account in which the amounts recorded as depreciation (*q.v.*) of the related asset are accumulated.

Amortization (1) Gradual reduction, redemption, or liquidation of the balance of an account according to a specified schedule of times and amounts. (2) Provision for the extinguishment of a debt by means of a debt service fund (*q.v.*).

Annual Pension Cost The annual expense to an employer for a pension plan, which is a function of annual required contribution (ARC), net pension obligation (NPO), interest, and adjustments.

Annual Required Contribution (ARC) An actuarially determined amount that the employer should contribute each year to a defined benefit pension plan to ensure full actuarial funding of the plan.

Annuity A series of equal money payments made at equal intervals during a designated period of time. In governmental accounting, the most frequent annuities are accumulations of debt service funds for term bonds and payments to retired employees or their beneficiaries under public employee retirement systems.

Annuity Agreements Assets given to an organization subject to an agreement that binds the organization to pay stipulated amounts periodically to the donor(s).

Annuity Serial Bonds Bonds for which the amount of annual principal repayments is scheduled to increase each year by approximately the same amount that interest payments decrease.

Apportionment A distribution made of a federal appropriation by the Office of Management and Budget into amounts available for specified time periods.

Appropriation Act, Bill, Ordinance, Resolution, or Order A legal action giving the administration of a government authorization to incur on behalf of the government liabilities for the acquisition of goods, services, or facilities to be used for purposes specified in the act, ordinance, or so on, in amounts not to exceed those specified for each purpose. The authorization usually expires at the end of a specified term, most often one year.

Appropriations Authorizations granted by a legislative body to incur liabilities for purposes specified in the Appropriation Act (*q.v.*). *Note:* An appropriation is usually limited in amount and as to the time when it may be expended. See, however, Indeterminate Appropriation.

Appropriations Budget Appropriations requested by departments or by the central administration of a government for a budget period. When the appropriations budget has been adopted in accord with procedures specified by relevant law, the budget becomes legally binding on the administration of the government for which the budget has been adopted.

Appropriations Used An account used in federal government accounting to indicate resources provided by current- or prior-period appropriations that were consumed during the current fiscal period.

Arbitrage Earning a higher interest rate from investing borrowed funds than is applicable to the entity's tax-exempt debt. Federal tax regulations require governments to rebate the investment earnings in excess of that permitted. See also Arbitrage Rebate.

Arbitrage Rebate Required repayment to the federal government arising from the arbitrage rules that prohibit the government from investing bond proceeds at interest rates higher than that applicable to the entity's tax-exempt debt.

Assess To value property officially for the purpose of taxation. *Note:* The term is also sometimes used to denote the levy of taxes, but such usage is not correct because it fails to distinguish between the valuation process and the tax levy process.

Assessed Valuation A valuation set on real estate or other property by a government as a basis for levying taxes.

Assessment (1) The process of making the official valuation of property for purposes of taxation. (2) The valuation placed on property as a result of this process.

Asset Impairment A significant, unexpected decline in the service utility of a capital asset (*q.v.*).

Assets Probable future economic benefits obtained or controlled by a particular entity as a result of past transactions or events.

Assets Limited as to Use Assets whose use is limited by contracts or agreements with outside parties (such as proceeds of debt issues, funds deposited with a trustee, self-insurance funding arrangements, and statutory reserve requirements) other than donors or grantors. The term also includes limitations placed on assets by the board of directors or trustees.

Attestation Engagements Services related to internal control, compliance, MD&A presentation, allowability and reasonableness of proposed contract amounts, final contract costs, and reliability of performance measures.

Audit The examination of documents, records, reports, systems of internal control, accounting and financial procedures, and other evidence for one or more of the following purposes:

1. To determine whether the financial statements or other financial reports and related items are fairly presented in accordance with generally accepted accounting principles or other established or stated criteria.
2. To determine whether the entity has complied with laws and regulations and other specific financial compliance requirements that may have a material effect on the financial statements or that may affect other financial reports or the economy, efficiency, or effectiveness of program activities.
3. To determine whether the entity is acquiring, protecting, and using its resources economically and efficiently.
4. To determine whether the desired program results or benefits established by the legislature or other authorizing body are being achieved.

Audit Committee A committee of the governing board whose function it is to help select the auditor, monitor the audit process, review results of the audit, assist the governing board in understanding the results of the audit, and participate with both management and the independent auditor in resolving internal control or other deficiencies identified during the audit.

Audit Findings Items identified by the auditors in the course of the audit, such as internal control weaknesses, instances of noncompliance, questioned costs, fraud, and material misrepresentations (by the auditee).

Auditor's Opinion or Report A statement signed by an auditor stating that he or she has examined the financial statements in accordance with generally accepted auditing standards (with exceptions, if any) and expressing his or her opinion on the financial condition and results of operations of the reporting entity, as appropriate.

Authority A government or public agency created to perform a single function or a restricted group of related activities. Usually such governments are financed from service charges, fees, and tolls, but in some instances they also have taxing powers. An authority may be completely independent of other governments, or in some cases it may be partially dependent on other governments for its creation, its financing, or the exercise of certain powers.

Auxiliary Enterprises Activities of a college or university that furnish a service to students, faculty, or staff on a user-charge basis. The charge is directly related but not necessarily equal to the cost of the service. Examples include college unions, residence halls, stores, faculty clubs, and intercollegiate athletics.

Available Collectible within the current period or soon enough thereafter to be used to pay liabilities of the current period.

B

Balance Sheet A statement that reports the balances of assets, liabilities, reserves, and equities of a fund, government, or not-for-profit entity at a specified date, properly classified to exhibit financial position of the fund or unit at that date.

Balanced Scorecard An integrated set of performance targets, both financial and nonfinancial, that are derived from an organization's strategies about how to achieve its goals.

Basic Financial Statements Term used in *GASBS 34* to describe required government-wide and fund financial statements.

Basis of Accounting The standard(s) used to determine the point in time when assets, liabilities, revenues, and expenses (expenditures) should be measured and recorded as such in the accounts of an entity. See Accrual Basis, Cash Basis, and Modified Accrual Basis.

Bearer Bond A bond that requires the holder to present matured interest coupons or matured bonds to the issuer or a designated paying agent for payment. Payments are made to the bearer since the issuer maintains no record of current bond ownership. *Note:* Federal law requires that all tax-exempt bonds issued since June 15, 1983, must be in registered form (see also Registered Bonds). However, some long-term bearer bonds remain outstanding.

Benchmarking The method of identifying a number that represents a target to which actual results are compared, or a basis for comparison; for example, industry averages.

Betterment An addition made to or change made in a capital asset that is expected to prolong its life or to increase its efficiency over and above that arising from maintenance (*q.v.*) and the cost of which is therefore added to the book value of the asset. *Note:* The term is sometimes applied to sidewalks, sewers, and highways, but these should preferably be designated as improvements or infrastructure assets (*q.v.*).

Blended Presentation The method of reporting the financial data of a component unit in a manner similar to that in which the financial data of the primary government are presented. Under this method the component unit data are usually combined with the appropriate fund types of the primary government and reported in the same columns as the data for the primary government except General Funds. See Discrete Presentation.

Block Grants Federal monies given to state or local governments with the discretion to administer for many projects and to many recipients and for which no matching requirement exists.

Board-Designated Funds Funds created to account for assets set aside by the governing board of an organization for specified purposes.

Board-Designated Net Assets Unrestricted net assets that the not-for-profit organization's board decides to set aside or "designate" for specific purposes.

Bond A written promise to pay a specified sum of money, called the *face value* or *principal amount,* at a specified date or dates in the future, called the *maturity date(s),* together with periodic interest at a specified rate. *Note:* The difference between a note and a bond is that the latter runs for a longer period of time and requires greater legal formality.

Bond Anticipation Notes (BANs) Short-term interest-bearing notes issued by a government in anticipation of bonds to be issued at a later date. The notes are retired from proceeds of the bond issue to which they are related. See also Interim Borrowing.

Bond Discount The excess of the face value of a bond over the price for which it is acquired or sold. *Note:* The price does not include accrued interest at the date of acquisition or sale.

Bond Indenture The contract between an entity issuing bonds and the trustees or other body representing prospective and actual holders of the bonds.

Bond Ordinance or Resolution An ordinance (*q.v.*) or resolution (*q.v.*) authorizing a bond issue.

Bond Premium The excess of the price at which a bond is acquired or sold over its face value. *Note:* The price does not include accrued interest at the date of acquisition or sale.

Bonded Debt That portion of indebtedness represented by outstanding bonds. See Gross Bonded Debt and Net Bonded Debt.

Bonds Authorized and Unissued Bonds that have been legally authorized but not issued and that can be issued and sold without further authorization. *Note:* This term must not be confused with the terms *margin of borrowing power* or *legal debt margin,* either one of which represents the difference between the legal debt limit of a government and the debt outstanding against it.

Book Value Value (*q.v.*) as shown by the books of account. *Note:* In the case of assets subject to reduction by valuation allowances, *book value* refers to cost or stated value less the appropriate allowance. Sometimes a distinction is made between *gross* book value and *net* book value, the former designating value before deduction of related allowances and the latter after their deduction. In the absence of any modifier, however, the term *book value* is understood to be synonymous with net book value.

Budget A plan of financial operation embodying an estimate of proposed expenditures for a given period and the proposed means of financing them. Used without any modifier, the term usually indicates a financial plan for a single fiscal year.

Budget Accounts Accounts used in federal agencies that are broad in scope, for which appropriations are made, and that are not the same as the standard general ledger accounts used for accounting purposes.

Budget Calendar A schedule of certain steps to be followed in the budgeting process and the dates by which each step must be completed.

Budget Document The instrument used by the budget-making authority to present a comprehensive financial program to the appropriating body. The budget document usually consists of three parts: (1) a message from the budget-making authority with a summary of the proposed expenditures and the means of financing them; (2) schedules supporting the summary; and (3) drafts of the appropriation, revenue, and borrowing measures necessary to put the budget into effect.

Budget Officer A person, usually in the central administrative office, designated to ensure that administrative policies are actually used in budget preparation and that the budget calendar and other legal requirements are met.

Budgetary Accounts Those accounts that reflect budgetary operations and condition, such as estimated revenues, appropriations, and encumbrances, as distinguished from proprietary accounts. See also Proprietary Accounts.

Budgetary Control The control or management of a government or enterprise in accordance with an approved budget for the purpose of keeping expenditures within the limitations of available appropriations and available revenues.

Budgetary Resources A term that includes new budgetary authority for the period plus unobligated budgetary authority carried over from the prior period and offsetting collections, if any, plus or minus any budgetary adjustments in a federal agency.

Budget Solvency A government's ability to generate enough revenue over its normal budgetary period to meet its expenditures and not incur deficit's.

Buildings A capital asset account that reflects the acquisition value of permanent structures used to house persons and property owned by a government. If buildings are purchased or constructed, this account includes the purchase or contract price of all permanent buildings and fixtures attached to and forming a permanent part of such buildings. If buildings are acquired by gift, the account reflects their appraised value at time of acquisition.

Business-Type Activities Commercial-type activities of a government, such as public utilities (e.g., electric, water, gas, and sewer utilities), transportation systems, toll roads, toll bridges, hospitals, parking garages and lots, liquor stores, golf courses, and swimming pools.

C

Callable Bond A type of bond that permits the issuer to pay the obligation before the stated maturity date by giving notice of redemption in a manner specified in the bond contract. Also called optional bond.

Capital Assets Assets of a long-term character that are intended to continue to be held or used, such as land, buildings, machinery, furniture, and other equipment. *Note:* The term does not indicate the immobility of an asset, which is the distinctive character of "fixture" (*q.v.*). Also called *fixed assets.*

Capital Budget A plan of proposed capital outlays and the means of financing them for the current fiscal period. It is usually a part of the current budget. If a capital program is in operation, it will be the first year thereof. A capital program is sometimes referred to as a capital budget. See also Capital Program.

Capital Expenditures See Capital Outlays.

Capital Improvements Fund A fund to accumulate revenues from current taxes levied for major repairs and maintenance to capital assets of a nature not specified at the time the revenues are levied. Appropriations of this fund are made in accord with state law at the time specific projects become necessary.

Capital Lease A lease that substantively transfers the benefits and risks of ownership of property to the lessee. Any lease that meets certain criteria specified in applicable accounting and reporting standards is a capital lease. See also Operating Lease.

Capital Outlays Expenditures that result in the acquisition of or addition to capital assets.

Capital Program A plan for capital expenditures to be incurred each year over a fixed period of years to meet capital needs arising from a long-term work program or otherwise. It sets forth each project or other contemplated expenditure in which the government is to have a part and specifies the full resources estimated to be available to finance the projected expenditures.

Capital Projects Fund (CPF) A fund created to account for all resources to be used for the construction or acquisition of designated capital assets by a government except those financed by proprietary or fiduciary funds.

Capitation Fees Fixed dollar amount of fees per person paid periodically by a third-party payor to a health care organization, regardless of services provided.

Cash Currency, coin, checks, money orders, and bankers' drafts on hand or on deposit with an official or agent designated as custodian of cash and bank deposits. *Note:* All cash must be recorded as a part of the fund to which it belongs. Any restrictions or limitations as to its availability must be indicated in the records and statements. It is not necessary, however, to have a separate bank account for each fund unless required by law.

Cash Basis The basis of accounting under which revenues are recorded when received in cash and expenditures (or expenses) are recorded when cash is disbursed.

Cash Discount An allowance received or given if payment is completed within a stated period of time.

Cash Equivalents Short-term, highly liquid investments that are both readily convertible into known amounts of cash and so near their maturity that they present insignificant risk of changes in value due to changes in interest rates.

Cash Solvency A government's ability to generate enough cash over a 30- or 60-day period to pay its bills.

Certificate of Participation (COP) A long-term debt instrument authorized for construction of municipal facilities, typically issued by a quasi-independent authority but secured by a long-term lease with a general-purpose local government.

Character A basis for distinguishing expenditures according to the periods they are presumed to benefit. See also Character Classification.

Character Classification A grouping of expenditures on the basis of the fiscal periods they are presumed to benefit. The three groupings are (1) current expenditures, presumed to benefit the current fiscal period, (2) debt service, presumed to benefit prior fiscal periods primarily but also present and future periods, and (3) capital outlays, presumed to benefit the current and future fiscal periods. See also Activity, Activity Classification, Expense, Function, Functional Classification, Object, and Object Classification.

Charitable Solicitation The direct or indirect request for money, credit, property, financial assistance, or other things of value on the representation that these assets will be used for a charitable purpose.

Charity Care Service provided by a health care organization to persons with a demonstrated inability to pay.

Check A bill of exchange drawn on a bank and payable on demand; a written order on a bank to pay on demand a specified sum of money to a named person, to his or her order, or to the bearer, from money on deposit to the credit of the maker. *Note:* A check differs from a warrant in that the latter is not necessarily payable on demand and may not be negotiable. It differs from a voucher in that the latter is not an order to pay.

Clearing Account An account used to accumulate total charges or credits for the purpose of distributing them later among the accounts to which they are allocable or for the purpose of transferring the net differences to the proper account. Also called *suspense account.*

Cognizant Agency for Audit Responsibilities The federal awarding agency that provides the predominant amount of direct funding to a nonfederal entity expending more than $25 million in federal awards, as provided by OMB *Circular A–133,* unless the OMB designates a different cognizant agency.

Collateralized Secured with the pledge of assets to minimize the risk of loss. Deposits, investments, or loans are often required to be collateralized.

Collections Works of art, historical treasures, or similar assets that are (1) held for public exhibition, education, or research in furtherance of public service rather than financial gain, (2) protected, kept unencumbered, cared for, and preserved, and (3) subject to an organizational policy that requires the proceeds of items that are sold to be used to acquire other items for collection.

Combining Financial Statement A financial statement that displays nonmajor governmental or enterprise funds in columns with totals that agree with those reported in the basic financial statements.

Commitment In federal government usage, a reservation of an agency's allotment in the estimated amount of orders for goods or services, prior to actually placing the orders. See also Obligation.

Common Rule Term given to OMB *Circular A–102* that describes administrative requirements that must be met by a state or local government receiving federal financial assistance.

Compliance Audit An audit designed to provide reasonable assurance that a government has complied with applicable laws and regulations. Required for every audit performed in conformity with generally accepted governmental auditing standards.

Component Units Separate governments, agencies, or not-for-profit corporations that, pursuant to the criteria in the GASB *Codification,* Section 2100, are combined with other component units to constitute the reporting entity (*q.v.*).

Comprehensive Annual Financial Report (CAFR) A government's annual report that contains three sections—introductory, financial, and statistical. A CAFR provides financial information beyond the general purpose external financial statements and conforms to guidance in the GASB *Codification.*

Conditional Promise to Give A promise to make a contribution to an organization that depends on the occurrence of a specified future and uncertain event to bind the promisor, such as obtaining matching gifts by the recipient.

Construction Work in Progress The cost of construction work that has been started but not yet completed.

Consumption Method A method of recording supplies as inventory when purchased and as expenditures when used or consumed. The alternative method is called the *purchases method.*

Contingency Fund Assets or other resources set aside to provide for unforeseen expenditures, anticipated expenditures, or an uncertain amount(s).

Contingent Liabilities Items that may become liabilities as a result of conditions undetermined at a given date, such as guarantees, pending lawsuits, judgments under appeal, unsettled disputed claims, unfilled purchase orders, and uncompleted contracts. Contingent liabilities of the latter two types are disclosed in balance sheets of governmental funds as Reserve for Encumbrances; other contingent liabilities are disclosed in notes to the financial statements.

Continuing Appropriation An appropriation that, once established, is automatically renewed without further legislative action, period after period, until altered or revoked. *Note:* The term should not be confused with *indeterminate appropriation* (*q.v.*).

Continuing Care Retirement Community (CCRC) A facility that provides residential care along with some level of long-term nursing or medical care, generally to elderly or retired persons.

Contractual Adjustments (or Allowances) The difference between the gross patient service revenue and the negotiated payment by third-party payors in arriving at net patient service revenue.

Contribution An amount given to an individual or to an organization for which the donor receives no direct private benefits. Contributions may be in the form of pledges, cash, securities, materials, services, or capital assets.

Control Account An account in the general ledger in which is recorded the aggregate of debit and credit postings to a number of identical or related accounts called *subsidiary accounts.* For example, the Taxes Receivable account is a control account supported by the aggregate of individual balances in individual property taxpayers' accounts.

Cost The amount of money or money's worth exchanged for property or services. *Note:* Costs may be incurred even before money is paid, that is, as soon as a liability is incurred. Ultimately, however, money or money's worth must be given in exchange. Again, the cost of some property or service may, in turn, become a part of the cost of another property or service. For example, the cost of part or all of the materials purchased at a certain time will be reflected in the cost of articles made from such materials or in the cost of services provided using such materials.

Cost Accounting The branch of accounting that provides for the assembling and recording of all elements of cost incurred to accomplish a purpose, to carry on an activity or operation, or to complete a unit of work or a specific job.

Cost Determination The use of statistical procedures to determine or estimate the cost of goods or services as opposed to accumulating such costs in a formal cost accounting system.

Cost Objective In federal terminology, an organization unit, function, activity, project, cost center, or pool established for the accumulation of costs.

Cost Unit A term used in cost accounting to designate the unit of product or service whose cost is computed. These units are selected for the purpose of comparing the actual cost with a standard cost or with actual costs of units produced under different circumstances or at different places and times. See also Unit Cost.

Coupon Rate The interest rate specified on interest coupons attached to a bond. The term is synonymous with nominal interest rate (*q.v.*) for coupon bonds.

Covered Payroll The amount of payroll on which contributions to a pension plan are based.

Credit Risk The risk that a debt issuer will not pay interest and principal when due. See also Default.

Cumulative Results of Operations A term generally used in federal agencies to refer to the net difference between expenses/losses and financing sources, including appropriations, revenues, and gains, since the inception of the activity.

Current A term applied to budgeting and accounting that designates the operations of the present fiscal period as opposed to past or future periods.

Current Assets Those assets that are available or can be made readily available to meet the cost of operations or to pay current liabilities. Some examples are cash, temporary investments, and taxes receivable.

Current Financial Resources Cash or items expected to be converted into cash during the current period or soon enough thereafter to pay current period liabilities.

Current Fund In governmental accounting, sometimes used as a synonym for General Fund.

Current Funds Funds whose resources are expended for operating purposes during the current fiscal period. Colleges and universities and voluntary health and welfare organizations often use fund types called Current Funds—Unrestricted and Current Funds—Restricted for Internal Purposes.

Current Liabilities Liabilities payable within a relatively short period of time, usually no longer than a year. See also Floating Debt.

Current Resources Resources (*q.v.*) to which recourse can be had to meet current obligations and expenditures. Examples are estimated revenues of a particular period not yet realized, transfers from other funds authorized but not received, and, in the case of certain funds, bonds authorized and unissued.

Current Special Assessments (1) Special assessments levied and becoming due during the current fiscal period from the date special assessment rolls are approved by the proper authority to the date on which a penalty for nonpayment is attached. (2) Special assessments levied in a prior fiscal period but becoming due in the current fiscal period from the time they become due to the date on which a penalty for nonpayment is attached.

Current Taxes (1) Taxes levied and becoming due during the current fiscal period from the time the amount of tax levy is first established to the date on which a penalty for nonpayment is attached. (2) Taxes levied in the preceding fiscal period but becoming due in the current fiscal period from the time they become due until a penalty for nonpayment is attached.

Customer Advances for Construction Amounts required to be deposited by a customer for construction projects undertaken by the utility at the request of the customer.

Customer Relationship Management (CRM) Systems that create an integrated view of a customer to coordinate services from all channels of the organization with the intent to improve long-term relationships.

Cycle Billing A practice to bill part of the customers each working day during a month instead of billing all customers as of a certain day of the month. It is followed by utilities, retail stores, and other organizations with a large number of credit customers.

D

Data Processing (1) The preparation and handling of information and data from source media through prescribed procedures to obtain specific end results such as classification, problem solution, summarization, and reports. (2) Preparation and handling of financial information wholly or partially by use of computers.

Debt A liability resulting from the borrowing of money or from the purchase of goods and services. Debts of governments include bonds, time warrants, notes, and floating debt. See also Bond, Notes Payable, Time Warrant, Floating Debt, Long-term Debt, and General Long-term Liabilities.

Debt-Financed Income Income from property that is subject to debt, such as rental income from a building that has been financed with a mortgage.

Debt Limit The maximum amount of gross or net debt that is legally permitted.

Debt Margin The difference between the amount of the debt limit (*q.v.*) and the net amount of outstanding indebtedness subject to the limitation.

Debt Service Fund (DSF) A fund established to finance and account for the payment of interest and principal on all tax-supported debt, serial and term, including that payable from special assessments.

Default Failure of a debtor to pay interest or repay the principal of debt when legally due.

Defeasance A transaction in which the liability for a debt is substantively settled and is removed from the accounts, even though the debt has not actually been paid. See also Legal Defeasance and In-Substance Defeasance.

Deferred Revenues or Deferred Credits In governmental accounting, items that may not be recognized as revenues of the period in which received because they are not "available" until a subsequent period.

Deferred Serial Bonds Serial bonds (*q.v.*) in which the first installment does not fall due for two or more years from the date of issue.

Deficiency A general term indicating the amount by which anything falls short of some requirement or expectation. The term should not be used without qualification.

Deficit (1) The excess of liabilities and reserved equity of a fund over its assets. (2) The excess of expenditures over revenues during an accounting period or, in the case of enterprise and internal service funds, of expense over revenue during an accounting period.

Defined Benefit Plan A pension plan that provides a specified amount of benefits based on a formula that may include factors such as age, salary, and years of employment.

Defined Contribution Plan A pension plan that specifies the amount or rate of contribution, often a percentage of covered salary, that the employer and employees must contribute to the members' accounts.

Delinquent Special Assessments Special assessments remaining unpaid on and after the date on which a penalty for nonpayment is attached.

Delinquent Taxes Taxes remaining unpaid on and after the date on which a penalty for nonpayment is attached. Even though the penalty may be subsequently waived and a portion of the taxes may be abated or canceled, the unpaid balances continue to be delinquent taxes until abated, canceled, paid, or converted into tax liens. *Note:* The term is sometimes limited to taxes levied for the fiscal period or periods preceding the current one, but such usage is not entirely correct. See also Current Taxes and Prior-Years' Tax Levies.

Deposit Warrant A financial document prepared by a designated accounting or finance officer authorizing the treasurer of a government to accept for deposit sums of money collected by various departments and agencies of the government.

Deposits Money deposited with a financial institution that must be released upon the "demand" of the depositor; for example, demand deposits (checking) and time deposits (savings accounts). These funds are generally insured by the Federal Deposit Insurance Corporation (up to a limit) and are distinguished from investments.

Depreciation (1) Expiration of the service life of capital assets other than wasting assets attributable to wear and tear, deterioration, action of the physical elements, inadequacy, and obsolescence. (2) The portion of the cost of a capital asset other than a wasting asset that is charged as an expense during a particular period.

Derivative A financial instrument or other contract that has one or more reference rates and one or more notional amounts (e.g., face amount), requires little or no initial investment, and requires or permits net settlement.

Derived Tax Revenues A classification of nonexchange transactions, such as income or sales taxes.

Designated A term that describes assets or equity set aside by action of the governing board; as distinguished from assets or equity set aside in conformity with requirements of donors, grantors, or creditors.

Diagnosis-Related Groups (DRGs) A case-mix classification scheme instituted by Congress in 1983 in relation to the Medicare program that is used to determine the reimbursement received by a hospital for inpatient services.

Payment is made based on the patient's diagnosis regardless of how much the hospital spends to treat a patient.

Direct Costs Costs incurred because of some definite action by or for an organization unit, function, activity, project, cost center, or pool; costs identified specifically with a cost objective (*q.v.*).

Direct Debt The debt that a government has incurred in its own name or assumed through the annexation of territory or consolidation with another government. See also Overlapping Debt.

Direct Expenses Those expenses that can be charged directly as a part of the cost of a product or service or of a department or operating unit as distinguished from overhead and other indirect costs that must be prorated among several products or services, departments, or operating units.

Direct Lobbying Testifying at legislative hearings, corresponding or conferring with legislators or their staffs, and publishing documents advocating specific legislative action.

Disbursements Payments in cash.

Discount on Taxes A cash discount offered to taxpayers to encourage early payment of taxes.

Discrete Presentation The method of reporting financial data of component units in a column(s) separate from the financial data of the primary government.

Disqualified Person A person who has substantial influence over the affairs of a not-for-profit organization, such as an officer or manager.

Donated Assets Noncash contributions (*q.v.*) that may be in the form of securities, land, buildings, equipment, or materials.

Donated Materials See Donated Assets.

Donated Services The services of volunteer workers who are unpaid or are paid less than the market value of their services.

Double Entry A system of bookkeeping that requires that for every entry made to the debit side of an account or accounts an entry for a corresponding amount or amounts to the credit side of another account or accounts be made. *Note:* Double-entry bookkeeping involves maintaining a balance between assets on the one hand and liabilities and equities on the other.

Due Diligence Formal disclosure and discovery of all relevant information about a transaction or organization, particularly about risks.

E

Earnings See Income and Revenue.

Economic Condition A composite of a government's financial health and its ability and willingness to meet its financial obligations and its commitments to provide services.

Economic Interest An interest in another organization because it holds or utilizes significant resources that must be used for the purposes of the reporting organization or the reporting organization is responsible for the liabilities of the other entity.

Economic Resources Measurement Focus Attention on measuring the total economic resources that flow in and out of the government rather than on measuring *current financial resources* only.

Economic Size The minimum possible size to be able to provide services without long-term damage to the organization's financial base.

Effective Interest Rate The rate of earning on a bond investment based on the actual price paid for the bond, the maturity date, and the length of time between interest dates, in contrast with the nominal interest rate (*q.v.*).

Effectiveness Measures Measures that relate cost to outcomes.

Efficiency Measures Measures that relate quantity or cost of resources used to unit of output.

Eligibility Requirements Specified characteristics that program recipients must possess or reimbursement provisions and contingencies tied to required actions by the recipient.

Encumbrances Accounts used to record the estimated amount of purchase orders, contracts, or salary commitments chargeable to an appropriation. The account is credited when goods or services are received and the actual expenditure of the appropriation is known.

Endowment A gift whose principal must be maintained inviolate but whose income may be expended.

Engagement Letter Written agreement between an auditor and the audited entity that describes the scope of work to be completed, among other things.

Enterprise Debt Debt that is to be retired primarily through the earnings of governmentally owned and operated enterprises. See also Revenue Bonds.

Enterprise Fund (EF) A fund established to finance and account for the acquisition, operation, and maintenance of governmental facilities and services that are entirely or predominantly self-supporting by user charges; or for when the governing body of the government has decided periodic determination of revenues earned, expenses incurred, and/or net income is appropriate. Governmentally owned utilities and hospitals are ordinarily accounted for by enterprise funds.

Entitlement The amount of payment to which a state or local government is entitled as determined by the federal government pursuant to an allocation formula contained in applicable statutes.

Entity Assets Those assets of a federal agency that the reporting entity has authority to use in its operations as opposed to holding but not available to spend.

Entitywide Perspective A view of the net assets of the organization as a whole, rather than as a collection of separate funds.

Entrepreneurial Budgeting A budgeting approach that positions budgeting at the highest level and merges strategic plans, incentives, and accountability into the budget to communicate to citizens as a package.

Entry (1) The record of a financial transaction in its appropriate book of account. (2) The act of recording a transaction in the books of account.

Equipment Tangible property of a more or less permanent nature (other than land, buildings, or improvements) that is useful in carrying on operations. Examples are machinery, tools, trucks, cars, furniture, and furnishings.

Escheats (Escheat Property) Private properties that revert to government ownership upon the death of the owner if there are no legal claimants or heirs.

Estimated Expenditures The estimated amounts of expenditures included in budgeted appropriations. See also Appropriations.

Estimated Other Financing Sources Amounts of financial resources estimated to be received or accrued during a period by a governmental or similar type fund from interfund transfers or from the proceeds of noncurrent debt issuance.

Estimated Other Financing Uses Amounts of financial resources estimated to be disbursed or accrued during a period by a governmental or similar type fund for transfer to other funds.

Estimated Revenues For revenue accounts kept on an accrual basis (*q.v.*), this term designates the amount of revenue estimated to accrue during a given period regardless of whether or not it is all to be collected during the period. For revenue accounts kept on a cash basis (*q.v.*), the term designates the amount of revenue estimated to be collected during a given period. Under the modified accrual basis (*q.v.*), estimated revenues are those that are measurable and available. See also Revenue, Cash Basis, Accrual Basis, and Modified Accrual Basis.

Estimated Uncollectible Accounts Receivable (or Current Taxes, Delinquent Taxes or Interest Receivable) That portion of receivables that it is estimated will never be collected. The account is deducted from the Accounts Receivable account on the balance sheet in order to arrive at the net amount of accounts receivable.

Excess Benefit Transaction A transaction that results in unfair benefits to a person who has substantial influence over a not-for-profit organization, for example, unreasonable compensation, sales of assets at bargain prices, and lease arrangements.

Exchange Transaction A transaction in which each party receives direct tangible benefits commensurate with the resources provided, for example, sales between a buyer and a seller.

Exchange-like Transactions A transaction in which the values exchanged, though related, may not be quite equal or in which the direct benefits may not be exclusively for the parties to the transaction, unlike a "pure" exchange transaction.

Exemption A statutory reduction in the assessed valuation of taxable property accorded to certain taxpayers, such as senior citizens and war veterans.

Expendable Assets and resources may be converted into cash and used in their entirety for purposes of the fund.

Expended Appropriation (Authority) A charge against an appropriation for the actual cost of items received; the appropriation is no longer available to acquire additional goods and services.

Expenditure Responsibility The responsibility of one public charity over another to which it has given a grant to ensure that the grant was used exclusively for the purpose for which it was made.

Expenditure An expenditure is recorded when liabilities are incurred pursuant to authority given in an appropriation (*q.v.*). If the accounts are kept on the accrual basis (*q.v.*) or the modified accrual basis (*q.v.*), this term designates the cost of goods delivered or services rendered, whether paid or unpaid, including expenses, provision for debt retirement not reported as a liability of the fund from which retired, and capital outlays. When the accounts are kept on the cash basis (*q.v.*), the term designates only actual cash disbursements for these purposes. *Note:* Encumbrances are not expenditures.

Expense A charge incurred, whether paid or unpaid, for operation, maintenance, interest, and other charges presumed to benefit the current fiscal period.

External Investment Pool Centrally managed investment portfolios (pools) that manage the investments of participants (e.g., other governments and not-for-profit organizations) outside the reporting entity of the government that administers the pool.

External Support Test One of two parts of the broad public support test to determine if an organization is a public charity rather than a private foundation. It is met if at least one-third of the organization's total revenue comes from the government or general public in the form of contributions, grants, membership dues, charges for services, or sales of merchandise.

Extraordinary Items Unusual and infrequent material gains or losses.

F

Face Value As applied to securities, the amount of liability stated in the security document.

Facilities and Administrative Costs (F&A) Costs that are not readily assignable to one program or cost objective in a college or university but are incurred for a joint purpose. These costs are called *indirect costs* in some OMB circulars. See also Indirect Costs.

Fair Value The amount at which a financial instrument could be exchanged in a current transaction between willing parties other than in a forced or liquidation sale.

Federal Financial Management Improvement Act of 1996 (FFMIA) Act of Congress in 1996 that requires each federal agency to maintain a financial management system that applies federal accounting standards and provides the information necessary to report whether the agency is in compliance with those standards.

Federated Fund-Raising Organization An organization composed of independent charitable organizations that have voluntarily joined together to raise and distribute money among themselves.

Feeder Organization An entity controlled by a not-for-profit organization and formed to carry on a trade or business for the benefit of an exempt organization and remit its profits to the exempt organization.

Fidelity Bond A written promise to indemnify against losses from theft, defalcation, and misappropriation of public funds by government officers and employees. See also Surety Bond.

Fiduciary Activities Activities in which the government acts in a fiduciary capacity either as an agent or trustee for parties outside the government, for example in the collection of taxes or amounts bequeathed from private citizens, as well as assets held for employee pension plans.

Fiduciary Funds Any fund held by a government in a fiduciary capacity for an external party, ordinarily as agent or trustee. Also called *trust and agency funds.*

Financially Accountable When a primary government either appoints a voting majority of an organization's governing board and can impose its will on the organization, or the organization can provide specific benefits to (or impose specific burdens on) the primary government. See Accountability.

Financial Audit One of the two major types of audits defined by the U.S. Government Accountability Office (see Performance Audit for the other major type). A financial audit provides an auditor's opinion that financial statements present fairly an entity's financial position and results of operations in conformity with generally accepted accounting principles or that other financial reports comply with specified finance-related criteria.

Financial Condition The probability that a government will meet its financial obligations as they become due and its service obligations to constituencies, both currently and in the future. See Financial Position.

Financial Position The adequacy of cash and short-term claims to cash to meet current obligations and those expected in the near future. See Financial Condition.

Financial Reporting Entity See Reporting Entity.

Fiscal Accountability Current-period financial position and budgetary compliance reported in fund-type financial statements of governments. See also Financial Accountability.

Fiscal Agent A bank or other corporate fiduciary that performs the function of paying, on behalf of the government or other debtor, interest on debt or principal of debt when due.

Fiscal Capacity A government's ongoing ability and willingness to raise revenues, incur debt, and meet its financial obligations as they become due.

Fiscal Period Any period at the end of which a government determines its financial position and the results of its operations.

Fiscal Year A 12-month period of time to which the annual budget applies and at the end of which a government determines its financial position and the results of its operations. For example, FY10 refers to the year that ends in 2010 (e.g., 7-1-09 to 6-30-10).

Fixed Assets See Capital Assets.

Fixed Charges Expenses (*q.v.*) the amount of which is set by agreement. Examples are interest, insurance, and contributions to pension funds.

Fixtures Attachments to buildings that are not intended to be removed and that cannot be removed without damage to the latter. *Note:* Those fixtures with a useful life presumed to be as long as that of the building itself are considered a part of the building; all others are classed as equipment.

Floating Debt Liabilities other than bonded debt and time warrants that are payable on demand or at an early date. Examples are accounts payable, notes, and bank loans. See also Current Liabilities.

Force Account Construction The determination of the cost of construction of buildings and improvements by some agency of the government.

Forfeiture The automatic loss of cash or other property as a punishment for not complying with legal provisions and as compensation for the resulting damages or losses. *Note:* The term should not be confused with *confiscation.* The latter term designates the actual taking over of the forfeited property by the government. Even after property has been forfeited, it cannot be said to be confiscated until the government claims it.

Franchise A special privilege granted by a government permitting the continuing use of public property, such as city streets, and usually involving the elements of monopoly and regulation.

Full Cost The total cost of providing a service or producing a good; the sum of both direct costs (*q.v.*) and indirect costs (*q.v.*).

Full Faith and Credit A pledge of the general taxing power for the payment of debt obligations. *Note:* Bonds carrying such pledges are usually referred to as *general obligation bonds.*

Function A group of related activities aimed at accomplishing a major service or regulatory responsibility for which a government is responsible. For example, public health is a function. See also Subfunction, Activity, Character, and Object.

Functional Classification A grouping of expenditures on the basis of the principal purposes for which they are made. Examples are public safety, public health, and public welfare. See also Activity, Character, and Object Classification.

Fund A fiscal and accounting entity with a self-balancing set of accounts recording cash and other financial resources together with all related liabilities and residual equities or balances, and changes therein, which are segregated for the purpose of carrying on specific activities or attaining certain objectives in accordance with special regulations, restrictions, or limitations.

Fund Accounting An accounting system organized on the basis of funds, each of which is considered a separate accounting entity. Accounting for the operations of each fund is accomplished with a separate set of self-balancing accounts that comprise its assets, liabilities, fund equity, revenues, and expenditures, or expenses, as appropriate. Resources are allocated to and recorded in individual funds based upon purposes for which they are to be spent and the means by which spending activities are controlled. Fund accounting is used by states and local governments and internally by not-for-profit organizations that need to account for resources the use of which is restricted by donors or grantors.

Fund Balance The portion of fund equity (*q.v.*) available for appropriation.

Fund Balance Sheet A balance sheet for a single fund. See Fund and Balance Sheet.

Fund Balance with Treasury An asset account of a federal agency representing cash balances held by the U.S. Treasury upon which the agency can draw. The Treasury will disburse cash on behalf of and at the request of the agency to pay for authorized goods and services.

Fund Equity The excess of fund assets and resources over fund liabilities. A portion of the equity of a governmental fund may be reserved (*q.v.*) or designated (*q.v.*); the remainder is referred to as *fund balance.*

Fund Financial Statements A category of the basic financial statements that assist in assessing fiscal accountability.

Fund Type A classification of funds that are similar in purpose and character.

Funded Deficit A deficit eliminated through the sale of bonds issued for that purpose. See also Funding Bonds.

Funded Ratio The ratio of actuarial value of assets to actuarial accrued liability (AAL) of a pension plan.

Funding The conversion of floating debt or time warrants into bonded debt (*q.v.*).

Funding Bonds See Refunding Bonds.

Funds Functioning as Endowments Funds established by the governing board of an institution, usually a college or university, to account for assets to be retained and invested. Also called *quasi-endowment funds.*

GAAP Hierarchy The chart from *SAS No. 69* amended by *SAS No. 91* that shows the relative weight to be placed on authoritative and other material for nongovernmental entities, state and local governments, and federal governmental entities.

Gains Increases in net assets from peripheral or incidental transactions of an entity.

General Capital Assets (GCA) Those capital assets of a government that are not recognized by a proprietary or fiduciary fund.

General Fund A fund used to account for all transactions of a government that are not accounted for in another fund. *Note:* The General Fund is used to account for the ordinary operations of a government that are financed from taxes and other general revenues.

General Long-Term Liabilities Long-term debt legally payable from general revenues and backed by the full faith and credit of a governmental entity. See Long-Term Debt.

General Obligation (GO) Bonds Bonds for whose payment the full faith and credit of the issuing body is pledged. More commonly, but not necessarily, general obligation bonds are considered to be those payable from taxes and other general revenues. In some states, these bonds are called *tax-supported bonds.* See also Full Faith and Credit.

General Property, Plant, and Equipment Property, plant, and equipment used to provide general government goods and services in a federal agency.

General Purpose Governments Governments that provide many categories of services to their residents, such as states, counties, municipalities, and townships. Typical services include public safety, road maintenance, and health and welfare.

General Revenues Revenues that are not directly linked to any specific function or do not produce a net revenue.

Generally Accepted Accounting Principles (GAAP) The body of accounting and financial reporting standards, conventions, and practices that have authoritative support from standards-setting bodies such as the Governmental Accounting Standards Board and the Financial Accounting Standards Board, or for which a degree of consensus exists among accounting professionals at a given point in time. Generally accepted accounting principles are continually evolving as changes occur in the reporting environment.

Generally Accepted Auditing Standards (GAAS) Standards prescribed by the American Institute of Certified Public Accountants to provide guidance for planning, conducting, and reporting on audits by certified public accountants.

Generally Accepted Government Auditing Standards (GAGAS) See Government Auditing Standards.

Gifts in kind Contributions of tangible items to a tax-exempt organization.

Government Auditing Standards (GAS) Auditing standards set forth by the Comptroller General of the United States to provide guidance for federal auditors, state and local governmental auditors, and public accountants who audit federal organizations, programs, activities, and functions. Also referred to as *generally accepted government auditing standards (GAGAS).*

Government-Mandated Nonexchange Transactions A category of nonexchange transactions, such as certain education, social welfare, and transportation services mandated and funded by a higher level of government.

Governmental Accounting The composite activity of analyzing, recording, summarizing, reporting, and interpreting the financial transactions of governments and agencies. The term generally is used to refer to accounting for state and local governments rather than the U.S. federal government.

Governmental Activities Core governmental services, such as protection of life and property (e.g., police and fire protection), public works (e.g., streets and highways, bridges, and public buildings), parks and recreation facilities and programs, and cultural and social services. Also includes general administrative support, such as data processing, finance, and personnel.

Governmental Assets (Liabilities) Assets (or liabilities) that arise from transactions of the federal government or an entity of the federal government with nonfederal entities.

Governmental Funds A generic classification used by the GASB to refer to all funds other than proprietary and fiduciary funds. The General Fund, special revenue funds, capital projects funds, debt service funds, and permanent funds are the types of funds referred to as *governmental funds.*

Government-wide Financial Statements Two statements prescribed by *GASBS 34* designed to provide a highly aggregated overview of a government's net assets and results of financial activities.

Grant A contribution by one entity to another, usually made to aid in the support of a specified function (for example, education), but sometimes for general purposes or for the acquisition or construction of capital assets.

Grants in Aid See Grant.

Grass-Roots Lobbying An appeal to the general public to contact legislators or to take other action regarding a legislative matter.

Gross Bonded Debt The total amount of direct debt of a government represented by outstanding bonds before deduction of any assets available and earmarked for their retirement. See also Direct Debt.

Gross Tax Levy The amount of the tax bill sent to the taxpayer without regard for any estimate of uncollectible taxes.

H

Health Maintenance Organization (HMO) A prepaid health care plan that functions as a broker of health care between the consumer/patient requiring services and health care providers. HMOs differ depending, in part, on whether or not the health care provider is an employee of the HMO. Similar to *preferred provider organizations (PPOs).*

Heritage Assets Federal capital assets (*q.v.*), such as the Washington Monument, that possess educational, cultural, or natural characteristics.

Historical Cost The amount paid or liability incurred by an accounting entity to acquire an asset and make it ready to render the services for which it was acquired.

Human Service Organization See Voluntary Health and Welfare Organization.

I

Imposed Nonexchange Revenues A category of nonexchange revenue, such as property taxes and most fines and forfeitures.

Improvements Buildings, other structures, and other attachments or annexations to land that are intended to remain so attached or annexed, such as sidewalks, trees, drives, tunnels, drains, and sewers. *Note:* Sidewalks, curbing, sewers, and highways are sometimes referred to as *betterments,* but the term *improvements other than buildings* is preferred. *Infrastructure assets* is also a term used.

Improvements Other than Buildings A capital asset account that reflects the acquisition value of permanent improvements, other than buildings, that add value to land. Examples of such improvements are fences and retaining walls. If the improvements are purchased or constructed, this account contains the purchase or contract price. If improvements are obtained by gift, it reflects fair value at time of acquisition.

Income A term used in accounting for governmental enterprises to represent the excess of revenues earned over the expenses incurred in carrying on the enterprise's operations. It should not be used without an appropriate modifier, such as operating, nonoperating, or net. See also Operating Income, Nonoperating Income, and Net Income. *Note:* The term *income* should not be used in lieu of *revenue* (*q.v.*) in nonenterprise funds.

Incremental Budgeting A budgeting approach that is simply derived from the current-year's budget by multiplying by a factor (i.e., an incremental increase equal to inflation) or by adding amounts expected to be required by salary and other cost increases and deducting expenses not needed when the scope of operations is reduced.

Indeterminate Appropriation An appropriation that is not limited to any definite period of time and/or to any definite amount. *Note:* A distinction must be made between an indeterminate appropriation and a continuing appropriation. A continuing appropriation is indefinite only as to time, an indeterminate appropriation is indefinite as to both time and amount. Even indeterminate appropriations that are indefinite only as to time are to be distinguished from continuing appropriations in that such indeterminate appropriations may eventually lapse.

Indirect Costs Costs incurred that cannot be identified specifically with a cost objective (*q.v.*) but benefit multiple cost objectives (e.g., a hospital cafeteria, central data processing department, and general management costs).

Indirect Expenses Those expenses that are not directly linked to an identifiable function or program.

Industrial Aid Bonds Bonds issued by governments, the proceeds of which are used to construct plant facilities for private industrial concerns. Lease payments made by the industrial concern to the government are used to service the bonds. Such bonds may be in the form of general obligation bonds (*q.v.*) or revenue bonds (*q.v.*). Also called *industrial development bonds (IDBs).*

Influencing Promoting, supporting, affecting, modifying, opposing, or delaying by any means. Often used in the context of "influencing" legislation or political candidates.

Infrastructure Assets Roads, bridges, curbs and gutters, streets, sidewalks, drainage systems, and lighting systems installed for the common good. See also Improvements.

Input Measures Measures of service efforts, or financial and nonfinancial resources used in a program or process.

In-Substance Defeasance A transaction in which low-risk U.S. government securities are placed into an irrevocable trust for the benefit of debtholders, and the liability for the debt is removed from the accounts of the entity even though the debt has not been repaid. See Defeasance and Legal Defeasance.

Intangible Assets Capital assets that lack physical substance, have a useful life of more than one reporting period, and are nonfinancial in nature.

Inter-Activity Transactions Interfund loans or transfers that occur between a governmental fund (or internal service fund) and an enterprise fund.

Interest and Penalties Receivable on Taxes The uncollected portion of interest and penalties due on taxes.

Interest Receivable on Investments The amount of interest receivable on investments, exclusive of interest purchased. Interest purchased should be shown in a separate account.

Interest Receivable—Special Assessments The amount of interest receivable on unpaid installments of special assessments.

Interfund Accounts Accounts in which transactions between funds are reflected. See Interfund Transfers.

Interfund Loans Loans made by one fund to another.

Interfund Transfers Amounts transferred from one fund to another.

Intergovernmental Revenue Revenue from other governments. Grants, shared revenue, and entitlements are types of intergovernmental revenue.

Interim Borrowing (1) Short-term loans to be repaid from general revenues during the course of a fiscal year. (2) Short-term loans in anticipation of tax collections or bonds issuance. See Bond Anticipation Notes, Tax Anticipation Notes, and Revenue Anticipation Notes.

Interim Statement A financial statement prepared before the end of the current fiscal year and covering only financial transactions during the current year to date.

Intermediate Sanctions Penalties imposed by the IRS in the form of excise taxes on private inurement to disqualified persons resulting from excess economic benefit transactions. For example, excessive salaries paid to a manager of a not-for-profit organization or rents higher than fair market value paid to a board member who owns the building the organization occupies.

Internal Control A plan of organization under which employees' duties are so arranged and records and procedures so designed as to make it possible to exercise effective accounting control over assets, liabilities, revenues, and expenditures. Under such a system, the work of employees is subdivided so that no single employee performs a complete cycle of operations. For example, an employee handling cash would not post the accounts receivable records. Moreover, under such a system, the procedures to be followed are definitely laid down and require proper authorizations by designated officials for all actions to be taken.

Internal Exchange Transactions A term (coined by the authors) that captures both the interfund and interactivity nature of reciprocal exchange transactions within an entity (formerly called *quasi-external transactions*).

Internal Service Funds (ISFs) Funds established to finance and account for services and commodities furnished by a designated department or agency to other departments and agencies within a single government or to other governments. Amounts expended by the fund are restored thereto either from operating earnings or by transfers from other funds, so that the original fund capital is kept intact. Formerly called a *working capital fund* or *intragovernmental service fund.*

Internal Support Test One of two tests of broad public support to determine if an organization is a public charity rather than a private foundation. The test is met if the not-for-profit organization does not receive more than one-third of its total support from investment income and unrelated business income.

Interperiod Equity A term coined by the Governmental Accounting Standards Board indicating the extent to which current-period revenues are adequate to pay for current-period services.

Intra-Activity Transactions Transactions that occur between two governmental funds (or between a governmental fund and an internal service fund) or between two enterprise funds.

Intra-Entity Transactions Exchange or nonexchange transactions between the primary government and its blended or discretely presented component units.

Intragovernmental Assets (Liabilities) Claims by or against a reporting entity that arise from transactions between that entity and other reporting entities.

Inventory A detailed list showing quantities, descriptions, and values of property and frequently units of measure and unit prices.

Invested in Capital Assets, Net of Related Debt One of the three categories of net assets reported by governments. It is the net capital assets less the debt relating to the acquisition or construction of the capital assets.

Investment Trust Funds Funds used to account for the assets, liabilities, net assets, and changes in net assets corresponding to the equity of the external participants.

Investments Securities and real estate held for the production of income in the form of interest, dividends, rentals, or lease payments. The term does not include capital assets used in governmental operations.

Irregular Serial Bonds Bonds payable in which the total principal is repayable, but the repayment plan does not fit the definitions of regular serial bonds, deferred serial bonds, or term bonds.

J

Job Order Cost Cost accounting system most appropriate for recording costs chargeable to specific jobs, grants, programs, projects, activities, or departments.

Joint Venture A legal entity that results from a contractual arrangement that is owned, operated, or governed by two or more participants as a separate and specific activity subject to joint control.

Jointly Governed Organizations A regional government or other multigovernmental arrangement that is governed by representatives.

Judgment An amount to be paid or collected by a government as the result of a court decision, including a condemnation award in payment for private property taken for public use.

Judgment Bonds Bonds issued to pay judgments (*q.v.*). See also Funding.

Judgments Payable Amounts due to be paid by a government as the result of court decisions, including condemnation awards in payment for private property taken for public use.

L

Land A capital asset account that reflects the carrying value of land owned by a government. If land is purchased, this account shows the purchase price and costs such as legal fees and filling and excavation costs that are incurred to put the land in condition for its intended use. If land is acquired by gift, the account reflects its appraised value at time of acquisition.

Lapse (Verb) As applied to appropriations, to terminate an appropriation. *Note:* Except for indeterminate appropriations (*q.v.*) and continuing appropriations (*q.v.*), an appropriation is made for a certain period of time. At the end of this period, any unexpended and unencumbered balance thereof lapses unless otherwise provided by law.

Leasehold The right to the use of real estate by virtue of a lease, usually for a specified term of years, for which a consideration is paid.

Legal Defeasance A transaction in which debt is legally satisfied based on certain provisions in the debt instrument (e.g., third-party guarantor assumes the debt) even though the debt has not been repaid. See also Defeasance and In-Substance Defeasance.

Legislation Action by Congress, a state legislative body, or a local council to establish laws, statutes, and ordinances.

Levy (Verb) To impose taxes, special assessments, or service charges for the support of governmental activities. (Noun) The total amount of taxes, special assessments, or service charges imposed by a government.

Liabilities Probable future sacrifices of economic benefits arising from present obligations of a particular entity to transfer assets or provide services to other entities in the future as a result of past transactions or events. *Note:* The term does not include encumbrances (*q.v.*).

Life Income Fund Funds, ordinarily of colleges and universities and not-for-profit organizations, established to account for assets given to the organization subject to an agreement to pay to the donor or designee the income earned by the assets over a specified period of time. Also called *pooled (life) income funds*.

Limited Obligation Debt Debt secured by a pledge of the collections of a certain specified tax (rather than by all general revenues).

Limited Purpose Governments See Special Purpose Governments.

Line Item Budget A detailed expense or expenditure budget, generally classified by object within each organizational unit and often classified within each object as to authorized number of employees at each salary level within each job classification, and so on.

Loans Receivable Amounts that have been loaned to persons or organizations, including notes taken as security for such loans.

Lobbying Communicating directly with a public official in either the executive or legislative branch of the state government for the purpose of influencing legislation.

Local Education Agency (LEA) A broad term that is used to include school districts, public schools, intermediate education agencies, and school systems.

Long-Run Solvency A government's ability in the long run to pay all of the costs of doing business.

Long-Term Budget A budget prepared for a period longer than a fiscal year, or, in the case of some state governments, a budget prepared for a period longer than a biennium. If the long-term budget is restricted to capital expenditures, it is called a *capital program* (*q.v.*) or a *capital improvement program*.

Long-Term Debt Debt with a maturity of more than one year after the date of issuance.

Losses Decreases in net assets from peripheral or incidental transactions of an entity.

Lump-Sum Appropriation An appropriation made for a stated purpose or for a named department without specifying further the amounts that may be spent for specific activities or for particular objects of expenditure. An example of such an appropriation would be one for the police department that does not specify the amount to be spent for uniform patrol, traffic control, and so on, or for salaries and wages, materials and supplies, travel, and so on.

M

Machinery and Equipment See Equipment.

Maintenance The upkeep of physical properties in condition for use or occupancy. Examples are the inspection of equipment to detect defects and the making of repairs.

Major Funds Funds are classified as major if they are significantly large with respect to the whole government. A fund is "major" if

(a) total assets, liabilities, revenues, or expenditures/expenses of the individual governmental or enterprise fund are at least 10 percent of the corresponding total of assets, liabilities, revenues, or expenditures/expenses for all funds of that category or type (total governmental or total enterprise funds), and

(b) total assets, liabilities, revenues, or expenditures/expenses of the individual governmental fund or enterprise fund are at least 5 percent of the corresponding total for all governmental and enterprise funds combined.

Major Programs All federal programs identified by the auditor through a risk-based process that will be audited as part of a single audit.

Management's Discussion and Analysis (MD&A) Narrative information, in addition to the basic financial statements, in which management provides a brief, objective, and easily readable analysis of the government's financial performance for the year and its financial position at year-end. An MD&A is required by *GASBS 34* for state and local governments and by FASAB's *SFFAC No. 3* for federal agencies.

Market Risk The risk of loss arising from increases in market rates of interest or other factors that reduce market value of securities.

Material Weakness A reportable condition of such magnitude that the internal control structure elements do not reduce the risk of material noncompliance to an acceptably low level.

Materiality An auditor's judgment as to the level at which the quantitative or qualitative effects of misstatements will have a significant impact on user's evaluations.

Matured Bonds Payable Bonds that have reached their maturity date but remain unpaid.

Matured Interest Payable Interest on bonds that has matured but remains unpaid.

Measurable Capable of being expressed in monetary terms.

Measurement Focus The nature of the resources, claims against resources, and flows of resources that are measured and reported by a fund or other entity. For example, governmental funds currently measure and report available financial resources, whereas proprietary and fiduciary funds measure and report economic resources.

Modified Accrual Basis Under the modified accrual basis of accounting, required for use by governmental funds (*q.v.*), revenues are recognized in the period in which they become available and measurable, and expenditures are recognized at the time a liability is incurred pursuant to appropriation authority.

Modified Approach An approach that allows the government to elect *not* to depreciate certain eligible infrastructure assets provided certain requirements are met.

Modified Cash Basis Sometimes same as Modified Accrual Basis, sometimes a plan under which revenues are recognized on the cash basis but expenditures are recognized on the accrual basis.

Mortgage Bonds Bonds secured by a mortgage against specific properties of a government, usually its public utilities or other enterprises. If primarily payable from enterprise revenues, they are also classed as revenue bonds. See also Revenue Bonds.

Municipal In its broadest sense, an adjective that denotes the state and all subordinate units of government. As defined for census statistics, the term denotes a city, town, or village as opposed to other units of local government.

Municipal Bond A bond (*q.v.*) issued by a state or local government.

Municipal Corporation A body politic and corporate established pursuant to state authorization for the purpose of providing governmental services and regulations for its inhabitants. A municipal corporation has defined boundaries and population and is usually organized with the consent of its residents. It usually has a seal and may sue and be sued. Cities and towns are examples of municipal corporations. See also Quasi-Municipal Corporation.

N

Net Assets The difference between total assets and total liabilities.

Net Bonded Debt Gross bonded debt (*q.v.*) less cash or other assets available and earmarked for its retirement.

Net Income A term used in accounting for governmental enterprises to designate the excess of total revenues (*q.v.*) over total expenses (*q.v.*) for an accounting period. See also Income, Operating Revenues, Operating Expenses, Nonoperating Income, and Nonoperating Expenses.

Net Pension Obligation (NPO) A component of annual pension cost that comprises (1) the transition pension liability (or asset), if any, and (2) the cumulative difference from the implementation date of *GASBS 27* to the current balance sheet date between the annual pension cost and the employer's actual contributions.

Net Position Net assets of a federal agency.

Net Revenue Available for Debt Service Gross operating revenues of an enterprise less operating and maintenance expenses but exclusive of depreciation and bond interest. *Net revenue* as thus defined is used to compute "coverage" of revenue bond issues. *Note:* Under the laws of some states and the provisions of some revenue bond indentures, net revenues used for computation of coverage are required to be on a cash basis rather than an accrual basis.

Nominal Interest Rate The contractual interest rate shown on the face and in the body of a bond and representing the amount of interest to be paid, in contrast to the effective interest rate (*q.v.*). See also Coupon Rate.

Nonaudit Work Work that is solely for the benefit of the entity requesting the work and does not provide for a basis for conclusions, recommendations, or opinions.

Nonentity Assets Those assets of a federal agency that the reporting entity is holding but are not available for the entity to spend.

Nonexchange Revenue See Derived Tax Revenues, Imposed Nonexchange Revenues, Voluntary Nonexchange Transactions, and Government-Mandated Nonexchange Transactions.

Nonexchange Transactions Transactions in which the donor derives no direct tangible benefits from the recipient agency, for example, a contribution to or support for a government or not-for-profit organization.

Nonexpendable The principal and sometimes the earnings of a gift that may not be expended. See also Endowment.

Nonexpenditure Disbursements Disbursements not chargeable as expenditures; for example, a disbursement made for the purpose of paying a liability previously recorded on the books.

Nonoperating Expenses Expenses (*q.v.*) incurred for nonoperating properties or in the performance of activities not directly related to supplying the basic service by a governmental enterprise. An example of a nonoperating expense is interest paid on outstanding revenue bonds. See also Nonoperating Properties.

Nonoperating Income Income of governmental enterprises that is not derived from the basic operations of such enterprises. An example is interest on investments or on bank time deposits.

Nonoperating Properties Properties owned by a governmental enterprise but not used in the provision of basic services for which the enterprise exists.

Nonoperating Revenue Revenue arising from transactions peripheral or incidental to the delivery of basic operations, including investment income, gains and losses, and unrestricted contributions.

Nonrevenue Receipts Collections other than revenue (*q.v.*), such as receipts from loans whose liability is recorded in the fund in which the proceeds are placed and receipts on account of recoverable expenditures.

Normal Cost The present value of benefits allocated to the current year by the actuarial cost method being used.

Not-for-Profit (Nonprofit) Organizations An entity that is distinguished from a business enterprise by these characteristics: (1) contributions by providers who do not expect commensurate returns, (2) operating purposes other than to earn a profit, and (3) absence of ownership interests. The AICPA prefers the term *not-for-profit* over *nonprofit.* The term *nongovernmental organization* (*NGO*) is used in an international context.

Notes Payable In general, an unconditional written promise signed by the maker to pay a certain sum in money on demand or at a fixed or determinable time either to the bearer or to the order of a person designated therein.

Notes Receivable A note payable held by an entity.

O

Object A basis for distinguishing expenditures by the article purchased or the service obtained (as distinguished from the results obtained from expenditures). Examples are personal services, contractual services, materials, and supplies.

Object Classification A grouping of expenditures on the basis of goods or services purchased, for example, personal services, materials, supplies, and equipment. See also Functional Classification, Activity Classification, and Character Classification.

Objects of Expenditure See Object.

Obligated Group A group of independent organizations that have joined together for a specific purpose, for example, to obtain financing in which case all parties are obligated in some way to repay the debt.

Obligation Generally, an amount that a government may be required legally to meet out of its resources. Included are actual liabilities, as well as unliquidated encumbrances. In federal usage, obligation has essentially the same meaning as encumbrance in state and local governmental accounting.

Obsolescence The decrease in the value of capital assets resulting from economic, social, technological, or legal changes.

Operating Budget A budget that applies to all outlays other than capital outlays. See Budget.

Operating Cycle The cycle of an organization that includes forecasting cash flows; collecting revenues; investing excess cash; tracking the performance and security of investments; making disbursements for various purposes; and monitoring, evaluating, and auditing cash flows.

Operating Expenses (1) As used in the accounts of governmental enterprises, those costs that are necessary to the maintenance of the enterprise, the rendering of services, the sale of merchandise, the production and disposition of commodities produced, and the collection of enterprise revenues. (2) Sometimes used to describe expenses for general governmental purposes.

Operating Fund The fund used to account for all assets and related liabilities used in the routine activities of a hospital. Also sometimes used by governments as a synonym for General Fund.

Operating Income Income of a governmental enterprise derived from the sale of its goods and/or services. For example, income from the sale of water by a municipal water utility is operating income. See also Operating Revenues.

Operating Lease A rental-type lease in which the risks and benefits of ownership are substantively retained by the lessor, and thus do not meet the criteria defined in applicable accounting and reporting standards for a capital lease (*q.v.*).

Operating Revenues Revenues derived from the primary operations of governmental enterprises of a business character.

Operating Statement A statement summarizing the financial operations of a government for an accounting period as contrasted with a balance sheet (*q.v.*) that shows financial position at a given moment in time.

Operational Accountability Information useful in assessing operating results and short- and long-term financial position and the cost of providing services from an economic perspective reported in entitywide financial statements.

Opinion Units In the *GASBS 34* reporting model, these are (1) governmental activities, (2) business-type activities, (3) aggregate discretely presented component units, (4) each major governmental and enterprise fund, and (5) the aggregate remaining fund information.

Order A formal legislative enactment by the governing body of certain local governmental entities that has the full force and effect of law. For example, county governing bodies in some states pass orders rather than laws or ordinances.

Ordinance A formal legislative enactment by the council or governing body of a municipality. If it is not in conflict with any higher form of law, such as a state statute or constitutional provision, it has the full force and effect of law within the boundaries of the municipality to which it applies. *Note:* The difference between an ordinance and a resolution (*q.v.*) is that the latter requires less legal formality and has a lower legal status.

Organization Unit Units or departments within an entity, such as police department or city attorney department.

Organizational Test A not-for-profit organization meets the organizational test if its articles of incorporation limit the organization's purposes to those described in IRC Sec. 501 and does not empower it to engage in activities that are not in furtherance of those purposes.

Original Cost The total of assets given and/or liabilities assumed to acquire an asset. In utility accounting, the original cost is the cost to the first owner who dedicated the plant to service of the public.

Other Appropriations Realized A budgetary account used in federal government accounting to record an agency's basic operating appropriations for a fiscal period.

Other Comprehensive Basis of Accounting (OCBOA) A term used to encompass bases of accounting that are not GAAP (*q.v.*). Bases included are cash, modified cash, regulatory basis, income tax basis, and substantial support criteria basis.

Other Financing Sources An operating statement classification in which financial inflows other than revenues are reported, for example, proceeds of long-term debt and transfers in.

Other Financing Uses An operating statement classification in which financial outflows other than expenditures are reported, for example, transfers out.

Other Postemployment Benefits (OPEB) Benefits, other than pensions, provided to employees subsequent to employment. Included would be items such as health care and life insurance.

Other Stand-Alone Government A legally separate governmental organization that does not have a separately elected governing body and is not a component unit.

Outcome Measures Accomplishments, or the results of services provided.

Outlays Sometimes synonymous with disbursements. See also Capital Outlays.

Output Measures Quantity measures reflecting either the total quantity of service provided or the quantity of service provided that meets a specified quality requirement.

Overhead Those elements of cost necessary in the production of an article or the performance of a service that are of such a nature that the amount applicable to the product or service cannot be determined accurately or readily. Usually they relate to those objects of expenditure that do not become an integral part of the finished product or service, such as rent, heat, light, supplies, management, or supervision.

Overlapping Debt The proportionate share of the debts of local governments located wholly or in part within the limits of the government reporting entity that must be borne by property within each government. *Note:* Except for special assessment debt, the amount of debt of each unit applicable to the reporting unit is arrived at by (1) determining what percentage of the total assessed value of the overlapping jurisdiction lies within the limits of the reporting unit and (2) applying this percentage to the total debt of the overlapping jurisdiction. Special assessment debt is allocated on the basis of the ratio of assessments receivable in each jurisdiction that will be used wholly or in part to pay off the debt to total assessments receivable that will be used wholly or in part for this purpose.

Oversight Agency The federal agency that makes the predominant amount of direct funding to the nonfederal entity receiving less than $25 million in federal awards. An oversight agency's responsibilities are similar to those of a cognizant agency but are less extensive.

P

Pay-As-You-Go Basis A term used to describe the financial policy of a government that finances all of its capital outlays from current revenues rather than by borrowing. A government that pays for some improvements from current revenues and others by borrowing is said to be on a *partial* or *modified pay-as-you-go basis.*

Penalty A legally mandated addition to a tax on the day it became delinquent (generally, the day after the day the tax is due).

Pension Trust Funds (PTFs) See Public Employee Retirement Systems.

Performance Audit One of the two major types of audits defined by the U.S. Government Accountability Office (see Financial Audit for the other type). A performance audit provides an auditor's independent determination (but not an opinion) of the extent to which government officials are efficiently, economically, and effectively carrying out their responsibilities.

Performance Budgeting Budget format that relates the input of resources and the output of services for each organizational unit individually. Sometimes used synonymously with program budget (*q.v.*).

Performance Indicator A measure of how well a health care organization has performed. Examples include "excess of revenues over expenses," "revenues and gains over expenses and losses," "earned income," and "performance earnings."

Permanent Endowments Gifts for which donors or other external agencies have stated that as a condition of the gift the principal must be maintained intact in perpetuity.

Permanent Funds Governmental-type funds used to account for public-purpose trusts for which the earnings are expendable for a specified purpose, but the principal amount is not expendable (i.e., an endowment).

Permanently Restricted Net Assets A term used in accounting for not-for-profit organizations indicating the amount of net assets whose use is permanently restricted by an external donor. See Endowment and Net Assets.

Perpetual Inventory A system whereby the inventory of units of property at any date may be obtained directly from the records without resorting to an actual physical count. A record is provided for each item or group of items to be inventoried and is so divided as to provide a running record of goods ordered, received, and withdrawn, and the balance on hand, in units and frequently also in value.

Petty Cash A sum of money set aside for the purpose of making change or paying small obligations for which the issuance of a formal voucher and check would be too expensive and time-consuming. Sometimes called a *petty cash fund,* with the term *fund* here being used in the commercial sense of earmarked liquid assets.

Planning-Programming-Budgeting System (PPBS) A budgeting approach that integrates planning, programming, and budgeting into one system; most popular in the federal government during the 1960s.

Plant Acquisition Adjustment See Acquisition Adjustment.

Political Activity Activity designed to influence legislation or that relates to a candidate's campaign for political office.

Political Organization Entities described in IRC Sec. 527, such as political action committees, political parties, and campaign committees for candidates for government office.

Pollution Remediation Obligations Obligations that arise from responsibilities related to the cleanup of hazardous waste resulting from existing pollution.

Pooled (Life) Income Fund See Life Income Fund.

Pooled Investments Investments that may be pooled or merged to simplify portfolio management, obtain a greater degree of investment diversification for individual endowments or trusts, and reduce brokerage, taxes, and bookkeeping expenses.

Popular Reports Highly condensed financial information, including budgets, summaries, and narrative descriptions.

Postaudit An audit made after the transactions to be audited have taken place and have been recorded or approved for recording by designated officials if such approval is required. See also Preaudit.

Posting The act of transferring to an account in a ledger the data, either detailed or summarized, contained in a book or documentary of original entry.

Preaudit An examination for the purpose of determining the propriety of proposed financial transactions and financial transactions that have already taken place but have not yet been recorded, or, if such approval is required, before the approval of the financial transactions by designated officials for recording.

Preferred Provider Organization (PPO) See Health Maintenance Organization.

Prepaid Expenses Expenses entered in the accounts for benefits not yet received. Prepaid expenses differ from deferred charges in that they are spread over a shorter period of time than deferred charges and are regularly recurring costs of operations. Examples of prepaid expenses are prepaid rent, prepaid interest, and premiums on unexpired insurance.

Prepayment of Taxes The deposit of money with a government on condition that the amount deposited is to be applied against the tax liability of a designated taxpayer after the taxes have been levied and such liability has been established. See also Taxes Collected in Advance and Deferred Revenues.

Primary Government A state government or general purpose local government. Also, a special-purpose government that has a separately elected governing body, is legally separate, and is fiscally independent of other state or local governments.

Prior-Years' Encumbrances See Reserve for Encumbrances—Prior Year.

Prior-Years' Tax Levies Taxes levied for fiscal periods preceding the current one.

Private Foundation An organization exempt from federal income taxes under IRC Sec. 501(a) that (1) receives its support from a small number of individuals or corporations and investment income rather than from the public at large and (2) exists to make grants to public charities.

Private-Purpose Trust Funds Funds that account for contributions received under a trust agreement in which the investment income of an endowment is intended to benefit an external individual, organization, or government.

Private Trust Fund A trust fund (*q.v.*) that will ordinarily revert to private individuals or will be used for private purposes, for example, a fund that consists of guarantee deposits.

Pro Forma For form's sake; an indication of form; an example. The term is used in conjunction with a noun to denote merely a sample form, document, statement, certificate, or presentation, the contents of which may be either wholly or partially hypothetical, actual facts, estimates, or proposals.

Program Budgeting A budget wherein inputs of resources and outputs of services are identified by programs without regard to the number of organizational units involved in performing various aspects of the program. See also Performance Budgeting.

Program Revenues Revenues linked to a specific function or program and reported separately from general revenues on the government-wide statement of activities.

Program-Specific Audit An audit of one specific federal program as opposed to a single audit of the whole entity.

Programs Activities, operations, or organizational units grouped together because they share purposes or objectives.

Project A plan of work, job, assignment, or task. Also refers to a job or task.

Promise to Give A pledge or promise to make a contribution that may be unconditional or conditional.

Propaganda Information that is skewed toward a particular belief with a tendency to have little or no factual basis.

Property Assessment A process by which each parcel of taxable real and personal property owned by each taxpayer is assigned a valuation.

Property Taxes Taxes levied by a legislative body against agricultural, commercial, residential, or personal property pursuant to law and in proportion to the assessed valuation of said property, or other appropriate basis. See Ad Valorem Property Taxes.

Proprietary Accounts Those accounts that show actual financial position and operations, such as actual assets, liabilities, reserves, fund balances, revenues, and expenditures, as distinguished from budgetary accounts (*q.v.*).

Proprietary Funds Sometimes referred to as *income-determination, business-like,* or *commercial-type* funds of a state or local government. Examples are enterprise funds and internal service funds.

Prospective Payment System (PPS) Medicare's system in which payments are based on allowed service costs for medical procedures within the same diagnosis-related group rather than on the length of the patient's hospital stay or actual cost of services rendered.

Public Authority See Authority.

Public Charity An organization exempt from taxes under IRC Sec. 501(a) that receives its support from the public at large rather than from a limited number of donors. Most often public charities are exempt from federal income taxes under IRC Sec. 501(c)(3).

Public Corporation See Municipal Corporation and Quasi-Municipal Corporation.

Public Employee Retirement Systems (PERS) The organizations that collect retirement and other employee benefit contributions from government employers and employees, manage assets, and make payments to qualified retirants, beneficiaries, and disabled employees.

Public-Purpose Trust Contributions received under a trust agreement in which the investment income or an endowment must be used to benefit a public program or function or the citizenry.

Public Trust Fund A trust fund (*q.v.*) whose principal, earnings, or both must be used for a public purpose, for example, a pension or retirement fund.

Purchase Order A document that authorizes the delivery of specified merchandise or the rendering of certain services and the making of a charge for them.

Purchases Method A method of recording supplies as Expenditures when purchased. If inventory levels have risen at the end of the month, the asset Supplies Inventory is debited and Fund Balance—Reserve for Inventory is credited. An alternative method is called the *consumption method.*

Purpose Restrictions Specifications by resource providers of the purposes for which resources are required to be used.

Q

Quasi-Endowments See Funds Functioning as Endowments.

Quasi-External Transaction See Internal Exchange Transactions.

Quasi-Municipal Corporation An agency established by the state primarily for the purpose of helping to carry out its functions, for example, a county or school district. *Note:* Some counties and other agencies ordinarily classified as quasi-municipal corporations have been granted the powers of municipal corporations by the state in which they are located. See also Municipal Corporation.

Questioned Cost A cost identified by an auditor in an audit finding that generally relates to noncompliance with a law, regulation, or agreement, when the costs are either not supported by adequate documentation or appear unreasonable. OMB cost circulars identify, for different kinds of organizations, which costs are allowable and unallowable.

R

Rate Base The value of utility property used in computing an authorized rate of return as authorized by law or a regulatory commission.

Realize To convert goods or services into cash or receivables. Also to exchange for property that is a current asset or can be converted immediately into a current asset. Sometimes applied to conversion of noncash assets into cash.

Rebates Abatements (*q.v.*) or refunds (*q.v.*).

Receipts This term, unless otherwise qualified, means cash received.

Recoverable Expenditure An expenditure made for or on behalf of another government, fund, or department or for a private individual, firm, or corporation that will subsequently be recovered in cash or its equivalent.

Refunding Bonds Bonds issued to retire bonds already outstanding. The refunding bonds may be sold for cash and outstanding bonds redeemed in cash, or the refunding bonds may be exchanged with holders of outstanding bonds.

Registered Bond A bond the owner of which is registered with the issuing government and that cannot be sold or exchanged without a change of registration.

Registered Warrant A warrant that is registered by the paying officer for future payment on account of present lack of funds and that is to be paid in the order of its registration. In some cases, such warrants are registered when issued; in others, they are registered when first presented to the paying officer by the holders. See also Warrant.

Regular Serial Bonds Bonds payable in which the total principal is repayable in a specified number of equal annual installments.

Regulatory Accounting Principles (RAP) The accounting principles prescribed by federal or state regulatory commissions for investor-owned and some governmentally owned utilities. Also called *statutory accounting principles (SAP)*. RAP or some SAP may differ from GAAP.

Reimbursement Cash or other assets received as a repayment of the cost of work or services performed or of other expenditures made for or on behalf of another government or department or for an individual, firm, or corporation.

Replacement Cost The cost as of a certain date of a property that can render similar service (but need not be of the same structural form) as the property to be replaced. See also Reproduction Cost.

Reportable Condition A significant deficiency in the design or operation of the internal control structure that could adversely affect the entity's ability to administer federal financial assistance programs in accordance with laws and regulations.

Reporting Entity The primary government and all related component units, if any, combined in accordance with GASB *Codification* Section 2100 constitute the governmental reporting entity.

Reproduction Cost The cost as of a certain date of reproducing an exactly similar new property in the same place.

Repurchase Agreement An agreement wherein a government transfers cash to a financial institution in exchange for securities and the financial institution agrees to repurchase the same securities at an agreed-upon price.

Required Supplementary Information (RSI) Information that is required by generally accepted accounting principles to be included with the audited annual financial statements, usually directly following the notes to the general purpose external financial statements.

Requisition A written demand or request, usually from one department to the purchasing officer or to another department, for specified articles or services.

Reserve An account that records a portion of the fund equity that must be segregated for some future use and that is, therefore, not available for further appropriation or expenditure. See also Reserve for Inventory and Reserve for Encumbrances.

Reserve for Encumbrances A segregation of a portion of fund equity in the amount of encumbrances outstanding. See also Reserve.

Reserve for Encumbrances—Prior Year Encumbrances outstanding at the end of a fiscal year are designated as pertaining to appropriations of a year prior to the current year in order that related expenditures may be matched with the appropriations of the prior year rather than appropriations of the current year.

Reserve for Inventory A segregation of a portion of fund equity to indicate that assets equal to the amount of the reserve are invested in inventories and are, therefore, not available for appropriation.

Reserve for Noncurrent Interfund Loans Receivable A reserve that represents the segregation of a portion of a fund equity to indicate that assets equal to the amount of the reserve are invested in a long-term loan to another fund and are, therefore, not available for appropriation.

Reserve for Revenue Bond Contingency A reserve in an enterprise fund that represents the segregation of a portion of net assets equal to current assets that are restricted for meeting various contingencies, as may be specified and defined in the revenue bond indenture.

Reserve for Revenue Bond Debt Service A reserve in an enterprise fund that represents the segregation of a portion of net assets equal to current assets that are restricted to current servicing of revenue bonds in accordance with the terms of a bond indenture.

Reserve for Revenue Bond Retirement A reserve in an enterprise fund that represents the segregation of a portion of net assets equal to current assets that are restricted for future servicing of revenue bonds in accordance with the terms of a bond indenture.

Reserve for Uncollected Taxes A reserve equal to the amount of taxes receivable by a fund. The reserve is deducted from Taxes Receivable, thus effectively placing the fund on the cash basis of revenue recognition.

Resolution A special or temporary order of a legislative body; an order of a legislative body requiring less legal formality than an ordinance or statute. See also Ordinance.

Resources Legally budgeted revenues of a state or local government that have not been recognized as revenues under the modified accrual basis of accounting as of the date of an interim balance sheet.

Restricted Assets Assets (usually of an enterprise fund) that may not be used for normal operating purposes because of the requirements of regulatory authorities, provisions in bond indentures, or other legal agreements, but that need not be accounted for in a separate fund.

Restricted Fund A fund established to account for assets the use of which is limited by the requirements of donors or grantors. Hospitals may use three types of restricted funds for internal purposes: specific purpose funds, endowment funds, and plant replacement and expansion funds. The governing body or administration cannot restrict the use of assets; they may only designate the use of assets. See Board-Designated Funds.

Restricted Net Assets The portion of the residual of assets and liabilities (i.e., net assets) that has been restricted in purpose or time by parties external to the organization.

Retirement Fund A fund out of which retirement annuities and/or other benefits are paid to authorized and designated public employees. The accounting for a retirement fund is the same as that for a pension trust fund (*q.v.*).

Revenue The inflow of economic resources resulting from the delivery of services or activities that constitute the organization's major or central operations rather than from interfund transfers (*q.v.*) and debt issue proceeds.

Revenue Anticipation Notes (RANS) Notes issued in anticipation of the collection of revenues, usually from specified sources, and to be repaid upon the collection of the revenues.

Revenue Bonds Bonds whose principal and interest are payable exclusively from earnings of a public enterprise. In addition to a pledge of revenues, such bonds sometimes contain a mortgage on the enterprise's property and are then known as *mortgage revenue bonds.*

Revenues Budget A legally adopted budget authorizing the collection of revenues from specified sources and estimating the amounts to be collected during the period from each source.

Revenues Collected in Advance A liability account that represents revenues collected before they are earned.

Revolving Fund See Internal Service Funds.

Risk-Based Approach This approach, used by auditors to determine which programs will be audited as part of the single audit, is a five-step process designed to select federal programs that are relatively large as well as likely to have problems. The auditors can use their professional judgment to classify programs that have been audited recently without audit findings, have had no significant changes in personnel or systems, or have a high level of oversight by awarding agencies as "low risk."

Risk Contract An insurance policy used to protect a prepaid health care plan from losses arising from excess of actual cost of providing health care over the fixed (capitation) fee.

S

Schedules (1) The explanatory or supplementary statements that accompany the balance sheet or other principal statements periodically prepared from the accounts. (2) The accountant's or auditor's principal work papers covering their examination of the books and accounts. (3) A written enumeration or detailed list in orderly form.

Scrip An evidence of indebtedness, usually in small denomination, secured or unsecured, interest bearing or noninterest bearing, stating that the government, under conditions set forth, will pay the face value of the certificate or accept it in payment of certain obligations.

Securities Bonds, notes, mortgages, or other forms of negotiable or nonnegotiable instruments. See also Investments.

Self-Supporting or Self-Liquidating Debt Debt obligations whose principal and interest are payable solely from the earnings of the enterprise for the construction or improvement of which they were originally issued. See also Revenue Bonds.

Serial Annuity Bonds Serial bonds in which the annual installments of bond principal are so arranged that the combined payments for principal and interest are approximately the same each year.

Serial Bonds Bonds the principal of which is repaid in periodic installments over the life of the issue. See Serial Annuity Bonds and Deferred Serial Bonds.

Service Capacity A government's ongoing ability and willingness to supply the capital and human resources needed to meet its commitments to provide services.

Service Efforts and Accomplishments (SEA) A conceptualization of the resources consumed (inputs), tasks performed (outputs), goals attained (outcomes), and the relationship among these items in providing services in selected areas (e.g., police protection, solid waste garbage collection, and elementary and secondary education).

Service-level Solvency A government's ability to provide services at the level and quality that are required for the health, safety, and welfare of the community and that its citizens desire.

Settlement Accounts Receivables (or payables) arising from differences between original payment estimates by third-party payors, cash received and paid, and final determinations in health care organizations.

Shared Revenue Revenue levied by one governmental unit but shared, usually on a predetermined basis, with another unit of government or class of governments.

Short-Term Debt Debt with a maturity of one year or less after the date of issuance. Short-term debt usually includes floating debt, bond anticipation notes, tax anticipation notes, and interim warrants.

Significant Deficiency A deficiency in internal control, or combination of deficiencies, that adversely affects the entity's ability to initiate, authorize, record, process, or report data reliably.

Single Audit An audit prescribed by federal law for state and local governments and not-for-profit organizations that expend federal financial assistance above a specified amount. Such an audit is to be conducted in conformity with the Office of Management and Budget *Circular A–133.* Such an audit is conducted on an organizationwide basis rather than on the former grant-by-grant basis. The Single Audit Act of 1984, as amended in 1996, and the circular cited impose uniform and rigorous requirements for conducting and reporting on single audits.

Sinking Fund See Debt Service Fund.

Sinking Fund Bonds Bonds issued under an agreement that requires the government to set aside periodically out of its revenues a sum that, with compound earnings thereon, will be sufficient to redeem the bonds at their stated date of maturity. Sinking fund bonds are usually also term bonds (*q.v.*).

Special Assessment A compulsory levy made against certain properties to defray part or all of the cost of a specific improvement or service that is presumed to be a general benefit to the public and of special benefit to such properties.

Special Assessment Bonds Bonds payable from the proceeds of special assessments (*q.v.*). If the bonds are payable only from the collections of special assessments, they are known as *special-special assessment bonds.* If, in addition to the assessments, the full faith and credit of the government is pledged, they are known as *general obligation special assessment bonds.*

Special Assessment Liens Receivable Claims that a government has on properties until special assessments (*q.v.*) levied against them have been paid. The term normally applies to those delinquent special assessments for the collection of which legal action has been taken through the filing of claims.

Special Assessment Roll The official list showing the amount of special assessments (*q.v.*) levied against each property presumed to be benefited by an improvement or service.

Special District An independent unit of local government organized to perform a single governmental function or a restricted number of related functions. Special districts usually have the power to incur debt and levy taxes; however, certain types of special districts are entirely dependent on enterprise earnings and cannot impose taxes. Examples of special districts are water districts, drainage districts, flood control districts, hospital districts, fire protection districts, transit authorities, port authorities, and electric power authorities.

Special District Bonds Bonds issued by a special district. See Special District.

Special Fund Any fund that must be devoted to some special use in accordance with specific regulations and restrictions. Generally, the term applies to all funds other than the General Fund (*q.v.*).

Special Items Operating statement items that are either unusual or infrequent and are within management control.

Special Purpose Governments Governments that provide only a single function or a limited number of functions, such as independent school districts and special districts. Formerly called *limited purpose governments.*

Special Revenue Funds (SRFs) Funds used to account for revenues from specific taxes or other earmarked revenue sources that by law are designated to finance particular functions or activities of government. After the fund is established, it usually continues year after year until discontinued or revised by proper legislative authority. An example is a motor fuel tax fund used to finance highway and road construction.

Special-Special Assessment Bonds See Special Assessment Bonds.

Spending Rate The proportion of total return that may prudently be used by an institution for current purposes.

Split-Interest Agreements Forms of planned giving by donors who divide the rights to investment income on assets and assets themselves with intended beneficiary organizations in a predetermined manner.

Statute A written law enacted by a duly organized and constituted legislative body. See also Ordinance, Resolution, and Order.

Statutory Accounting Principles (SAP) See Regulatory Accounting Principles.

Stewardship Investments Beneficial investments of the federal government in items such as nonfederal physical property (property financed by the federal government but owned by state or local governments), human capital, and research and development.

Stewardship Land Federal land other than that included in general property, plant, and equipment (e.g., national parks).

Stores Materials and supplies on hand in storerooms subject to requisition and use.

Straight Serial Bonds Serial bonds (*q.v.*) in which the annual installments of a bond principal are approximately equal.

Subactivity A specific line of work performed in carrying out a governmental activity. For example, replacing defective street lamps would be a subactivity under the activity of street light maintenance.

Subfunction A grouping of related activities within a particular governmental function. For example, police is a subfunction of the public safety function.

Subsidiary Account One of a group of related accounts that support in detail the debit and credit summaries recorded in a control account, for example, the individual property taxpayers' accounts for taxes receivable in the general ledger. See also Control Account and Subsidiary Ledger.

Subsidiary Ledger A group of subsidiary accounts (*q.v.*) the sum of the balances of which is equal to the balance of the related control account. See also Control Account and Subsidiary Account.

Support The increase in net assets arising from contributions of resources or nonexchange transactions and includes only amounts for which the donor receives no direct tangible benefits from the recipient agency.

Surety Bond A written promise to pay damages or to indemnify against losses caused by the party or parties named in the document through nonperformance or through defalcation. An example is a surety bond given by a contractor or by an official handling cash or securities.

Surplus Receipts A term sometimes applied to receipts that increase the balance of a fund but are not a part of its normal revenue, for example, collection of accounts previously written off. Sometimes used as an account title.

Suspense Fund or Account A fund or account established to account separately for certain receipts pending the distribution or disposal thereof. See also Agency Funds.

Sweep Accounts Arrangements in which a bank automatically "sweeps" cash that exceeds the target balance into short-term cash investments.

Syndicate, Underwriting A group formed for the marketing of a given security issue too large for one member to handle expeditiously after which the group is dissolved.

T

Tax Anticipation Notes (TANs) Notes (sometimes called *warrants*) issued in anticipation of collection of taxes usually retirable only from tax collections and frequently only from the proceeds of the tax levy whose collection they anticipate.

Tax Certificate A certificate issued by a government as evidence of the conditional transfer of title to tax-delinquent property from the original owner to the holder of the certificate. If the owner does not pay the amount of the tax arrearage and other charges required by law during the special period of redemption, the holder can foreclose to obtain title. Also called *tax sale certificate* and *tax lien certificate* in some jurisdictions. See also Tax Deed.

Tax Deed A written instrument by which title to property sold for taxes is transferred unconditionally to the purchaser. A tax deed is issued on foreclosure of the tax lien (*q.v.*) obtained by the purchaser at the tax sale. The tax lien cannot be foreclosed until the expiration of the period during which the owner may redeem his or her property through paying the delinquent taxes and other charges. See also Tax Certificate.

Tax Expenditure A revenue loss attributable to provisions of federal tax laws that allow a special exclusion, exemption, or deduction from gross income or that provide a special credit, a preferential rate of tax, or a deferral of tax liability.

Tax Increment Debt Debt secured by an incremental tax earmarked for servicing the debt, such as a half-cent sales tax, or payable from taxes derived from incremental growth in the tax base that was financed by the tax increment debt.

Tax Levy See Levy.

Tax Levy Ordinance An ordinance (*q.v.*) by means of which taxes are levied.

Tax Liens Claims that governments have on properties until taxes levied against them have been paid. *Note:* The term is sometimes limited to those delinquent taxes for the collection of which legal action has been taken through the filing of liens.

Tax Liens Receivable Legal claims against property that have been exercised because of nonpayment of delinquent taxes, interest, and penalties. The account includes delinquent taxes, interest, penalties receivable up to the date the lien becomes effective, and the cost of holding the sale.

Tax Rate The amount of tax stated in terms of a unit of the tax base, for example, 25 mills per dollar of assessed valuation of taxable property.

Tax Rate Limit The maximum rate at which a government may levy a tax. The limit may apply to taxes raised for a particular purpose or to taxes imposed for all purposes and to a single government, a class of governments, or all governments operating in a particular area. Overall tax rate limits usually restrict levies for all purposes and of all governments, state and local, having jurisdiction in a given area.

Tax Roll The official list showing the amount of taxes levied against each taxpayer or property. Frequently, the tax roll and the assessment roll are combined but even in these cases the two can be distinguished.

Tax Supplement A tax levied by a local government that has the same base as a similar tax levied by a higher level of government, such as a state. The local tax supplement is frequently administered by the higher level of government along with its own tax. A locally imposed, state-administered sales tax is an example of a tax supplement.

Tax-Supported Debt All debt secured by pledges of tax revenues.

Tax Title Notes Obligations secured by pledges of the government's interest in certain tax liens or tax titles.

Taxable Property All property except that which is exempt from taxation; examples of exempt property are property owned by governments and property used by some religious and charitable organizations.

Taxes Compulsory charges levied by a government for the purpose of financing services performed for the common benefit. *Note:* The term does not include either specific charges made against particular persons or property for current or permanent benefits such as special assessments or charges for services rendered only to those paying such charges as, for example, sewer service charges.

Taxes Collected in Advance A liability for taxes collected before the tax levy has been made or before the amount of taxpayer liability has been established.

Taxes Levied for Other Governments Taxes levied by the reporting government for other governments, which, when collected, are to be paid over to these governments.

Taxes Paid in Advance Same as Taxes Collected in Advance. Also called *prepaid taxes.*

Taxes Receivable—Current The uncollected portion of taxes that a government has levied but that are not yet delinquent.

Taxes Receivable—Delinquent Taxes remaining unpaid on and after the date on which a penalty for nonpayment is attached. Even though the penalty may be subsequently waived and a portion of the taxes may be abated or canceled, the unpaid balances continue to be delinquent taxes until paid, abated, canceled, or converted into tax liens.

Temporarily Restricted Net Assets A term used in accounting for not-for-profit organizations indicating the amount of net assets temporarily restricted by an external donor for use in a future period or for a particular purpose. See Net Assets.

Term Bonds Bonds the entire principal of which matures on one date.

Term Bonds Payable A liability account that records the face value of general obligation term bonds issued and outstanding.

Term Endowments Assets for which donors or other external agencies have stipulated, as a condition of the gift, that the principal is to be maintained intact for a stated period of time (or term).

Termination Benefits Benefits provided to employees as a result of the voluntary or involuntary termination of employment.

Third-Party Payor Term used in health care organizations to refer to the entity other than the patient/client that pays for services such as an insurance company or federal insurance program.

Time Requirements Restrictions that relate to the period when resources are required to be used or when use may begin.

Time Warrant A negotiable obligation of a government having a term shorter than bonds and frequently tendered to individuals and firms in exchange for contractual services, capital acquisitions, or equipment purchases.

Total Quality Management (TQM) A management approach in which an organization seeks to continuously improve its ability to meet or exceed customer demands, where *customer,* in government or not-for-profit organization usage, may be broadly defined to include such parties as taxpayers, service recipients, students, and members.

Total Return A comprehensive measure of rate of investment return in which the sum of net realized and unrealized appreciation or shrinkage in portfolio value is added to dividend and interest yield.

Transfers See Interfund Transfers.

Trial Balance A list of the balances of the accounts in a ledger kept by double entry (*q.v.*), with the debit and credit balances shown in separate columns. If the totals of the debit and credit columns are equal or their net balance agrees with a control account, the ledger from which the figures are taken is said to be "in balance."

Trust and Agency Funds See Agency Funds, Trust Funds, and Fiduciary Funds.

Trust Funds Funds consisting of resources received and held by the government as trustee, to be expended or invested in accordance with the conditions of the trust. See also Endowment, Private-Purpose Trust Funds, and Public-Purpose Trust.

U

Unallotted Balance of Appropriation An appropriation balance available for allotment (*q.v.*).

Unamortized Discounts on Bonds Sold That portion of the excess of the face value of bonds over the amount received from their sale that remains to be written off periodically over the life of the bonds.

Unamortized Premiums on Bonds Sold An account that represents that portion of the excess of bond proceeds over par value and that remains to be amortized over the remaining life of such bonds.

Unapportioned Authority The amount of a federal appropriation made by the Congress and approved by the President but not yet apportioned by the Office of Management and Budget. See Other Appropriations Realized and Apportionment.

Unbilled Accounts Receivable An account that designates the estimated amount of accounts receivable for services or commodities sold but not billed. For example, if a utility bills its customers bimonthly but prepares monthly financial statements, the amount of services rendered or commodities sold during the first month of the bimonthly period would be reflected in the balance sheet under this account title.

Unconditional Promise to Give A promise to make contributions to an organization that depends only on the passage of time or demand by the promisee for performance.

Underwriting Syndicate See Syndicate, Underwriting.

Undistributed Change in Fair Value of Investments An account used by a cash and investment pool to accumulate realized and unrealized gains and losses on sales of investments pending distribution to pool participants. See Undistributed Earnings.

Undistributed Earnings An account used by a cash and investment pool to accumulate investment earnings pending distribution to pool participants.

Unearned Income See Deferred Revenues.

Unencumbered Allotment That portion of an allotment not yet expended or encumbered.

Unencumbered Appropriation That portion of an appropriation not yet expended or encumbered.

Unexpended Allotment That portion of an allotment not yet expended.

Unexpended Appropriation The equity of a federal agency provided by an appropriation that has not yet been expended.

Unfunded Actuarial Liability See Actuarial Accrued Liability.

Unit Cost A term used in cost accounting to denote the cost of producing a unit of product or rendering a unit of service, for example, the cost of treating and purifying a thousand gallons of sewage.

Unliquidated Encumbrances Encumbrances outstanding.

Unrealized Revenue See Accrued Revenue.

Unrelated Business Income Gross income from trade or business regularly carried on by a tax-exempt organization less directly connected expenses, certain net operating losses, and qualified charitable contributions that is not related to its exempt purpose. If more than $1,000, the income is subject to federal income tax at corporate tax rates.

Unrestricted Assets Assets that may be utilized at the discretion of the governing board of a not-for-profit entity.

Unrestricted Funds Funds established to account for assets or resources that may be utilized at the discretion of the governing board.

Unrestricted Net Assets The portion of the excess of total assets over total liabilities that may be utilized at the discretion of the governing board of a governmental or not-for-profit entity. See Net Assets, Temporarily Restricted Net Assets, and Permanently Restricted Net Assets.

User Charge A charge levied against users of a service or purchasers of a product.

Utility Plant Acquisition Adjustment An account that captures the premium paid on a utility plant purchased by a government. Similar to goodwill except that the premium is the difference between the purchase price and the depreciated original cost of the utility rather than the difference between the purchase price and fair value.

V

Value As used in governmental accounting, this term designates (1) the act of describing anything in terms of money or (2) the measure of a thing in terms of money. The term should not be used without further qualification. See also Book Value, Face Value, and Fair Value.

Variance Power The unilateral power of an organization to redirect donated assets to a beneficiary different than the third party initially indicated by the donor.

Voluntary Health and Welfare Organization Not-for-profit organizations that receive contributions from the public at large and provide health and welfare services for a nominal or no fee. Also known as *human service organizations.*

Voluntary Nonexchange Transactions A category of nonexchange transaction that includes certain grants and entitlements and most donations.

Voucher A written document that evidences the propriety of transactions and usually indicates the accounts in which they are to be recorded.

Voucher System A system that calls for the preparation of vouchers (*q.v.*) for transactions involving payments and for the recording of such vouchers in a special book of original entry (*q.v.*), known as a *voucher register,* in the order in which payment is approved.

Vouchers Payable Liabilities for goods and services evidenced by vouchers that have been preaudited and approved for payment but not paid.

W

Warrant An order drawn by the legislative body or an officer of a government on its treasurer, directing the latter to pay a specified amount to the person named or to the bearer. It may be payable on demand, in which case it usually circulates the same as a bank check, or it may be payable only out of certain revenues when and if received, in which case it does not circulate as freely. See also Registered Warrant and Deposit Warrant.

Warrants Payable The amount of warrants outstanding and unpaid.

Work Order A written order authorizing and directing the performance of a certain task and issued to the person who is to direct the work. Among the items of information shown on the order are the nature and location of the job, specifications of the work to be performed, and a job number that is referred to in reporting the amount of labor, materials, and equipment used.

Working Capital Fund See Internal Service Funds.

Y

Yield Rate See Effective Interest Rate.

Z

Zero-Based Budgeting (ZBB) A budget based on the concept that the very existence of each activity, as well as the amounts of resources requested to be allocated to each activity, must be justified each year.

Governmental and Not-for-Profit Organizations

AAA — **American Accounting Association** An organization of accounting educators and practitioners involved in education whose objectives are to contribute to the development of accounting theory, to encourage and sponsor accounting research, and to improve the quality of accounting education.

ABFM — **Association for Budgeting and Financial Management** A section of the American Society for Public Administration that advances the science, processes, and art of public administration as it relates to budgeting and financial management.

ACE — **American Council on Education** An organization founded in 1918 to influence public policy on higher education issues through advocacy, research, and program initiatives.

AFGI — **Association of Financial Guaranty Insurors** The trade association of the insurers and reinsurers of municipal bonds and asset-backed securities.

AGA — **Association of Government Accountants** An association formed in 1950 to serve the professional development of governmental finance professionals by providing education, research, and professional certifications, such as the certified government financial manager (CGFM).

AHA — **American Hospital Association** An association organized in the early 1900s by hospital administrators to promote economy and efficiency in hospital management. Its current mission is to take a leadership role in public policy, representation and advocacy, and health services.

AICPA — **American Institute of Certified Public Accountants** The professional organization to which certified public accountants (CPAs) belong. In addition to providing educational and lobbying services on behalf of its members, the AICPA is responsible for promulgating auditing standards applicable to private companies, governments, and not-for-profit organizations.

APPA — **American Public Power Association** The national trade association representing state and local government-owned electric utilities.

ASBOI — **Association of School Business Officials International** A professional association of school business management professionals that provides programs and services to promote the highest standards of school business management practices, professional growth, and the effective use of educational resources.

BBB Wise Giving Alliance A 2001 merger of the National Charities Information Bureau and the Philanthropic Advisory Service of the Council of Better Business Bureaus Foundation.

CBO — **Congressional Budget Office** An office of the legislative branch of the federal government established in 1974 that gathers information for the House and Senate budget committees with respect to the budget submitted to the executive branch, appropriations bills, other bills providing budget authority, tax expenditures, and other analysis.

CSG — **Council of State Governments** An association of state financial officers that forecasts policy trends for states, commonwealths, and territories and champions state sovereignty.

FAF — **Financial Accounting Foundation** The organization that finances and appoints members of the Financial Accounting Standards Board and Governmental Accounting Standards Board.

FASAB — **Federal Accounting Standards Advisory Board** The nine-member standards-setting body that recommends federal governmental accounting and financial reporting standards to the U.S. Comptroller General, Secretary of the Treasury, and Director of the Office of Management and Budget.

FASAC — **Financial Accounting Standards Advisory Council** The council that advises the Financial Accounting Standards Board on policy matters, agenda items, project priorities, technical issues, and task forces.

FASB — **Financial Accounting Standards Board** The designated organization in the private sector for establishing standards of financial accounting and reporting since 1973.

GAO — **Government Accountability Office** An agency of the legislative branch of the federal government responsible for prescribing accounting principles for federal agencies; the auditing arm of Congress.

GASAC — **Governmental Accounting Standards Advisory Council** The council that advises the Governmental Accounting Standards Board on policy matters, agenda items, project priorities, technical issues, and task forces. Its members are broadly representative of preparers, attestors, and users of financial information.

GASB — **Governmental Accounting Standards Board** The independent agency established under the Financial Accounting Foundation in 1984 as the official body designated by the AICPA to set accounting and financial reporting standards for state and local governments.

GFOA — **Government Finance Officers Association** An association of government finance managers founded in 1906 as the Municipal Finance Officers Association to promote the professional management of governments. The GFOA administers the Certificate of Achievement program to reward excellence in financial reporting, budgeting, and other areas.

GRA **Governmental Research Association** A national organization, founded in 1914, of individuals professionally engaged in governmental research.

HFMA **Healthcare Financial Management Association** A not-for-profit organization of financial management professionals employed by hospitals and other health care providers established in 1946 to provide professional development opportunities, influence health care policy, and communicate information and technical data.

ICMA **International City/County Management Association** An organization founded in 1914 that is the professional and educational organization for appointed administrators serving cities, towns, counties, and regional entities around the world.

IPSASB **International Public Sector Accounting Standards Board** An independent standards-setting body, designated by the International Federation of Accountants (IFAC) to develop high quality accounting standards for use by public sector entities around the world.

NABL **National Association of Bond Lawyers** An organization of bond lawyers that educates its members and others in the laws relating to state and municipal bonds.

NACo **National Association of Counties** An organization created in 1935 by county officials to provide legislative, research, technical, and public affairs assistance to members and ensure that the concerns of over 3,000 counties in the United States are heard at the federal level of government.

NACUBO **National Association of College & University Business Officers** A not-for-profit professional organization founded in 1962 representing chief administrative and financial officers at colleges and universities whose mission is to promote sound management and financial practices at institutions of higher education.

NAFOA **Native American Finance Officers Association** An association of tribal officers, controllers, treasurers, accountants, auditors, financial advisors, tribal leaders, and others that provides educational forums and resources about finance and accounting best practices.

NASACT **National Association of State Auditors, Comptrollers, and Treasurers** An organization formed in 1915 for state officials who deal with the financial management of state government.

NASBO **National Association of State Budget Officers** The professional organization for state budget and finance officers through which the states and U.S. territories have collectively advanced state budget practices since 1945.

NASRA **National Association of State Retirement Administrators** An organization comprised of directors of the nation's public retirement systems for the 50 states, the District of Columbia, and U.S. territories.

NCSL **National Conference of State Legislatures** A bipartisan association that serves the legislators and staffs of the nation's states, commonwealths, and territories by providing research, technical assistance, and opportunities for policy makers to exchange ideas on state issues.

NFMA **National Federation of Municipal Analysts** An association chartered in 1983 to promote professionalism in municipal credit analysis and to further the skill level of its members through educational programs and industry communication.

NGA **National Governors' Association** A bipartisan organization of the nation's governors founded in 1908 to promote visionary state leadership, share best practices, and speak with a unified voice on national policy.

NLC **National League of Cities** An organization founded in 1924 as the American Municipal Association to represent municipal governments and strengthen and support cities.

OMB **Office of Management and Budget** An office of the executive branch of the federal government that has responsibility for establishing policies and procedures for approving and publishing financial accounting principles and standards to be followed by executive branch agencies. It also has the authority to control the size and nature of appropriations requested of each Congress.

PCIE **President's Council on Integrity and Efficiency** A federal agency established by executive order that is comprised of all presidentially appointed Inspectors General, as well as other federal agency members. Its charge is to conduct interagency and interentity audits and inspect and investigate projects in order to effectively and efficiently deal with government-wide issues of fraud, waste, and abuse.

SIFMA **Securities Industry and Financial Markets Association** A merger of The Bond Market Association and The Securities Industry Association representing member firms in all financial markets with the broad mission to strengthen markets and support investors.

USCM **U.S. Conference of Mayors** A nonpartisan organization established in 1932 representing U.S. cities with populations of 30,000 or more. The conference aids the development of effective national urban policy, strengthens federal–city relationships, ensures that federal policy meets urban needs, and provides mayors with leadership and management tools of value in their cities.

For contact information, go to *http://www.msu.edu/~kattelus* under "Government and Nonprofit Resources."

Index